Doubt in Islamic Law

This book considers an important and largely neglected area of Islamic law by exploring how medieval Muslim jurists resolved criminal cases that could not be proved beyond a doubt. Intisar A. Rabb calls into question a controversial popular notion about Islamic law today, which is that Islamic law is a divine legal tradition that has little room for discretion or doubt, particularly in Islamic criminal law. Despite its contemporary popularity, that notion turns out to have been far outside the mainstream of Islamic law for most of its history. Instead of rejecting doubt, medieval Muslim scholars largely embraced it. In fact, they used doubt to enlarge their own power and to construct Islamic criminal law itself. Through a close examination of legal, historical, and theological sources and a range of illustrative case studies, this book shows that Muslim jurists developed a highly sophisticated and regulated system for dealing with Islam's unique concept of doubt, which evolved through the deployment of legal maxims from the seventh to the sixteenth century.

Intisar A. Rabb is Professor of Law at Harvard Law School and a director of its Islamic Legal Studies Program. She also holds an appointment as a professor of history (affiliated) and as Susan S. and Kenneth L. Wallach Professor at the Radcliffe Institute for Advanced Study at Harvard University.

Cambridge Studies in Islamic Civilization

Other titles in the series are listed at the back of the book.

Doubt in Islamic Law

A History of Legal Maxims, Interpretation, and Islamic Criminal Law

INTISAR A. RABB
Harvard Law School

CAMBRIDGE
UNIVERSITY PRESS

CAMBRIDGE
UNIVERSITY PRESS

32 Avenue of the Americas, New York, NY 10013-2473, USA

Cambridge University Press is part of the University of Cambridge.

It furthers the University's mission by disseminating knowledge in the pursuit of education, learning, and research at the highest international levels of excellence.

www.cambridge.org
Information on this title: www.cambridge.org/9781107080997

First published 2015

Printed in the United States of America

A catalog record for this publication is available from the British Library.

Library of Congress Cataloging in Publication Data
Rabb, Intisar A., author.
Doubt in Islamic law : a history of legal maxims, interpretation, and Islamic criminal law / Intisar A. Rabb.
pages cm – (Cambridge studies in islamic civilization)
Includes bibliographical references and index.
ISBN 978-1-107-08099-7 (hardback)
1. Criminal law (Islamic law) – Interpretation and construction. 2. Belief and doubt. 3. Legal certainty. 4. Legal maxims (Islamic law) – History. 5. Islamic law – Interpretation and construction. I. Title.
KBP3821.R33 2014
345′.06–dc23 2014021442

ISBN 978-1-107-08099-7 Hardback

in honor of my brother

Contents

Acknowledgments

Like stone soup, this book accumulated essential ingredients from many generous contributors. If my preoccupation with doubt was the improbable rock at the center, its vessel was a traveling one that benefited from the ideas, exchanges, and challenges of numerous teachers and colleagues over the course of the past decade and no less than five institutions. Every stop offered a remarkable intellectual community, the conversations and insights from each reflected in the pages of this book. The brevity with which I acknowledge them does not reflect the profundity of my appreciation.

Hossein Modarressi provided steady and probing mentorship throughout – illuminating sources and posing arguments that would have otherwise remained elusive or unaddressed, and leading me to identify both common threads and uncommon points in Islamic law and history – all with a tremendous amount of patience and care. While the mistakes are mine, he enriched this book beyond measure through his exacting erudition (and pen!), his generous integrity, and his own meticulous example as a scholar and teacher.

At Princeton, Michael Cook shared his historical insight, contagious curiosity, and critical comments through instructive conversations and often humorous notes in the margins of various drafts. Kim Scheppele added keen sociological perspectives in ways that prompted me to explore broader questions of comparative law and society, with one eye on what the legal texts said and the other on what they did *not* say. Many others contributed at Princeton during my time there and afterward, including Seven Ağir, Azar Ashraf, Najam Haider, Andras Hamori, Hendrik Hartog, Nancy Khalek, Amineh Mahallati, Asma Sayeed, Laura Weinrib, and M. Qasim Zaman.

At Yale, James Whitman unfailingly offered valuable observations and conscientious feedback from his wide-ranging knowledge of comparative legal history – as he pushed me to identify, reconstruct, and question untold but important aspects of Islamic legal history with serious questions of comparative law in mind. William Eskridge and Daniel Markovits supplied useful comments at various stages and raised important questions, as did Aslı Bali, Owen Fiss, Anthony Kronman, Darryl Li, Aziz Rana, and all who participated in the Thomas Lecture, including James A. Thomas himself.

At Boston College, Paulo Barrozo, Mary Bilder, and Vlad Perju engaged the work with helpful comments and conversations, as did the participants of the Legal History Roundtable.

At NYU, Marion Katz gave detailed feedback on the entire manuscript, as did Daniel Hulsebosch and William Nelson, along with the members of the Golieb Legal History colloquium. The book further gained from conversations with Rachel Barkow, Erin Murphy, and Everett Rowson.

At Harvard, a stellar set of colleagues, students, and libraries made it a delightful place to visit and to eventually call home, bringing my travels to an end. Roy Mottahedeh offered valuable exchanges on significant aspects of early Islamic law and social history. Lani Guinier gave generous feedback on multiple occasions as I worked to lay out the book's arguments for a broader audience. In addition, the work benefited from conversations with William Alford, Christine Desan, Charles Donahue, Einer Elhague, Noah Feldman, the late Wolfhart Heinrichs, Baber Johansen, Adriaan Lanni, John Manning, Martha Minow, Carol Steiker, and the participants of the Law School "junior" faculty workshop as well as the all-school faculty workshop.

Elsewhere, Judge Thomas Ambro gave a master chef's lesson on how legal ingredients mix in the real world during my time serving as his law clerk. Others who added richly include Mohammad Fadel, Wael Hallaq, Sherman Jackson, Racha El Omari, Ahmed El Shamsy, Wahba al-Zuhayli, and Adnan Zulfiqar; my teachers at Mofid University and other scholars in Qum; and participants at several other sessions at which portions of the manuscript were presented – including at the annual meetings of the American Society for Legal History, the Law and Society Association, and the Middle East Studies Association; at the NYU–Abu Dhabi Institute, and the Princeton Islamic Studies Colloquium; and at workshops at Fordham Law School, Hofstra University School of Law, NYU, Shahid Beheshti University, UCLA, UC-Davis, University of Pennsylvania, and Yale Law School.

A group of editors helped pull the varied elements together. At Cambridge University Press, Marigold Acland first accepted the book and solicited the helpful reviews of the anonymous readers, Sarika Narula helped arrange some mechanics of production, and William Hammell adroitly shepherded it to completion. Hanna Siurua devoted many hours to careful examinations of all that went into the pot with her superbly intelligent edits, as did Meagan Froemming with hers. And editors at the *Vanderbilt Journal of Transnational Law* and the *Journal of Islamic Law and Society* graciously allowed me to include portions of earlier published articles.

Several institutional awards of financial and other support facilitated the research necessary for this project: Princeton's Department of Near Eastern Studies, Center for the Study of Religion, Council of the Humanities, Law and Public Affairs Program, Institute for International and Regional Studies, and University Center for Human Values; as well as the Naples Road Fellowship and research funding from each of the five institutions noted above at which I studied or worked. It may go without saying, but historical work of this sort would never have been possible without the commendable preservations, beautiful atmospheres, and helpful staffs at the libraries and archives that I consulted and at which I worked – especially Firestone Library in Princeton – as well as libraries in Cambridge (Langdell and Widener Libraries at Harvard), Damascus (Maktabat al-Asad), Istanbul (ISAM and Süleymaniye Kütüphanesi), London (SOAS and the British Library), New Haven (Sterling Library at Yale), and Qum (Kitābkhanah-i Marʿashī).

Last, but certainly not least, was the vital contribution at the start: my family – my parents in particular – who first taught me about principles and doubt.

Introduction

This book is about doubt in Islamic law. Specifically, it is a history of the concept of doubt in Islam's system of criminal law, a concept that reveals much about the nature and complexities of Islamic law itself – also known as *sharīʿa*. This history calls into question a popular notion about Islamic law – which some have upheld and promoted and others have criticized and opposed. The notion is that Islamic law is a divine legal tradition that has little room for discretion or doubt, particularly in Islamic criminal law.

Despite its contemporary popularity, that notion turns out to have been far outside the mainstream of Islamic law for most of its history. Instead of rejecting doubt, medieval Muslim scholars largely embraced it. In fact, these scholars – the expert jurists who articulated the main contours and rules of Islam's legal system – held doubt so closely that it came to be at the heart of Islamic criminal law. Moreover, these scholars embraced doubt in ways that helped them construct the system of Islamic law, which they simultaneously claimed to have divine origins. This account examines that process of construction-through-interpretation by exploring some of the thorniest issues in Islamic law: those involving Islamic criminal law. More often than not, the difficult interpretive questions of crime and punishment facing Muslim jurists were characterized by doubt.

AN EARLY EPISODE OF DOUBT

One early episode in Islamic legal history illustrates the problems posed by doubt. Not long after Islam's advent in the seventh century, a type of early police force in a small Arabian town was out patrolling. Members of this patrol came across a man in the town ruins holding a blood-stained knife and standing over the body of another man who had apparently just been stabbed to death. The patrol arrested the man with the knife. Upon arrest, he immediately confessed: "I killed him."

The suspect was brought before ʿAlī, the beloved cousin and son-in-law of the Prophet Muḥammad (who had died less than three decades before in 632). ʿAlī was the fourth caliph according to the Sunnī account of successors to the Prophet and the first Imām in the competing Shīʿī account. He presided over criminal trials in his capacity as leader of the young Muslim community from 656 to 661, as had the Prophet before him. Upon hearing the defendant's story, ʿAlī reportedly sentenced him to death, in accordance with the Islamic law of retaliation for homicide and personal injury: a life for a life.

Before the sentence was carried out, another man rushed forward, telling the executioners not to be so hasty. "Do not kill him. *I* did it," he announced. ʿAlī turned to the condemned man incredulously. "What made you confess to a murder that you did not commit?" he asked. The man explained that he thought ʿAlī would never take his word over that of the patrolmen who had witnessed a crime scene wherein all signs had pointed to him as the perpetrator. In reality, the man explained, he was a butcher who had just finished slaughtering a cow. Immediately after the slaughter, he needed to relieve himself, so he entered the area of the ruins, bloody knife still in hand. Upon return, he came across the dead man and stood over him in concern. It was then that the patrol encountered him. Figuring that he could not plausibly deny having committed the crime, he confessed to the "obvious" and decided to leave the matter in God's hands.

The second man offered a corroborating story. He explained that *he* was the one who had murdered a man for his money and then fled upon hearing sounds of the patrol approaching. On his way out, he passed the butcher entering the area and then watched the events unfold just as the butcher had described them. Once the butcher was condemned to death, however, the second man felt compelled to step forward. He did not want the blood of *two* men on his hands.[1]

1 Ibrāhīm b. Hāshim al-Qummī (mid-third/ninth century), *Qaḍāyā Amīr al-Muʾminīn ʿAlī b. Abī Ṭālib*, ed. Fāris Ḥassūn Karīm (Qum: Muʾassasat Amīr al-Muʾminīn, 1382/2003), 88–89, 238 (paraphrased). Both Sunnī and Shīʿī scholars cite this as an example of exemplary *ḥudūd* jurisprudence. See, for example, Ibn Qayyim al-Jawziyya (d. 751/1350), *al-Ṭuruq al-ḥukmiyya fī ʾl-siyāsa al-sharʿiyya*, ed. Muḥammad Jamīl Ghāzī (Cairo: Maṭbaʿat al-Madanī, 1978), 82–84 (quoting *Qaḍāyā ʿAlī* and *ʿAjāʾib* [*aḥkām Amīr al-Muʾminīn* = *Qaḍāyā ʿAlī*, as given in the edition of Muḥsin Amīn al-ʿĀmilī, *ʿAjāʾib aḥkām Amīr al-Muʾminīn ʿAlī b. Abī Ṭālib* (Qum?: Markaz al-Ghadīr liʾl-Dirāsāt al-Islāmiyya, 2000)]);

This episode, which we may call the *Case of the Falsely Accused Butcher*, depicts the difficulties that medieval Muslim judges faced when attempting to apply Islamic criminal law without the benefit of being able to discern the *facts*, the *law*, or the *morality* of punishment with any certainty. As for the facts, confession or witness testimony typically sufficed to establish guilt in Islamic criminal law.[2] But here, ʿAlī was presented only with circumstantial and contradictory evidence. As for the Islamic law of homicide, the Qur'ān and other foundational texts contained clear rules that retaliation applied to intentional murder.[3] But those rules did not cover the case before ʿAlī. As for the morality (and, consequently, legitimacy) of punishment, given scriptural commands to punish and despite uncertainties about the law and the facts, ʿAlī had to decide whether to enforce punishment or avoid it. He chose to avoid punishment.[4]

The question is why. The answer is shrouded by a tangled web that took Muslim jurists centuries to weave and, therefore, takes serious historical

Muḥammad b. Yaʿqūb al-Kulaynī (d. 329/940–1), *Kāfī*, ed. ʿAlī Akbar al-Ghaffārī (Tehran: n.p., 1377/1957–8), 7:289 (quoting the story from Ibrāhīm b. Hāshim al-Qummī, as received through that author's son, ʿAlī b. Ibrāhīm al-Qummī). For a detailed account of the role and debates surrounding ʿAlī against the first three caliphs in the question of succession to the Prophet, see Wilferd Madelung, *The Succession to Muḥammad: A Study of the Early Caliphate* (Cambridge: Cambridge University Press, 1997).

2 For a basic overview of Islamic criminal procedure, see Ṣubḥī Maḥmaṣānī, *Falsafat al-tashrīʿ fī 'l-Islām*, 5th ed. (Beirut: Dār al-ʿIlm li'l-Malāyīn, 1980; orig. 1946), 325–76 (English trans. Farhat Ziadeh, *The Philosophy of Jurisprudence in Islam* (Leiden: Brill, 1961)). See further Part III.

3 For an accessible overview of Islamic substantive criminal law, see generally Rudolph Peters, *Crime and Punishment in Islamic Law* (Cambridge: Cambridge University Press, 2005) (describing Islam's three categories of offenses: (1) *ḥudūd* – fixed, nondiscretionary crimes and penalties, including four agreed-upon offenses, namely, illicit sexual relations, false accusations of illicit sexual relations, theft, and intoxication, as well as three offenses of disputed status, namely, apostasy, blasphemy, and highway robbery; (2) *qiṣāṣ* – the laws of murder and personal injury; and (3) *taʿzīr* – discretionary penalties). See further Chapter 1.

4 The story (likely apocryphal) is not clear about the outcome in the case, but it conveys the impression that ʿAlī released the first man and pardoned the second, without further analysis as to why. That analysis was left to later Muslim jurists. On a strict textualist analysis of foundational texts establishing confession as probative evidence, the story could mean that when the second man confessed, ʿAlī might have made a determination of his guilt with certainty. But on a pragmatic analysis, the story could mean that even that confession had become subject to doubt given that the butcher's confession had initially yielded the same degree of certainty but moments later was reversed by the retraction and competing confession. Muslim jurists citing this and other cases as precedent for issues of doubt in matters of fact, law, and the moral propriety of punishment sought to explain why ʿAlī and other founding figures chose to, as they termed it, embrace doubt and avoid punishment in such cases.

work to unravel. To cut to the center first: Muslim jurists made doubt – and avoidance of punishment on its basis – a central pillar of Islamic criminal law. As myriad episodes like the *Case of the Falsely Accused Butcher* entered the corpus of early Islamic legal literature, perhaps carefully selected or constructed by later jurists as episodes worthy of preservation for their instructive fact patterns, Muslim jurists *retrospectively* explained such cases with reference to doubt. Taking cases such as that one as a precedent, those jurists then *prospectively* promoted a surprisingly extensive tendency of extending the benefit of the doubt to the accused. They packaged that tendency in the form of a directive calling on judges to "avoid criminal punishments in cases of doubt: *idraʾū ʾl-ḥudūd biʾl-shubahāt*."[5] I call this statement Islamic law's "doubt canon" – one of many Islamic legal maxims that were rooted in past cases and gained the status of an oft-repeated principle of interpretation that medieval Muslim jurists sought to apply to future cases.[6]

For the reader familiar with American criminal law, it is important to note here that the Arabic term for "doubt" in this canon, *shubha*, was a term of art. It assumed a much more expansive meaning than the common conception of reasonable doubt in American law. Rather than representing a principally fact-based standard of proof, the Islamic doctrine covered factual uncertainties, legal ambiguities, and even extralegal considerations that I call "moral doubt." Moreover, the Islamic doctrine of doubt corresponds to analogous American doctrines as seemingly disparate as the principle of legality; the presumption of innocence; legal ambiguity and the corresponding rule of lenity; the requirement for proof beyond a reasonable doubt and lesser standards of proof; *mens rea* requirements;

[5] Multiple treatises collecting Islamic legal maxims – a rich body of legal literature so far underexplored in both Sunnī and Shīʿī law – typically analyze criminal law doctrine through this doubt canon as did *fiqh* works before them. See, for example, Ibn ʿAbd al-Salām (d. 660/1262), *al-Qawāʿid al-kubrā*, 2nd ed., ed. Nazīh Kamāl Ḥammād and ʿUthmān Jumuʿa Ḍumayriyya (Damascus: Dār al-Qalam, 2007), 2:279–80; Shihāb al-Dīn al-Qarāfī (d. 684/1285), *Anwār al-burūq fī anwāʾ al-furūq* (Beirut: Dār al-Maʿrifa, 197-?), 4:1307, no. 240; Jalāl al-Dīn al-Suyūṭī (d. 911/1505), *al-Ashbāh waʾl-naẓāʾir fī qawāʿid wa-furūʿ al-Shāfiʿiyya*, ed. Muḥammad al-Muʿtaṣim biʾllāh al-Baghdādī (Beirut: Dār al-Kitāb al-ʿArabī, 1998), 236–38; Ibn Nujaym (d. 970/1563), *al-Ashbāh waʾl-naẓāʾir*, ed. Muḥammad Muṭīʿ al-Ḥāfiẓ (Damascus: Dār al-Fikr, 1983), 142.

[6] For a comparison between legal canons in Islamic law and American law, see my "Islamic Legal Maxims as Substantive Canons of Construction: *Ḥudūd*-Avoidance in Cases of Doubt," *Islamic Law and Society* 17, 1 (2010), 63–125. Elsewhere, I have called the statement "the Islamic rule of lenity," when emphasizing the aspects of legal ambiguity inherent in the concept of *shubha*. See my "The Islamic Rule of Lenity: Judicial Discretion and Legal Canons," *Vanderbilt Journal of Transnational Law* 44 (2011), 1299–1351.

mistake, ignorance, impossibility, and other potentially mitigating circumstances; and even mercy. In addition, the concept of *shubha* covers notions particular to Islamic law, such as "contractual doubt" and "interpretive doubt."[7]

This expansive meaning of doubt in Islamic law is doubly perplexing because doubt seems somehow misplaced in a religious legal tradition that posits God as a divine Lawgiver who asserts absolute supremacy over the law and who "legislated" a series of harsh criminal sanctions.[8] Indeed, given the ever-present specter of doubt, Muslim jurists obsessed over devising an "economy of certainty."[9] But if Islamic law is a textualist legal tradition requiring Muslims to apply the rule of God rather than the discretion of men (as Islamic theorists maintain that it is), how did doubt – about textual meaning as well as matters that were atextual and otherwise uncertain in nature – come to be so central and confer so much discretion on the jurists? Moreover, why did this occur? The remainder of this book seeks to untangle the means and motives behind the growth of doubt in Islamic criminal law, historically and in comparative perspective.

THE SIGNIFICANCE OF DOUBT

Before discussing those means and motives, it is worth considering why doubt is so significant as a subject of inquiry today beyond the counter-intuitive fact of its existence in popular and theoretical perceptions of Islamic law. I suggest three main reasons, each related to the relevance of doubt's history to the present.

One reason has to do with contemporary developments in the Muslim world, where Islamic law is spreading not only in constitutions and civil codes, but in criminal matters as well. Since the 1970s, more than thirty-eight countries have introduced constitutions with a clause declaring Islamic law to be "a source" or "the source" of state law.[10] During this

7 For a detailed discussion of the various types of "doubt" folded into the doubt canon, see Chapters 5 and 6.

8 See Chapter 1, Section B.1.

9 Aron Zysow, *The Economy of Certainty: An Introduction to the Typology of Islamic Legal Theory* (Atlanta, GA: Lockwood Press, 2013), 1 ("From a very early period … Muslims came to treat the question of legitimacy along explicitly epistemological lines. Certainty and probability were the fundamental categories with which they approached every question of law. This concern with epistemology sets Islamic law apart from other legal systems that treat the problem of legitimacy in institutional terms.").

10 See my "We the Jurists: Islamic Constitutionalism in Iraq," *University of Pennsylvania Journal of Constitutional Law* 10 (2008), 527–79, at 527, n. 1; and for updates, my "The

same period, at least a dozen states have adopted Islamic penal codes as well – in countries ranging from Iran, Pakistan, and Saudi Arabia to provinces in Malaysia, Northern Nigeria, and now Syria.[11] More recently, in the wake of the tumultuous Arab uprisings that began in 2010, there is great uncertainty about the fate of democracy and the rule of law, in no small part because of the raging battles between authoritarian secularist regimes and rebel Islamists who promote ill-defined or ill-conceived versions of Islamic law to oppose them.[12]

Least Religious Branch? Judicial Review and the New Islamic Constitutionalism," *UCLA Journal of International and Foreign Affairs* 17 (2013), 72–132, at nn. 1 and 17.

11 One example is the draft criminal code of the Maldives, written in consultation with Professor Paul Robinson at the University of Pennsylvania Law School based on early Islamic legal sources, submitted to the Maldivian Government in 2006 for review, and passed into law in 2014. See Paul Robinson et al., "Codifying Sharīʿa: International Norms, Legality & the Freedom to Invent New Forms," *Journal of Comparative Law* 2, 1 (2007), 1–53. Other Islamic penal codes include those of Afghanistan (2004), Brunei (2014), Iran (1979, 1981, rev. 2013), Kuwait (1960, 1970), Libya (1972), Oman (1974), Pakistan (1979, as well as uncodified applications in the Swat Valley), Qatar (2004), Sudan (1983, 1991), United Arab Emirates (1988), and Yemen (1994), as well as provinces in Malaysia (Kelantan, 1993), Nigeria (multiple Northern states, 1999–2000), and Indonesia (Aceh, 2009). Non-codified practices are reported in Algeria (since 1993), Egypt (since 2012), Iraq (in 2014), Northern Mali (since 2012), Somalia (since the 1990s), and Syria (since 2011). For general discussion, see further M. Cherif Bassiouni, "Crimes and the Criminal Process," *Arab Law Quarterly* 12 (1997), 269–86; Rudolph Peters, "The Islamization of Criminal Law: A Comparative Analysis," *Die Welt Des Islams* 34 (1994), 246–74. For country-specific studies, see, for example, Ziba Mir-Hosseini, "Criminalising Sexuality: Zinā Laws as Violence Against Women in Muslim Contexts [in Iran]," *Sur* 8, 15 (2011), 7–34; Philip Ostien, ed., *Sharia Implementation in Northern Nigeria, 1999–2006: A Sourcebook* (Ibadan, Nigeria: Spectrum Books, 2007); Abdel Salam Sidahmed, "Problems in Contemporary Applications of Islamic Criminal Sanctions: The Penalty for Adultery in Relation to Women [in Sudan]," *British Journal of Middle Eastern Studies* 28 (2001), 187–204; Mohammad Hashim Kamali, "Punishment in Islamic Law: A Critique of the Hudud Bill of Kelantan, Malaysia," *Arab Law Quarterly* 13 (1998), 203–34; Asifa Quraishi, "Her Honor: An Islamic Critique of the Rape Laws of Pakistan from a Woman-Sensitive Perspective," *Michigan Journal of International Law* 18 (1996–97), 287–320; A. Jahangir and H. Jilani, *The Hudood Ordinances* [of Pakistan]*: A Divine Sanction?* (Lahore: Rhotac Books, 1988).

12 See, for example, Said A. Arjomand, "Middle Eastern Constitutional and Ideological Revolutions and the Rise of Juristocracy," *Constellations* 19 (2012), 204–15; Malika Zeghal, *Constitution-Drafting and Islam in Tunisia* (forthcoming); Karim Mezran, "Constitutionalism and Islam in Libya," in *Constitutionalism in Islamic Countries: Between Upheaval and Continuity*, ed. Rainer Grote and Tillmann J. Röder (Oxford: Oxford University Press, 2012), 513–33; Alex Warren and Lin Noueihed, *The Battle for the Arab Spring: Revolution, Counter-Revolution and the Making of a New Era* (New Haven, CT: Yale University Press, 2012). For a comparison of pre- and post-revolutionary activity, see further Nathan Brown, *When Victory Is Not an Option: Islamist Movements in Arab Politics* (Ithaca, NY: Cornell University Press, 2012) (examining the inability of Islamists to participate in politics before the Arab uprisings); and Nathan Brown, *Arab Constitutions in the 21st Century: A New Beginning or an Unhappy Ending?*

The emergence of such ill-conceived versions of Islamic law in recent times has prompted, more than anything, fears of its punishments. In fact, those punishments have come to define the face of "*sharīʿa*" itself – often left untranslated in order to highlight the exoticism and danger that it can evoke in the popular imagination. On this view, *sharīʿa* is no more than a religious code that expresses the will of an angry and vengeful god intent on oppressing women, amputating hands, and executing apostates. Indeed, reports of summary executions and other violence on the part of state actors in Iran, Northern Nigeria, and Saudi Arabia disproportionately meted out to women and religious minorities fuel this perception. Furthermore, reports of violence by non-state actors in Afghanistan, Mali, and Syria seem to reflect a view that enforcing Islamic criminal punishments as expansively as possible is a religious obligation with early Islamic origins that authorizes extralegal violence. On that view, it is no wonder that *sharīʿa* inspires fear of its spread not only in the Muslim world but throughout the globe. In the light of history, however, these views present a distortion of the theory and practice of Islamic criminal law, a distortion ironically adopted by the most vociferous proponents and opponents of "*sharīʿa*" alike.

In point of fact, new Islamic constitutions and codes do require many judges in the Muslim world to apply Islamic law in their decisions,[13] in ways deeply connected to Islamic legal history. Some judges in these Islamic constitutional countries tend to appeal to conceptions of Islamic law drawn from its foundational texts and from understandings of Islam's ever-authoritative "founding period," which stretched from the seventh to the eleventh century.[14]

(New Haven, CT: Yale Law School Dallah Albaraka Lectures on Islamic Law and Civilization, 2014).

13 See, for example, *Constitution of the Arab Republic of Egypt*, art. 2 (1971, 1980, 2011, 2012, 2014) (including two additional clauses in the 2012 version – arts. 4 and 219, expanding the role of *sharīʿa* – which ultimately failed to appear in the subsequent version, although Article 2 survived). For analysis of the formation and execution of Egypt's "article 2" jurisprudence, see Clark Lombardi, "Egypt's Supreme Constitutional Court: Managing Constitutional Conflict in an Authoritarian, Aspirationally 'Islamic' State," *Journal of Comparative Law* 3 (2008), 234–53; Clark Lombardi, *State Law as Islamic Law in Modern Egypt: The Incorporation of the Sharīʿa into Egyptian Constitutional Law* (Leiden: Brill, 2006).

14 For example, *Egyptian Supreme Constitutional Court Case* No. 62, Judicial Year 19, 12 SCC 92–110 (Nov. 2006) (citing and applying Qurʾānic verses and legal canons on contractual performance to uphold a challenged property law statute); *Case No. 23*, 12 SCC 307–13 (Apr. 2007) (citing Qurʾānic verses and historical juristic interpretations of family law provisions to uphold an Art. 2 "*sharīʿa* clause" challenge to alimony requirements of personal status law reforms); *Case No. 45*, 12 SCC 1359–72 (Nov. 2009) (citing legal

As I use the phrase, the founding period for Islamic law begins with the legal developments articulated and attributed to the Prophet and other authoritative figures during Islam's first three centuries (seventh–ninth centuries): the "early founding period," or simply, the "early period." Authoritative figures during this first phase included the Prophet's companions for Sunnīs, his family members – especially the Imāms – for the Shīʿa, the associates of each group, and other learned scholars who took charge of matters of Islamic law and religion. Some of these scholars were the early jurists whom Islamic legal historians later dubbed the "founders" of Sunnī Islam's multiple legal schools. The founding period ends with a second phase that saw the systematization and "textualization" of Islamic substantive law, legal theory, and core legal maxims during the next two centuries (tenth and eleventh centuries): the "late founding period."[15] This second phase

canons and Islamic principles in upholding personal status law reforms requiring that marriages be registered to be recognized as valid). For an annotated translation of one SCC case, see Nathan J. Brown and Clark B. Lombardi, "Translation: The Supreme Constitutional Court of Egypt on Islamic Law, Veiling and Civil Rights: An Annotated Translation of Supreme Constitutional Court of Egypt Case No. 8 of Judicial Year 17 (May 18, 1996)," *American University International Law Review* 23 (2006), 379–436 (analysis), 437–60 (translation). For an analysis suggesting that these judges continued this approach after the regime change of July 3, 2013, see Nathan Brown, "Egypt: A Constitutional Court in an Unconstitutional Setting" (unpublished paper presented at New York University Law School Constitutional Transitions Colloquium, Oct. 23, 2013).

15 Rather than the more common but contested term among Islamic law specialists, "formative period," I use "founding period" to refer to legal developments from the beginning of Islam through the systematization and textualization of Islamic substantive law, legal theory, and core legal maxims for the reasons stated here. On the contested definitions and alternative designations of the "formative period" particularly as applied to Sunnī law, see, for example, Noel Coulson, *A History of Islamic Law* (Edinburgh: Edinburgh University Press, 1964) (dating that period to the beginning of the fourth/tenth century); Norman Calder, *Studies in Early Muslim Jurisprudence* (Oxford: Clarendon Press, 1993) (identifying the rise of the short law compendium, the *mukhtaṣar*, and the beginning of the period of *taqlīd* as the end of the formative period at the fourth/tenth to fifth/eleventh centuries); Mohammad Fadel, "The Social Logic of *Taqlīd* and the Rise of the *Mukhtaṣar*," *Islamic Law and Society* 3, 2 (1996), 195–233 (noting that the rise of the *mukhtaṣar* in Mālikī law did not occur until the seventh/thirteenth century and offering a different account of its meaning: as a "codification" and systematization of Islamic law into a system of knowable rules between non-binding common law and civil law); Jonathan Brockopp, *Early Mālikī Law: Ibn ʿAbd Al-Ḥakam and His Major Compendium of Jurisprudence* (Leiden: Brill, 2000) (dating the formative period to a time between the third/ninth and fifth/eleventh centuries with the rise of the *mukhtaṣar* and with jurists self-consciously referring to themselves as members of eponymically named schools of law); Wael Hallaq, *The Origins and Evolution of Islamic Law* (Cambridge: Cambridge University Press, 2005) (revising Joseph Schacht's placement of the end of formative period in the third/ninth century, placing it in the fourth/tenth century, and defining it as "that historical period in which the legal system arose from rudimentary beginnings and then developed to the point at which its constitutive features had acquired an identifiable shape").

coincides with the so-called closing of the gates of *ijtihād*, a phrase that Sunnī Muslim jurists created to signal the settling of their legal schools and to suggest that they were applying God's rule rather than human interpretive discretion.[16] The history of doubt demonstrates that at least one significant foundational text and legal maxim was still in formation and flux during this founding period, suggesting that others were as well.

After this period, it is not that interpretation ended as the theory of closed gates suggests. Rather, Sunnī jurists sought to close the canon of foundational texts in their efforts to systematize Islamic law and place it more on a foundation of shared *textual* bases of authority than it had been in the previous era – when regional or judicial practice, charismatic authority, and local norms often prevailed. Put differently, the so-called gate-closing of Islam's late founding period signified the moment when Sunnī Muslim jurists – in the process of their attempts at systematizing Islamic law and legal theory – turned increasingly to the authority of texts and authoritative modes of interpretation, by which they simultaneously added to the textual corpus in textualizing legal maxims such as the doubt canon.

While the centuries of Islam's founding may now seem quite remote, the notion that Muslims look to that period as a source of legal authority should not sound strange to anyone familiar with the American legal tradition. Americans frequently appeal to the Founding Fathers from the eighteenth century to make arguments about the meaning of the U.S. Constitution today. Similarly, given the enormous weight of Islam's early period for defining power and authority in the Muslim world today, anyone interested in uncovering the possibilities and perils of Islamic law in modern times is best served by understanding its history. In short, inasmuch as harsh punishment presents the most barbed and thus challenging face of Islamic law, to understand Islamic criminal law's past is to better grasp its present. This book pursues that task.

A second reason relates to the importance of doubt in the structure of criminal justice more broadly, not only for Islamic law but also for

[16] The phrase led many modern historians incorrectly to accept that fiction as an actual end of interpretation in Islamic law. For further discussion of the "gates of *ijtihād*" and the "regime of *taqlīd*," see Chapter 5, nn. 90–93 and accompanying text. See also, for example, Baber Johansen, "Legal Literature and the Problem of Change: The Case of the Land Rent," *Islam and Public Law*, ed. Chibli Mallat (London: Graham and Trotman, 1993), 29–47 (repr. in Baber Johansen, *Contingency in a Sacred Law: Legal and Ethical Norms in the Muslim Fiqh* (Leiden: Brill, 1999), 446–64) (arguing that legal change after this period came through commentaries and *fatāwā* literature, while the basic texts of the law treatises preserved the traditional opinions).

American law when both are examined comparatively. As comforting as certainty may be, in law it is much too often elusive.[17] Doubt pervades "open-textured" laws and becomes alarming when it arises in criminal law.[18] In this high-stakes area of law, the criminal process could result in unjustified deprivations of life, liberty, or property flowing from dubious convictions.[19] A challenge to any system of criminal law, doubt – if unheeded by operation of the doubt canon in Islamic law – could result in the wanton loss of life or limb. In short, attention to doubt in Islamic and other comparative contexts is important because criminal law tends to center on certainty, which is often in short supply, and because the stakes of getting criminal law decisions wrong are so high.

Before authorizing punishment, other legal traditions typically require knowledge of a crime's commission beyond a reasonable doubt. Roman law began with the legal maxim stipulating that there could be "*nulla poena sine lege*: no punishment without law."[20] Roman law further

[17] See Frederick Schauer, "An Essay on Constitutional Language," in *Interpretive Law and Literature: A Hermeneutic Reader*, ed. Sanford Levinson and Steven Mailloux (Evanston, IL: Northwestern University Press, 1988), 133–54 (describing the difficulty of achieving certainty in legal interpretation). On the "psychological comforts" derived from popular perceptions that textualist "plain meaning" rules necessarily lead to certain, predictable results, see Peter Linzer, "The Comfort of Certainty: Plain Meaning and the Parol Evidence Rule," *Fordham Law Review* 71 (2002), 799–839.

[18] H. L. A. Hart, *The Concept of Law*, 2nd ed. (Oxford: Oxford University Press, 1994) (orig. 1961), 125–28 (highlighting inevitable indeterminacies in general rules, standards, and principles that, "however smoothly they work over the great mass of ordinary cases, will, at some point where their application is in question, prove indeterminate"). See also Friedrich Waismann, "Verifiability," *Proceedings of the Aristotelian Society*, Supplementary Volume 19 (1945), 119–50 (introducing the term "open texture," popularized by Hart, to describe potentially unlimited uncertainties of meaning that arise from an inability to anticipate every possible application of a statement).

[19] See, for example, *United States v. Bass*, 404 U.S. 336, 349 (1971) (noting an "instinctive distaste against men languishing in prison unless the lawmaker has clearly said they should") (quoting Henry J. Friendly, "Mr. Justice Frankfurter and the Reading of Statutes," reprinted in Henry J. Friendly, *Benchmarks* (Chicago: University of Chicago Press, 1967), 196–234, at 209). For the earliest iteration of this theme in U.S. federal law, see *United States v. Hudson & Goodwin*, 11 U.S. (7 Cranch) 32, 34 (1812) (barring federal common law crimes).

[20] For a standard history, see Adolf Schottlaender, *Die geschichtliche Entwicklung des Satzes*: Nulla poena sine lege (Breslau: n.p., 1911). For more recent comparative studies, see Georges Martyn, Anthony Musson, and Heikki Pihlajamäki, eds., *From the Judge's Arbitrium to the Legality Principle: Legislation as a Source of Law in Criminal Trials* (Berlin: Duncker und Humblot, 2013); Stefan Vogenauer and Stephen Weatherill, eds., *The Harmonisation of European Contract Law: Implications for European Private Laws, Business and Legal Practice* (Oxford; Portland, OR: Hart, 2006), esp. 1:584–89 (early continental usage of the principle of legality and *in dubio pro reo* as "benign interpretation") and 2:729–30, 839–41 (early English interpretations).

absorbed the Aristotelian principle "*in dubio pro reo*: [when] in doubt, [judge] in favor of the accused," and this legal maxim took on a life of its own in German and other Continental European contexts.[21] Early English jurors devised strategies to avoid findings of guilt in all but the most egregious criminal offenses.[22] For instance, they expanded the scope of the old "benefit of the clergy" doctrine, which originally exempted members of the Church from the criminal jurisdiction of secular courts, to allow first-time offenders in fourteenth-century ecclesiastical courts to receive more lenient sentences.[23] Prosecutors consistently "downcharged" crimes or "downgraded" the value of stolen goods to arrive at a milder sentence than the statute would have required.[24] Finally, judges regularly barred criminal convictions when the evidence caused significant uncertainty about culpability or fairness.[25] Taken together, the lasting judicial iteration of these schemes became the common law rule of lenity and standard of reasonable doubt: equitable principles of narrowing construction and requirements for factual proof that had become regular English judicial practice by the early eighteenth century.[26] These practices migrated to American law, with Justice John Marshall famously invoking the

21 See Walter Stree, *In dubio pro reo* (Tübingen: Mohr, 1962), esp. chapter 1; Daniela Demko, "*In dubio pro reo* – im Zweifel für den Angeklagten," in *Zweifelsfälle*, ed. Christine Abbt and Oliver Diggelmann (Bern: Stämpfli, 2007), 155–70; Martina Wilke and Heike Pfann, *In dubio pro reo: Risikoklassifikation und risikospezifische Suche nach Risikoentschärfungsoperatoren* (MA thesis, Heidelberg University, 2006). My thanks to Stefan Vogenauer for kindly suggesting these and the previous footnote's references.

22 Jerome Hall, *Theft, Law, and Society* (Boston: Little, Brown, 1935), 92–95 (noting that juries used to "invent technicalities in order to avoid infliction of the capital penalty").

23 See Leona Christine Gabel, *Benefit of Clergy in England in the Later Middle Ages* (New York: Octagon Books, 1969) (orig. 1929); Peter Benson Maxwell, *On the Interpretation of Statutes* (London: W. Maxwell & Son, 1875), 239. See also John Hamilton Baker, *An Introduction to English Legal History*, 4th ed. (London: Butterworths, 2002) (orig. 1971), 513–15 (overview); J.M. Beattie, *Crime and the Courts in England, 1660–1800* (Princeton, NJ: Princeton University Press, 1986), 141–45 (examples); John Langbein, "Shaping the Eighteenth-Century Criminal Trial: A View from the Ryder Sources," *University of Chicago Law Review* 59 (1983), 1–136, at 36–41 (further examples).

24 John Langbein, *The Origins of the Adversary Criminal Trial* (Oxford: Oxford University Press, 2003), 334–35 (citing, inter alia, William Blackstone, *Commentaries on the Laws of England* (Oxford: Clarendon Press, 1765–1769), 4:239); Leon Radzinowicz, *A History of English Law and Its Administration from 1750* (London: Stevens & Sons, 1948), 83–106, 138–64.

25 For the development of reasonable doubt jurisprudence in the English common law and in continental European law, see James Q. Whitman, *The Origins of Reasonable Doubt* (New Haven, CT: Yale University Press, 2008); see also Langbein, *Adversary Criminal Trial*, 334–36.

26 There is debate about when lenity became prevalent, but agreement that it was in full force by the eighteenth century. See Livingston Hall, "Strict or Liberal Construction of Penal

American rule of lenity in *United States v. Wiltberger* in the early nineteenth century: "The rule that penal laws are to be construed strictly is perhaps not much less old than construction itself."[27]

Centuries earlier, comparable doctrines of doubt prevailed in Arabia, North Africa, and other major centers of the new Muslim empire in the form of the doubt canon. As the *Case of the Falsely Accused Butcher* well illustrates, when adjudicating criminal cases, Muslim judges and jurists faced the same *factual*, *legal*, and *moral* doubts that afflicted judges and jurors in European and other legal traditions. The Muslim juristic response was to build an extensive doctrine of doubt, the contours of which have not been explored previously.

The history, justifications, and structures underlying doubt in classical Islamic law were quite different from those of law in the modern world, whether in Muslim-majority lands or in the West. These differences make the comparative examination of Islamic law potentially illuminating for concepts in modern Islamic and American criminal law. Why and how doubt emerged in such different institutional and historical contexts cannot be understood without uncovering the Islamic history of doubt. Other scholars have unearthed that history in the American context. This book takes up that task for Islamic contexts.[28]

A third reason for focusing on the Islamic history of doubt is that it has been nearly forgotten despite its surprising centrality to early Islamic criminal law and to the role of Muslim jurists in constructing it. This history reveals that the doubt canon was one of many legal maxims that historically – in the hands of jurists – played a central, but currently underappreciated role in the construction of Islamic law. Legal maxims, also known as canons of construction, are "rules of thumb used ... to enable interpreters to draw inferences from the language, format, and subject matter" of ambiguous legal texts.[29] Common to many legal traditions – including Roman law, common

Statutes," *Harvard Law Review* 48 (1935), 748–74, at 750, nn. 12–13 (tracing the consistent use of the rule of lenity back to mid-seventeenth-century England); Langbein, *Adversary Criminal Trial*, 335 (noting that the rule predated the eighteenth century but did not become prevalent until then); Whitman, *Reasonable Doubt*, 185–200.

[27] *United States v. Wiltberger*, 18 U.S. 35, 43 (1820); see also *In re Winship*, 397 U.S. 358, 312–63 (1970).

[28] In so doing, it also invites criminal law scholars and comparatists to consider further doubt's broader past and to understand better its present – particularly when it comes to recognizing and considering the value (or lack thereof) of maintaining American divisions of doubt (heuristically separating, inter alia, questions of law from questions of fact and both from considerations of mercy).

[29] William N. Eskridge Jr., Philip Frickey, and Elizabeth Garrett, *Legislation: Statutes and the Creation of Public Policy*, 4th ed. (St. Paul, MN: West, 2006), 847–48. For definitions of

law, and civil law – legal maxims typically express policies of law developed over the course of many cases, which then could be used to decide novel issues when existing legal texts were not dispositive. Islamic legal maxims (*qawāʿid fiqhiyya*) are established principles that ostensibly served these same functions. Stated in concise, pithy form, at least some of these legal maxims have been invoked by Muslim jurists since as early as the seventh century.

The history of doubt is a significant example of the operation and growth of one Islamic legal maxim, as it interacted with other legal maxims and sociolegal rules.[30] Islam's doubt canon spread quickly, achieving a place of prominence in Islamic law very early in its history. Within decades of the Prophet's death, the doubt canon had become so central to Islamic criminal law that, by the end of Islam's first century, the leading jurist of the law school of Kūfa, Ibrāhīm al-Nakhaʿī (d. ca. 96/717), could refer to it as axiomatic.[31] Jurists of succeeding generations did likewise,[32] with leading scholars in every major center of the growing Muslim empire invoking the principle by the middle of the eighth century. By the turn of the ninth century, one scholar announced that the doubt canon was one of the few principles on which all Muslim jurists had reached consensus.[33] Thereafter, the canon was so well entrenched that it featured in popular literature as celebrated as the *Arabian*

various categories of Islamic legal maxims, see ʿAlī Aḥmad al-Nadwī, *al-Qawāʿid al-fiqhiyya* (Damascus: Dār al-Qalam, 1418/1998); for definitions of American legal maxims in what remains a leading treatise in that field, see Jabez Gridley Sutherland, *Statutes and Statutory Construction*, ed. Norman J. Singer, 5th ed. (Chicago: Callaghan, 1992) (orig. 1891); and for Roman legal maxims, see Peter Stein, *Regulae Iuris: From Juristic Rules to Legal Maxims* (Edinburgh: Edinburgh University Press, 1966).

30 For more on the definitions and history of Islamic legal maxims into which the study of doubt fits, see Appendix C ("A Prehistory of Doubt") and Wolfhart Heinrichs, "*Qawāʿid* as a Genre of Legal Literature," in *Studies in Islamic Legal Theory*, ed. Bernard Weiss (Leiden: Brill, 2002), 365–84. For a broad account of the role of doubt as a central feature of Islamic history, including but not limited to law, see Thomas Bauer, *Die Kultur der Ambiguität: Eine andere Geschichte des Islams* (Berlin: Verlag der Weltreligionen, 2011).

31 Several second/eighth- and third/ninth-century sources record Ibrāhīm al-Nakhaʿī's citation of the doubt canon on anonymous authority (i.e., *kānū yaqūlūn*). See Abū Yūsuf (d. 182/798), *Kitāb al-Kharāj*, ed. Muḥammad Ibrāhīm al-Bannā' (Cairo: Dār al-Iṣlāḥ, 1981), 303; ʿAbd al-Razzāq al-Ṣanʿānī (d. 211/826), *Muṣannaf*, ed. Ḥabīb al-Raḥmān al-Aʿẓamī (Beirut: Dār al-Kutub al-ʿIlmiyya, 1972), 8:430; Ibn Abī Shayba (d. 235/849), *Muṣannaf*, ed. Muḥammad b. Ibrāhīm al-Laḥīdān and Ḥamad b. ʿAbd Allāh al-Jumuʿa (Riyadh: Maktabat al-Rushd, 2004), 9:359, no. 28966.

32 That is, both proto-Sunnī and Shīʿī jurists (including Abū Ḥanīfa, Mālik, Shāfiʿī, Qāḍī Nuʿmān, and Ibn Bābawayh), as well as earlier authorities in both camps whose opinions are quoted in works such as the *Muṣannaf*s of ʿAbd al-Razzāq and Ibn Abī Shayba on the Sunnī side, and ʿAlī as quoted in the records of his judgments collected by Ibrāhīm b. Hāshim al-Qummī, *Qaḍāyā Amīr al-Muʾminīn*, on the Shīʿī side. See further Chapter 4 and Appendix B.

33 See Ibn al-Mundhir (d. 319/930), *al-Ijmāʿ* (Beirut: Dār al-Jinān, 1986), 132 (*wa-ajmaʿū ʿalā* [...] *darʾ al-ḥadd biʾl-shubahāt*).

Nights.[34] It also featured in noteworthy historical chronicles, such as the one set to verse by an Andalusian historian from a town in what is today Portugal: "The rule of 'avoiding punishment in cases of doubt' / Is a *ḥadīth* reported by all scholars of reputable clout."[35] A *ḥadīth* is a report of the words or actions of Prophet Muḥammad, and it is a foundational text of Islamic law, second only to the Qur'ān.[36] The historian-poet's lyrical statement is thus telling: by the twelfth century in which that historian wrote, and even before, Muslim jurists had come to regard the doubt canon as being prophetic in origin.

It was by no means inevitable that doubt would become central to Islamic criminal law, or for that matter that any such legal maxim would have become as accepted or widespread. Against the Andalusian historian's insistence to the contrary, the doubt canon was once not even regarded as a foundational text, that is, as an authentic prophetic *ḥadīth*.[37] For this reason, the doubt canon was the subject of intense controversy, once vehemently opposed by a minority of jurists who adopted a strict textualist approach to interpretation in Islamic law.[38]

Here, again, a look at analogous debates in American law is instructive. Despite their enormous differences, the American and Islamic legal traditions share at least one significant structural feature: they both place major emphasis on lawmaking only by (an) authorized legislator(s) (that is, "legislative supremacy") based substantially on foundational texts, which in turn manifests as an emphasis on textual fidelity, especially in criminal law.[39] Some

[34] See *Alf layla wa-layla*, ed. Ṭāwūs Ḥājjī Bālṭayyib (Tunis: Wizārat Shu'ūn al-Mar'a wa'l-Usra, n.d.), night 298. For an English account of the *Arabian Nights* story, see Maribel Fierro, "Idra'ū l-ḥudūd bi-l-shubuhāt: When Lawful Violence Meets Doubt," *Hawwa* 5, 2–3 (2007), 208–238, at 208–209. See also Qāḍī al-Tanūkhī (d. 384/994), *Nishwār al-muḥāḍara wa-akhbār al-mudhākara*, ed. 'Abbūd al-Shāljī (Beirut: Dār Ṣādir, 1971–73), 252–54 for an English translation, see D. S. Margoliouth, trans., *The Table Talk of a Mesopotamian Judge* (London: Royal Asiatic Society, 1922) (recording the story wherein Abū Yūsuf used the doubt canon to benefit Hārūn al-Rashīd's family).

[35] Abū al-Ḥasan Ibn Bassām al-Shantarīnī (d. 542/1147), *al-Dhakhīra fī maḥāsin ahl al-Jazīra*, ed. Iḥsān 'Abbās (Beirut: Dār al-Thaqāfa, 1979), 7:355–57 ("*Inna dar'a 'l-ḥudūdi bi'l-shubahāt / la-ḥadīthun rawāhu kullu 'l-thiqāt.*").

[36] For definitions of *ḥadīth* (often equated with or used as a means for discovering the Sunna), see Chapter 1, note 14 and accompanying text.

[37] Throughout, I use "foundational text(s)" or "primary text(s)" to refer to the two basic textual sources in Islamic law: the Qur'ān and the Sunna. See Chapter 1, Section B.

[38] See Part IV.

[39] Central is the principle that only (a) properly authorized legislator(s), whether human or divine, may make laws; and those laws are expressed through legal texts. See Abū al-Ḥasan al-Māwardī (d. 450/1058), *Kitāb al-ḥudūd min al-Ḥāwī al-kabīr*, ed. Ibrāhīm b. 'Alī Ṣanduqjī (Beirut: n.p., 1995), 1:101 (explaining that fixed criminal laws are called *ḥudūd* because of the specified (*maḥdūd*) acts and sanctions designed to prevent people

scholars have pointed out that legal maxims are controversial because they seem to have no specific textual pedigree and can be used as tools in the hands of willful judges to insert their own preferences into the law beyond the literal words of a text. Such objections to legal maxims arose in American law in famously colorful terms, notable here for their resonance with analogous debates in Islamic law. Karl Llewellyn, a prominent American legal realist, vehemently attacked legal maxims for being wholly indeterminate.[40] He complained that for every maxim supporting one interpretation, there was a countermaxim supporting the opposite view. And to prove it, he mapped out a damning thrust-and-parry chart of contradictory maxims commonly used in the courts.[41] His idea was that judges used maxims selectively to reach predetermined results, and he complained that this practice was illegitimate. Llewellyn's critique transformed American legal maxims from supposedly neutral principles that guided and constrained legal interpretation to "conclusory explanations appended after the fact to justify results reached on other grounds."[42] In response, the ensuing decades saw scholars advancing theories of legal interpretation beyond a formalism that appealed only to legal texts and legal canons, theories thereby insulated from Llewellyn-style attacks by more sophisticated understandings of legislative processes and interpretive functions.[43]

from committing specific crimes, just as the outer borders (*ḥudūd*) of a house prevent trespass). Compare *McBoyle v. United States*, 283 U.S. 25, 27 (1931) ("Although it is not likely that a criminal will carefully consider the text of the law before he murders or steals, it is reasonable that a fair warning should be given ... of what the law intends to do if a certain line is passed. To make the warning fair, so far as possible the line should be clear."). For elaboration on this argument, see further my "Islamic Rule of Lenity," 1299–351.

40 Karl N. Llewellyn, "Remarks on the Theory of Appellate Decision and the Rules or Canons about How Statutes Are to be Construed," *Vanderbilt Law Review* 3 (1950). On the legal realist attacks against formalist jurisprudence, beginning in the 1920s and 1930s, see Brian Leiter, "American Legal Realism," in *The Blackwell Guide to the Philosophy of Law and Legal Theory*, ed. Martin P. Golding and William A. Edmundson (Malden, MA; Oxford: Blackwell, 2005), 50–56.

41 Llewellyn, "Rules or Canons," 401–406.

42 Geoffrey P. Miller, "Pragmatics and the Maxims of Interpretation," *1990 Wisconsin Law Review* (1990), 1179–1227, at 1180.

43 Most notable in the attempt to rehabilitate interpretation from the realist critique was the 1950s emergence of the legal process theory of Henry M. Hart Jr. and Albert M. Sacks, *The Legal Process*, ed. William N. Eskridge Jr. and Philip P. Frickey, 10th ed. (Eagan, MN: Foundation Press, 1994) (orig. 1958), and the rise of "new textualism" in the 1980s, as elucidated by John Manning, "Second-Generation Textualism," *California Law Review* 98 (2010), 1287–1318. For an overview of the major periods of statutory interpretation, see Eskridge et al., *Legislation*, 689–846. For a small sampling of further discussion in the vast statutory interpretation literature that usefully focuses on interpretation and legal canons, see Richard A. Posner, "Statutory Interpretation – In the Classroom and in the Courtroom," *University of Chicago Law Review* 50 (1983), 800–23; Frank Easterbrook,

Given similar controversies over legal maxims in Islamic law, what was the basis on which Muslim jurists wielded such seemingly text-flouting discretion in the form of an invocation of doubt, how did the practice become so prevalent, and why? It is primarily in response to these questions that this book explores the nearly forgotten concept of doubt so central to Islamic criminal law. It explores the methods by which Muslim jurists deployed the doubt canon and justified its extensive use during the period stretching from the seventh to the sixteenth century in central Islamic lands. *My fundamental claim is that medieval Muslim jurists, claiming to be textualists, deployed doubt (alongside other extratextual legal maxims) to form a pragmatic method of interpretation that increased their institutional power over law. To accomplish this interpretive task, they articulated ideals of moral values, legal processes, and interpretive authority by which they sought to define the legitimate use of force in Islamic criminal law.*

MEANS AND MOTIVES BEHIND DOUBT

Back to the means and motives. How could Muslim jurists both claim to be textualists and depart from the texts? Why did they? In the course of answering these questions, my goal is to systematically uncover the means and, in the process, to suggest some of the motives for which Muslim jurists managed to convert doctrines of doubt into textual rules.

First, the means. I claim that over the course of eight centuries and through many interpretive debates, Muslim jurists collectively *canonized*, *textualized*, and *generalized* an Islamic doctrine of doubt rooted in early judicial practice. That is, they identified a doctrine of doubt applied in early cases, which – with repetition as a matter of judicial practice – became a legal maxim in its standard, oft-repeated form. These jurists then converted a judicial practice of avoiding punishments in doubtful cases into a legal text requiring it. To accomplish this "textualization" of the canon, the jurists asserted that the Prophet Muḥammad himself had uttered the statement calling on judges to "avoid criminal punishments in cases of doubt."[44] By giving it a prophetic pedigree, these jurists rendered the

"Statutes' Domains," *University of Chicago Law Review* 50 (1983), 533–52; David L. Shapiro, "Continuity and Change in Statutory Interpretation," *New York University Law Review* 67 (1992), 921–60; Einer Elhauge, *Statutory Default Rules: How to Interpret Unclear Legislation* (Cambridge, MA: Harvard University Press, 2008).

44 For discussion of the fairly complex debates about the origins and authenticity of the doubt canon as a *ḥadīth*, see further Chapter 2, and my "Islamic Legal Maxims."

canon into a normative legal text. Having equipped the canon with a textual basis of authority, these same jurists then generalized its import and defined the underlying concept by elaborating a centuries-long, evolving jurisprudence of doubt.

Second, the motives. What explains this radical transformation of the Islamic doctrine of doubt from judicial practice into binding legal text, and its expansion to a general principle that came to dominate and even define Islamic criminal law and procedure? The answer is complex. It has to do with what we may call both external, contextual factors and internal, textual factors relevant to Islamic legal interpretation. External to the Muslim jurists' interpretive project was the overarching structure of institutional power to define Islamic law, over which they were in constant negotiation with ruling authorities. There are two critical points worth noting here to understand the import of that negotiation. First, medieval Muslim jurists, and thus definitions of Islamic law, were neither integrated into nor controlled by the state in the way modern states exert monopoly over law. Second, those jurists were legal scholars distinct from a separate class of state-appointed judges, even though some jurists wore both hats. Thus, there was an interplay between jurists, who defined the law, ruling authorities, who enforced it, and judges, who looked to jurists for definitions of law and to rulers for enforcement of their decisions. Given this configuration of criminal law as an area of public law involving all three types of actors, doubt is an important lens through which we may determine *how* institutional actors historically arrived at mainstream Islam's well-known institutional arrangements that attempted to balance relations between Muslim jurists and political rulers. These institutional structures are laid out in Part I.

Internal to their interpretive project, I argue, was Muslim jurists' use of textual interpretation to define and articulate Islamic legal rules and, in the process, to negotiate institutional relations and a code of moral conduct. This framework applied to Sunnī and Shīʿī jurists alike. Muslim jurists accomplished this task by focusing on three main factors, all of which were presented as their attempts to faithfully serve the divine Lawgiver: the *moral values* to which jurists elected to accord preference in light of changing sociopolitical contexts surrounding criminal law and doubt, the *legal processes* that Muslim jurists designed in multiple schools of interpretation in order to define a "jurisprudence of doubt," and the meaning of textualism and jurists' theology-driven theories of the scope of their own *interpretive authority*.

ORGANIZATION OF THIS BOOK

This book has four parts, each comprising two chapters. After Part I lays the foundation for the content and institutional structures framing Islamic criminal law, each subsequent part explores the three factors noted above by outlining key moments in the jurists' construction of that law through the expansion and eventual contraction of doubt.

In Part I, on institutional structures, Chapter 1 provides the basic outlines of Islamic criminal law through discussion of a landmark case from the Sunnī corpus of reports on the Prophet's lifetime in the early seventh century: the *Case of Māʿiz*. This chapter also reveals the significance of that case to a central theme running through the history of Islamic legal interpretation: debates between Muslim strict textualists and pragmatic textualists as pitched on the battlefield of doubt. Chapter 2 provides an overview of how, within that framework, Muslim jurists came to canonize, textualize, and eventually generalize doubt. It further addresses related institutional questions of how those jurists and political officials divided and shared authority over the public law arena of crime and punishment.

Part II examines the social and moral context surrounding the emergence of the doubt canon in the long founding period of the seventh through eleventh centuries. During this time, the jurists transformed doubt from a judicial practice into a foundational legal text just as they completed the process of systematizing the jurisprudence of Islam's multiple legal schools.[45] Chapter 3 addresses concerns of hierarchy in Islamic criminal law and abuse of the doubt canon to privilege the well-connected and the powerful in the context of the social realities of the medieval Muslim elite. Chapter 4 then examines the competing policies of criminal law enforcement and avoidance that resulted from Muslim jurists' desire to implement God's law despite their moral discomfort with capital punishment, and their related push for a better definition of Islamic criminal procedure by way of the doubt canon.

Part III delves more into the legal process involved in the Sunnī "jurisprudence of doubt," that is, the majority of medieval Muslim jurists' use of doubt to articulate the criminal laws and procedures for situations not addressed by the foundational texts. Chapter 5 identifies ways in which the

[45] On the systematization and "corporate" character of these legal schools in Sunnī law, see Sherman Jackson, *Islamic Law and the State: The Constitutional Jurisprudence of Shihāb al-Dīn al-Qarāfī* (Leiden: Brill, 1996). On the stages of development and systematization of Shīʿī law, see Hossein Modarressi, *An Introduction to Shīʿī Law: A Bibliographical Study* (London: Ithaca Press, 1984), 23–58.

founders of Islam's various legal schools tentatively folded doubt into definitions of criminal law in their legal treatises written between the eighth and tenth centuries, during which time they considered the relevance of doubt to criminal liability on a case-by-case basis. Chapter 6 traces the entrenchment and rapid expansion of doubt to become *the* dominant guiding principle of Islamic criminal law beginning in the eleventh century. This chapter also follows medieval Muslim jurists' elaboration of the concept of doubt in later periods, as they added new types of doubt and theories to justify them both in the course of writing new treatises in the old style of commentaries and by authoring works in a new genre of Islamic legal literature: treatises of legal maxims.

Part IV is about opposition to the doubt canon. This part investigates the relationship between textualism and doubt in the Sunnī and Shīʿī legal corpora to assess the failure of a minority of Muslim jurists who opposed the doctrine of doubt to offer convincing arguments against the majority's theory of divine delegation of interpretive authority, which accommodated both discretion and doubt. Chapter 7 explores how Sunnī strict textualists either grudgingly accepted or altogether rejected doubt, but never managed to prevail in removing doubt from the center of the interpretive process for Islamic criminal law. Chapter 8 examines the theological tenor of similar arguments in Shīʿī law, where strict textualists outright rejected the validity of doubt as an expansive canon, but where doubt persisted nonetheless.

In the end, this history of doubt in Islamic law presents a model of interpretation that substantially adds to conventional narratives of Islamic legal history. This book demonstrates that, instead of a single factor explaining its trajectory, Islamic legal interpretation was driven by several factors continuously at work alongside one another to help shape its main institutional structures. Beyond those *institutional structures* (Part I), three factors were key: *morality and social context* (Part II), *legal-process* concerns attempting to link text with context by articulating jurisprudential schemes to resolve doubt (Part III), and the scope of *interpretive authority* as determined by a theology of divine delegation – or the lack thereof – for Muslim jurists to construe Islam's foundational texts (Part IV).

ON SOURCES AND METHODS

This book contributes to the fields of Islamic legal history and comparative law by combining approaches from intellectual and social history with insights from modern theories of constitutional and statutory interpretation in American law. Importantly, it seeks to expand existing studies of Islamic law in terms of methodology, subject matter, and sources.

Most studies of Islamic law examine *either* intellectual history (focusing on legal doctrine) *or* social history (focusing on legal actors), and none are informed by comparative constitutional and statutory interpretation theory in any depth. In joining these approaches, this book takes Islamic law as a system of law that has much to gain from and offer to comparative law and interpretive legal theory. It speaks to issues of interpretation with which all legal systems are concerned. The book also draws on constitutional and statutory interpretation theory in American law, a field that has witnessed significant advances in recent years. Starting from the basic insight that interpretation helps define and manage institutional relations in a constitutionally defined set of structures in the American context, my study seeks to better detail ways in which interpretation helps define and manage institutional relations in the quite different structures of Islamic contexts. Further, my study uses the doubt canon to identify and examine comparable processes of interpretation and institutional relations as they play out through interpretation in Islamic criminal law. While this book is a history of Islamic law first and foremost, comparative work occurs through its theoretical approach and through articulation of that history in legal conceptual terms drawn from American legal theory, explicit reference to which is highlighted in Chapters 4 and 8, and otherwise in the margins where most relevant.

This book also differs from most studies of Islamic law by tracing the history and use of the doubt canon as one of many legal maxims important to the construction of Islamic law. English-language scholarship on Islamic legal maxims is sparse. Most studies of Islamic law tend to portray a bipartite arrangement that includes substantive legal rules (*furūʿ al-fiqh*) and formalist jurisprudence (*uṣūl al-fiqh*), without much attention to legal maxims (*qawāʿid al-fiqh*) as the third major genre of Islamic law. Moreover, there have been no English-language monograph-length studies of any single Islamic legal maxim, and the handful of articles in recent years that raise preliminary questions about Islamic legal maxims do so mainly with respect to Sunnī law only.[46] Counter to that treatment in English-language scholarship, in recognition of the importance of legal

[46] See Mohammad Hashim Kamali, "Legal Maxims," in *Sharīʿah Law: An Introduction* (Oxford: Oneworld, 2008), 141–61; Mohammad Hashim Kamali, "Legal Maxims and Other Genres of Literature in Islamic Jurisprudence," *Arab Law Quarterly* 20, 1 (2006), 77–101; see also Wolfhart Heinrichs, "Ḳawāʿid Fiḳhiyya," in *EI*² Supplement (Leiden: Brill, 2008–), 517–18. For a translation of a Persian article providing an overview of

maxims, the body of literature on the subject in Arabic and other Near Eastern languages has seen rapid growth in recent decades. These publications, however, are of limited historical insight because they build on the traditional doctrinal approach of medieval Islamic treatises on the subject: identifying core legal maxims, discussing the legal bases for each, and providing examples of their application in particular schools of law.[47] To be sure, a number of Arabic and Persian publications have focused on individual legal maxims, including a few on the doubt canon itself.[48] But such works also tend to catalog and describe those legal maxims without addressing their origins, interpretive differences, or institutional and social contexts.

In contrast, this book examines the role of doubt in Islamic law and jurisprudence in surrounding sociopolitical contexts, that is, with an eye on law and society, for which it draws on a wide range of sources. From the corpus of Islamic legal literature, I have consulted the earliest extant sources of Islamic law for their treatments of legal maxims, including *ḥadīth* collections, legal treatises, judicial manuals, and jurisprudential works from the first three centuries of Islamic law – all from both Sunnī and Shīʿī circles. I also consulted the main sources for each legal school in the later sources for the period under review, including – for the first time – consideration of treatises on legal maxims that arose toward the end of Islam's founding period in addition to the later renditions of the types of

legal maxims in Shīʿī law, see Muṣṭafā Muḥaqqiq Dāmād, "The Codification of Islamic Juridical Principles," *Ḥikmat* 1, 1 (1995), 89–107. For applications of legal maxims in contemporary criminal law contexts, see Luqman Zakariyah, *Applications of Legal Maxims in Islamic Criminal Law with Special Reference to Shariah Law in Northern Nigeria (1999–2007)* (PhD diss., University of Wales, 2009), and a series of articles building on it.

47 For a partial list, see Heinrichs, "*Qawāʿid* as a Genre of Legal Literature."

48 I am aware of five articles and four monographs on the doubt canon (besides my own). The articles include Riḍā Ustādī, "Qāʿidah-i darʾ," *Fiqh-i Ahl-i Bayt* 34 (1382/2005), 46–71 (Part 1), and vol. 37 (1383/2005), 71–94 (Part II); Muḥammad Bahrāmī, "Barrasī va taḥlīl-i fiqhī va ḥuqūqī-i qāʿidah-i '*Tudraʾ al-ḥudūd biʾl-shubahāt*,'" *Dīdgāhhā-yi ḥuqūqī* 5–6 (1376/1997–8), 19–56; [Muḥammad] Mūsawī Bujnūrdī, "Dū qāʿidah-i fiqhī: Qāʿidah-i '*Tudraʾ al-ḥudūd biʾl-shubahāt*,'" *Faṣlnāmah-i dīdgāhhā-yi ḥuqūqī* 8 (1365/1986–7), 11–36; Muḥammad Muḥammadī Gīlānī, "Āshināʾī bā qāʿidah-i '*al-Ḥudūd tudraʾ biʾl-shubahāt*,'" *Majallah-i qaḍāʾī va ḥuqūqī-i dādgustarī-i Jumhūrī-i Islāmī-i Īrān* 5, 15–16 (1375/1996–7), 25–30; and Maribel Fierro, "When Lawful Violence Meets Doubt," 208–38. The monographs include Saʿīd Manṣūrī, *Qavāʿid-i fiqh: Bakhsh-i jazāʾī – fiqh-i taṭbīqī-i qāʿidah-i darʾ* (Tehran: Tadbīr, 1375/1997); Saʿīd b. Misfir al-Daghghār al-Wādiʿī, *Athar al-shubahāt fī darʾ al-ḥudūd* (Riyadh: Maktabat al-Tawba, 1998); ʿAqīla Ḥusayn, *al-Shubahāt al-musqiṭa liʾl-ḥudūd aw al-ẓurūf al-mukhaffifa waʾl-aʿdhār al-musqiṭa liʾl-ʿuqūbāt al-mutarattaba ʿalā jarāʾim al-ḥudūd: Dirāsa fiqhiyya muqārana ʿalā ʾl-madhāhib al-Sunniyya* (Beirut: Dār Ibn Ḥazm, 2003); Muḥammad Ḥasan al-Rabbānī, *Qāʿidat al-darʾ* (Qum: Muʾassasat al-Nashr al-Islāmī al-Tābiʿa li-Jāmiʿat al-Mudarrisīn, 1428/2007–2008). Among these works, Maribel Fierro's article is an exception as it takes a law and society approach.

sources just mentioned.[49] Supplementing the legal literature, I have further consulted relevant sources that provide richer context for the intellectual and social history of doubt: biographical dictionaries of jurists and judges, heresiographical works of early Islamic figures, historical chronicles, literary sources, and theological works.

Furthermore, this book covers a wide chronological and geographical range, spanning the seventh through sixteenth centuries in the central Islamic lands. The specific geographical focus is on the major centers of the Muslim world during its early period: the "eastern" lands of Egypt, Iran and Iraq, and Greater Syria, and the "western" lands of present-day North Africa and Spain. A study this broad-ranging does not offer a comprehensive picture of Islamic criminal law's application, nor do the available sources allow it. The sources also do not allow general conclusions about whether the jurists' efforts to constrain political excess were successful. What the sources do allow is an assessment of the evolving role of doubt in Islamic legal history, of which the history of Islamic legal maxims is a significant part. By the sixteenth century, the period with which this book concludes, doubt appeared to be far more pervasive and of far more benefit to the historical evolution of Islamic law and society than certainty.

To be sure, certainty has long provided a firm theoretical starting point for Muslim jurists seeking to define Islamic law. But from a legal historical perspective, it is doubt that provides the lens through which scholars today can comprehend the moral, interpretive, and institutional means by which early Muslim jurists constructed Islamic criminal law. As one legal philosopher trenchantly remarked about American law, "quixotic quests for certainty are likely to interfere with more fruitful quests for an intelligent understanding of the causes and management of uncertainty."[50] This observation applies no less to Islamic law. Accordingly – with an eye on the high-stakes, constitutional consequences of interpretive difficulties associated with crime and punishment – this study of Islamic legal interpretation and criminal law is not about certainty. It is about uncertainty, ambiguity, and doubt.

[49] Specifically, I examined the sources for the major Sunnī and Shīʿī schools, with some reference to minority schools (including the Ibāḍī, Ismāʿīlī, Ẓāhirī, and Zaydī traditions) where significant to the larger narrative.

[50] Schauer, "Constitutional Language," 153.

PART I

ISLAMIC INSTITUTIONAL STRUCTURES AND DOUBT, FIRST/SEVENTH–TENTH/SIXTEENTH CENTURIES

I

The God of Severity and Lenity

A. THE RECURRING *CASE OF MĀʿIZ*

A man by the name of Māʿiz was a zealous new convert who wished to confess to the crime of adultery. He lived in Medina, not long after the Prophet had arrived there from Mecca to take up leadership over the community in the year 622. By his own account, Māʿiz had committed adultery. Feeling remorseful, he came to the Prophet, who presided over criminal cases in his capacity as new leader of the small town. Māʿiz confessed, begging the Prophet to punish him.

This was a serious matter. If his confession were to be believed, Māʿiz had violated the Islamic law against adultery and would be liable for punishment by flogging, imprisonment, or even – according to the interpretation of most later Muslim jurists – death. The Qurʾān prohibits fornication and adultery (both called *zinā*) and directs judges to flog "those who commit *zinā*, whether female or male, one hundred times each."[1] In addition, although stoning was not a Qurʾānic punishment, early Muslims understood the Sunna to also authorize death by stoning for adultery convictions.[2]

The Prophet initially sent Māʿiz away, declining to hear the case. Māʿiz came back a second time and a third, each time renewing his confession and requesting punishment, each time with the same result. On the fourth time, the Prophet finally spoke. He asked some of Māʿiz's neighbors whether the defendant was of sound mind, to which they replied that he was. The Prophet then suggested that Māʿiz had not committed adultery within the full meaning of the term, but perhaps had merely "kissed or winked or looked at" another woman. Māʿiz

[1] Qurʾān, 24:2. See also Qurʾān, 17:32 ("Do not come close to fornication or adultery (*zinā*). It is a shameful act, sinful, and it paves the way to other evils."

[2] On the introduction of reports about stoning as a Qurʾānic punishment, see Hossein Modarressi, "Early Debates on the Integrity of the Qurʾān: A Brief Survey," *Studia Islamica* 77 (1993), 5–39.

> insisted that he was of sound mind and had committed adultery within the full meaning of the term.[3]
>
> Eventually, the Prophet found Māʿiz guilty, but did not punish him. In fact, he seems to have said nothing about the punishment initially. Not waiting for specific instructions from the Prophet, the townspeople themselves decided to enforce the harsher of the punishments: death by stoning. When they informed the Prophet of what they had done, he exclaimed in dismay that they "should have let Māʿiz go!" He further remarked that if Māʿiz had repented, "God surely would have accepted his repentance."[4]

From his statements, it appears that the Prophet had been reluctant to punish Māʿiz. It was quite possible that Māʿiz would repent of the crime, a prospect for which the Prophet preferred to avoid punishment.[5] In other words, the Prophet – who of all people should have been beholden to following God's commands – was willing to set aside a strict reading of the text. Even though he had convicted Māʿiz, the Prophet had "doubt" – as later Muslim jurists would term it – about whether punishment was due.

The *Case of Māʿiz* was of central concern to Sunnī Muslim jurists and, together with other early cases, to the development of Islamic criminal law itself. The case was featured in the criminal law sections of all major Sunnī *ḥadīth* collections from the eighth through eleventh centuries.[6] These *ḥadīth* collections, the vast majority of which discuss the *Case of Māʿiz* in sections on criminal law, in turn provided the raw materials for major treatises of Islamic law and politics from the eighth century to the present

3 For an early report of the case, see Ibn Abī Shayba, *Muṣannaf*, 9:413–14, 418 (nos. 29240, 29241, 21254). See also Muḥammad b. Ismāʿīl al-Bukhārī, *Ṣaḥīḥ*, no. 6438, in Aḥmad b. ʿAlī Ibn Ḥajar al-ʿAsqalānī, *Fatḥ al-bārī: sharḥ Ṣaḥīḥ al-Bukhārī*, ed. Ṭāhā ʿAbd al-Raʾūf Saʿd et al. (Cairo: Maktabat al-Kulliyyāt al-Azhariyya, 1994).

4 See Ibn Abī Shayba, *Muṣannaf*, 9:413–14, 418.

5 The other ninth-century sources collecting prophetic reports of early "cases" like these are replete with similar stories of individual confessions and hesitance to punish. See, for example, Bukhārī, *Ṣaḥīḥ*, no. 6437 (reporting that a man came to the Prophet confessing to having committed a serious crime multiple times, until the Prophet responded that his participation in congregational prayers indicated repentance, so God had forgiven him).

6 For a precanonical collection, see Ibn Abī Shayba, *Muṣannaf*, 9:550; for a canonical collection, see Bukhārī, *Ṣaḥīḥ*, no. 6438. See also Māwardī, *Kitāb al-ḥudūd min al-Ḥāwī*, 1:206–207, n. 1, which lists other major *ḥadīth* sources, including collections by ʿAbd al-Razzāq (d. 211/826), Aḥmad Ibn Ḥanbal (d. 241/855), Dārimī (d. 255/869), Abū Dāwūd (d. 275/889), Tirmidhī (d. 279/892), Ibn Mājah (d. 303/915), Ibn al-Mundhir (d. 319/930), Ṭaḥāwī (d. 321/933), Ṭabarānī (d. 360/970), al-Ḥākim al-Naysābūrī (d. 405/1015–6), and Bayhaqī (d. 458/1066).

day.[7] Disputes about this case also appeared in manuals for judging, advisory opinions on criminal law issued by expert jurists to resolve difficult cases, collections of legal maxims, and historical chronicles and biographical dictionaries that offer anecdotal evidence of Islamic criminal trials and punishment. In short, in Sunnī discussions of Islamic criminal law, the *Case of Māʿiz* was ubiquitous.

But *why* so much ado about Māʿiz?

B. FOUNDATIONS BENEATH MĀʿIZ: ISLAMIC CRIMINAL LAW

The *Case of Māʿiz* was significant because the Prophet's apparent inclination to avoid punishment seemed to challenge the idea of God as the supreme Lawgiver, which was the starting point of Islamic law. That is, through the message of Islam, the Prophet sought to establish a new moral-legal order with God as legislator and himself as exponent of divine law. That law took shape in the form of the Qurʾān and the Prophet's words and actions elaborating on it (the Sunna). In that vein, several verses in the Qurʾān instruct Muslims to "obey God and his Messenger,"[8] promising eternal reward for those who do so.[9] An important *ḥadīth* further elaborates a theological-jurisprudential duty of obedience: "The 'right'

[7] For a sampling of discussions in legal treatises, in chronological order, see Abū Yūsuf (d. 182/798), *Ikhtilāf Abī Ḥanīfa wa-Ibn Abī Laylā*, ed. Abū al-Wafāʾ al-Afghānī (Hyderabad: Maṭbaʿat al-Wafāʾ, 1357/1938–9), 156; Abū Yūsuf, *Kitāb al-Āthār*, ed. Abū al-Wafāʾ al-Afghānī (Hyderabad: Lajnat Iḥyāʾ al-Maʿārif al-Nuʿmāniyya, 1355/1936–7), 157; Muḥammad b. Idrīs al-Shāfiʿī (d. 204/820), *Kitāb al-Umm*, ed. Aḥmad Badr al-Dīn Ḥassūn (n.p.: Dār Qutayba, 1996), 7:498; Abū Bakr al-Rāzī al-Jaṣṣāṣ (d. 370/981), *Aḥkām al-Qurʾān*, ed. Muḥammad al-Ṣādiq Qamḥawī (Beirut: Dār Iḥyāʾ al-Turāth al-ʿArabī, n.d.), 2:108, 3:263–64; Abū al-Ḥasan al-Māwardī, *Kitāb al-ḥudūd min al-Ḥāwī*, 1:206–207; Abū al-Ḥusayn Aḥmad b. Muḥammad al-Qudūrī (d. 428/1037), *Tajrīd: al-Mawsūʿa al-fiqhiyya al-muqārana*, ed. Muḥammad Aḥmad al-Sirāj and ʿAlī Jumuʿa Muḥammad (Cairo: Dār al-Salām, 2004), 11:5891, 5949–50; Ibn Ḥazm, *al-Muḥallā biʾl-āthār*, ed. ʿAbd al-Ghaffār Sulaymān al-Bandārī (Beirut: Dār al-Kutub al-ʿIlmiyya, 1988), 8:252, 12:18–22; Burhān al-Dīn al-Marghīnānī (d. 593/1197), *al-Hidāya: sharḥ Bidāyat al-mubtadiʾ*, ed. Muḥammad Muḥammad Tāmir and Ḥāfiẓ ʿĀshūr Ḥāfiẓ (Cairo: Dār al-Salām, 2000), 2:735–36; Ibn Abī al-Qāsim (d. 624/1226), *al-Wāḍiḥ fī sharḥ Mukhtaṣar al-Khiraqī*, ed. ʿAbd al-Malik b. ʿAbd Allāh b. Duhaysh (Beirut: Dār Khiḍr, 2000), 4:413; Ibn al-Qayyim, *Ṭuruq*, ed. Nāyif b. Aḥmad al-Ḥamad (Mecca: Dār ʿĀlam al-Fawāʾid, 1428/2007), 87; Ibn Abī al-ʿIzz (d. 792/1390), *al-Tanbīh ʿalā mushkilāt al-Hidāya*, on the margins of *Hidāya* by Burhān al-Dīn al-Marghīnānī, ed. Anwar Ṣāliḥ Abū Zayd (Beirut: Dār al-Kutub al-ʿIlmiyya, 2007), 4:128.

[8] See Qurʾān, 3:32, 132; 5:92; 8:1, 20, 46; 24:54; 47:3; 49:14; 58:13; 64:12; see also Qurʾān, 4:59 (adding instructions for Muslims to also obey "those in authority among you: *wa-ulī ʾl-amri minkum*").

[9] See Qurʾān, 4:13, 69; 24:52; 33:71; 48:17.

(*ḥaqq*) of God vis-à-vis His servants is that they worship Him and do not associate any partners with Him, and the 'right' of individuals vis-à-vis God is that whoever refrains from associating partners with Him will not be punished."[10] These statements – located in Islam's foundational texts – reflect the desires of early Muslims to build a community that cohered around an ideal of submission to the will of a God represented by the Prophet and others in positions of authority who, at Islam's inception, were both political and religious-moral leaders. Building on these fundamentals, Muslims across time have conceived of God as the sole Legislator,[11] and of implementing His law (as expounded by the Prophet) as their sacred duty.[12] In other words, Islam was a tradition that promoted a core idea of *divine legislative supremacy*.

Yet the nuance with which medieval Muslim jurists approached that ideal is shrouded in a history not of certainty, but of doubt. Those dynamics played out notably in Islamic criminal law.

[10] See Bukhārī, *Ṣaḥīḥ*, in Ibn Ḥajar al-ʿAsqalānī, *Fatḥ al-bārī*, 12:8–9, no. 2856. See also Muslim b. al-Ḥajjāj (d. 261/875), *Ṣaḥīḥ*, ed. Muḥammad Fu'ād ʿAbd al-Bāqī (Cairo: Dār Iḥyā' al-Kutub al-ʿArabiyya, 1375/1955–6), 1:58–59, nos. 48–51 (with variations); Tirmidhī, *Sunan* (n.p.: 1965–69), 7:298–99; Ibn Mājah, *Sunan*, ed. Maḥmūd Muḥammad Maḥmūd Ḥasan Naṣṣār (Beirut: Dār al-Kutub al-ʿIlmiyya, 1998), 5:668–69, no. 4296.

[11] The conception comes directly from the Qur'ān, which states repeatedly, "The Law comes only from God: *Ini 'l-ḥukmu illā li'llāh*." Qur'ān, 6:57, 12:40, 12:67; see also ibid., 6:62 ("Surely, the law belongs to God [alone]: *alā lahu 'l-ḥukm*"). Islamic jurisprudential literature and Muslim political movements, from the seventh century through the twenty-first century, regularly deploy derivative statements proclaiming divine sovereignty. See Bernard Weiss, *The Spirit of Islamic Law* (Salt Lake City: University of Utah, 1998), 36 (citing, inter alia, "God is the [sole] Lawgiver: *al-Ḥākim huwa 'llāh*.").

[12] Muslim theologians and jurists had a relatively straightforward answer to the old philosophical question of why follow the law: God required it through Islam's foundational texts – namely, the Qur'ān and prophetic edicts. The only step necessary to trigger the positivist "rule of recognition" for the authoritativeness of those texts was to recognize God as a deity who sent Muḥammad as His Prophet. On the general regard for the Qur'ān and Sunna as Islamic sources of "positive" law, see Hugh Kennedy, *The Prophet and the Age of the Caliphates: The Islamic Near East from the Sixth to the Eleventh Century*, 2nd ed. (Harlow: Pearson Education, 1986), 45. On the rule of recognition, see Hart, *Concept of Law*, 94–95 ("[The] 'rule of recognition' ... specif[ies] some feature or features possession of which by a suggested rule is taken as a conclusive affirmative indication that it is a rule of the group to be supported by the social pressure it exerts. The existence of such a rule of recognition ... may, as in the early law of many societies, be no more than the fact that an authoritative list or text of the rules is to be found in a written document or carved on some public monument.... [Reducing all rules to writing in one place] is not itself the crucial step, though it is a very important one: what is crucial is the acknowledgement of reference to the writing or inscription as *authoritative*, i.e., as the *proper* way of disposing of doubts as to the existence of the rule.").

1. The Theory of Islamic Criminal Law as Divine Legislation

In Islamic criminal law, issues concerning the authority to interpret and enforce the law are pronounced. Muslims believed God to have legislated in the foundational sources a series of fixed, mandatory criminal sanctions called *ḥudūd* laws. The term *ḥudūd* (sg. *ḥadd*) refers to both the major crimes and their associated punishments in Islamic criminal law. According to Islamic legal theory, God Himself specified these laws in Islam's foundational legal texts, the Qur'ān and the Sunna. Moreover, as sole Lawgiver, He required strict adherence to these laws and barred discretion over matters of punishment for their violation. Observing that legislation was a matter of fulfilling "God's rights."[13]

For Muslims, Sunnīs and Shī'a alike, *ḥudūd* laws represented a subset of divine legislation, the expression of which the Prophet and other authority figures were merely a conduit. Not even the Prophet, much less Shī'ī Imāms or Sunnī authority figures – including judges and jurists – had the discretion to diverge even slightly from the letter of the *ḥudūd* laws. The Qur'ān and the Sunna together were taken as normative and thus form the foundational, or "constitutional," sources of legislation for Islamic law.[14] In theory, those foundational, constitutional sources were both first and final.

[13] While "*ḥudūd*" refers to punishments in the context of Islamic criminal law, in the conventional language of the jurists it came to refer to the laws surrounding the prohibitions as well, in that the commission of specific criminal acts triggered fixed punishments. For more detailed overviews of *ḥudūd* and other types of criminal law, see sources listed in the Introduction, notes 2 and 3. On the notion of God's rights (*ḥuqūq Allāh*), see Anver M. Emon, "*Ḥuqūq Allāh* and *Ḥuqūq al-'Ibād*: A Legal Heuristic for a Natural Rights Regime," *Islamic Law and Society* 13, 3 (2006), 325–91; Miriam Hoexter, Shmuel N. Eisenstadt, and Nehemia Levtzion, eds., *The Public Sphere in Muslim Societies* (Albany, NY: State University of New York Press, 2002); Weiss, *Spirit of Islamic Law*, 181–84; Miriam Hoexter, "*Ḥuqūq Allāh* and *Ḥuqūq al-'Ibād* as Reflected in the *Waqf* Institution," *Jerusalem Studies in Arabic and Islam* 19 (1995), 133–56; Mohammad Hashim Kamali, "Fundamental Rights of the Individual: An Analysis of *Ḥaqq* (Right) in Islamic Law," *American Journal of Social Sciences* 10, 3 (1993), 340–65; Baber Johansen, "Sacred and Religious Elements in Hanafite Law – Function and Limits of the Absolute Character of Government Authority," in *Islam et politique au Maghreb*, ed. Abdallah Hamoudi et al. (Paris: Centre National de la Recherche Scientifique, 1981), 281–303. See further sources cited in Emon, "*Ḥuqūq Allāh*," 330, nn. 12–17.

[14] Alongside these foundational sources, Muslim jurists identified an additional two "interpretive" sources for a set of four main sources of Islamic law. For Sunnīs, the four principal sources of law include the Qur'ān, Sunna (prophetic practice – typically contained in reports of the Prophet's words and actions, called *ḥadīth*), consensus (*ijmā'*), and analogical reasoning (*qiyās*); and for the Shī'a, they include the Qur'ān, Sunna (normative prophetic and imāmic practice), consensus, and reason (*'aql*). For discussions, see Mohammad Hashim Kamali, *Principles of Islamic Jurisprudence*, rev. ed. (Cambridge: Islamic Texts

Within that rubric, Muslim jurists argued that *ḥudūd* laws were so explicit and specific that adherence to them provided a prime example of upholding divine legislative supremacy. In private law, these same jurists often contended that God had permitted wide latitude for human discretion by the generality with which guidelines regulating commercial law or family law arrangements, for example, were phrased. But for the public-law arena of criminal law, the jurists concluded that the specificity of the foundational texts meant that no one – neither political nor religious-legal authorities – could make or alter *ḥudūd* laws. The theory was clear: *ḥudūd* laws came from God, and humans were barred from exercising any discretion over them. As one prominent eleventh-century Muslim jurist put it, "it is impermissible to increase or decrease" the scope of *ḥudūd* crimes or their associated punishments.[15]

2. Three Types of Criminal Offenses: *Ḥudūd*, *Qiṣāṣ*, and *Taʿzīr*

The well-ordered theory of Islamic criminal law as a set of explicit divinely legislated crimes with specific penalties was at odds with the reality. In the practice of medieval Muslim jurists and judges, *ḥudūd* laws were neither entirely specific nor exhaustive, and they did not always find their origins in the recognized foundational texts.

To begin with, medieval Muslim jurists found it difficult to determine the proper or *legitimate* definition and application of criminal laws because of the often indeterminate nature of Islamic legal texts.[16] The Qur'ān was a single, static text but sparse on details of law.[17] The more

Society, 1991), 16–116, 228–305; Bernard Weiss, *The Search for God's Law* (Salt Lake City: University of Utah, 1992), 151–258; Modarressi, *Introduction to Shīʿī Law*, 2.

15 Abū al-Ḥasan al-Māwardī, *Kitāb al-ḥudūd min al-Ḥāwī*, 1:100–101.

16 Other scholars have recognized the link between Muslim jurists and legitimacy. For example, Noah Feldman, *Fall and Rise of the Islamic State* (Princeton, NJ: Princeton University Press, 2008), 2; Wael Hallaq, *Authority, Continuity, and Change in Islamic Law* (Cambridge: Cambridge University Press, 2001), 159–83. But none has examined closely those jurists' use of interpretation to define institutional roles, the elaboration of that process in significant part through criminal law, or the reasons that explain or justify these moves. In the course of arguing that Muslim jurists used specific interpretive maneuvers to expand their power over criminal law and to limit that of the executive, this chapter explores how jurists came to be so central to defining the law, and the next four chapters will – through examining the growth of the doubt doctrine – demonstrate how and why they pursued this strategy in one area of law.

17 See Roy P. Mottahedeh, introduction to *Lessons in Islamic Jurisprudence* by Muḥammad Bāqir al-Ṣadr (Oxford: Oneworld, 2003), 1 ("[O]ut of over six thousand verses in the Qur'ān, there were only five hundred verses with legal content. … Out of these five hundred verses, there are about one hundred and ninety that deal with non-ritual aspects of the law.").

detailed body of Sunna was known through collections of scattered *ḥadīth* reports of often dubious authenticity and ambiguous meaning. Moreover, the *ḥadīth* reports often conflicted with one another, and sometimes added to or diverged from Qur'ānic legislation.[18]

Muslim jurists attempted to address the indeterminacies of the texts by delineating three types of criminal offenses: fixed crimes and punishments that according to the theory were specified by the foundational texts (*ḥudūd*), laws of retaliation and financial compensation for homicide and personal injury also drawn from the texts (*qiṣāṣ*), and discretionary penalties for offenses not addressed by the texts (*ta'zīr*).[19] Even with this framework, Muslim jurists and judges were hard-pressed to apply each category with the certainty and specificity that the theory of Islamic criminal law demanded.

The absence of a single code clearly detailing the boundaries of Islamic criminal law presented constant challenges to early Muslim jurists' attempts to define and apply it. The relevance of these challenges to the construction of Islamic law's entire interpretive enterprise cannot be overstated. When jurists and judges attempted to apply these wily sources to specific cases, they discovered that the texts were significantly vague about the scope and definitions of punishable crimes, and resoundingly silent as to whether and how to punish undesirable behavior not mentioned in the texts. Case in point: the purportedly textual basis of *ḥudūd* laws notwithstanding, Muslim jurists did not agree on what this category of criminal offense entailed.[20]

18 The Sunna, the Prophet's life example, is recorded in thousands of disparate reports of the Prophet's words and actions (*ḥadīth*; these include – for Twelver Shīʿī Muslims – reports from a series of twelve Imāms who succeeded the Prophet). For further discussion of the sources of Islamic law, see Kamali, *Principles of Islamic Jurisprudence*, 16–55, 58–60; Modarressi, *Introduction to Shīʿī Law*, 3–4.

19 For overviews of Islamic criminal law and procedure, see Peters, *Crime and Punishment*, and Maḥmaṣānī, *Falsafat tashrīʿ fī 'l-Islām*, as well as ʿAbd al-Qādir ʿAwda, *al-Tashrīʿ al-jināʾī al-Islāmī* (Beirut: Dār al-Kitāb al-ʿArabī, 1968); Ramsīs Behnām, *al-Naẓariyya al-ʿāmma liʾl-qānūn al-jināʾī* (Alexandria: Munshaʾāt al-Maʿārif, 1968); M. Cherif Bassiouni, ed., *The Islamic Criminal Justice System* (London: Oceana, 1982).

20 Medieval Muslim jurists classified crimes differently over time and by school. For one of the earliest classifications, see ʿAbd Allāh Muḥammad al-Jubūrī (d. 157/774), *Fiqh al-Imām al-Awzāʿī* (Baghdad: Maṭbaʿat al-Irshād, 1977), 2:30 (listing six *ḥudūd* crimes: illegal sexual relations, defamation, theft, wine drinking, apostasy, and highway robbery. For a late eleventh-century Shāfiʿī treatment, see Abū Ḥāmid al-Ghazālī (d. 505/1111), *al-Wajīz fī fiqh al-Imām al-Shāfiʿī*, ed. ʿAlī Muʿawwaḍ and ʿĀdil ʿAbd al-Mawjūd (Beirut: Dār al-Arqam, 1997), 2:163 (listing seven *ḥudūd* crimes: the previous six along with rebellion). For a twelfth-century Mālikī treatment, see Ibn Rushd al-Ḥafīd (d. 595/1198), *Bidāyat al-mujtahid* (Beirut: Dār al-Kutub al-ʿIlmiyya, 2000), 2:297 (listing eight *ḥudūd* crimes: the seven listed by Ghazālī plus retaliation laws for murder or personal injury (*qiṣāṣ*)). For further discussion of medieval criminal law classifications, juristic debates about which

a. Ḥudūd *Laws: Serious Felonies, Egregious Moral Wrongs*

Muslim jurists agreed that *ḥudūd* laws criminalized at least four acts: (1) illicit sexual relations (*zinā*: both fornication and adultery),[21] (2) defamation (*qadhf*: specifically, slanderous accusations of sexual impropriety),[22] (3) theft (*sariqa*), and (4) wine drinking (*shurb al-khamr*). But there was considerable disagreement about the associated sanctions for each act, on a scale ranging from corporal to capital punishment.[23] For illicit sexual relations, the Qur'ān specified penalties of home confinement or flogging (100 lashes).[24] Muslim jurists understood the *ḥadīth* corpus to authorize stoning for adultery, a norm that the second caliph, ʿUmar, reportedly affirmed emphatically: that those who committed adultery were to receive a penalty of death by stoning.[25] The Qur'ān specified a punishment of flogging (80 lashes) for defamation.[26] It specified a punishment of hand-amputation for theft.[27] And it specified no punishment for wine drinking. Instead, early jurists looked to the *ḥadīth* corpus to determine that a punishment of flogging should apply. The amount was set at 40 lashes according to prophetic practice, but was later increased by the caliph ʿUmar to 80 lashes.[28]

offenses count as *ḥudūd* laws, and contemporary accounts assessing these classical categorizations, see Peters, *Crime and Punishment*, 60–65.

21 Qur'ān, 17:32 ("Do not come close to [committing] *zinā*. It is a shameful act, sinful, and it paves the way to other evils.").

22 For the general prohibition against defaming the character of chaste women, see Qur'ān, 24:4. For the specific rules addressing accusations of illicit behavior against a spouse, see Qur'ān, 24:6–9 ("For those who levy false charges against their spouses, and have no evidence but their own [accusation], their solitary testimony requires four sets of testimony, [sworn with an oath] that, by God, they are solemnly telling the truth, and a fifth [statement] that they solemnly invoke God's curse on themselves if they are lying. But it would avert the punishment from the wife if she bears witness [with an oath] repeated four times that, by God, her husband is lying, and a fifth [statement] that she solemnly invokes God's wrath on herself if [her accuser] is telling the truth.").

23 See Peters, *Crime and Punishment*, 53–65.

24 See Qur'ānic verses and discussion accompanying note 1.

25 See Modarressi, "Early Debates," 5–39, and discussion accompanying note 2.

26 Qur'ān, 24:4–5 ("And those who levy false charges against chaste women but fail to produce four witnesses [to verify their claim] are to be flogged eighty times, and their testimony is never again to be accepted, for they are wicked transgressors – [that is] unless they repent and mend [their conduct], for God is oft-forgiving, most merciful.").

27 Qur'ān, 5:38–39 ("As to the thief, both male and female, cut off their hands as punishment for what they have done and as an example from God. And God is the almighty, the wise. But if the thief repents after his crime and corrects [his conduct], then God accepts his repentance. For God is oft-forgiving, most merciful.").

28 On the post-prophetic designation of the sanction for wine drinking, see Shāfiʿī, *Umm* (1996), 6:144, 179–81. See Peters, *Crime and Punishment*, 64 (explaining this punishment with reference to the early Islamic notion – attributed to ʿUmar – that a person who drinks

Over time, Muslim jurists collectively also treated a set of three further acts as *ḥudūd* crimes and designated them as capital offenses: (5) highway robbery (*ḥirāba* or *qaṭʿ al-ṭarīq*), (6) apostasy (*ridda*), and (7) blasphemy (which they held to be the equivalent of apostasy and treated as a new and more grave form of defamation, or *qadhf*). The Qurʾān prohibited highway robbery and specified four options for punishment: cross-amputation, crucifixion, exile, or death.[29] As for apostasy and blasphemy, on the one hand, the Qurʾān unequivocally condemned apostasy as an egregious moral-spiritual wrong, but attached no specific criminal punishment to it or to blasphemy. On the other hand, the Qurʾānic laws of war commanded Muslims to fight enemy apostates, and these commands were bolstered by *ḥadīth* statements authorizing the killing of apostates who were also enemy combatants. Extending these rules from moral admonitions and the laws of war to criminal law, Muslim jurists criminalized apostasy and blasphemy alike. They counted statements of disbelief or disrespect against God, the Prophet, or his companions and family members as defamation tantamount to apostasy, and considered both capital crimes.[30]

In contrast to their treatment of the laws of war, though some jurists counted it as an eighth crime, most Muslim jurists treated rebellion (*baghy*) as a type of political resistance, which is not itself banned by the textual sources. These jurists tolerated rebellion as a form of resistance to political

is more likely to get drunk and then commit defamation, for which the Qurʾānic punishment is eighty lashes).

29 Qurʾān, 5:33 ("The punishment for those who wage war against God and His Messenger, and who strive with all their might and main to sow discord through the land, is execution or crucifixion, that their hands and feet be cut off from opposite sides, or exile. That is their disgrace in this world, and they will have a heavy punishment in the next world, except for those who repent before being captured, in which case: know that God is oft-forgiving, most merciful."). That the ruler possessed discretion to choose the punishment from this menu of options made this offense fall outside the strict sense of nondiscretionary *ḥudūd* crimes that were accompanied by specific, fixed punishments. Many Muslim jurists typically treated highway robbery within this category of offense nonetheless.

30 On the post-prophetic treatment of blasphemy as apostasy and as a death-eligible crime, see my "Negotiating Speech in Islamic Law and Politics: Flipped Traditions of Expression," in *Islamic Law and International Human Rights Law*, ed. Anver M. Emon et al. (Oxford: Oxford University Press, 2012), 144–67, at 146–47. For Ḥanafī and Shāfiʿī objections to treating apostasy as a death-eligible crime, see Rudolph Peters and Gert J. J. de Vries, "Apostasy in Islam," *Die Welt des Islams* 17, 1/4 (1976–77), 1–25, at 5–6. For contemporary Muslim jurists' critiques of apostasy laws as contrary to Qurʾānic law and on arguments that the relevant *ḥadīth* are either inauthentic or inapplicable outside contexts of war, see, for example, Mohamed S. El Awa, *Punishment in Islamic Law* (Indianapolis: American Trust Publications, 1993), 49–56, 61–62; Khaled Abou El Fadl, *Rebellion and Violence in Islamic Law* (Cambridge: Cambridge University Press, 2001), 32.

injustice, provided there was a legitimate cause.[31] When there was no legitimate cause, rebels were to be treated as "domestic terrorists," that is, as perpetrators of the crime of highway robbery, and penalized accordingly.[32]

Altogether, this list entailed a range of some four to eight crimes that counted as *ḥudūd* laws. Importantly, at least half of these crimes and associated punishments derived not from explicit and specific foundational texts, but from a significant degree of juristic interpretation, which would spark a nontrivial amount of doubt in the theory and application of *ḥudūd* laws.

b. Qiṣāṣ *Laws: Criminal Law of Homicide and Personal Injury*

Homicide and personal injury formed the second type of offense – falling somewhere between *ḥudūd* laws and torts. Though the modern tendency is to regard murder as the quintessential crime, Islamic law historically regulated homicide and injuries by rules of retaliation, or "talion," common to the antique and medieval world. These rules are familiar from their origins in the Biblical and Near Eastern context: "an eye for an eye, a tooth for a tooth,"[33] and modified by Muslim scripture.[34] As Muslim jurists understood the relevant Qur'ānic verses, intentional or reckless acts that resulted in personal injury or death were subject to laws of in-kind retaliation (*qiṣāṣ* or *qawad*), which could be commuted to payment of

[31] For a nuanced discussion of the complex jurisprudence on the legality of rebellion, see Abou El Fadl, *Rebellion and Violence*.

[32] For highway robbery as "domestic terrorism," see Sherman Jackson, "Domestic Terrorism in the Islamic Legal Tradition," *The Muslim World* 91 (2001), 293–310.

[33] Matthew, 5:38–42; Exodus, 21:22–25. For a discussion of the historical theory and applications of the concept, see Yung Suk Kim, "Lex Talionis in Exodus 21:22–25: Its Origin and Context," *Journal of Hebrew Scriptures* 6, 3 (2006), 2–11. For discussions of the concept in modern criminal law theory, see further Nico H. Frijda, "Lex Talionis: On Vengeance," in *Emotions: Essays in Emotion Theory*, ed. Stephanie H. M. van Goozen, Nanne van de Poll, and Joseph A. Sergeant (Oxford: Psychology Press, 1994), 263–89; Jeremy Waldron, "Lex Talionis," *Arizona Law Review* 34 (1992), 25–52.

[34] Qur'ān 5:45 ("And we prescribed for them [in previous laws] a life for a life, an eye for an eye, a nose for a nose, an ear for an ear, and a tooth for a tooth, and for other wounds, retaliation [or compensation]. But whoever forgoes [retaliation], it will be better for him ...."). See also Qur'ān, 2:178–79 ("O you who believe, prescribed for you is retaliation for those murdered: the free for the free, the slave for the slave, and the female for the female. But whoever pardons his brother of any [injurious] act, that [pardon] should be followed by appropriate payment to him, delivered with good conduct. This is a lightening of and a mercy [from the old prescription] from your Lord. And whoever transgresses after that will receive a grievous punishment. There is life for you in *qiṣāṣ*, O people of understanding, so that perhaps you might learn God-consciousness [also: restraint]."), 4:92 (outlining the laws of homicide, including compensatory rules for accidental homicide).

financial compensation (*diya*) in cases of pardon by the victim or victim's family. Financial compensation rules also applied to cases of unintentional personal injury or homicide. The amount of compensation for each injury was specified by the jurists based on general guidelines set by the Prophet.

In one sense, Muslim jurists treated homicide as only a quasi-fixed crime, and in another sense, they treated it as a tort.[35] They considered it a grave offense punishable by death, but most held that murder did not formally count as a part of *ḥudūd* laws because the sanction entailed more than one option.[36] Also, unlike *ḥudūd* laws, the Islamic laws of talion relied on the use of judicial discretion within a juridical framework for their precise determination, and encouraged the victim or the victim's family to exercise their own discretion to pardon the offender and to accept a specified amount of financial compensation in lieu of retaliation.[37]

c. Taʿzīr *Laws: Misdemeanors, Moral Wrongs*

Acts that did not fit under the *ḥudūd* or *qiṣāṣ* frameworks included a wide range of behaviors that jurists deemed morally undesirable but that were unspecified in the foundational texts. Laws regulating this category of offenses were called *taʿzīr*, which meant "censure" or "reprimand." Unspecified crimes meant unspecified sanctions, and such offenses were typically handled case by case – similar to common law crimes and punishments that took shape through the tremendous discretion of early Anglo-American judges in both definitions of crimes and decisions to punish.[38]

[35] For a discussion comparing the Islamic law of talion to tort law, see J. N. D. Anderson, "Homicide in Islamic Law," *Bulletin of the School of Oriental and African Studies* 13 (1951), 811–28.

[36] A minority of jurists placed the laws of homicide and personal injury in the category of *ḥudūd* laws. See, for example, Ibn Rushd al-Ḥafīd, *Bidāyat al-mujtahid*, 2:577; Badr al-Dīn al-ʿAynī (d. 855/1451), *al-Bināya: sharḥ al-Hidāya*, ed. Ayman Ṣāliḥ Shaʿbān (Beirut: Manshūrāt Muḥammad ʿAlī Bayḍūn, 2000), 6:190 (citing Fakhr al-Islām al-Bazdawī (d. 482/1089), *Mabsūṭ*).

[37] For a discussion of Islamic law's attempts to ameliorate pre-Islamic practices of privately administered talion that fueled ongoing tribal wars, see Peters, *Crime and Punishment*, 38–53 ("The origins of [talion] go back to the pre-Islamic custom of feuding, which allowed revenge for killing and bodily harm on all members of the tribe of the perpetrator. This often resulted in feuds that could last for generations. These feuds would cease if the victim's family would accept compensation, to be paid collectively by all members of the tribe. With the advent of Islam, this institution of revenge was drastically modified. . . . The most important reforms were that revenge in kind could only be taken on the person of the offender and only after due trial.").

[38] On common law crimes, see generally John H. Langbein, Renee Lettow Lerner, and Bruce P. Smith, *A History of the Common Law: The Development of Anglo-American Legal Institutions* (New York: Aspen Publishers, 2009).

These discretionary offenses were not completely unspecified. They were often counted as "moral wrongs" – *malum in se* acts that Muslims knew or should have known to be prohibited. In criminal law, the per se immorality of the act was sufficient to trigger criminal liability, notwithstanding claims of mistake.[39] Adding to the presumption of constructive knowledge of the immorality and illegality of these acts, Muslim jurists increasingly specified them as illegal in their legal treatises penned over time. Political authorities also legislated against these offenses through administrative decrees. In this sense, these offenses also became *malum prohibitum* – acts explicitly prohibited by law. Muslim jurists honored those decrees, consistent with early judicial practices and related arguments of necessity, tacitly acknowledging that political authorities enjoyed the widest ambit of jurisdiction and discretion over this class of crimes when matters involved public order. That is, the agents of the caliph, rather than the jurists, were authorized to prosecute and penalize such acts, which were taken to compromise public safety, which the caliphs possessed ultimate responsibility to ensure.[40]

In point of fact, Muslim jurists were not wholly absent from the definition and decision making surrounding *taʿzīr* offenses. They sought to retain some jurisdiction over defining these offenses as well as specifying sentence ranges for them, typically by attempting to set *ḥudūd* and *qiṣāṣ* laws as the upper limits for prohibited acts and for sentencing, and counterdefining *taʿzīr* offenses on that basis.[41] To that end, they encapsulated the theory of proportional punishment for non-*ḥudūd* offenses in a legal maxim: "*Taʿzīr* penalties must be less than *ḥudūd* penalties."[42] Jurists also developed a legal maxim that "any offense not specifically criminalized by

39 On the moral wrong doctrine, see Chapter 5, note 22 and accompanying text.

40 Māwardī explained that these types of unspecified offenses were punishable at the discretion of a judge or caliphal official according to the policy preferences of the political authority (*siyāsa*) if certain acts constituted behavior that threatened to compromise public order or the public interest (*maṣlaḥa*), which the caliph was charged with upholding. See Abū al-Ḥasan al-Māwardī, *al-Aḥkām al-sulṭāniyya*, ed. Muḥammad Fahmī al-Sirjānī (Cairo: al-Maktaba al-Tawfīqiyya, 1978), 250, 266–69; see also Abū al-Ḥasan al-Māwardī, *Kitāb al-ḥudūd min al-Ḥāwī*, 2:1022 (maintaining that the ruler *must* apply *taʿzīr* punishments in instances that affect the public interest).

41 For an early discussion, see Abū al-Ḥasan al-Karkhī (d. 340/952), *Uṣūl*, in *Taʾsīs al-naẓar* by Abū Zayd ʿUbayd Allāh b. ʿUmar al-Dabūsī, ed. Zakariyyā ʿAlī Yūsuf (Cairo: Maṭbaʿ al-Imām, 1972?), 217–18.

42 For a basic treatment in Sunnī law, see Māwardī, *al-Aḥkām al-sulṭāniyya*, 267; al-Shaykh Niẓām et al., *al-Fatāwā al-ʿĀlamgīriyya* (Bulaq: n.p., 1975), 2:167–70 (*taʿzīr taʾdīb dūn al-ḥadd*). For a discussion from the perspective of Shīʿī law compared to contemporary Iranian law, see Sayyid Muḥammad Amīn Hāshimī, "Taʿzīr dūn al-ḥadd," *Fiqh-i Ahl-i Bayt* 57 (2010), 178–228. For further discussion of the proportionality principle for discretionary penalties, see Chapter 3, note 12 and accompanying text.

ḥudūd laws deserved a *taʿzīr* penalty."[43] It is worth noting that juristic formulations for *taʿzīr* laws may seem perfunctory, given that the history of Islamic criminal law is replete with violations of those very standards.[44] Yet it is significant that Muslim jurists articulated rules for discretionary penalties at all. They likely did so – as I will argue – in an attempt to set standards of legitimacy that could in turn rein in executive excess, if not in fact or by force, then by virtue of the moral delegitimation of unbridled punishment.[45] Put differently, Muslims jurists regarded even discretionary criminal laws as guided by God but plagued by doubt, and they attempted to regulate them accordingly.

3. *Ḥudūd*, *Qiṣāṣ*, and *Taʿzīr*, and Doubt

What does all of this have to do with doubt and with the *Case of Māʿiz*? Doubt was connected to the ideal of divine legislative supremacy as much as punishment was in that case. Following God's laws meant close adherence to the letter of the *ḥudūd* laws, which Muslims look to Islam's foundational texts to specify. Any doubt about the definition of a criminal law or the culpability of an accused offender would lead jurists to avoid punishment, by operation of the doubt canon. For worse than inadvertently failing to apply God's clear law was to make new laws by applying unspecified norms as if they were *ḥudūd* laws, or to enforce *ḥudūd* laws wrongfully against individuals whose culpability was not certain.

Moreover, doubt was also a consequence of the harshness of criminal punishments. Violations of Islamic criminal laws triggered severe punishments – ranging from reprimand, fines, and shaming to imprisonment, corporal punishment, and death.[46] The harshness and irrevocability of

[43] ʿAbd al-Fattāḥ al-Ḥusaynī al-Marāghī (d. 1250/1835), *al-ʿAnāwīn* (Qum: Muʾassasat al-Nashr al-Islāmī, 1417–18/1996–98), 2:627, no. 4 (*kull mā lam yarid fīh ḥadd min al-sharʿ fī ʾl-maʿāṣī, fa-fīh al-taʿzīr*).

[44] To take just two examples from the Seljūq period and the Mamlūk period, respectively, see generally Christian Lange, *Justice, Punishment and the Medieval Muslim Imagination* (Cambridge: Cambridge University Press, 2008), and Yossef Rapoport, "Legal Diversity in the Age of *Taqlīd*: The Four Chief *Qāḍīs* under the Mamlūks," *Islamic Law and Society* 10 (2003), 2.

[45] For further discussion of the moral values underlying *ḥudūd* jurisprudence, see Part II.

[46] See Peters, *Crime and Punishment*, 30–38, listing the penalties as follows: reprimand (*taʾdīb*); fines (*ghurm*, *arsh*); public exposure to shame (*tashhīr*), which may include shaving the head and parading around town on the back of a donkey, often facing backward; banishment (*nafy*, *taghrīb*); imprisonment (*ḥabs*); flogging (*jald*); amputation of the hand and/or foot from opposite sides (*qaṭʿ*, *al-qaṭʿ min khilāf*); in-kind retaliation (*qiṣāṣ*) or financial compensation (*diya*) for personal injuries and murder; the death penalty

these punishments – especially in the capital context – prompted jurists to find means to avoid punishment, lest they be responsible for the consequences of getting it wrong. Doubt provided the vehicle and the justification for doing so.

From the earliest periods in Islamic history, the very real specter of unjustified and excessive punishment rankled Muslim jurists. In advocating for the ideal of divine legislative supremacy, they also promoted themselves as the only qualified exponents of God's law. In that context, the jurists saw excessive punishment both as a moral wrong for which they might be accountable if they authorized it and as a means of social control that shifted power from them to the ruling authorities.[47] For these reasons, very early in Islamic history, jurists were not only concerned with their own role in applying God's law but also keen on regulating the ruling authorities' role.

These are the ends to which Muslim jurists extensively invoked the doctrine of doubt. In response to political excesses in punishment, and despite its apparent specificity to *ḥudūd*, jurists applied the doubt canon widely.[48] That is, they applied the doubt canon to *ḥudūd* laws as well as to the *qiṣāṣ* framework and *taʿzīr* penalties. In doing so, they adopted the doubt doctrine as the guiding principle of Islamic criminal law, represented in the oft-repeated formulation of the doubt canon: "Avoid imposing criminal sanctions in cases of doubt: *idraʾū ʾl-ḥudūd biʾl-shubahāt.*" Here, the avoidance imperative of the doubt canon was the inverse of the enforcement imperative of the foundational texts, yet the former took precedence over the latter: whenever jurists feared divergence from the criminal law texts, even inadvertently, doubt cautioned avoidance of punishment.

Within this tripartite scheme of Islamic criminal law, there was no doubt that Māʿiz had committed a *ḥadd* crime. On the strictest reading of the law, his confession made this scenario just the sort of case in which punishment would have signaled adherence to a clear divine legislative directive. Yet the Prophet seemed to prefer that Māʿiz not be punished.

(*qatl*) through various methods, including stoning or lapidation (*rajm*) for adultery; and other non-punitive legal consequences (for example, a bar on testifying in court).

47 See, for example, Jonathan P. Berkey, *The Formation of Islam: Religion and Society in the Near East, 600–1800* (Cambridge: Cambridge University Press, 2003), 84–85 (noting that the Umayyad and ʿAbbāsid dynasties both indulged in excesses, often garnering complaints regarding disparate and excessive applications of punishment); see further Lange, *Justice* (detailing the particularly violent Seljūq use of punishment for social control).

48 See Mottahedeh, *Lessons*, 6–8 (noting the jurists' formation of a "pious opposition" against the political rulers, seeking to restrict as much as possible the caliphal reach over Islamic law writ large). See further Chapters 2 and 3.

This left jurists who wished to understand the Prophet's stance with a puzzle: How might they resolve conflicting aspects of the foundational texts, where – as here – the divine textual rule against adultery seemed to conflict with a prophetic preference to avoid punishment? The answer was not so simple as to say that the Qur'ān trumps the Sunna, for the Qur'ān did not authorize the capital punishment in the first place. Nor was it as simple as saying that capital punishment was illegitimate, for the death penalty persisted in the medieval Muslim jurists' imagination as divinely sanctioned. Rather, the answer required devising ways to deal with interpretation and "doubt" that arose in this case about the facts, the law, and the propriety of punishment. For Sunnīs, understanding the *Case of Māʿiz* would be an essential part of devising a general theory of Islamic legal interpretation and a specific theory of Islamic criminal law. Both would aid Muslim jurists in their attempts to interpret Islamic law and to resolve recurring questions of doubt.

C. DEBATES ABOUT MĀʿIZ

Understood from the foundations of Islamic criminal law, the *Case of Māʿiz* was significant because of a "foundational doubt" about the requisite procedures and the value or necessity of punishment in an early application of *ḥudūd* laws. The case combined features of both certainty and ambiguity: it had a solid textual provenance in the *ḥadīth* corpus, but a deep textual ambiguity about its meaning.

In the legal literature, the ongoing debates about Māʿiz emerged in large part because Muslim jurists could not agree on the normative significance of the case. They generally agreed on what happened: Māʿiz was punished despite the Prophet's objections.[49] They also agreed that the case was

[49] To be sure, there is some question in the various *ḥadīth* reports about what happened: whether Māʿiz had committed adultery once or multiple times; whether he was the same unnamed "man from the tribe of Aslam" about which a similar scenario appears in the Sunnī *ḥadīth* corpus; whether the Prophet authorized punishment and then regretted it; if so, whether stoning was the authorized punishment; whether Māʿiz had in fact repented verbally or merely by trying to escape once the punishment had commenced; and whether the Prophet's reason for rebuking the townspeople was an orientation toward mercy, or something else. Gaps of this kind in the "record" are typical for early cases, which were reported in the *ḥadīth* collections with extremely sparse details about the litigants' conversations, the case outcomes, and the reasoning behind the judgment or punishment. These gaps created the sort of foundational doubt that provided jurists with room for interpretive maneuvering about both law and facts, reflexively. That is, later jurists often filled in gaps about *what happened* with normative rules about *what*

important: its provenance in the founding period with the Prophet presiding as judge made it a source of normative guidance for future generations. But they found the case unclear regarding which outcome (punishment or release) and, therefore, which interpretive approach would have been correct.

One approach, which I call "strict textualism," advocated looking only at the Qur'ānic text (and sometimes consensus-based *ḥadīth*) to determine matters of guilt and punishment. According to this approach, the townspeople were correct to punish Māʿiz. He had violated the textual prohibition against adultery, as the Prophet had concluded in his pronouncement of guilt. The townspeople were merely enforcing the sanction that they believed (even if incorrectly) to be required by the Qur'ānic text. Even though a modern lawyer might expect the judge to order the punishment, on this medieval reading, all that strict textualists needed to authorize punishment in the Islamic context was the conviction itself. With a conviction, they believed that the divine text authorized punishment in a way that superseded any authority that the judge (including the Prophet acting as judge) might have had to ignore the logical consequences of his verdict. In other words, the idea of divine legislative supremacy was represented in the *text* rather than in judicial discretion – even the sort extending from Prophetic authority. This reading explained why the people had carried out the punishment over the objection of the Prophet. This approach gave rise to the strict textualist rule that judges should *enforce punishments* whenever caliphal officials could provide judges with some evidence that a crime had been committed.

The second approach, which I call "pragmatic textualism," suggested that even Qur'ānic textual rules were qualified by contextual concerns that affected whether convictions and punishments were warranted in

should have happened based on doctrines that they later devised through combining legal text with social context at the time of their systematic writings of legal treatises, especially from the fifth/eleventh century onward. The *Case of Māʿiz*, and the evolution of the doubt doctrine from it and like cases, provides a powerful illustration of this process. For notes on how analogous notions of "foundational doubt" operated in public law contexts of international American constitutional law, notably due to three structural factors shared with Islamic law, see Jack Goldsmith and Daryl Levinson, "Law for States: International Law, Constitutional Law, Public Law," *Harvard Law Review* 122 (2009), 1791–1868, at 1794 (noting that "constitutional law suffers from the same kinds of foundational uncertainty and contestation over meaning that are viewed as characteristic of international law," due to the lack of a centralized legislature to issue laws, a judicial institution with final say over the meanings of laws, or a powerful enforcement authority to execute laws).

particular cases.[50] Jurists adopting this view read the Qurʾānic text pragmatically in the context of the Prophet's objection to punishing Māʿiz, to conclude that his objection should have carried the day. For them, the Prophet had identified countervailing considerations – having to do with repentance and rehabilitation, mercy, and antipathy toward imposing the death penalty on dubious grounds – all of which should have prevented punishment. This approach gave rise to the pragmatic rule that judges should *avoid punishments* whenever such countervailing considerations threw the propriety of punishment into "doubt."

These two interpretive approaches produced opposite normative outcomes. That is, the precedential rule arising out of the *Case of Māʿiz* differed radically depending on whether jurists evaluated it according to textual or pragmatic (contextual) criteria. The first option, *enforcing punishment*, seemed to accord best with the text. The second option, *avoiding punishment*, seemed to depart from the text and to be responsive to extratextual context.

Yet most jurists – claiming to be textualists – understood the case to require the second option: avoiding punishment. What was the basis for their claim and the tenor of the debates by which the strictly textualist jurists begged to differ? Answers to these complex questions form the detailed narrative of this book. Sunnī jurists began to answer as follows.

1. The Case for Enforcing Punishment: Strict Textualism

For the jurists who maintained that the townspeople had properly enforced the punishment against Māʿiz, it was God Himself who had required the sanction. God was the sole legislator. The dictates of His texts therefore bound both the Prophet and the townspeople.[51] That is, not even the Prophet could depart from the rule requiring punishment.

[50] I borrow the concept, though not the more cumbersome term of "contextual textualism," from William N. Eskridge Jr., "No Frills Textualism," *Harvard Law Review* 119 (2005–2006), 2014–76, at 2041 (reviewing Adrian Vermeule, *Judging Under Uncertainty* (Cambridge, MA: Harvard University Press, 2006)). See also William N. Eskridge Jr. and Philip P. Frickey, "Statutory Interpretation as Practical Reasoning," *Stanford Law Review* 42 (1990), 321–84. For an application to Shīʿī law, see Chapter 8. I also use pragmatic and contextual (and sometimes extratextual) interchangeably, because of the conceptual overlap between those terms in this context.

[51] Most Sunnī jurists – even pragmatists – cited the *Case of Māʿiz* as one of the few early precedents supporting the claim that stoning was a divinely legislated punishment for adultery, even though they argued that it was not appropriately enforced in this case. Traces of this dispute in the surviving juristic literature are scant and objections to stoning – as in Khārijī objections to the punishment – are rejected by most mainstream jurists. However, see, for example, Jaṣṣāṣ, *Aḥkām al-Qurʾān*, 2:108, 3:263–64.

Strict textualists adopting this view looked to the *Case of Māʿiz* alongside other early cases both to justify their interpretive approach and to distill specific legal precepts about when to enforce punishment.

Their argument was colorfully advanced by the Muslim jurist known as Dāwūd al-Ẓāhirī (d. 270/883–4) – that is, Dāwūd "The Literalist" – who established the most strictly textualist school in Islamic law.[52] To begin with, he argued, God required judges to appeal *only* to the Qur'ān and authentic, clear reports of the Sunna without permitting human interpretation.[53] Further, a judge was not to express personal preferences or exercise any discretion in such cases.[54] Finally, he advocated a general approach to criminal law – among other areas of law – that entailed applying each rule according to the plain meaning of the text. Whenever a crime was established, judges were to enforce the associated punishment.[55] Considerations of mercy, moral concerns, or contextual facts were irrelevant.

For proof, textualist jurists looked to the Qur'ān itself, which – when specifying the adultery prohibition and punishment – commanded: "Do not let mercy dissuade you from imposing the punishment."[56] Textualists also looked to reports of other early cases that more clearly showed instances in which the Prophet acknowledged that even he was required to apply the punishments specified in the Qur'ānic texts, without exercising discretion of his own. For example, in the *Case of the Makhzūmī Thief*,[57]

[52] For an outline of Ẓāhirī legal theory see ʿĀrif Khalīl Muḥammad Abū ʿĪd, *Imām Dāwūd al-Ẓāhirī wa-atharuh fī 'l-fiqh al-Islāmī* (Kuwait: Dār al-Arqam, 1984). See further the Ẓāhirī manual of jurisprudence that Devin Stewart attributes to Dāwūd's son. Devin Stewart, "Muḥammad b. Dā'ūd al-Ẓāhirī's Manual of Jurisprudence, *al-Wuṣūl ilā maʿrifat al-uṣūl*," in *Studies in Islamic Legal Theory*, ed. Bernard Weiss (Leiden: Brill, 2002), 99–160.

[53] Stewart, "Muḥammad b. Dā'ūd al-Ẓāhirī's Manual," 157–58 (noting that, according to Ẓāhirī doctrine, allowing "interpretation" would permit each judge to rule "according to whim, [yielding results] opposite those determined by the whim of [other judges]").

[54] Ibid., 156–57 (making a case against interpretation by quoting the Qur'ānic verse 4:105, "We have revealed the Book unto you with the truth so that you may judge between mankind by that which God shows you. Do not be a pleader for the treacherous," and commenting that God did not say, "by that which you think for yourself" or "by that to which your preferences and perceptions lead you").

[55] Muḥammad b. Ḥasan al-Shaṭṭī (d. 1307/1890), *Risāla fī madhhab al-Imām Dāwūd al-Ẓāhirī* (Damascus: Maṭbaʿat Rawḍat al-Shām, 1330/1911–2), 25 (collecting legal opinions attributed to Dāwūd b. ʿAlī from various Ḥanbalī works, including the strict enforcement of criminal punishment even in cases where a criminal defendant who confessed to a crime subsequently retracted the confession).

[56] Qur'ān, 24:2. For analysis in a medieval legal-exegetical treatise on the import of Qur'ānic verses for issues of law, see Abū Bakr Ibn al-ʿArabī (d. 543/1148), *Aḥkām al-Qur'ān* (Beirut: Dār al-Fikr, n.d.), 3:340–48.

[57] For additional discussion of this case, see Chapter 4.

the Prophet had convicted a woman of theft. In that case, the elite members of society petitioned the Prophet to avoid punishment and to let the convict go. The petitioners were members of Muḥammad's family, as was the woman convicted of stealing. The Prophet responded that even *his* hands were tied from pardoning the woman, when the evidence proved her guilt. "Would you intervene in a matter involving God's laws?" he asked. "I swear by God that even if Fāṭima [my own daughter] had stolen, I would cut off her hand!"[58] Here, the Prophet was referring to the Qur'ānic punishment for theft.[59] The *Case of Māʿiz* and the *Case of the Makhzūmī Thief* were both founding cases that textualist judges understood to mean that even the Prophet's authority was restricted to the text. Like him, all judges were bound to a version of divine legislative supremacy that required them to follow the strict meaning of the text.[60]

2. The Case for Avoiding Punishment: Pragmatic Textualism

The jurists who used the *Case of Māʿiz* to conclude that punishment should have been avoided believed that several contextual considerations should have overridden the apparent textual commands supporting punishment, and that Māʿiz should have been released. Accordingly, they read this case to support a prospective rule of avoiding punishments in similar cases of doubt. Moreover, they invoked the *Case of Māʿiz* to support the doubt canon that called on judges to "avoid criminal punishments in cases of doubt."[61] Was this placing "spirit over text," as textualists might charge?[62]

58 The term for "God's laws" here is *ḥudūd Allāh*. The early, Qur'ānic meaning of the term was simply "limits" or "divine rules." The term only later came to mean "Islamic criminal law." For reports of this case, see Bukhārī, *Ṣaḥīḥ*, no. 6887; Muslim, *Ṣaḥīḥ*, no. 1688; Abū Dāwūd al-Sijistānī, *Sunan*, ed. Muḥammad ʿAbd al-ʿAzīz al-Khālidī (Beirut: Dār al-Kutub al-ʿIlmiyya, 1996), 4:133, nos. 4373–74; Aḥmad b. Shuʿayb al-Nasāʾī, *al-Sunan al-kubrā*, ed. Ḥasan ʿAbd al-Munʿim al-Shalabī (Beirut: Muʾassasat al-Risāla, 2001), 4:330; Aḥmad b. al-Ḥusayn al-Bayhaqī (d. 458/1066), *al-Sunan al-kubrā*, ed. Muḥammad ʿAbd al-Qādir ʿAṭāʾ (Beirut: Dār al-Kutub al-ʿIlmiyya, 1994), 8:267, no. 17004.

59 Qur'ān, 5:38. For problems that Muslim jurists faced in interpreting the verse and determining the associated punishment, see Bernard Weiss, *Spirit of Islamic Law*, 104–109.

60 See Ibn Ḥazm, *Muḥallā*, 8:252. For further discussion, see Chapter 7.

61 For example, Māwardī, *Kitāb al-ḥudūd min al-Ḥāwī*, 1:206–207; Qudūrī, *Tajrīd*, 11:5891, 5949–50; Marghīnānī, *Hidāya* (2000), 2:735–36. For further discussion, see my "Islamic Rule of Lenity," 1327–49.

62 This formulation recalls language from the *Church of Holy Trinity v. United States*, 143 U.S. 457 (1892), which presented a conflict between strictly textual readings and a purposive reading that went beyond the text. See *Holy Trinity*, 143 U.S. at 459 ("[W]e

Against strict textualist accusations to the contrary, pragmatic textualists asserted that *they* were more faithful to the divine legislative intent. That is, the divine intent behind Islam's adultery rules was not to solicit judges' blind obedience in carrying out punishments. Rather, the intent behind adultery rules and other criminal laws was to elicit moral consciousness, which would be served by repentance (signifying rehabilitation) as much as it would be by punishment.

For example, one pragmatic textualist – the prominent eleventh-century Ḥanafī jurist Qudūrī – argued that the *Case of Māʿiz* stood for the proposition that crimes could be established by confessions only if the defendant freely confessed four separate times that he or she had committed the crime. Moreover, for Qudūrī, the case indicated that if a defendant retracted his or her confession even once before the punishment was completed, the authorization to enforce the punishment would lapse. The same would be true if one of the four witnesses required by the Qurʾān to prove an adultery charge perjured him- or herself before the punishment was carried out. Applying these rules to Māʿiz, Qudūrī argued that Māʿiz's attempted escape was tantamount to a retracted confession, and perhaps to repentance as well.[63]

This reading, against the accusations of "spirit over text," explained why the Prophet blamed the townspeople for not letting Māʿiz go. This reading also clarified that the proper judicial response to a criminal case where there was a conviction accompanied by the possibility of repentance was to avoid punishment. In defending this view, Qudūrī and the majority of medieval Muslim jurists claimed, like Dāwūd, to be textualists devoted to the principle of divine legislative supremacy. Further, the mainstream pragmatic jurists asserted that the literalists and strict textualists, not they, had impermissibly used the text to justify an outcome that the divine lawgiver had not intended. The divine intent, they held, was not punishment for punishment's sake, but punishment only when there was no doubt – on a pragmatic, contextual reading – that punishment was in fact due.[64]

cannot think Congress intended to denounce with penalties a transaction like that in the present case. It is a familiar rule, that a thing may be within the letter of the statute and yet not within the statute, because not within its spirit, nor within the intention of its makers.").

63 For example, Qudūrī, *Tajrīd*, 11:5949–50.

64 The looming question would be how to define doubt, which was expansive, as described at length in Part III.

3. The Significance of Māʿiz

Stepping back to assess the jurists' institutional concerns in their debates about Māʿiz, it is fair to say that the *Case of Māʿiz* was about the antipathy of *both* sets of jurists toward doubt – the strict textualists and the pragmatic textualists alike. Although their strategies for resolving doubt differed, both framed their arguments about the fate of Māʿiz as a search for legislative intent.

Consider another significant aspect of the *Case of Māʿiz*. In many ways, that case may be compared with famous interpretive debates about an episode in the American context that one scholar described as "not only a case," but a "marker for an entire legal tradition, . . . [which emphasizes] that there is far more to law than the plain meaning of authoritative legal texts . . . ."[65] Yet it is important to bear in mind that, in contrast to the American context, in historical Islamic contexts, there were no constitutionally defined institutions of law and governance. Instead, an informal constitutional arrangement unfolded whereby a class of scholar-jurists assumed the power to interpret *sharīʿa* as a system of law, and monarchical rulers called caliphs assumed the power to enforce it. Between them were judges, whom the caliph appointed and who looked to the jurists for authoritative formulations of law.[66] This much about the general arrangement of institutions and law and governance in early Islamic history is well known.

[65] Frederick Schauer, "Constitutional Invocations," *Fordham Law Review* 65 (1997), 1295–1312, at 1307 (describing *Holy Trinity*, 143 U.S. 457 (1892), discussed in note 62). For similar observations focusing on the use of legislative history as an extratextual source of interpretation, see Adrian Vermeule, *Judging Under Uncertainty*, 88 (observing that most judicial and academic commentary on legislative history and statutory interpretation theory begins with *Holy Trinity* as "the leading case in the legislative history debate," known for "endorsing countertextual interpretive techniques"); Antonin Scalia, *A Matter of Interpretation: Federal Courts and the Law* (Princeton, NJ: Princeton University Press, 1997), 3, 18–23 (describing *Holy Trinity* as the "prototypical case involving the triumph of supposed 'legislative intent' ... over the text of the law"); William N. Eskridge Jr., *Dynamic Statutory Interpretation* (Cambridge, MA: Harvard University Press, 1994), 209 (labeling the case a "sensation" that inaugurated a trend of judicial use of legislative history).

[66] See Wael Hallaq, *Sharīʿa: Theory, Practice, Transformations* (Cambridge: Cambridge University Press, 2009), 159–80; Feldman, *Fall and Rise*, 2–4 (arguing that a "separation of powers" obtained between the three institutions of jurists, caliphs, and judges). To be sure, many other officials operated with criminal law jurisdiction outside of this scheme. However, this tripartite scheme provided the central pivots for law and order, and even in those contexts, the caliphal officials were in principle subject to juridical articulations of law to set the upper limits of punishment. See note 42.

Less familiar is the idea that jurists helped define the boundaries of institutional power through interpretation of – among other areas – criminal law. Their ability to claim fidelity to ideals of textualism and divine legislative supremacy was key to the jurists' role in constructing matters of law and governance. That brand of fidelity conferred on them the legitimacy to make pronouncements shaping the institutions in charge of articulating law and implementing governance.[67] That type of fidelity also explained the importance of attaching the text-based doubt canon to early textual precedents such as the *Case of Māʿiz* in order to define its contours with reference to more text. In short, whenever jurists debated criminal law texts such as the disputed *Case of Māʿiz*, they were not only interpreting early precedents and the accompanying scope of doubt but also defining and redefining their own power over public law against that of other institutional actors – as further elaborated in the next chapter.

CONCLUSION

Islamic law has always regarded itself as a system of divine law. But to state it as such is to repeat a nameless formulation that has tended to obscure the agency of those who defined the contours of Islamic law historically. Close investigation of the historical record of Islamic criminal law reveals the nuance by which Muslim jurists approached that ideal. The *Case of Māʿiz* illustrates how.

For early and medieval Muslim jurists alike, the *Case of Māʿiz* represented a structural-interpretive question of how Muslim jurists could honor Islam's principle of divine legislative supremacy when applying abstract standards to concrete facts. Did a violation of a clear Qurʾānic-legislative prohibition against adultery absolutely warrant punishment? Where there was some evidence to prove commission of the crime, what justified departure from the seemingly clear directive to punish? In other words, taking Qur'ān and *ḥadīth*-based criminal laws as expressions of divine legislative intent in cases such as this, what did God require?

In attempts to answer these questions, Muslim jurists debating the fate of Māʿiz tried to make sense of the divergence between Qurʾānic legislation

[67] For a comparative sense of the types of legitimacy to which Muslim jurists appealed, see Richard H. Fallon Jr., "Legitimacy and the Constitution," *Harvard Law Review* 118 (2005), 1849–51 (outlining an "overall" legitimacy that combines legal, sociological, and moral criteria for judicial authority).

as to the law and popular and prophetic responses as to the punishment. These jurists manifested in their debates about Māʿiz a certain antipathy toward doubt, and devised different interpretive strategies to resolve it – ranging from strict to pragmatic textualism. Yet the key factor is that both sets of jurists framed their arguments about the fate of Māʿiz as a commitment to textualism and a search for divine legislative supremacy.

As these medieval Muslims debated how best to realize the divine legislative supremacy ideal, their contestations suggested an inverse relationship between the domain of certainty about divine intent from the *texts and theory* of Islamic law and an ever-widening domain of doubt about its *application*. In seeking to navigate the domain of doubt, the jurists' interpretive theories took shape through construction of a solid text-based authority to back their extensive use of the doubt canon, a process to which we now turn.

2

The Rise of Doubt

Doubt turns out to be a stage on which the well-known contests between political authorities and jurists over the power and authority to interpret Islamic law played out over the course of Islamic legal history. Tensions between the ideal of divine legislative supremacy and the reality of doubt made questions of who had the power to interpret Islamic criminal law unavoidable. The foundational texts required the ruling authorities to enforce criminal laws, and Muslim jurists themselves emphasized the mandatoriness of enforcing *ḥudūd* laws in particular. But when it came to applying those laws, evidentiary infirmities of the type that arose in the infamous *Case of Māʿiz* prompted jurists to invoke the doubt canon to caution against punishment. The jurists asserted that they, rather than the political rulers, possessed both the religious-moral authority and the institutional competence to determine when avoidance rather than enforcement was appropriate under Islamic law. They established a judicial practice of invoking the doubt canon in this process, a principle that gained virtually unassailable authority once they could cite it as a foundational text.

A. THE CANONIZATION OF DOUBT: JUDICIAL PRACTICE

From the beginning – or at very least soon after Islam's advent – the doubt canon was a central principle of Islamic criminal law, notable as a widespread judicial practice. The canon was certainly known to early *ḥadīth* collectors and jurists alike. But as I have shown at length elsewhere, for three centuries, none of them thought the doubt canon as we now know it to have been prophetic in origin.[1]

Jurists all across the young Islamic empire cited the doubt canon broadly in their writings without attributing it to the Prophet directly. In seventh- and eighth-century Iraq, followers of the two leading jurists of Kūfa, Ibrāhīm al-Nakhaʿī (d. ca. 96/717) and Abū Ḥanīfa (d. 150/767), expounded the canon in the form that has been popularized among most subsequent jurists: *idraʾū ʾl-ḥudūd biʾl-shubahāt*. One of Abū Ḥanīfa's two most famous students, Muḥammad b. al-Ḥasan al-Shaybānī (d. 189/804), recorded the canon in his *Kitāb al-Āthār*, a book of traditions he learned from his teacher, who in turn drew on the opinions of Ibrāhīm al-Nakhaʿī.[2] Abū Ḥanīfa's other prominent student, Abū Yūsuf (d. 182/798), also recorded the canon in his *Kitāb al-Kharāj*, a book ostensibly about tax policy that also covered other public laws such as criminal law.[3]

[1] See my "Islamic Legal Maxims," 69–70, 100.

[2] Muḥammad b. Ḥasan al-Shaybānī, *Kitāb al-Āthār*, ed. Khadīja Muḥammad Kāmil (Karachi: Idārat al-Qurʾān waʾl-ʿUlūm al-Islāmiyya, 1998–99), 136 (*bāb dirāʾ* [*sic*] *al-ḥudūd*) (citing version 2, in Appendix A). Shaybānī does not mention the standard version in this work, in which he records traditions that he learned from Abū Ḥanīfa, but he tells us that his teacher adopted a variant of version 2, wherein Ibrāhīm al-Nakhaʿī attributes the saying to ʿUmar. There is a problem in his citation: the content is consistent with ʿAbd al-Razzāq's record of a report from Ibrāhīm al-Nakhaʿī (on anonymous authority), but the chain is consistent with Ibn Abī Shayba's attribution of the report to Ibrāhīm al-Nakhaʿī from ʿUmar. Nevertheless, the basic point remains that Abū Ḥanīfa adopted the canon from his teacher.

[3] Abū Yūsuf records several versions, including a form of the standard version (which he attributes to "Companions and Successors"). See Abū Yūsuf, *Kitāb al-Kharāj*, 303 (Arabic text: *idraʾū ʾl-ḥudūd biʾl-shubahāt mā ʾstaṭaʿtum, waʾl-khaṭaʾ fī ʾl-ʿafw khayr min al-khaṭaʾ fī ʾl-ʿuqūba*, combining the standard version with the addition that appears in various *ḥadīth* versions (*mā ʾstaṭaʿtum*) plus the rationale adduced in the last part of version 2 (*al-khaṭaʾ fī ʾl-ʿafw* ...)), 305 (Arabic text: *idraʾū ʾl-ḥudūd ʿan al-muslimīn mā ʾstaṭaʿtum, fa-idhā wajadtum liʾl-muslim makhrajan fa-khallū sabīlah fa-inna ʾl-imām la-in yukhṭiʾ fī ʾl-ʿafw khayr lah min an yukhṭiʾ fī ʾl-ʿuqūba*, that is, version 2 together with the familiar *isnād* transmitted directly to Abū Yūsuf rather than through the intermediate Wakīʿ: Yazīd b. Abī Ziyād – Zuhrī – ʿUrwa – ʿĀʾisha), 303 (Arabic text: *idraʾū ʾl-ḥudūd ʿan ʿibād Allāh mā ʾstaṭaʿtum*, that is, version 3 together with the truncated *isnād* (al-Aʿmash – Ibrāhīm [al-Nakhaʿī]), as it appears in Ibn Abī Shayba's version), 304–305 (Arabic text: *la-an uʿaṭṭil al-ḥudūd fī ʾl-shubahāt aḥabb* [or *khayr*] *min an uqīmahā fī ʾl-shubahāt*, that is, version 7, also with the *isnād* later identified by Ibn Abī Shayba: Manṣūr – Ibrāhīm (al-Nakhaʿī) – [...] – ʿUmar). The saying appears in other editions with formulations close to the standard one, that is, using *shubahāt*; but this is likely an interpolation of what later came to be so standard that the copyist easily thought that it belonged in the wording. See, for example, the edition of Aḥmad Muḥammad Shākir (Cairo: al-Maṭbaʿa al-Salafiyya, 1347/1929), 181 (Arabic text: *idraʾū ʾl-ḥudūd ʿan al-muslimīn* [*biʾl-shubahāt*] *mā ʾstaṭaʿtum* ..., with brackets in the original text and a note from the editor that the *shubahāt* phrase inside the brackets appears in a Taymūriyya manuscript of this work).

Moreover, there are colorful stories of instances in which Abū Yūsuf and a third student of Abū Ḥanīfa, Zufar b. Hudhayl (d. 158/774), applied the canon as well.[4] In one episode, Zufar was verbally attacked by a man named ʿAbd al-Wāḥid b. Ziyād for his fellow Ḥanafīs' use of the canon. Reportedly, when ʿAbd al-Wāḥid encountered Zufar, he complained, "You [Ḥanafīs] have circulated a ridiculous saying (*ḥadīth*) among the people." "And what is that?" Zufar asked. ʿAbd al-Wāḥid responded, "You say, 'avoid criminal punishments in cases of doubt: *idraʾū ʾl-ḥudūd biʾl-shubahāt*,' but when you are faced with the harshest punishments, you rule that they are to be enforced despite the existence of doubt." Taken aback, Zufar asked, "How so?" ʿAbd al-Wāḥid replied, "The Prophet said that a Muslim is not to be put to death for the homicide of a non-Muslim (*kāfir*), but you say that [a Muslim may be put to death for killing] non-Muslims who have a covenant of protection to live in Muslim lands (*dhimmī*s)." Here, Zufar is reported to have retracted the early Ḥanafī ruling that said as much.[5]

Elsewhere in Iraq, the doubt canon found broad application by Sufyān al-Thawrī (d. 161/778), a contemporary of Abū Ḥanīfa and his associates, who founded his own school. Sufyān al-Thawrī held, for instance, that the *ḥadd* punishment for *zinā* (fornication or adultery) was to be avoided in a case in which a man had intimate relations with a slave woman who belonged to him but who had a contract to purchase her freedom, which rendered intimate relations with her illicit.[6] Sufyān al-Thawrī also held that no *ḥadd* punishment was to apply to a man who had sexual relations with a slave woman

[4] For the infamous case involving Abū Yūsuf's purported misuse of doubt, see Chapter 3.

[5] Bayhaqī, *Sunan*, 8:31, no. 15700; see also Shams al-Dīn al-Dhahabī (d. 748/1348), *Siyar aʿlām al-nubalāʾ*, ed. Ḥusayn al-Asad and Shuʿayb al-Arnaʾūṭ (Beirut: Muʾassasat al-Risāla, 1981), 8:40–41 (entry for Zufar b. Hudhayl, reporting the story as related by ʿAbd al-Raḥmān al-Mahdī (d. 198/813)). For the early Ḥanafī rule that a Muslim is eligible for the death penalty for intentionally killing a non-Muslim, see Shaybānī, *Āthār*, 218–19 (mentioning capital liability for Muslims who kill several categories of non-Muslims living in Muslim lands as *dhimmī*s, that is, including non-Muslims living under a covenant of protection, Christians, Jews, and – according to one narration – Zoroastrians: *muʿāhad, naṣrānī, yahūdī, mājūs*).

[6] ʿAbd al-Razzāq, *Muṣannaf*, ed. Ayman Naṣr al-Dīn al-Azharī (Beirut: Manshūrāt Muḥammad ʿAlī Bayḍūn; Dār al-Kutub al-ʿIlmiyya, 2000), 8:430 (*yudraʾ ʿanh al-ḥadd*). Classical Islamic family law generally recognized marriage and creation of a master-slave relationship as the two legal instruments rendering permissible sexual relations between two people. Not every scholar recognized the second. It was disputed by prominent jurists and theologians in Islam's early period, that is, the first/seventh through the third/ninth century. See, for example, Muwaffaq al-Dīn Ibn Qudāma (d. 620/1223), *al-Mughnī*, ed. ʿAbd Allāh b. ʿAbd al-Muḥsin al-Turkī and ʿAbd al-Fattāḥ Muḥammad al-Ḥilw (Cairo: Hajar, 1986), 9:552 (noting an objection from al-Ḥasan al-Baṣrī (d. 110/728)); ʿAbd al-Qāhir al-Baghdādī (d. 429/1037), *Kitāb Uṣūl al-dīn* (Beirut: Dār al-Āfāq al-Jadīda, 1981), 336 (noting the

whom he had purchased with capital supplied by his business partner.[7] In both cases, the *ḥadd* sanction was to be avoided because the defendant had partial ownership of the slave woman in question, which created a reasonable basis for the defendant to believe that sexual relations between them were licit. The reasonable belief on the part of the offender(s) was enough to create a punishment-avoiding "doubt" on the part of the judge.[8]

In Medina, Mālik b. Anas (d. 179/795) invoked the doubt canon, holding that the *ḥadd* punishment for *zinā* was to be avoided when a man had sex with a slave woman without having the full ownership that would permit him to do so legally.[9] Likewise, Mālik maintained that the canon would also serve to avert punishment from a man who permitted his slave woman to have sex with another man, or from a man who had sex with his son's or daughter's slave woman – both acts that were illegal.[10]

In Egypt, Ibn al-Qāsim (d. 191/806), Mālik's student and the jurist best known for shaping early Andalusian Mālikī law, applied the doubt canon to avoid punishment for *zinā* against a man who denied consummating his marriage despite having been alone with his wife after the wedding, but who allegedly had sex with another woman instead. If he did consummate the marriage and then was proved to have had intimate relations with

objections of a group of early Muʿtazilī rationalist theologians). Similarly, known Sunnī and Shīʿī jurists-cum-exegetes came down against any blanket permissibility of master-slave sexual relations with skepticism. See Ṭabarī (d. 310/923), *Jāmiʿ al-bayān ʿan taʾwīl āy al-Qurʾān* (also known as *Tafsīr al-Ṭabarī*), ed. Ṣalāḥ ʿAbd al-Fattāḥ al-Khālidī and Ibrāhīm Muḥammad al-ʿAlī (Damascus: Dār al-Qalam; Beirut: al-Dār al-Shāmiyya, 1997), 8:151–69 (interpreting Qurʾān, 4:24, and other verses to require a slave woman's consent before sexual relations with her master are deemed permissible); Muḥammad Ḥusayn al-Ṭabāṭabāʾī (d. 1403/1983), *al-Mīzān fī tafsīr al-Qurʾān* (Beirut: Muʾassasat al-Aʿlamī liʾl-Maṭbūʿāt, n.d.), 4:266–68 (alluding to the opinion of "some exegetes" who generalized the meaning of the Qurʾānic verse 4:24 to refer not to slave women but to chaste women, implying a position against the notion that master-slave relationships automatically validate sexual relations). For an opinion with similar implications from a minority group, see Abū Muḥammad ʿUthmān b. ʿAbd Allāh al-ʿIrāqī (mid-sixth/twelfth century), *al-Firaq al-muftaraqa* (Ankara: n.p., 1961), 16 (quoting the Khārijī group called the Ḥamziyya, who considered the enslavement of prisoners of war illegal altogether).

7 See ʿAbd al-Razzāq, *Muṣannaf* (1972), 8:255 (*duriʾa ʿanh al-ḥadd biʾl-shubha*).

8 Sufyān al-Thawrī applied the doubt canon in several other instances, though not always with reference to it. For instance, he avoided enforcing the *ḥadd* punishment against a man who consummated a marriage with a woman who never agreed to the marriage in the first place and where there were no witnesses or any other signs of a valid marriage. See ʿAbd al-Razzāq, *Muṣannaf* (1972), 6:207. For other instances, see Muḥammad Rawwās al-Qalʿahjī, *Mawsūʿat fiqh Sufyān al-Thawrī* (Beirut: Dār al-Nafāʾis, 1990), 241–44.

9 See Mālik b. Anas, *Muwaṭṭaʾ*, narration of Yaḥyā b. Yaḥyā al-Laythī, ed. Bashshār ʿAwwād Maʿrūf (Beirut: Dār al-Gharb al-Islāmī, 1996), 3:393.

10 Ibid. (invoking the doubt canon with anonymous phrasing: *duriʾa ʿanh al-ḥadd* and *yudraʾ ʿanh al-ḥadd*).

another woman, the act would constitute adultery, for which the punishment due would be stoning. If no marriage took place, the act would be fornication, punishable by flogging. Ibn al-Qāsim noted that, by operation of the doubt canon, the *ḥadd* punishment was to be avoided altogether until and unless the man admitted to consummating the marriage or to having sex with another woman without consummation of his marriage, or unless witnesses could be found to testify to the latter fact.[11]

In Egypt, Muḥammad b. Idrīs al-Shāfiʿī (d. 204/820), too, applied the doubt canon. His application of the canon is particularly striking because his work of jurisprudence, *al-Risāla*, emphasizes appeals to *textual* sources for legal authority (Qur'ān and *ḥadīth*, especially, and consensus to a lesser degree).[12] From his insistence on text, one would have expected him to invoke the doubt canon only if it were an authentic *ḥadīth*. Yet he invoked the doubt canon on *anonymous authority*, like his contemporaries elsewhere. In a case of conflicting testimony concerning stolen goods, he opined that if two of four witnesses testified that the item stolen was a certain garment of particular value and the other two maintained that it was a different garment of some other value, the *ḥadd* punishment for theft (hand amputation) would not apply. To be sure, the two sets of testimony were sufficient to establish that the alleged thief had committed a crime, but the conflict in testimony created doubt as to *which* item was stolen. In such cases, Shāfiʿī held, the *ḥadd* punishment was to be waived altogether "because we avoid *ḥudūd* punishments in cases of doubt," particularly for

11 Saḥnūn, *al-Mudawwana al-kubrā* (Beirut: Dār Ṣādir, n.d.), 16:236 (*yuqāl idra'ū 'l-ḥudūd bi'l-shubahāt*). For a related ruling using a similar formula, see ibid., 16:276 (citing the doubt canon in a similarly anonymous formula – *qad qīla idra'ū 'l-ḥudūd bi'l-shubahāt* – when considering whether grandparents could be held criminally liable for taking money from their grandchildren).

12 Muḥammad b. Idrīs al-Shāfiʿī, *al-Risāla*, ed. Muḥammad Nabīl Ghanāyim and ʿAbd al-Ṣabūr Shāhīn (Cairo: Markaz al-Ahrām li'l-Tarjama wa'l-Nashr, Mu'assasat al-Ahrām, 1988). This attention to Shāfiʿī's textualism is not to signal agreement with Joseph Schacht's assumption that any early jurist would use a *ḥadīth* if he or she knew of one, or to his placement of the origins of doubt in second/eighth-century Kūfa along with most other maxims. See Joseph Schacht, *The Origins of Muhammadan Jurisprudence* (Oxford: Clarendon Press, 1950), 180–89. For further elaboration, see my "Islamic Legal Maxims," 71–74, nn. 17–25. Rather, it is to argue precisely the opposite. As argued elsewhere in this book, there was a material change from early forms of authority to which jurists appealed (where citation of principles deemed to be Sunna did not always take the form of a prophetic *ḥadīth*, particularly when they were so widely diffused as to be considered self-evident policies attested by continuous community practice) to later textual forms of authority (which saw increasing reliance on *ḥadīth* texts used to make or bolster one's arguments against divergent views and practices).

blood punishments.[13] Though he was not subject to blood punishment, the perpetrator would not get off scot-free: he was to pay the value of the less valuable of the disputed garments to the owner in restitution.[14] Also in Egypt, al-Layth b. Saʿd (d. 175/791) is said to have applied the doubt canon whenever a perpetrator was ignorant of the illegality of the crime. In such instances, the offender's ignorance was sufficient to create judicial doubt about whether the law had been intentionally violated.[15]

Jurists in the other major centers of the Islamic empire also invoked the doubt canon in Iraq, Syria, the Ḥijāz, and other corners of the proto-Sunnī world.[16] Even Aḥmad Ibn Ḥanbal (d. 241/855) noted that the canon applied to women suspected of *zinā* who claimed that they had been raped. That is, he cited a *ḥadīth* in which the Prophet declined to punish a woman for having illicit sexual relations given the possibility of a lack of voluntariness on her part.[17]

Meanwhile, the doubt canon was widespread among the followers of ʿAlī, too, in the proto-Shīʿī world. Most tellingly, the canon features in a work of ʿAlī's judgments collected in Kūfa in the third/ninth century. We have already encountered the *Case of the Falsely Accused Butcher* from

[13] Shāfiʿī, *Umm* (1996), 7:52–53 (justifying his decision "from the standpoint that we avoid criminal punishments in cases of doubt, and this is the strongest [case] for avoiding punishment: *min qibal annā nudriʾ al-ḥudūd biʾl-shubha wa-hādhā aqwā mā yudraʾ bih al-ḥadd*").

[14] Ibid.

[15] Al-Layth b. Saʿd (d. 175/791), who was highly regarded by Shāfiʿī, was called the "Imām of Egypt" during his lifetime. He received his legal training in Mecca and Medina under Mālik but subsequently charted his own path. He is said to have avoided enforcing *ḥudūd* punishments when a perpetrator was ignorant of the illegality of the crime, for example, a man marrying two sisters or taking on a fifth wife (see Ibn Ḥazm, *Muḥallā*, 11:247), or a man taking money to which he was not entitled from the spoils of war (see Ibn Qudāma, *Mughnī*, 8:470; Muḥammad b. Aḥmad al-Qurṭubī, *al-Jāmiʿ li-aḥkām al-Qurʾān* (Cairo: Dār al-Shaʿb, 1961?), 4:260), because of the presence in each case of a doubt as to culpability. In the first two cases, ignorance of the law diminishes culpability for clearly prohibited acts, while in the last case, the man's partial ownership interest in the spoils of war exculpates him from the accusation of stealing property to which he is not in fact entitled.

[16] Though early sources for practices in Mecca and Syria are sparser than those for Medina and Iraq, there are indications that jurists followed practices of *ḥudūd* avoidance in cases of doubt there as well. See, for example, ʿAbd al-Razzāq, *Muṣannaf* (2000), 7:210; Wakīʿ (d. 306/917), *Akhbār al-quḍāt*, ed. Saʿīd Muḥammad al-Laḥḥām (Beirut: ʿĀlam al-Kutub, 2001), 617 and 53 (providing a corrupted version of the doubt canon in a letter of investiture attributed to ʿUmar, appointing Abū Mūsā al-Ashʿarī to the judgeship in Kūfa and used by Sunnīs as a model for judicial requirements everywhere).

[17] Ibn Ḥanbal (d. 241/855), *Musnad*, ed. ʿAbd Allāh al-Darwīsh (Beirut: Dār al-Fikr, 1991), 5:416. He thought – like other early *ḥadīth* scholars – that the saying was of dubious authenticity, and it is unclear whether he thought this singular case to be precedential for others. This ambivalence later revealed itself in his school's traditionist jurisprudence, which assumed differing degrees of opposition to the doubt canon.

that collection.[18] In another case, a man gave his wife a slave woman and then had sex with the latter. When the wife complained to ʿAlī, accusing her husband of illicit sexual relations, she immediately began to fear the harsh consequences of the punishment against her husband. She fell on her sword – perjuring herself, retracting her testimony, and thereby seeking to avoid the punishment against her husband. ʿAlī avoided the punishment given the doubt created by the conflicting testimony.[19] These are just two of many instances of ʿAlī's deference to doubt.[20] In all such instances, early Muslim jurists advised judges to apply the rule of *ḥudūd* avoidance when facing doubt-ridden facts. Intriguingly, they did so without citation to the Qurʾān or to the corpus of *ḥadīth*.

It was not that the doubt canon was unknown as a *ḥadīth* text. To the contrary, these same jurists knew of *ḥadīth* versions of the canon, which they sometimes mentioned in the course of offering general accounts of Islamic criminal law.[21] But they did not regard those versions as authentic *ḥadīth*. Likewise, *ḥadīth* collectors included nonstandard versions of the canon in their collected volumes. But *ḥadīth* critics charged with assessing the authenticity of prophetic reports never conferred on the standard form of the canon their stamp of approval through inclusion in their collections.[22] Indeed, an analysis of the various chains of transmission reveals that none goes back to the Prophet reliably, though some went back to Companions and other early legal authorities.[23] The jurists used the canon nevertheless.

18 See Introduction, note 1 and accompanying text.

19 See Qummī, *Qaḍāyā*, 253–54 (*fa-udriʾ ʿanh al-ḥadd*). One source has it that ʿAlī advised his faithful companion, Mālik al-Ashtar, to follow the wisdom of the doubt canon in a celebrated letter of investiture and advice upon sending him to be governor of Egypt. See Ibn Shuʿba (d. fifth/eleventh century?), *Tuḥaf al-ʿuqūl*, ed. ʿAlī Akbar al-Ghaffārī (Tehran: Maktabat al-Ṣadūq, 1376), 126–49, at 128. This source is dubious, and the doubt canon does not appear in the version of the letter recorded in al-Sharīf al-Raḍī (d. 406/1015), *Nahj al-balāgha*, ed. Ṣubḥī al-Ṣāliḥ (Beirut: Dār al-Kitāb al-Lubnānī, 1967), 426–45, no. 53. Yet its presence in *Tuḥaf* indicates that the canon was known in the circles that Ibn Shuʿba frequented in the fourth/tenth or fifth/eleventh century. More importantly, the doubt canon appears in Ibn Bābawayh's fourth/tenth-century work (*Faqīh*, 4:53), which records traditions that were widely known and accepted as authentic in the mainstream Shīʿī community from at least a generation before his time.

20 For a list, see Appendix B, Cases 18–25.

21 See, for example, note 3 (this chapter) for various versions of the canon in Abū Yūsuf, *Kitāb al-Kharāj*, 303. See further Appendix A.

22 For a full list, see Appendix A.

23 Instead, the *ḥadīth* versions of the saying (listed in Appendix A) differ in textual formulation and often attribution – frequently going back to an early Companion and to the Prophet only on dubious authority that failed to meet the most stringent requirements of authenticity in *ḥadīth*-critical circles.

One might suppose that jurists of this early period relied on the doubt canon because they viewed statements of the Prophet's Companions or Imāms, alongside those of the Prophet himself, as authoritative sources of law.[24] One might further suppose that text-conscious jurists such as Shāfiʿī cited the canon because they, too, viewed the statements of the Prophet's Companions as authoritative, despite their rhetoric to the contrary.[25] But even Shāfiʿī, like the other jurists applying the canon, appealed not to a Companionate saying but to widespread practice – announcing simply that "*we* avoid *ḥudūd* punishments in cases of doubt."[26] His anonymous citation signals that the doubt canon was an axiomatic, widely circulating, accepted legal principle requiring no attribution. In other words, this canon functioned – as do canons in other legal traditions – as a kind of "super-precedent" for which specific attribution was either uncommon or unnecessary.[27]

[24] Nineteenth- and twentieth-century European scholars of Islamic law developed a theory of the "backgrowth of *isnāds*," which posited a need for retroactive attribution of prophetic chains of transmission to Companionate reports or else to wholly invented reports. This theory has since become a starting point for *ḥadīth* studies. See Ignaz Goldziher, *Muslim Studies*, ed. and trans. S.M. Stern and C.R. Barber (Chicago: Aldine Atherton, 1971), 2:76ff.; Schacht, *Origins*, 22, 165–66; and Joseph Schacht, "A Revaluation of Islamic Traditions," *Journal of the Royal Asiatic Society* 81, 3–4 (1949), 143–54, at 147–51. For further development of the theory, see generally G.H.A. Juynboll, *Muslim Tradition: Studies in Chronology, Provenance and Authorship of Early Ḥadīth* (Cambridge: Cambridge University Press, 1983); G.H.A. Juynboll, "Some Notes on Islam's First *Fuqahāʾ* Distilled from Early *Ḥadīṯ* Literature," *Arabica* 39, 3 (1992), 287–314, at 299–300. For a review of this and subsequent theories and an alternative view, see Harald Motzki, *The Origins of Islamic Jurisprudence: Meccan Fiqh before the Classical Schools*, trans. Marion H. Katz (Leiden: Brill, 2002), 1–49.

[25] Christopher Melchert contests the dominant view that Shāfiʿī represents the third/ninth-century culmination of a gradual move away from reliance on various early authorities to an exclusive reliance on prophetic reports. See Christopher Melchert, "The Traditionist-Jurisprudents and the Framing of Islamic Law," *Islamic Law and Society* 8, 3 (2001), 383–406, at 401; Christopher Melchert, *The Formation of the Sunni Schools of Law, 9th–10th Centuries C.E.* (Leiden: Brill, 1997), 48 (noting that the impulse to cite prophetic reports is visible in the third/ninth century and before among Ḥanafīs).

[26] See note 13 (emphasis added).

[27] See my "Islamic Legal Maxims," 65. See further William N. Eskridge Jr. and John Ferejohn, "Super-Statutes," *Duke Law Journal* 50 (2001), 1215–76 (defining "super-statutes" as special laws that "successfully penetrate public normative and institutional culture in a deep way"); William N. Eskridge Jr. and John Ferejohn, *A Republic of Statutes: The New American Constitution* (New Haven, CT: Yale University Press, 2010). Compare Michael Gerhardt, "Super Precedent," *Minnesota Law Review* 90 (2006), 1294–331 (relating the concept of "super-statutes" from Eskridge and Ferejohn to "super-statutes" or "super-stare decisis" to describe laws so deeply entrenched in the legal system as to be inexorable commands that are especially hard to overturn); Michael Gerhardt, *The Power of Precedent* (New York: Oxford University Press, 2008) (same).

If anything, it was the anonymous authority of the oft-repeated doubt canon that reflected the legal authority of *judicial practice* during the early period. That is, anonymity here reflected a view that punishment avoidance by means of doubt was a widespread, accepted judicial practice that lay well within the spirit and even the firm directives of Islamic law even if it did not come directly from the Prophet or other early authorities as a foundational *legal text*. This point about the origins of the doubt canon is significant and bears broad implications for *ḥadīth*-focused studies of Islamic law.[28] It is not just that the weight of authority required to validate and use early Islamic traditions was in flux, as many contemporary scholars emphasize. It is also that widespread judicial practice was an authoritative basis for early Islamic law, without regard to *ḥadīth* chains of transmission.

In sum, the early jurists' widespread use of the doubt canon suggests a particularly significant feature of the history and operation of early Islamic law, given that the authenticity of the doubt canon as a prophetic *ḥadīth* did not determine its normativity for law. This fact suggests that early Islamic law was more practice-based than textual – a conception of Islamic law that was to change radically in the fourth/tenth century with extraordinary implications for the scope of doubt and of juristic power.

B. THE TEXTUALIZATION OF DOUBT: FOUNDATIONAL TEXT

The anonymous use of the doubt canon was not to last. Over the years, the doubt canon became so firmly entrenched as a principle of Islamic criminal law that by the tenth century, Muslim jurists asserted that it must have issued from the Prophet himself. But whereas earlier legal experts were content to

[28] For example, instead of following the Goldziher-Schacht theory of the backgrowth of *isnād*s to study to what extent medieval jurists participated in or were aware of schemes to manufacture *ḥadīth*, contemporary scholars interested in the operation of Islamic law and society can identify legal maxims by observing the extent of their application in judicial practice, regardless of *ḥadīth* attribution. For a critique of revisionist Islamic historiography and its characteristic skepticism in *ḥadīth* studies, see Fred M. Donner, *Narratives of Islamic Origins: The Beginnings of Islamic Historical Writing* (Princeton, NJ: Darwin Press, 1998). Compare Jonathan Brown, "Critical Rigor vs. Juridical Pragmatism: How Legal Theorists and *Ḥadīth* Scholars Approached the Backgrowth of *Isnāds* in the Genre of *ʿIlal al-ḥadīth*," *Islamic Law and Society* 14, 1 (2008), 1–41 (investigating collections of flawed reports (*kutub al-ʿilal*) to conclude that the introduction of fabricated *ḥadīth* assumed by the Goldziher-Schacht theory of the backgrowth of *isnād*s was known and accounted for by discarded *ḥadīth*). This is not to suggest that such studies are not useful in their own right for the many early reports cited as *ḥadīth*, but they do not shed light on the likely sizeable field of legal maxims from the early period that fall outside that rubric altogether.

rely on widespread judicial practice as evidence for that idea, later jurists seemed to need the authority of prophetic reports. The *ḥadīth* basis for such legal maxims – alluded to above as marginal to their early usage – became indispensable by the tenth century. This shift was a product of what has been called the triumph of Sunnī traditionalism.[29] That is, *ḥadīth*-minded scholars had prevailed in asserting that Islamic laws had to be backed by prophetic *ḥadīth* rather than earlier forms of authority, of which judicial practice was just one.[30] It is likely that the anonymity and ubiquity of the doubt canon together with the traditionalist triumph occasioned the shift in the jurists' treatment of the canon, resulting in the move from broad acceptance of the canon as a *judicial practice* to heavy citation of it as a *foundational text*.

During this period, the doubt canon now appeared with prophetic attributions among most of its proponents. In Baghdad, the Ḥanafī jurist Jaṣṣāṣ (d. 370/981) referred to it without fanfare as a *ḥadīth* in his legal treatise. Before him, the Qayrawānī scholar Khushanī (d. 361/971 or 371/981) recorded an incident in which the Cordovan Mālikī jurist ʿAbd al-Mālik b. Ḥabīb (d. 238/853) reportedly attributed the canon to the Prophet.[31] Thereafter, most jurists cited the doubt canon in its

[29] See, for example, George Makdisi, "The Significance of the Sunnī Schools of Law in Islamic Religious History," *International Journal of Middle East Studies* 10, 1 (1979), 1–8, at 7–8 (dating the triumph to the founding of the Ḥanbalī school and the failure of the theological Inquisition in the third/ninth century with the articulation of a "moderate traditionism" in the fourth/tenth century that would accompany the demise of Ẓāhirī strict textualist-traditionism a century later). Compare Berkey, *Formation of Islam*, 148–49 ("The popularity of traditionalism manifested itself repeatedly in Baghdad in the late ninth, tenth, and eleventh centuries ... [as] a principled opposition to practices not associated with the Prophet," partially "in response to Shīʿī claims"); Melchert, *The Formation of the Sunni Schools of Law*, 48–49 (outlining further elements of traditionism).

[30] The focus on *ḥadīth* has been described as Shāfiʿī's triumph in particular, though some scholars now question whether Shāfiʿī was in fact responsible for this theory. Committed Sunnī traditionism is best exemplified by Ḥanbalism, which was founded by Aḥmad Ibn Ḥanbal (d. 241/855), some fifty to one hundred years after the other enduring Sunnī schools, or by Ẓāhirism, which waned after the fifth/eleventh century. For an analysis of the shift in the role of *ḥadīth* from one of many supporting bases for legal conclusions to canonical sources for law, see Jonathan Brown, *The Canonization of al-Bukhārī and Muslim: The Formation and Function of the Sunnī Ḥadīth Canon* (Leiden: Brill, 2007).

[31] See Jaṣṣāṣ, *Aḥkām al-Qurʾān*, 3:330; Muḥammad b. al-Ḥārith al-Khushanī (d. 361/971 or 371/981), *Akhbār al-fuqahāʾ waʾl-muḥaddithīn*, ed. Sālim Muṣṭafā al-Badrī (Beirut: Dār al-Kutub al-ʿIlmiyya, 1999), 186–91. Despite Maribel Fierro's claim that Khushanī also recorded an earlier prophetic attribution, such attribution seems highly unlikely, as contemporaneous sources from earlier periods indicate that no other second/eighth- or third/ninth-century figure deemed the canon to be prophetic. True, another prominent Cordovan Mālikī jurist, Muḥammad b. Aḥmad al-ʿUtbī (d. 255/869), reported that, in a case in which a man suffering from extreme hunger sold his wife to another man for funds, Mālik's student ʿAbd al-Raḥmān b. al-Qāsim invoked the doubt canon to avoid

standardized form (*idra'ū 'l-ḥudūd bi'l-shubahāt*) as a prophetic *ḥadīth* in Ḥanafī, Mālikī, Shāfiʿī, and Shīʿī works, even though the "founders" of all of these schools had previously cited and employed the canon without a prophetic attribution.[32] Among Sunnīs, only the strict textualists, typically called "traditionists" or "traditionalists,"[33] were consistently attuned to the nonprophetic pedigree of the doubt canon and used that fact as a means to reject the canon both as a *ḥadīth* (in attribution) and as a substantive legal canon (in application). Among the Shīʿa, the Akhbārī strict textualist jurists, also called "traditionalists," recognized the authenticity of the canon as a *ḥadīth*, but they limited its application nonetheless.[34] The strict textualist opposition notwithstanding, most Muslim jurists after the early period saw the doubt canon as so securely entrenched that it likely seemed a necessary feature of law and therefore inevitably prophetic. It had completed its transformation into a super-precedent, a foundational text central to Islam's criminal law system.

punishment and used the word *ḥadīth*. See Ibn Rushd al-Jadd (d. 520/1126), *al-Bayān wa'l-taḥṣīl*, ed. Muḥammad Ḥajjī (Beirut: Dār al-Gharb al-Islāmī, 1984), 16:324 (quoting the *ʿUtbiyya*: *Qad jā'a 'l-ḥadīth idra'ū 'l-ḥudūd bi'l-shubahāt*). But ʿUtbī's citation of the canon appears in Khushanī's work. By Khushanī's time, and in his work, the canon had already become recognized as a prophetic *ḥadīth*. Moreover, it is not clear that ʿUtbī's use of the term *ḥadīth* is to be taken in the developed technical sense of a "prophetic report" rather than as a general statement, which the term also denoted in earlier periods. Finally, one would expect that if Ibn al-Qāsim in fact cited the canon as a prophetic *ḥadīth* in one place as in the above reference, he would have done so elsewhere, such as when relating Mālik's opinions to Saḥnūn (d. 240/854) or in his notebook from which ʿUtbī copied. But this seems not to have been the case: As recorded in the *Mudawwana*, Ibn al-Qāsim recounted the canon to Saḥnūn twice, but both times on decidedly anonymous authority (*yuqāl* and *qad qīla*). See ʿUmar b. ʿAbd al-Karīm al-Jīdī, *Mabāḥith fī 'l-madhhab al-Mālikī bi 'l-Maghrib* (Rabat: al-Hilāl al-ʿArabiyya, 1993), 70–72 (noting that, in compiling the *Mudawwana*, Saḥnūn relied on Ibn al-Qāsim, with whom he verified opinions from a notebook recording Mālik's sayings and legal opinions from his student Asad b. al-Furāt (d. 213/828), and that ʿUtbī also relied on Ibn al-Qāsim by copying Saḥnūn's notebooks and those of other students of Mālik for his compilation of Mālikī opinions in the *ʿUtbiyya*).

32 See Part III.

33 Although there is sometimes overlap between these two terms, I use "traditionist" to refer to collectors of *ḥadīth* reports and scholars of *ḥadīth* criticism (that is, *muḥaddithūn* – many from the first three centuries) and "traditionalist" to refer to legal scholars who followed a jurisprudence and a "theology-lite" based directly on those traditions, with the result that they saw the role of reason and the scope of human discretion in legal interpretation to be severely constrained (that is, Sunnī *ahl al-ḥadīth*, Shīʿī Akhbārīs, and others – many from later periods). For a discussion making a similar distinction and offering further definitions in the Sunnī context, see Asma Sayeed, *Women and the Transmission of Religious Knowledge in Islam* (Cambridge: Cambridge University Press, 2013), 3, n. 3; 7–8, and sources cited therein.

34 See Chapter 7 (on Ḥanbalī and Ẓāhirī textualism) and Chapter 8 (on Akhbārī textualism).

From the canonization to the textualization of doubt, medieval Muslim jurists continuously operated against a backdrop of the divine legislative supremacy ideal. To be sure, they differed on how to achieve that ideal. Strict textualists regarded the widespread use of doubt as tantamount to juridical legislation. But most jurists conceived of themselves as restraining their own discretion and that of the political authorities in deference to criminal laws specified by God. For them, the doctrine of divine legislative supremacy meant that the ambiguity and severity endemic to Islamic criminal law required jurists to proceed with caution – to "avoid punishments in cases of doubt." As it was canonized through early judicial practice and then textualized as a *ḥadīth*, the doubt canon took on ever-expanding significance. Rather than representing the inverse of *ḥudūd* laws, doubt had become part and parcel of the textual corpus of Islamic criminal law itself.

On the flip side of divine legislative supremacy, punishment avoidance also provided a way for jurists to emphasize other early moral imperatives of fairness, to mitigate their own moral anxieties about enforcing punishments that were unauthorized, and to rein in the discretion of political authorities. These moral aspects of doubt are discussed in Part II. Before getting there, it is worth considering how Muslim jurists gained the institutional authority and wherewithal to define doubt in the first place.

C. THE INTERPRETATION OF DOUBT: ON INSTITUTIONAL STRUCTURES AND LEGITIMACY

In elaborating this account of Muslim jurists' broad interpretive legal authority, the point is not to recount a detailed history of how early Muslim jurists came to wield tremendous power over definitions of Islamic law.[35] Rather, the point is to emphasize the bases on which those jurists successfully asserted their interpretive power: *religious morality* and *institutional competence*. In criminal law, these two elements alternately competed with and complemented the *enforcement power* of the caliphs. They also provided the basis for the popularly recognized epistemic authority that conferred legitimacy on juristic interpretations of Islamic law. The story begins with the Prophet.

[35] For useful histories, see generally Hallaq, *Sharīʿa*; M. Qasim Zaman, *Religion and Politics under the Early ʿAbbāsids: The Emergence of the Proto-Sunnī Elite* (Leiden: Brill, 1997).

During his lifetime, the Prophet Muḥammad embodied both religious and political leadership. His guidance assumed multiple institutional functions: political leadership (governance), moral-societal directives (legislation), and dispute resolution (adjudication). The *Hijra* – the young Muslim community's migration in 622 from the town of Mecca to the town of Medina some two hundred miles north – was all-important in the history of Islamic law and governance. In Mecca, the Prophet enjoyed only charismatic religious authority over followers with whom his message of morality and societal ethics resonated. But in Medina, he gained political and legal authority as well.[36] With Muḥammad's death in 632, the religious and political functions split, and the tasks of governance, legislation, and adjudication ceased to be combined in a single person.[37]

The Prophet's death caused a crisis in leadership, which would radically change the political organization of the young Muslim community.[38] A series of four caliphs took over political leadership, appointing judges and performing other executive-governance functions.[39] But they lacked the divinely designated prophetic authority to assert an exclusive prerogative to define Islamic law.[40] Unlike the Prophet, most – if not all – were not immune to correction on points of Islamic law. For example, one of Muḥammad's former companions successfully challenged the second

[36] Tellingly, the Islamic calendar begins not when the Prophet first received revelation; it begins at the *Hijra* (AH denoting *Anno Hegirae*) – that is, with his migration to Medina – precisely because at that point he became the head of state. For general overviews of law and governance during Muḥammad's lifetime, see Kennedy, *The Prophet and the Age of the Caliphates*, 50–81; Hallaq, *Sharīʿa*, 27–71.

[37] See Kennedy, *The Prophet and the Age of the Caliphates*, 50.

[38] See, for example, Mahmoud M. Ayoub, *The Crisis of Muslim History: Religion and Politics in Early Islam* (Oxford: Oneworld, 2003), 7 (labeling the Prophet's death the first "crisis of Muslim history"); Madelung, *Succession to Muḥammad*.

[39] See, for example, Abū al-ʿAbbās al-Qalqashandī (d. 821/1418), *Ṣubḥ al-aʿshā fī ṣināʿāt al-inshāʾ* (Cairo: al-Muʾassasa al-Miṣriyya al-ʿĀmma, 1981) (orig. 1964), 10:21, 79, 359 (reproducing the famous letter of appointment and investiture from the second caliph, ʿUmar b. al-Khaṭṭāb, to the judge Abū Mūsā al-Ashʿarī, containing instructions on general policies for judging). See also al-Sharīf al-Raḍī, *Nahj al-balāgha*, no. 53 (reproducing the famous letter explicating judicial and governing policies from the fourth caliph and first Shīʿī Imām, ʿAlī, to Mālik al-Ashtar upon sending him to Egypt to take over as governor).

[40] See Kennedy, *The Prophet and the Age of the Caliphates*, 50–81, noting that these caliphs exercised political authority by virtue of most Muslims having agreed to "elect" a single leader after the Prophet. See also Wael Hallaq, *Origins and Evolution of Islamic Law*, 38–39; Roy P. Mottahedeh, *Loyalty and Leadership in an Early Islamic Society*, rev. ed. (London: I. B. Tauris, 2001) (orig. Princeton, NJ: Princeton University Press, 1980), 12–21.

caliph, ʿUmar b. al-Khaṭṭāb, in an arbitration proceeding over the destruction of borrowed property. Even though the decision was against him, the caliph was so impressed with the arbiter's reasoning and scholarly acumen that he appointed him a judge.[41] Such anecdotes suggest that early Muslims understood the first four caliphs to be leading members of the learned circles of the Prophet's former companions and family members.[42] The extent of their religious-legal authority depended on their individual scholarly competence in articulating norms drawn from their long association with the Prophet.[43]

The assassination of ʿAlī, the fourth caliph and first Shīʿī Imām, just three decades after the Prophet's death inaugurated a dramatic shift in community leadership from scholarly competence to monarchical rule. Muʿāwiya was the infamous governor of Syria and cousin of the slain third caliph, ʿUthmān, who would initiate the shift. Seeking to avenge ʿUthmān's killing, Muʿāwiya rallied troops to march against ʿAlī – whom he accused of taking insufficient measures to bring the assassin to justice. Ultimately, Muʿāwiya succeeded in wresting control from ʿAlī, who was killed in battle by a defector from his own troops.[44] Muʿāwiya then established the Umayyad dynasty, the first in a series of monarchical dynasties that presided over the Muslim world in one form or another until the end of the Ottoman Empire in 1924.[45]

As the caliphate violently passed on to Muʿāwiya, he and his successors usually acknowledged that they had little basis to assert power to define Islamic law, including Islamic criminal law.[46] Yet they continued to use the

[41] Wakīʿ, *Akhbār al-quḍāt*, 357 (recounting the judicial appointment story of Shurayḥ (d. ca. 76/695–6 or 80/699–700)).

[42] See Hallaq, *Origins and Evolution of Islamic Law*, 29–56. For a contrary view, see Patricia Crone and Martin Hinds, *God's Caliph: Religious Authority in the First Centuries of Islam* (Cambridge: Cambridge University Press, 1986), 2–3 (arguing that caliphs after Abū Bakr saw themselves not just as political authorities but as religious authorities as well). Compare Hossein Modarressi, *Crisis and Consolidation in the Formative Period of Shīʿite Islam* (Princeton, NJ: Darwin Press, 1993), 29.

[43] Hallaq, *Origins and Evolution of Islamic Law*, 34–56.

[44] Kennedy, *The Prophet and the Age of the Caliphates*, 70–80 (describing the motivations of the defecting group, the "Khawārij").

[45] For a survey of Muslim dynasties, including a list of Umayyad and ʿAbbāsid rulers, see Clifford E. Bosworth, *The New Islamic Dynasties*, 2nd ed. (New York: Columbia University Press, 2004).

[46] That much was evident from their episodic but always unsuccessful attempts to control the jurists. See Zaman, *Religion and Politics*, 90 (describing the failed proposal of the vizier Ibn al-Muqaffaʿ (d. 137/755 or 139/756) to place interpretive authority over Islamic law in the hands of the caliph by requiring jurists to write an Islamic legal code).

title of caliph, which literally meant "deputy" or "representative."[47] But the term had lost the sense of religious morality with the transformation of the caliphate from an office of moral stewardship to a position of power based on the sword, the purse, and tribal loyalties.[48]

Afterward, the ruling authorities across the medieval Muslim world and across time tended to use their power over discretionary penalties to be maximally expansive in criminal punishment. The Umayyads and ʿAbbāsids were known for their excesses in punishment.[49] Christian Lange has detailed the Seljūq sultan's extensive use of harsh criminal justice to assert social control. And Yossef Rapoport has similarly detailed instances in which Mamlūk sultans used the juristic framework itself to do the same.[50] In short, while more in-depth studies remain to be done, there is substantial indication that political authorities were often only marginally responsive to the juristic protestations against their actions.

Within half a century of Islam's advent, as political leadership had passed from a charismatic prophet to a militaristic caliph, religious leadership shifted almost entirely to the scholarly, learned class comprising the Prophet's close family members and companions. After ʿAlī's assassination, this religious-scholarly class – known as the jurists – maintained that continuous study and application of the Prophet's life provided them with a special degree of religious morality and institutional competence to discern its meaning, that is, to "say what the law is."[51] In Sunnī terms, circles of learned Companions of the Prophet and succeeding scholar-jurists were

[47] Ibn Manẓūr (d. 711/1311), *Lisān al-ʿArab* (Beirut: Dār Ṣādir, 1997), 2:299–303 (s.v. "kh-l-f").

[48] Ayoub, *Crisis*, 54–57 (arguing that this transformation to tribal loyalty began with ʿUthmān). Compare Louise Marlow, *Hierarchy and Egalitarianism in Islamic Thought* (Cambridge: Cambridge University Press, 2002), 14–16, 28 (detailing a social egalitarian bent during the early Islamic period that became explicitly hierarchical during ʿUthmān's time and arguing that Muʿāwiya's assumption of leadership based on bloodlines ended "the opportunity for social equalising" on the basis of piety criteria).

[49] See, for example, Berkey, *Formation of Islam*, 84–85 (noting complaints of excessive Umayyad and ʿAbbāsid applications of punishment).

[50] See generally Lange, *Justice*; Rapoport, "Legal Diversity," 210–28; and Chapter 1, note 44 and accompanying text.

[51] See my "We The Jurists," 542. See also Chibli Mallat, *The Renewal of Islamic Law: Muhammad Baqer as-Sadr, Najaf and the Shiʿi International* (Cambridge: Cambridge University Press, 1993), 79 (calling the "constitutional question of who ultimately holds the power to 'say what the law is' … the essential problem of contemporary Islamic law," and quoting Chief Justice John Marshall's famous exposition of the "Judicial Power" under Article III of the U.S. Constitution in *Marbury v. Madison*, 5 U.S. (1 Cranch) 137, 177 (1803)).

like religious "heirs to the Prophet."[52] Among the Shīʿa – who had the same tradition, though conceived and deployed in very different ways – separate circles of learned members of the Prophet's family looked to the Imāms, who were regarded as the rightful successors to the Prophet and his actual and religious heirs.[53] In both communities, the religious morality once articulated by the Prophet had turned into the institutional competence of the jurists to determine the legal content of that morality.[54]

Importantly, history suggests that the general populace agreed with the jurists. That is, the scholarly claim to interpretive authority over Islamic law resonated with the political and religious sensibilities of a sufficient number of factions that the jurists were ultimately successful in their claim.[55] The jurists – armed only with the soft power of popular perceptions of religious and epistemic legitimacy – relied on caliphal enforcement of their proclamations of law. Reflexively, caliphs – possessed of the coercive power of the sword and the purse – could ensure political stability only by ostensibly agreeing to enforce juristic interpretations of law.[56] In this way legitimacy – if not law enforcement – depended on the jurists' interpretation, extending from their ultimately successful claims to religious morality and institutional competence to interpret God's law.

Criminal law was a significant manifestation of this entire arrangement because, as one of few areas of public law, it was a domain of shared jurisdiction between jurists and caliphs. In public law especially, the

[52] For discussions in the context of Sunnī law, see Feldman, *Fall and Rise*, 26. For the tradition on which these discussions are based (Ar.: *al-ʿulamāʾ [hum] warathat al-anbiyāʾ*), see Bukhārī, *Ṣaḥīḥ*, no. 1376; Abū Dāwūd, *Sunan* ed. Muḥammad Muḥyī al-Dīn ʿAbd al-Ḥamīd (Cairo: al-Maktaba al-Tijāriyya al-Kubrā, 1935), 3:317, no. 3641; Ibn Mājah, *Sunan*, ed. Muḥammad Fuʾād ʿAbd al-Bāqī (Cairo: Dār Iḥyāʾ al-Kutub al-ʿArabiyya, 1952–53), 1:81, no. 223; Dārimī (d. 255/869), *Sunan*, ed. ʿAbd Allāh Hāshim Yamānī al-Madanī (Cairo: Dār al-Maḥāsin liʾl-Ṭibāʿa, 1966),1:83, no. 349. For Shīʿī law, see Liyakat N. Takim, *The Heirs of the Prophet: Charisma and Religious Authority in Shi'ite Islam* (Albany: State University of New York Press, 2006).

[53] See Modarressi, *Crisis and Consolidation*, 27–29 (noting that the early mainstream Imāmī Shīʿī community believed the authority of the Imāms to have been founded on their being pious scholars). For further studies, see also Wilferd Madelung, *Religious Schools and Sects in Medieval Islam* (London: Variorum Reprints, 1985); Etan Kohlberg, "*al-Uṣūl Al-Arbaʿumiʾa*," *Jerusalem Studies in Arabic and Islam* 10 (1987), 128–66.

[54] On the moral and "epistemological" basis for juristic authority and legitimacy, see generally Hallaq, *Authority*, esp. 1–23, 55–57, 85, and passim; see also Zysow, *Economy of Certainty*, 1.

[55] This fact led to an uneasy balance between jurists and government officials over law as well as to more intense discussions in legal-religious circles about what the law was. See Mottahedeh, *Lessons*, 6–8.

[56] See Hallaq, *Sharīʿa*, 159–83, 197–221, esp. 199.

caliphs and the jurists depended on one another. In presenting themselves as best qualified to interpret Islamic criminal law, jurists readily acknowledged that they lacked the effective power to enforce it. By tacit agreement, the caliphs ceded most interpretive authority to the jurists and retained control over judicial appointments, policing, and law enforcement of all types – fixed, retaliatory, and discretionary.[57] For their part, the jurists developed Islamic criminal law norms – and the expanding arena of doubt – independently of caliphal involvement and control.[58] Between the two, judges who were not themselves jurists were to consult the expert jurists in all types of criminal law matters.[59]

Against this backdrop, interpretations of Islamic criminal law and of doubt highlight the means by which the jurists constructed the boundaries of the post-prophetic judicial, legislative, and political functions of early Muslim societies. Medieval Islam was unlike modern American law, in which three branches are well defined and in dialogue with one other in contests over institutional functions, with an active legislature able to change the law from time to time.[60] In Islamic law, divine legislative supremacy was the ultimate ideal – meaning juridical deference to a Lawgiver who legislated once in the seventh century. Yet as in any society, Muslims had to confront novel situations in criminal law. In their institutional contexts, textual interpretation took on exaggerated importance – a situation not unlike that of medieval common law. To ensure legitimacy, after the tenth century Muslim jurists expended increasing efforts to draw a connection to *texts* as a means of assessing the intent of God. The effect on the actual implementation of criminal punishment is unclear.

[57] Hallaq, *Sharīʿa*, 197–199 (describing this tripartite scheme as a "Circle of Justice" in which jurists, caliphs, and judges formed coequal arcs necessary to complete the circle). On criminal law enforcement in varied contexts, see further Kristen Stilt, *Islamic Law in Action: Authority, Discretion, and Everyday Experiences in Mamluk Egypt* (Oxford: Oxford University Press, 2011); Delfina Serrano, "Twelve Cases on the Application of Penal Law under the Moravids," in *Dispensing Justice in Islam: Qadis and Their Judgments*, ed. Muhammad Khalid Masud, Rudolph Peters, and David S. Powers (Leiden: Brill, 2006), 473–93; Rapoport, "Legal Diversity," 210–28.

[58] For accounts of the early schools, beginning in the Umayyad reign and lasting until the formalization of legal doctrine under the early ʿAbbāsids, see generally Nurit Tsafrir, *The History of an Islamic School of Law: The Early Spread of Ḥanafism* (Cambridge, MA: Islamic Legal Studies Program at Harvard Law School, 2004); Motzki, *Origins*.

[59] Hallaq, *Origins and Evolution of Islamic Law*, 38–39 (citing an instance where an Egyptian judge was appointed despite his lack of knowledge of inheritance laws).

[60] On the dialogic nature of the communication between American courts, Congress, and executive agencies, see discussions in American statutory interpretation debates, for example, in sources cited in Chapter 1, note 65.

But regardless of whether jurists dictated outcomes, what is important is that their interpretations helped set the institutional frameworks for what could be called Islamic law. In that respect, their interpretations provided the baseline against which caliphs operated – walking the fine line between expansive criminal punishment and appeals to jurist-defined legitimacy.[61]

CONCLUSION

In the end, Muslim jurists used interpretation to define institutional roles separated not by constitutional structure but by institutional function. In the exercise of their interpretive power to guide *judicial functions*, they could readily claim that their reliance on texts made them wholly subordinate to a divine legislator.[62] Yet as we will see, that same power to define the law entailed something of a *legislative function*, cloaked by claims to textualism.[63] Moreover, that the jurists had ceded the *executive-enforcement function* to the caliphs would bear important consequences for the extent to which succeeding jurists constructed expansive theories of doubt in attempts to impugn the legitimacy of excessive punishments and thus curtail them.

A textual basis for doubt would allow jurists to argue that their push against punishment came directly from God and the Prophet and thus honored the divine legislative supremacy ideal. In this way, the jurists could decline to authorize punishments that they deemed improper. They

[61] Whether the jurists were able to rein in caliphs successfully is a matter worthy of further study. While the historical sources suggest that caliphs punished wantonly, the nature of the sources leaves no way of determining conclusively whether punishment would have been more or less expansive without the presence of jurists and the jurisprudence of doubt. My hunch is that it would have been more expansive, given evidence of individual cases in which jurists were able to appeal to the doubt canon to absolve a defendant from liability and punishment. Regardless, it is clear that doubt matters as an aspirational ideal central to the structure of Islamic criminal law, and that caliphal punishment did not carry precedential value for Islamic law, while narrowing juristic interpretations did.

[62] For an elaboration of a similar idea in American statutory interpretation, see Jane Schacter, "The Changing Structure of Legitimacy in Statutory Interpretation," *Harvard Law Review* 108 (1995), 593–663 (noting that, when judges interpret text, they are implicitly defining their own role "by outlining the goal and methodology of the interpretive enterprise, and by taking an institutionalist stance in relation to the legislature").

[63] In addition to the textualization of doubt, Muslim jurists adopted changing definitions of "text" in the course of their definitions and invocations of the doubt canon. For discussion, see further Chapters 5, 6, and 8.

sought to accomplish regulation and authorization of criminal punishment by interpreting early prophetic precedents alongside the doubt canon to *narrow* the range of valid instances of criminal law enforcement in favor of a *broad* policy of punishment avoidance. Importantly, these jurists' interpretive maneuvers responded to competing assertions of power from both the ruling authorities and from dissenting strict textualists, both of whom – for different reasons – wished to enforce criminal law *broadly*. The *Case of Māʿiz*, outlined in the laṣt chapter, vividly illustrates this phenomenon. The next two chapters introduce a number of other cases from the early founding period to examine the rationales behind it.

PART II

MORALITY AND SOCIAL CONTEXT, FIRST/SEVENTH–FIFTH/ELEVENTH CENTURIES

3

Hierarchy and *Ḥudūd* Laws

The social context within which the doubt canon emerged was one that early Muslim jurists found to be fraught with decidedly "un-Islamic" mores, especially during the first three centuries of Islam's founding period. After the Prophet's death and the crisis of succession thereafter, questions of morality became increasingly sharp as political officials and religious-scholarly figures competed for authority over the legitimate interpretation of and effective power over Islamic law. Criminal law was representative of the problems surrounding issues of morality, power, and authority. From the jurists' perspective, the status hierarchies rampant in Arab society began to seep into the practice of Islamic criminal law. Further, the ruling authorities regularly over-enforced Islamic criminal law against their foes and under-enforced the law for their friends. Doubt was a way of curbing both practices and restoring a moral order of egalitarianism and other values that the earliest Muslim jurists took to characterize Islamic criminal law.

A. EARLY ISLAMIC VALUES: EGALITARIANISM AND DETERRENCE

In the seventh-century Arabian society in which it emerged, Islam sought to create a new social-moral order. Beyond establishing an "uncompromising monotheism" and the Prophet's authority as the apostle of God,[1] a major

[1] See Kennedy, *The Prophet and the Age of the Caliphates*, 47.

feature of the new order was an emphasis on certain moral precepts.[2] These precepts found clear expression in Islamic criminal law.

In criminal law, monotheism's ideal of divine legislative supremacy meant establishing a criminal justice system that set moral standards meant to be applied in an egalitarian way. As later Muslim commentators saw it, God wished to correct the moral ills of seventh-century Arabia, where acts generating social harms were rampant and laws applied disparately. On the Muslim commentators' account, murder, highway robbery, theft, wine drinking, apostasy, and the range of sex crimes were criminalized because they contravened a moral order that God wished to establish uniformly. The Qur'ān itself sets out punishments for many – though not all – of these acts,[3] to signal the gravity of each act as a moral offense. Moreover, the Qur'ān cautions against a general policy of avoiding punishments where warranted merely out of lenient attitudes or a reluctance to enforce the law.[4] By deterring a short list of bad acts, these criminal laws were intended to promote adherence to "Islamic" moral ideals. To further

[2] Narratives of this earliest period of Islamic history are a matter of considerable scholarly debate, the contours of which are marginal to the discussion here, which proceeds from areas of broad agreement concerning early Islamic history. For textbook historical accounts, in addition to Kennedy (*The Prophet and the Age of the Caliphates*), see further Ira Lapidus, *A History of Islamic Societies* (Cambridge: Cambridge University Press, 2002) (orig. 1988); Fred Donner, *Early Islamic Conquests* (Princeton, NJ: Princeton University Press, 1981); Marshall Hodgson, *The Venture of Islam* (Chicago: University of Chicago Press, 1974) (orig. 1961), 1:188–230. For alternative accounts, see Madelung, *Succession to Muḥammad* (presenting a narrative from common Sunnī sources that yield conclusions more in line with the early Shīʿī interpretation of the succession dispute than with later Sunnī, potentially revisionist, narratives); Patricia Crone, *Roman, Provincial, and Islamic Law: The Origins of the Islamic Patronate* (Cambridge: Cambridge University Press, 2002) (testing a hypothesis of Roman borrowing through examining the institution of tribal clientage); Robert Hoyland, *Seeing Islam as the Others Saw It: A Survey and Evaluation of Christian, Jewish, and Zoroastrian Writings on Early Islam* (Princeton, NJ: Darwin Press, 1997) (presenting translations of contemporaneous source materials by observers of Islam outside of its community together with analyses of those sources).

[3] Scholars in the field have acknowledged that the Qur'ān does not designate punishments for every act it censures. For example, as noted, although medieval Muslim jurists counted them as *ḥudūd* crimes, the Qur'ān mentions no punishment for apostasy or wine drinking, and stoning is not a Qur'ānic punishment for adultery. See Chapter 1.

[4] Qur'ān, 24:2 (The passage refers to *zinā*: "As for those who commit *zinā*, whether female or male, flog them one hundred times each, and let not compassion for them stay you in a matter of obedience to God if you believe in God and the Last Day; and let a party from the community be witness to the punishment: *wa'l-zāniyatu wa'l-zānī fa-'jlidū kulla wāḥidin minhumā mi'ata jaldatin wa-lā ta'khudhkum bihimā ra'fatun fī dīni 'llāhi in kuntum tu'minūna bi'llāhi wa'l-yawmi 'l-ākhiri wa'l-yashhad ʿadhābahumā ṭā'ifatun min al-mu'minīn.*").

elucidate this concept, Muslim jurists set out to justify Islamic criminal law in primarily moral terms.

1. Islamic Criminal Law Rationales 1: Deterrence as Morality

Islamic criminal law was justified primarily in terms not of retribution or repentance but of *deterrence* of behaviors that God had designated as immoral. Early Muslim jurists pointed to the morality-cum-deterrence rationales explicitly. There was agreement between the pragmatists and strict textualists on this approach. The early pragmatic jurists Abū Yūsuf and Shāfiʿī announced pointedly that "criminal laws aim to *deter*."[5] Further, the strict textualist jurist Dāwūd al-Ẓāhirī explained that prohibitions against fornication, theft, and defamation were legislated to deter people from mixing bloodlines, taking private property, and impugning honor, respectively.[6] In so saying, he was offering an early formulation of the set of five fundamental values that Muslim jurists took all of Islamic law to promote: the preservation of life, religion, sanity (or intellect), honor, and property (commonly referred to as the five "objectives" or "essential principles" of Islamic law: *maqāṣid al-sharīʿa* or *al-ḍarūriyyāt al-khamsa*).[7]

A secondary rationale for Islamic criminal law was *spiritual expiation* for perpetrators.[8] In the Islamic tradition, repentance on the part of the offender was as laudatory as retribution initiated by the state. But aside from *qiṣāṣ* rules of retribution in cases of personal injury and murder, jurists largely left the criminal law implications (or sincerity) of repentance

[5] Abū Yūsuf, *Āthār*, 157 (*al-ḥudūd wuḍiʿat liʾl-zajr*) (emphasis added); Shāfiʿī, *Umm* (1996), 7:330 (same). For a useful discussion of a range of opinions detailing justifications for Islamic criminal law, see Ibn Nujaym, *al-Baḥr al-rāʾiq: sharḥ Kanz al-daqāʾiq* (Cairo: n.p., 1983?), 5:4–5.

[6] Dāwūd al-Ẓāhirī (d. 270/883–4), *ʿUyūn al-masāʾil*, quoted by Shaṭṭī, *Risāla*, 27.

[7] In Sunnī law, see, for example, Abū Ḥāmid al-Ghazālī, *al-Mustaṣfā min ʿilm al-uṣūl*, ed. Ibrāhīm Muḥammad Ramaḍān (Beirut: Dār al-Arqam, 1997?), 1:289–90 (developing the five objectives of the law and listing them as *nafs*, *dīn*, *ʿaql*, *nasab* [or *ʿirḍ*], and *māl*); Shāṭibī (d. 790/1388), *al-Muwāfaqāt fī uṣūl al-aḥkām*, ed. Muḥammad Muḥyī al-Dīn ʿAbd al-Ḥ amīd (Cairo: Muḥammad ʿAlī Ṣabīḥ, 1969–70), 2:2ff. (same). In Shīʿī law, see, for example, Miqdād al-Suyūrī (d. 826/1423), *Naḍd al-qawāʿid al-fiqhiyya*, ed. ʿAbd al-Laṭīf al-Kūhkamarī et al. (Qum: Maktabat Āyat Allāh al-ʿUẓmā al-Marʿashī, 1403/1982–3), 60–63 (same). For discussion, see further Muhammad Khalid Masud, *Islamic Legal Philosophy: A Study of Abū Isḥāq al-Shāṭibī's Life and Thought* (Islamabad: Islamic Research Institute, 1977).

[8] Abū Yūsuf, *Āthār*, 157 (reporting a prophetic *ḥadīth*: *al-ḥudūd kaffārāt li-ahlihā*); cf. Qudūrī, *Tajrīd*, 11:5949–50.

and retribution in God's hands.[9] Instead of using either to justify criminal law, they took for granted that God had determined the "just deserts" for bad acts in ways that accounted for both. That is, they assumed that God had identified bad acts and set punishments for them through *ḥudūd* and *qiṣāṣ* laws, and they believed that He would evaluate claims of repentance and administer any further retribution due in the afterlife. Indeed, Qur'ānic legislation of criminal laws signaled as much.[10]

The emphasis on specified crimes and fixed punishments defining *ḥudūd* laws left the category of criminal laws for which God had not designated punishments – the realm of discretionary (*ta'zīr*) penalties – open to some question. To determine the appropriate punishment for unspecified crimes, Muslim jurists took guidance from the first and second types of criminal laws (*ḥudūd* and *qiṣāṣ* laws), and used those categories as a framework to apply the deterrence-cum-morality rationale behind those laws to this tertiary category. That is, the jurists used *ḥudūd* and *qiṣāṣ* laws as a baseline in their attempts to develop rules proportionate to the moral harm involved in unspecified crimes. Abū Yūsuf summed it up as follows: "*Ḥudūd* laws were legislated for deterrence of grave moral offenses (*fawāḥish*) and other crimes. The more morally corrupt the act (*afḥash*), the greater the measure of deterrence required."[11] Applying these rules to *ta'zīr* penalties created an otherwise unstated rule of proportionality for Islamic criminal law.[12]

9 Abū Yūsuf, *Āthār*, 157 (noting that repentance usually does not void criminal liability).

10 For mention of punishment in the afterlife, see, for example, Qur'ān, 24:23 (on defamation: "Those who slander chaste women, indiscreet but believing, are cursed in this life and in the hereafter; for them is a grievous Penalty"); Qur'ān, 5:33–34 (on highway robbery: "The punishment for those who wage war against God and His Messenger, and who strive with all their might and main to sow discord through the land, is execution or crucifixion, that their hands and feet be cut off from opposite sides, or exile: that is their disgrace in this world, and they will have a heavy punishment in the next world, except for those who repent before being captured, in which case, know that God is oft-forgiving, most merciful"); Qur'ān, 2:217 (on apostasy: "Tumult and oppression are worse than slaughter. Nor will they cease fighting you until they turn you back from your faith if they can. And if any of you turn back from your faith and die in unbelief, their works will bear no fruit in this life and in the Hereafter; they will be companions of the fire and abide therein."). For further connections between this-worldly and afterworldly punishment, see generally Lange, *Justice*.

11 Abū Yūsuf, *Āthār*, 252.

12 For Sunnī law, see, for example, Aḥmad b. al-Naqīb al-Miṣrī al-Shāfiʿī (d. 769/1367), *'Umdat al-sālik wa-'uddat al-nāsik*, in Muḥammad al-Zuhrī al-Ghamrāwī, *Anwār al-masālik: sharḥ 'Umdat al-sālik*, ed. Yūsuf 'Alī Badīwī (Damascus: Dār al-Ṭabbā', 1996), 468 (noting that *ta'zīr* punishments may not exceed the lowest *ḥadd* punishment, that is,

2. Islamic Criminal Law Rationales 2: Moral Egalitarianism

In addition to deterring acts deemed immoral, Islamic criminal law placed a heavy accent on moral egalitarianism – a principle of uniform treatment under the law that stressed preference on the basis of good character and moral excellence rather than bloodlines and wealth.[13] The cultural context in which Islam emerged was one in which tribal values accompanied a type of entrenched egalitarianism, apparent in the very limited authority that tribal leaders commanded.[14] Status and hierarchy came through lineage and competition. Arabs drew prestige from their bloodlines and they gained further respect through performing meritorious acts of honor and bravery.[15]

Against this backdrop, the Qur'ān attempted to bolster the spirit of egalitarianism while replacing worldly criteria for social status, tribal preference, and upward mobility with spiritual-moral criteria for the same. In one frequently repeated verse, it announces:

> O people! We have created you from a male and a female and fashioned you into peoples and tribes that you may know one another; surely, the most noble of you in the sight of God is the most God-conscious of you: *yā ayyuhā 'l-nāsu innā khalaqnākum min dhakarin wa-unthā wa-jaʿalnākum shuʿūban wa-qabāʾila li-taʿārafū inna akramakum ʿinda 'llāhi atqākum.* (Qur'ān, 49:13)[16]

forty lashes for free people and twenty lashes for slaves); see also M. Y. Izzi Dien, "Taʿzīr," in *EI*², 10:406. For Shīʿī law, see, for example, ʿAlī b. Mūsā al-Riḍā (d. 203/818) (attributed), *Fiqh al-Riḍā*, in *YF* (defining *taʿzīr* as less than *ḥudūd* punishments, that is, 20 to 99 lashes, and *ta'dīb* (disciplinary penalties for minor crimes or misdemeanors) as 3 to 10 lashes); Ṭūsī (d. 460/1067), *al-Nihāya fī mujarrad al-fiqh wa'l-fatāwā* (Tehran: Chāpkhānah-i Dānishgāh, 1342/1963), 2:752 (recommending separation and 12 lashes, which is one-sixteenth of the *ḥadd* punishment for *zinā*, for consummation of a marriage between a free man and an enslaved woman if the couple failed to obtain permission to marry); al-ʿAllāma al-Ḥillī (d. 726/1325), *Qawāʿid al-aḥkām*, in *YF*, 23:406–12 (same). For further sources, see Chapter 1, note 42.

13 Marlow, *Hierarchy*, 2, 4–5 (noting broad types of egalitarianism in Arab monotheism along with Arab tribalism – which was fiercely competitive in the face of the lack of formal institutional hierarchies – marking acquired merit (*ḥasab*) and inherited merit or genealogy (*nasab*) as organizing principles and containing social and wealth inequalities that could be challenged by show of individual merit).

14 See Patricia Crone, *Slaves on Horses: The Evolution of the Islamic Polity* (Cambridge: Cambridge University Press, 1980), 19–20; Charles Lindholm, "Kinship Structure and Political Authority: The Middle East and Central Asia," *Comparative Studies in Society and History* 28, 2 (1986), 334–35.

15 See Peri Bearman et al., "Ḥasab wa-nasab," in *EI*², 3:238–39. See also Mottahedeh, *Loyalty and Leadership*, 98–104.

16 For a history of exegetical commentaries on this verse, see Roy P. Mottahedeh, "The Shuʿûbîyah Controversy and the Social History of Early Islamic Iran," *International Journal of Middle East Studies* 7, 2 (1976), 161–82.

Several other verses stress that "sons and wealth" will not elevate anyone's spiritual station, no matter how much they may elevate one's social station. And still other verses praise those who "believe and do good works," promising them great rewards for their embodiment of moral excellence.[17] Many Muslims took these verses to unquestionably require broad-stroked egalitarianism for rules of Islamic law (including rules of Islamic criminal law), in contrast to the pre-Islamic tribal structures and to the social hierarchies that emerged soon after Islam's advent.[18]

Further, in the Islamic historical sources, examples abound of prophetic and post-prophetic attempts to replace the old pre-Islamic Arabian formula for tribal egalitarianism with a Qur'ānic egalitarianism of piety.[19] In fact, political authorities that refused to govern with policies tending to increase social mobility based on morality rather than hierarchy met with fierce consequences. As we will see in the next section, contravention of this Islamic egalitarianism of moral preference led to regicide, revolution, and unrest.

B. SOCIAL STATUS AND POLITICAL POWER: OVERCRIMINALIZATION OF POLITICAL OPPONENTS

1. Islamic Moral Values: Aspirational Ideals

The lofty ideals of the social-moral values undergirding *ḥudūd* laws and the spiritual-moral egalitarianism expressed in Islam's earliest texts remained largely aspirational. Muḥammad advanced them, and the later literary sources depict the second and fourth caliphs, ʿUmar and ʿAlī, to have insisted on egalitarian principles in their governmental policies and moral exhortations.[20] Derogation from these principles in the second half

[17] See Marlow, *Hierarchy*, 2–3 (citing Qur'ān, 26:88–89, 18:47, 2:247, and 49:13 for the first category, and 16:75, 32:18, and 4:95 for the second).

[18] Ibid. (referring to distinctions between and among Arab tribes, and between Arabs and non-Arabs, as well as to other types of social hierarchies). Marshall Hodgson refers to jurists who shared these sentiments as the "piety-minded." Hodgson, *Venture*, 1:241–79.

[19] Marlow, *Hierarchy*, 2–3.

[20] With Islam came a notion of *Islamic* egalitarianism (by which early caliphs treated all members of the Muslim community as equal in rank), as a replacement to pre-Islamic practices of tribal egalitarianism (by which tribal leaders conferred preference on members based on tribal pedigree and personal prowess). ʿUmar modified the blanket Islamic egalitarianism in favor of a doctrine of first-mover preference based on the length of one's history with Islam (*sābiqa*), by which he conferred more rewards on "early comers" in their conversion to Islam than on those who converted later. ʿAlī inaugurated egalitarian fiscal policies for all Muslims regardless of conversion history. See further Martin Hinds,

of the reign of the third caliph, ʿUthmān, led to his assassination.[21] It also led to a vast amount of social unrest and political restructuring. Once Muʿāwiya – who saw himself as the rightful successor to ʿUthmān and the avenger of his murder – seized the caliphate from ʿAlī, "the opportunity for social equalising" on the basis of piety criteria came to an end.[22] Muʿāwiya adopted a structure of political governance based on kinship ties and inaugurated the first of many dynasties based on bloodlines, supported by political and military structures built on these same bloodlines and tribal loyalties.[23]

Predictably, this turn was neither absolute nor without challenge. Some groups, such as one group of the followers of ʿAlī who would later become the group known as the Imāmī Shīʿa, advocated a concept of precedence that combined moral-spiritual excellence with familial ties to the Prophet.[24] Others, such as the puritanical Khārijīs who withdrew their support for

"Kufan Political Alignments and Their Background in the Mid-Seventh Century A.D.," *International Journal of Middle East Studies* 2, 4 (1971), 346–67, at 347 (on "early comers"); Marlow, *Hierarchy*, 14–16 (on the notion of *sābiqa* and on ʿAlī's fiscal policies); Reuben Levy, *The Social Structure of Islam*, 2nd ed. (Cambridge: Cambridge University Press, 1957) (orig. *The Sociology of Islam* (1931–33)), 55–57 (for anecdotes quoting early sources recounting ʿUmar's brand of egalitarianism). Both models of Islamic egalitarianism enjoyed significant community buy-in, as policies on their bases seem to have equalized chances for upward mobility among converts regardless of genealogy, such that the absence of either model was intolerable in the early period – a fact marked by the unrest that resulted from ʿUthmān's reversion to tribal preferences during the second half of his reign. For discussion and contrasts of pre-Islamic with Islamic ideals of egalitarianism and social preference, see further Michael Morony, *Iraq after the Muslim Conquest* (Princeton, NJ: Princeton University Press, 1984), 261–62; Riḍwān al-Sayyid, *al-Umma wa'l-jamāʿa wa'l-sulṭa* (Beirut: Dār al-Iqra', 1984), 117 (*naẓarāt fī jadaliyyāt al-ʿilāqa bayna 'l-namūdhajayn al-siyāsiyyayn al-ta'rīkhiyyayn al-Īrānī al-qadīm wa'l-islāmī al-wasīṭ*).

21 For a study of the factions aligned against ʿUthmān in the lead-up to his murder, see Martin Hinds, "The Murder of the Caliph ʿUthmān," in *Studies in Early Islamic History*, ed. Jere Bacharach, Lawrence Conrad, and Patricia Crone (Princeton, NJ: Darwin Press, 1996), 29–55, at 52–53. For further details on ʿUthmān's policies, see Kennedy, *The Prophet and the Age of the Caliphates*, 69–75; Hodgson, *Venture*, 1:212–17.

22 Kennedy, *The Prophet and the Age of the Caliphates*, 69–75 (citing Crone, *Roman, Provincial and Islamic Law*, 89); Ira Lapidus, "The Arab Conquests and the Formation of Islamic Society," in *Studies on the First Century of Islamic Society*, ed. G. H. A. Juynboll (Carbondale: Southern Illinois University Press, 1982), 49–72 (describing how differences of status among Arabs became greater than they had been in the past); see also Marlow, *Hierarchy*, 14, nn. 3–4, and the sources cited therein.

23 For standard overviews, see Kennedy, *The Prophet and the Age of the Caliphates*, 82–123 (Umayyads), 124–99 (ʿAbbāsids); Berkey, *Formation of Islam*, esp. Part II (emergence of Islam through the ʿAbbāsid Revolution).

24 On early Imāmī political and theological doctrines surrounding the Imāmate, see generally Modarressi, *Crisis and Consolidation*, especially 29–31. See also Wilferd Madelung, *Religious Trends in Early Islamic Iran* (Albany, NY: Bibliotheca Persica, 1988), 786; Etan Kohlberg, "The Evolution of the Shīʿa," in *Belief and Law in Imāmī Shīʿism*

ʿAlī, advanced a notion of strict adherence to God's law (as they defined it) as the essential qualification for leadership, that adherence being the mark of spiritual-moral excellence.[25] Still others, such as the group that came to be known as the Zaydī Shīʿa, held that leadership should devolve to a competent leader from the Prophet's family who exhibited some degree of spiritual-moral excellence and was willing to assume leadership by way of revolution and rebellion.[26] These factions remained a constant threat to each ruling authority as long as they laid claim to leadership.[27]

2. Criminal Law Enforcement: Social Control

As a result of the political implications of competing religious claims to moral authority, the Umayyads and their successors treated potential political adversaries harshly. Each reign was marked by efforts to maintain control in the face of competing claims to leadership. Any perusal of the historical chronicles gives the impression of a series of political intrigues and power struggles over these very questions.[28] Part of the struggle for

(Aldershot: Variorum Reprints, 1991), 1–21; Etan Kohlberg, "Imām and Community in the Pre-Ghayba Period," in *Belief and Law*, 25–53.

25 On the history and changing political and legal doctrine of the Khārijīs, who came to adopt a more quietist attitude as Ibāḍīs, see Tadeusz Lewicki, "The Ibádites in Arabia and Africa," *Cahiers d'histoire mondiale* 13, 1 (1971), 51–130, esp. 51–80; John C. Wilkinson, *The Imamate Tradition of Oman* (Cambridge: Cambridge University Press, 1987), 1–17; Madelung, *Religious Trends*, 54–76.

26 On early Zaydī political and theological doctrines, see Madelung, *Religious Trends*, 86–92. Compare Najam Haider, *The Origins of the Shīʿa: Identity, Ritual, and Sacred Space in Eighth-Century Kūfa* (Cambridge: Cambridge University Press, 2011), 17–21, 189–214. On developed doctrines, see generally Bernard Haykel, *Revival and Reform in Islam: The Legacy of Muhammad al-Shawkani* (Cambridge: Cambridge University Press, 2003).

27 For a brief discussion, see Marlow, *Hierarchy*, 40. For an excellent, concise summary of the various religio-political tendencies discussed in brief here, see W. Madelung, "Imāma," in *EI*[2], 3:1163–69; Mottahedeh, *Loyalty and Leadership*, 19–20.

28 See especially Abū al-Faraj al-Iṣbahānī, *Maqātil al-Ṭālibiyyīn*, ed. Aḥmad Ṣaqr (N.p.: al-Maktaba al-Ḥaydariyya, 1423/2002–3) (recording the ʿAlid revolts against the Umayyads and ʿAbbāsids); see also Abū al-Ḥasan al-Ashʿarī, *Maqālāt al-Islāmiyyīn wa-ʾkhtilāf al-muṣallīn*, ed. Muḥyī al-Dīn ʿAbd al-Ḥamīd (Beirut: al-Maktaba al-ʿAṣriyya, 1990), 1:136–65 (listing the multiple rebellions within the first two centuries of Islam's rise). Other representative examples include Ibn Jarīr al-Ṭabarī, *Taʾrīkh al-rusul waʾl-mulūk*, ed. Muḥammad Abū al-Faḍl Ibrāhīm (Cairo: Dār al-Maʿārif, 1960–77; English translation in forty vols., *History of al-Ṭabarī* (Albany: State University of New York Press, 1989–2007) (covering pre-Islamic history through the year 301–2/915); Masʿūdī, *Murūj al-dhahab wa-maʿādin al-jawhar*, ed. Yūsuf Asʿad Dāghir (Beirut: Dār al-Andalus, 1965–66) (ʿAbbāsid period); Ibn al-Jawzī, *al-Muntaẓam fī tawārīkh al-mulūk waʾl-umam*, ed. Muḥammad ʿAbd al-Qādir ʿAṭāʾ and Muṣṭafā ʿAbd al-Qādir ʿAṭāʾ (Beirut: Dār al-Fikr, 1992) (recounting the Prophet's biography and post-prophetic Islamic history through the ʿAbbāsid period).

power involved harshly punishing anyone who would disturb the existing societal order and thus challenge the political leadership through crime, rebellion, or other means. Political opponents and petty criminals were put to death and punished in other severe ways never authorized by the Islamic sources.[29] Within that context, punishments were meted out on the basis of political threat or disfavor, just as absolution from punishment was doled out on the basis of political allegiance and favor.

In most sectors of Umayyad society, social hierarchy triumphed and quietism set in. This quietism lasted until the Umayyad regime was toppled by the ʿAbbāsid Revolution, which was backed by the strength of an ʿAlid religious claim whose moral effect on politics was fleeting at best. The regime had changed, but the basic setup was similar: like the Umayyads, the ʿAbbāsids accorded preferential treatment to members of the elite and treated those with competing religio-political claims to leadership harshly.[30]

In the end, the Qur'ānic value of egalitarianism centering on preference by moral excellence became a spiritual ideal reserved mostly for the next world. As for this world, social preference tended to run parallel to tribal affinities, and society's elite members enjoyed disproportionate access to wealth, power, and prestige.[31] All of this would have nontrivial effects on Islamic criminal law.

C. HIERARCHY IN *ḤUDŪD* LAWS: UNDERCRIMINALIZATION OF THE ELITE

Given the sociopolitical influence of the elite, it was perhaps inevitable that their claim to social privilege would find its way into the law. Notwithstanding the attempts of medieval Muslim jurists to maintain

[29] For a vivid discussion of examples from the central Islamic lands in the fifth/eleventh through seventh/thirteenth centuries, see Lange, *Justice* (drawing heavily on instances presented in Ibn al-Jawzī's *Muntaẓam*). For a catalog of instances of punishment practices drawn from historical chronicles and literary sources, see ʿAbbūd al-Shāljī, *Mawsūʿat al-ʿadhāb* (Beirut: al-Dār al-ʿArabiyya li'l-Mawsūʿāt, 198?). For a list of "Islamic" punishments as distinct from "non-Islamic" ones, see Peters, *Crime and Punishment*, 33–38, 44–68.

[30] On the connection between social hierarchy and political quietism in regimes that favored the elite, see Marlow, *Hierarchy*, 90, 93–116. Exceptions included some Khārijīs and Zaydīs, whose theological doctrines *required* rebellion, before they settled down in later periods. See Madelung, *Religious Trends*, 54–76 (Khārijī doctrines), 77–86 (Zaydī doctrines); Lewicki, "Ibádites," 55–56, 62–64 (describing Khārijī "fanaticism" and "quietism" or "moderation" and the subsequent rapprochement of moderates, who came to be known as Ibāḍīs, with the Umayyad caliph ʿAbd al-Mālik).

[31] For a similar conclusion, see Marlow, *Hierarchy*, 174–75.

independence from government officials and to promote egalitarian ideals, these same jurists were nonetheless part of the elite.[32] Thus, for example, jurists shaped marriage laws in ways that facilitated maintaining the integrity of bloodlines and the status hierarchies that formed the basis for political patronage and social privilege.[33] Some even identified and ratified the distinct social strata that they found in Arab societies.[34] But when a group of those jurists tried to fold status hierarchies into criminal law, they met with stiff resistance from their peers.

1. The Elite-Leniency Maxim

Just when most jurists came to regard the doubt canon as a prophetic *ḥadīth*, some jurists began to circulate a countermaxim encouraging *ḥudūd* avoidance for those of high status even when there was no doubt about criminal culpability. The new saying advised judges to "overlook the

[32] Quite a number of jurists worked closely with the government as judges and caliphal advisors, as recorded in judicial biographies and chronicles such as that of Wakīʿ, *Akhbār al-quḍāt*. Aside from the well-known example of the close relationship between Abū Yūsuf and the caliph Hārūn al-Rashīd, two prominent examples of such partnerships are those of Ibn Shubruma (d. 144/761), ibid., 512–17, 557–82, and Ibn Abī Laylā (d. 148/765), ibid., 573–82, with the second ʿAbbāsid caliph Abū Jaʿfar al-Manṣūr (r. 136–58/754–75) and his nephew ʿĪsā b. Mūsā, who governed in Kūfa. For a discussion and further examples, see Zaman, *Religion and Politics*, esp. 70–118 (describing close interactions between scholars and early ʿAbbāsid caliphal officials); Zaman, "The Caliphs, the *ʿUlamāʾ*, and the Law: Defining the Role and Function of the Caliph in the Early ʿAbbāsid Period," *Islamic Law and Society* 4, 1 (1997), 1–36 (pointing out that the caliph had a certain measure of judicial authority to interpret the law or to choose particular interpretations of it during this early period); Norman Calder, *Studies in Early Muslim Jurisprudence*, 134, 141–45, 156 (noting that Abū Yūsuf sought to describe the caliph's "discretionary powers" in financial matters and in other spheres of administration). See also Tsafrir, *Early Spread of Ḥanafism*, 17ff and passim (discussing the role of state patronage in early Muslim societies in support of juristic endeavors, especially in Iraq).

[33] The legal doctrine requiring equality between marital partners for a valid marriage (*kafāʾa*, most famously adopted by the Ḥanafīs) included socio-genealogical status. For a treatment of how this status-reinforcing doctrine played out in the social history of the ʿAlids and their intermarriage with members of various Qurashī clans, see Teresa Bernheimer, *The ʿAlids: The First Family of Islam, 750–1200* (Edinburgh: Edinburgh University Press, 2013), 32–50.

[34] See Marlow, *Hierarchy*, 7 (quoting Nāṣir al-Dīn al-Ṭūsī's (d. 672/1274) quadripartite model of social hierarchies to be observed in the law); ibid., 2–4 (arguing that the Qurʾān does not necessarily attempt to abolish social hierarchies in the present world, however meaningless it insists they are for the next; also arguing that the Qurʾān can be understood to endorse existing forms of worldly inequality in Arab society, such as slavery, the social superiority of men over women, and the idea of divine favor bestowed on some individuals or peoples over others).

faults of the nobles."[35] As historian Louise Marlow has pointed out, this phrase was one of many sayings that tended to reflect and reinforce new status hierarchies. Ibn Qutayba used it as proof of divine sanction for ethnic inequalities, and Ṭurṭūshī similarly used it to argue for divine endorsement of social hierarchies.[36] In fact, the saying was so widespread that it, like other common sayings in the first two centuries, was considered a matter of "necessary cultural knowledge" for the educated and religious elite.[37]

When applied to criminal law, this directive amounted to a lenient stance toward crimes committed by members of the elite that stood in direct contradiction to the policy of enforcing *ḥudūd* laws in deference to divine legislative supremacy. It also contradicted the import of the doubt canon, which advocated punishment avoidance in cases of *doubt*, not in cases of elite *status*. Marlow has argued convincingly that this saying, which we may call the "elite-leniency maxim," emerged after a shift away from the early Islamic egalitarian ideals, given that the saying contrasts markedly with the Qurʾānic view of "moral preference," which is to be taken as a reflection of the values of the earliest community.[38] In other words, there were tensions between early Islamic ideals of moral egalitarianism and Arab recognition of social hierarchy.

Notwithstanding the tension between the doubt canon and the elite-leniency maxim, some jurists started to circulate a single maxim that

[35] See Ibn Rāhawayh, *Musnad*, ed. ʿAbd al-Ghafūr b. ʿAbd al-Ḥaqq al-Balūshī (Medina: Maktabat al-Īmān, 1412/1990–1), 2:567, no. 1142 (*aqīlū dhawī ʾl-hayaʾāt zallātihim*); Nasāʾī, *Sunan*, 4:310–11, nos. 7293, 7296, 7298 (*aqīlū dhawī ʾl-hayaʾāt ʿatharātihim*), 7297 (depicting the Prophet applying the maxim to a case of a master inflicting personal injury on his slave), 7295 (*tajāwazū ʿan zallat dhī ʾl-hayʾa*); Ibn Ḥibbān (d. 354/965), *Ṣaḥīḥ*, ed. Shuʿayb al-Arnaʾūṭ and Ḥusayn Asad (Beirut: Muʾassasat al-Risāla, 1407/1987), 1:296 (*aqīlū dhawī ʾl-hayaʾāt zallātihim*); Bayhaqī, *Sunan*, 8:334, no. 17405 (*aqīlū dhawī ʾl-hayaʾāt ʿatharātihim*); Ibn Abī al-Dunyā (d. 281/894), *Makārim al-akhlāq*, ed. Majdī al-Sayyid Ibrāhīm (Cairo: Maktabat al-Qurʾān, 1411/1990), 1:32, no. 62 (*aqīlū ʾl-kirām ʿatharātihim*); Bukhārī, *al-Adab al-mufrad*, ed. Muḥammad Fuʾād ʿAbd al-Bāqī (Beirut: Dār al-Bashāʾir, 1409/1989), 1:165, no. 465 (*aqīlū dhawī ʾl-hayaʾāt ʿatharātihim*); Sulaymān b. Aḥmad al-Ṭabarānī (d. 360/970), *al-Muʿjam al-awsaṭ*, ed. Ṭāriq b. ʿIwaḍ Allāh b. Muḥammad and ʿAbd al-Muḥsin b. Ibrāhīm al-Ḥusaynī (Cairo: Dār al-Ḥaramayn, 1415/1995), 6:54, no. 5774 (*aqīlū ʾl-kirām ʿatharātihim*) and 7:302, no. 7562 (*aqīlū dhawī ʾl-hayaʾāt zallātihim*); ʿAlī b. Abī Bakr al-Haythamī (d. 807/1405), *Majmaʿ al-zawāʾid* (Cairo: Dār al-Rayyān liʾl-Turāth; Beirut: Dār al-Kutub, 1407/1986–7), 6:282 (quoting the latter version from Ṭabarānī); ʿAlī b. Abī Bakr al-Haythamī, *Mawārid al-ẓamʾān*, ed. Muḥammad ʿAbd al-Razzāq Ḥamza (Beirut: Dār al-Kutub al-ʿIlmiyya, n.d.), 364, no. 1520 (*aqīlū dhawī ʾl-hayaʾāt zallātihim*); Badr al-Dīn al-ʿAynī, *ʿUmdat al-qārī: sharḥ Ṣaḥīḥ al-Bukhārī* (Cairo: Idārat al-Ṭibāʿa al-Munīriyya, 1348/1929–30), 14:256 (*aqīlū dhawī ʾl-hayaʾāt ʿatharātihim*). For further citations and discussion, see Marlow, *Hierarchy*, 27–28, n. 78.

[36] Marlow, *Hierarchy*, 16–17.

[37] Ibid., 17.

[38] Ibid., 13–17.

combined the two sayings: "Avoid criminal punishments in cases of doubt and overlook the faults of the nobles." The incompatibility of the two sayings was not lost on all jurists. Many saw the first part of this combined maxim to advise *ḥudūd* avoidance in cases of doubt generally, but the second part to counsel against *ḥudūd* enforcement as applied to elite members of society for crimes that would warrant harsh punishment even in cases in which there was no doubt.

To ease the contradiction, a number of jurists introduced a version of the elite-leniency maxim that carried a "*ḥudūd* exception" into the combined maxim.[39] As with the doubt canon, there are many versions of the elite-leniency maxim.[40] The relevant difference between the versions is the occasional inclusion of the "*ḥudūd* exception," which stipulates that any avoidance of punishment for the *minor* faults or misdemeanors of high-status members of society should not apply to their *major* faults, that is, to *ḥudūd* crimes. For such serious moral offenses, the *ḥudūd* exception emphasizes that those of high status are subject to punishment like anyone else. In other words, the versions of the elite-leniency maxim that include the *ḥudūd* exception tended toward rules of *ḥudūd* enforcement rather than avoidance and gave shape to the demands of Islamic egalitarianism.[41] By introducing this exception to the elite-leniency maxim, one group of jurists sought to deauthorize the elite-favoring second half of the combined saying.

[39] Other jurists refused to recognize the elite-leniency maxim as a valid Islamic legal maxim at all. Still other jurists acknowledged the validity of the elite-leniency maxim but restricted its import to misdemeanors rather than crimes – the latter of which the Lawgiver required to be enforced. See note 35.

[40] There are three differences in terminology: (1) the term used for "overlook" is variously *aqīlū*, *ajīzū*, *tajāwazū*, or *iḥtabalū*; (2) the term used to refer to those of high status is alternately *al-kirām*, *dhawū 'l-haya'āt* or *hay'a*, *dhū 'l-murū'a* and *dhawū 'l-murū'āt*, *dhawū 'l-sakhā'*, or even *dhawū 'l-buyūt* (as in Muḥammad Amīn b. Faḍl Allāh al-Muḥibbī, *Khulāṣat al-athar fī a'yān al-qarn al-ḥādī 'ashar* (Beirut: Maktabat Khayyāṭ, 1966), 4:422 – though this author or the teacher who related it to him apparently copied or paraphrased the term incorrectly); (3) the terms used for "faults" or "misdemeanors" include *'atharāt* and *zallāt*. For a list of several versions, see al-Muttaqī al-Hindī (d. 975/1567), *Kanz al-'ummāl* (Aleppo: Maktabat al-Turāth al-Islāmī, 1969?), nos. 12975–84, 12987–88. The second set of terms (*kirām*, *dhawū 'l-haya'āt*, etc., loosely translating as "those of high status") is perhaps most interesting, as it raises questions about just which class of people the saying is intended to encompass. For an excellent discussion of class distinctions in Islamic history (through the eighth/fourteenth century), see generally Marlow, *Hierarchy*.

[41] Indeed, those who include the doubt canon with the elite-leniency maxim in their collections tend to cite the version of the latter that appended the *ḥudūd* exception. See, for example, Abū Dāwūd, Ibn Ḥanbal, Bayhaqī, Dāraquṭnī, Ṭabarānī, and Ibn 'Adī, who record only the version with the *ḥudūd* exception. For specific examples, see note 53.

The strategy of introducing the *ḥudūd* exception to the combined saying cut across interpretive and theological boundaries. The jurists who endorsed the *ḥudūd* exception included both Sunnīs and Shīʿīs. The Ismāʿīlī judge Qāḍī Nuʿmān (d. 363/974) did so,[42] as reportedly did the Sunnī traditionist-jurist Ibn ʿAdī (d. 365/976),[43] as well as the Imāmī traditionist-jurist Ibn Bābawayh (d. 381/991–2).[44] Their new saying went as follows: "avoid criminal punishments in cases of doubt and overlook the faults of the nobles except in cases of a criminal violation of one of God's *ḥudūd* laws: *idraʾū ʾl-ḥudūd biʾl-shubahāt wa-aqīlū ʾl-kirām ʿatharātihim illā fī ḥadd min ḥudūd Allāh*."

This combined maxim is of particular interest for two reasons. First, it is doubtful that it existed in this form in the early period. Like the doubt canon, it came from early judicial practices attributed to the Prophet rather late in Islamic legal history. But unlike the doubt canon, this maxim combined two very different judicial practices and accompanying moral principles. Therefore, the existence of this combined maxim gives further insight into the fluid construction and application of Islamic legal maxims in criminal law over time. Second, this combined version begs the question whether the doubt canon emerged originally as a tool to benefit the elite and in contrast to the emphasis on divine legislative supremacy and the moral ideals that jurists placed on that canon.[45] Evaluating the first question helps answer the second.

2. Combining Doubt with Elite Leniency: Attribution and Circulation

On the origins of the combined maxim, at least four considerations indicate a late emergence. First, there are no contemporaneous reports of

[42] See Qāḍī Nuʿmān (d. 363/974), *Daʿāʾim al-Islām*, ed. A. A. A. Fyzee (Cairo: Dār al-Maʿārif, 1951 & 1960), 2:466, no. 1653 (also cited in Ḥusayn b. Muḥammad Taqī al-Nūrī al-Ṭabarsī, *Mustadrak al-Wasāʾil* (Qum: Muʾassasat Āl al-Bayt li-Iḥyāʾ al-Turāth, 1407/1986–7), 18:26, no. 21911). For Qāḍī Nuʿmān's biography and life as a judge in the early Fāṭimid empire, see Ismail K. Poonawala, "Al-Qāḍī al-Nuʿmān and Ismāʿīlī Jurisprudence," in *Mediaeval Ismāʿīlī History and Thought*, ed. Farhad Daftary (Cambridge: Cambridge University Press, 1996), 117–43.

[43] On the attribution of the saying to Ibn ʿAdī, see note 46.

[44] See Ibn Bābawayh (d. 381/991–2), *Kitāb man lā yaḥduruh al-faqīh*, ed. ʿAlī Akbar al-Ghaffārī (Qum: Jamāʿat al-Mudarrisīn fī ʾl-Ḥawza al-ʿIlmiyya, 1994), 4:53, no. 90.

[45] This theory is the argument advanced by Maribel Fierro in her article "When Lawful Violence Meets Doubt," 233 (arguing that episodes in which high-status offenders used the doubt canon to escape punishment provide the background "context [that] makes sense of Ibn ʿAdī's variant of the saying . . .").

the combined maxim in the early *ḥadīth* reports, biographical dictionaries, or other literature from the first three centuries. Second, there is no reliable reference to the combined maxim in the earliest source in which Sunnī scholars place it: a lost work of Ibn ʿAdī that purportedly referenced the combined maxim, albeit typically without a transmission chain. Tellingly, the combined maxim is not to be found in his known work on *ḥadīth* transmitters, *al-Kāmil*, where one might expect it.[46] Third, significantly, Qāḍī Nuʿmān appears to have taken the combined maxim from an earlier source that had combined the two different sayings. Finally, it is worth noting that both parts of the combined maxim were in wide circulation during Islam's early period (the first three centuries), but they were quite distinct in attribution, circulation, and application.

To trace the origin of the combined maxim, consider its first part: the doubt canon. Recall that, in the early period, the doubt canon itself was a non-prophetic saying attributed to Companions or adduced anonymously. As a "*ḥadīth*," alternative versions of the canon had a Kūfan pedigree and, among the Sunnī canonical *ḥadīth* collections, appeared only in the works of Ibn Mājah and Tirmidhī. It was only as a maxim that the doubt canon circulated widely among jurists in Iraq, the Ḥijāz, and elsewhere.[47] In the

[46] The very attribution of this saying to Ibn ʿAdī is problematic. Badr al-Dīn al-ʿAynī is the earliest known reference and the only one to give a chain of transmission (see Appendix A, version 11), though he does not provide his source. See ʿAynī, *ʿUmdat al-qārī*, 20:259. Several authors cite a notebook of *ḥadīth* (*juz*ʾ) ascribed to Ibn ʿAdī wherein this statement reportedly appeared with a simple attribution to Ibn ʿAbbās. For example, Jalāl al-Dīn al-Suyūṭī, *Jāmiʿ al-aḥādīth*, ed. Aḥmad ʿAbd al-Jawwād and ʿAbbās Aḥmad Ṣaqr (Beirut: Dār al-Fikr, 1998), 1:135, no. 793, whence al-Muttaqī al-Hindī, *Kanz al-ʿummāl*, 5:309, no. 12972; ʿAbd al-Raʾūf al-Munāwī, *al-Taysīr: sharḥ al-Jāmiʿ al-ṣaghīr*, ed. Muṣṭafā Muḥammad al-Dhahabī (Cairo: Dār al-Ḥadīth, 2000), 1:156, no. 314; Shams al-Dīn al-Dhahabī, *Siyar*, 8:36–37, n. 2 (s.v. Zufar b. Hudhayl) (with the editor's note quoting without citing Suyūṭī). But that notebook seems to have been lost. Further, there is also confusion among later scholars about the proper attribution and source of this saying. For instance, although Munāwī attributes it to Ibn ʿAdī in his *Taysīr* when commenting on Suyūṭī's *al-Jāmiʿ al-ṣaghīr*, he mentions in his *Fayḍ* that ʿAbd al-Razzāq, rather than Ibn ʿAdī, narrates this tradition on the authority of Ibn ʿAbbās. But this latter mention is incorrect as no such attribution appears in ʿAbd al-Razzāq's *Muṣannaf*. See Muḥammad Ḥasan Ḍayf Allāh, *Fayḍ al-qadīr* (Cairo: Maktaba wa-Maṭbaʿat Muṣṭafā al-Bābī al-Ḥalabī, 1964), 2:142. Finally, one commentator notes that this version of the saying is in Ibn ʿAdī's *Kāmil*. See the editor's note in Ibn Rushd al-Jadd, *Bayān*, 16:324, n. 169. But my examination of *al-Kāmil* revealed no such *ḥadīth* in that book. See Yūsuf al-Biqāʿī, ed., *Muʿjam aḥādīth ḍuʿafāʾ al-rijāl min Kitāb al-Kāmil* (Beirut: Dār al-Fikr, 1988); see also Fierro, "When Lawful Violence Meets Doubt," 218, n. 33 (noting that her search for this *ḥadīth* in *al-Kāmil* was also inconclusive).

[47] See Ibn Mājah, *Sunan* (1998), 4:161, no. 2545; Tirmidhī, *Sunan*, 5:112–13, no. 1424. For further discussion, see Chapter 2 and Appendix A. Worth noting is that, although Ibāḍīs

Shīʿī context, versions of the doubt canon appear in Ibn Bābawayh's collection, which also draws mostly on Kūfan *ḥadīth* reported on the authority of scholars in Qum.[48] In short, the canon seems to have a solid Kūfan pedigree as a *ḥadīth*, and was otherwise a canon that reflected widespread judicial practice.

In contrast, its transmission chains place the elite-leniency maxim outside of Kūfa, where the doubt canon seems to have originated. For Sunnīs, the elite-leniency maxim circulated in the Ḥijāz (Mecca, Medina, and Ṭā'if), usually alongside other Ḥijāzī sayings calling on Muslims to overlook the faults of fellow Muslims.[49] Mainstream Shīʿīs either were not familiar with or did not accept the elite-leniency maxim. Neither Ibn Bābawayh nor any other collector of mainstream Shīʿī *ḥadīth* in Kūfa or elsewhere recorded that saying.[50] This fact suggests that Shīʿī scholars at that time did not regard it as a *ḥadīth* or, more pointedly, as a valid principle of law.

As for the second part of the combined maxim, the elite-leniency formulation, both Sunnī and Shīʿī *ḥadīth* transmitters present largely uniform views of its source and spread, neither of which align well with the origins and circulation of the doubt canon. In every available record of the elite-leniency maxim, its chains of transmission differ from the transmission chains for the doubt canon. In early Sunnī *ḥadīth* collections, the elite-leniency maxim originates from the Prophet via ʿĀ'isha and then Abū Bakr b. ʿAmr b. Ḥazm

developed a separate jurisprudence of doubt, they relied on Ibn Mājah and Tirmidhī's reports of the doubt canon as a prophetic report to do so. See Muḥammad Muṣṭafā ʿAbbūd Āl Harmūsh, *Muʿjam al-qawāʿid al-fiqhiyya al-Ibāḍiyya* (Oman: Wizārat al-Awqāf wa'l-Shu'ūn al-Dīniyya, 2010?), 1:361–63.

48 Ibn Bābawayh, *Faqīh*, 4:53, no. 90. See also al-Nūrī al-Ṭabarsī, *Mustadrak al-Wasā'il*, 18:26, no. 21912 (listing the doubt canon as it has been popularized, attributed to ʿAlī without an *isnād* (from Ibn Bābawayh, *Muqniʿ* (Qum: Mu'assasat al-Imām al-Hādī, 1994), 437)).

49 Especially the "*taʿāfaw* saying," which encourages people to overlook each other's faults so long as offenses have not been brought before the court, in which case adjudication and punishment become mandatory. See ʿAbd al-Razzāq, *Muṣannaf* (1972), 10:229, no. 18937 (*taʿāfaw fī-mā baynakum qabla an ta'tūnī fa-mā balaghanī min ḥadd fa-qad wajab*); see also Abū Dāwūd, *Sunan*, ed. Muḥammad ʿAbd al-ʿAzīz al-Khālidī (Beirut: Dār al-Kutub al-ʿIlmiyya, 1996), 3:137, no. 4376; Nasā'ī, *Sunan*, 7:12, nos. 7331–32; Ṭabarānī, *al-Muʿjam al-awsaṭ*, 6:210, no. 6212; al-Ḥākim al-Naysābūrī, *al-Mustadrak ʿalā 'l-Ṣaḥīḥayn* (Cairo: Dār al-Ḥaramayn, 1997), 4:537, no. 8236; Bayhaqī, *Sunan*, 8:575, no. 17611.

50 The elite-leniency maxim appears elsewhere in the Shīʿī *ḥadīth* corpus. For example, al-Ḥurr al-ʿĀmilī (d. 1104/1692), *Wasā'il al-Shīʿa* (Qum: Mu'assasat Āl al-Bayt li-Iḥyā' al-Turath, 1490/1988–9), 11:534, records a version of the saying from Kulaynī's work, *al-Kāfī*. For inclusion of that saying in later collections, see further Ibn Abī Jumhūr al-Aḥsā'ī (d. early tenth/sixteenth century), *ʿAwālī 'l-la'ālī*, ed. Mujtabā al-Arāqī (Qum: Maṭbaʿat Sayyid al-Shuhadā', 1983–85), 1:236; Ḥusayn al-Ṭabāṭabā'ī al-Burūjirdī (d. 1380/1961), *Jāmiʿ aḥādīth al-Shīʿa* (Qum: Maṭbaʿat Mihr, 1992), 23:328 (citing Ibn Bābawayh, *Faqīh*).

or one of his sons.[51] Further, the elite-leniency maxim is altogether missing in the works of Ibn Abī Shayba, ʿAbd al-Razzāq, Shāfiʿī, Abū Yūsuf, Mālik, and most others who wrote or recorded juristic opinions during that period – the same jurists who had included the doubt canon in their works. In mainstream Shīʿī *ḥadīth* collections, the elite-leniency maxim originates with Jaʿfar al-Ṣādiq rather than the Prophet.[52] Qāḍī Nuʿmān does not record the simple version of the saying at all.

In sum, the doubt canon and the elite-leniency maxim originated and circulated alongside each other during the early period, in parallel and in different cities rather than in combination in the same cities, such that one might have expected them to be uttered in the same breath as the combined maxim suggests. That is, one group of *ḥadīth* scholars cited the doubt canon while a completely different set of scholars cited the elite-leniency maxim.[53] This early separation between the two would change when *ḥadīth* scholars and legal scholars began to combine the two maxims. How and why did this occur?

As a recorded *ḥadīth*, the doubt canon and the elite-leniency maxim appear in combination first in Qāḍī Nuʿmān's *Daʿāʾim*, which is a law

[51] See my "Islamic Legal Maxims," 77–86. One of the few textualist-traditionist jurists of the early period to mention the elite-leniency maxim, Ibn Rāhawayh (d. 238/853), records that maxim but not the doubt canon – a typical example of the lack of overlapping citations to the doubt canon and the elite-leniency maxim in the early period. Ibn Rāhawayh, *Musnad*, 2:567 (*aqīlū dhawī ʾl-hayaʾāt zallātihim*, without the *ḥudūd* exception). On Ibn Rāhawayh's jurisprudence and biography, see Susan Spectorsky, "*Ḥadīth* in the Responses of Isḥāq b. Rāhwayh," *Islamic Law and Society* 8, 3 (2001), 407–31; see also Susan Spectorsky, trans., *Chapters on Marriage and Divorce: Responses of Ibn Ḥanbal and Ibn Rāhwayh* (Austin: University of Texas Press, 1993), esp. 1–59; ʿAbd al-Ghafūr b. ʿAbd al-Ḥaqq al-Balūshī, *al-Imām Isḥāq b. Rāhawayh wa-kitābuh al-Musnad* (Medina: Maktabat al-Īmān, 1990).

[52] See al-Ḥurr al-ʿĀmilī, *Wasāʾil al-Shīʿa*, 11:534, no. 3 (*ajīzū* [or *aqīlū*] *li-ahl al-maʿrūf ʿatharātihim wa-ʾghfirūhā lahum fa-inna kaffa ʾllāh ʿazza wa-jalla ʿalayhim hākadhā, wa-awmaʾa bi-yadih kaʾannah bihā yazull shayʾan*, with the following chain: Abū ʿAbd Allāh [Jaʿfar al-Ṣādiq] – Sayf b. ʿUmayra – Ismāʿīl b. Mihrān – Aḥmad b. Muḥammad b. Khālid – a group of Shīʿī traditionists: *ʿidda min aṣḥābinā*).

[53] Whereas the *ḥadīth* versions of the doubt canon appear in Ibn Mājah's and Tirmidhī's collections, the elite-leniency maxim appears in the collections of Abū Dāwūd and Nasāʾī. See Abū Dāwūd, *Sunan* (1996), 3:137, no. 4375; Nasāʾī, *Sunan*, 6:468–69, nos. 7253–58. For other contemporaneous sources and references through the fifth/eleventh century, see Ibn Rāhawayh, *Musnad*, 2:567; Ibn Ḥanbal, *Musnad*, 6:181; Abū Yaʿlā (d. 307/918), *Musnad*, ed. Ḥusayn Salīm Asad (Damascus: Dār al-Maʾmūn liʾl-Turāth, 1984–94), 8:363–64, no. 4953; Ibn Ḥibbān, *Ṣaḥīḥ*, 1:296; Ṭabarānī, *al-Muʿjam al-awsaṭ*, 3:277, no. 3139; 6:54, no. 5774; and 7:302, no. 7562; Dāraquṭnī (d. 385/995), *Sunan*, ed. Shuʿayb al-Arnaʾūṭ et al. (Beirut: Muʾassasat al-Risāla, 2004), 3:207; Bayhaqī, *Sunan*, 8:579–80, nos. 17627–79. For later sources, from the ninth/fifteenth and tenth/sixteenth centuries, see ʿAynī, *ʿUmdat al-qārī*, 14:256; al-Muttaqī al-Hindī, *Kanz al-ʿummāl*, 5:121–24.

manual that draws on a collection of reports not only from Kūfa, where the doubt canon first appeared as a *ḥadīth*, but also from the Ḥijāz, where we know the elite-leniency maxim was circulating.[54] Qāḍī Nuʿmān seems to have copied the elite-leniency maxim from an earlier Ḥijāzī source, which had included them both. In his *Daʿāʾim*,[55] Qāḍī Nuʿmān often splices together *ḥadīth* of different provenance or omits chains altogether to support a particular legal proposition.[56] This seems to have been a common enough practice in his time. In this case, the sources suggest that it was not Qāḍī Nuʿmān but someone from whom he copied his *ḥadīth* who spliced the two sayings together to form the combined maxim. Intriguingly, it seems to have been early Zaydī scholars who first joined the two statements, providing a source – even if inadvertently – for Qāḍī Nuʿmān and the apocryphal combined maxim.[57]

[54] Qāḍī Nuʿmān extracted the reports in *Daʿāʾim*, from which he omitted transmission chains, mostly from his massive work of law-related *ḥadīth*, *Kitāb al-Īḍāḥ*, which gathered – among other sayings – *ḥadīth* attributed to the Prophet's family together with their transmission chains. See Qāḍī Nuʿmān, *Kitāb al-Iqtiṣār*, ed. ʿĀrif Tāmir (Beirut: Dār al-Aḍwāʾ, 1996), 9–10; cf. Qāḍī Nuʿmān, *Īḍāḥ*, ed. Muḥammad Kāẓim Raḥmatī (Beirut: Muʾassasat al-Aʿlamī, 2007) (providing the surviving fragments of *ḥadīth* on ritual law). See also Poonawala, "Al-Qāḍī al-Nuʿmān," 121, 128 (noting the Zaydī and Mālikī components that Qāḍī Nuʿmān added to the *Daʿāʾim*); Wilferd Madelung, "The Sources of Ismāʿīlī Law," *Journal of Near Eastern Studies* 35 (1976), 29–40 (noting the Imāmī and Zaydī components). *Kitāb al-Īḍāḥ* is mostly lost, but from the surviving portion on ritual law, Madelung has reconstructed the sources on which Qāḍī Nuʿmān drew, and locates them in the late second and early third centuries in sources circulating outside of Qum – as a synthesis between Imāmī and Zaydī Shīʿī law, materially based on the authoritative sources of both but emphasizing the authority of the Imāms in line with the Twelver Shīʿī tendency and against that of the Zaydīs.

[55] *Daʿāʾim* is the most authoritative compendium of law for Ṭayyibī Ismāʿīlīs. It is also a source of Imāmī Shīʿī *ḥadīth*, as Qāḍī Nuʿmān recorded traditions attributed to Imām Jaʿfar al-Ṣādiq and because some Imāmī scholars counted Qāḍī Nuʿmān as one of their own. See Madelung, "Sources of Ismāʿīlī Law," 29; see also al-Nūrī al-Ṭabarsī, *Mustadrak al-Wasāʾil*, 18:26, no. 21911 (citing Qāḍī Nuʿmān, *Daʿāʾim*, no. 1653).

[56] Madelung, "Sources of Ismāʿīlī Law," 29 ("He usually quotes only a single tradition on any question in support of actual doctrine, or simply formulates it himself ....").

[57] Interestingly, the doubt canon itself did not appear as a prophetic *ḥadīth* in most Zaydī works until the modern period. Compare Ibn al-Murtaḍā (d. 840/1437), *Kitāb al-Azhār* and *al-Baḥr al-zakhkhār* in addition to al-Nāṭiq biʾl-Ḥaqq's *Kitāb al-Taḥrīr* (no citations to the doubt canon in any of these works) with Muḥammad b. ʿAlī al-Shawkānī's *Nayl al-awṭār*, ed. Muḥammad Ḥallāq and ʿIzz al-Dīn Khaṭṭāb (Beirut: Dār Iḥyāʾ al-Turāth al-ʿArabī, 1999), 7:109 (with citations to the doubt canon as a *ḥadīth*), and ʿAlī b. Ismāʿīl al-Ṣanʿānī, *Kitāb Raʾb al-ṣadʿ* (Beirut: Dār al-Nafāʾis, 1990), 3:1390, 1393, 1405 (with citations to the doubt canon, though not as a *ḥadīth*). On modern Zaydīs and particularly Shawkānī's appropriation of Sunnī *ḥadīth* (as here with the doubt canon), see generally Haykel, *Revival and Reform in Islam*.

In substantial part, Qāḍī Nuʿmān's sources differed from those informing Ibn Bābawayh, who recorded traditions on the authority of scholars in Kūfa, who in turn mainly reported traditions circulating in Qum (the main Imāmī center of learning since the third/ninth century) and nearby Rayy. By contrast, Qāḍī Nuʿmān's sources tended not to pass through Qum, coming instead from the written accounts of scholars in the Ḥijāz, Kūfa, and other parts of Iraq.[58] There was, however, a small amount of overlap. Qāḍī Nuʿmān and Ibn Bābawayh could have garnered the doubt canon from a common source available to both of them at the time the former wrote *al-Īḍāḥ* (that is, between 297/909 and 322/934, during the first Fāṭimid caliph al-Mahdī's reign) and/or *al-Daʿāʾim* (around 349/960). This is because further investigation into eighth- and ninth-century sources suggests a Zaydī provenance. The canon was cited by Zaydism's eponymous founder, Zayd b. ʿAlī (d. 122/740), according to the *Amālī*, a book of his teachings recorded by his grandson.[59] It seems clear that Qāḍī Nuʿmān copied the combined maxim from that book.[60] There, the saying had already been combined and attributed to the Prophet: *qāla Rasūl Allāh ... idraʾū ʾl-ḥudūd biʾl-shubahāt wa-aqīlū*

[58] Apparently, Qāḍī Nuʿmān's choice of sources was dictated by their availability to him in North Africa (Ifrīqiya and Egypt), signaling that he had access neither to many of the works used by Qummī scholars nor to those Imāmī scholars themselves. The sources he names in the extant portion of *al-Īḍāḥ* rarely overlap with those used by the Imāmī traditionists, though a small percentage of the reports he cites is identical to *ḥadīth* reports of the fifth and sixth Imāms cited in the canonical Imāmī collections. See Madelung, "Sources of Ismāʿīlī Law," 30–31.

[59] See Zayd b. ʿAlī (d. 122/740), *Musnad*, collected and compiled by ʿAbd al-ʿAzīz b. Isḥāq al-Baghdādī (d. 363/973–4) (Ṣanʿāʾ, Yemen: Maktabat al-Irshād, 1990), 297–304 (not including the doubt canon in his *kitāb al-ḥudūd*); Aḥmad b. ʿĪsā b. Zayd (d. 248/869), *Amālī* (also called *Kitāb al-ʿUlūm*), collected and commented upon by Muḥammad b. Manṣūr b. Yazīd al-Murādī al-Kūfī ([Yemen]: Yūsuf b. al-Sayyid Muḥammad al-Muʾayyad al-Ḥasanī, 1401/1981), 211 (citing both the doubt canon and the elite-leniency maxim). See also Ṣanʿānī, *Kitāb Raʾb al-ṣadʿ*, 3:1390–1405.

[60] We know that Qāḍī Nuʿmān tended to copy material from *written* Shīʿī sources for his works on law. The transmission chain (Muḥammad – Ḥusayn b. Naṣr – Khālid – Ḥuṣayn [b. Mukhāriq] – Jaʿfar [al-Ṣādiq] – his father [Muḥammad al-Bāqir]), which appears in Qāḍī Nuʿmān's *Daʿāʾim*, provides specific evidence that this combined saying – recorded as a *ḥadīth* report – was copied from a book. See Hossein Modarressi, *Tradition and Survival: A Bibliographical Survey of Early Shīʿite Literature* (Oxford: Oneworld, 2003), 275–76 (noting that Abū Junāda al-Salūlī [Ḥuṣayn in the above chain], a late second/eighth-century Kūfan transmitter of *ḥadīth* from Jaʿfar al-Ṣādiq [as he appears in the above chain] and Mūsā al-Kāẓim, authored a work called *Kitāb Jāmiʿ al-ʿilm*, and that this work appears to have been quoted extensively in Aḥmad b. ʿĪsā's *Amālī*, always through the same chain of transmitters as above: Ḥusayn b. Naṣr b. al-Muzāḥim – Khālid – al-Ḥuṣayn b. Makhāriq – that is, the same chain noted in the copy of Aḥmad b. ʿĪsā's *Amālī* available to me in reference to *ḥadīth* taken from this work and quoted by Qāḍī Nuʿmān in his *Daʿāʾim*).

ʾl-kirām ʿatharātihim illā min ḥadd. It seems to have been not uncommon for *ḥadīth* on similar topics to have appeared side by side in early notebooks. It was also not uncommon for later copyists to divide the running text of these multiple *ḥadīth* sometimes incorrectly, as here, and to attribute them to the Prophet as if they were a combined *ḥadīth* with an attached chain of transmission, also as here. Put differently, Qāḍī Nuʿmān did not do the combining himself, especially given the fact that the only other time the doubt canon appears in his works it does so in the form used by other early scholars: as an anonymous statement that bears no relation to the elite-leniency maxim or any other saying.[61] Rather, Qāḍī Nuʿmān most likely copied the combined saying from an earlier Zaydī work, where the *ḥadīth* were already – perhaps inadvertently – combined and attributed to the Prophet.[62]

The same process of combining different maxims may have occurred in the Sunnī context, where there was also a lack of overlap between the doubt canon and the elite-leniency maxim. As noted above, jurists of the early period regularly cited and applied the doubt canon. But they rarely, if ever, cited or applied the elite-leniency maxim to validate the practice of avoiding criminal sanctions when it came to the elite.[63]

Exceptionally for jurists, who tended to cite *either* the doubt canon *or* the elite-leniency maxim, Aḥmad Ibn Ḥanbal recorded both. He seems to have grappled with but overcome the problem of incompatibility between the two by rejecting the prophetic attribution of the doubt canon,[64] and by adopting the version of the elite-leniency maxim that contained the *ḥudūd*

[61] Related works by Qāḍī Nuʿmān include the lost *Kitāb al-Ikhbār* [*sic*] (which also omits chains of transmission and other details included in his *Īḍāḥ*); its abridgment, *Kitāb al-Iqtiṣār*, which survives; and a didactic poem (*urjūza*) called *al-Muntakhaba* ("Selected"). Madelung, "Sources of Ismāʿīlī Law," 29ff. On the doubt canon, in *Kitāb al-Iqtiṣār*, 146, Qāḍī Nuʿmān simply reports at the end of the chapter on *ḥudūd* that "punishments are to be avoided in cases of doubt: *wa-yudraʾ al-ḥadd biʾl-shubha*" without *isnād* or attribution. The most we can glean from this mention is that the fuller tradition, using the term *shubha* or *shubahāt* for doubt, most probably appeared, if at all, in *Kitāb al-Īḍāḥ*.

[62] For further discussion, see my "Islamic Legal Maxims," 90–93.

[63] Abū Bakr b. Muḥammad b. ʿAmr b. Ḥazm, a *ḥadīth* scholar and a Medinese judge under ʿUmar II, is said to have promulgated the *ḥadīth* in Medina, although he and other jurists applied it in forms that supported enforcing rather than avoiding *ḥudūd* laws. See my "Islamic Legal Maxims," 93.

[64] To be sure, Ibn Ḥanbal acknowledged that the Prophet had avoided enforcing a *ḥadd* punishment in at least one instance when he declined to punish a woman charged with *zinā*, because she claimed that she had been raped. But Ibn Ḥanbal rejected the notion that the Prophet's decision in that case had a more general import as a maxim of prospective and general application, as other jurists read the doubt canon. See Ibn Ḥanbal, *Musnad*, 5:416.

exception meant to require *ḥudūd* enforcement against the elite. While both the doubt canon and the elite-leniency maxim were known by his time,[65] Ibn Ḥanbal's treatment suggests that the lack of overlap between them in the *ḥadīth* collections and juristic works was not fortuitous. As an opponent of gratuitous *ḥudūd* avoidance, he would have viewed the doubt canon as spurious and the elite-leniency maxim as wholly unacceptable without a *ḥudūd* exception. Though other scholars disagreed with him about the doubt canon, most came to signal agreement with his hostility to the elite-leniency maxim. Accordingly, the elite-leniency maxim virtually disappeared from subsequent legal literature,[66] while the doubt canon figured prominently.

3. Class-Based Distinctions in the Law: On Practice versus Theory

With this survey, we are now in a better position to revisit the social context of the doubt canon in order to answer the question about whether it emerged in order to benefit the elite. To be sure, in the literary memory of Muslim historians, some government-friendly jurists used and abused the doubt canon to benefit the elite. Yet the juridical record of contemporaneous legal literature shows that the vast majority of jurists railed against elite-favoring practices and constructed the jurisprudence of doubt to oppose them.

Enter the notion of a "touch of class." In light of the historical record – when read separately from the juridical record – it stands to reason that another historian who has examined the doubt canon concluded that its two versions (the judicial practice and the prophetic statement) reflected a historical trend of favoring the social elite in criminal proceedings. Maribel

[65] In addition to being scattered through the Sunnī *ḥadīth* corpus, the elite-leniency maxim also appeared regularly in compilations of sayings and proverbs from the early Islamic period, notably without the *ḥudūd* exception. See, for example, Abū ʿUbayd al-Qāsim b. Sallām (d. 224/838), *Kitāb al-Amthāl*, ed. ʿAbd al-Majīd Qaṭāmish (Mecca: Jāmiʿat al-Malik ʿAbd al-ʿAzīz, 1980), 1:52, no. 68. For further citations of this maxim from the early Islamic period and from the pre-Islamic period, see Marlow, *Hierarchy*, 27–28, n. 78 (and sources cited therein).

[66] An exception appears, perhaps predictably, in later Ḥanbalī literature, when Ibn al-Qayyim cites the elite-leniency maxim with its *ḥudūd* exception, as had Ibn Ḥanbal. See the collection of his *fiqh* opinions: *Jāmiʿ al-fiqh*, ed. Yusrī al-Sayyid Muḥammad (Mansoura, Egypt: Dār al-Wafāʾ, 1428/2007), 6:414 (citing and commenting on a citation of the saying as a *ḥadīth* by the fifth/eleventh-century Ḥanbalī luminary Ibn ʿĀqil: *aqīlū dhawī ʾl-hayaʾāt ʿatharātihim illā ʾl-ḥudūd*).

Fierro posits that the canon was a principle employed (or perhaps designed) to benefit the upper class and that this was done under the aegis of a rule of prophetic attribution. This, to her, was the "touch of class" that affected Islamic criminal law just as it had informed other areas of Islamic law.[67] Indeed, the historical sources report several cases of jurists using the doubt canon to benefit those of high status.

a. The Abū Yūsuf Episode: Using Doubt to Curry Political Favor

One of the elite-favoring uses of doubt involved the prominent Ḥanafī jurist Abū Yūsuf and the indiscretions of a young prince. According to the story, Abū Yūsuf was a poor, orphaned, no-name jurist who came to Baghdad after Abū Ḥanīfa's death and during the reign of Hārūn al-Rashīd, the famous ʿAbbāsid caliph. At that time, one of the local leaders had violated an oath and was looking for a juristic opinion as to how to expiate the violation, which was taken to be a grave sin. When the leader encountered Abū Yūsuf, the jurist told him that he had not technically violated his oath, and no expiation was due. Pleased, the official gave Abū Yūsuf a sizeable sum of money and secured a house for him in town close to his own.

One day, this same official went to Hārūn and found him depressed. The caliph explained that his sadness had to do with a religio-legal matter regarding which he needed a jurist to render an opinion, so the man immediately suggested Abū Yūsuf. When the latter arrived, he noticed a young man with an air of royalty who appeared to be locked in his room. The young man gestured at Abū Yūsuf in an appeal for help, but the jurist could not make out what he wanted. He proceeded to his appointment with the caliph.

"What is your opinion," Hārūn asked, "concerning an *imām* [leader] who witnessed [another] man committing *zinā*; must [the perpetrator] receive the *ḥadd* punishment?" Surmising that the caliph must be referring to one of his family members – the young man whom he had passed on the way – Abū Yūsuf replied, "No." Hārūn prostrated in joy. Abū Yūsuf explained that his opinion was consistent with the Prophet's instructions to "avoid criminal punishments in cases of doubt: *idraʾū ʾl-ḥudūd biʾl-shubahāt*." Judicial knowledge is insufficient evidence to establish a crime, he said; with no direct or corroborating evidence (that is, a confession or

67 See Fierro, "When Lawful Violence Meets Doubt," 229–38, esp. 237 ("The 'touch of class', the influence that social rank and status had in the application of the law can … be observed in the equality or inequality of punishments regarding Muslims and dhimmīs" as well as in the use of the doubt canon by elite jurists to favor political friends).

four eyewitnesses to the act), the matter was sufficiently doubtful to avoid the *ḥadd* sanction. (We are reminded of ʿAlī's decision regarding the murder in Medina discussed in the Introduction, plus – here – the intrigues and favors of royalty.) In gratitude, the caliph bestowed upon Abū Yūsuf a considerable amount of money and favor on behalf of the offending prince. According to the lore, this episode eventually led to Abū Yūsuf's judicial appointment and ensured his continuing elite status.[68] The anecdote is obviously a stylized narration. Its effect is to feature the doubt canon in its popular form as a prophetic saying subject to abuse by the elite.[69]

b. The Ibn Ḥabīb Episode: Using Doubt to Intervene for the Elite

In another episode, the prominent Cordovan jurist ʿAbd al-Malik Ibn Ḥabīb (d. 238/853) reportedly invoked the doubt canon to save his brother Hārūn from an accusation of blasphemy due to questionable statements that the latter had made.[70] When it comes to *ḥudūd* laws legislated and made mandatory by God, the jurist stated, the Prophet commanded "avoid[ing] criminal punishments against members of [his] community in cases of doubt: *idraʾū ʾl-ḥudūd ʿan ummatī biʾl-shubahāt*," as did his Companions, commanding avoidance of criminal punishments against Muslims to the extent possible: *idraʾū ʾl-ḥudūd ʿan al-muslimīn mā wajadtum lahum* ... (*makhrajan*).[71]

In this case, Hārūn b. Ḥabīb (ʿAbd al-Malik's brother) had made a statement denigrating the religious Muslims of his time in favor of Christians, whom he deemed more trustworthy. When two neighbors approached him to inquire whether he was of sound mind, he said, "I am fine, except that I have become so sick that even if I murdered Abū Bakr and ʿUmar [the first two caliphs, ranked by later Sunnī creed as most preferred in spiritual rank after the Prophet] ... I would not deserve

68 This story is repeated relatively frequently in the literary sources. See Tanūkhī, *Nishwār al-muḥāḍara*, 252–54; see also Ibn Khallikān, *Wafayāt al-aʿyān* (Beirut: Dār al-Thaqāfa, 1968), 6:381–82; Ibn al-Wardī, *Taʾrīkh Ibn al-Wardī* (Najaf: al-Maṭbaʿa al-Ḥaydariyya, 1969), 1:281 (reporting this event under the year 181 AH); and Abū ʿAbd Allāh al-Yāfiʿī, *Mirʾāt al-janān wa-ʿibrat al-yaqẓān fī maʿrifat ḥawādith al-zamān* (Beirut: Muʾassasat al-Aʿlamī liʾl-Maṭbūʿāt, 1390/1970), 1:383 (quoting Ibn Khallikān and reporting this event under the year 182 AH).

69 Scholars have recently taken note of this story in contexts discussing the doubt canon. See Fierro, "When Lawful Violence Meets Doubt," 231–32; Lange, *Justice*, 192.

70 Khushanī, *Akhbār*, 186–91.

71 There is an ellipsis in the text; I have filled it with the text of the *ḥadīth* as recorded in the Sunnī *ḥadīth* collections. See Appendix A, version 2.

this!"[72] The person who heard the first statement along with the two neighbors accused him of blasphemy and sent a letter to the reigning caliph, ʿAbd al-Raḥmān b. al-Ḥakam (ʿAbd al-Raḥmān II, r. 206–38/822–52), offering written testimony to that effect. Fortunately for Hārūn, his brother ʿAbd al-Malik was one of the jurists whom the caliph and judges called upon for advice on particularly difficult questions of law. The caliph wrote to ask the judge of Cordova along with Ibn Ḥabīb and his fellow expert jurists to investigate the blasphemy charge, which – if proved – carried a penalty of death.

Ibn Ḥabīb made three arguments to highlight the doubt and uncertainty surrounding the case in an ultimately successful effort to save his brother Hārūn from the death penalty. Two arguments cast doubt on the merits of the blasphemy charge and one concerned the evidence. On the merits, Ibn Ḥabīb argued that all his brother had done with the first statement was to censure the Muslims of his time for what he had perceived as rampant corruption. This, the jurist argued, should not be a prosecutable offense, because the sentiment actually fell in line with the prophetic prediction of increasingly corrupt societies across time (*fasād al-zamān*).[73]

The second statement was more problematic. Admittedly, Ibn Ḥabīb said, his brother's words could be construed as either praiseworthy or ill advised. Muslim ascetics had been known to use such figures of speech, as when the pious Uways al-Qaranī told a disciple to stand before God in prayer as if he had just destroyed the heavens and the earth – meaning, in a state of such attention and repentance that he was truly aware of presenting himself to God as a humble and lowly creature. If his brother, in mentioning the murder of the illustrious Companion-caliphs, meant something of this kind, then the statement was praiseworthy. Yet it was no secret that this esoteric meaning was unlikely. Instead, people popularly used such figures of speech for emphasis to express in exaggerated terms the extent of their hardships in life (*li-shiddat al-karb*). This second meaning was common to "fools and ignoramuses," who were merely complaining about what God had meted out to them. It was ill advised, Ibn Ḥabīb admitted, and thus could warrant some kind of disciplinary punishment

[72] Khushanī, *Akhbār*, 187. To preserve the sense of the original text, I have removed the honorific "may God be pleased with them," which appears to be an interpolation that followed the common later practice of including a blessing in any mention of the early Companions.

[73] Ibid.

(*ʿuqūba*), but it was not a case involving *ḥudūd* laws. That is, there was no legal rule prohibiting people from complaining of hardship. Granted, the Prophet discouraged it, but God never legislated any *ḥadd* sanction against it. In fact, the Qurʾān relates stories of Jacob (who complained at losing Joseph) and Job (who complained of the hardship that he suffered for eighteen years) without any absolute condemnation. When God censured them for complaining, Jacob said that he had committed a sin – not a crime – and asked for forgiveness; Job was never considered an apostate nor was he punished. To the contrary, he was held up as a paragon of patience! Read in this light, the jurist concluded, Hārūn's statement was ill advised, but it was not a criminal offense such that it warranted the *ḥadd* sanction for blasphemy.

Finally, Ibn Ḥabīb argued in the alternative that, even if Hārūn's alleged statements rose to the level of criminal wrongdoing on the merits, any *ḥadd* punishment should be avoided because the accusation rested on insufficient evidentiary grounds. Islamic criminal procedure barred certain types of testimony in criminal adjudication; among them was testimony that did not allow the defendant to confront his or her accuser. Before conviction and sentencing, the court must identify the witnesses who testified against the accused and give the latter the opportunity to defend himself.[74] At bottom, Ibn Ḥabīb concluded, his brother had committed no *ḥadd* crime. The doubt canon works to avert punishments of bad acts that God had specifically criminalized whenever their commission has not been proved beyond doubt; how much more should the tendency to avoid punishment apply when dealing with *un*specified crimes that are full of doubt concerning criminality or culpability? With these arguments, featuring the doubt canon and cleverly highlighting areas of doubt, Ibn Ḥabīb saved his brother from the *ḥadd* punishment of death.[75]

In the account, Ibn Ḥabīb insists that he would make the same arguments for anyone and that his arguments had nothing to do with the fact that the case involved his brother or, presumably, the high social rank of their family. But perhaps he doth protest too much, because his

[74] Ibid., 190 (*fa-law kānat al-ʿuqūba tajib ʿalā Hārūn wa-wajaba an yusammā lah man shahida bihā ʿalayh wa-yubsiṭ lah al-madfaʿa li-dhālik wa-yuwassiʿuh min al-ʿadl mā wasaʿa ʾl-muslimīn*).

[75] See ibid., 191. The brother received a lesser, discretionary punishment; he was imprisoned until the caliph died, after which the latter's son and successor, Caliph Muḥammad I (r. 238–73/852–86), freed him.

jurisprudence in other contexts is revealing. Ibn Ḥabīb seems to have generally been in favor of the death penalty in his role as consultant to the judge of Cordova.[76] When asked about the blasphemy case of the nephew of the royal concubine ʿAjab – someone of relatively high status but not related to him – Ibn Ḥabīb was not so intent on avoiding the punishment. In that case, he made none of the arguments he had advanced for his brother Hārūn, though those proceedings arose just after those involving Hārūn. To the contrary, Ibn Ḥabīb was one of the jurists in favor of imposing the death penalty on ʿAjab's nephew, with the result that the blasphemy charge stuck and the concubine's nephew was executed.[77]

c. The Ṣāliḥ b. Quddūs Episode: Legal Doubt versus Caliphal Offense

In an earlier blasphemy case in Iraq, the defendant had not been as fortunate as Hārūn turned out to be, though the doubt canon was still at play in the legal arguments invoked in the case. During the time of the ʿAbbāsid caliph al-Mahdī (r. 158–69/ 775–85), a Baṣran litterateur named Ṣāliḥ b. ʿAbd al-Quddūs (d. 167/783) was one of the poets accused of masked religious infidelity (*zandaqa*), that is, of secretly holding non-Islamic theological beliefs. Upon hearing allegations that the poet had rejected the Prophet in some of his poetry, al-Mahdī summoned him to answer a charge of blasphemy. In one version of the story, Ṣāliḥ denied having authored the offending verses, swearing that he had never uttered any blasphemous statements: "By God, I never joined others with God even for the blink of an eye. So be mindful of God! Don't shed my blood on the basis of doubt, for the Prophet instructed us to 'avoid criminal sanctions in cases of doubt.'" He then recited the Qurʾān until the caliph had a change of heart. The caliph was so impressed by the poet's eloquence and wisdom that he commanded that Ṣāliḥ be set free (*amara bi-takhliyat sabīlih*).

Just before the poet left, however, al-Mahdī asked him to recite some poetry to him, and Ṣāliḥ readily obliged. He recited until he came to the following lines:

[76] For the full story, see Fierro, "When Lawful Violence Meets Doubt," 230–31; Fierro, *La heterodoxia en al-Andalus durante el periodo omeya* (Madrid: Instituto Hispano-Arabe de Cultura, 1987), 63–70 and sources cited therein.

[77] For this story, see Fierro, "When Lawful Violence Meets Doubt," 230; see also Fierro, *La heterodoxia*, 57–63 and sources cited therein for a fuller account.

An old man does not abandon his ways *Wa'l-shaykhu lā yatruku akhlāqahū*	Until his body is buried in the earth *ḥattā tawārā fī tharā ramsihī*
No sooner does he repent than he reverts to his folly *Idhā 'r'awā 'āda ilā jahlihī*	Like a sickly man who falls back to his weakness *ka-dhī 'l-ḍannā 'āda ilā nuksihī* . . .[78]

Taken aback, the caliph reversed his decision to accept the poet's claims of innocence and perhaps rehabilitation. Al-Mahdī gathered from these lines that Ṣāliḥ would never give up his blasphemous ways and decided to rule on his case harshly. Ṣāliḥ was executed and crucified on a bridge.[79]

This time, invocation of the doubt canon was not enough to spare his life. But it is noteworthy that the canon was again recognized and invoked in the highest circles with al-Mahdī, as it had been under the governing authorities Hārūn al-Rashīd (the 'Abbāsid caliph) and 'Abd al-Raḥmān II (the Spanish Umayyad caliph). Ṣāliḥ's citation of the doubt canon represented another instance of at least an attempt by a member of the elite to use the doubt canon to avoid punishment regardless of the merits of the case (or even when guilt was presupposed, as it had been with the caliph Hārūn's son and with Hārūn, the brother of Ibn Ḥabīb).[80]

[78] I have drawn on the version recorded in a critical edition of Ṣāliḥ's poetry contained in a monograph on his life and writings. See 'Abd Allāh al-Khaṭīb, *Ṣāliḥ b. 'Abd al-Quddūs al-Baṣrī* (Baghdad: Dār Manshūrāt al-Baṣrī, 1967), 116–52, at 43 (in "*Dīwān Ṣāliḥ b. 'Abd al-Quddūs*"). Note that *ar'awā* literally means "to abandon," but it is rendered here as "repent." For an alternative translation, see Fierro, "When Lawful Violence Meets Doubt," 238 ("An old man cannot change his ways until he is in the grave and . . . when the old man abandons his mistakes, he does not fail to come back to them, like a convalescent who falls sick again").

[79] See al-Khaṭīb al-Baghdādī (d. 463/1071), *Ta'rīkh Baghdād*, ed. Muṣṭafā 'Abd al-Qādir 'Aṭā' (Beirut: Dār al-Kutub al-'Ilmiyya, 1997), 9:303, no. 4844 (s.v. Abū al-Faḍl al-Baṣrī [= Ṣāliḥ b. 'Abd al-Quddūs]); Ibn 'Asākir (d. 571/1176), *Ta'rīkh Madīnat Dimashq* (Beirut: Dār al-Fikr, 1995), 23:347–55, no. 2819 (s.v. Abū al-Faḍl al-Baṣrī); Ibn Khallikān (d. 681/1282), *Wafayāt al-a'yān*, 2:492 (s.v. Ṣāliḥ b. 'Abd al-Quddūs). For discussions in secondary sources, see Fierro, "When Lawful Violence Meets Doubt," 238 (citing Ignaz Goldziher, "Sâlih b. 'Abd al-Kuddus und das Zindîkthum während der Regierung des Chalifen al-Mahdî," in *Transactions of the Ninth International Congress of Orientalists* (London, September 1892), ed. E. Delmar Morgan (London: printed for the Committee of Congress, 1893), 104–29; Melhem Chokr, *Zandaqa et zindiqs en Islam au second siècle de l'Hégire* (Damascus: Institut français de Damas, 1993), 222–31; Josef van Ess, *Theologie und Gesellschaft im 2. und 3. Jahrhundert Hidschra: Eine Geschichte des religiösen Denkens im frühen Islam* (Berlin: Walter de Gruyter, 1991–97), 2:15–20).

[80] Fierro recounts additional episodes in "When Lawful Violence Meets Doubt," 1–2, 229–30, describing, in addition to these three cases, the following: (1) Andalusian judge Ibn Abī 'Īsā (d. 339/950) avoiding the *ḥadd* punishment for wine drinking according to a Ḥanafī rule disallowing punishment for a single confession (citing Bunnāhī [also known as 'Alī b. 'Abd Allāh al-Nubāhī (d. after 798/1389–90) – on whom, see M. Bencherifa, "al-Bunnāhī lā

How might we understand these episodes within the history of doubt, in light of theories that the doubt canon was deployed, and perhaps invented, to make such regard for the elite possible? Based on these and other episodes, Fierro has argued that the two versions of the doubt canon show that the standard form of the doubt canon was elite-regarding. For her, the *ḥadīth* version that advises judges to "avoid criminal punishments as much as you can" was a vague formulation that preceded the more specific, standard form of the directive to "avoid criminal punishments in cases of doubt." The benefit of the latter directive was to provide a more technical term for doubt (*shubahāt*). Accordingly, she argues, it may be that the latter formulation replaced the former in an attempt to curtail the canon's arbitrary and elite-favoring aspects through more objective and law-regarding standards (contained in the technical term for "doubt"). The more technical version would help those who might be called establishment jurists to avoid the censure of more respected, independent jurists who were not interested in working with the political authorities or in reifying social status; that is, of the "pious opposition."[81] However, the

al-Nubāhī," in *Académia: Revue de l'Académie du Royaume du Maroc* 8 (1998), 71–89; A. Carmona, "Al-Nubāhī (or more probably, al-Bunnāhī)," in *EI*[2] Supplement, 7:679], *al-Marqaba al-ʿulyā de al-Nubahi: La atalaya suprema sobre el cadiazgo y el muftiazgo*, ed. and trans. Arsenio Cuellas Marqués and Celia del Moral (Granada: Universidad de Granada, 2005), 89–91, 222–25); (2) Zīrid vizier Simāja avoiding the *ḥadd* punishment in a similar scenario (citing Ibn al-Khaṭīb (d. 776/1374), *Kitāb aʿmāl al-aʿlām*, ed. Évariste Lévi-Provençal (Rabat: al-Maṭbaʿa al-Jadīda, 1353/1934), 268–69; E. García Gómez, "Sobre la diferencia en el castigo de plebeyos y nobles," *Al-Andalus* 36 (1971), 73–74); and (3) Umayyad governor of Baṣra Khālid al-Qasrī (d. 126/743) urging a high-status thief to avoid punishment by simply denying criminal wrongdoing, which would provide the requisite basis to trigger the doubt canon (citing *Alf layla wa-layla*, night 298; Muḥammad b. Diyāb al-Itlīdī (d. late eleventh/seventeenth century), *Nawādir al-khulafāʾ al-musammā iʿlām al-nās bi-mā waqaʿa liʾl-Barāmika maʿa Banī al-ʿAbbās*, ed. Ayman ʿAbd al-Jābir al-Buḥayrī (Cairo: Dār al-Āfāq al-ʿArabiyya, 1998), as related by Abū Saʿīd ʿAbd al-Mālik al-Aṣmaʿī (d. 216/831)).

81 Fierro is suggesting that *shubahāt* is more of a technical term and thus more limited than *mā ʾstaṭaʿtum*. She posits that the latter preceded the former, which emerged as a response to the "pious opposition" of jurists such as Ibn Ḥanbal, Ibn Mājah, and Tirmidhī (and later Ibn Ḥazm), who were concerned that the law be applied in an egalitarian way. See Fierro, "When Lawful Violence Meets Doubt," 227, 236 (noting traditions forbidding Muslims from interceding on behalf of their high-status peers). While her argument about the technical nature of the term accords with subsequent juristic usage, it was not designated as technical in the early period, and, arguably, for the likes of Ibn Ḥazm, the *shubahāt* version provides a framework no more or less arbitrary than any other version of the canon from the early period. More importantly, the two versions are contemporaneous with one another but circulated in different scholarly circles, as I have demonstrated here. Furthermore, as I argue below, the elaboration of *shubha* came later: jurists who invoked it did not endow it with any marked precision until the fourth and fifth centuries. See Chapters 5, 6, and 8.

full picture of doubt is more textured. Notwithstanding their support for the general proposition that elite status seeped into Islamic criminal law, these episodes do not depict the entire story of doubt when measured against the juristic and historical corpus of literature related to it. At most, these narratives underscore the extent to which social stratification was a fact of life in early Islamic societies and show that government-related officials – including some jurists – reportedly used statements such as the doubt canon and the elite-leniency maxim (without its *ḥudūd* exception) to exploit the law in order to justify preferential treatment, even in the criminal context.

To be sure, the literary and prosopographical sources in which these stories appear likely record the most spectacular of such encounters, memorable precisely for their exceptional sociopolitical valence or the unique cunning on display. Further, as is typical in Islamic historiography, we do not look to anecdotes for, nor do we expect from them, a comprehensive sampling of the course of historical events. Nevertheless, this sampling is useful inasmuch as it provides a window onto relatively early understandings of Islamic law and society surrounding the elite's encounter with criminal law and social status in the seventh and eighth centuries. Yet those notions stand in sharp contrast to the theory of Islamic criminal law offered in the works of *ḥadīth* and law from the same period and afterward.

Fierro's distinction between the different formulations is important, even if it does not fully support her theory about the elitist origins and use of doubt. In noting the differences between the two forms of the canon and in calling attention to the legalistic tenor of what came to be the standard "doubt" (*shubahāt*) version, her intervention may explain why the standard version became central to the later juristic literature. Indeed, when they textualized doubt, both *ḥadīth* scholars and jurists grafted a prophetic attribution onto the standard version rather than to the existing *ḥadīth* versions, signaling their preference for the more legalistic formulation.

Yet none of these facts suggests that doubt (*shubha*) was a well-defined "technical term" during the early period (the sources suggest that it was not), or that the standard juristic version came later (the sources suggest that it did not).[82] Instead, the sources indicate that the differences in the form of the doubt canon in the early period were a matter not of *sequence*,

[82] For a contrasting view, see Fierro, "When Lawful Violence Meets Doubt," 225 ("Although he objects to the Prophetic saying with the standard formula, Abū Bakr b. al-ʿArabī does use *shubha* as a technical term."), 222 (suggesting that early Ḥanafīs were "responsible for the formulation of the saying that was to become standard, in which *mā istaṭaʿtum* was replaced by a more technical expression (*bi-l-shubuhāt*)").

but of *genre*. My analysis of the first three centuries of *ḥadīth* and legal literature revealed that the *ḥadīth* versions and the standard version of the doubt canon circulated in two completely different arenas, simultaneously, as was also the case with the doubt canon and the elite-leniency maxim. *Ḥadīth* scholars concerned with one set of criteria for recording traditions included in their collections a set of reports different from the canon deployed by jurists committed to another set of criteria for expounding law. Thus, *ḥadīth* scholars cited the various versions of the canon but never mentioned the standard version, which did not meet their criteria for *ḥadīth* reliability; meanwhile, legal scholars consistently cited the standard version when articulating and applying the law.

That these various sayings were known and cited in different circles, depending on whether scholars were acting in the capacity of *ḥadīth* reporters or of jurists, clarifies an important feature of Islam's early legal system and the nature of its foundational texts. With the doubt canon, both camps knew of both of its versions. Jurists, however, did not regard their formulation as prophetic in origin. They nevertheless cited and applied the doubt canon as a substantive principle of criminal law that drew on earlier precedent. In other words, though the wording was not authoritative, the precedent from judicial practice – as expressed in the canon – was.

What of the other versions of the doubt canon combining the standard version with the elite-leniency maxim? The existence of this version in Ibn ʿAdī's work, Fierro suggests, provides corroboration for the historical trend of elite favoritism in criminal laws.[83] Here is where timing does come into play. Although the elite-leniency maxim is as old as the doubt canon, the combined version attributed to Ibn ʿAdī and Qāḍī Nuʿmān is not. It came later, through the splicing together of these two different sayings from two different regions – as posited above. Additionally, even if the doubt canon and the elite-leniency maxim were known in the same region at the same time by the mid-third/ninth century, as indicated by Ibn Ḥanbal's reference to both, was the prescriptive value of the elite-leniency maxim taken as a license to apply the doubt canon in a way that authorized avoiding *ḥudūd* punishments for those of high social status? Perhaps so in the version of the elite-leniency maxim that lacked the *ḥudūd* exception, but emphatically not in the version with that exception. For this reason, Ibn Ḥanbal cites the version of the elite-leniency maxim that includes the

[83] See Fierro, "When Lawful Violence Meets Doubt," 218, 233–34 (noting that Ibn ʿAdī's version of the combined maxim "echoes the clash between the egalitarianism of religious law and the hierarchical structure of society"; citing Marlow, *Hierarchy*, 1–3, 25–27).

ḥudūd exception, making clear that any societal norms that ordinarily allowed for excusing the elite for minor faults and misdemeanors did not exempt them from *ḥudūd* liability. Rather than using doubt to *benefit the elite*, it is more likely that Ibn Ḥanbal and other jurists cited the doubt canon to *curb elite privilege* in the application of *ḥudūd* laws through insisting on using the combined version that did carry a *ḥudūd* exception to the elite-leniency maxim.

CONCLUSION

In sum, whereas the "arbitrary" and "objective" (in Fierro's words) versions of the doubt canon circulated side by side in the early period through the ninth century, the widespread elite-leniency maxim was disregarded by jurists in the *ḥudūd* context. Also, that maxim was certainly not appended to the doubt canon in the early *ḥadīth* context. Instead, the elite-leniency maxim was attached to the doubt canon only after the principle of mandatory, egalitarian *ḥudūd* enforcement had won out. Accordingly, the more popular combined maxim carried a *ḥudūd* exception to the elite-leniency portion of the saying designed to underscore, not subvert, the principle that the elite were not exempt from criminal liability. This understanding of the origins and applications of the doubt canon and associated legal maxims accords well with the jurists' emphasis on the early Islamic values of divine legislative supremacy and egalitarian moral values through criminal law enforcement except in cases of doubt. This understanding also prompts consideration of the notion that the historical sources recording abuse of the doubt canon in favor of the elite tell only half of doubt's story. The other half concerns the theory and practice of doubt jurisprudence from the legal sources.

Chapter 4 illustrates how the majority of early Muslim jurists outlined a criminal law jurisprudence that actively opposed orientations toward the kinds of preferential treatment and arbitrary justice reflected in the historical and literary sources. Far from using doubt as an elite-favoring tool, the jurists' rejection of hierarchy and arbitrariness in *ḥudūd* laws pushed them to develop a criminal law system that used doubt to promote early Islamic moral ideals and to mediate between notions of severity and lenity.

4

Doubt as Moral Concern

The competing realities of moral egalitarianism and social hierarchy in Islam's first three centuries provide a fitting sociopolitical context for understanding trends in *ḥudūd* jurisprudence related to doubt in the last two centuries of the founding period. The episodes displaying hierarchy in *ḥudūd* laws appeared primarily in historical sources describing political events. But all of these episodes were legally non-precedential.[1] The precedential cases appeared in the *ḥadīth* collections and other foundational sources of law from the early period. It is to these sources that later jurists looked when attempting to identify and interpret the earliest ideals and realities of *ḥudūd* laws and to apply them to resolve doubt. Strikingly, the jurists' analysis resulted in firm support both for *ḥudūd* avoidance and for *ḥudūd* enforcement, with the result that their early outlines of Islamic criminal law oscillated between the two.

The question is why. What about the social and political context of early Islamic law and society made it necessary for jurists to invoke or oppose the doubt canon? As we have seen, one theory has it that the doubt canon emerged from the elite, was subject to exploitation by the elite, and

[1] In Islamic legal theory, only directives based on Islam's foundational legal sources are binding. To take shape as a part of actual Islamic jurisprudence, somewhat like in common law, those directives typically do not take on specific meaning and precedential weight until they are used by judges to decide legal cases and/or are repeated in judgments, advisory opinions, and juristic treatises that provide restatements of law. For discussions, see generally Jackson, *Islamic Law and the State*; Abou El Fadl, *Rebellion and Violence*. Cf. Johansen, "Legal Literature and the Problem of Change."

was therefore a creature of the arbitrariness of the elite. On that view, juristic opposition to the canon was meant to curb its abuse.[2] That view suggests a fundamental conflict between one tendency to invoke the canon and thereby avoid *ḥudūd* punishments and an opposite tendency to suppress the canon and lean instead toward *ḥudūd* enforcement. Yet that portrayal does not convincingly explain or reflect the concerns of the juristic community writing during Islam's founding period, members of which both invoked and limited the reach of doubt in their treatment of early Islamic criminal law. A better explanation would have to investigate where the doubt doctrine fell along a spectrum that ranged from *ḥudūd* enforcement to avoidance in the sociopolitical context of the early period, during Umayyad and early ʿAbbāsid rule.

My investigation of that spectrum complicates the picture, revealing that moral concern, more than social status, was at play in the construction of the early Islamic doctrine of doubt. To be sure, the social status of jurists played a major role in shaping early Islamic criminal law and the jurisprudence of doubt. Yet there was no one-to-one correspondence between social status and support for *ḥudūd* avoidance. Another factor played a significant role – namely, a high degree of moral concern on the part of many jurists responding to shifting social and political developments in the young Muslim community. This moral concern stemmed from the juristic community's desire to adhere to the divine legislative will in a way that both recognized the divine legislative supremacy ideal and the divine moral imperatives culled from Islam's foundational texts, while at the same time grappling with political excesses in punishment.

Inevitably plagued by doubt, medieval Muslim jurists stood at the intersection of legal authority and moral values in the realms of politics and law. The following discussion traces the outlines of the contests between the two realms. On the one hand, the jurists approached *ḥudūd* enforcement with an eye to sociopolitical realities evident in the literary and historical sources. On the other hand, they looked to moral-legal values drawn from the foundational sources of Islamic law to anchor new rationales for *ḥudūd* avoidance. Accordingly, this chapter presents the competing values surrounding issues of morality and authority in early Islamic societies, which are then used as a means to explain the

[2] Fierro, "When Lawful Violence Meets Doubt," 236. Fierro counts Ibn Ḥanbal among the scholarly "pious opposition," who considered the "as much as you can" wording of the *ḥadīth* version of the doubt canon subject to too few constraints and too much abuse by the elite by the mid-second/eighth century.

opposing tendencies in juristic debates about *ḥudūd* enforcement and *ḥudūd* avoidance. The chapter ends by drawing attention to the great compromise reached between ruling and juristic authorities over issues of morality and legal authority by the ninth and tenth centuries and the role of Islamic criminal law as a form of public law central to developing that new order.

Before delving into the early cases to elucidate this claim, it is worth pausing to consider the nature of the sources. The usual disclaimer applies when drawing on sources that are not contemporaneous with the events that they describe. Although the cases presented here purport to detail events from the Prophet's time and immediately afterward, reports of them are available in written sources only from the late Umayyad and early ʿAbbāsid periods, at the earliest, and they do not claim to be transcripts of actual criminal proceedings. Rather than taking them as verbatim representations of what actually happened, we can understand them to indicate the ideas that later generations of scholars came to associate with Islam's earliest period. We can also take them to represent the arguments that resonated in early juristic circles as normative.[3] This is not to suggest that these accounts are entirely fictional, but rather that, as with all

[3] I take my cue from Roy Mottahedeh, who observed the high regard that one medieval Muslim society accorded to oaths through observing their portrayal in anecdotal, legal, and historical-political literature. The point was not whether the anecdotes told involving oath taking were historical, but that they clearly signified a premium on not violating oaths as they attributed negative consequences for piety, social cohesion and political loyalties to doing so. To take just one example, anecdotes about political leaders and notables taking personal oaths of obligation suggest not that these leaders aimed to bind their followers but that they could secure the compliance of their followers through existing loyalties. Likewise, a certain type of oath of fealty to the leader (*bayʿa*) was essential for political loyalty, and the juristic or social sanctions for breaking that oath were the "only device for ensuring loyalty when all other sanctions belonged to the established government." See Mottahedeh, *Loyalty and Leadership*, 53, 61, and passim. In a similar vein, numerous other social and intellectual historians have looked to the traditions to make observations about social conventions and normative arguments that carried weight in the premodern societies that preserved them. See, for example, Marlow, *Hierarchy*, 13 (adopting a similar approach in the context of maxims). This approach, and thus this chapter, is not directly concerned with questions of origins, authenticity, or historical accuracy. Rather, it is meant to complement critical investigations of the sources of the type conducted in Chapters 2 and 3 that seek to closely evaluate and comment on the provenance and circulation of certain reports or intellectual schools extracted from the earliest available written sources that point to or verify yet earlier trends. Excellent examples of this latter approach include Motzki, *Origins*; and Rudolph Peters, "Murder in Khaybar: Some Thoughts on the Origins of the *Qasāma* Procedure in Islamic Law," *Islamic Law and Society* 9, 2 (2002), 132–67.

historiography, they are interpretations that partly reveal the historical circumstances and values of the community recounting them.[4]

This exercise is useful for our purposes of identifying the societal values and moral concerns present in early Islamic legal history, interested as we are in the juristic ideals of that time. As one scholar aptly put it,

> just as looking at how men and women dress and act when they are trying to look their best tells us something important about ideals of beauty, so looking at legal doctrine when judges pretty it up for public display tells us something important about ideals of justice.... [Legal opinions] embody the aspirations of legal institutions, showing us what judges do when they want to get things right for a special occasion.... If the question one is asking is what ideals the law embodies, then one should look at those settings most likely to provide the ideal point of view.[5]

Legal maxims do this work of providing the ideal point of view in Islamic law to an even greater extent than do legal opinions in the common law context about which that scholar spoke. They express the essence of established Islamic legal opinions that have become accepted as normative for legal pedagogy and practice, which explains why they are of such central concern in this book.

Like general legal maxims of the early Islamic period, the cases recorded in the juristic literature of that period show that "a number of different social ideals were in competition in the early second century, and that the exponents of each were eager to claim the authority of the past."[6] Some reflect the sentiments of egalitarianism and judicial subservience, and they were expressed by calls to enforce *ḥudūd* laws strictly. Others reflect a deeper

[4] For discussions of Islamic historiographical literature, see, for example, Stephen Humphreys, *Islamic History: A Framework for Inquiry*, rev. ed. (Princeton, NJ: Princeton University Press, 1991) (orig. 1983), esp. chap. 3 (describing the character of early Islamic historiography and surveying major approaches to the field in contemporary scholarship); Donner, *Narratives of Islamic Origins*, esp. 1–31 (introduction: surveying approaches to Islamic history and historiography in contemporary scholarship and critiquing the radically skeptical approach in favor of one that looks to the Islamic sources for a "kernel" of historical truth); Tayeb El-Hibri, *Reinterpreting Islamic Historiography: Hārūn al-Rashīd and the Narrative of the ʿAbbāsid Caliphate* (Cambridge: Cambridge University Press, 1999) (arguing that early Arab history writing should be viewed as a register not of facts but of anecdotes for moralizing); Chase Robinson, *Islamic Historiography* (Cambridge: Cambridge University Press, 2003) (suggesting that Muslim historians who received patronage produced written accounts that aimed to present facts in order to legitimate the sponsoring regime or to give answers that belief required, though noting that their accounts *could* coincide with historical fact).

[5] Kim Lane Scheppele, *Legal Secrets: Equality and Efficiency in the Common Law* (Chicago: University of Chicago Press, 1988), 316–17.

[6] Marlow, *Hierarchy*, 13.

moral discomfort about imposing the harshest of sanctions, namely, the death penalty, and this discomfort materialized in measures to avoid *ḥudūd* punishments altogether. And still others reveal compromise attempts to strike a balance between the two tendencies in light of the police power of the ruling authorities and the moral concerns of the jurists. These early cases, I argue, demarcate an area of *public morality* over which political jurisdiction and *ḥudūd* enforcement may have been warranted to shelter an area of private action where concealment and avoidance were key. It is through discussion of these early cases that later jurists negotiated competing moral values. In what follows, I present these competing tendencies in criminal law jurisprudence by focusing on early cases that are of recurring importance in the later legal literature.[7] Throughout, I argue that these cases should be read against the backdrop of an increasingly stratified social context (in terms of sociopolitical status), which challenged the ideals of the earliest community to which the scholarly community recounting these cases aimed to hearken back.

By reviewing the early cases, I aim to show that they express some of the core moral concerns of the early Muslim community arising from important social and political developments of the time – namely, opposition to the use of social position for unequal and arbitrary application of the law, attention to religious imperatives to adhere to divine commands, and the resulting moral concern of the jurists charged with defining or interpreting Islamic criminal law. The jurists' rulings were also a protection against encroachments by the ruling authorities on their own jurisdiction, inasmuch as they took themselves to be more able exponents of God's law. These concerns resulted in a certain insistence on *ḥudūd* enforcement in some instances and on *ḥudūd* avoidance in others, as revealed through myriad criminal cases circulating among the jurists during Islam's first three centuries, attributed to the Prophet and other early authorities acting as judges during this early founding period of Islamic law.[8]

[7] See note 8.

[8] I designate these episodes "landmark cases," because they come from the first three centuries of Islamic rule – wherein reports that were sometimes subsequently attributed to the Prophet and taken to have prospectively precedential weight were actively being gathered. It is to these cases that jurists writing in the tenth and eleventh centuries, and afterward, hearken back. The selection of cases, particularly of those contained in Sunnī *ḥadīth* literature, is based on an analysis of the usage of jurists in *fiqh* works from this early period (for example, treatises by Shāfiʿī, Mālik, Abū Yūsuf, and Shaybānī), *fiqh* works composed after the third/ninth century, and *fiqh*, *fatāwā*, and *qawāʿid* works from the fifth/eleventh through ninth/fifteenth centuries in Būyid, Seljūq, Fāṭimid, Andalusian, and Mamlūk lands, as discussed in the next three chapters. Additionally, a comparison of the cases selected here with the full range of

A. *ḤUDŪD* ENFORCEMENT: MORAL EGALITARIANISM AND DIVINE LEGISLATIVE SUPREMACY

1. Fraud: The *Case of the Makhzūmī Thief*

One early episode illustrates well the jurists' fixation on Islam's egalitarian ideals: the aforementioned *Case of the Makhzūmī Thief*. According to reports of that case, the Prophet had convicted a woman of theft for borrowing goods and then denying that she had done so. The conviction made her eligible for the *ḥadd* punishment of hand amputation. Before the punishment, the elite members of society petitioned the Prophet to avoid punishment and let the convict go. She belonged to the prominent Makhzūm clan within the Prophet's tribe of Quraysh, and its members did not want to see one of their own punished.[9] Leading members of the clan designated one Makhzūmī clansman, Usāma b. Zayd, to approach the Prophet on the woman's behalf in an attempt to avert the requisite sanction. In their estimation, Usāma had the greatest chance of success given his relationship to the Prophet: he was the son of the Prophet's own adopted son. But the Prophet responded quite unfavorably, exclaiming, "Usāma, would you intervene in a matter involving God's laws [lit. one of the *ḥudūd* laws of God]?" The Prophet ordered the sentence to be carried out and then publicly addressed the people, in rebuke and admonition:

> Surely, those who came before you were destroyed because [it was their practice that], when a person of high status (*sharīf*) stole, they would let him go; but when a commoner (*ḍaʿīf*) stole, they would impose the *ḥadd* punishment on him. I swear by God that even if Fāṭima [my own daughter] had stolen, I would cut off her hand.[10]

cases and rulings contained in second/eighth- and third/ninth-century *ḥadīth* collections shows that these cases offer a useful sample of major types if not frequency of issues that arise in *ḥadīth* works as they relate to interpretive moves and maxims in Islamic criminal law. For a list of cases, see Appendix B.

9 On the stature of the Makhzūmī clan within the Qurashī tribe, see Zubayr b. Bakkār, *Jamharat nasab Quraysh*, ed. Maḥmūd Muḥammad Shākir (Cairo: Maktabat Dār al-ʿUrūba, 1381/1962), 284; Abū ʿAbd Allāh al-Zubayrī, *Nasab Quraysh*, ed. E. Lévi-Provençal (Cairo: Dār al-Maʿārif, 1953), 247; Ibn Ḥazm, *Jamharat ansāb al-ʿArab*, ed. ʿAbd al-Salām Muḥammad Hārūn (Cairo: Dār al-Maʿārif, 1962), 124. See also M. Hinds, "Ma<u>kh</u>zūm, Banū," in *EI*[2], 6:137–40; Bernheimer, *ʿAlids*, 60–63 (noting intermarriages between ʿAlids and Makhzūmīs as indicants of marital suitability for those of the same social-genealogical status, as necessitated by the principle of equality in marriage, *kafāʾa*).

10 Abū Dāwūd, *Sunan* (1996), 4:133, no. 4373 (that she had stolen in the narration by al-Layth b. Saʿd); no. 4374 (that she used to borrow goods without returning them in the narration by Maʿmar, or that she stole a thick cloth (*qaṭīfa*) from the Prophet's house in the narration by Masʿūd b. al-Aswad); see also Bukhārī, *Ṣaḥīḥ*, no. 6887 (in *bāb iqāmat al-ḥ udūd ʿalā ʾl-sharīf waʾl-waḍīʿ*); Muslim, *Ṣaḥīḥ*, no. 1688; Nasāʾī, *Sunan*, 4:330; Bayhaqī,

In so saying, the Prophet prohibited in no uncertain terms disparities in *ḥudūd* enforcement based on social status or familial relations – recognizing neither acquired nor inherited merit as legitimate bases for deciding issues of Islamic law.[11]

The Prophet's allusion to Fāṭima is significant for reasons beyond the obvious familial connection and caution against nepotism on that basis. Her mention brought into play the deep religious and cultural valence that Fāṭima enjoyed rather uniquely in Muslim societies across time and space. At the time the *ḥadīth* scholars and jurists recorded this case in the eighth and ninth centuries and after, Fāṭima had long been recognized as the single most revered woman in Islamic history among Sunnīs and Shīʿa alike, for her piety and for reasons centered on but also going beyond her familial tie to the Prophet.[12] Imagining even Fāṭima as *ḥadd*-eligible, then, was the most emphatic declaration possible to signal that *ḥudūd* laws were to be enforced in an egalitarian manner, regardless of social status or lineage. Like the *Case of Māʿiz*, the *Case of the Makhzūmī Thief* was a founding case from the early period that later Muslim jurists understood to mean that even the Prophet's authority was restricted when it came to Islamic criminal law, especially where – unlike the *Case of Māʿiz* – there was no doubt that caused him to avoid punishment.

2. Theft: The *Case of Ṣafwān*

A second case, in which issues of the offender's status were not immediately apparent (though those of the victim's status were), spoke further to jurists' general concern with the Qur'ānic imperative to obey the divine law. This famous incident involved the early convert Ṣafwān b. Umayya, who stayed in Mecca after most Muslims had migrated to Medina years after the Prophet began preaching the message of Islam. The emigrants

Sunan, 8:287, no. 17004 (citing Bukhārī and Muslim, and noting that they recorded the version of al-Layth b. Saʿd).

11 For discussions of both types of merit (*ḥasab* and *nasab*), see Chapter 3, note 13 and accompanying text.

12 See Denise L. Soufi, *The Image of Fatima in Classical Muslim Thought* (PhD diss., Princeton University, 1997) (describing universal regard for and veneration of Fāṭima as the exemplar for Muslim women in terms of societal role, intellectual competence, and piety). Moreover, Fāṭima was the progenitor of the ʿAlid line of descent, which has been called the "peerless aristocracy of Islam," more elite than other relatives of the Prophet (*sharīf*s). See Bernheimer, *ʿAlids*, 161–65 (noting that familial boundaries were upheld through marriages as recorded in genealogies, records of which were well maintained during the early period and throughout ʿAbbāsid rule).

made known their attitude that those who remained in Mecca were wrong to do so, and the continuing negative sentiment against those latecomers is said to have eventually prompted Ṣafwān to join the emigrants in Medina some two hundred miles to the north. On his way, he stopped to rest in a mosque, napping with his head on his cloak. He awoke only to discover that a man had come and stolen his cloak. Ṣafwān pursued the thief immediately and, having captured him, dragged him to the Prophet for criminal prosecution. The Prophet ruled that the man was to have his hand amputated, in accordance with the Qur'ānic *ḥadd* punishment for theft. At this, Ṣafwān balked: "I never intended this [outcome]!" he exclaimed. "I hereby gift him the cloak." Notwithstanding Ṣafwān's elite status, the Prophet rejected his attempt to determine the outcome of the case.[13] He responded, "If only you had done so before you came to me!" In one version of the story, the Prophet ordered that the *ḥadd* punishment be enforced, rejecting Ṣafwān's belated attempt to avert it.[14]

Later Muslim jurists typically cite this case for the proposition that criminal matters, once adjudicated, are final (but that before adjudication, a change in ownership status could avert the associated punishment).[15] In this case, the matter had already been adjudicated, and it was the Prophet's duty – as the political and judicial authority charged with implementing the divine law – to enforce the punishment in deference to divine legislative

[13] Before Islam, Ṣafwān was a prominent merchant, who is said on some accounts to have opposed the Muslims at Badr and then tried to escape to Syria with a caravan carrying a considerable amount of silver that he owned. See Patricia Crone, *Meccan Trade and the Rise of Islam* (Princeton, NJ: Princeton University Press, 1987), 87; see also Kennedy, *The Prophet and the Age of the Caliphates*, 43, who groups Ṣafwān among the "die-hard leaders" of that city who resisted the Prophet's overtures for reconciliation until the Prophet's eventual conquest of that city, after which he finally returned, reconciled, and eventually converted.

[14] Shāfiʿī, *Umm*, ed. Muḥammad Zuhrī al-Najjār (Cairo: Maktabat al-Kulliyyāt al-Azhariyya, 1961), 131 (*hallā qabla an ta'tīnī bih*); cf. ʿAbd al-Razzāq, *Muṣannaf* (2000), 10:229, no. 18938 ("O Messenger of God, would you [still] cut off [this man's] hand for my cloak that I now gift to him?"). There are many versions of this narrative, with slight variations. The variant quoted here records the cloak as having been stolen from under Ṣafwān's head; another has it that Ṣafwān left the cloak atop his waiting camel outside. For the latter version, see ʿAbd al-Razzāq, *Muṣannaf* (2000), 10:229, no. 18938; see also Nasā'ī, *Sunan*, 4:4330, no. 7371 (similar to ʿAbd al-Razzāq's version). But this latter version is problematic as a model case (and thus disfavored by the jurists in their later citations), because the thief would not have taken the cloak from a secure location, which is a key condition for the application of the *ḥadd* punishment as against a more lenient discretionary punishment. For a collection of versions, see Bayhaqī, *Sunan*, 8:287, nos. 17002–17003.

[15] For further discussion, see Chapters 5 and 6.

supremacy.[16] This case represents an instance of jurists who adopted this position showing that political and judicial authorities alike were accountable and subordinate to the dictates of the divine law, again without exception for the elite. Legal process was key. If even the Prophet could not avoid applying sanctions once the process revealed that an offender had clearly violated the law, no one could.

3. Wine Drinking: The *Case of the Drunken Orphan*

A third case, pointedly emphasizing the moral imperative to obey the divine law and further emphasizing egalitarian ideals, is reported to have occurred some years after *Ṣafwān's Case*. The *Case of the Drunken Orphan* concerned a man who brought his nephew to one of the leading Companions of the Prophet, Ibn Masʿūd (d. 32/652–3), while he was presiding as Kūfa's first governor and judge.[17] The man asked Ibn Masʿūd to punish the young man for drunkenness. The nephew protested on grounds that his uncle was derelict in his duties as a guardian: "You neither disciplined me [to thereby teach me right from wrong] nor covered my sin," he complained. Here he was alluding to a general sentiment against revealing indiscretions publicly, which applied to members of all classes and was not reserved to the special preferences that the elite-leniency maxim advised for the elite.[18]

In his deliberations, Ibn Masʿūd referred to instances in which the Prophet had reportedly enforced *ḥudūd* punishments against anyone who violated the law, even though it pained him deeply. When the Prophet had faced the very first case of theft (likely a reference to the *Case of the Makhzūmī Thief*), Ibn Masʿūd said, he had grimly accepted that his personal qualms about the severity of the sanction "could not stop [him] from" enforcing punishment.[19] Drawing on this precedent, Ibn Masʿūd sentenced the young man reluctantly but decidedly. It pained

16 A minority – who take this case as a precedent for *ḥudūd* avoidance – deny that the Prophet imposed the *ḥadd* sanction. See, for example, Qudūrī, *Tajrīd*, 11:5986–87.

17 This would have occurred during the reign of ʿUmar or in the first part of ʿUthmān's reign, before the beginning of complaints about the latter's nepotism. There is some dispute about when Ibn Masʿūd, a prominent companion in Sunnī records, assumed the judgeship in Kūfa or even who was the first judge there. Regardless, he appears to have been the first judge with any lasting effect. For reports of his judicial decisions, see Wakīʿ, *Akhbār al-quḍāt*, 354–55.

18 For extended discussions of the elite-leniency maxim (advising judges to "overlook the faults of the nobles"), see Chapter 3.

19 Al-Ḥākim al-Naysābūrī, *Mustadrak*, 4:24.

him, too, he said, to punish the young man. But he found himself constrained from avoiding punishment because the guilt was not contested. True, "God is [quick to] pardon and loves pardon," Ibn Masʿūd quoted, but whenever a *ḥadd* violation is brought to the presiding authority (*walī ʾl-amr*), he must enforce the designated punishment.[20]

Even as Ibn Masʿūd observed that concerns with divine legislative supremacy and egalitarianism required him to enforce the sanction, he endorsed the system of concealing faults to which the nephew had referred – but only *before* crimes had been raised to the courts. The Prophet, Ibn Masʿūd advised, had indeed encouraged people *not* to bring *ḥudūd* matters to the courts:

> Do not be helpers to Satan on behalf of your brother. It is improper for the *imām*, when a *ḥadd* crime is raised to him, to do anything but enforce [punishment]. God is [quick to] pardon and loves pardon, so pardon and overlook [the faults of others]! Do you not wish for God to forgive you? For God is oft-forgiving, most merciful.[21]

This general impetus toward concealing minor crimes reflects a strong tradition of privacy in early Islamic law, first expressed in Qurʾānic verses and prophetic statements prohibiting spying and regulating entry into others' homes. This was a system of "public virtue, private vice": misdemeanors could be overlooked so long as they remained private, but once raised to the courts – and thus made public – they had to be punished in an egalitarian manner.[22]

[20] Bayhaqī, *Sunan*, 8:331, no. 17391. This narrative is similar to a story related about ʿAbd al-Raḥmān, son of ʿUmar, whom his brother dragged to court in Egypt for drunkenness. There, the governor-judge ʿAmr b. al-ʿĀṣ enforced the *ḥadd* sanction secretly, and when ʿUmar heard about it, he enforced it again publicly in Medina. It could be that ʿUmar doubted whether ʿAmr ever enforced the punishment, as no one witnessed it or could testify to it. Alternatively, he may have insisted on public punishment for the reason cited above – namely, because mere compassion could not warrant departure from proper *ḥudūd* enforcement. See Ibn Taymiyya, *Majmūʿ al-fatāwā*, ed. ʿAbd al-Raḥmān b. Muḥammad b. Qāsim al-ʿĀṣimī al-Najdī al-Ḥanbalī and his son Muḥammad (Beirut: Maṭābiʿ Muʾassasat al-Risāla, 1997), 14:287 (citing the tradition in the course of his commentary on Qurʾān, 24:2: *wa-lā taʾkhudhkum bi-himā raʾfa*).

[21] Al-Ḥākim al-Naysābūrī, *Mustadrak*, 4:24 (noting here, as he does in the remainder of his work, that he includes this *ḥadīth* in his collection as authentic according to the *methodology* of Bukhārī and Muslim, even though those two scholars did not include it in their collections).

[22] See Michael A. Cook, *Commanding Right and Forbidding Wrong in Islamic Thought* (Cambridge: Cambridge University Press, 2000), 80–82, 100, 380. For the Qurʾānic verses, see Qurʾān, 49:12 (prohibiting spying), 2:189, 24:27 (listing regulations on entering a home).

This sentiment – that Muslims should conceal their own minor faults and those of others – was repeated so often that it became a widely diffused norm of privacy.[23] In criminal law, the concealment imperative was frequently available to petty offenders who had not yet been prosecuted. For example, an episode that we may call the *Case of ʿAmmār's Thief* involved an incident of theft in the presence of Ibn ʿAbbās and other Companions, including a man by the name of ʿAmmār. While traveling through the valley of Muzdalifa, a thief stole ʿAmmār's leather bag and fled. ʿAmmār pursued him and managed to reclaim the bag. Deciding not to prosecute, ʿAmmār announced: "I am overlooking his crime so that God will overlook mine."[24]

ʿAlī echoed these sentiments when he became caliph. At one point, after reluctantly accepting the confession of a woman of her own sexual misconduct, he made an exasperated plea to whoever "commits a sin: Repent to God privately! By God, repentance to God in private is better than destroying yourself and casting off His concealment [of you]!"[25] In so saying, ʿAlī was amplifying his instructions to Mālik al-Ashtar in his celebrated letter of investiture upon sending him to govern Egypt:

> The people farthest from you and the most despicable are the ones most intent on exposing the shortcomings of others. People [inevitably] have shortcomings, and the authorities are the most appropriate to conceal them. So do not expose that which is hidden from you, and guard [the people's] privacy to the extent possible. God will guard that which you wish to be kept private from your subjects.... Overlook anything that is not [already] apparent to you. And do

23 On privacy norms in Islamic law, see Eli Alshech, "'Do Not Enter Houses Other Than Your Own': The Evolution of the Notion of a Private Domestic Sphere in Early Sunnī Islamic Thought," *Islamic Law and Society* 11, 3 (2004), 291–332; Cook, *Commanding Right*, 80–82. For a useful discussion of how privacy laws played out in sodomy cases, see Seema Saifee, "Penumbras, Privacy, and the Death of Morals-Based Legislation: Comparing U.S. Constitutional Law with the Inherent Right of Privacy in Islamic Jurisprudence," *Fordham International Law Journal* 27 (2003), 370–454 (describing privacy laws that barred the medieval Muslim authorities from pursuing and prosecuting nonpublic sex crimes, with comparison to recent changes in American law announced by the Supreme Court in *Lawrence v. Texas*, 539 U.S. 558 (2003)).

24 Ibn Abī Shayba, *Muṣannaf*, 9:282–83 (*astur ʿalayh laʿalla Allāh an yastur ʿalayya*). In another version, ʿIkrima tells the story and criticizes the others for releasing the thief, to which Ibn ʿAbbās retorts, "You have no compassion. If it were you, *you* would be happy to be released!" Ibid., 9:282 (*Lā umma lak. Ammā law kunta anta, la-sarraka an yukhallā sabīluk!*). In a similar vein, Abū Bakr reportedly said that if he were arrested for wine drinking or theft, he would "hope that God would overlook [his crime]." Ibid., 9:283 (literally, "would have loved that God 'cover' his crime: *la-aḥbabtu an yasturah Allāh*").

25 Qummī, *Qaḍāyā*, 80, 85–87.

> not be quick to believe the backbiting informant [who tells you about people's faults], for such informants are treacherous, even if they resemble [sincere] advisors.[26]

More generally, the concealment impetus benefitted Muslims who chose to commit nonviolent crimes in the privacy of their own homes, as illustrated in the following *Case of Private Drinking*. ʿUqba b. ʿĀmir al-Juhanī (d. 58/677–8), a Companion who served as Muʿāwiya's governor in Egypt (r. 44–47/665–67), was presiding:

> His secretary, Dukhayn al-Ḥajrī, explained to him that he had neighbors who drank wine, and he proposed to summon the police (*shuraṭ*) to arrest them. ʿUqba told him not to do this, but rather to counsel and threaten them [verbally]. He did so, but to no effect, so he again proposed to call the police. ʿUqba once more told him not to and quoted a tradition he had heard from the Prophet: "Whoever keeps hidden what would disgrace a believer (*man satara muʾminan*), it is as though he had restored a buried baby girl (*mawʾūda*) to life from her tomb."[27]

In such scenarios, the concealment impetus served as a commoner's replacement for the status-regarding and hierarchical elite-leniency maxim.[28] By emphasizing personal culpability and concealment, later jurists were attempting to stress the spiritual-moral element of *ḥudūd* violations at the individual, private level and to limit the divine imperative to enforce punishment to matters of public vice.[29] Through advocating a general principle of concealment, jurists aimed to ensure that anyone could avoid punishment by keeping their indiscretions private while

26 Al-Sharīf al-Raḍī, *Nahj al-balāgha*, no. 53. The version by Ibn Shuʿba also includes the doubt canon – though as noted in Chapter 2, note 19, this source is of dubious provenance. See Ibn Shuʿba, *Tuḥaf al-ʿuqūl*, 126–49, at 128 (advising al-Ashtar to accept excuses "and avoid criminal sanctions in case of doubt: *wa-ʾdraʾ al-ḥudūd biʾl-shubahāt*").

27 Cook, *Commanding Right*, 81 (citations omitted, noting that the *ḥadīth* refers to the pre-Islamic practice of female infanticide (*waʾd*), which the Qurʾān attempted to strictly prohibit). For further discussion of privacy and concealment of faults in an exhaustive survey of the duty to command right and forbid wrong in Islamic thought, see ibid., 80ff and passim.

28 For discussion, see further Chapter 3.

29 For example, Fakhr al-Dīn al-Zaylaʿī (d. 743/1343), *Tabyīn al-ḥaqāʾiq*, ed. Aḥmad ʿIzzū ʿInāya (Beirut: Dār al-Kutub al-ʿIlmiyya, 2000), 3:341–42, who argued that the Qurʾānic law itself encourages *zinā* to be concealed given the fact that the existence of four witnesses to the act is rare (if not impossible); Ibrāhīm b. Muḥammad al-Bājūrī (d. 1277/1860), *Ḥāshiyat Fatḥ al-qarīb* (Beirut: Dār al-Maʿārif, 1974), 384, who affirmed that anyone who commits *zinā* or a related crime should repent privately, for "whoever publicizes or makes known his sexual transgression incurs [eligibility for] the *ḥadd* punishment." For further elucidation of medieval jurists' arguments along these lines, see Marion Holmes Katz, "The *Ḥadd* Penalty for *Zinā*: Symbol or Deterrent? Texts from the Early Sixteenth Century," in *The Lineaments of Islam: Studies in Honor of Fred McGraw Donner* (Leiden: Brill, 2012), 351–76.

discouraging public disregard of the moral code designated by Islamic criminal law.[30]

All of these cases emphasize the duty to obey the law by enforcing *ḥudūd* punishments once a crime is established publicly. No intervention or status, personal qualms about severity, or baseless pleas for lenience were to be entertained. Accordingly, Usāma's attempt to intervene on behalf of his fellow clanswoman failed in the *Case of the Makhzūmī Thief*; Ṣafwān was unable to avoid punishment with his belated attempt to change the legal facts by "gifting" his stolen cloak to the thief after sentencing in the *Case of Ṣafwān*; and the orphan's attempt to avoid punishment in the face of admitted guilt was ineffective in the *Case of the Drunken Orphan*.[31] Despite the attempts to avoid them, *ḥudūd* punishments were applied in these and similar cases.[32]

30 Some later jurists even insisted that prohibitions that offended no clear private interest, so-called victimless crimes such as wine drinking, were not instituted for their own sake or for any intrinsic moral value, but primarily for the preservation of public order. See, for example, Aḥmad al-Wansharīsī (d. 914/1508), *ʿUddat al-burūq fī jamʿ mā fī ʾl-madhhab min al-jumūʿ waʾl-furūq*, ed. Ḥamza Abū Fāris (Beirut: Dār al-Gharb al-Islāmī, 1990), 683–84 (describing this opinion as a Mālikī view).

31 Such attempts to retroactively change facts did not always fail. In fact, after the early period, a change in legal facts at any stage of the proceedings – at the trial stage, after sentencing, or even in the midst of carrying out the sentence – tended to justify *ḥudūd* avoidance. For instance, the late ninth/fifteenth-century North African Mālikī jurist Wansharīsī reports a case from eighth/fourteenth-century Andalusia in which the judge al-Ṣughayyir maintained that post hoc changes to legal facts sufficed to create *ḥadd*-averting doubt, as when someone confesses to adultery and then subsequently denies it. Aḥmad al-Wansharīsī, *al-Miʿyār al-muʿrib waʾl-jāmiʿ al-mughrib ʿan fatāwā ahl Ifrīqiya waʾl-Andalus waʾl-Maghrib*, ed. Muḥammad Ḥajjī (Rabat: Wizārat al-Awqāf waʾl-Shuʾūn al-Islāmiyya, 1981), 4:493–95. For discussion, see David S. Powers, *Law, Society, and Culture in the Maghrib, 1300–1500* (Cambridge: Cambridge University Press, 2002), 62–63.

32 The sources portray another series of cases from Yemen that indicate either local ignorance about the details of new Islamic laws or a transitional period in which those laws had not yet been set. In one instance, a criminal defendant's guilt was not contested for a sex crime but the associated punishment was, at a time when stoning had not yet become settled as the appropriate punishment for adultery. In that case, which receives considerable attention in later juristic literature, an early convert from Yemen came to the Prophet, asking him to judge between him and a man who accused the convert's son of committing *zinā* with his (the accuser's) wife. The father explained his son's case, contesting not his guilt, but the sentence: "My son is this man's servant (*ʿasīf*) and committed *zinā* with his wife. I ransomed my son with a hundred sheep and a slave girl of mine. But when I then asked the more knowledgeable people [about the matter], they informed me that my son was to receive one hundred lashes and be exiled for a year and that this man's wife should be stoned." Reportedly, the Prophet reluctantly responded that the latter opinion was correct, ruling that the husband was to return the sheep and the slave, and the son was to be flogged

The jurists' interest in recounting these cases was twofold. First, no doubt, the decisions provided support for the notion that sociopolitical status could not absolve a defendant of criminal culpability. This they could use against those Umayyads who typically skirted the law or attempted to intervene in judicial affairs on that basis. These cases set the precedent that, like the Prophet, all Muslim judges were bound to uphold an ideal of divine legislative supremacy through enforcing criminal punishments of proved crimes without exception for members of the elite. Accordingly, these cases provided support for the stance that political and judicial authority alike were legitimate only as long as each followed God's law with attention to its egalitarian and other moral imperatives. In the context of Umayyad and ʿAbbāsid excesses, the jurists reporting these cases were indicating their strong opposition to the growing influence of status hierarchies on the applications of Islamic law of their times.

Second, the examples would also have served to temper caliphal assertions of absolute control over criminal law by protecting a wide juristic sphere of authority on moral-religious grounds. The jurist's duty, they could argue from these precedents, was to argue in favor of enforcing the law according to the facts of the case. Claims that the jurists were barred from considering external factors would have been helpful in alleviating the enormous pressure from high-status offenders and interceding members of the sociopolitical elite, who were known to repeatedly try to persuade judges to avoid punishments based on extralegal considerations.[33] Moreover, their uniform "stand in favour of privacy [was] reinforced by a marked element of hostility and mistrust directed against the state. It is not out of concern for privacy that [one jurist, for example,] refuses to have anything to do with [the caliph] al-Mahdī's suggestion that they join forces .... What we have here is rather a characteristic example of [the jurist's] sullenness toward the authorities – his 'Staatsverdrossenheit', as van Ess has dubbed it."[34]

If Muslim jurists were casting about for support for the argument that their hands were tied by the dictates of the law, these cases provided it and – counterintuitively – thereby expanded their jurisdiction over penal law. By keeping the memory of the egalitarian and moral ideals alive

with one hundred lashes and exiled for a year. "He then instructed Unays to go to the accused wife and, if she confessed, to stone her." Bukhārī, *Ṣaḥīḥ*, no. 6440.

[33] In addition to these cases discussed in the legal treatises, see the cases from the historical chronicles, discussed in Chapter 3.

[34] Cook, *Commanding Right*, 82 (quoting van Ess, *Theologie und Gesellschaft*, 1:224; other citations omitted).

through elevating these criminal law stories to core founding precedents, these jurists could present themselves as the agents best equipped morally and intellectually to define Islamic criminal law. From that standpoint, they could successfully insist that the ruling authorities had religious legitimacy only as long as they supported the jurists in recognition of that authority to define Islamic criminal law.[35]

This portrayal of juristic authority in epistemic-moral terms against the state is not new. It is a restatement of the settled scholarly view of early Islamic political and legal theory that proto-jurists formed a "pious opposition" to the political excesses of the Umayyads and their successors. As one scholar put it:

> The pious opposition to the Umayyads not only shrank the caliph's authority to promulgate legal rulings, it also created a number of circles in which a more intense discussion of religious matters took place, and their members were the forerunners of the ulema, the specialists in religious learning so prominent in the later Islamic Middle East. . . . The distance between the "pious opposition" and government also accounts for the development of the independent *fatwā* or opinion . . . . Conscientious Muslims went to the legally minded among the forerunners of the ulema and got opinions. . . . Although later dynasties often appointed muftis, many muftis sought to remain and succeeded in remaining largely independent because people were free to choose their authorities and because a mufti who kept his distance from the government gained prestige among ordinary Muslims. The independence of the mufti was a significant part of the formation and persistence of a semi-independent community of jurists.[36]

What is new here is a picture of how these notions of juristic authority functioned and were elaborated in criminal law contexts, with Muslim jurists acting as oppositional agents to the state. In essence, they emphasized early precedents requiring strict enforcement of *ḥudūd* sanctions as a way of giving expression to values of egalitarianism and divine legislative supremacy. It bears repeating that whether the events recounted took place historically is immaterial to their utility for informing the later construction of Muslim jurists' interpretive authority.[37] What matters is that the jurists of the tenth and eleventh centuries, seeking to shore up their authority, invoked these early cases as precedents in their moral oppositional project.

[35] On the epistemological basis for juristic authority in Islamic law, see Chapter 2, note 52 and accompanying text.
[36] Mottahedeh, *Lessons*, 7–8.
[37] See discussion above, note 3 and accompanying text.

The more the politics of power drove political authorities to disregard Islam's early moral imperatives, the more concerned the scholarly classes became with insisting on criminal law enforcement against the elite. Thus, while jurists acknowledged instances in which *ḥudūd* liability could be removed, they insisted that "it is improper for the *imām* to neglect them [that is, *ḥudūd* laws, altogether]."[38] As later theorists would frame it, subservience to divine law was both the *raison d'être* for political authority and its legitimating factor. In Islamic contexts, these cases reflect jurists' attempts to define their own moral-interpretive authority against that of the political elite through interpretation of Islamic criminal law. Both morality and interpretation were packaged as mere adherence to Islamic egalitarianism and to the divine legislative supremacy ideal.

B. *ḤUDŪD* AVOIDANCE: DEATH IS DIFFERENT AND OTHER MORAL CONCERNS

Muslim jurists did not always emphasize the mandatoriness of enforcing *ḥudūd* sanctions. In building the textual authority and relevance of the doubt canon, jurists cited a rash of reports in which the Prophet and his companions or family members advised *ḥudūd avoidance* rather than enforcement. By appealing to this set of reports, jurists also expressed a certain amount of moral concern with arbitrarily and wantonly enforcing harsh sanctions.

The process of articulating formal doctrines of doubt first came through juristic readings of early judicial practices. Muslim jurists of the tenth and eleventh centuries systematically emphasized early precedents in favor of avoiding punishment in their legal treatises. For them, the point was to demonstrate that criminal matters were not always what they seemed, which is another way of saying that criminal cases frequently produced factual and legal doubt. From reviewing dozens of early cases, jurists concluded that extensive doubt permeated criminal cases. This doubt was enough, they concluded, to require heightened procedures before authorizing convictions and punishment. As shorthand for those additional procedures and for the early cases to which they alluded, it was the doubt canon that the jurists cited as a means of avoiding punishment. In the jurists' estimation, the trend of

[38] Bayhaqī, *Sunan*, 8:414, no. 17060 ("Avoid *ḥudūd* [punishments], though it is improper for the *imām* to suspend them [completely]: *idra'ū 'l-ḥudūd wa-lā yanbaghī li'l-imām an yu'aṭṭil al-ḥudūd*"). Notably, this *ḥadīth* – attributed to the Prophet via 'Alī – comes from a fifth/eleventh-century source that appears to have reconciled the two traditions of *ḥudūd* enforcement and avoidance, as discussed below. See Appendix A, version 10.

judicial practices from the early period illustrated how often the founding figures had avoided punishment. Their frequent avoidance helped later jurists determine how Māʿiz, for example, should have fared retrospectively and how criminal defendants like Māʿiz should be treated prospectively.

The infamous *Case of Māʿiz* was the most-cited precedent for punishment avoidance – which may seem counterintuitive at first blush. In that case, the Prophet reluctantly accepted Māʿiz's confession that he had committed *zinā* but objected to the townspeople's execution of Māʿiz – ostensibly, as later jurists would interpret it, because he had doubt.[39] The later jurists' frequent citation of this case to support punishment avoidance was counterintuitive given that Māʿiz was put to death. Yet most jurists cited the case in this way because they read the Prophet to have concluded that the punishment was improper. That is, despite the fact of Māʿiz's punishment, the Prophet's objection supported jurists' widespread policy of avoiding punishment, especially where capital punishment was at issue. They cited "doubt" as the operative legal cause for avoidance – even when, as in *Māʿiz's Case*, guilt was not in question.[40] Of the dozens of other cases cited in this vein, consider the following three.[41]

1. Rape: The *Case of the Mysterious Pregnancy*

One case hails from first/seventh-century Yemen, a generation after Māʿiz. The local judge, Yemeni native Abū Mūsā al-Ashʿarī (d. ca. 42/662), was asked to preside over a criminal case where a man, likely the accused woman's husband, accused a woman of committing adultery. Recall that adultery was a capital crime as early Muslims had come to understand it.[42]

The woman's situation looked suspicious. She was pregnant and her husband had perhaps been absent in the lead-up to the pregnancy, such that there was no easy exit from the accusation of an extramarital affair. Moreover, the changing neighborhood conditions of the time may well have provided the space for her to have committed the act.[43] The woman swore an oath that she had not committed any act of infidelity. Instead, she claimed that she woke up one night to find a man on top of herself; she did

39 For an extended discussion of the *Case of Māʿiz*, see Chapter 1.
40 For example, Abū Yūsuf, *Ikhtilāf*, 156–57; Qudūrī, *Tajrīd*, 11:5891, 5949–50.
41 For a collection of some twenty-five early criminal cases demonstrating trends of alternative avoidance and enforcement of Islamic criminal punishment, see Appendix B.
42 See Chapter 1.
43 See note 47.

not know him, and he fled soon after.[44] Essentially, she claimed to have been raped.[45] "I swear by God," she declared to Abū Mūsā,

> I have not taken a lover or become intimate with any male companion since I converted to Islam. However, at some point, when I was sleeping in the privacy of my own home – by God – I woke up to find a man atop me, leaving in me a fire. I looked at him to identify him [but] was left with no idea as to who he was from among all of God's creatures!"[46]

Abū Mūsā was perplexed. If the woman had confessed to adultery, the textual rule might have guided him to convict her. But she had not, leaving him as nonplussed as she presented herself to be. He needed to consult a more informed and authoritative jurist. He wrote to the caliph-cum-jurist ʿUmar in Medina, asking how he should proceed. In response, ʿUmar summoned Abū Mūsā along with the accused woman and a few witnesses from her town to vouch for her character. Standing before ʿUmar, the woman recounted her story, and repeated her denial. As the Prophet had with Māʿiz, ʿUmar asked the witnesses about her character and mental state. They vouched for her and praised her generously. The facts did not decisively resolve the case.

The situation was as follows: The woman neither had admitted guilt nor was known to be of bad moral character. At most, she was subject to an accusation of infidelity given the circumstantial facts of pregnancy and the possible means to commit the crime in the rapidly urbanizing Yemeni society.[47] For Abū Mūsā and ʿUmar both, it was clear that some sex crime had taken place. But it was not clear that the woman was culpable. To the contrary, it may have even been the case that the woman was not a perpetrator of adultery, but a victim of rape, as she claimed. ʿUmar remarked that he feared God's wrath "if [he] sentenced this woman to

[44] It is unclear from the facts recounted in the report whether she was married and who brought the accusation, but I infer from the fact that ʿUmar referred to the potential penalty as death that later jurists reporting the case understood the alleged offense to have been adultery. Her husband, or another family member, would likely have made the accusation. See Ibn Abī Shayba, *Muṣannaf*, 9:360–61, no. 27970.

[45] A common strategy for Muslim women of the fifth/eleventh century to contest adultery accusations in other contexts was to claim that they were raped. See, for example, Serrano, "Twelve Cases," 475, 491.

[46] Ibn Abī Shayba, *Muṣannaf*, 9:360–61, no. 27970.

[47] On privacy in Islamic law, see Alshech, "'Private Domestic Sphere," 317 (noting that pre-Islamic Arabs craved privacy but that existing social and architectural norms – as in the fact that Ḥijāzī homes lacked screens or doors – often frustrated that desire). On the urban conditions experienced for the first time with the Arabs' rapid migration to the garrison towns, including towns in Yemen, accompanying the spread of Islam, see Lapidus, *Islamic Societies*, 45–53.

death." Instead of punishing her, he fed her, clothed her, and instructed her people to treat her well.[48]

In another version of the story, it was a pregnant woman who herself came to ʿUmar in a small area called Mina near Mecca, riding atop a donkey and crying profusely. When she reached ʿUmar, he asked her, "Why are you crying?" and further commented that "perhaps you have been raped."[49] She told him that she was typically a heavy (and presumably early) sleeper, but that one night she had been able to stay up to perform the night prayer before sleeping. "I swear by God that, when I woke up, a man was atop me; I looked at him to identify him but had no idea who he was from among all of God's creatures!" ʿUmar remarked that he feared God's wrath "if [he] sentenced this woman to death."[50] Accordingly, he ruled that no *ḥadd* punishment applied because the woman neither admitted to being guilty nor was she known to be of bad moral character. Here, too, a sex crime had clearly taken place; but it was not clear that the woman was criminally culpable. Instead, she may have been a victim – a possibility for which the punishment was to be avoided.

Later Muslim jurists took both versions of this case to be an instance of factual doubt. ʿUmar's questioning regarding the defendant's mental state and her character paralleled the Prophet's questioning of Māʿiz about the facts. In this case, the doubts arose not from a confession but from the probity of circumstantial evidence. Was the pregnancy, without a confession or witnesses, sufficient to convict the woman of adultery? Given her claims of rape, the answer was doubtful at best. It was due to factual doubt, the jurists reporting this case concluded, that ʿUmar avoided punishment.

48 Ibn Abī Shayba, *Muṣannaf*, 9:360–61, nos. 27891 and 27970. For discussion of the jurists' antipathy toward capital punishment read into scenarios such as this one, see notes 62–63 and accompanying text.

49 The Mālikī jurist Shihāb al-Dīn al-Qarāfī understood the term used (*imraʾa ḍakhma*) to mean that she was "pregnant" as in the first version. See Shihāb al-Dīn al-Qarāfī, *al-Dhakhīra fī furūʿ al-Mālikiyya* (Beirut: Dār al-Gharb al-Islāmī, 1994), 12:60. For a similar version in an earlier Mālikī source, see Saḥnūn, *Mudawwana*, 7:2444 (equating sex with a sleeping woman to rape).

50 Ibn Abī Shayba, *Muṣannaf*, 9:361, no. 27891. The meaning of ʿUmar's actual comment is somewhat obscure. The text in the *Muṣannaf* says that ʿUmar made reference to his fear of the fire looming as large as two sizable mountains in the Ḥijāz (called Akhshabān?) or to his fear that any mistake in imposing the death penalty would be as if those mountains themselves would be set aflame (*khashaytu ʿalā ʾl-Akshabayn al-nār*). The editor notes that in other variants, his remark could be read to mean the following: "If I killed this woman standing between these two mountains, God would punish them [the people]." Ibid., n. 1 (citing Bayhaqī, *Sunan*, 8:336).

2. Adultery: The *Case of the Absentee Husband*

A second type of doubt combines the decisions of the second and fourth caliphs, ʿUmar and ʿAlī, acting in their capacities as judge and advisor, respectively. This time, the doubt was not about the fact of the conviction, but the propriety of punishment for considerations wholly external to the acts in question.

Similar to the first case, reports of this case note that a man had gone traveling for two years and returned to find his wife pregnant. The husband accused his wife of adultery. When he brought the case to ʿUmar to adjudicate, ʿUmar determined that the woman was guilty and sentenced her to death. When ʿAlī heard about the decision, he rushed to ʿUmar, saying, "if this is your decision as to the woman, then what will happen to her [unborn] son?" ʿAlī managed to convince ʿUmar to delay the sentence until the woman gave birth. Once the son was born, he convinced ʿUmar to postpone the sentence until the baby was no longer reliant on nursing for sustenance. During this time, perhaps as ʿAlī had intended, the husband claimed paternity of the child, effectively rescinding the earlier accusation of adultery.

ʿUmar observed this turn of affairs with surprise and regret. He had initially sentenced the woman to death. If he had carried out the punishment, he would have been at fault, because the husband claimed the child and dropped the basis for criminal liability and punishment. ʿUmar expressed his appreciation to ʿAlī and retracted the punishment order.[51] He remarked: "If it were not for ʿAlī, [I] would be at a loss!"[52] In other words, ʿUmar was saying that, had he carried out the sentence earlier, the later paternity claim would have retroactively rendered the punishment erroneous, and ʿUmar would have suffered the spiritual brunt of that decision.

In the end, this case was more about avoiding capital punishment through sentence postponement and through the formalities surrounding paternity than it was about the fact of the wife's infidelity. Sexual relations

[51] Qummī, *Qaḍāyā*, 119 (with editor's notes citing variants in later Shīʿī sources, including works by prominent Shīʿī jurists Mufīd and al-ʿAllāma al-Ḥillī, as well as works by prominent Sunnī scholars Bayhaqī, Bāqillānī, and Ibn Ḥajar).

[52] Ibid. (*law lā ʿAlī la-halaka ʿUmar*) (citing variants). This same sentiment appears elsewhere in Zaydī law, recorded in the same period and appended to a different scenario in which ʿAlī instructs ʿUmar to avoid punishment based on evidentiary infirmities. See Aḥmad b. ʿĪsā b. Zayd, *Amālī*, 4:204.

were fluid in pre- and early Islamic societies, which the Qur'ān's sexual ethics sought to regulate.[53] In a society where social status and entitlements were determined on the basis of family membership and tribal pedigree, paternity was an important matter, one whose assignment was challenged by illicit sexual relations that resulted in pregnancies and, eventually, children unclaimed by their fathers or tribes. To resolve this problem where the facts were dubious, Muslim jurists adopted the infamous "paternity maxim," the origins and function of which scholars have debated at length.[54] In brief, this maxim stipulated that "The child belongs to the marital bed: *al-walad li'l-firāsh.*" This simple formulation allowed judges to assign paternity of a child born from a married woman's illicit sexual relationship to her husband in order to avoid the criminal and social consequences of the child's bastardization. In this case, once the husband claimed the child, the punishment for adultery would no longer have been authorized. In other words, the husband's eventual "admission" of paternity – however dubious – eventually served to cancel the punishment order altogether. For Muslim jurists, then, the demands behind concerns underlying the paternity maxim took precedence over the punishment-enforcement imperative, leading them to avoid punishment later justified by doctrines of doubt.[55]

[53] For an excellent discussion, see Harald Motzki, "*Wal-muḥṣanātu mina n-nisā'i illā mā malakat aimānukum* (Koran 4:24) und die koranische Sexualethik," *Der Islam* 63 (1986), 192–218.

[54] Among English-speaking scholars, Joseph Schacht first made reference to this maxim in a half-page discussion in his book *Origins of Muhammadan Jurisprudence*, 181–82; see also Crone, *Roman, Provincial and Islamic Law*, 10, 96ff (collecting Schacht's references in five other works and challenging his attribution of this maxim to Roman law). Several scholars have focused on this maxim in their treatments of early *ḥadīth* literature to question Schacht's initial characterization of it. See Harald Motzki, ed., *Ḥadīth: Origins and Developments* (Aldershot: Ashgate Variorum, 2004), 304; Harald Motzki, *Origins*, 126, 128–30; Harald Motzki, "The *Muṣannaf* of ʿAbd al-Razzāq al-Ṣanʿānī as a Source of Authentic *Aḥādīth* of the First Century A.H.," *Journal of Near Eastern Studies* 60 (1991), 1–21, at 18. See also Uri Rubin, "'Al-Walad li-l-Firāsh': On the Islamic Campaign against 'Zinā,'" *Studia Islamica* 78 (1993), 5–26; G. H. A. Juynboll, "Notes on Islam's First *Fuqahā*'"; Crone, *Roman, Provincial and Islamic Law*, 10, 96ff. For an application of the paternity maxim to determine the murky parentage of known historical figures, see Elizabeth Urban, "The Identity Crisis of Abū Bakra: *Mawlā* of the Prophet, or Polemical Tool?" in *The Lineaments of Islam: Studies in Honor of Fred McGraw Donner*, ed. Paul Cobb (Leiden: Brill, 2012), 121–49, esp. 131, 136, 144.

[55] For a case that similarly deals with paternity under the guise of an adultery claim, see Qummī, *Qaḍāyā*, 264, version 2 (addressing circumstances of a slave driver having sex with a slave woman while the actual master or owner was gone, and noting that ʿAlī returned the slave woman to her previous owner but imposed no punishment, commanding instead simply that the son born of their intimate relations stay with the slave driver, to whom he assigned paternity). For additional cases reporting ʿAlī's practices of punishment avoidance, in

This case was a typical display of ʿAlī's superior approach to criminal law from an early Shīʿī source reporting his decisions, as later picked up by Sunnī jurists who also saw ʿAlī as an exemplar of justice. In his decision making, ʿAlī used various procedural strategies to advise ʿUmar to avoid punishment even after the adultery conviction. Later Sunnī jurists read ʿAlī to have possessed a special judicial acumen (*firāsa*) that guided his decisional advice in such cases.[56] These jurists further regarded this case as yet another instance of the rule of giving legal effect to ʿAlī's sort of judicial acumen – of which the *Case of the Falsely Accused Butcher* was illustrative. His actions extended from that judicial acumen, which manifested as demands for procedural tools used to avoid capital punishment, and which later Muslim jurists identified as a function of "doubt."[57]

3. Murder: The *Case of the Falsely Accused Butcher*

A third set of evidentiary doubts surrounded the probity of witness testimony in reports about the early case of murder in Medina. ʿAlī had presided over the *Case of the Falsely Accused Butcher*, recounted in the Introduction.[58] That case presented the question whether the Qurʾānic rule of retaliation, which permitted the death penalty for anyone convicted of murder, applied to a man convicted of the crime based on circumstantial evidence or applied instead to a second man who confessed to having committed the crime after the conviction of the first man.[59] ʿAlī ultimately concluded that the he could not sentence either alleged perpetrator to death – neither the convict nor the confessor. Later jurists attributed his avoidance of capital punishment to their developed notion of doubt.[60]

addition to the *Case of the Falsely Accused Butcher* detailed in the Introduction and below, see Appendix B, case nos. 20 (*Case of the Absent Slave Owner*), 21 (*Case of a Framed Rape*), 22 (*Case of the Orphan and the Jealous Wife*), 23 (*Case of Sex with a Wife's Slave Woman*), 24 (*Case of Sex in Prison*), and 25 (*Case of Sex while Traveling*).

56 See Ibn al-Qayyim, *Ṭuruq* (2007), 3, 43–80.

57 Ibid.

58 See Introduction, note 1 and sources cited therein.

59 For the Qurʾānic law of retaliation, see Qurʾān, 2:178–79, 4:92, and 5:45. For a discussion of the Islamic "reforms" to ancient Near Eastern practices, see Peters, *Crime and Punishment*, 40.

60 It is unclear whether either or both of the men received a lesser punishment, as occurred in many other cases where the *ḥadd* punishment was dropped. This episode is analogous to another early case of rape, the *Case of the Falsely Accused Passerby*, wherein the sources report that a man raped a woman while she was on her way to the mosque to perform the early morning prayer. One man tried to pursue the rapist on the woman's behalf, but another group attempting to help her arrested that man while the rapist got away. At trial,

This case presented a new type of doubt. Whereas *Māʿiz's Case* dealt with doubt about criminal culpability with a confession, and the previous case addressed doubt about criminal culpability from circumstantial evidence, this case highlighted problems of circumstantial evidence and confessions together. Given the possibility that both were false, as he apparently determined here, ʿAlī avoided the punishment altogether.

Later jurists read this case to support the rule that judges should avoid enforcing the death penalty even when the ordinarily acceptable forms of evidence seemed dispositive. Typically, murder convictions required either a confession or two eyewitnesses, preferably corroborated by knowledge of the witnesses' credibility or of circumstances pointing to the reliability of the testimony.[61] Here, there was the perfect trifecta in any competition for good evidence: a confession, testimony of multiple "eyewitnesses," and corroboration by strong circumstantial evidence. Yet even then, ʿAlī – with his superior judicial acumen – perceived cause for doubt. For the jurists, this case provided both evidence and justification for the doubt doctrine and its general policy of punishment avoidance particularly in capital cases. For them, this case was demonstration that judges could never reach evidentiary *certainty* about guilt.

How might these cases, exhibiting policies of *ḥudūd avoidance*, be explained against the backdrop of the imperative for *ḥudūd enforcement* in the previous section? One distinguishing factor has to do with the relationship between these crimes and issues of status. In the previous set of cases, litigants typically tried to intervene on the basis of social status in order to avoid punishment – attempts that jurists firmly rejected. In this set of cases – where jurists sought to avoid punishment – the defendants seemed to be nameless and ordinary, or even low-status, members of the Muslim community. Yet this distinction does not tell us why, if egalitarianism and divine legislative supremacy were dominant concerns that drove policies of enforcement, jurists should then wish to avoid punishment.

A second distinguishing factor has to do with the certainty of the guilt determination and the propriety of punishment. In the first set of cases, guilt was not at issue. The crimes had been established by either confession

the presiding judge (said, erroneously, to be the Prophet) convicted the arrestee, then canceled punishment when the actual rapist showed up admitting to the crime, saying, "Don't stone him; stone me! *I* am the one who committed the crime against her!" The judge concluded that the first man was not guilty and the second had repented through his admission. See Ibn al-Qayyim, *Ṭuruq* (2007), 84–89 (citing multiple versions and discussing discrepancies between them).

61 See Peters, *Crime and Punishment*, 51.

or witness testimony, and the only question presented was whether elite status or some other excuse gave the presiding judges cause for avoiding punishment. The jurists' answer, roundly, was "no." In this set of cases, evidence that some crime had taken place also seemed to be uncontested, but Muslim jurists nevertheless located evidentiary infirmities that created "doubt" about the culpability of the accused and thus the propriety of punishment. Their actions still present the question of why, if a crime was proved, jurists declined to enforce punishment in the second set of cases that they cited as due in the first set of cases.

The third, much more significant distinguishing factor between these two sets of cases better explains why. This factor has to do with the severity of punishment. The first set of cases involved fraud, theft, and wine drinking – all nonviolent crimes. *Ḥudūd* enforcement for those crimes involved punishments ranging from flogging to hand-amputation – harsh by modern standards, but ordinary in medieval times, and short of capital punishment. By contrast, the second set of cases involved crimes that either were violent or otherwise violated even more closely held moral values of the early Muslim community than did the first set of crimes, as signaled by the severity of punishment: Muslims designated rape, adultery, and murder as capital crimes.

Indeed, contrary to Fierro's theory of the elite origins of doubt, status hierarchies seemed to lie outside of the juristic concerns at the heart of the bulk of the cases emphasizing *ḥudūd* avoidance.[62] So did issues of factual truth. Instead, the jurists' reluctance to punish likely had to do with the final and irrevocable nature of the death penalty as punishment. In short, they had come to conceive of death as different.[63] This "death-is-different" conception

[62] Fierro, "When Lawful Violence Meets Doubt," 233ff.

[63] The American experience with the death penalty, from which I draw the title of this section, well articulates the "difference" of death. When placing a moratorium on the death penalty in 1972, the Supreme Court cited the need for procedure, in light of the fundamentally different nature of the death penalty, and to avoid executions that were so arbitrary as to be "wanton and freakish" in nature. *Furman v. Georgia*, 408 U.S. 238 (1972) (imposing what was to become a four-year moratorium on the death penalty). In his concurrence, Justice Brennan explained that this outcome had to do with the fact that "[d]eath is a unique punishment, … in a class by itself." Ibid., 286–89 (Brennan, J., concurring). See also ibid., 306 (Stewart, J., concurring) ("The penalty of death differs from all other forms of criminal punishment, not in degree but in kind."). When capital punishment was reinstated in the 1970s, the Court subjected it to heightened procedures above those of ordinary crimes. See *Gregg v. Georgia*, 428 U.S. 153, 188 (1976) (joint opinion of Stewart, Powell, and Stevens, JJ.) (calling the "penalty of death … different in kind from any other punishment" and "unique"); *Woodson v. North Carolina*, 428 U.S. 280, 305 (1976) (joint opinion of Stewart, Powell, and Stevens, JJ.) ("[The] penalty of death is qualitatively different from a sentence of imprisonment, however long."). For an analysis of the consequences of

manifested as an antipathy toward *ḥudūd* enforcement in capital cases in favor of a broad-based policy of *ḥudūd* avoidance in cases of doubt.

C. THE GENERALIZATION OF DOUBT: LEGITIMACY AND MORAL CONCERN

The doubt-based strategy of *ḥudūd* avoidance spread beyond the capital context to encompass ordinary crimes. This spread accompanied Muslim jurists' increasingly oppositional stance toward the political authorities, which they were able to express through the ever more elaborate Islamic doctrine of doubt.

Muslim jurists historically had been skittish about any involvement with political authorities, including judging, which they deemed potentially corrupting for people of moral conscience. Though some jurists certainly served as state-appointed judges and assumed other government posts, they were a distinct minority. Many who were nominated for official judgeships or other positions stubbornly refused to serve, preferring to remain independent of the political apparatus. The sources are replete with instances of Muslim jurists' recoil at being nominated to judge. Famously, Abū Ḥanīfa was said to have endured torture for his refusals.[64] The main chronicle for the early history of judges opens with prophetic cautions *against* judging.[65] That source also presents instances of judges refusing the position or accepting it only with great reluctance.[66] This animus against judging represented just one aspect of the Muslim jurists' moral concerns about applying God's law, and getting it right.

The jurists' general antipathy about judging, I suggest, was exacerbated in *capital* contexts – a fact that helps explain the rise of the doubt doctrine in Islamic law. When it came to the death penalty, Muslim jurists feared answering in the afterlife for wrongful deaths occasioned by authorizing

America's constitutional and procedural decisions to regulate rather than abolish the death penalty, see Carol S. Steiker and Jordan M. Steiker, *Entrenchment and/or Destabilization? Reflections on (Another) Two Decades of Constitutional Regulation of Capital Punishment* (forthcoming).

64 For a discussion of this episode and his extreme antipathy toward the ruling authorities, as well as his censure of judges such as his rival Ibn Abī Laylā who "colluded" with them, see Muḥammad Abū Zahra, *Abū Ḥanīfa: Ḥayātuh wa-ʿaṣruh, ārāʾuh wa-fiqhuh*, 2nd ed. (Beirut: Dār al-Fikr al-ʿArabī, 1965?), 37–48, esp. 47.

65 See Wakīʿ, *Akhbār al-quḍāt*, 19–61 (opening with a section on *ḥadīth* and other "reports announcing the gravity of assuming a judicial post over people and that whoever assumes [such a post] has been [metaphorically] slaughtered without a knife").

66 Ibid., 23–24, 112, 145–48.

punishments that were not in fact warranted.[67] Moreover, against the backdrop of excessive executions in the Seljūq culture of political violence, Muslim jurists were signaling through increased rules of procedure something about the extent to which they had come to see the death penalty as *different* from punishments for ordinary crimes.

Practically, their special orientation toward avoiding capital crimes manifested in the jurists' call for *more procedure* than the foundational texts of Islamic law ordinarily required.[68] Procedures for non-capital crimes – including theft, intoxication, and sexual slander – ordinarily required two witnesses or a voluntary confession.[69] A conviction for ordinary crimes warranted punishment that ranged from public flogging to hand-amputation: harsh, but not deadly. By contrast, the Qurʾān required four eyewitnesses to sex crimes, which it designated as serious moral offenses and which Muslims understood to be capital offenses.[70] Convictions for murder – also a serious moral harm, an act of extreme violence against another, and potentially a capital crime – similarly required heightened procedures of proof.[71]

Moreover, as evidenced in the latter set of cases (detailing *ḥudūd* avoidance), Muslim jurists analyzing the early cases determined that more procedure – beyond the Qurʾānically mandated increased witness requirements for sex crimes – was necessary for *all* capital crimes: adultery, rape, and murder.[72] Again, the *Case of Māʿiz* is illustrative. From the Prophet's exclamation upon learning of the defendant's execution, "you should have let Māʿiz go" [or in one version: "if only you had let

[67] See Baber Johansen, "Vom Wort- zum Indizienbeweis: Die Anerkennung des richterlichen Folter in islamischen Rechtsdoctrinen des 13. und 14. Jahrhunderts," *Ius Commune* 28 (2001), 1–46, esp. 11–12 (noting medieval Muslim jurists' fears of the legal and physical consequences of punishment for false convictions: namely, the doctrine that the judge responsible would suffer the same punishment in the afterlife as he had falsely inflicted in this life). Cf. Lange, *Justice*, 101–15 (noting the connection between this-worldly sins and fear of otherworldly punishment).

[68] For extensive discussion, see Chapter 5.

[69] Abū al-Ḥasan al-Māwardī, *Adab al-qāḍī*, ed. Muḥyī Hilāl al-Sarḥān (Baghdad: Riʾāsat Dīwān al-Awqāf; Maṭbaʿat al-ʿĀnī, 1392/1972), 2:3–32.

[70] For the four-witness requirement for sex crimes, see Qurʾān, 4:15, and for the related four-oath procedure of mutual imprecation (plus a fifth invoking God's wrath for lying) for spousal accusations of *zinā*, called *liʿān*, see Qurʾān 24:7, 9.

[71] Another procedure contained in the *ḥadīth* corpus, but not in the Qurʾān, was the elaborate process of swearing multiple oaths to assign liability for homicide in order to assign responsibility for paying blood money for homicide where evidence was lacking to prove murder. On this fifty-oath procedure, called *qasāma*, see Peters, "Murder in Khaybar," 132–67.

[72] See Chapter 1.

him go"], most later jurists understood the case to require judges to question offenders about possible deficiencies that would remove *ḥadd* liability.[73]

These same jurists rapidly extended the policy of heightened procedures to ordinary crimes as well. In addition to encouraging perpetrators of minor offenses to conceal their crimes, the jurists read *ḥudūd* offenses narrowly – restricting the extent to which an accused offender could be prosecuted – and outlining heightened procedures required to secure a conviction.[74] They instituted a host of additional evidentiary safeguards, including rules restricting the acceptance of confessions, disallowing verdicts based on judicial knowledge alone, and limiting the use of circumstantial evidence.[75] More generally, some jurists maintained that the "*ḥadd* punishment is to be avoided" whenever the accused retracts his or her confession or repents.[76]

By themselves, the Qur'ānic rules of increased witness requirements for sex crimes did not lead to the heightened procedures imposed for other offenses. To accomplish this addition of heightened procedures to ordinary crimes, Muslim jurists repeatedly cited the early judicial practices as precedent along with the doubt canon as a foundational text. After the tenth-century textualization of doubt, judges and jurists could more easily

[73] See, for example, Ibn Abī al-ʿIzz, *Tanbīh*, 4:128.

[74] For example, when discussing various so-called fixed *ḥudūd* crimes, jurists interpreted the foundational texts to severely limit criminal liability. Concerning sex crimes, for instance, many jurists restricted the definition of fornication to a consensual sex act between a man and a woman, and most determined that judges could enforce punishment only following sworn, uniform testimony from four witnesses to the act of penetration along with details as to the time, manner, and place of the act. See, for example, Abū Ibrāhīm Ismāʿīl b. Yaḥyā al-Muzanī, *Mukhtaṣar*, ed. Ḥusayn ʿAbd al-Ḥamīd Nīl (Beirut: Dār al-Kutub al-ʿIlmiyya, 1993), 9:276; Ibn Bābawayh, *Hidāya*, in *YF*, 23:19; Marghīnānī, *Hidāya*, ed. Muḥammad ʿAdnān Darwīsh (Cairo: Muḥammad ʿAlī Ṣabīḥ, 1966), 4:129. For theft, Muslim jurists authorized judges to convict only when there was a minimum actionable amount, when the theft had been completed, and when there was a lack of mitigating circumstances (such as destitution or famine) that might excuse the act. For detailed discussions of the procedures attached to these and other crimes, see Chapters 5 and 6.

[75] For examples in Sunnī law, see, for example, Shams al-A'imma al-Sarakhsī (d. 483/1090), *Mabsūṭ*, ed. Abū ʿAbd Allāh Muḥammad Ḥasan Ismāʿīl al-Shāfiʿī (Beirut: Dār al-Kutub al-ʿIlmiyya, 2001), 9:43–106. For examples in Shīʿī law, see, for example, Ibn Idrīs al-Ḥillī, *Kitāb al-Sarā'ir* (Qum: Mu'assasat al-Nashr al-Islāmī, 1410/1989–90), 3:537, 4:432 (noting exceptions to the Sunnī bar on judicial determinations by private knowledge for offenses against *ḥuqūq Allāh*). For basic overviews of criminal procedure, see Peters, *Crime and Punishment*, 8–19; Maḥmaṣānī, *Falsafat al-tashrīʿ*, 325–76.

[76] See Abū Yūsuf, *Ikhtilāf*, 156–57 (*yudra' ʿanh al-ḥadd*, noting that he and Abū Ḥanīfa shared this view, but that Ibn Abī Laylā held the opposite view – that is, that the *ḥadd* punishment was to apply with confessions, which he determined could not be retracted).

justify their support for a general policy of punishment avoidance and heightened procedures in cases of doubt. Only when combined with a textual rule of doubt, read through the lens of early judicial practices as a call for more procedure, did the basic Qurʾānic rule of increased procedure for serious crimes lead to a textual rule of increased procedure for ordinary crimes. In this way – through a robust doctrine of doubt – multiple confessions, judicial investigations into mitigating circumstances, avoiding textual ambiguity, and other criminal procedures became part and parcel of Islamic criminal law across the board.

Further demonstrating the jurists' preference to avoid rather than enforce punishment, the doubt canon also assumed formulations that sounded like the old Blackstonian quotation that it is better to let ten guilty men go free than to punish one unjustly. Thus one version stated: "Avoid *ḥudūd* punishments against Muslims to the extent possible; if there is any way out, then release [the convict], as it is better that the *imām* make a mistake in pardoning than in punishing."[77] The second caliph ʿUmar reportedly said when acting in his capacity as a judge, "If you come to me [with a criminal dispute, I would] question to the utmost extent possible, for I would rather make a mistake in pardoning than make a mistake in punishing."[78] So it was that, in Seljūq times, Muslim judges appealed to a textually grounded doubt canon as a way to alleviate moral concerns that came with authorizing punishments that they deemed illegitimate at the hands of political authorities. Together, these judicial practices and the textual doubt canon could allow a morally anxious judge to claim – in the face of pressures from political officials to issue execution orders on doubtful facts – that his hands were constrained by the Islamic law of doubt. Thus, the jurists expressed their concerns through a doubt doctrine that decreased legitimation of punishments until and unless there was factual or legal certainty of a crime and moral certainty of the propriety of its punishment. Such certainty was exceedingly rare.[79]

[77] ʿAbd al-Razzāq, *Muṣannaf* (1972), 10:166, no. 18698; Ibn Abī Shayba, *Muṣannaf*, 9:360, no. 28972; Tirmidhī, *Sunan*, 5:112–13, no. 1424; *al-Musnad al-jāmiʿ*, 2:41–42, no. 16799; Dāraquṭnī, *Sunan*, 4:62–63, no. 3097; Bayhaqī, *Sunan*, 8:413, nos. 17057–58.

[78] Bayhaqī, *Sunan*, 8:414, no. 17061. Cf. Ibn Abī Shayba, *Muṣannaf*, 9:359, no. 28963.

[79] Notably, although Muslim jurists used the doctrine of doubt to express discomfort with the arbitrariness of capital punishment, they were careful to note that they were not attempting to vitiate criminal punishment altogether. Instead, these jurists took criminal law prohibitions to be justified – Bentham style – as rules aiming to *deter crime*. See, for example, Shāfiʿī, *Umm* (1996), 8:288 (describing the two purposes of *ḥudūd* laws as deterrence and spiritual purification or rehabilitation); Māwardī, *Kitāb al-ḥudūd min al-Ḥāwī*, 1:99 ("*Ḥudūd* are punishments by which God deters (*zajara bihā*) people from

These types of moral concerns about judging and doubt were not unique to medieval Muslim jurists and judges. Their Christian counterparts in England and continental Europe were themselves morally anxious when it came to dealing with doubt, and likewise created procedures designed to allay those concerns. Shared across these disparate contexts, morality-based responses to doubt were clearly regular features of criminal law in medieval religious communities, even when their precise motives and means markedly differed.

As comparative legal historian James Whitman has argued, the reasonable doubt doctrine that eventually emerged out of medieval Christian contexts was "designed [not] to make it more difficult for jurors to convict, [but to make it] *easier*, by assuring jurors [as well as witnesses and judges] that their souls were safe if they voted to condemn the accused."[80] In the modern scheme, *finding facts* particular to criminal elements became the equivalent of establishing guilt "beyond a reasonable doubt," without special regard for truth or moral concern about the soul of the one responsible for convicting a defendant.[81] This observation is thus significant inasmuch as it radically differs from modern understandings of reasonable doubt as a safeguard for defendants' rights. It is also significant in the extent to which it sheds light on the differing trajectories of doubt rooted in the medieval Islamic and Christian worlds.

In early European and English approaches to doubt, there were parallels to the Islamic jurisprudence of doubt. Medieval European and English judges and jurors initially declined to punish in the face of doubt out of

committing prohibited [acts] and encourages them to follow [His] commands."). They also acknowledged a retributive justification for criminal sanctions for defendants like Māʿiz, who requested criminal punishment believing it to provide this-worldly divine retribution that would expiate sins and result in forgiveness. Māwardī, *Kitāb al-ḥudūd min al-Ḥāwī*, 1:100. For further discussion of justifications for Islamic criminal law, see Chapter 3. For a meditation on difficulties raised by alternative justifications for and alternatives to punishment in the context of contemporary criminal law responses to mass atrocities, see Martha Minow, *Between Vengeance and Forgiveness* (Boston: Beacon Press, 1998), 9–24.

80 Whitman, *Reasonable Doubt*, 4, 11, 194 ("[T]he underlying concern was not with protecting the defendant at all. It was with protecting the jurors."). Cf. Charles Donahue Jr., "Proof by Witnesses in the Church Courts of Medieval England: An Imperfect Reception of the Learned Law," in *On the Laws and Customs of England: Essays in Honor of Samuel E. Thorne*, ed. Morris S. Arnold et al. (Chapel Hill: University of North Carolina Press, 1981), 127–58.

81 For more on the somewhat contrasting notions that modern American liberalism relies on constitutional due-process values to align questions of reasonable doubt with defendants' rights, but that the reasonable doubt doctrine emphasizes fact-based inquiries that sometimes obscure truth within the context of procedural norms such as the exclusionary rule that may otherwise prejudice defendants, see Whitman, *Reasonable Doubt*, 203, 207, 334–36.

concern for their own souls. They feared – in addition to the legal and physical consequences that sometimes obtained from demonstrably false verdicts – the spiritual consequences of unjust verdicts, particularly when criminal convictions triggered punishments of death.[82] Against this backdrop, heightened procedures for criminal trials grew out of a world of moral anxieties facing judges about the very act of judging. The idea was that God Himself was "the great avenger of justice."[83]

Promoting that view, the Church defined a complex rubric of procedures that formed part of its moral "theology of doubt," which episodically shifted to allow legal actors to alternately avoid and enforce punishment. Initially, the Church introduced procedures designed to absolve the misgivings of legal actors of the Middle Ages concerned about the stakes of getting convictions wrong. An example was the use of the Ordeals, by which God Himself became the divine arbiter of right and wrong. When the Church abolished the Ordeals at the Fourth Lateran Council of 1215, it aimed to transform judges from "ministers of bloodshed" to "ministers of the law."[84] On the Continent, these developments occasioned an almost immediate shift from judges to *witnesses* as the bearers of moral responsibility for punishing serious crime. Following rigorous canon procedure provided cover for the thirteenth-century European judge, who could assert whenever he condemned a defendant to death: "It is the law that kills him, and not I."[85] In England, the Church developments occasioned a shift from judges to *jurors* as the bearers of this same moral responsibility, accompanying the rise of the jury in the same century. The English judge could make a similar claim about the law, deflecting both responsibility and doubt. The shift of doubt and moral responsibility from judges to witnesses and jurors in many criminal cases meant that "royal jurisdiction had finally displaced divine jurisdiction."[86]

[82] See James Fitzjames Stephen, *A History of the Criminal Law of England* (London: Routledge, 1996) (orig. 1883), 1:573 ("[Medieval judges often dreaded] the responsibility – which to many men would appear intolerably heavy and painful – of deciding . . . upon the guilt or innocence of a prisoner.") (quoted in Whitman, *Reasonable Doubt*, 11).

[83] See Whitman, *Reasonable Doubt*, 11 (noting the work of "anthropologists and historians of religion [demonstrating that] . . . anyone in the premodern world involved in the killing of another person subjected himself to the risk of bad luck, bad karma, bad fate, or some kind of vengeful divine retribution" (citations omitted), and quoting Adam Smith in his *Moral and Political Philosophy*, ed. Herbert W. Schneider (New York: Harper and Row, 1970), 192–93, 198–99 (on God as the "great avenger of justice")).

[84] Whitman, *Reasonable Doubt*, 51–90, esp. 90.

[85] Ibid., 91–124, esp. 94, 105.

[86] Ibid., 126–57, esp. 138.

This shift had been workable for a few centuries, when generalized procedures shielded the newly responsible legal actors from personal responsibility for the harshest consequences of their decisions. But when the state instituted procedures that again placed the moral responsibility for specific punishment decisions on English jurors, to name one party, in the sixteenth and seventeenth centuries, the latter found their consciences taxed once again and devised new strategies to avoid corporal and capital punishment in the face of doubt.[87]

Over the course of these several centuries, multiple punishment avoidance strategies manifested whenever judges, witnesses, or jurors perceived their own moral responsibility for conviction in the face of doubt. For example, witnesses often refused to testify, and juries found strategies to avoid findings of guilt in ordinary crimes that they did not feel warranted capital punishment.[88] Juries also expanded the scope of the old "benefit of the clergy" doctrine, allowing first-time offenders in fourteenth-century ecclesiastical courts to receive lighter sentences in formulations available to literate members of the Church.[89] Moreover, prosecutors frequently "downcharged" crimes or "downgraded" the value of stolen goods to arrive at more lenient sentences than the statute would ordinarily require.[90] And judges regularly barred criminal convictions or construed criminal laws narrowly where they had doubt about the relationship between the evidence and criminal culpability or fairness of punishment for an alleged crime.[91]

Taken together, the lasting judicial iteration of the multifaceted procedural manifestations of doubt took on multiple forms that persist in some form in modern American criminal law: heightened standards and burdens of proof; the void-for-vagueness doctrine for criminal law, and its "junior version," the rule of lenity; the presumption of innocence; the principle of legality; the rule against federal common law crimes; doctrines of mistake to absolve criminal liability; and of course the reasonable doubt doctrine. Possessed of only a general awareness of the roots of reasonable doubt and

[87] Ibid., 161.

[88] Hall, *Theft, Law, and Society*, 92–95 (noting that juries used to "invent technicalities in order to avoid infliction of the capital penalty").

[89] See Gabel, *Benefit of Clergy in England in the Later Middle Ages*. See also Introduction, note 23 and sources cited therein.

[90] Langbein, *Adversary Criminal Trial*, 334–35 (citing, inter alia, Blackstone, *Commentaries*, 4:239; Radzinowicz, *History*, 83–106, 138–64).

[91] For the development of these reasonable doubt practices in English common law and in continental European law, see Whitman, *Reasonable Doubt*, 334–36. For the development of lenity practices, see Introduction, note 26 and sources cited therein.

lenity, Justice John Marshall famously stated in his nineteenth-century invocation of the American rule of lenity: "The rule that penal laws are to be construed strictly is perhaps not much less old than construction itself."[92]

While medieval Muslims and Christians shared moral concerns and devised punishment avoidance procedures to alleviate doubt, it is clear that the shape of, impetus behind, and goals targeted by their respective doubt-based procedures were quite different. The differences between medieval Islamic and Christian treatments of doubt have to do with differences in theology and institutional structure. In contrast to the prominent role medieval Muslim jurists played in constructing the law, their English and European counterparts were not autonomous or even first actors in that task. The latter group had more scholastic and less singular power to legitimately define law. Moreover, it was two competing and highly centralized institutions that defined law for English and European judges: the Church and the Crown. The Crown eventually won the jurisdictional battle over criminal procedure, but by then, the Church had developed a moral theology that absolved most legal actors of the consequences of doubt – which together led to procedures that would allow doubt to facilitate rather than bar convictions.[93]

In contrast, medieval Muslim judges and jurists – lacking a centralized authority in the form of a unified church or state to define the law without their input – continued to see doubt as a matter of moral concern that, in turn, informed the scope of what they saw as their divinely delegated

[92] *United States v. Wiltberger*, 18 U.S. 35, 43 (1820). For recent applications of the lenity rule, see *Burrage v. United States*, 134 S. Ct. 881, 891 (2014) rejecting the government's reading of a statute that rendered a defendant subject to a sentencing enhancement for distributing cocaine that "result[ed] in" death, where the defendant contributed to but did not cause a death, and noting that, "[e]specially in the interpretation of a criminal statute subject to the rule of lenity, we cannot give the text a meaning that is different from its ordinary, accepted meaning, and that disfavors the defendant") (citations omitted); *United States v. Santos*, 553 U.S. 507, 512 (2008) (applying the rule of lenity to a money-laundering statute that left in doubt whether the statute's prohibition on using "proceeds" from unlawful activity applied to profits or receipts from illegal gambling activities). On the reasonable doubt doctrine, see *In re Winship*, 397 U.S. 358, 362, 363 (1970) ("[P]roof of a criminal charge beyond a reasonable doubt is constitutionally required.... The standard provides concrete substance for the presumption of innocence – that bedrock 'axiomatic and elementary' principle whose 'enforcement lies at the foundation of the administration of our criminal law.'") (citations omitted).

[93] Whitman, *Reasonable Doubt*, 131 ("[T]he kings of England were involved in political conflicts both with the church and with a recalcitrant, and sometimes rebellious, feudal nobility. In the early days of the development of English law, those conflicts expressed themselves largely as conflicts over jurisdiction....").

power to define Islamic law, theology, and morality in criminal law and other arenas. Wracked by doubt and quite aware of their institutional position as exponents of Islamic law in "pious opposition" to the state, particularly in matters of criminal punishment, they pursued at least three goals when defining a jurisprudence of doubt. They used doubt to alleviate a deep sense of moral concern with false convictions, to rein in rather than work with the political rulers in punishment, and to construct a version of Islamic law in line with their ideals of divine legislative supremacy. With no moral theology to absolve doubt and no state to assert absolute control over the authorization of punishment, medieval Muslim jurists had both moral and institutional reasons to deploy a procedure-laden, robust doctrine of doubt. The modern situation is quite different. It was only much later that the breakdown of traditional moral and institutional structures would lead to the wholesale dismissal of doubt in most modern Islamic criminal law contexts – a fact underscored by this examination of its forgotten history.

CONCLUSION

The reports discussed in this chapter were early "landmark cases" that were carefully selected, packaged, and retold in abundance by *ḥadīth* collectors and jurists of the eighth and ninth centuries (as models for basic criminal law adjudication) and by jurists of the tenth and eleventh centuries (as foundations for a more sophisticated criminal law jurisprudence). That each set of cases emphasizes the propriety of punishment suggests ongoing moral concerns driving the jurists' selective preservation of these reports. While they had claimed the moral-epistemic authority to interpret Islamic law and its subsidiary doctrine of doubt, they were also cognizant of the harsh realities of institutional violence at risk of going unregulated in the political sphere. Those realities had both this-worldly consequences and afterworldly ones – particularly when the punishment at issue involved death. Moreover, jurists thought themselves accountable before God in exercising their assumed interpretive agency to authorize punishment, for which they required clear sanction from the foundational texts. In short, they wished to assume interpretive authority over the law but were concerned about the consequences of not getting it right.

Medieval Muslim jurists looked to these early cases because they needed a *ḥudūd* jurisprudence from the founding period that could inform both their jurisprudential concern with upholding divine legislative supremacy and their moral concern with taking life and with adhering to other moral values expressed by early Islamic criminal law. The tension between the two imperatives – enforcement versus avoidance – and the resulting moral concerns led to the main feature of doubt jurisprudence: a requirement of *ḥudūd* enforcement whenever violations were public, proved with certainty, and without mitigating factors to remove criminal liability; and of *ḥudūd* avoidance otherwise. These tensions further helped shape two central characteristics of Islamic criminal law: (1) that it was an area of *shared jurisdiction* between the jurists and the ruling authorities, and (2) that it was subject to *more procedure* in forms that resembled but went far beyond the safeguards for criminal defendants that arose in the medieval origins of Anglo-American reasonable doubt doctrines and death-is-different jurisprudence.

More broadly, Islamic legal interpretation depended on interpretive methodologies developed by a diverse set of jurists as they navigated sociopolitical realities that intersected with a host of moral concerns extending from the application of Islamic criminal law. Jurists and political rulers promoted two different sets of interests on issues of morality and authority over the law. Where the latter institutionalized hierarchical norms and sought to maximize their authority over the law and the public sphere, the former sought to curb them. Acting as a "pious opposition" to what they perceived as excesses in punishment, jurists opposed the state's status-reinforcing *under*criminalization, by which high-status offenders were absolved of criminal liability. And in the process of elaborating the law, their moral concerns around imposing the death penalty also led them to oppose fairness-disregarding *over*criminalization.

Actual punishment was likely often harsh and may have been only marginally responsive to the jurists' ameliorative concerns, as political authorities seemed – to understate the case – less concerned about the moral-legal imperatives so occupying the jurists' attention. But political punishment could not be justified through Islamic law, nor could it offer precedential value for its prospective application, which was governed by the complex matrix of Islamic criminal law that was in turn heavily informed by doctrines of doubt. The details of this jurisprudence are taken up in the next two chapters.

PART III

THE JURISPRUDENCE OF DOUBT, SECOND/EIGHTH–TENTH/SIXTEENTH CENTURIES

5

Early Doubt: Doubt as an Element of Islamic Criminal Law

For medieval Muslim jurists to navigate between competing precedents for punishment avoidance and enforcement with any sense of legitimacy in the Sunnī world, they had to develop a criminal law jurisprudence that offered guidance to judges on when to invoke doubt. This chapter shows how the collective attempt to accomplish this task by early Muslim jurists became the first construction of Islam's "doubt jurisprudence." Often, the early jurists made little reference to doubt, instead cataloging model cases of *ḥudūd* avoidance and enforcement. After the textualization of doubt that coincided with the end of the founding period, as demonstrated in the next chapter, later Muslim jurists systematically elaborated this early Islamic doubt jurisprudence with explicit reference to the doubt canon.

This chapter examines Sunnī juristic conceptions of doubt during the first three centuries of Islamic history.[1] The authors of the legal manuals outlining these concepts were the same jurists who recorded the prophetic reports of criminal cases discussed in the last chapter. That chapter addressed the moral concerns motivating the jurists' alternating emphasis on criminal law enforcement and avoidance. This chapter turns from a consideration of motives to a reexamination of means. It looks at how early Sunnī pragmatic jurists who favored doubt interpreted the foundational texts in tandem with precedents from early judicial practice on the doctrine of doubt to define Islamic criminal law. Notably plural, the jurists' arguments developed differently in each circle that recognized a nascent doctrine of doubt, and gave rise to distinct notions of Ḥanafī, Mālikī, and Shāfiʿī doubt as an element of Islamic criminal law itself.

[1] For treatments of early and late Shīʿī law, see Part II and Chapter 8 in Part IV, respectively.

A. EARLY ḤANAFĪ CRIMINAL LAW

We begin with the early Ḥanafīs. They provide a useful starting point because Abū Ḥanīfa was the oldest of the main "founders" of the Sunnī legal schools and because his associates played a key role in first popularizing the doubt canon.[2]

Ḥanafīs were exceptional among early legal schools by virtue of the considerable state patronage they received from the young ʿAbbāsid regime.[3] Because of their close ties to political power, the historical literature sometimes paints them as wielding the doubt canon to benefit their own associates without respect for legal rules.[4] But regardless of whether some Ḥanafīs *in fact* abused the doubt canon, politics did not dictate their *normative* approach to criminal law. As jurists charged with defining Islamic criminal law, Ḥanafīs had to grapple with the same precedents balancing norms of judicial subservience and moral concerns that preoccupied other jurists outside of the political establishment in the early community. Accordingly, Ḥanafīs gradually developed rather exacting rules of criminal law enforcement and of doubt-based avoidance.

1. *Ḥudūd* Enforcement

On *ḥudūd* enforcement, Ḥanafīs took no "lenient" stance when it came to the circumstances surrounding the subjective question of intent. Where there was no objective basis for avoiding punishment, Abū Ḥanīfa generally rejected subjective claims about intent both during the commission of a crime (opting for objective criteria for *mens rea*) and after the fact (opting for rules recognizing the finality of judicial decisions rather than repentance).

[2] See Chapter 1.

[3] For the background political context in which Ḥanafism formed and developed in Iraq, Khurāsān, and elsewhere, see Tsafrir, *Early Spread of Ḥanafism*, 20–21, 27–34; Wilferd Madelung, "The Early Murjiʾa in Khurāsān and Transoxania and the Spread of Ḥanafism," *Der Islam* 59 (1971), 32–39.

[4] See Chapter 3. Compare Fierro, "When Lawful Violence Meets Doubt," 229–33. For an analysis of the standing and institutionalization of the Mālikī school in Andalusia under the Western Umayyads, similar to the early Ḥanafī state patronage in the East, see Maribel Fierro, "Proto-Malikis, Malikis, and Reformed Malikis in al-Andalus," in *The Islamic School of Law: Evolution, Devolution, and Progress*, ed. Peri Bearman, Rudolph Peters, and Frank E. Vogel (Cambridge, MA: Islamic Legal Studies Program at Harvard Law School, 2005), 57–76.

a. Mens Rea*: Objective Indicia of Voluntariness, Knowledge, Effects*

To begin with, early Ḥanafīs approached criminal cases with objective inquiries about a defendant's state of mind. Ignoring the subjective state of mind often barred defendants from escaping judgments of guilt, and it frequently allowed state-backed Ḥanafī jurists to recommend punishment. Examples are found in issues concerning voluntariness, knowledge, and intent.

Voluntariness: Sexual Coercion Voluntariness was a key component of criminal culpability in cases of rape – though Muslim jurists discussed this component not on the part of the victim but on that of the alleged perpetrator.[5] Abū Ḥanīfa recognized that a man accused of rape had to have acted voluntarily to be criminally culpable. Accordingly, defendants who wished to overcome a rape accusation could attempt to argue that they were themselves "victims" of a third party forcing them to commit rape, in order to demonstrate their lack of voluntariness. Abū Ḥanīfa generally rejected such attempts. He maintained that – except in limited circumstances – a man who committed rape could not claim to be a victim of third-party coercion as a defense. For Ḥanafīs, biology dictated that a man could not be coerced into committing rape because arousal was a prerequisite to sex, and arousal was an indication of voluntariness.[6] If a man was truly in fear of his life or limb, Ḥanafīs concluded, fear would overcome his will or ability to have sex.[7] They set forth a general rule of per se criminal liability against perpetrators of rape who claimed that their actions were coerced, and advised enforcing criminal punishment.

An exception to this general rule arose in cases where a person endowed with political authority was the third party doing the coercing. Ḥanafīs maintained that criminal liability would not attach in such cases not

[5] This approach contrasts with that of modern American law, which initially required proof that the accuser did not consent, but then, finding that subject inquiry too unwieldy, focused on the objective indications of the use of force. For discussion, see note 104 and accompanying text.

[6] See Abū al-Ḥasanāt al-Laknawī (d. 1304/1887), *al-Nāfiʿ al-kabīr* (*sharḥ al-Jāmiʿ al-ṣaghīr*), on the margins of Shaybānī, *al-Jāmiʿ al-ṣaghīr* (Karachi: Idārat al-Qurʾān wa'l-ʿUlūm al-Islāmiyya, 1407/1987), 230 (*lā yutaṣawwar illā baʿd intishār al-āla wa-hādhā āyat al-ṭawʿ*); Qudūrī, *Tajrīd*, 11:5898 (*min ṭabʿ al-Ādamī idhā khāfa zāla intishāruh fa-lammā lam yazul ʿalimnā annah ghayr khāʾif wa-qawluhum annah qad lā yazūl al-intishār maʿa 'l-khawf amr nādir jarat al-ʿāda bi-khilāfih*).

[7] Qudūrī, *Tajrīd*, 11:5896 (*al-khawf yunāfī 'l-shahwa wa'l-intishār fa-lammā wujida minh dalla ʿalā 'khtiyārih*).

because of the facts, but because of the power dynamics involved.[8] The person wielding political authority (*sulṭān*) – as the putative representative of the caliph – was the authority ultimately responsible for enforcing criminal laws.[9] If he was the one violating those laws, crimes would be regarded as having been committed in the absence of *any* legitimate authority to enforce punishment.[10] That situation would be akin to crimes committed in non-Muslim territory (*dār al-ḥarb*), a domain outside of the jurisdiction of Islamic law where there generally was no liability for violations of *ḥudūd* laws.[11]

Not all Ḥanafīs agreed on this exception to criminal liability for coerced rape. One later Ḥanafī jurist insisted that criminal punishment should be enforced even when the political authority did the coercing.[12] In such

[8] For an analogous outcome in American criminal law, consider the exclusionary rule, which excludes improperly obtained evidence as a way to temper the power dynamics by which state officials act against individuals. For an accessible treatment of the rule, see Potter Stewart, "The Road to *Mapp v. Ohio* and Beyond: The Origins, Development, and Future of the Exclusionary Rule in Search-and-Seizure Cases," *Columbia Law Review* 83 (1983), 1365–404.

[9] The term used in these discussions is *sulṭān* – meant less to connote an individual political ruler than the person endowed with authority over public law, which typically refers to ruling authorities. Mohammad Fadel, "Public Authority (*Sulṭān*) in Islamic Law," in *Oxford International Encyclopedia of Legal History*, ed. Stanley N. Katz (Oxford: Oxford University Press, 2009), 5:3–6.

[10] Shaybānī, *al-Jāmiʿ al-ṣaghīr*, 230 (calling the legitimating authority the *imām*). There is some difference about whether Abū Ḥanīfa made an exception for coercion by the ruling authorities (in which case *ḥadd* liability was to be voided) or denied such an exception (in which case the *ḥadd* punishment was due even if the political authority or someone else coerced the act of *zinā*). It is generally understood that Abū Ḥanīfa initially held the first opinion, but subsequently adopted the latter. See Qudūrī, *Tajrīd*, 11:5896–97. For further discussion of this problem and coercion in Islamic law more generally, see Khaled Abou El Fadl, "The Common and Islamic Law of Duress," *Arab Law Quarterly* 6, 2 (1991), 121–59, esp. 147–48; Mairaj Syed, *Coercion in Classical Islamic Law and Theology* (PhD diss., Princeton University, 2011).

[11] See Qudūrī, *Tajrīd*, 11:5896. Laknawī further justifies the rule on the bases that the coerced individual has no higher authority to which to appeal and that if a person fears for his life with no available option to him other than obeying the political authority even by committing a criminal act, that level of fear creates the possibility that the act is fully involuntary. He also notes that this rule changed from Abū Ḥanīfa's time, when there was a single political ruler, to subsequent times, when there were multiple "usurping" (*mutaghallib*) sultans – which meant that there was no clear government with authority over *ḥudūd* crimes, resulting in a rule that *ḥadd* avoidance should apply across the board. Laknawī, *Nāfiʿ*, on the margins of Shaybānī, *al-Jāmiʿ al-ṣaghīr*, 230.

[12] See Qudūrī, *Tajrīd*, 11:5897 (citing the doubt canon in its standard form: *idraʾū ʾl-ḥudūd biʾl-shubahāt*, and referring to this potential category of *shubha* as *shubhat al-imām*). Interestingly, Qudūrī here espoused a creative solution to soften the rigid *ḥudūd* enforcement rule. He posited that *ḥudūd* liability is not canceled in such instances. Yet the legal

instances, he said, "we do not see cause for doubt."[13] Because he regarded arousal as an objective indication of voluntariness, this jurist was adamant that a rape perpetrator could not claim sultanic coercion as a basis for legal doubt.[14] Moreover, the sources suggest a moral rationale at play.

This was a dispute about more than facts. Ḥanafīs questioned whether third-party coercion to commit rape was possible and whether it resulted in criminal culpability based on understandings of human biology as well as on power politics and moral concerns. All Muslim jurists regarded rape as an egregious criminal act as well as a morally reprehensible act. But while some were concerned with checking political power, others exhibited concern with checking moral wrongs as violations of God's law. For those interested in checking political power, coercion could serve as an excuse. But for those concerned with upholding God's law along moral dimensions, a person being coerced to commit rape on pain of death should have sacrificed his own life rather than violate the bodily integrity of the victim, which was clearly a violation of the divine law.[15] In this way, competing political and moral concerns informed Ḥanafī rules of criminal-law enforcement in cases of sexual violence.[16]

After Abū Ḥanīfa set forth the rule of strict liability for rape with the exception of coercion only if orchestrated by a person endowed with political authority, his students Abū Yūsuf and Shaybānī changed this rule to remove *ḥudūd* liability in all cases of coercion. For them, political developments had quickly rendered the limited quality of the "*sulṭān* exception" obsolete.[17] Not long after Abū Ḥanīfa's death, ongoing rivalries and rebellions called into question rules based on a political order with a singular political ruler endowed with authority over public law. These events forced subsequent Ḥanafīs to concede that, from as early as the First Civil War (35–40/656–61), it was rarely – if ever – the case that a single ruler exercised the type of force and authority over the Muslim community

establishment may excusably avoid enforcing punishment given the absence of anyone with the legitimate political authority to sanction the punishment. In that sense, the act in question becomes similar to Muslims committing *zinā* in non-Muslim lands, where *moral* culpability remains even though the *ḥudūd* sanctions are not applied.

13 See ibid. (*lā nusallim wujūd al-shubha*).

14 See ibid. (*al-mukhtār lā yu'aththir fīh al-ikrāh*).

15 See Abou El Fadl, "Common and Islamic Law of Duress," 127–29, n. 112.

16 For further discussion of duress, see ibid., 127–29 (describing the Ḥanafī distinction between compelling duress, which vitiates voluntariness and removes liability, and pressure that may be regarded as "incomplete compulsion," which is less constraining and does not remove liability).

17 See Qudūrī, *Tajrīd*, 11:989 (attributing the "new" opinion to Abū Ḥanīfa as well).

that Abū Ḥanīfa's rulings had contemplated.[18] In other words, the universal Islamic political ideal to recognize a single ruler at any given time was far from reality.[19] Against this backdrop, the new ruling changed the strict liability rule, introducing wider room for the use of coercion-based "doubt" to avoid punishment.

Knowledge: Sex with a Prohibited Partner Alongside the narrow voluntariness requirement, Abū Ḥanīfa recognized a thin knowledge requirement for criminal culpability. Like other jurists, he maintained that full criminal liability often required that a defendant commit a crime with knowledge of its illegality. As a corollary, a person who committed a criminal act on the mistaken belief that his actions were legal could avoid criminal punishment.

This mistake-of-law defense applied broadly to "victimless crimes," that is, those involving no harm against the bodily integrity or property – that is, "individual interests" (*ḥuqūq al-nās*) – of another party. For instance, if a man divorced his wife three times (which rendered the divorce final), and the couple then had sex during her divorce waiting period, Abū Ḥanīfa ascribed no criminal liability to either if the husband claimed that he "thought [sex with his wife] was legal."[20] Likewise, there would be no criminal liability on a man who had sex with a slave woman belonging to a

[18] Laknawī, *Nāfiʿ*, 230. Arguably, ʿAbbāsid caliphs such as Hārūn al-Rashīd were far more powerful than the earliest caliphs, as they were heads of a more centralized state. Yet the diffusion of the empire and constant contests for power among factions with relative autonomy made putatively stronger ʿAbbāsid caliphs less powerful and their authority less singular than that of the earliest caliphs. For further discussion, see Chapter 2.

[19] As one scholar has remarked, the surprising element of political leadership in early Muslim lands was not that it shifted easily from one ruler to another given the vastness of the empire from an early period and the competing factional claims to leadership, but the frequency with which those in effective control over the community sought to maintain the fiction of a single caliph as a symbol of unity of all Muslims. See Mottahedeh, *Loyalty and Leadership*, 19.

[20] Shaybānī, *al-Jāmiʿ al-ṣaghīr*, 228. *Ḥudūd* liability was to be canceled in a similar scenario if a man had sex with his wife after telling her, "you are free" (*khaliyya* or *bariyya*) or "you are in charge of your own affairs" (*amruk bi-yadik*), when these are phrases that she (erroneously, in the husband's estimation) interprets as initiation of divorce, from which point she enters her divorce waiting period. Here, there is to be no *ḥadd* liability for the couple subsequently having sex even if the husband says that he was under the firm impression that the action was *not* legal. Laknawī explains that this conclusion has to do with a difference of opinion among the Companions concerning whether figurative speech (*kināya*) could result in divorce. Laknawī, *Nāfiʿ*, on the margins of *Shaybānī, al-Jāmiʿ al-ṣaghīr*, 228. Laknawī was likely recognizing the difference as "interpretive doubt" – about which see Chapter 6. But Abū Ḥanīfa likely did not and instead held that figurative speech did not effect divorce, given the thrust of his *not* recognizing that type of doubt.

member of his household (for example, his mother, father, son, or wife) and similarly claimed that he thought it was legal.[21]

However, mistake defenses would typically fail for crimes considered egregious moral wrongs, where excuses merely amounted to claims of mistakes of fact.[22] For example, Abū Ḥanīfa maintained that a man who had sex with a woman who happened to be staying in his house, claiming that he thought she was a permissible sex partner, which she turned out not to be, would be criminally liable for *zinā*. The reason was that he was in a position to ascertain her identity rather than commit a crime with the potential for incest – which the Muslim community regarded as an offense even more egregious than an ordinary sex crime.[23] In this way, Abū Ḥanīfa recognized a knowledge requirement but narrowed its scope based on a moral wrong doctrine.

Intention: Defamation's Effects Also in addition to a narrow voluntariness doctrine and a thin knowledge requirement, Abū Ḥanīfa restricted punishment avoidance in one important area of criminal law by again

[21] Shaybānī, *al-Jāmiʿ al-ṣaghīr*, 228–29 (noting, however, that paternity for any resulting child would not be established, except in a case of someone sleeping with a slave woman belonging to his son, in which case paternity would be established and the offender would be obligated to pay his son the value of the slave woman). Shaybānī does not cite it, but this rule likely comes from the fact that there is a legitimate textual claim for the man's supposition that sex with the son's slave woman was licit, namely, the common *ḥadīth* that all other jurists cite (and that later Ḥanafī jurists cite as well) in which the Prophet told a son that "your father owns [or has rights over] you and your property: *anta wa-māluk li-abīk*." Thus, the footnote in this text – wherein the editor explains that it is because fathers *actually* own their sons' property – is incorrect.

[22] In the analogous – though now little-used – moral-wrong doctrine, common law jurists maintained that a criminal defendant could claim "a *reasonable* mistake regarding an attendant circumstance and yet still demonstrate moral culpability worthy of punishment. The basis of the moral-wrong doctrine is that 'there should be no exculpation for mistake where, if the facts had been as the actor believed them to be, his conduct would still be ... immoral.'" Joshua Dressler, *Understanding Criminal Law*, 6th ed. (Danvers, MA: LexisNexis, 2012), 158–59 (citing *Bell v. State*, 668 P.2d 829, 833 (Alaska Ct. App. 1983)). Criminal law experts locate that rule in the infamous nineteenth-century English case, *Regina v. Prince*, L.R. 2 Cr. Cas. Res. 154 (1875) (holding the defendant guilty for "unlawfully tak[ing] or caus[ing] to be taken" an unmarried girl under the age of 16 years from her parents' home, despite the jury's finding that the defendant reasonably believed the 14-year-old girl in question to be 18 years of age). But see *A Minor v. Director of Public Prosecutions*, [2000] A.C. 428, 476 (H.L.) (disavowing *Prince*).

[23] Here and elsewhere, Abū Ḥanīfa and his associates called for *ḥudūd* enforcement whenever incest was involved. See Qudūrī, *Tajrīd*, 11:5899. This rule does not appear in contemporaneous works of Shaybānī or Abū Yūsuf, nor in Jaṣṣāṣ's *Aḥkām* or Dabūsī's *Isrār*. However, later Ḥanafīs uniformly cite and discuss this rule, attributing it to Abū Ḥanīfa and offering extended explanations. Qudūrī's discussion, for instance, runs a full eight pages, from 11:5899 to 11:5907.

preferring an objective to a subjective inquiry as to criminal intent. For defamation cases, early Ḥanafīs asked about the *effects* of potentially defamatory statements rather than the speaker's *mens rea*. For example, most non-Ḥanafī jurists regarded the statement "You are not from [a certain] tribe" to be a defamatory statement of lineage denial if intentionally made and directed at a person about whom it was factually incorrect. A speaker could be absolved of criminal liability if he could prove that he did not have a defamatory intent.[24] For Abū Ḥanīfa, by contrast, intention in defamation actions was irrelevant. A mere statement cannot have the effect of denying tribal affiliation or lineage, because it is factually incorrect. People are in fact born of two parents, not a tribe.[25] The result was to limit *ḥadd* liability in such cases.

But Ḥanafīs expanded criminal liability in contexts where there was the threat of another type of egregious moral wrong: blasphemy. Abū Ḥanīfa and his followers infamously tended to advocate *ḥudūd* enforcement for statements deemed blasphemous – regardless of whether the speaker intended them as such.[26] For instance, the Ḥanafīs deemed it blasphemous for a person to doubt his faith but then say, "I am a believer, God willing,"[27] or to say, "I am bored of Islam,"[28] or "I am Satan," even if joking.[29] Likewise, if a person commits a sin but nevertheless affirms him- or herself to be a Muslim, it is blasphemous for another person to then say to that person, "Damn you and your Islam!"[30] In addition, if two men argue, and one of them exclaims, "There is no power or strength except in God" – a common saying among Muslims – and the other responds, "'There is no power [except in God]' has nothing to do with this," Ḥanafīs regarded the respondent's statement as

24 For discussion, see my "Negotiating Speech in Islamic Law and Politics," 151.

25 Abū Yūsuf, *Ikhtilāf*, 163 (noting that the rival Iraqi judge and jurist Ibn Abī Laylā would impose the *ḥadd* sanction here). For other instances of mixed rulings on *ḥudūd* enforcement and avoidance for the crime of defamation, see Shaybānī, *al-Jāmiʿ al-ṣaghīr*, 235–38. Cf. Qudūrī, *Tajrīd*, 11:5955–56 (*al-taʿrīḍ biʾl-qadhf*).

26 For examples, see al-Shaykh al-Niẓām et al. (fl. eleventh/seventeenth century), *al-Fatāwā al-ʿĀlamgīriyya*, ed. ʿAbd al-Laṭīf Ḥasan ʿAbd al-Raḥmān (Beirut: Dār al-Kutub al-ʿIlmiyya, 2000), 2:537–83. This work was composed between 1075/1664 and 1083/1672, and it collects blasphemy cases and statements from, inter alia, Qāḍī Khān (d. 592/1196), *Fatāwā Qāḍī Khān* (Cairo: Maṭbaʿat Muḥammad Shāhīn, 1282/1865), and Burhān al-Dīn Maḥmūd b. Aḥmad al-Bukhārī al-Marghīnānī (d. 616/1219), *al-Muḥīṭ al-burhānī fī ʾl-fiqh al-Nuʿmānī*, ed. Aḥmad ʿIzzū ʿInāya (Beirut: Dār Iḥyāʾ al-Turāth al-ʿArabī, 2003).

27 Al-Shaykh al-Niẓām et al., *al-Fatāwā al-ʿĀlamgīriyya* (2000), 2:257.

28 Ibid., 2:300.

29 Ibid., 2:301.

30 Ibid., 2:257 (Per. *laʿnat bar tu va bar musalmānī-yi-tu* [Ar. *laʿnat Allāh ʿalayk wa-ʿalā Islāmik*]).

blasphemous.[31] In all of these instances and others, Ḥanafīs rather uniquely opted for a stance of enforcing punishment.[32]

b. Finality

In addition to restricting *mens rea* requirements, early Ḥanafīs also detailed rules for enforcing punishment once judgment was rendered. This "rule of finality" affected the availability of repentance as a means of post-conviction relief from punishment. Unlike other prominent jurists of their time,[33] early Ḥanafīs generally maintained that repentance did not cancel *ḥadd* liability once a final judgment had been rendered.[34]

For a textual basis, these Ḥanafīs relied on the *Case of Māʿiz* and other reported instances of stoning, in which the punishment was enforced even after the defendant had repented or expressed remorse.[35] But, as we saw with the debates about Māʿiz, this was not the only reading of his case. To guide their textual reading, Ḥanafīs identified two rationales for enforcing punishment when judgment was final, notwithstanding a defendant's desire to repent – perhaps through expressing remorse or retracting his or her confession. First, *ḥudūd* sanctions were legislated primarily for deterrence.[36] If repentance always removed *ḥadd* liability, every perpetrator

31 Ibid., 2:273 (Per. *lā ḥawl bi-kār nīst or lā ḥawl rā chih konam* [Ar: *lā tanfaʿ lā ḥawl*]).

32 For further discussion, see my "Negotiating Speech in Islamic Law and Politics," 144–67.

33 For example, Shāfiʿī, *Umm* (1996), 6:131 (concluding that *ḥadd* liability could be canceled even after a judge had rendered a guilty verdict and started to carry out the sentence, against the notion of finality that "announcing the sentence is the functional equivalent of carrying it out: *khurūj ḥukm al-ḥākim qabla maḍāʾ al-ḥadd ka-maḍāʾ al-ḥadd*").

34 Exceptions for Ḥanafīs included repentance after apostasy and highway robbery, based on a Qurʾānic directive. This example – where the Ḥanafī rule is qualified by textual bases – challenges the Shāfiʿī accusation that the Ḥanafīs ignored the text in favor of rational principles (*aṣl, uṣūl*). In using *ḥadīth* for law, Ḥanafīs purported to reject statements posing as *ḥadīth* whenever they contradicted principles extracted from known, settled texts. This maneuver was their way of mediating between *ḥadīth* of disputed reliability, allowing them in some ways to avoid issues of authenticity, as noted by Ahmed El Shamsy, *From Tradition to Law: The Origins and Early Development of the Shāfiʿī School of Law in Ninth-Century Egypt* (PhD diss., Harvard University, 2009), 19–24 (now published as *The Canonization of Islamic Law: A Social and Intellectual History* (Cambridge: Cambridge University Press, 2013)). For further discussion of Abū Ḥanīfa's position as to the authoritativeness of *ḥadīth*, see ʿAbd al-Majīd Maḥmūd ʿAbd al-Majīd, *al-Ittijāhāt al-fiqhiyya ʿinda aṣḥāb al-ḥadīth fī ʾl-qarn al-thālith al-hijrī* (Cairo: Maktabat al-Khānjī, 1399/1979), 460–62.

35 See Abū Yūsuf, *Āthār*, 157 (reporting and commenting on the *Case of Māʿiz*, arguing that the *ḥadd* sanction was enforced, even though Māʿiz had repented); cf. Qudūrī, *Tajrīd*, 11:5949–50 (also citing the case of the woman from the Ghāmidī tribe).

36 See Abū Yūsuf, *Āthār*, 157. For further discussion of the deterrence rationale, see Chapter 3.

would express remorse and those sanctions would never apply.[37] Second, and only secondarily, *ḥudūd* sanctions serve as spiritual expiation for perpetrators.[38] Because repentance generally does not cancel the requirement for expiation in other contexts, by analogy, neither should it cancel *ḥadd* liability.[39] In these ways, in contrast to their stance cautioning *ḥudūd* avoidance when objective criteria of contracts were at issue (as elaborated below), early Ḥanafīs created mechanisms to enforce punishment in cases where subjective considerations were at play.

2. *Ḥudūd* Avoidance

a. *Defining Criminal Elements*

As suggested above, Abū Ḥanīfa made determinations about the propriety of *ḥudūd* enforcement or avoidance by first defining the criminal elements for each offense. True to the common understanding of his jurisprudence, he appealed to rational precepts to do so.[40] Two examples suffice: his treatment of drinking a certain type of alcoholic beverage popular in his day, and his assessment of liability for theft where ownership changes in the course of a criminal proceeding.

The Drinking Debate: Contextual Interpretation The first, rather infamous example involves heated disputes over a certain beerlike drink called *nabīdh*.[41] The dispute boiled down to ambiguities about the scope of the Qurʾān's prohibition on wine (*khamr*): did the prohibition outlaw only wine drinking, or did the prohibition extend beyond the strict text to include all intoxicants? Abū Ḥanīfa and many Iraqi jurists famously

[37] Abū Yūsuf, *Āthār*, 157.

[38] Ibid. (reporting a prophetic *ḥadīth*: *al-ḥudūd kaffārāt li-ahlihā*). For further discussion of other justifications for Islamic criminal law, see Chapter 3.

[39] Abū Yūsuf, *Āthār*, 157 (citing apostasy as the exceptional case in which repentance will void criminal liability because of clear statements in the foundational texts to that effect, namely, Qurʾān, 6:38: *qul li-ʾlladhīna kafarū in yantahū yughfar lahum mā qad salaf*, and the *ḥadīth*: *al-islām yajubbu mā qablah*). See also Qudūrī, *Tajrīd*, 11:5953 (citing, for the same purpose, Qurʾān, 6:38, a *ḥadīth*, and a rational argument that repentance cancels *ḥadd* liability).

[40] See El Shamsy, *From Tradition to Law*, 14–24.

[41] *Nabīdh* was an infused alcoholic drink produced by soaking dried or fresh fruits until the water became fermented and sweet, and it was of particular concern in the literature. Other drinks included *ṭilāʾ*, which Iraqi proto-Ḥanafī jurists permitted along with *nabīdh*, and *fuqqāʿ*, which the Shīʿa specifically prohibited. For classifications of the other types of intoxicating beverage typically discussed by early jurists, see Haider, *Origins of the Shīʿa*, 139–41.

read the text *narrowly* and *contextually* to conclude that *nabīdh* was permissible.

The Ḥanafīs first argued that the text prohibiting wine had to be interpreted in light of the surrounding context in which it was revealed. For them, it was significant that *nabīdh* was a common drink ingested during the time of the Prophet in Medina.[42] On their reading of the early history, prominent Companions such as ʿUmar and Abū Dharr and many Successors reportedly continued to drink *nabīdh* after the Prophet's death.[43] Moreover, the illustrious Companion-jurist Ibn Masʿūd (d. 32/653), while in Kūfa, reportedly deemed the drink legal as well – even if he did not himself partake of it.[44]

Many subsequent jurists in Iraq followed suit, taking that early practice to mean that the ban on wine did not prohibit *nabīdh*.[45] Abū Ḥanīfa's teacher Ibrāhīm al-Nakhaʿī regarded *nabīdh* as perfectly legal,[46] as did Abū Ḥanīfa's student Abū Yūsuf.[47] Several other Iraqi judges also deemed it legal, including many outside of Abū Ḥanīfa's circle. For example, one of Abū Ḥanīfa's rivals, the famous jurist and judge Ibn Abī Laylā (d. 148/765), reportedly drank *nabīdh* liberally.[48] Likewise, the renowned judge Shurayḥ (d. ca. 76/695–6 or 80/699–700) deemed it legal,[49] as did the prominent judge Sharīk (d. 177/793–4).[50]

42 Jaṣṣāṣ, *Aḥkām al-Qurʾān*, 1:385. For definitions, see P. Heine, "Nabīdh," in *EI*², 7:840, and sources cited therein.

43 Jaṣṣāṣ, *Aḥkām al-Qurʾān*, 1:385.

44 See Wakīʿ, *Akhbār al-quḍāt*, 594.

45 Ibid.

46 See Abū Yūsuf, *Āthār*, 224 (reporting anecdotes in which Ibrāhīm and Ibn Masʿūd drank *nabīdh* and noting that they used to send a servant to the market to buy it in large jars).

47 Ibid., 224–26; Wakīʿ, *Akhbār al-quḍāt*, 652. On his life and judicial decisions, see further Wakīʿ, *Akhbār al-quḍāt*, 650–57, 678. By his time, there was apparently some pushback, as it has been noted that people used to shun him and gossip about him for drinking *nabīdh*. See Joseph Schacht, "Abū Yūsuf," in *EI*², 1:164–65.

48 Wakīʿ, *Akhbār al-quḍāt*, 573–82 (s.v. Ibn Abī Laylā); Joseph Schacht, "Ibn Abī Laylā," in *EI*², 3:687–88. The reports of his drinking capacity are so exaggerated that they verge on the ludicrous. Some say that he never let anyone give testimony unless they drank *nabīdh* and that he always had a few glasses before going out to judge himself. See Wakīʿ, *Akhbār al-quḍāt*, 576, 578.

49 See Wakīʿ, *Akhbār al-quḍāt*, 372 (also permitting *ṭilāʾ*, an intoxicant made by reducing juice to one-third or one-half of its essence), 523.

50 See ibid., 590 (reporting that, in response to a group of Medinese who prohibited *nabīdh*, Sharīk ruled that there was no bar to drinking it), 593–94 (noting that Sharīk permitted people to drink it if it agreed with them but advised them not to drink so much that they got drunk). The same exaggerated story that is told about Ibn Abī Laylā is told about Sharīk: that he would judge only after consuming three helpings of *nabīdh* to the point that he

But there was significant dissent. Leading jurists in the Ḥijāz (including Mālik and Shāfiʿī) were against drinking *nabīdh*, and a handful of Iraqi jurists agreed.[51] The Kūfan judge and jurist Ibn Shubruma (d. 144/761)[52] read several prophetic and other traditions alongside the Qurʾānic ban on wine as textual support for a general ban on intoxicants.[53] The clearest proof for him was the *ḥadīth* stating that "anything that intoxicates is wine."[54] In fact, by Abū Ḥanīfa's time, a majority of the jurists were against *nabīdh*.[55]

Why did scholars reading the same texts differ so radically on the import? Ḥanafī jurists' support for *nabīdh* amounted to an objection to the textualism of *nabīdh* opponents. For Ḥanafīs, the texts did not speak for themselves, and a proper interpretation of the law of intoxicants required balancing competing principles from both texts and context, including history and local practice.[56]

According to Ḥanafīs, the prophetic reports that *nabīdh* opponents cited in defense of prohibition did not actually support their point. First, drinking was a widespread practice and thus a matter of general community concern (*ʿumūm al-balwā*). According to an established interpretive

mixed up the court proceedings. It is said that he even composed a poem in its praise. Wakīʿ, *Akhbār al-quḍāt*, 595–96, 600.

51 See, for example, Saḥnūn, *Mudawwana*, 7:2459 (reporting Mālik's opinion defining *khamr* as all intoxicants).

52 Wakīʿ, *Akhbār al-quḍāt*, 512–27, 557–82, esp. 567 (s.v. Ibn Shubruma).

53 He narrated some of the same traditions that Shāfiʿī had narrated to that effect. See ibid., 516–17, 523–24, listing several traditions with multiple chains, including the following: (1) "Whatever intoxicates is [the equivalent of] wine: *mā askara fa-khamr*"; (2) "Whatever intoxicates is prohibited: *mā askara fa-ḥarām*"; (3) "Every intoxicant is prohibited and every intoxicant is [the equivalent of] wine: *kull muskir ḥarām wa-kull muskir khamr*"; (4) "Every drink that only increases in excellence upon being left to sit is prohibited: *kull sharāb lā yazīd ʿalā ʾl-tark illā jawda fa-huwa ḥarām*"; (5) "Wine is prohibited *per se*, in small quantity and in large quantity, as is any other drink that intoxicates: *ḥurrimat al-khamr bi-ʿaynihā qalīluhā wa-kathīruhā waʾl-sakar min kull sharāb*"; (6) that raisin *nabīdh* (*nabīdh min al-zabīb*) is the equivalent of wine; (7) that Ibrāhīm [al-Nakhaʿī] permitted *nabīdh*. Ibn Shubruma apparently used his office as judge to enforce his views, with the approval of the governor, ʿĪsā b. Mūsā. One report has it that the governor wanted to prohibit *nabīdh*, but was told at one point that it was impossible because Kūfa's leading jurist (Ibn Abī Laylā) permitted it. Ibid., 576. Another report has it that a judge by the name of "Shurayḥ" – by which the narrator may mean Sharīk (d. 179/795–6), as the famous Iraqi judge Shurayḥ b. al-Ḥārith al-Kindī died well before the judge Ibn Shubruma (d. 144/761) – lifted the latter's stiff prohibition of *nabīdh* after his death. See ibid., 523.

54 Ibid., 523.

55 Ibid., 524 (*rakhkhaṣa fī ʾl-nabīdh waʾl-umma ʿalā ghayr dhālik*).

56 For a more detailed discussion, see ʿAbd al-Majīd, *Ittijāhāt*, 61–67 (on basic differences between traditionists and Iraqi jurists who adopted *raʾy* as a type of pragmatic reasoning), 246–54 (on traditionist criteria for authentic *ḥadīth* and the Ḥanafī and Mālikī additions to those criteria), and 460–62 (on Abū Ḥanīfa's stance toward *ḥadīth*).

principle, any prohibition of such widespread concern would have been made known by a *clear statement* of law, rather than a few isolated reports. Moreover, knowledge of a blanket prohibition would have been reflected in widespread and continuous community practice (*tawātur*) from the time of the Prophet.[57] But any claim of consensus or continuous practice would have been belied by the reports of the permissive judgments and practices of ʿUmar, Abū Dharr, Ibn Masʿūd, and other Companions.

On those facts, Ḥanafīs took the lack of a clear statement prohibiting *nabīdh* to suggest at least tacit permission of the drink. Moreover, one report of an early case presents the Prophet deciding whether to punish a man who was drunk from having had his fill of a "mixed drink" called *khalīṭayn* – a kind of fermented beverage made from the dates of two different types of palm.[58] The Prophet prohibited the drink on the spot (though the report says nothing about punishment). Nevertheless, Ḥanafīs drew from this report the lesson that the Prophet's ad hoc prohibition of excessive drinking in this case indicated the lack of a blanket prohibition of intoxicants in other cases.[59]

Second, Ḥanafīs contended, opponents of *nabīdh* such as Ibn Shubruma and Shāfiʿī used texts only selectively to support their position, ignoring equally reliable reports to the contrary. According to another established interpretive principle, equally reliable reports should be read to avoid potential conflicts as much as possible. Thus, the report equating intoxicants with wine should be read in a way that does not contradict reports permitting non-wine intoxicants such as *nabīdh*.[60] Accordingly, Ḥanafīs concluded that non-wine intoxicants were called *khamr* in a figurative sense when they *in fact* intoxicate, not because they have the *capacity* to intoxicate.[61]

Finally, Ḥanafīs found their opponents' opinions surrounding intoxicants to amount to an admission that not even they thought the *nabīdh* ban to be a textually grounded prohibition. All Muslim jurists considered people who declared lawful what God had unambiguously prohibited to

[57] See Jaṣṣāṣ, *Aḥkām al-Qurʾān*, 1:387.

[58] For the *ḥadīth*, see al-Ḥākim al-Naysābūrī, *Mustadrak*, 4:416, no. 8129; Bayhaqī, *Sunan*, 8:317, no. 17301; Ṭaḥāwī, *Sharḥ maʿānī ʾl-āthār*, ed. Muḥammad Zuhrī al-Najjār, Muḥammad Sayyid Jād al-Ḥaqq, and Yūsuf ʿAbd al-Raḥmān al-Marʿashlī (Beirut: ʿĀlam al-Kutub, 1994), 3:156 (*ḥadīth* cited in Jaṣṣāṣ, *Aḥkām al-Qurʾān*, 1:386, 387). Cf. Qudūrī, *Tajrīd*, 12:6080.

[59] Jaṣṣāṣ, *Aḥkām al-Qurʾān*, 1:386.

[60] Ibid.

[61] Ibid. (calling the equation a figurative metaphor: *tashbīh*, *majāzan*).

be unbelievers (*kāfir*, pl. *kuffār*), and the jurists further agreed that this rule applied to people who declared wine to be legal, given the clear statement against it in the Qur'ān. Yet even jurists such as Shāfiʿī, who insisted that *nabīdh* was unlawful, refrained from declaring people who deemed it lawful to be unbelievers. Instead, Shāfiʿī simply called them morally corrupt (*fāsiq*, pl. *fussāq*). For Abū Ḥanīfa, Shāfiʿī's shift in terminology for *nabīdh* permitters was an acknowledgment of the lack of a clear statement of prohibition in Islam's foundational texts.[62]

In the end, early Ḥanafīs concluded that the text against wine drinking proved an insufficient basis for a ban on *nabīdh* drinking. Moreover, they added that the historical and practice-based context suggested that no such ban was justified.[63]

Theft Liability: Continuing Legal Effects Abū Ḥanīfa took a similar contextualist view of criminal liability with respect to the point in a crime's commission at which criminal liability would attach. Recall *Ṣafwān's Case*, in which a man stole Ṣafwān's cloak, and Ṣafwān wished to prosecute him but then changed his mind after presenting the case to the Prophet for adjudication. He decided to give the cloak to the thief and forego any claims he had to the property. In response to Ṣafwān's attempt to drop charges in the middle of the decision-making process, the Prophet said, "if

[62] Jaṣṣāṣ, *Aḥkām al-Qur'ān*, 1:387. The Shāfiʿī accommodation of the divergent Ḥanafī position was obviously necessary here to avoid summarily excommunicating the Iraqi jurists and their sizable following from the community of Muslims.

[63] The same approach to interpretation appeared in other criminal law rulings, creating rifts with more textualist Shāfiʿī jurists on such matters as the criminality of male sodomy. The dominant Shāfiʿī opinion regards acts of male sodomy as *zinā*, making married men convicted of male sodomy death-eligible for adultery. See Abū Ḥāmid al-Ghazālī, *al-Wasīṭ fī 'l-madhhab*, ed. Aḥmad Maḥmūd Ibrāhīm and Muḥammad Muḥammad Tāmir (Cairo?: Dār al-Salām, 1997), 6:440–41. Mālikīs tended to categorize male – but not female – sodomy under the rubric of *zinā*. See Ibn ʿAbd al-Barr, *al-Kāfī fī fiqh ahl al-Madīna al-Mālikī* (Beirut: Dār al-Kutub al-ʿIlmiyya, 2002?), 2:1069, 1073. And one of the two Ḥanafī opinions (that of Abū Ḥanīfa) maintained that male sodomy was not a *ḥadd* crime, while the other opinion (that of Abū Yūsuf and Shaybānī) held that it was. See Qudūrī, *Tajrīd*, 11:5910–16 (presenting and adopting the former opinion); Ibn Nujaym, *al-Baḥr al-rā'iq*, 5:17 (presenting both opinions and adopting the latter). Abū Ḥanīfa's stance, that male sodomy did not warrant *ḥudūd* sanctions, was based on his notion that those acts did not fit the *conventional* (rather than linguistic) meaning of *zinā*, which he took to be sex between a man and a woman. See Shaybānī, *Āthār*, 230 (noting that Abū Ḥanīfa allowed discretionary punishments for such acts, in contrast to Abū Yūsuf and Shaybānī, who maintained that *ḥudūd* punishments were warranted). On the disagreement between Abū Ḥanīfa and his two disciples on male sodomy, see Lange, *Justice*, 200ff., and on bestiality, see Qudūrī, *Tajrīd*, 11:5917–18.

only you had done so [that is, gifted the stolen item to the thief] before. . . ." Early Ḥanafīs read this statement to mean that the Prophet indeed avoided punishment but signaled irritation at having to do so in the middle of the trial.[64] Ordinarily, the consequences for theft included both a mandatory fixed penalty of hand-amputation (*wujūb al-qaṭ'*) and return of the stolen item. However, gift of the stolen item to the thief would cancel *ḥadd* liability, rendering the situation equal to one in which there had been no theft in the first place.[65] On this reading, because the thief had come to own the stolen item, enforcing the sentence would have been tantamount to punishing the new owner for taking his own property.[66]

As we will see, this reading of *Ṣafwān's Case* is diametrically opposed to that of more textualist-minded jurists such as Shāfi'ī. Where Shāfi'ī underscored the mandatoriness of *ḥudūd* enforcement, Abū Ḥanīfa argued that criminal liability attached not when criminal acts were committed but if criminality continued without settlement or other resolution.[67]

Explaining their divergent opinion, Ḥanafīs registered a threefold objection to other jurists' reliance on the doubt-ridden text on which the contrary opinion was based. They first raised a question of authenticity: Ḥanafīs viewed the report of the Prophet's objection in *Ṣafwān's Case* to be of unreliable attribution to the Prophet.[68] They next identified an ambiguity regarding meaning. They pointed out that the actual outcome of the case was unclear. A number of narrations end with Ṣafwān pleading with the Prophet not to cut off the hand of the thief since he was now the owner of the cloak and the Prophet responding, "if only you had done so before you came to me!"[69] In all but one version, the report is silent on whether the Prophet actually carried out the sentence.[70] The idea that the sentence was actually enforced comes from a version of the report associated with a single narrator[71] – which, under Ḥanafī principles, provides a dubious basis for

64 See Qudūrī, *Tajrīd*, 11:5987.
65 Ibid., 11:5985–86.
66 See ibid., 11:5985 (noting that the *ḥadd* liability for a prima facie case of theft is simply a presumption (*aṣl*) that is rebutted when the legal requisites for liability change; also noting that Shaybānī adopted Abū Ḥanīfa's position, but that Abū Yūsuf took the opposite view).
67 The major exception involves repentance (*tawba*), which Shāfi'ī – but not Abū Ḥanīfa – held to cancel *ḥadd* liability, as noted above.
68 Qudūrī, *Tajrīd*, 11:5986 (noting that the *ḥadīth*, as narrated in Mālik's *Muwaṭṭa'*, is *mursal*, because Ṣafwān b. 'Abd Allāh did not narrate from Ṣafwān b. Umayya).
69 Ibid., 11:5987 (*hallā qabla an ta'tīnī bih*). For the Shāfi'ī discussion of this same episode, see Chapter 4, note 14.
70 Qudūrī, *Tajrīd*, 11:5987.
71 Ibid. (*khabar al-wāḥid*).

such a harsh rule. Placing the reports together, the holding of the case is simply disputed.[72] In such instances, where the facts and import of a reported case were inconclusive, Ḥanafīs concluded that the proper course of action would be to suspend judgment on the authenticity of the report (*tawaqquf*) and to decline enforcement of the *ḥudūd* punishments.[73] Third, they saw a problem of competing presumptions. Even if the report was taken to mean that the sentence was enforced, it still would not control the question whether gifting a stolen item would remove *ḥadd* liability. For them, the report could not serve as evidence to trump the judicial presumption (*aṣl*) that transfer of ownership occurs by gift and acceptance (which would remove *ḥadd* liability), because it was silent on whether the thief actually accepted the gift.[74] Thus, it is possible that the punishment was enforced because Ṣafwān attempted to gift the cloak but the thief refused it. For all of these reasons, Abū Ḥanīfa preferred to avoid punishment where neither attribution nor meaning were clear and where neither was certain enough to override competing judicial presumptions.[75]

Notwithstanding his rule of finality as applied to repentance, here and in other cases, Abū Ḥanīfa evaluated each alleged offense with respect to its continuing legal effects at the time of the trial and even after the verdict, not at the time of the alleged events. This rule worked alongside the rule of finality, leaving wide room for accommodating doubt about criminal liability and thereby avoiding *ḥudūd* sanctions.

b. Primacy of Contracts

In Abū Ḥanīfa's view, competing rules of contract law often created the types of doubt that would also bar criminal liability. Assuming a rather unique stance, he held that the legal permissions that ordinarily flowed from a contract were enough to remove *ḥadd* liability even when a contract was materially defective and even when the social-moral consequences were significant. For example, he held that no *ḥadd* liability for *zinā* would result from a marriage between two close relatives, even though he otherwise viewed incestuous relations as extremely odious. For him,

[72] Ibid. (*ghayr muttafaqa*).

[73] Ibid. (*wajaba 'l-tawaqquf ḥattā yuʿlam aṣl al-khabar*).

[74] Ibid. (*laysa fīh annah aqbaḍah iyyāhā*).

[75] For similar arguments with respect to defamation and other crimes, see ibid., 11:5987–90 (noting, for example, that someone accused of defamation for alleging that a woman committed *zinā* (at time A) although she did not actually commit it until sometime later (at time B) would have *ḥadd* liability canceled by the woman's subsequent actions rendering the criminal elements for defamation – including falsity of the statement – incomplete).

such unions proceeded with the *form* of a marital union, which created the *semblance of a contract* (*shubhat al-ʿaqd*). Even though this type of contract was defective and thus voidable (*fāsid*), the contractual semblance was enough to defeat criminal liability for *zinā* (defined as sex outside of a marriage contract).

Ordinarily, the early Islamic law of contract provided protection from liability for defective commercial transactions entered into under the mistaken belief that any subsequent acts were carried out under color of a valid contract. The semblance of a contract sufficed to absolve liability even for improper transactions, as long as the defect was subsequently corrected. Abū Ḥanīfa extended this commercial law norm to family law, then further extended it to provide protection against criminal liability as well. In this example, the semblance of a contract would exculpate a couple from criminal liability for *zinā*, even if they knew that they were not valid marriage partners in the first place.[76] By deeming knowledge of the defect irrelevant to *ḥadd* liability, Abū Ḥanīfa designated a place of primacy to the enforcement of contract law over that of criminal law.

He applied a similar logic to the question of legality concerning a merchant having sexual relations with a slave woman held temporarily, on security. Traditional Islamic commercial law considered slaves to be a form of property, thus allowing debtors to entrust slave women to their creditors to guarantee payment of debt. As with monetary guarantees, ownership in such cases devolved to the creditor only in case of default and only following certain judicial procedures. A separate rule permitted master-slave sexual relations,[77] on the notion that the master-slave relationship created a semblance of a contractual family law association that, like a marriage contract, established legal entitlements to sexual enjoyment in cases of mutual consent.[78] But the permissive rule about master-slave

[76] Ibn Nujaym, *Ashbāh*, 1:128 (noting Abū Ḥanīfa's rule of *ḥadd* avoidance by "contractual doubt: *shubhat al-ʿaqd*," even when the contracting parties knew of the illegality and did not claim a mistake).

[77] For the basic regulations of sexual permissions within the context of marriage and of slavery in classical Islamic family law, see Chapter 2, n. 6.

[78] Kecia Ali raises questions about whether this entitlement (which, like ownership in general, is termed *milk*) falls under slave or property law on the one hand or contract law in the context of Islamic family law on the other hand within the classical sources themselves. Her reading aligns with the former (that the entitlement falls under slave or property law). See Kecia Ali, *Marriage and Slavery in Early Islam* (Cambridge, MA: Harvard University Press, 2010), 37–40, 44–46, 63–64, and passim (concluding that the Islamic laws of marriage and slavery were often considered forms of male ownership and authority over women). A more sophisticated view from the sources for early Islamic law is the latter (that the entitlement falls under contract or

relations did not apply to slave women held on security, because there was no full master-slave relationship.

What of cases where the creditor mistakenly believed that it was legal for him to have intimate relations with the slave woman he was holding on guaranty? Here Abū Ḥanīfa's treatment of criminal law and family law becomes extremely interesting. When discussing *criminal law*, Abū Ḥanīfa – like other jurists – held that the creditor would incur *ḥadd* liability because he had no legal basis to justify his actions. But when discussing *commercial law*, Abū Ḥanīfa considered this same scenario to be a case of *ḥadd*-averting doubt! In his view, the deposit-loan agreement created the semblance of a contract, which conferred on the creditor at least partial ownership of and therefore a legal basis, along with consent, to be intimate with the slave woman. This contractual semblance in turn provided a legal basis for his mistaken belief in his authority within a (temporary) master-slave relationship to licitly have sex with the slave woman.[79]

These examples illustrate how, for Abū Ḥanīfa, a single case could have two aspects – one criminal and the other commercial – and that the two

family law), based in part on the fact that *milk* – often translated as ownership or possession – linguistically refers to a legitimate right of access or "entitlement." See Ibn Manẓūr, *Lisān al-ʿArab*, 6:92 (s.v. "m-l-k"). The term has been used as such in legal terminology for marriage and other contexts. See Ṭabarī, *Tafsīr*, 8:151–65 (discussing the active and passive readings of *iḥṣān* as applied to *muḥṣanāt* or *muḥṣināt* in Qur'ān 4:3, 4:23, 4.24, 5:5, 5:25, 24:4, and 24:33). Motzki has argued – following Ṭabarī – that the Qur'ān provides evidence for this view. Qur'ān 4:24 permits men to have sexual relations (or marriage) with women considered *milk al-yamīn*, a term that refers to women over whom men have acquired a contract that gives rise to a relationship of *milk*, that is, a master-slave relationship. Qur'ān 24:33 forbids slave masters from forcing slave women into having sexual relations. Put together, these verses indicate that the master-slave relationship creates a status through which sexual relations *may become licit*, provided both parties consent. In other words, those called *milk al-yamīn* are *eligible* for marriage (or sexual relations) just as are free, believing women. Both require a further consensual agreement and neither category of woman can be forced to have sex without her consent – a condition whose violation the sources see as tantamount to the crime of *zinā* and/or rape. In sum, these rules render the validation of master-slave sexual relations more akin to family law under the rubric of contract law than to slave law under the rubric of property law. For a slightly different analysis of these same issues in terms of the Ḥanafī law of contracts as "commercial" versus "social" exchange, see Baber Johansen, "The Valorization of the Human Body in Muslim Sunnī Law," in *Law and Society in Islam*, ed. Baber Johansen, Amy Singer, and Devin Stewart (Princeton, NJ: Markus Wiener, 1996), 71–112, especially 75–85.

79 This rule of Abū Ḥanīfa is explained in Ibn al-ʿAlāʾ al-Anṣārī (d. 786/1384–5), *al-Fatāwā al-Tātārkhāniyya*, ed. Sajjād Ḥusayn (Karachi: Idārat al-Qur'ān wa'l-ʿUlūm al-Islāmiyya, 1990–), 5:108–16 (discussing the differences in the rules *fī kitāb al-rahn* and *fī kitāb al-ḥudūd*); Ibn ʿĀbidīn, *al-Radd al-muḥtār ʿalā 'l-Durr al-mukhtār*, ed. ʿĀdil Aḥmad ʿAbd al-Mawjūd and ʿAlī Muḥammad Muʿawwaḍ (Beirut: Dār al-Kutub al-ʿIlmiyya, 1994–98), 12:61–84; Ibn Nujaym, *Ashbāh*, 1:128; see also Qāḍī Khān, *Fatāwā*, 3:480–89.

could be governed by distinct sets of laws with differing legal outcomes. On the one hand, Islamic *criminal* law generally defines *zinā* as sexual relations between two people in the absence of a valid legal relationship, as between an unrelated man and woman, between siblings, or between a slave master and a slave woman of whom the master has only partial ownership. On the other hand, Islamic *commercial* law validates such relations whenever there is a contract or, according to Abū Ḥanīfa, the semblance of one. In such cases, when competing areas of law yielded contradictory legal rulings, Abū Ḥanīfa privileged contract law, voiding *ḥadd* liability and espousing a rule of *ḥudūd* avoidance on the basis of the doubt created by the semblance of a contract.

Abū Ḥanīfa's privileging of contract law led him to espouse a general rule of *ḥudūd* avoidance in criminal cases involving contracts, even if known to be defective. He thus expanded the meaning of "doubt" to cover contracts for sex that other jurists would have considered prostitution.[80] Further, he extended this rule to cover cases in which marriages that were valid in non-Ḥanafī schools provided a semblance of a contract that, although invalid in Ḥanafī law, was a sufficient basis for Ḥanafī jurists to identify doubt that would caution avoidance of *ḥudūd* sanctions.[81] In all of these cases, Abū Ḥanīfa directed judges to avoid *ḥudūd* punishments on the basis of contract law.

3. Early Ḥanafī Doubt: Focus on Context and Contracts

For early Ḥanafīs, the juristic debates were not about leniency per se. Abū Ḥanīfa and other early jurists were concerned with delineating circumstances warranting either *ḥudūd* enforcement or *ḥudūd* avoidance. In the course of reviewing the early Ḥanafī jurisprudence of doubt, it becomes clear that Abū Ḥanīfa's approach to criminal law was informed by interpretive principles that were pragmatically textualist and that

[80] Most other jurists – including Abū Ḥanīfa's two companions, many mainstream Ḥanafīs, and members of other legal schools – rejected this approach. See, for example, Qudūrī, *Tajrīd*, 11:5908–909; Ibn Nujaym, *al-Baḥr al-rā'iq*, 5:16.

[81] On the same logic, marriages validated in non-Ḥanafī schools gave rise to instances of *ḥadd*-averting doubt, not because Ḥanafīs recognized the validity of those marriages on bases that gave rise to reasonable mistakes of law, but because those types of marriages could yield the semblance of a marriage contract. Specifically enumerated are marriages without witnesses (which were permitted according to a Mālikī rule), temporary marriages (which were permitted according to an early Meccan opinion attributed to Ibn ʿAbbās, shared by the Shīʿa), or sexual relations with a slave woman with the permission of her master (which were permitted, again, according to an early Meccan rule). See Ibn Nujaym, *Ashbāh*, 1:128.

placed primacy squarely on some competing social-moral values over others. In particular, he was so oriented toward vindicating private agreements that he essentially placed contracts on par with foundational texts. By viewing contracts as another type of validating "text," Abū Ḥanīfa's privileging of commercial law instruments vastly expanded the scope of *ḥudūd* avoidance in his jurisprudence.

Abū Ḥanīfa's rulings did not always set the norm for his school.[82] To the contrary, dissent from his doctrines was so regular a feature of Ḥanafī law, and disagreement among his disciples so common, that after the second/eighth century, Ḥanafism seems to be largely the legal legacy of one of his disciples, Muḥammad al-Shaybānī (d. 189/804).[83] Nevertheless, all those who subscribed to Ḥanafism in that period and afterward are fairly deemed Ḥanafī, inasmuch as Abū Ḥanīfa's students shared a sense of school affiliation and an interpretive technique, even when they differed from the conclusions of their teacher and of each other.[84]

[82] Only a minority of later Ḥanafīs followed Abū Ḥanīfa's views on contractual doubt (*shubhat al-ʿaqd*), often implicitly. Qudūrī, for example, indicates that he would adopt that category in discussions where he agrees with Abū Ḥanīfa's positions in illustrative cases involving contractual doubts (for example, for *ḥudūd* avoidance in cases of prostitution and of marrying a prohibited partner (*maḥram*)). See Qudūrī, *Tajrīd*, 11:5901–07. Other jurists seem to accept contractual doubt as a mistake of law (*shubhat al-maḥall*), which is regarded as a type of *ḥadd*-averting *legal* doubt and therefore sometimes called *shubha ḥukmiyya*. See, for example, Zaylaʿī, *Tabyīn al-ḥaqāʾiq*, 3:566. Still others accepted contractual doubt outright, identifying it as marital ambiguity (*shubhat al-nikāḥ* or *shubhat al-milk*). These jurists adopted Abū Ḥanīfa's rule that *ḥadd* liability is canceled in cases of incestuous marriage. See Kāsānī (d. 587/1191), *Badāʾiʿ al-ṣanāʾiʿ fī tartīb al-sharāʾiʿ*, ed. Aḥmad Mukhtār ʿUthmān (Cairo: Zakariyyā ʿAlī Yūsuf, 1968), 9:4150 (defining types of doubt according to categories of contract: *ḥaqīqat al-milk* versus *shubhat al-milk*, *ḥaqq al-milk* or *ḥaqīqat al-nikāḥ* versus *shubhat al-nikāḥ*, and *shubhat al-ishtibāh fī mawḍiʿ al-ishtibāh fī ʾl-milk waʾl-nikāḥ*).

[83] To reflect the often radically divergent opinions of Abū Ḥanīfa and his students, Christian Lange introduces the idea of two separate currents of Ḥanafism – followers of Abū Ḥanīfa and followers of Abū Yūsuf and Shaybānī – on the issue of male sodomy; he refers to these currents as the "pro-*ḥadd*" and "anti-*ḥadd*" factions. Lange, *Justice*, 201. Aside from specific areas of convergence and divergence, Ḥanafīs after the early period typically referred to the six books authored by Shaybānī, collectively called *ẓāhir al-riwāya* (that is, *al-Mabsūṭ*, *al-Jāmiʿ al-kabīr*, *al-Jāmiʿ al-ṣaghīr*, *al-Siyar al-kabīr*, *al-Siyar al-ṣaghīr*, and *al-Ziyādāt*), as the authoritative positions of the Ḥanafī school. See Maḥmaṣānī, *Falsafat al-tashrīʿ*, 45–48.

[84] Tsafrir, *Early Spread of Ḥanafism*, xi. In recognition of the divergent strands and our incomplete knowledge of early Ḥanafī doctrines, Tsafrir calls those associated with second/eighth-century Ḥanafism a "Ḥanafī circle" rather than a "Ḥanafī school." She dates the onset of a "school" to a period between the third/ninth century – marked by the Ḥanafīs' collaboration with the government in the Inquisition about the createdness of the Qurʾān (*miḥna*) – and the fourth/tenth century – with the elaboration of Ḥanafī legal theory (*uṣūl al-fiqh*). Ibid., xii–xiii.

Significantly, one of the internal disagreements among Ḥanafī jurists cast the commercial law aspect of Abū Ḥanīfa's doubt jurisprudence into relief. His two most prominent students, Abū Yūsuf and Shaybānī, objected strenuously, for instance, to the idea of *ḥadd*-averting "contractual doubt," as did most subsequent Ḥanafīs.[85] For them, a marriage contract between close relatives was not just defective and void*able* (*fāsid*); it was per se *void* (*bāṭil*), because the two parties were ineligible to enter into the contract in the first place.[86] In other words, the prohibition against incest means that any agreement purporting to create a marriage contract between close relatives is not legally cognizable and *ḥudūd* punishments for *zinā* must be enforced.[87] To say otherwise would amount to "playing with the law" and playing with Muslim scripture itself, according to one scholar.[88]

Subsequent Ḥanafīs followed one of the two Ḥanafī currents – typically adopting definitions of doubt attributed to Abū Ḥanīfa or to his two principal students. While these Ḥanafīs continued to assess whether *ḥudūd* enforcement was warranted, they invoked the doubt canon early and often. Recall that the first known attribution of the canon to the Prophet comes from the pen of the Ḥanafī jurist Jaṣṣāṣ (d. 370/981).[89] Indeed, virtually all Ḥanafīs thereafter firmly accepted the doubt canon as prophetic. They disagreed only about how expansively the canon applied, in line with the two currents of Ḥanafī thought on questions of *ḥadd* liability, usually on a case-by-case basis. By the fifth/eleventh century, illustrious Ḥanafī jurists such as Qudūrī (d. 428/1037) and Sarakhsī (d. 483/1090) had begun to transform the case-by-case determinations of *ḥudūd* avoidance into a systematic discourse about doctrines of doubt through delineating model cases giving rise to *ḥudūd* avoidance.

85 See Ibn Nujaym, *Ashbāh*, 1:128. For more discussion on the role that these "two companions," together with a third student, Zufar b. al-Hudhayl, played in forming Ḥanafī doctrine, see Tsafrir, *Early Spread of Ḥanafism*, 20–36.

86 In fact, jurists such as Ibn al-Humām insisted that there are only two types of *shubha*: mistake of law (*shubha fī 'l-maḥall* or *shubha ḥukmiyya*) and mistake of fact (*shubha fī 'l-fiʿl* or *shubhat al-ishtibāh*). Ibn al-Humām, *Fatḥ al-qadīr* (Beirut: Dār Ṣādir, 1972?), 5:249–52; 5:253 (rejecting Abū Ḥanīfa's category of contractual doubt (*shubhat al-ʿaqd*)). Compare Ibn Nujaym, *al-Baḥr al-rāʾiq*, 5:5.

87 See Ibn Nujaym, *al-Baḥr al-rāʾiq*, 5:16 (discussing contracts for incestuous marriages, incestuous master-slave relations, and temporary contracts for sex).

88 Ibn Abī al-ʿIzz, *Tanbīh*, 4:148.

89 Jaṣṣāṣ, *Aḥkām al-Qurʾān*, 3:330. For discussion, see Chapter 2, note 31 and accompanying text.

Notably, the fifth/eleventh-century period leading up to Qudūrī's, Sarakhsī's, and other Ḥanafī jurists' formulations of their school's doctrine was a time of increased adherence to school-specific doctrines and expansion of those doctrines through juridical commentaries and glosses. This increase in adherence to school-specific doctrines and interpretive principles is also known in contemporary scholarship on Islamic legal history as the "regime of *taqlīd*."[90] Many contemporary scholars had long tagged *taqlīd* as nothing more than "blind imitation" and pejoratively dubbed the fourth/tenth century a period of stagnation and of the "closing of the gates of *ijtihād*."[91] But more recent scholarship on Islamic legal history has sought to reevaluate the definition and function of *taqlīd*, seeing it as a doctrine meant to ensure the rule of law in much the same way that common law precedent does. That is, against the backdrop of a disintegrating center of authority in the late ʿAbbāsid empire of the fifth/eleventh century, *taqlīd* meant adherence to particular legal doctrines and interpretive methods within increasingly corporatized legal schools. In short, *taqlīd* was a way for Muslim jurists to secure the legal stability, continuity, and predictability needed for a functioning legal system that a radically decentralized and delegitimized state could not assure.[92]

Whatever the precise sociolegal function of the regime of *taqlīd*, the end of the founding period that heralded it in certainly accompanied more systematization of Islamic law. It was at that point that the disciplines of *ḥadīth* studies, substantive law (*fiqh*), jurisprudence (*uṣūl al-fiqh*), and theology (*kalām*) became professionalized disciplines – now constituted by scholars operating in distinct, self-identifying groups, each with developed doctrines and particular methodological principles. During this period, the

[90] See Jackson, *Islamic Law and the State*, xx–xxii, 81–88.

[91] See, for example, Maḥmaṣānī, *Falsafat al-tashrīʿ*, 105–107 (noting that jurists had come to a tacit consensus in the early fourth/tenth century on the "closing of the doors of *ijtihād*," which led to societal retrogression and stagnation that manifested in the law in a dogged reliance on abridged law manuals (*mukhtaṣars*)); Schacht, *Introduction*, 70–71; Fazlur Rahman, *Islam*, 2nd ed. (Chicago: University of Chicago Press, 1979) (orig. London, 1966), 77–78; J. N. D. Anderson, *Law Reform in the Muslim World* (London: Athlone Press, 1976), 7.

[92] See Wael Hallaq, "Was the Gate of *Ijtihād* Closed?" *International Journal of Middle East Studies* 16, 1 (1984), 3–41; Hallaq, "On the Origins of the Controversy About the Existence of Mujtahids and the Gate of *Ijtihād*," *Studia Islamica* 63 (1986), 129–41; Mohammad Fadel, "The Social Logic of *Taqlīd* and the Rise of the *Mukhtaṣar*," *Islamic Law and Society* 3, 2 (1996), 195–233; Sherman Jackson, "*Taqlīd*, Legal Scaffolding and the Scope of Legal Injunctions in Post-Formative Theory: *Muṭlaq* and *ʿĀmm* in the Jurisprudence of Shihāb al-Dīn al-Qarāfī," *Islamic Law and Society* 3, 2 (1996), 165–92; Jackson, *Islamic Law and the State*, 81–88.

radical legal and theological pluralism of Islam's early period was reduced to the relatively few known, enduring schools of Islamic law and theology.[93] Also during this period, the doubt canon remained the central governing principle of criminal law, except that it was no longer an outgrowth of loosely defined judicial practice. Instead, Ḥanafī jurists – to take the example under discussion here – recognized three specific categories of uncertainty to which the doubt canon applied by repeating and offering rationales for the early cases, in the course of offering textual bases for the canon and for the rules of their doubt jurisprudence. Once they had come to some broad settlement on meanings of doubt during the age of *taqlīd*, Ḥanafī jurists next moved into a phase in which they further distilled these principles of Islamic law in collections of legal maxims beginning in the tenth/sixteenth century. These developments are taken up in the next chapter.

B. EARLY MĀLIKĪ CRIMINAL LAW

In approaching questions of *ḥudūd* avoidance and enforcement, early Mālikīs invoked the doubt canon much more liberally than did Ḥanafīs and their colleagues from other schools. Their liberal invocation of the doubt canon is striking, because the canon seems better known for its Iraqi usage, while Mālik lived in the Ḥijāz and his students spread first to Egypt and Andalusia.[94] Nevertheless, Mālik unmistakably rooted his doubt jurisprudence firmly in his view that the prophetic Sunna was reflected in Medinan practice (*ʿamal*).[95] For him, that practice meant that determinations of *ḥadd* liability turned in significant part on evidentiary matters in

93 On the proliferation of dozens, if not hundreds, of Islamic legal schools in the earliest period, see George Makdisi, *Rise of Colleges: Institutions of Learning in Islam and the West* (Edinburgh: Edinburgh University Press, 1981), 2–4 (noting approximately 500 proto-Sunnī schools, most of which slowly died out by the third/ninth century). On the coalescence of some five Sunnī schools, see Maḥmaṣānī, *Falsafat al-tashrīʿ*, 325–76.

94 Maribel Fierro posits that Iraqi Ḥanafīs brought the doubt canon into circulation and remained its greatest champions. See Fierro, "When Lawful Violence Meets Doubt," 222–26.

95 For overview of Mālikī law and the doctrine of relying on the "practice of the people of Medina" as the determinant of the Sunna, see Umar Faruq Abd-Allah Wymann-Landgraf, *Mālik and Medina: Islamic Legal Reasoning in the Formative Period* (Leiden: Brill, 2013) (revised version of his *Mālik's Concept of ʿAmal in the Light of Mālikī Legal Theory*, PhD diss., University of Chicago, 1978); Yasin Dutton, *Original Islam: Malik and the Madhhab of Madina* (London: Routledge, 2007); Yasin Dutton, "*ʿAmal* v. *Ḥadīth* in Islamic Law: The Case of *Sadl al-Yadayn* (Holding One's Hands by One's Sides) When Doing the Prayer," *Islamic Law and Society* 3, 1 (1996), 13–40; Mohammad Fadel, *Adjudication in the Mālikī Madhhab: A Study of Legal Process in Medieval Islamic Law* (PhD diss., University of Chicago, 1995).

the courtroom, which led him and his students often to direct judges to *find* doubt through a process of judicial investigation.

1. *Ḥudūd* Enforcement

To determine questions of *ḥudūd* enforcement, Mālik focused on *mens rea*, proof of which he held to require a mix of subjective and objective indicia of intent. While subjective facts such as ignorance or mistake could provide valid excuses, Mālik typically required defendants to prove them.

a. Mens Rea*: Quasi-Objective Indicia of Intent*

Circumstantial evidence often provided quasi-objective indicia of criminal intent, regarding which Mālik placed the burden on the accused to demonstrate innocence or on the judge to find doubt. In defamation cases, Mālik held that implicitly defamatory statements would trigger full *ḥadd* liability.[96] Liability would attach, for example, to one man saying to another, "*I* am not the promiscuous one."[97] Local language conventions made it clear that the speaker was implying that the addressee was promiscuous.[98] Moreover, Mālik found his conclusion to be backed by a Medinan precedent. During the reign of the second caliph, ʿUmar b. al-Khaṭṭāb, one man reportedly told another, "By God, *my* mother and father were not promiscuous." When ʿUmar asked about the statement in adjudicating a defamation accusation, the speaker said he had simply been praising his parents. ʿUmar responded that there were better ways to praise and flogged him.[99] Similarly, if a man called another *mukhannath*, which typically means "effeminate," Mālik held that the speaker became *ḥadd*-eligible, because the conventional meaning of the word was defamatory. The speaker could avoid criminal liability by swearing an oath that he did not mean the statement in a derogatory way. Or he could swear that he meant to pay a spiritual compliment, with *mukhannath* referring to being "bent or impotent before God" – so long as the claim was somewhat

[96] Saḥnūn, *Mudawwana*, 7:2429 (reporting Mālik's saying that *fī 'l-taʿrīḍ al-ḥadd kāmilan*).

[97] Ibid. (*mā anā bi-zān*).

[98] Ibid. Some of these rules reflected and implicitly preserved status hierarchies based on ethnic groups. Thus, Mālik held that if a person addressed an Arab man with "O Abyssinian!" (that is, Black man), he would be *ḥadd*-eligible because the term amounted to placing the addressee outside of his own "race" or "group" (*jins*, literally: genus) – the equivalent of denying his lineage, which Arabs diligently recorded. But if the addressee were a client of another tribe with non-Arab origins (*mawlā*) and was called a Berber, a Persian, a Roman, or a Nabatean, this would incur no *ḥadd* liability. Ibid., 7:2435.

[99] Mālik, *Muwaṭṭa'*, 2:392.

plausible.[100] Thus, a judge might accept an oath if the target of the statement was in fact effeminate or soft-spoken (*ta'annuth*, *līn*, *istirkhā'*). But if the addressee had none of those characteristics, the judge was to reject the oath and enforce the *ḥadd* punishment, based on an objective evaluation of the evidence rather than implausible statements made to avoid punishment.[101] In all of these cases, it was as if the circumstantial factors created a rebuttable presumption of guilt – the removal of which hinged on plausible claims of noncriminal intent.

Consider another example: rape. Mālik deemed rape to be a strict liability offense – where claims of mistake or lack of *mens rea* provided no excuse.[102] But Mālik also took pregnancy to provide unambiguous circumstantial evidence of sex and left it to an unmarried pregnant woman to prove rape in order to avoid criminal liability for illicit sex outside of marriage.[103] As in common law contexts, in Islamic law contexts rape was notoriously hard to prove. It required evidence of force, such as indications that the woman had been crying or had called for help during the act.[104] Mālikī reliance on circumstantial evidence resulted in a virtually impossible burden for the victim to meet, turning rape law on its head.[105]

What explains his jurisprudence? In short, Mālik's approach to *ḥudūd* liability centered on his Medinan practice-based understanding of Sunna.

[100] That (*mukhannath bi-'llāh*) is another conventional, but less frequent, usage. See Edward W. Lane, *Arabic-English Lexicon* (Cambridge: Islamic Texts Society, 1984) (orig. London: Williams and Norgate, 1863), 1:814–15 (s.v. "kh-n-th").

[101] Saḥnūn, *Mudawwana*, 7:2440.

[102] Ibid., 7:2444 (equating sex with a sleeping or insane woman to rape, according to 'Alī b. Abī Ṭālib, Ibn Mas'ūd, Sulaymān b. Yasār, Rabī'a, and 'Aṭā').

[103] See ibid., 7:2465 (noting that reliable two-witness testimony of *ḥadd* liability trumps victim testimony attempting to avoid such liability).

[104] For a review and critique of the force requirement in common law contexts, see, for example, Kit Kinports, "Rape and Force: The Forgotten *Mens Rea*," *Buffalo Criminal Law Review* 4 (2001), 755–99; Susan Estrich, *Real Rape: How the Legal System Victimizes Women Who Say No* (Cambridge, MA: Harvard University Press, 1987), 57–71 (critiquing the old "force" standard in rape cases). For similar observations on modern applications of Islamic law in Pakistan, see Quraishi, "Her Honor: An Islamic Critique of the Rape Laws of Pakistan," 287–320.

[105] The standard does not always seem to have been as high as Mālikīs came to regard it. See, for example, Mālik, *Muwaṭṭa'*, 2:390; Appendix B, case no. 14 and accompanying citations (reporting an early case in which 'Umar had ruled that there was no *ḥadd* liability for a woman who came to him crying and claiming to have been raped); Appendix B, case no. 15 (depicting the Prophet [*sic*; more likely, a Baghdādī governor] avoiding the *ḥadd* punishment for both the alleged perpetrator and the victim, without requiring strong evidence).

For criminal law, that meant heavy reliance on circumstantial evidence, which created rebuttable presumptions of guilt alleviated by judicial findings of doubt.

b. Criminal Elements and Convention

In defining other criminal elements, Mālik characteristically looked to the practice of the people of Medina. For him, Medinan practice – rather than *ḥadīth* authenticity – was the best arbiter of confusions surrounding the content of the Sunna, even in determining *ḥudūd* liability.[106] For example, he drew on practice-based definitions of Sunna to define *zinā* as sexual intercourse between a man and a woman. On that notion, anal sex with a woman was *zinā*, but bestiality was not; and the former would incur *ḥadd* liability while the latter would not.[107]

Weighing in on the drinking debate, Mālik defined the prohibition of *khamr* to include any intoxicating beverage. He cited the report that "any intoxicant is wine" and further looked to Medinan practice to affirm it.[108] Consistent with his permissive admission of either direct or circumstantial evidence, Mālik held that criminal liability for drinking attached when the accused confessed, or when witnesses testified that they had seen a defendant drinking or smelled intoxication on his breath.[109]

Like Abū Ḥanīfa, Mālik also adopted a rule of finality – this time to bar intervention rather than repentance. He cited the *Case of Ṣafwān* for the proposition that *ḥadd* liability was due whenever the criminal elements were proved. And because he believed the definitions of and evidence for crimes to be clear from the practice of the people in Medina, whenever

[106] Like Shāfiʿī, Mālik sought to bring order to the growing chaos brought about by disputed views of the Sunna on the basis of conflicting *ḥadīth* and some of the Iraqi juristic opinions that – in his view – could not claim to be rooted in the Sunna, based as they were in *ra'y* without the benefit of Medinan practice. For further discussion, see El Shamsy, *From Tradition to Law*, 10. For a discussion of Mālik's limitations on variant opinions that emerge from Ḥanafī-style *ra'y*, see ibid., 24–28. For a discussion of the differences between Shāfiʿī and Mālik on substantive areas of law (mostly noncriminal), revealing their interpretive differences vis-à-vis *ḥadīth*, see Shāfiʿī, *Umm*, ed. Rifʿat Fawzī ʿAbd al-Muṭṭalib ([Mansoura]: Dār al-Wafā', 2008), 8:513–779 (*kitāb ikhtilāf Mālik wa'l-Shāfiʿī*).

[107] Saḥnūn, *Mudawwana*, 7:2420 (on bestiality).

[108] Ibid., 7:2459–60 (quoting Ibn al-Qāsim).

[109] Ibid., 7:2459. Compare Ibn Rushd al-Jadd, *Bayān*, 16:324–25 (noting that minor or false conflicts in evidence for some crimes would not serve to absolve criminal liability – as when two witnesses testified that they saw a man drinking an intoxicant but disagreed as to whether it was *nabīdh* or *khamr* – in which case Mālikīs would regard the elements of the crime to have been satisfied either way).

quasi-objective indications of criminal intent were proved, *ḥadd* liability attached, and no intervention was allowed.[110]

2. *Ḥudūd* Avoidance

a. *Defining Criminal Elements*

When assessing the contours of criminal liability and of doubt, Mālik considered many of the same questions that faced Abū Ḥanīfa and other early jurists. Some are by now familiar. Doubt about the propriety of a man having sex with a jointly owned slave woman meant no *ḥadd* liability.[111] Similarly, for accusations of theft, doubt about ownership meant no *ḥadd* liability.[112] The same went for spouses who stole from each other in a house they shared, or servants who stole from their masters when they had free access to the house.[113] In all of these cases, Mālik identified a *plausible* doubt as to whether the accused had a legitimate – albeit erroneous – justification for his or her actions as a valid basis for invoking the doubt canon.[114]

For Mālik, any deficiency in the elements necessary to complete a crime (that is, "elemental doubt") voided criminal liability. Thus, he held that there was no *ḥadd* liability for mere attempts. For example, no *ḥadd* liability would apply to a thief who gathered materials with the clear intention to take someone else's property but did not remove them from a secure location (that is, mere attempt); to a man found with an alcoholic drink in his hands who was not actually observed sipping the beverage; or to a couple discovered alone in a compromising position who did not actually have sex.[115] For Mālik, the actors in all of these

110 Mālik, *Muwaṭṭa'*, 2:397 (citing *Ṣafwān's Case*).

111 See ibid. (discussing sexual relations between master and slave, when the man shares ownership of the slave with a business partner). Compare ʿUtbī, in Ibn Rushd al-Jadd, *Bayān*, 16:165, defining this instance as *ḥadd*-averting doubt – *yuqaddar bi-hādhihi 'l-shubha wa-duri'a ʿanh al-ḥadd bihā fa-kharajat min an takūn jināya* – because of the uncertainty regarding the views of early scholars Ibn al-Qāsim and Saḥnūn on the basic precept (*aṣl*) as to whether joint ownership (*sharika*) created doubt.

112 Ibid., 2:293 (citing instances of a father taking his son's or daughter's belongings).

113 Mālik, *Muwaṭṭa'*, 2:402–404, calling it fraud (*khalsa* or *khiyāna*) rather than theft.

114 See, for example, ibid., 2:393 ("The *ḥadd* is averted by [the permission given]: *duri'a ʿanh al-ḥadd bi-dhālik*" in the case of a man who has sex with another man's slave woman with his permission; "the *ḥadd* is averted from . . . : *yudra' ʿanh al-ḥadd*" a man who has sex with his son's or daughter's slave woman); ibid., 7:2411–12 (noting that *ḥadd* liability could be removed from a man accused of having sex with another man's slave woman if he could swear an oath to establish a claim of sale or marriage that would make such relations licit – which, regardless of the truth of the claim, created doubt sufficient to avoid the *ḥadd* sanction).

115 Ibid., 2:406.

scenarios exhibited bad intents, not bad acts; and the law punished only the latter.[116]

b. Finding Doubt: The Judicial Role

Within just a few generations, Mālikī law spread to Egypt and Andalusia, bringing with it an approach to criminal law that placed evidentiary inquiry about doubt at its center.[117] Most notable was the enterprising Egyptian jurist, ʿAbd al-Raḥmān b. al-Qāsim (d. 191/806), who studied under Mālik and became the main conduit for his teachings[118] – including a rather unique approach to criminal law recorded in a treatise called the *Mudawwana*.[119]

116 Cf. Abou El Fadl, *Rebellion and Violence*, 241–44 (noting that, as the jurists developed the term, *baghy* (rebellion) did not itself connote criminal liability, particularly if rebels had a valid – if erroneous – interpretation of law (*taʾwīl*) underlying their acts).

117 Through primarily Ibn al-Qāsim and his students, Mālikī law spread from Medina to Egypt, then to North Africa and Andalusia, with some pockets of Mālikīs in Baghdad during the early period as well. For an analysis of Mālikī law in Egypt and the "oldest systematic handbook of the Mālikī school," see Jonathan Brockopp, *Early Mālikī Law*, esp. 66, quoting Joseph Schacht, "On Some Manuscripts in the Libraries of Kairouan and Tunis," *Arabica* 14 (1967), 225–58, at 240 (citing the manuscripts listed in Carl Brockelmann, *Geschichte der arabischen Litteratur* (Leiden: Brill, 1996–)). For a fuller list, see Fuat Sezgin, *Geschichte des arabischen Schrifttums* (Leiden: Brill, 1967–2007), vol. 1.

118 Ibn al-Qāsim was the main informant for both the *Mudawwana* and the *ʿUtbiyya*, which – together with the *Mawwāziyya* by Muḥammad b. al-Mawwāz al-Iskandarī (d. 269/882) and the *Kitāb al-Wāḍiḥa* of Ibn Ḥabīb (d. 238/362) – form the canonical works of Andalusian Mālikī law (*ummahāt*). Of these four works, the only two to survive are the *Mudawwana*, published as an independent work, and the *ʿUtbiyya*, quoted in Ibn Rushd al-Jadd's *al-Bayān waʾl-taḥṣīl* and preserved in part in manuscript form. For the manuscripts, see Alfonso Carmona, "The Introduction of Mālik's Teachings in al-Andalus," in Bearman et al., *The Islamic School of Law*, 41–56, at 50, n. 109 (citing bibliographies for the manuscripts in Qayrawān). The other two are available only in brief quotations in later books. See Jīdī, *Mabāḥith*, 63–66; Ana Fernández Félix, *Cuestiones legales del islam temprano: La ʿUtbiyya y el proceso de formación de la sociedad islámica andalusí* (Madrid: Consejo Superior de Investigaciones Científicas, 2003).

119 The *Mudawwana* – known as the "second source [of Mālikī law]: *al-aṣl al-thānī*" after the *Muwaṭṭaʾ* – provided the basis for judicial decisions and advisory opinions in Mālikī law. Jīdī, *Mabāḥith*, 63–66. Asad b. al-Furāt (d. 213/828) and Saḥnūn recorded the work, based on Ibn al-Qāsim's reports of Mālik's opinions along with some additions of his own. Though there is some question as to whether Asad recorded the *Mudawwana* (see Miklos Muranyi, *Die Rechtsbücher des Qairawāners Saḥnūn b. Saʿīd: Entstehungsgeschichte und Werküberlieferung* (Stuttgart: Deutsche Morgenländische Gesellschaft and F. Steiner, 1999), x, 18, 37–38), it is clear that the work was considered the most important compendium of Mālikī law in Andalusia by the first few decades of the third/ninth century. For a comprehensive review of Mālikī luminaries and doctrines from the second/eighth through fifth/eleventh

According to Ibn al-Qāsim, Mālik was the first jurist to explicitly call upon judges to investigate criminal cases with an eye to *finding doubt* and to avoiding *ḥudūd* punishments. The judge, Ibn al-Qāsim explained, was to inquire about the time and manner of an alleged offense to ensure that the accused met the technical definition of the crime before coming to a ruling on *ḥadd* liability. For support, he cited the *Case of Māʿiz*. In that case, he noted that the Prophet had asked the defendant whether he had perhaps merely "kissed or winked or looked at a woman" and "confessed" to *zinā* only because he mistakenly thought that such acts met the technical meaning of adultery.[120] Mālik understood this case to have set a precedent requiring judges to similarly query defendants about the precise circumstances surrounding alleged crimes, investigating each case for the presence of *ḥadd*-averting doubt.[121]

Ibn al-Qāsim further explained that judicial investigation of doubt should focus on issues of evidence and *mens rea*. In matters of evidence, Ibn al-Qāsim advised judges to readily set aside statements from initial witnesses, given the ever-present specter of false testimony.[122] Thus, if two witnesses testified against a man accused of theft, but two other witnesses then testified that someone else was the culprit, this created a doubt by which the judge should avoid the *ḥadd* punishment.[123] In a similar vein, if a thief confessed to stealing but claimed to have only a single silver coin of the stolen money left, the thief could receive a discretionary punishment,

centuries based on manuscript evidence from the Qayrawān Library, see Muranyi, *Beiträge zur Geschichte der Ḥadīt und Rechtsgelehrsamkeit der Mālikiyya in Nordafrika bis zum 5. Jh. d. H.: Bio-bibliographische Notizen aus der Moscheebibliothek von Qairawān* (Wiesbaden: Harrassowitz, 1997).

120 See Appendix B, case no. 13.

121 Saḥnūn, *Mudawwana*, 7:2463 (that is, *mā yudraʾ bih al-ḥadd ʿanh*). Thus, it may be that the value of a stolen item may not have risen to the level that would have warranted the *ḥadd* sanction of hand-amputation, though the act itself otherwise would have counted as a *ḥadd* crime.

122 *Shahādat al-zūr*, as false or coerced testimony, was a significant issue in Muslim evidentiary contexts from the earliest periods. For an analysis, see ʿAbd al-Majīd, *Ittijāhāt*, 549–50. Likewise, false testimony was *the* major issue plaguing analogous medieval Christian contexts of proof, accounting for many of the shifting procedures of the criminal trial. See Whitman, *Reasonable Doubt*, 114–16, and passim.

123 Saḥnūn, *Mudawwana*, 7:2479 (noting that if the first two witnesses were upright and spoke to the best of their knowledge, their mistake was to be overlooked, they were not to be disciplined with punitive measures for the mistake, and their testimony was to be accepted thereafter; but that if they were not known to be upright, they could receive a discretionary punishment, could be held liable for paying recompense for the cut limb if they retracted their testimony after the sentence had been carried out, and were not to be allowed to testify thereafter).

but the judge was to avoid enforcing the *ḥadd* punishment. The lack of solid evidence that the man stole the minimum of three silver coins required to complete the elements of theft created a *ḥadd*-averting doubt.[124] Finally, if a thief stole an item worth three silver coins of debased money, the judge was to avoid the *ḥadd* sanction on the basis of doubt as to whether the theft satisfied the minimum value requirement. In such cases generally, Ibn al-Qāsim explained, "I prefer to avoid the *ḥadd* sanction because of the presence of doubt."[125]

In matters of *mens rea*, Mālik required not only intent to commit a crime, but also knowledge of its illegality *and* of the *ḥadd* sanction. Accordingly, before he would attach *ḥadd* liability to two closely related individuals who married one another, Ibn al-Qāsim advised judges to ascertain whether the offenders both entered into the marriage purposefully, with knowledge that they were prohibited partners for one another, *and* were aware that they were subject to the *ḥadd* penalty of lashing as a consequence.[126] Likewise, if a couple got married during a woman's divorce waiting period, admitted to having known of the illegality of doing so, but claimed not to know that they were liable for a *ḥadd* penalty as a result, their lack of knowledge about the penalty alone created "doubt" about the presence of full *mens rea* to commit the crime. This doubt sufficed for a judge to avoid the *ḥadd* punishment.[127]

Judges were also to investigate whether an alleged criminal offender was generally ignorant about the law – in which case punishment was to be avoided. For instance, if a man gave permission to a friend to have sex with his slave woman, not knowing that it was illegal to grant such permission, judges were to avoid enforcing the *ḥadd* punishment against the slave owner because of the "doubt" about culpability created by his ignorance about the law.[128] They were also to avoid punishing the friend who had sex with the slave woman regardless of whether he believed it was legal

[124] ʿUtbī, *ʿUtbiyya*, in Ibn al-Rushd al-Jadd, *Bayān*, 16:220.

[125] Ibn al-Rushd al-Jadd, *Bayān*, 16:210 (*aḥabb ilayya an yudraʾ al-ḥadd biʾl-shubha*). For a contrary Mālikī view, see ibid. (reporting that Ibn al-Mawwāz held the opposite view).

[126] Saḥnūn, *Mudawwana*, 7:2411 (noting that marriage to classes of per se prohibited partners, if purposeful and with knowledge of the prohibition (*ʿāmidan ʿārifan biʾl-taḥrīm*), would incur *ḥadd* liability – a rule that included marriage to a fifth wife, a thrice-divorced former wife, a foster or actual sister, and a woman otherwise barred from marriage (*maḥram*)).

[127] Ibid., 7:2419 (commenting that Mālik – had he ruled on the issue – would have avoided enforcing the *ḥadd* sanction (*yudriʾ al-ḥadd*) because of the similarity to the precedent established by ʿUmar, who avoided the *ḥadd* punishment but required a man who had married a fifth wife to separate from her and ruled that the couple could never be licit to each other thereafter).

[128] Ibid., 7:2417–18 (*duriʾa ʿanh al-ḥadd biʾl-shubha*).

because the owner's purported permission created a legal basis for the friend's belief in its legality and for judges' resultant "doubt" about the propriety of punishment.[129]

The same heightened *mens rea* requirement applied to cases of alleged theft – such as situations in which a father took money from his son. Ibn al-Qāsim saw such situations as filled with doubt about the legality of the action and advised judges to apply the doubt canon.[130] He further expanded that basic rule to other contexts – finding doubt in scenarios in which theft was allegedly committed by spouses, by servants who shared their master's house, or by guests staying in a house even if the owner had locked up his or her belongings so that a guest would have had to break the lock to take them.[131] In all of these scenarios, Ibn al-Qāsim found "doubt" in the ambiguous status of ownership and access.[132] Taken together, these rules reflected Ibn al-Qāsim's view – which came to be common among later Mālikī and other jurists – that *ḥadd* liability attaches whenever there is a *lack of doubt* concerning ownership or permissibility of use.

3. Early Mālikī Doubt: Focus on Judicial Investigation

In sum, Mālik maintained that anything short of a completed crime – the elements of which were defined by "Medinan practice–based" notions of the Sunna – triggered *ḥudūd* avoidance. While he did not mention "doubt" directly, he and his followers detailed several instances of *ḥudūd* avoidance in the language of the doubt canon: "We avoid punishments in cases where ...." Ibn al-Qāsim's broad allowance for *ḥudūd* avoidance balanced the potentially harsh effects of Mālik's admission of circumstantial evidence for *ḥudūd* liability and his insistence on objective indicia of criminal intent. So did his requirement that judges investigate cases with an eye to the propriety of *ḥudūd* avoidance, which Ibn al-Qāsim translated into a requirement for judges to *find* doubt.

Ibn al-Qāsim invoked the doubt canon liberally. In the process, he expanded the scope of doubt on evidentiary and procedural grounds by creating a heightened *mens rea* requirement: identifying mistakes and

129 Ibid. (*yudra' 'anh al-ḥadd jāhilan kāna 'lladhī waṭa'a aw 'āliman* – excusing *ḥadd* liability but requiring the offender to pay the value of the slave woman).

130 Ibid., 7:2472 (*wa-qad qīla: idra'ū 'l-ḥudūd bi'l-shubahāt*).

131 Ibid., 7:2469.

132 Ibid., 7:2472 (further concluding that, while a wife who took property from a house shared with her husband would not be *ḥadd*-eligible, a wife who took her husband's property from a house other than the one they shared would).

ignorance as doubt, and specifying various types of evidentiary doubt.[133] He reportedly even once invoked the doubt canon to avoid punishment against a man suffering from extreme hunger who sold his wife to another man for the money.[134]

Other Mālikī jurists followed suit. The prominent Cordovan Mālikī jurist Muḥammad b. Aḥmad al-ʿUtbī (d. 255/869) quoted Ibn al-Qāsim extensively on issues of doubt in his writings. Other prominent Mālikī jurists of the time, including Ashhab (d. 204/819), Ibn Ḥabīb (d. 238/853), and Ibn al-Mawwāz (d. 269/882), did likewise, paying particular attention to issues of evidentiary doubt.[135] Further, we have already seen how Ibn Ḥabīb invoked the doubt canon to save his brother Hārūn from capital punishment for blasphemy.[136] These episodes were applications of the judicial rule against applying *ḥadd* sanctions except in the presence of incontrovertible evidence that all elements of a crime had been completed.

As these reports of Mālikī jurists of the first generations demonstrate, by the mid-second/eighth and third/ninth centuries, the doubt canon was a regular part of Mālikī jurisprudence and was pervasive among the highest echelons of the Muslim societies and juristic circles in which the Mālikīs operated. By the fourth/tenth century, Mālikīs also regarded the doubt canon as a sound prophetic *ḥadīth*.[137] Subsequent Mālikīs expanded on this line, from Ibn ʿAbd al-Barr and Abū al-Walīd al-Bājī of the fifth/eleventh century to the famous Ibn Rushds – the grandfather and the grandson – of the sixth/twelfth century.[138] Then and thereafter, the doubt canon featured centrally in Mālikī law as its jurists systematized

[133] See, for example, Saḥnūn, *Mudawwana*, 7:2417–18, 2459–60, 2472 (quoting Ibn al-Qāsim and citing the doubt canon).

[134] See Ibn Rushd al-Jadd, *Bayān*, 16:324–25 (reporting this story about Ibn al-Qāsim on the authority of ʿUtbī).

[135] For examples, see Ibn Abī Zayd al-Qayrawānī (d. 386/996), *al-Nawādir wa'l-ziyādāt* (Beirut: Dār al-Gharb al-Islāmī, 1999), 9:95–101 (quoting, inter alia, Ibn al-Mawwāz, *Kitāb Ibn al-Mawwāz* [= *al-Mawwāziyya*]; Ibn al-Qāsim in ʿUtbī, *ʿUtbiyya* (esp. *kitāb al-daʿwā*); and Ibn Ḥabīb, *Kitāb Ibn Ḥabīb* [= *al-Wāḍiḥa*]).

[136] See Chapter 3, notes 70–75 and accompanying text; Appendix B, case no. 4 and accompanying citations.

[137] See, for example, Ibn Abī Zayd, *Nawādir*, 9:95–101.

[138] See Ibn Rushd al-Ḥafīd, *Bidāyat al-mujtahid*, 2:324 (claiming universal consensus on the authenticity and applicability of the doubt canon as a prophetic *ḥadīth* regarding doubts on *zinā* charges). See also Qarāfī (d. 684/1285), *Anwār al-burūq fī anwāʾ al-furūq* (Beirut: Dār al-Maʿrifa, 197-?), 4:1307–309; Qarāfī, *Dhakhīra*, 12:50–51, 60 (applying the doubt canon as a *ḥadīth* and as a legal maxim of judicial practice to several cases); Ibn Farḥūn (d. 799/1396–7), *Tabṣirat al-ḥukkām*, ed. Jamāl Marʿashlī (Beirut: Dār al-Kutub al-ʿIlmiyya, 2001), 2:88; Wansharīsī, *Miʿyār*, 2:431, 4:493–95 (quoting an opinion of a judge attributing the maxim to the Prophet); Dasūqī (d. 1230/1815), *Ḥāshiya* (Cairo:

the school's methodology and, with it, developed theories of doubt presented in the legal maxims literature.[139] These later developments are addressed in the next chapter.

C. EARLY SHĀFIʿĪ CRIMINAL LAW

Shāfiʿī is a suitable ending point, because he attempted to provide a comprehensive theory of Islamic legal interpretation in response to what he deemed the inadequate approaches of the Ḥanafīs and the Mālikīs, that is, the jurists of the other principal Sunnī legal schools of his time.[140] He aimed to bring order to the growing chaos of pluralistic, divergent and often, in his view, wrong-headed statements of law espoused by his colleagues.[141]

As a former pupil-turned-critic of Mālik and of Muḥammad b. al-Ḥasan al-Shaybanı, the student of Abu Ḥanıfa, Shafiʿı's interpretive

Dār Iḥyā' al-Kutub al-ʿArabiyya, 198-?), 4:337 (*wa-qad warada 'dra'ū 'l-ḥudūd bi'l-shubahāt ...*); Ṣāliḥ b. ʿAbd al-Samīʿ al-Ābī al-Azharī, *al-Thamr al-dānī ʿalā Risālat al-Qayrawānī*, ed. Aḥmad Muṣṭafā Qāsim al-Ṭaḥṭāwī (Cairo: Dār al-Faḍīla, 2007), 617 (citing the doubt canon as a Prophetic *ḥadīth*).

139 To be sure, not all Mālikīs agreed on when to avoid punishment. Ashhab, for example, frequently disagreed with Ibn al-Qāsim in instances where the latter would have counseled punishment avoidance. For example, against Ibn al-Qāsim, Ashhab would have advocated enforcement of the punishment for theft in the case of a man taking property from his grandson, in contrast to father-from-son takings. The later Mālikī jurist Abū al-Walīd al-Bājī explained that Ashhab based his opinion on a view of the crime from the perspective of rights to the property, not the so-called doubt concerning the secure location. That is, the grandfather-thief has no obligation to provide for his grandson, so he has no claim of right to the latter's property that might offer the type of doubt to which a father could appeal to avoid *ḥadd* liability. For the same reason, Ashhab held that a son would receive the *ḥadd* punishment for theft for taking his father's goods: the son also has no claim of right that would create doubt about ownership of his father's property as he lacks an obligation to care for his father financially: *lā shubha lah fī māl al-ab [li-annah] lā nafaqa lah minh*. See Abū al-Walīd al-Bājī, *al-Muntaqā: sharḥ Muwaṭṭa' Mālik*, ed. Muḥammad ʿAbd al-Qādir Aḥmad ʿAṭā' (Beirut: Dār al-Kutub al-ʿIlmiyya, 1999), 9:232.

140 The other two principal Sunnī schools postdated Shāfiʿī by some decades: Ḥanbalism – the school of Aḥmad Ibn Ḥanbal (d. 241/855) – and Ẓāhirism – the school founded by Dāwūd al-Ẓāhirī (d. 270/883–4). The even stricter textualism of these two schools led them to largely reject the doubt canon, as outlined in Chapter 7.

141 For a discussion of interpretive trends before Shāfiʿī and the major differences between those who practiced a type of "pragmatic" reasoning (*ahl al-ra'y*) and those who relied on the text of *ḥadīth* reports as bases for law (*ahl al-ḥadīth*), see ʿAbd al-Majīd, *Ittijāhāt*, 31–92. For a more in-depth discussion of Iraqi *ra'y* as a form of systematic legal reasoning based on rational propositions and counterpropositions that generated countless hypothetical cases (*masā'il*) through which Ḥanafī law was articulated, see El Shamsy, *From Tradition to Law*, 14–24.

approach was more textualist than those of the other two schools.[142] To him, Abū Ḥanīfa was insufficiently textualist, and as a result, his associates produced multiple, contradictory opinions.[143] Likewise, Shāfiʿī found Mālik's practice-based arguments to be unacceptable. Shāfiʿī viewed the appeal to the "living tradition" of the Prophet through the practice of the people of Medina to be a weak, subjective, and provincial basis for identifying the Sunna.[144] Moreover, Shāfiʿī objected to the fact that Mālikīs also produced more than one interpretation of practice, which led to contradictory opinions within the school, thus calling into question the integrity of their methods. Most problematic for Shāfiʿī was the fact that both Ḥanafī and Mālikī approaches often conflicted with authentic reports of prophetic practice.[145]

A more objective basis for knowing the Sunna, Shāfiʿī maintained, was to look to the text of the reports of it.[146] Even on this premise, Shāfiʿī needed to devise a way of dealing with conflicting reports, such as the

142 For a useful literature review of Shāfiʿī studies and analysis of Shāfiʿī's works, see Joseph E. Lowry, *Early Islamic Legal Theory: The Risāla of Muḥammad ibn Idrīs al-Shāfiʿī* (Leiden: Brill, 2007), esp. 8–16. For discussions of Shāfiʿī's critiques of his contemporaries, see ibid., 275–318; El Shamsy, *From Tradition to Law*, 49–55 (against Mālik), 57 (against Ḥanafī *ra'y*).

143 Ḥanafīs appealed to a type of "juridical intuition" of a pragmatic-rational mind, which has been called *dhawq al-sharīʿa* (literally: "a taste for the law") and even *firāsa* (discussed in Chapter 7, section A, as "judicial acumen"). See further Ibn al-Qayyim, *Ṭuruq* (2007), 3.

144 For multiple definitions of Sunna, see ʿAbd al-Majīd, *Ittijāhāt*, esp. 11–12.

145 For discussion, see El Shamsy, *From Tradition to Law*, 29 (describing the fluidity of opinions generated by those who subscribed to legalist-minded interpretation (*ahl al-ra'y*), which created uncertainties that rankled with Shāfiʿī and the ʿAbbāsid state alike – resulting in Ibn al-Muqaffaʿ's proposal to codify the law into a single book with singular opinions), 49–50 (citing a criminal law debate to reveal the plurality of opinions in Shāfiʿī's attempt to show that "not only [had] jurists and governors – both carriers of the normative ʿ*amal* in the Mālikī framework – disagreed on individual issues, but also . . . these sources in fact contradict the Mālikī position that claims to be based on them . . . .").

146 See Majid Khadduri, introduction to *al-Imām Muḥammad ibn Idris al-Shāfiʿīs al-Risāla fī Uṣūl al-Fiqh: Treatise on the Foundations of Islamic Jurisprudence* (Cambridge: Islamic Texts Society, 1987), 42–43 ("Not only did he reject the use of sources that [he deemed un-Islamic], such as custom and personal opinion, but he also defined the method by which legal reasoning was restricted within the framework of authoritative [*ḥadīth*] sources."); El Shamsy, *From Tradition to Law*, 54 ("Al-Shāfiʿī's solution for safeguarding the integrity of the revealed message was to isolate the sacred past as a clearly defined and uniquely normative category. This past was enshrined in and accessible through verifiable reports – primarily the Qur'ān and the Sunna, of which other sources such as consensus (*ijmāʿ*) and the opinions of the Companions were derivations. The circumscribed sacred past [as contained in *ḥadīth*] thus provided an unchanging and authoritative measuring stick – a *canon* – by means of which the jurists could evaluate and categorize new cases.").

early precedents in criminal law depicting competing tendencies toward *ḥudūd* enforcement and avoidance. To that end, he introduced rules designed to systematize legal interpretation and to bring a measure of coherence to it through his book, the *Risāla*, which is widely – though incorrectly – considered the first work of Islamic legal theory or jurisprudence (*uṣūl al-fiqh*).[147] That approach translated into his substantive law rulings, as laid out in his treatise, the *Umm*, which – as it was compiled later in his life – contains and explains his most developed legal opinions.[148] These interpretive differences would have a nontrivial effect on his jurisprudence of doubt for criminal law.[149]

1. *Ḥudūd* Enforcement

As a consequence of his textualist orientation at a time before the doubt canon was a recognized "text," Shāfiʿī focused more on *ḥudūd* enforcement than on doubt when interpreting the foundational texts for Islamic criminal law. To be sure, he recognized the competing tendencies of *ḥudūd* enforcement and avoidance in earlier precedents from judicial practices reported in the *ḥadīth* collections, and he occasionally invoked the doubt canon. But it

[147] See generally Shāfiʿī, *Risāla* (discussed earlier, Chapter 2, section A); and for an English translation, see now Muḥammad b. Idrīs al-Shāfiʿī, *The Epistle on Legal Theory*, ed. and trans. Joseph Lowry (New York: New York University Press, 2013). For scholarly assertions of Shāfiʿī's influence on the Islamic jurisprudential canon, see Khadduri's introduction to *Shāfiʿī's al-Risāla*, 40 (calling him the "founder of *uṣūl al-fiqh*"); Coulson, *A History of Islamic Law*, Chapter 4 (calling him the "chief architect" of Islamic law). For the more convincing arguments against this designation, see Wael Hallaq, "Was al-Shāfiʿī the Master Architect of Islamic Jurisprudence?" *International Journal of Middle East Studies* 25, 4 (1993), 587–605, esp. 588 (arguing that Shāfiʿī's designation as "founder of *uṣūl al-fiqh* was a later creation" as "his *Risāla* had very little, if any, effect during most of the 9th century"); Joseph E. Lowry, "Does Shāfiʿī Have a Theory of 'Four Sources' of Law?" in *Studies in Islamic Legal Theory*, ed. Bernard Weiss (Leiden: Brill, 2002), 23–50; Joseph E. Lowry, *Early Islamic Legal History*, 16 ("It can no longer be sensibly maintained that Shāfiʿī founded the discipline of *uṣūl al-fiqh* or that the *Risāla* simply constitutes the first work of this discipline, because the *Risāla* is not a work of *uṣūl al-fiqh* at all."); El Shamsy, *From Tradition to Law*, 5 (arguing that Shāfiʿī's role in the gradual shift in Islamic law from oral tradition to systematic science came "in the context of and through engagement with various strands of legal thought in his age, and formed part of broader cultural and societal transformations," and that his writings merely formed one of the earliest enduring expressions of that process).

[148] See Shāfiʿī, *Umm* (2008), 7:319.

[149] For standard works that detail the formation, history, and doctrinal differences between the main Sunnī schools of thought, see generally Coulson, *History of Islamic Law*; Maḥmaṣānī, *Falsafat al-tashrīʿ*, 325–76; Christopher Melchert, *Formation of the Sunni Schools of Law*; Hallaq, *Sharīʿa*, 27–158.

was clear that, in his view, instances of doubt and *ḥudūd* avoidance were derivative of the legal framework calling for *ḥudūd* enforcement. Understanding of that framework began with the text.

a. Defining Criminal Elements

For Shāfiʿī, the text of the Qurʾān provides a starting point, if not the ending point, as in the verse commanding hand-amputation for "the thief, male or female . . . as their due for their crime, an exemplary punishment imposed by God."[150] For him, such scriptural texts were dispositive, although he held that they could be fully understood only when read alongside related, authentic prophetic reports.[151]

Shāfiʿī's treatment of the *Case of Ṣafwān* illustrates how he understood the Qurʾānic text in light of the prophetic reports. Shāfiʿī acknowledged what he regarded as the mistaken Ḥanafī and Mālikī conclusions that punishment was not due (and perhaps had not been enforced) in that case.[152] He also deemed their interpretations to have disregarded the rules governing the basic elements of theft, including elements of timing and criminal culpability. For him, the prophetic reports specified that *ḥadd* liability is established when four elements of theft are completed: (1) the taking of the minimum actionable amount of a quarter of a gold coin (*dīnār*), or its equivalent of three or ten silver coins (*dirhams*), (2) from a secure location, (3) by someone who did not own and was not otherwise entitled to the property.[153] Further, Shāfiʿī read other reports to require that (4) these elements be completed *at the time of the offense*, not subject to

150 Qurʾān, 5:38 (*al-sāriqu wa'l-sāriqatu fa-'qṭaʿū aydiyahumā jazāʾan bi-mā kasabā nakālan min Allāh* . . .). This is Shāfiʿī's "starting point" quite literally; he begins the chapter on criminal law with a citation to and discussion of this verse in the course of discussing his methodological approach generally, namely, the need to read Qurʾānic verses in light of authentic *ḥadīth*. See Shāfiʿī, *Umm* (2008), 7:319.

151 Shāfiʿī, *Umm* (2008), 7:319. Shāfiʿī rejects definitions based on the apparent meaning of the Qurʾān without reference to the traditions – rejecting, for instance, claims that *any* taking constitutes theft without regard to the traditions in which the Prophet defines theft as actionable with respect to a certain minimum value of goods stolen. See ibid., 7:325.

152 See above, Chapter 4.

153 Shāfiʿī, *Umm* (2008), 7:324, 372–73 (citing the *ḥadīth*, "Hand-cutting is due for [theft of goods worth] one-quarter of a *dīnār* or more: *al-qaṭʿ fī rubʿ dīnār fa-ṣāʿidan*"). Here, Shāfiʿī is apparently reconciling multiple *ḥadīth* reports, which state alternatively that the minimum amount is one-quarter of a gold *dīnār* or three silver *dirhams*, by equating the two; he is implicitly rejecting additional *ḥadīth* stating that the minimum amount is five or ten *dirhams*. By contrast, Abū Ḥanīfa surmised that all reports on the matter were authentic, and adopted the highest stated amount (that is, three or ten *dirhams*) as the minimum actionable amount out of a principle of precaution. For a citation of all four traditions and discussion of the dispute between Shāfiʿī and Abū Ḥanīfa, see ʿAbd al-Majīd,

revision once a judge had issued a guilty verdict and sentenced the offender.[154] For Shāfiʿī, whenever the *ḥadīth*-defined elements of theft were complete, criminal liability attached and there was no room for doubt or *ḥudūd* avoidance.

It is within this framework that Shāfiʿī interpreted *Ṣafwān's Case* to be one of *ḥudūd* liability and enforcement rather than avoidance. As Shāfiʿī understood it, the accused thief was *ḥadd*-eligible because he met the basic elements at the time of the offense: He took Ṣafwān's cloak, which presumably was worth more than one-quarter of a gold coin and to which he was not entitled, from a secure location.[155] All of these elements were completed *at the time of the crime*, notwithstanding Ṣafwān's attempt to change the element of ownership *after* the verdict by gifting the cloak to the thief.[156] In this way, Shāfiʿī used *Ṣafwān's Case* as a prophetic precedent to clarify the detailed meaning of the Qur'ānic verse on theft.

It is not that Shāfiʿī decided to favor *ḥudūd* enforcement because he had a penchant for punishment. To the contrary, he noted that the timeliness element present in *Ṣafwān's Case* could have the opposite effect, sometimes mitigating or barring punishment altogether. For example, if a slave committed theft, and his master freed him before judgment was rendered, was the slave to receive a full *ḥadd* punishment? The Qur'ān stipulated that slaves who committed crimes were liable for only half of the ordinary *ḥudūd* punishments.[157] Coupling that stipulation with the tradition-drawn timeliness rule, which led Shāfiʿī to look at the status of the offender

Ittijāhāt, 557. For the various positions, see Ṭabarī, *Tafsīr*, 3:220–22, noting that some scholars relied on the apparent meaning of the text (*ẓāhir al-āya*) to hold that no minimum value was required and that, initially, there were no *ḥadīth* in which the Prophet turned anyone away for stealing only a single *dirham*.

154 Shāfiʿī, *Umm* (2008), 7:326 (*al-ḥadd innamā wajaba yawm kāna 'l-fiʿl*), 346 (noting that a judge should always look into the status of the offender at the time of the theft: *fa-'nẓur abadan ilā 'l-ḥāl allatī yasruq fīhā 'l-sāriq*).

155 Ibid., 7:377 (extracting from this case a rule that anyone in a public place who sleeps on his belongings thereby creates a secure location for purposes of theft determination).

156 Ibid., 7:378 (noting that the *ḥadd* sanction would be due even if the stolen item was gifted to the thief before the *ḥadd* sentencing or even if the thief had gained a partial ownership interest in the stolen item). This view goes against the common understanding of *Ṣafwān's Case* – by which the Prophet's questioning of Ṣafwān as to why he did not gift the cloak to the thief before the verdict was taken as indication that a change of ownership status after the theft but before sentencing could change the sentence.

157 Ibid., 7:367. For the Qur'ānic verse legislating a half-punishment in the context of *zinā*, see Qur'ān, 4:25 ("As to slave women who become respectable married women [lit.: 'chaste through marriage'], if they commit an indecency, then they are to receive half the punishment of free married women: *fa-idhā uḥṣinna fa-in atayna bi-fāḥishatin fa-ʿalayhinna niṣfu mā ʿalā 'l-muḥṣanāti min al-ʿadhāb*").

at the time of the offense, he concluded that the recently freed ex-slave was to receive only half of the standard *ḥadd* punishment.[158]

Relatedly, Shāfiʿī concluded that slaves who stole from their masters might not be liable for punishment at all. On this point, Shāfiʿī cited an early precedent in which ʿUmar ruled that a slave could not be punished for stealing his mistress's mirror, worth eight silver coins. Shāfiʿī explained that slaves and masters take from one another's property regularly, making ownership standards unclear. More to the point, only three of the four requisite elements he identified for theft are met when slaves steal from their masters: Such scenarios included a taking, a lack of an ownership interest, and the timeliness element. But the additional element – taking from a secure location – was not met. Unlike in *Ṣafwān's Case*, in this case, the victim – the woman of the house – lived with the perpetrator and gave him free access to the household. As such, Shāfiʿī found that the criminality of the "taking" was "not free from doubt."[159] Accordingly, he determined that the act could be not be categorized as theft and at most could be regarded as fraud, dishonesty, or breach of trust – none of which meet the definition for the fixed *ḥadd* crime of theft or for its associated punishment.[160]

Another example concerns the famous drinking debate, which was particularly heated between Shāfiʿī and jurists in Iraq. Shāfiʿī agreed with jurists such as Mālik who deemed *all* intoxicating drinks to be prohibited based on the Qurʾānic prohibition of wine alongside prophetic reports to that effect.[161] Yet as Abū Ḥanīfa had made clear, many Iraqis did not regard as illegal intoxicating drinks made from dates and other substances or prepared in certain ways.[162] The latter group of jurists attempted to restrict criminal liability only to drinking to the point of intoxication, not

[158] In addition to slaves, other classes entitled to decreased or delayed *ḥudūd* punishments include pregnant women, terminally ill defendants, sickly individuals who would die if punished because of extreme heat or cold, etc. In a famous case of a terminally ill man found guilty of having committed *zinā*, the Prophet reportedly ordered that he be hit lightly twice with a plant that had fifty burrs on it – thus satisfying the formal requirement of 100 lashes. Shāfiʿī, *Umm* (2008), 7:343–45. Like all other jurists, Shāfiʿī noted that majority is a requisite element for *ḥudūd* liability, but unlike some jurists, he held that gender made no difference. See ibid., 7:374–75.

[159] Ibid., 7:382–84 (*laysa bi-ghayr shubha*).

[160] Ibid.

[161] All but the Ḥanafīs regarded the prohibition as a general one. For Shāfiʿī's view, see his *Umm* (2008), 7:365 ("Every drink that intoxicates is prohibited: *kull sharāb askara fa-huwa ḥarām*," citing multiple traditions to that effect as well as the precedent of ʿUmar, who flogged someone for drinking *ṭilāʾ*, an alcoholic beverage produced by simmering grape juice until it is reduced to one-third or one-half of its original volume).

[162] On the non-wine intoxicants *nabīdh*, *ṭilāʾ*, and *fuqqāʿ*, see note 41.

the mere drinking of a beverage that would be intoxicating in large amounts.[163] To counter this argument, Shāfiʿī cited more than two dozen reports intended to prove that the Qurʾānic prohibition of wine extends to all intoxicants.[164] By insisting that the text could resolve the debate, Shāfiʿī was taking aim at Abū Ḥanīfa and the other Iraqi jurists, whom he accused of arbitrarily permitting certain types of intoxicants in order to accommodate an Iraqi penchant for drinking in contravention of clear texts against it.

As for the punishment for intoxication, Shāfiʿī readily acknowledged that no Qurʾānic text or prophetic report stipulated a *ḥadd* punishment of eighty lashes. The early reports record the Prophet announcing a sentence of forty lashes, though incidents of actual enforcement were infrequent and ill attested.[165] ʿUmar increased the number to eighty after assuming the leadership post as caliph, because he noticed that drinking was becoming a regular phenomenon. He reasoned that "whoever drinks gets drunk, and whoever gets drunk talks nonsensically, and whoever speaks nonsensically makes defamatory remarks . . ." – for which an additional forty lashes were due.[166] In essence, ʿUmar doubled the punishment because he believed that serious harm to the public sphere would result from widespread incidents of drinking during his reign. The change stuck. Shāfiʿī's acceptance of the doubled punishment suggests that he saw ʿUmar's ruling as a legitimate textual basis for the law. That is, he counted Companions' policies such as this one to constitute *ḥadīth* reports that were foundational "texts" as authoritative as prophetic or divine legislation.[167]

In all of these cases, Shāfiʿī seems more concerned with textual fidelity and methodological consistency in the interpretation of Islamic criminal

[163] Shāfiʿī criticized Abū Ḥanīfa for relying on a *ḥadīth* with an unknown narrator in its chain to support this opinion, and accused him of ignoring the evidence that Shāfiʿī presented in the form of reports indicating a prohibition on *anything* that intoxicates. Shāfiʿī, *Umm* (2008), 7:365–66.

[164] See ibid., 7:363–66, 438–49.

[165] For example, one reported event occurred after the Battle of Ḥunayn, when the Prophet sentenced Khālid b. al-Walīd to be flogged for drinking. When Abū Bakr assumed leadership over the community following the Prophet's death, he was unaware of the precise rules on wine drinking and therefore had to ask those who were at Ḥunayn about what had transpired. When they informed him, he reportedly followed the precedent of imposing forty lashes. See Shāfiʿī, *Umm* (2008), 7:447.

[166] See ibid. Sunnī sources note that ʿUmar arrived at this decision through consultation with ʿAlī. The latter's inclusion likely follows a common practice of inserting ʿAlī into controversial decisions to serve sectarian purposes. For further discussion and a theory on the polemical use of *ḥadīth* for sectarian purposes, see Modarressi, "Early Debates," 5–39.

[167] ʿAbd al-Majīd notes that this held true for the group of traditionists (*ahl al-ḥadīth*) generally, but not for Ẓāhirīs, who regarded only prophetic statements as authoritative. See ʿAbd al-Majīd, *Ittijāhāt*, 359–61.

law than with any general policy toward enforcement or avoidance of punishment.[168] As a part of that project, he worked to identify and appeal to what he deemed authentic texts to determine matters of criminal liability. As a result, doubt – which was then merely a judicial evidentiary rule rather than a *ḥadīth* – was sidelined from his understanding of substantive criminal law.

b. Against Lenience

Shāfiʿī's interest in ascertaining textual standards for criminal law manifested starkly in his opposition to what he perceived to be a Ḥanafī tendency toward lenience. One example arose in their dispute over how to treat recidivists. For cases of repeated stealing, Ḥanafīs maintained that *ḥadd* penalties were due upon commission of a first and a second theft (that is, amputation of the right hand and then the left foot), but not for subsequent thefts.[169] They supported their position with a reading of the Qurʾānic verse on theft that took local conventions into account. That is, while the verse mentions only amputating "hands," local conventions regarded the word in question as referring to the *right* hand.[170] The punishment of amputating the left foot on a second offense came not from that verse but by way of analogy to a separate verse detailing a punishment of cross-amputation for highway robbers.[171] After a second offense, then, Ḥanafīs advised

[168] For similar arguments with respect to his general jurisprudence, see generally Lowry, *Early Islamic Legal Theory*; El Shamsy, *From Tradition to Law*. See also Khadduri, introduction to *Shāfiʿī's al-Risāla*, 43 ("Shāfiʿī's method of jurisprudence was concerned less with developing the law that existed in his age than with systematizing a body of law that had already reached a high degree of growth. Thus, in the *Risāla*, Shāfiʿī paid less attention to the problem of developing new principles of law than to the problem of how to demonstrate that all the principles and rules that existed in his time were derived from recognized Islamic sources.").

[169] Notably, the Qurʾānic verse also tolerates the opposite – amputation of the left hand and the right foot – as it does not specify which hand and foot but merely says that "hands and feet [can be] amputated from opposite sides." See Qurʾān, 5:33 (*aw tuqaṭṭaʿa aydīhim wa-arjulahum min khilāf*).

[170] See Qudūrī, *Tajrīd*, 11:6004 (noting agreement that *aydiyahumā* means *aymānihimā*, and that Ibn Masʿūd's variant reading includes the latter term), 6010–11 (analogizing to brigandage).

[171] One of the punishments for highway robbery is cross-amputation of a hand and a foot. Most jurists took this particular option to cover acts of theft committed in the course of highway robbery. See Qurʾān, 5:33 ("The penalty for those who wage war against God and His messenger, and who strive to make mischief in the land is execution, crucifixion, that their hands and feet be cut off from opposite sides, or exile: *innamā jazāʾu ʾlladhīna yuḥāribūna ʾllāha wa-rasūlahu wa-yasʿawna fī ʾl-arḍi fasādan an-yuqattalū aw yuṣallabū aw tuqaṭṭaʿa aydīhim wa-arjulahum min khilāfin aw yunfaw min al-arḍ.*"). Although the verse does not specify which hand or foot, jurists understood it to refer to the right hand and left foot – perhaps because they had in mind the theft

imprisoning a recidivist offender along with a discretionary punishment – which a judge could impose within a range of a minimum punishment of flogging to a maximum of death.[172] Yet although they allowed it, Ḥanafīs seemed to shy away from encouraging maximal punishment, or even the multiple amputations that Shāfiʿī advocated. Pragmatically, Ḥanafīs argued that to punish a recidivist repeatedly with further amputations would render the offender unable to function or to make a living, generally leading to "personal ruin."[173] Further, Ḥanafīs argued that ʿAlī and other luminaries had ruled that there was no *ḥadd* liability after a second offense.[174] ʿAlī reportedly put it this way: "I [would] feel guilty before God if I left [a thief] without the hands by which he eats or feet by which he walks."[175]

Shāfiʿī deemed this Ḥanafī reading of Qurʾānic texts and their pragmatic use of early precedents to be an unfounded basis for Islamic criminal law. First, he said, Ḥanafī jurists got this matter wrong because they departed from the requirements of detailing Islamic law on the basis of *authentic* texts. Recidivists, he maintained, were to receive the same punishments as first-time offenders, receiving a sentence for amputation of a different extremity

traditions' specification of the right hand for theft. For juristic interpretations, see generally Abou El Fadl, *Rebellion and Violence.*

172 Shāfiʿī, *Umm* (2008), 7:329 (reporting that the Ḥanafīs required that a thief be imprisoned and discretionarily punished: *ḥubisa wa-ʿuzzira*); cf. Qudūrī, *Tajrīd*, 11:6010–11. Though later jurists of the fifth/eleventh century defined discretionary punishments as less severe than *ḥadd* sanctions, this distinction was not dominant in the early period when Abū Ḥanīfa wrote and in fact rarely applied to punishments enforced under the jurisdiction of the political authorities. The latter frequently applied *more severe* punishments under the rubric of their discretion (*taʿzīr*, *siyāsa*); and in Ottoman administrative terminology, for example, the terms for discretionary punishment could themselves mean the death penalty. See C.E. Bosworth, "Siyāsa," in *EI*², 9:693–94; Izzi Dien, "Taʿzīr," in *EI*², 10:406; Bernard Lewis, "Siyāsa," in *In Quest of an Islamic Humanism: Arabic and Islamic Studies in Memory of Mohamed al-Nowaihi*, ed. A. H. Green (Cairo: American University in Cairo Press, 1984), 3–14 (quoting varied uses of *siyāsa* from early Islamic sources). Similarly, in Shīʿī law, third-time offenders were to receive the death penalty – though this rule was based on imāmic traditions rather than falling explicitly under the rubric of *taʿzīr*. See, for example, ʿAlī b. Mūsā al-Riḍā (attributed), *Fiqh al-Riḍā*, 23:3 (noting that this Islamic "three-strikes" rule applied only on the fourth offense for wine drinking); Yaḥyā b. al-Ḥasan b. Saʿīd al-Ḥillī (d. 698/1298–9), *Nuzhat al-nāẓir fī ʾl-jamʿ bayna ʾl-ashbāh waʾl-naẓāʾir*, in *YF*, 40:151, 163 (listing examples).

173 Shāfiʿī, *Umm* (2008), 7:332 (*li-ʿillat al-istihlāk maʿa khilāf al-sunna waʾl-athar*); cf. Qudūrī, *Tajrīd*, 11:6010–11.

174 Ḥanafīs were aware of but rejected traditions stating otherwise. See Qudūrī, *Tajrīd*, 11:6007.

175 Shāfiʿī, *Umm* (2008), 7:331. Cf. ʿAbd Allāh b. Maḥmūd al-Mawṣilī (d. 683/1284), *al-Ikhtiyār li-taʿlīl al-mukhtār* (Cairo: Maktaba wa-Maṭbaʿat Muṣṭafā al-Bābī al-Ḥalabī, 1951?), 341–51, citing *ḥadīth* from Ibn Abī Shayba, *Muṣannaf*; Dāraquṭnī, *Sunan*; and Bayhaqī, *Sunan.*

for each time they stole. The only limitation on that rule would have to be found in authentic reports of the Prophet and his successors. In Shāfiʿī's reading of the texts, not only did those reports contain no such limitation, they supported his position. He cited, for example, an early report in which Abū Bakr ordered left-hand amputation for a thief whose right hand and left foot had already been cut off,[176] alongside other traditions in which the Prophet reportedly commanded as much.[177] Moreover, Shāfiʿī accused the Ḥanafīs of regularly attributing traditions to ʿAlī – useful for his authoritative status – that were generally "unreliable" and indeed "despicable."[178] For instance, Ḥanafīs reported that ʿAlī ordered a thief's foot to be amputated in the middle (rather than at the ankle, against the norm of causing needless pain) and that he shaved off only the fingertips of minors who stole (despite the norm against *ḥadd* liability for minors).[179] To Shāfiʿī, the Ḥanafīs were selectively reading reports in order to adopt a lenient stance on recidivism directly at odds with the duty to enforce criminal law.

Second, Shāfiʿīs maintained, the Ḥanafīs got it wrong because they folded atextual, pragmatic arguments into their reasoning. Criminal sanctions are harsh, Shāfiʿī said, because they are meant first to deter people from committing crimes and second to serve as spiritual expiation for offenders.[180] If this was true, it made no sense for the Ḥanafīs to be concerned that the severity of the punishment would "ruin" the offender. Would the Ḥanafīs, Shāfiʿī queried, make the same argument about the death penalty, which would be the "utmost ruin" that a person could face?[181] That is, would they seek to avoid capital punishment because it would bring about a capital offender's personal ruin?[182] The not-so-subtle

[176] He held that if the thief continued to steal, he should be punished at the discretion of the judge (*taʿzīr*). See Shāfiʿī, *Umm* (2008), 7:327. For a fuller treatment, see Ghamrāwī, *Anwār al-masālik*, 494, and accompanying text by Ibn al-Naqīb (mentioning only the right hand and the left foot).

[177] See Dāraquṭnī, *Sunan*, 3:181, no. 292 (reporting that the Prophet said about the thief, "If [a thief] steals once, amputate his hand; if he steals again, amputate his foot; if he steals again, amputate his [other] hand; and if he steals [yet] again, amputate his [other] foot: *in sariqa fa-ʾqṭaʿū yadah, thumma in sariqa fa-ʾqṭaʿū rijlah, thumma in sariqa fa-ʾqṭaʿū yadah, thumma in sariqa fa-ʾqṭaʿū rijlah*"). As Qudūrī notes, Ṭaḥāwī concluded that this report had no authoritative basis, as the traditionists he consulted were unable to trace its source: *kull man laqaynāh min ḥuffāẓ al-ḥadīth yunkirūnah wa-yadhkurūna annahum lam yajidū lah aṣlan*. See Qudūrī, *Tajrīd*, 11:6011.

[178] See Shāfiʿī, *Umm* (2008), 7:330 (*ghayr thābit, mustankar*).

[179] See ibid.

[180] See ibid. See further discussion in Chapter 3.

[181] Shāfiʿī, *Umm* (2008), 7:330 (*aqṣā ghāyat al-istihlāk*).

[182] Ibid. (*wa-daraʾū ʾl-ḥudūd hāhunā li-ʿillat al-istihlāk*).

subtext was that jurists should be principled enough to advise criminal law enforcement when warranted by the facts in deference to divine legislative supremacy, and he believed that Ḥanafīs had fallen short of that ideal.

The governing principle in Shāfiʿī's criminal law jurisprudence, as in other areas of his jurisprudence, was that authentic texts were to control legal outcomes. For him, the texts specified that repeat offenses required repeat punishments.[183] This same principle governed Shāfiʿī's elaboration of rules for *zinā*, intoxication, and other crimes.[184] An orientation toward lenience therefore was not, for him, a valid reason for violating the letter of the law in order to avoid *ḥudūd* sanctions.[185]

2. *Ḥudūd* Avoidance

Matters of evidence often fell outside of the text. It is here that the doubt canon came in for Shāfiʿī.

a. Mens Rea*: Subjective Indicia of Voluntariness, Knowledge, Intent*

Shāfiʿī addressed instances of doubt most directly in his discussion of "factors that merit *ḥudūd* avoidance for *zinā* and [factors] that do not."[186] He identified voluntariness, knowledge, and criminal intent as essential elements of criminal liability, and then labeled coercion, ignorance, and lack of criminal intent as factors that would cast doubt on the presence of those elements, thereby cautioning *ḥudūd* avoidance.[187]

183 Ibid., 7:330–31.

184 In the same way that he argued for theft, after laying out the elements of each of the other crimes and then considering factors that do not arise in the simple statements of the definition, Shāfiʿī steadily added certain across-the-board elements intended to articulate more precisely when the law requires *ḥudūd* enforcement. For example, on *zinā*, see Shāfiʿī, *Umm* (2008), 6:330–36 (observing that non-Muslims in Muslim lands are subject to Islamic criminal laws rather than to their own laws), 7:394–95 (arguing that an adulteress is to receive a penalty of death by stoning even if she has committed the offense with a servant or a laborer (*ʿasīf*)).

185 An exception concerns the *ḥadd* for drunkenness, for which, Shāfiʿī said, a reliable report indicated that prophetic practice abrogated the rule requiring the death penalty after the third offense. See Shāfiʿī, *Umm* (2008), 7:363–65 (noting a prophetic saying imposing the rule and a subsequent instance in which the Prophet did not apply the death penalty, as a permanent dispensation or suspension of the original rule (*rukhṣa*)).

186 Ibid., 7:394 (*mā yudraʾ fīh al-ḥadd fī ʾl-zinā wa-mā lā yudraʾ*).

187 Ibid., 7:395 (*ikrāh*: *idhā ʾstakrah al-rajul al-marʾa*, and *jahāla*: *fa-in iddaʿā ʾl-jahāla bi-anna lahā zawj, in-qālat balaghanī mawt zawjī wa-ʿtadadtu thumma nakaḥtuh*).

By "coercion," Shāfiʿī by and large referred to rape or coerced sex.[188] He stipulated that "if a man rapes a woman, the *ḥadd* sanction is [to be] imposed on him but not on the woman, because she has been coerced."[189] A modern criminal lawyer might observe that there would have been no criminal liability or punishment to be "avoided" for the rape victim, because the criminal elements – including criminal intent and voluntariness – would not have been met. But Shāfiʿī framed the outcome as *ḥudūd* avoidance because it cast "doubt" on the woman's criminal culpability for having sex outside of marriage. This treatment was typical of other early jurists' approach to coercion: it created evidentiary doubt for accusations of *zinā* against the victim.[190]

By "ignorance," Shāfiʿī referred to an amalgam of factors related to mistakes of fact, mistakes of law, and lack of criminal intent. Prime examples arose in issues of marriage and family law. Islamic legal rules governing appropriate marriage partners are complex, generally barring close relatives from marrying each other.[191] Understanding these rules was difficult for the layperson because of the frequent marriages and

[188] Rape could occur by coercion by a third party, who forces a man to rape a woman. On this definition, Shāfiʿī reportedly held that if a man was forced to rape a woman, neither would receive the *ḥadd* punishment as both would have been coerced. This stance contradicts the general Ḥanafī position because of disputed facts: Ḥanafīs interpret the so-called coerced man's arousal to indicate a degree of voluntariness, reasoning that true coercion elicits deep-seated fear, which would prevent the arousal necessary for the rape. The exception to the Ḥanafī rule of liability occurs in situations when the political authority coerces the act, in which case Ḥanafīs remove *ḥadd* liability on the notion that the coerced man had no recourse for appeal or relief from political authorities regardless of his arousal. For further discussion of the Ḥanafī position, see above, notes 5–15, and accompanying text.

[189] Shāfiʿī, *Umm* (2008), 7:395 (that is, *mustakraha*, noting that the perpetrator is also fined a sum commensurate with customary dowry amounts (*mahr mithl*) plus a sum for any injuries for a free woman (*arsh*) or whatever decrease in value has been occasioned by the loss of virginity for a slave woman (*naqṣ min thamanihā*)).

[190] It is unclear whether he based this requirement on *ḥadīth* texts, such as the *Case of the Mysterious Pregnancy* discussed in Chapter 4 (see Appendix B, case no. 14 and sources cited therein). He well might have, if attempting to pursue a consistent methodology of legal interpretation according to textual bases; but it is impossible to tell for sure, as he does not mention textual bases here. Ibid., 7:395.

[191] In addition to the rule against marrying close family members, Shāfiʿī lists other prohibited marriage partners, not all of which were adopted by other legal schools. See, for example, ibid., 5:79–81 (against marriages designed to satisfy the rule against a fourth remarriage with the same person after three consecutive divorces without remarrying someone else in between (*nikāḥ muḥallil*) and against temporary marriages (*nikāḥ al-mutʿa*)), 76–77 (against parents agreeing to marry off their daughters through the pre-Islamic practice of trading daughters in marriage (*shighār*)), 12–13, 22, 23 (against marriage without a guardian, two witnesses, or dowry).

remarriages in early Muslim societies, which produced interweaving family ties.[192] Accordingly, Shāfiʿī limited the *ḥadd* liability of couples who got married either not knowing, because of their poor understanding of the legal impediments, that they were prohibited partners (a mistake of law), or not knowing that they were closely related (a mistake of fact).[193] In such instances, if the couple was arrested on *zinā* charges, judges were to avoid imposing the *ḥadd* punishment provided the partners swore an oath that they had not *knowingly* violated the law.[194] Only if the couple admitted to knowing *both* the facts *and* the law was the *ḥadd* sanction to be enforced.[195]

As for "criminal intent," Shāfiʿī took the position that in defamation claims, for example, criminal liability turned on the intention behind allegedly defamatory statements. Where statements merely implied sexual impropriety or lineage denial, Shāfiʿī generally held that *ḥadd* liability attached only when the person making the statement *intended* to defame.[196] When in doubt, the judge was to ask a person accused of defamation to swear an oath that he had a wholly lawful purpose behind

[192] See Bernheimer, *ʿAlids*, 32–50. See further Asad Ahmed, *The Religious Elite of the Early Islamic Ḥijāz: Five Prosopographical Case Studies* (Oxford: Unit for Prosopographical Research, 2011).

[193] That is, family members who fall within prohibited degrees of relations for marriage by virtue of blood ties, foster relations, or some other legal status making them ineligible marriage partners (*maḥram*) – including women who have an existing marital relationship, a wife's daughters from a previous marriage, and a wife's sisters or nieces. See Shāfiʿī, *Umm* (1961), 5:23–27 (listing categories of close relatives in prohibited degrees for marriage). This rule was so central to the mores of the Muslim community by Shāfiʿī's time that it needed no citation. Nevertheless, in his efforts to provide textual support for each rule, Shāfiʿī cites an incident in which ʿAbd Allāh b. ʿUmar wanted to conclude a marriage between Ṭalḥa b. ʿUmar and Bint Shayba b. Jubayr, even though they were closely related. Abān b. ʿUthmān refused to attend the wedding, saying that his father (the third caliph) had told him that the Prophet had explicitly prohibited such unions. See ibid., 5:78–79 (*ḥadīth*: *lā yankiḥ al-maḥram wa-lā yunkaḥ wa-lā yukhṭab*).

[194] Ibid. (*fa-in iddaʿā ʾl-jahāla ... uḥlif wa-duriʾa ʿanh al-ḥadd*). Cf. ibid., 7:392–93 (applying the same limitation of *ḥadd* liability to a woman with a missing husband who may have mistakenly thought that she was eligible to remarry – having received news that her previous husband had died in battle). On the symbolic importance of oaths even outside of procedural matters, see Mottahedeh, *Loyalty and Leadership*, 46, 61, and passim.

[195] Shāfiʿī, *Umm* (2008), 7:393 (*wa-law anna rajulan ukhidha maʿa ʾmraʾa fa-jāʾa bi-bayyina annah nakaḥahā wa-qāla nakaḥtuhā wa-ana aʿlam anna lahā zawjan aw annahā fī ʿidda min zawj aw annahā dhāt maḥram wa-ana aʿlām annahā muḥarrama fī hādhihi ʾl-ḥāl uqīma ʿalayh ḥadd al-zānī, wa-kadhālik in qālat hiya dhālika ...* [*aw*] *in qālat qad ʿalimtu annī dhāt zawj wa-lā yaḥill liya ʾl-nikāḥ, uqīma ʿalayhā ʾl-ḥadd*).

[196] Muzanī, *Mukhtaṣar*, 9:277.

the statement to which the person bringing an action took offense.[197] By introducing voluntariness, knowledge, and criminal intent as essential criminal elements, Shāfiʿī expanded the scope of punishment avoidance when there was doubt about whether, as a matter of fact, those elements of *mens rea* were missing.[198]

Like Mālik, Shāfiʿī did not mention doubt specifically in his treatment of substantive criminal law. However, he relied on the doubt canon when deciding issues of evidence – sometimes explaining that "we avoid criminal punishments in cases of doubt."[199]

b. Proving the Elements at Trial

In addition to facts surrounding *mens rea* elements, Shāfiʿī's recognition of doubt focused on evidentiary proof at trial. Early Islamic criminal cases, informal as they were, typically included four parties: the accused, the accuser (the victim, a witness, or a ruling authority), witnesses, and a judge.[200] To initiate a criminal proceeding, the accuser was to bring a claim against the accused before a judge with an accusation that had a minimum level of credibility (*tuhma*). Establishing liability for most *ḥudūd* crimes required a confession or two reliable witnesses – both offering a detailed and identical description of the underlying events in the presence of the accused. *Zinā* proceedings required multiple confessions or the testimony of four witnesses, who likewise had to offer uniform testimony as to the time, manner, and place of the act.[201] In contrast to commercial law contexts, a single witness plus an oath was typically deemed

[197] Ibid. (giving the example of someone who calls an Arab a "Nabatean," although the addressee's parents were not, and then swears that he meant only to refer to the addressee's geographical place of origin, not to deny the paternity of his Arab father).

[198] Shāfiʿī implicitly folds these *mens rea* requirements into his idea of criminal liability for the other types of crimes – theft, wine drinking, and defamation (the traditional *ḥudūd* crimes), as well as apostasy and highway robbery (which he also considers *ḥudūd* crimes) and *qiṣāṣ* (rules of murder and personal injury). Shāfiʿī, *Umm* (2008), 7:327.

[199] Ibid., 7:52–53 (noting the lack of criminal liability when witnesses offer conflicting testimony about the theft and the item allegedly stolen, because "we avoid criminal punishments in cases of doubt").

[200] See Peters, *Crime and Punishment*, 79–92. This arrangement mirrored the general parameters of medieval trials in other polities. For the common law and continental contexts, see Whitman, *Reasonable Doubt*, 96.

[201] Shāfiʿī, *Umm* (2008), 7:391 (specifying that the witnesses must see the act, as the well-known *ḥadīth* puts it, "like an eyeliner stick going into a kohl container: *annahum ra'aw dhālika minh yadkhul fī dhālika minhā dukhūl al-mirwad fī 'l-mikḥala*"). Unlike most jurists – who required multiple confessions, drawing on Māʿiz's case and analogizing to the four-witness requirement – Shāfiʿī required only a single confession.

insufficient evidence to establish crimes.[202] Likewise, in contrast to other, noncriminal law contexts in which women could testify (two women in place of one man),[203] in *ḥudūd* proceedings women's testimony was typically inadmissible.[204]

For Shāfiʿī, any deficiency in meeting these evidentiary burdens created doubt as to whether the criminal elements were completed. Thus, when it came to drinking, although Shāfiʿī maintained that Islamic law forbids drinking *any* intoxicant, he held that no liability would attach to drunkards unless they confessed to drinking an intoxicant or witnesses testified against them.[205] Circumstantial evidence of drunkenness was not enough.

Worth emphasizing is that Shāfiʿī did not understand doubt to refer to circumstances of textual or interpretive ambiguity, as later jurists even within his own school would.[206] Rather, Shāfiʿī saw doubt as an evidentiary and fact-based inquiry about whether the textually defined, known elements of a crime had been completed. It was only where "there is

202 Ibid., 387–88, 391 (particularly for theft or highway robbery).

203 For insightful reflections on the sociopolitical background of evidentiary disparities between men's and women's testimony, see Mohammad Fadel, "Two Women, One Man: Knowledge, Power and Gender in Medieval Sunni Legal Thought," *International Journal of Middle East Studies* 29 (1997), 185–204. Cf. Asma Sayeed, "Gender and Legal Authority: An Examination of Early Juristic Opposition to Women's Ḥadīth Transmission," *Islamic Law and Society* 16, 2 (2009), 115–50.

204 Shāfiʿī, *Umm* (2008), 7:388 (*lā yajūz fī 'l-ḥudūd shahādat al-nisā'*), 387 (discussing cases of *zinā*), 389 (same). Exceptions are cases of theft in which only a single male witness is available and the stolen item is present in the criminal proceedings; in such cases the accuser could produce a single witness and swear an oath and/or two women could testify in place of a second male witness. Even then, such testimony was considered defective, and those convicted through these means were permitted to pay back the value of the stolen goods on the day of the theft to avoid amputation. The other major exception allowing women's testimony in *ḥudūd* matters involved issues considered unique to women's areas of competence, such as issues of gender, childbirth, etc. For a discussion of these categories and their social significance, see Fadel, "Two Women, One Man," 185–204.

205 Shāfiʿī, *Umm* (2008), 7:446, adding that the witnesses would have to establish that the accused knew of the prohibition against drinking a particular intoxicant as a concession to unwitting Ḥanafī *nabīdh*-drinkers who had reason to believe in its legality. Specifically, he notes that punishment may also be due if a person admits to drinking a substance they knew to be prohibited by saying, "I drank an intoxicant," or admits to drinking from a container from which he knew others had drank and become intoxicated. In cases of doubt about whether the substance was intoxicating (*fa-ammā idhā ghāba maʿnāh*), neither the *ḥadd* punishment nor the discretionary punishment (*taʿzīr*) was to be enforced.

206 For instance, he insisted that judges should not regard marriages of disputed validity to be instances of doubt by which the *ḥudūd* punishments for invalid marriages could be avoided. See ibid., 7:361–62. Later Shāfiʿīs would reverse course, deeming marriages of disputed validity to be legitimate bases for *ḥadd*-averting doubt. For further discussion, see Chapter 4.

uncertainty about whether the law was violated" that judges were not to enforce punishment – "neither a *ḥadd* sanction nor any [lesser] discretionary sanction."[207] In essence, Shāfiʿī concluded, an act is "either a *ḥadd* crime or [it is] permissible," and accused offenders could be punished only if there was certainty.[208]

3. Early Shāfiʿī Doubt: Focus on Evidentiary Standards

The focus of Shāfiʿī's criminal law jurisprudence was on certainty, not doubt. He aimed to get the rules of criminal liability right and declared the mandatoriness of *ḥudūd* enforcement whenever bad acts met text-based definitional elements of crimes. For him, issues of doubt that would caution avoidance of punishment arose only in evidentiary matters when it came to proving the crime or criminal culpability.

Despite his apparently narrow, procedure-limited approach to doubt, Shāfiʿī arguably laid the foundations for expanding the scope of doubt and of *ḥudūd* avoidance in two major ways. First, he extended the doctrine of doubt by way of analogy from text-based precedents, "out of precaution" (*iḥtiyāṭ*), to cover acts not strictly covered by the texts. For example, he applied ʿUmar's ruling against *ḥadd* liability for servants who took the property of the master of the house to similar cases: spouses who took each other's property, children who took their parents' property and vice versa, anyone who took property from someone else living in the same house, and people who borrowed property held in security but then denied that it belonged to the original owner.[209] This extension by analogy gave subsequent Shāfiʿī jurists malleable tools for introducing a robust jurisprudence of doubt into their school's criminal law rules.[210] Second, more remarkably, Shāfiʿī's insistence on textual authority provided a strong justification for later jurists' ample advocacy of punishment avoidance in both substantive and procedural criminal law once the doubt canon had transformed into an authentic *ḥadīth* text in the tenth century. In the end,

[207] Ibid. 7:446. See above, note 205.

[208] Ibid. (*innamā yuʿāqab al-nās ʿalā ʾl-yaqīn*).

[209] Ibid., 7:782 (extending the rule – out of the principle of precaution (*ʿalā ʾl-iḥtiyāṭ*) – and applying it to fraud (*khalsa, ikhtilās*), based on a case in which Zayd b. Thābit said that the sanction of amputation for theft did not apply to fraud: *laysa fī khalsa qaṭʿ*).

[210] Even here, Shāfiʿī had shifted to a more open stance toward doubt – perhaps by virtue of the influence of other schools. He had earlier held that spouses *could* be *ḥadd*-eligible for stealing from each other if each partner had attempted to secure his or her belongings. Muzanī, *Mukhtaṣar*, 9:279 (citing *kitāb ikhtilāf Abī Ḥanīfa waʾl-Awzāʿī* and adopting Shāfiʿī's earlier, more restrictive view as more sound).

as much as he was influenced by the other Sunnī schools, Shāfiʿī succeeded in influencing them,[211] most notably by overlaying his *ḥadīth*-based textualism onto Ḥanafī rationalist and Mālikī practice-based interpretive methods when it came to doubt.[212]

Once the doubt canon became a text at the end of the founding period, its scope expanded radically in the Shāfiʿī school to the point that doubt became central to every question of criminal law. After that point, the doubt canon appears prominently in almost every Shāfiʿī treatise on substantive law as well as in Shāfiʿī manuals of judicial procedure and political theory.[213] One example of a jurist who wrote on doubt in all three genres was the illustrious fifth/eleventh-century jurist, teacher, and government advisor Abū al-Ḥasan al-Māwardī (d. 450/1058). He noticeably expanded the scope of the doubt canon in his legal treatise, his manual for judges, and his work on political-governance theory. Other Shāfiʿī jurists followed suit and moreover featured

[211] For analysis of Mālikī and Ḥanafī influences on Shāfiʿī and of Shāfiʿī's critiques of and influence on the other schools, see El Shamsy, *From Tradition to Law*, 7, 47–76, 121–27, and 186–207.

[212] Lowry defends the "middle of the road" view of Shāfiʿī as neither fully traditionist nor fully rationalist, but as straddling a line between the two. See Lowry, *Early Islamic Legal Theory*, 13, 313–16. For specific examples of Shāfiʿī's text-based interpretive principles, see El Shamsy, *From Tradition to Law*, 186–207.

[213] See, for example, Māwardī, *al-Aḥkām al-sulṭāniyya*, 254 (attributing the doubt canon to the Prophet and folding it into his treatise on political theory); Ghazālī, *Wasīṭ*, 6:443–44 (quoting the standard formula of the canon and attributing it to the Prophet as a *ḥadīth*). For further applications, see, for example, Shīrāzī (d. 476/1083), *al-Tabṣira fī uṣūl al-fiqh*, ed. Muḥammad Ḥasan Haytū (Damascus: Dār al-Fikr, 1980), 1:485 (indicating that the Prophet said both *idraʾū ʾl-ḥudūd biʾl-shubahāt* and *idraʾū ʾl-ḥudūd mā ʾstaṭaʿtum*); al-Qaffāl al-Shāshī, *Ḥilyat al-ʿulamāʾ fī maʿrifat madhāhib al-fuqahāʾ*, ed. Yāsīn Aḥmad Ibrāhīm Darādika (Amman: Maktabat al-Risāla al-Ḥadītha; Mecca: Dār al-Bāz, 1998), 8:7–15; Rāfiʿī (d. 623/1226), *al-ʿAzīz: sharḥ al-Wajīz*, ed. ʿAlī Muḥammad Muʿawwaḍ and ʿĀdil Aḥmad ʿAbd al-Mawjūd (Beirut: Dār al-Kutub al-ʿIlmiyya, 1997), 11:144–50 (citing the doubt canon as a prophetic *ḥadīth*, for example, on p. 145); Nawawī (d. 676/1277), *Minhāj al-ṭālibīn*, ed. Aḥmad b. ʿAbd al-ʿAzīz al-Ḥaddād (Beirut: Dār al-Bashāʾir, 2000), 3:206; Nawawī, *al-Majmūʿ: sharḥ al-Muhadhdhab*, ed. Muḥammad Najīb al-Muṭīʿī (Cairo: al-Maktaba al-ʿĀlamiyya, 1971), 18:375, 385; Nawawī, *Rawḍat al-ṭālibīn*, ed. ʿĀdil Aḥmad ʿAbd al-Mawjūd and ʿAlī Muḥammad Muʿawwaḍ (Beirut: Dār al-Kutub al-ʿIlmiyya, 1992), 7:306–13; Shirbīnī (d. 922/1560), *al-Mughnī al-muḥtāj ilā maʿrifat maʿānī alfāẓ al-Minhāj*, ed. ʿAlī Muḥammad Muʿawwaḍ and ʿĀdil Aḥmad ʿAbd al-Mawjūd (Beirut: Dār al-Kutub al-ʿIlmiyya, 1994), 5:442–45; Ibn Ḥajar al-Haytamī (d. 974/1567), *Tuḥfat al-muḥtāj bi-sharḥ al-Minhāj*, ed. ʿAbd Allāh Maḥmūd Muḥammad ʿUmar (Beirut: Dār al-Kutub al-ʿIlmiyya, 2001), 4:118–21 (citing the doubt canon as a prophetic *ḥadīth*, for example, on p. 118, and as a *khabar ṣaḥīḥ* on pp. 119–20); Bājūrī, *Ḥāshiya*, 2:383–90 ([*fī*] *ʾl-qāʿida fī ʾl-shubahāt al-dāriʾa liʾl-ḥudūd*: "on the legal maxim regarding *ḥudūd*-averting doubt").

the doubt canon as the central criminal law principle in their collections of legal maxims beginning in the seventh/thirteenth century.[214] This expanded jurisprudence is covered in the next chapter.

CONCLUSION

By and large, early Muslim jurists deployed the doubt canon with no uniform definition of doubt. Instead, they approached questions of *ḥudūd* avoidance with a casuistic eye, looking to individual early cases for precedential guidance and proceeding to determine instances of *ḥudūd* avoidance or enforcement largely on a case-by-case basis. One strand of Ḥanafīs notably emphasized the moral side of substantive criminal law questions. By placing primacy alternately on the value of contracts and on the egregiousness of incest, they created rules for criminal liability that determined when they would recognize or ignore certain notions of doubt. Mālikīs became strong proponents of the doubt canon in procedural criminal law, often prompting judges to investigate in order to *find* doubt and to avoid criminal punishments on that basis. And early Shāfiʿīs used doubt to help define substantive criminal law texts and to shape procedural criminal law where those texts were silent or of uncertain meaning as applied to specific offenders.

These differences notwithstanding, all of these early jurists recognized doubt (or its absence) as a material criminal law element and a central feature of early Islamic criminal law proceedings in one form or another, even before the recognition of the doubt canon itself as a text. Relatedly, these early jurists – pragmatic though they were – revealed their textualist bent by typically locating their rulings in an authoritative legal text. But they also revealed how unsettled the meaning of "text" was during this time by counting judicial practices, local conventions, contracts, and various other instruments beyond the foundational texts as sufficient "textual" grounds for their determinations of doubt. The shift to a more limited definition of text would occur in the following generations, accompanying the fourth/tenth-century textualization of doubt. Along with that shift, a fuller theory of doubt would also emerge. Whereas early jurists relegated determinations of criminal liability to courts on a case-by-case basis, later jurists developed a fuller theory of doubt through the rubric of legal maxims literature, as elaborated in the next chapter.

[214] For Shāfiʿī treatises on legal maxims including the doubt canon, see, for example, Ibn ʿAbd al-Salām, *Qawāʿid*, 2:279–80; Suyūṭī, *Ashbāh*, 236–38.

6

Sunnī Doubt: Substantive, Procedural, and Interpretive Doubt

After the textualization of the doubt canon in the tenth and eleventh centuries, Muslim jurists developed an increasingly sophisticated jurisprudence of doubt. At the founding period's end in the eleventh century, perspectives on doubt appeared as follows: As a *ḥadīth*, the doubt canon could be invoked regularly in considerations of the new and sometimes "hard cases" of criminal law adjudication. Its increased use, and increasing opposition to it among political officials and among jurists who were strictly textualist, required pragmatic juristic proponents of the canon to provide clearer, more detailed, notions of the types of doubt that warranted *ḥudūd* avoidance and of the rationales that justified the practice.

Agreement on the centrality of doubt among its proponents did not translate into general agreement on its meaning or appropriate use. This chapter examines the variations that developed around Islamic legal doctrines of doubt, along with the rationales that drove them. As before, we begin with the doctrines of doubt developed in the Ḥanafī school.

A. ḤANAFĪ DOUBT: ATTENTION TO SUBJECTIVITY AND INTENT

1. Overview of Ḥanafī Doubt

Once the doubt canon had acquired the luster of prophetic authority as a *ḥadīth* after the fourth/tenth century, Ḥanafī jurists folded doubt into their very definitions of substantive criminal laws and featured the doubt canon at the center of their treatise chapters on criminal law. In the process, they moved from a casuistic approach to doubt to a theory that further emphasized subjective considerations of *mens rea* and the continuing primacy of contracts.

In Central Asia, the writings of the great jurist Abū Zayd al-Dabūsī (d. 430/1039) on criminal law were illustrative of the post-tenth-century jurisprudence of doubt. As one of the first jurists to author both a treatise on legal maxims and a treatise on substantive law, he organized his substantive law work around legal maxims such as the doubt canon. Thus, in the criminal law chapter of his treatise, he devoted a section of his treatment of each crime to detailing instances of doubt that would give rise to *ḥudūd* avoidance.[1]

For sex crimes (*zinā*), when addressing the role of doubt, Dabūsī first identified the major points of difference between Ḥanafīs and other jurists. One of the scenarios of doubt that he raised is by now familiar: a woman enters a marriage contract that is indisputably defective, for example, by getting married during her waiting period following a divorce from a previous marriage; both she and her spouse know of the illegality of consummating the marriage.[2] For Dabūsī, this was an example of Abū Ḥanīfa's "contractual doubt," where the form of the contract – albeit defective – gives sufficient basis for a determination of legality to advise judges to avoid punishment.[3] This scenario was an example of an instance where doubt arose in substantive criminal law.

[1] See Abu Zayd al-Dabūsī (d. 430/1039), *Kitāb al-Asrār*, in *Debbusi'nin "El-Esrar fi'l-Usul ve'l-Furu" Adlı Eserinin Tahkik ve Tahlili*, ed. Salim Özer (PhD diss., Erciyes Üniversitesi [in Kayseri, Turkey], 1997), 151–1945, at 1213–33. Dabūsī divides his discussion of each crime into sections on substantive elements and on evidentiary or procedural elements. Falling between these two sections in each chapter is a discussion of doubt (*faṣl al-shubha*), often with an added section on carrying out the sentence. For instance, the sections in the chapter on *zinā* are as follows: *faṣl al-rukn wa'l-maḥall* (substantive elements), *faṣl al-sharṭ* (offender characteristics and attendant circumstances), *faṣl al-ḥukm* (legislated punishment), *faṣl al-shubha* (mitigating doubts), and *faṣl man yajib ʿalayh wilāyat al-iqāma* (officials responsible for executing the sentence). On doubt, see ibid., 1220–23 (*faṣl al-shubha*).

[2] Ibid., 1220.

[3] See Chapter 5 (discussing contractual doubt: *shubhat al-ʿaqd*). But see Dabūsī, *Asrār*, 1221 (noting rejection of this rule by Abū Ḥanīfa's students Abū Yūsuf, Shaybānī, and Zufar, who viewed such contracts as per se *void* (*bāṭil*) rather than merely defective and voidable (*fāsid*)). Further examples include (1) prostitution (lit., a contract to rent a woman for sex); (2) a temporarily insane man having sex with a slave woman, then coming to his senses after the fact and attempting to buy or marry her to make the act licit; (3) a man having sex with a slave woman belonging to his wife; (4) a man admitting to having sex with a woman who denies it; and (5) a woman having sex with a minor or insane man. Ibid., 1221–23. Note

Dabūsī detailed instances in which doubt could enter evidentiary matters related to sex crimes as well.[4] For example, if someone confesses to having committed fornication, and four witnesses offer corroborating testimony, a judge's determination of guilt seems fairly reasonable. Indeed, Shaybānī concluded as much: a confession with corroborating testimony is certain evidence of guilt. But Dabūsī came to the opposite conclusion, based on Abū Yūsuf's opinion that the witness testimony in that scenario would have been inadmissible, as witnesses may only testify *in lieu of confession* or to resolve *genuine factual disputes*. Excluding witness testimony here would leave a single confession, which was insufficient to establish liability for sex crimes, as *zinā* liability required a minimum of four confessions. For Dabūsī, then, following Abū Yūsuf, single confessions always created a type of evidentiary or "self-incriminating doubt" (*shubhat al-iqrār*) sufficient to trigger the doubt canon.[5]

Dabūsī held that matters became more complicated when establishing criminal liability for sex crimes by relying on witness testimony alone.[6] For example, if two sets of four witnesses testified that a man committed adultery, one set identifying a particular woman as his partner and the other identifying a different woman, the conflict in testimony would create doubt over the particularities of the crime but not the fact that the accused perpetrated it. That trivial sort of doubt, Dabūsī concluded, would not cancel criminal punishment, and the authorities were to enforce the death penalty against the convict. But if five of those witnesses subsequently perjured themselves (leaving only three witnesses to the alleged crime), those five would be collectively responsible for a quarter of the blood money, to be paid to the convict's family in compensation for wrongful death. Furthermore, the perjurers could be eligible for the *ḥadd* punishment for defamation, though their conflicting testimony could be viewed as

that the "currents" of Ḥanafī thought do not always break down as pitting Abū Ḥanīfa against his two students. For instance, the second scenario here shows Abū Ḥanīfa and Shaybānī agreeing with each other against the opinion of Abū Yūsuf. For a discussion of these Ḥanafī currents, see Lange, *Justice*, 200–201, and discussion in Chapter 5, note 63.

4 Dabūsī, *Asrār*, 1223 (describing methods of proof (*ḥujja*)).

5 Ibid., 1229 (*fa-tabqā 'l-shubha wa'l-ḥudūd tusqaṭ bi'l-shubahāt*). As with the Ḥanafī rule excluding criminal liability for state-directed rape, this doctrine is comparable to the exclusionary rule of American criminal law. In this context, it is not that the confessions were obtained improperly, but that witness testimony had improperly entered the criminal proceedings. This scenario illustrates a principle of Islamic law that in such cases a judge is to exclude evidence from consideration of guilt and to use doubt jurisprudence to avoid imposing the punishment. See Chapter 5, note 8 and accompanying citations.

6 See ibid., 1239–43 (*faṣl al-shubha*: listing other evidentiary scenarios).

so unreliable as to introduce another type of "testimonial doubt" based on witness unreliability by which punishment was to be avoided.[7]

In discussing theft, Dabūsī defined a familiar set of three material elements required to trigger *ḥadd* liability: (1) a taking, (2) from a secure location, (3) of a minimum actionable amount.[8] But he quickly followed that definition with an emphasis on the doubt canon – that punishment is to be avoided when there is some "external element indicating doubt."[9] Here, Dabūsī noted different opinions among Ḥanafī jurists and adopted a somewhat more narrow reading of doubt. One example concerned attempted theft. If someone entered a secure location, gathered valuable items in preparation for stealing them, and even threw them onto the street and exited the premises intending to collect the goods on the other side, would he or she be *ḥadd*-eligible if arrested upon exit? Zufar would have said no, because the throwing out would create a "doubt of material element defect" or simply "elemental doubt" (*shubhat al-ʿadam*) as to whether there was a taking.[10] Dabūsī, however, thought differently. For him, the perpetrator would be *ḥadd*-eligible because his or her actions would have signaled a clear intent, "dangerous proximity," and a "substantial step" toward completing the crime.[11] To be sure, Dabūsī

[7] Ibid., 1240 (noting that, while Abū Ḥanīfa and Abū Yūsuf would hold the perjurers themselves eligible for the *ḥadd* punishment for defamation, Shaybānī would not, on the notion that – given the directly contradictory testimony with no corroborating evidence – the perjurers could not be regarded as reliable either in their accusation of adultery or in their retraction of it).

[8] Ibid., 1193. Here, he continues to follow the strategy of the earliest treatise writers by first laying out the core elements of the crime before discussing instances of doubt.

[9] Ibid., 1200.

[10] Ibid., 1199.

[11] Though the three modern American tests of "dangerous proximity," "equivocality," and a "substantial step" were unknown to medieval Muslim jurists, Dabūsī's analysis presages similar requirements. For applications of those tests, see, for example, *People v. Rizzo*, 246 N.Y. 334 (1927), a New York case noting that attempt liability requires acts that have a "dangerous proximity to success" (citing Justice Holmes, dissenting in *Hyde v. United States*, 225 U.S. 347, 387 (1912); *King v. Barker*, [1924] N.Z.L.R. 865, 874–75 ("A criminal attempt is an act which shows criminal intent on the face of it. The case must be one in which *Res ipsa loquitur* [the things speaks for itself]. . . . To buy a box of matches with intent to use them in burning a haystack is not an attempt to commit arson, for it is in itself and in appearance an innocent act. . . . But he who takes matches to a haystack and there lights one of them and blows it out on finding that he is observed, has done an act which speaks for itself, and he is guilty of criminal attempt accordingly.")); American Law Institute Model Penal Code, § 5.01(1) (1962) ("A person is guilty of an attempt to commit a crime if, acting with the kind of culpability otherwise required for commission of the crime, he . . . purposely does or omits to do anything which, under the circumstances as he

acknowledged this type of elemental doubt; he simply excluded from that category criminal attempts that were completed but for the last step.[12]

Another type of doubt highlighted in theft cases would "remove [*ḥadd* liability] *after* the completion of the crime by some [evidentiary] contingency."[13] Here, the old facts of *Ṣafwān's Case* are illustrative. If a thief were to come into ownership of a stolen item after a conviction and sentencing for theft but before execution of the sentence, Dabūsī opined that the *ḥadd* punishment was to be avoided.[14] Dabūsī countered Shāfiʿī's strong critique of this view point by point. According to Dabūsī's reading of the case, the Prophet did not exclaim to Ṣafwān, "If only you had [gifted the stolen item to the thief] before you came to me," out of any compunction about applying the punishment, for enforcing *ḥudūd* sanctions was a known obligation performed out of deference to the divine will (following the divine legislative supremacy ideal). Rather, the Prophet made that statement because he did not want the crime to be known publicly when it was no longer an offense for which the victim wanted redress. Moreover, the report does not make clear that the Prophet did *not* in fact enforce the *ḥadd* punishment in that case.[15] The defect here was another type of elemental doubt, that is, a "doubt raised by impossibility." Judges were to avoid punishment for crimes that had been rendered impossible by cancellation of one of the material elements – in this case, lack of ownership through Ṣafwān's gift of the cloak to the otherwise guilty perpetrator.

As for crimes involving wine consumption, Dabūsī took on the challenge of defending the Ḥanafī acceptance of *nabīdh* and other non-wine intoxicating drinks. To begin, he acknowledged but interpreted away prophetic reports that Shāfiʿī had adduced for the contrary rule. Then, drawing on Ḥanafī law, Dabūsī discussed intra-Ḥanafī differences as to when various intoxicating beverages give rise to the type of doubt that

believes them to be, is an act or omission constituting a substantial step in a course of conduct planned to culminate in his commission of the crime."). For a general treatment of attempt, and lesser punishment for it in American law, see further Stephen Schulhofer, "Attempt," in *Encyclopedia of Crime and Justice* (New York: Free Press, 1983), 1:97.

12 See Dabūsī, *Asrār*, 1205 (defining *shubhat al-ʿadam* as "a deficiency in an element or condition [required for completion of the crime]: *nuqṣān al-sabab waʾl-sharṭ*), 1200 (discussing the punishment for highway robbery, and noting that when there is an elemental deficiency (*shubhat al-ʿadam*), the doubt canon applies to avoid the *ḥadd* sanction: *waʾl-shubha tudriʾ al-ḥadd*).

13 Ibid., 1205 (*shubha musqiṭa baʿd tamām al-ʿilla bi-sharṭihā*) (emphasis added).

14 Ibid.

15 Ibid., 1205–206. For further discussion, see Qudūrī, *Tajrīd*, 11:5989–90 (noting that at least one narration reports that the Prophet did not apply any *ḥadd* sanction).

would reverse *ḥadd* liability.[16] One scenario supposed a non-Muslim who, living outside of Islamic territories, waged war against Muslims, then converted to Islam and migrated to Muslim lands but continued to drink wine and claimed not to know of its illegality under Islamic law. Zufar held that this man would technically be *ḥadd*-liable because claims of ignorance would not excuse his failure to ask about the drinking norms in Islamic lands once he had entered them. Ignorance here was not an excuse because the man would have had what might be deemed constructive knowledge of the prohibition.[17] But Dabūsī was of the opinion that the *ḥadd* sanction should be avoided for *equitable concerns*,[18] following the precedent from the earlier period, when ʿUmar avoided imposing a *ḥadd* sanction against a recent convert who swore that he had not heard of the Qurʾānic prohibition on drinking.[19] In Dabūsī's view, the claimed ignorance yielded enough doubt – call it doubt created by "ignorance of the law" – to present the abiding possibility that enforcing a *ḥadd* sanction would be unjust.[20]

In this way, throughout his treatise, Dabūsī highlighted doubt and differences of opinion regarding what defines it, identifying many instances on which reasonable jurists both within his school and beyond it could

16 See Dabūsī, *Asrār*, 1244–50 (*kitāb al-ashriba*).

17 Ibid., 1250–51 (*fa-ammā fī-mā tusqaṭ biʾl-shubahāt fa-lā li-anna ʾl-dalīl law qāma wa-fīh shubha māniʿa ʾl-ḥadd fa-kayfa idhā lam yaqum* . . .).

18 Ibid., 1250 (*istiḥsān*).

19 Ibid. For other discussions of doubt in matters involving laws of retaliation, spiritual expiation for violations of ritual law, and coercion cases, respectively, see ibid., 231–34 (*masāʾil al-shubha al-musqiṭa liʾl-kaffāra*), 1122 (*kitāb al-diyāt: faṣl al-shubha biʾl-āla*), 996–1007 (*kitāb al-ikrāh*).

20 Cf. Abū Zayd al-Dabūsī, *Taʾsīs al-naẓar*, ed. Muṣṭafā Muḥammad al-Qabbānī al-Dimashqī (Beirut: Dār Ibn Zaydūn; Cairo: Maktabat al-Kulliyyāt al-Azhariyya, n.d.), 32–33 (requiring external corroboration of circumstantial evidence that yields clear signs of drinking before *ḥadd*-eligibility, in line with Shaybānī and against Abū Ḥanīfa and Abū Yūsuf). Dabūsī and the earlier scholar ʿUbayd Allāh b. al-Ḥusayn al-Karkhī (d. 340/952) are regarded as the first Ḥanafīs to pen works of legal maxims, titled *Taʾsīs al-naẓar* and *Uṣūl*, respectively (see, for example, Heinrichs, "Ḳawāʿid Fiḳhiyya," 12:517). In fact, those works list presumptions (*uṣūl*) of Ḥanafī law that include but are not limited to legal maxims reflecting both substantive rulings and methodological principles particular to that school. These presumptions are short statements of law explaining or justifying dominant Ḥanafī positions and differentiating them from the positions of other schools in disputed areas. Each stated presumption is accompanied by examples of application. These works are also examples of *takhrīj al-furūʿ ʿalā ʾl-uṣūl* literature, the stated purpose of which is to show the relationship between interschool presumptions and methodological principles, and which were closely related to maxims literature during this period. For an overview of *takhrīj* literature, see generally Ahmad Atif Ahmad, *Structural Interrelations of Theory and Practice in Islamic Law: A Study of Six Works of Medieval Islamic Jurisprudence* (Leiden: Brill, 2006).

disagree. Notably, the disagreements were never about whether doubt was *ḥadd* averting or whether jurists should actively look for doubts when considering criminal cases, even if the claimed basis for doubt seemed implausible. Rather, the disagreements were about whether and when doubt arose in particular cases. These questions were addressed in discussions surrounding the doubt canon, which prompted Dabūsī and like-minded jurists to define the scope of doubt on substantive, procedural, and interpretive grounds.

Meanwhile in Baghdad, the leading Iraqi Ḥanafī jurist, Aḥmad b. Muḥammad al-Qudūrī (d. 428/1037), also treated doubt as central to criminal law. Geographically closer to non-Ḥanafī jurists with whom he had to interact, Qudūrī had reason to defend Ḥanafī positions in inter-school disagreements about criminal liability and doubt.

Taking just one area of criminal law, consider his extensive treatment of doubt with respect to sex crimes. After briefly defining the basic elements of *zinā*, Qudūrī outlined six scenarios that should give rise to doubt but that had become subjects of major controversy between Shāfiʿīs and Ḥanafīs. These scenarios concerned the questions of whether a man would be *ḥadd*-liable for (1) third-party coerced rape: coercing another man to commit *zinā* or to rape a woman; (2) mistaken sexual relations with an illicit partner: having sex with a woman on the erroneous belief that he had a legal relationship with her; (3) legally barred sexual relations: having sex with a woman with whom he could not legally enter into a marriage contract; (4) prostitution: paying a woman for sex; (5) male sodomy; and (6) bestiality. Qudūrī was certain that almost all of these scenarios were matters in which *ḥudūd* punishment was to be avoided.[21]

In arguing against Shāfiʿī positions to the contrary, Qudūrī relied heavily on the doubt canon. On the question of prostitution, Qudūrī toed Abū Ḥanīfa's line that "contractual doubt" (*shubhat al-ʿaqd*) sufficed to require *ḥudūd* avoidance. Because of the semblance of a contract, sex acts in exchange for payment did not meet the definitional elements of *zinā*, which required illicit sex acts outside of any authorizing contract or relationship.[22] Furthermore, Qudūrī pointed to an early precedent – one

[21] The exception is the question of third-party coerced rape, for which Qudūrī adopted Abū Ḥanīfa's stance (rather than that of his two students) that fear prevents desire and arousal, and therefore the presence of either signifies voluntariness in the so-called coerced sex. Qudūrī, *Tajrīd*, 11:5896–98. To be sure, he recognized the validity of the doubt canon, but he failed to see it as applicable here because of objective interpretations of questions of fact. See ibid. (quoting the doubt canon as a prophetic *ḥadīth*: *idraʾū ʾl-ḥudūd biʾl-shubahāt*).

[22] Ibid., 11:5903, 11:5908–909.

that even Shāfiʿī would consider textual proof – to back his position. A report relates that during the time of the second caliph, ʿUmar, a woman sought water from a shepherd, who refused to give it to her until she had sex with him. When she did, a criminal charge against both parties was brought before the caliph. ʿUmar avoided the *ḥadd* punishment against the woman.[23] The most likely explanation is that his avoidance of punishment stemmed from the fact that the woman acted out of coercion or duress: she agreed to the arrangement out of necessity, not voluntarily or with criminal intent. Another explanation – especially if one considers that ʿUmar may have avoided enforcing the *ḥadd* sanction against both parties (a point on which the sources are unclear) – is that this report should be understood to mean that the caliph recognized the exchange as a de facto, though defective, marriage contract that thereby created the semblance of a contract and therefore doubt about *ḥadd* liability under Ḥanafī law, even if the woman was already married.[24]

Qudūrī applied a similar analysis to questions of male sodomy. After providing textual and pragmatic arguments against considering male sodomy a capital *ḥadd* offense as Shāfiʿī did,[25] Qudūrī directly introduced an early notion of "interpretive doubt" (labeled as such by later jurists).[26] The very fact of different juristic opinions as to whether male sodomy fell under the technical definition of the *ḥadd* crime called *zinā* created doubt, in Qudūrī's view, about the appropriateness of the sanction if not the legality of the practice. This doubt automatically required avoidance of the ḥ*add* punishment, for fear that it would not be authorized by God.[27] For Qudūrī, this view of reasonable but conflicting juristic interpretation as the locus of doubt was not limited to sex crimes; it would apply to questionable areas of criminality in every other area of criminal law.[28]

Leading Ḥanafī scholars of the ensuing years further centralized the role of doubt in Ḥanafī criminal law, both in the "East" (Central Asia and Persia) and in the "West" (Iraq and Syria). The great Transoxanian jurist Shams al-Aʾimma al-Sarakhsī (d. 483/1090) elaborated a doubt jurisprudence in his celebrated work of law, *Kitāb al-Mabsūṭ*, which became a

[23] Ibid., 11:5908–909 (*fa-daraʾa ʿanhā ʾl-ḥadd*).
[24] Ibid.
[25] Ibid., 11:5909 (citing Qurʾān, 4:16; requiring only some type of discretionary punishment (*adhā*) on two men who engage in male sodomy; and making a linguistic argument that male sodomy (*liwāṭ*) is distinct from fornication or adultery (*zinā*) by convention).
[26] See Section B for "interpretive doubt" (*shubhat al-khilāf*).
[27] See Qudūrī, *Tajrīd*, 11:5910 (here: *shakk*).
[28] For an analysis of *Ṣafwān's Case*, see Chapter 4.

leading treatise of Ḥanafī law. With an eye toward doubt, he outlined the elements of each crime necessary for *ḥudūd* enforcement based on clear statements in foundational texts and declared all other cases to be instances of doubt that would trigger *ḥudūd* avoidance.[29] His list of model scenarios that triggered the doubt canon built on the lists that Qudūrī and previous scholars had devised,[30] and it included (1) a man having sex with the slave woman of a relative within the household on the mistaken belief that doing so was legal;[31] (2) sex between a Muslim and a non-Muslim;[32] and (3) a man having sex with a slave woman belonging to a free woman on the claim or mistaken belief that he had bought her.[33]

The Syrian scholar Abū Bakr b. Masʿūd al-Kāsānī (d. 587/1191) – whose family had immigrated to Aleppo from Central Asia – expanded the scope of doubt jurisprudence even further, making the *absence of doubt* a core material element of the very definition of the crime of *zinā*. He defined *zinā* as

> voluntary non-anal sexual relations between a man and a woman [living] in Muslim territory, provided they are subject to [the jurisdiction of] Islamic law, and in the absence of the existence of an actual or a **semblance** of a master-slave or marital relationship (*ḥaqīqat al-milk*, ***shubhat al-milk***, *ḥaqq al-milk*, *ḥaqīqat al-nikāḥ*, or ***shubhat al-nikāḥ***), and in the absence of doubt or mistake in areas of legitimate confusion about either (***shubhat al-ishtibāh*** *fī mawḍiʿ al-ishtibāh fī ʾl-milk waʾl-nikāḥ*).[34]

In this passage, Kāsānī not only defined *zinā*, but also weighed in on varied centuries-long juristic debates about the elements and conditions required to meet the legal definition of the crime of *zinā* and to secure a conviction and prompt *ḥudūd* enforcement. His "definition" was actually a restatement of Ḥanafī law, giving certain conclusory remarks about doubt in opposition to divergent positions in the Shāfiʿī school.[35]

29 See Sarakhsī, *Mabsūṭ*, 9:41ff.
30 Ibid., 9:61, 66 (on rape, coerced sex, and prostitution).
31 Ibid., 9:61, 65 (disagreeing with Zufar that the *ḥadd* punishment is due in such cases, opining instead that an offender's subjective belief in the legality of his acts creates the type of doubt warranting *ḥudūd* avoidance because he had some reasonable basis to think that his acts were legal, and citing as possible textual support Qurʾān, 93:1 and early cases).
32 Ibid., 9:63.
33 Ibid., 9:66 (*daraʾa ʿanh al-ḥadd*).
34 Kāsānī, *Badāʾiʿ al-ṣanāʾiʿ*, 9:4150 (emphasis added).
35 Later jurists would offer competing definitions that added or dropped certain elements for *ḥadd* liability on accusations of *zinā*. Nasafī (d. 710/1310), for example, offered a simple definition of vaginal sex without a legally validating relationship (*milk*) and without doubt (*shubha*), and Zaylaʿī combined this definition with that of Kāsānī for the following formulation: "voluntary – from both male and female perspectives – vaginal sex of a

Kāsānī then specifically enumerated several types of doubt: (1) "elemental doubt": missing criminal elements, such as the absence of majority, sanity, or heterosexuality;[36] (2) "contractual doubt": defective contracts, such as marriages between legally barred partners, a man having sex with a jointly owned slave woman, or marriage to a woman during her divorce waiting period from a prior marriage;[37] (3) "mistake doctrine": mistakes of law, such as a man having sex with a slave woman belonging to his parents or held on security for another transaction, provided the mistake is plausible in that it rests on some legal basis that could fairly be said to have given rise to the belief of legality;[38] and mistakes of fact in some situations – as in when the wrong woman is "delivered" on the wedding night after an arranged marriage (as seems to have been typical enough, at least in jurisprudential discussions) held essentially in absentia.[39]

fully competent legal agent with a [naturally] desired partner whether now or in the past without a legally validating relationship or the semblance of one [committed] in Islamic territory: *waṭ' mukallaf ṭā'i'an mushtahāt ḥālan aw māḍiyyan fī 'l-qubul bi-lā shubhat milk fī dār al-Islām aw tamkīnih min dhālika aw tamkīnihā.*" Here, Zaylaʿī has added language to cover new scenarios, such as male rape, and reformulations to cover existing ones (such as "natural desire" to exclude bestiality and necrophilia). Ibn Nujaym commented that Nasafī's definition was incomplete and underinclusive, and that Zaylaʿī's definition – with some modification – would be more accurate, offering the following formulation: "voluntary sex of a [male] legal agent in the vagina of a [naturally] desired [woman] without a legally validating relationship (*milk*) or the semblance of one: *al-zinā al-mūjiba li'l-ḥadd = waṭ' mukallaf fī qubul al-mushtahāt ʿārin min milkih wa-shibhih ʿan ṭawʿ*. Commenting on Ibn Nujaym's definition, Ibn ʿĀbidīn in turn attempted to collapse the definition even further. The basic definition of *ḥadd*-incurring *zinā*, he said, is "penetration of a penis into the vagina of a [naturally] desired woman: *kawn al-ḥashafa fī qubul mushtahāt.*" He held that the additional "elements" are merely conditions that are not part and parcel of the essence of the act. For a discussion of these positions, see Ibn Nujaym, *al-Baḥr al-rā'iq*, 5:4ff.

36 Kāsānī, *Badā'iʿ al-ṣanā'iʿ*, 9:4150–53 (noting that the following categories of people would not be *ḥadd*-eligible: minors and the insane, those who engage in male sodomy, necrophiliacs, rape victims, and non-Muslims (*ḥarbī*)).

37 Ibid., 9:4253–55, noting intra-Ḥanafī debates on the rule, namely, Abū Ḥanīfa's opinion that such marriages required *ḥudūd* avoidance and the dissent of his two students Abū Yūsuf and Shaybānī, but concluding that in all cases, claims of ignorance typically suffice as evidence for lack of criminal intent as dictated by the doubt canon (*li-annah yudra'* [*al-ḥudūd*] *bi'l-shubahāt*).

38 Ibid., 9:4156–57. Thus, having sex with a slave woman belonging to a sibling would not give rise to *ḥudūd* avoidance, because there is no text that could create the impression that there is any automatic right to enjoyment of a sibling's "property."

39 Ibid., 9:4158–59, noting that this is *not* the contested category of legal doubt (*shubhat al-ishtibāh*) as some claim, but doubt that rests on some legal basis and thus requires *ḥadd* aversion; also noting Abū Ḥanīfa's and Abū Yūsuf's opinion that there is no *ḥudūd* avoidance in cases of illicit sex based on mistaken identity when the man could simply have asked about the identity of the woman he claims to have believed was licit; and finally, noting Zufar's contrary opinion based on what he deemed to be a type of reasonable

Kāsānī named only two of these categories specifically – mistakes of law (*shubhat al-ishtibāh*) and contractual doubt (*shubhat al-ʿaqd*) – but his aim is clear. Any instance of doubt – whether based on objective factors surrounding substantive material criminal elements or on subjective ones reflecting the offender's state of mind – was subject to *ḥudūd* avoidance by operation of the doubt canon. In sum, "*ḥudūd* sanctions are punishments for completed crimes," he explained, which "do not exist in cases of doubt." He concluded simply that the operative "principle in considering doubt in criminal law is the *ḥadīth* 'avoid *ḥudūd* punishments in cases of doubt.'"[40]

In Central Asia, Kāsānī's contemporary Burhān al-Dīn al-Marghīnānī (d. 593/1197) gave doubt an equal place of prominence in his treatment of criminal law in his treatise, which would become the most widespread and enduring work of Ḥanafī law next to that of Sarakhsī.[41] In the *Hidāya*, Marghīnānī opened the section on criminal law not by laying out the disputed or requisite elements of the definition of *zinā* (as did his forebears), but by outlining evidentiary standards of proof necessary to secure a conviction. These evidentiary standards were stringent and textually grounded in the Qurʾān: *zinā* convictions required four reliable witnesses to the act who offered uniform testimony as to the time, manner, and place, along with an exhibited understanding of the technical meaning of *zinā*.[42]

supposition to give rise to a legal basis for *ḥadd*-averting *shubha* (*li-annah yudraʾ ʿanh al-ḥadd*).

40 Ibid., 9:4150 (*idraʾū ʾl-ḥudūd biʾl-shubahāt*).

41 Marghīnānī's *Hidāya* was the subject of multiple commentaries, supercommentaries, and glosses spreading from Central Asia to Arab lands, from Turkish lands to the Indian subcontinent, and beyond. Despite the considerable dispute about some of his rulings by Ḥanafīs themselves, Marghīnānī's work gained central prominence in Western legal and colonial circles in the Muslim areas of the Indian subcontinent because of an eighteenth-century English translation used to facilitate British colonial rule in India. Interestingly, the English translation – as the translator himself explains – is based on a Persian translation of the Arabic original, which explains the Persianized forms of his English renderings of technical legal terms from the Arabic. In November 2000, a group of scholars gathered to discuss Marghīnānī at a conference organized by the Uzbekistan Academy of Sciences near his birthplace. For further discussion of Marghīnānī and the legacy of his work arising out of that conference, see Y. Meron, "Marghīnānī: His Method and His Legacy," *Islamic Law and Society* 9, 3 (2002), 410–16. For the eighteenth-century English translation, see Charles Hamilton, trans., *The Hedàya, or Guide: A Commentary on the Mussulman Laws*, translated by the order of the Governor-General and Council of Bengal [Warren Hastings] (London: T. Bensley, 1791) (repr., *The Hedaya: Commentary on the Islamic Law* (New Delhi: Kitāb Bhavan, 1985)).

42 Marghīnānī, *Hidāya* (2000), 2:735–36 (quoting Qurʾān, 4:15: "Produce four witnesses from among yourselves [to prove accusations of *zinā*]: *fa-ʾstashhidū ʿalayhinna arbaʿatan*

Marghīnānī's standards also relied on the textual precedent of the *Case of Māʿiz*. In Marghīnānī's reading, the Prophet's repeated questioning of Māʿiz set in place the requirement that judges investigate the evidence for broad possibilities of doubt. Judges were not to simply accept testimony or confessions at face value, but were to engage in judicial investigation, that is, to ask each witness about what he saw, the method by which the sex act was performed, where it occurred, at what time, and with whom.[43] "It may be that some act other than [the legal definition of *zinā*] occurred," Marghīnānī explained, "or that the act was committed in non-Muslim lands [for which there would be no *ḥadd* liability], or at a certain time [during which the perpetrators would not be liable], or that there was otherwise some doubt of which the accused or the witnesses were unaware . . . ."[44] In short, judges were to exert the utmost effort to investigate the circumstances surrounding an alleged crime and the character of the witnesses with the express aim of avoiding *ḥudūd* sanctions.[45]

Why should judges aim to avoid *ḥudūd* sanctions when *ḥudūd* enforcement was certainly a competing moral-legal imperative? For Marghīnānī, the avoidance imperative had overcome the enforcement imperative when properly understood. The Prophet himself directed judges to "avoid *ḥudūd* sanctions as much as you can."[46] And the doubt canon, by his time, was a clear prophetic *ḥadīth* that further directed judges to "avoid criminal sanctions in cases of doubt."[47]

In view of these "texts," for Marghīnānī, doubt and avoidance had to be central to any criminal law definition that contemplated enforcement. That is, he regarded the absence of doubt (*ʿadam al-shubha*) to be a necessary material element of the definition of *zinā*,[48] which he defined as "a man having vaginal sex with a woman without a legally validating relationship or the semblance of one [read: without 'contractual

minkum," and Qurʾān, 24:4: defining defamation as making accusations of *zinā* without producing four witnesses to prove it: *thumma lam yaʾtū bi-arbaʿati shuhadāʾ*; citing a *ḥadīth* requiring four witnesses: *iʾti bi-arbaʿa yashhadūna ʿalā ṣidq maqālatik*; and explaining that the four-witness requirement gives meaning to the doctrine of concealment (*satr*) and publicity in that there would be *ḥadd* liability only for sex crimes so public that they were open to four witnesses observing the illicit acts).

43 Ibid., 2:736 (*iḥtiyāṭ*).

44 Ibid.

45 Ibid. (*yastaqṣī fī dhālik iḥtiyāṭan liʾl-darʾ*).

46 Ibid. (*idraʾū ʾl-ḥudūd mā ʾstaṭaʿtum*).

47 Ibid., 2:748 (*idraʾū ʾl-ḥudūd biʾl-shubahāt*).

48 Ibid., 2:248 (*taʿarrī ʿan al-milk wa-shubhatih*).

doubt']."[49] He then listed (as had Kāsānī) several scenarios in which doubts might arise to head off *ḥudūd* enforcement.[50]

In defining doubt, Marghīnānī delineated two types of legal doubt: "legal uncertainty" (*shubha fī 'l-fiʿl*) and "legal ambiguity" (*shubha fī 'l-maḥall*).[51] The first type, which was subjective, was akin to mistake of law doctrine, sometimes called "practical doubt." It referred to the defendant's mistaken belief that there was some legal basis legitimating his actions. Abū Ḥanīfa's "contractual doubt" was a version of this subjective legal doubt.[52] The second type was objective; it was the equivalent of a textual ambiguity. It referred to objectively uncertain meanings of text, as in conflicting laws where one text rendered an act legal and another marked the same act as illegal.[53] Within this framework, Marghīnānī specified several scenarios in which these types of doubt played out on both substantive and procedural grounds in *zinā* and other crimes.[54]

After Marghīnānī, subsequent generations of Ḥanafī jurists regularly elaborated on his two-pronged formulation. In the seventh/thirteenth and eighth/fourteenth centuries, Abū al-Barakāt al-Nasafī (d. 710/1310) and his students followed Marghīnānī's categories and scenarios of doubt. Nasafī's work reads like an abridgment of Marghīnānī's treatment of categories of doubt.[55] In his commentary on Nasafī's work, produced in Cairo, Fakhr al-Dīn al-Zaylaʿī (d. 743/1343) took a similar tack with slight

[49] Ibid. (lit.: without an ownership or legal entitlement, and without quasi-ownership status: *waṭ' al-rajul al-mar'a fī 'l-qubul fī ghayr al-milk wa-shubhat al-milk*).

[50] Ibid.

[51] Ibid.

[52] Ibid. (*maʿnāh an yaẓunn ghayr al-dalīl dalīlan wa-lā budda min al-ẓann li-yataḥaqqaq al-ishtibāh*). He also recognized a third type of doubt – Abū Ḥanīfa's "contractual doubt" (saying that it is established by contract – *tathbut bi'l-ʿaqd*) – but counted it under the first category, because a contract provides a legal basis (*dalīl*) that gives rise to the belief of legality when an act is in fact illegal. In his criticism of Marghīnānī's work, the Ḥanbalī scholar Ibn Abī al-ʿIzz (d. 792/1390) considered this category bogus, because for him it played with the Qur'ānic definitions of contract. For this view, he noted that the Qur'ān defines marriage as between a man and an eligible woman – certain eligible categories of which it further specifies. Accordingly, he concluded, attempts to marry legally barred women may not give rise to a contract and should not then create any type of doubt. See Ibn Abī al-ʿIzz, *Tanbīh*, 4:148–49.

[53] Marghīnānī, *Hidāya* (2000), 2:248 (*al-thāniya tataḥaqquq bi-qiyām al-dalīl al-nāfī li'l-ḥurma fī dhātih wa-lā tatawaqqaf ʿalā ẓann al-jānī wa-ʿtiqādih*).

[54] Ibid., 2:748–55. He applied a similar analysis to wine drinking and other areas of law on substantive and procedural grounds, but none of his discussions of *ḥudūd* avoidance are as detailed as his treatment of *zinā*.

[55] Nasafī (d. 710/1310), *Kanz al-daqā'iq*, ed. Abū al-Ḥusayn ʿAbd al-Majīd al-Murādzihī al-Khāshī (Zāhidān, Iran: Mu'assasat Usāma, 2003), 1:563–66.

modifications.[56] He provided a model case to exemplify each category of doubt and slightly reordered the categories. Specifically, he placed Abū Ḥanīfa's category of "contractual doubt" under a broad, renamed heading of objective "legal doubt" (*shubha ḥukmiyya*), on the notion that both refer to situations in which the objective basis for the legal rule itself is uncertain.[57]

In the ninth/fifteenth century, other Ḥanafī jurists followed suit, again taking Marghīnānī as a starting point. Badr al-Dīn al-ʿAynī (d. 855/1451), an originally Turkish scholar who became a judge and a prison official in Cairo, wrote commentaries on works by Marghīnānī and Nasafī, following each of their treatments of doubt.[58] His contemporary Egyptian colleague Ibn al-Humām (d. 861/1457) also commented on Marghīnānī's formulation of doubt.[59]

2. Legal Maxims Literature: A Restatement of Ḥanafī Doubt Jurisprudence

Ibn Nujaym (d. 970/1563) famously translated Ḥanafī doubt jurisprudence into the language of legal maxims. He authored what came to be Ḥanafism's principal work on legal maxims, *al-Ashbāh wa'l-naẓā'ir*. The title technically refers to "similar legal cases," and in the work he collected legal maxims that had been used by his predecessors to distinguish, explain, and guide varied outcomes in cases with seemingly similar facts.

The doubt canon features in Ibn Nujaym's collection as one of the most essential legal maxims, and his treatment of it is similar to the way in which other maxims-treatise writers discuss legal maxims. That is, Ibn Nujaym noted the standard form of the doubt canon, detailed the legal bases for it (as an unassailably authentic prophetic report by his time), and explained the circumstances to which it applies in Ḥanafī law. To that end, he essentially provided a restatement of the Ḥanafī doctrine of doubt.[60] To wit, he noted that Ḥanafīs had settled on three categories of doubt: (1) legal doubt,

[56] See Zaylaʿī, *Tabyīn al-ḥaqā'iq*, 3:539–68.

[57] Ibid., 3:566–67.

[58] See ʿAynī, *Bināya*; ʿAynī, *Ramz al-ḥaqā'iq fī sharḥ Kanz al-daqā'iq* (Sakkhar, India: al-Maktaba al-Nūriyya al-Raḍawiyya, 1982).

[59] See Ibn al-Humām, *Fatḥ al-qadīr*, 5:249–53.

[60] Restatements often serve not only to restate, but also to codify principles for reform – not always successfully. While the scholarly literature on codes and restatements typically refers to modern experiments, the phenomenon of restatement through codification arguably applies to earlier restatements of the law through legal maxims treatises of the type Ibn Nujaym and others of his era authored as well. For accessible critiques of reform

(2) factual doubt, and (3) contractual doubt.[61] He further observed that all Ḥanafīs recognized the first two as triggering *ḥudūd* avoidance by operation of the doubt canon, but that the third type was disputed – having been first proposed by Abū Ḥanīfa but rejected by many of his school's adherents. Ibn Nujaym then provided details for each.

a. Legal Doubt: Mistake of Law Is an Excuse, if Reasonable

In Ibn Nujaym's treatment, legal doubt covers cases in which the law is unclear to the legal agent. It emerges when a person has a *reasonable basis* for believing that an illegal act is legal. To be reasonable, the belief must rest on some legal "text" – broadly construed. The paradigmatic example in the Islamic legal literature is the case of a father taking his son's property on the mistaken belief that he is entitled to do so. The text of a prophetic report declares that "a son and his property belong to (or are under the care of) his father," which could readily provide the basis for the father's belief in his entitlement to the property – albeit mistaken.[62] A second common example is the case of a man having sex with a jointly owned slave woman out of the mistaken belief that doing so was legal. In his defense, the part-owner could appeal to the early rule allowing sexual relations between master and slave as a reasonable basis for his belief that the act was legal, and he would have a colorable claim under Ḥanafī law. Although the early rule did not have explicit Qur'ānic or prophetic

through restatement in nineteenth- and twentieth-century American law and in Islamic law throughout the former Ottoman lands, respectively, see, for example, Lawrence Friedman, *A History of American Law*, 3rd ed. (New York: Simon and Schuster, 2005), 302–308; Wael Hallaq, "Can the Sharīʿa be Restored?" in *Islamic Law and the Challenges of Modernity*, ed. Yvonne Yazbeck Haddad and Barbara Freyer Stowasser (Walnut Creek, CA: AltaMira Press, 2004), 21–53, esp. 23–26.

61 Ibn Nujaym, *Ashbāh*, 1:128 (*shubhat al-fiʿl/ishtibāh*, *shubhat al-maḥall*, and *shubhat al-ʿaqd*). As we will see, jurists used quite different terms to refer to similar concepts of doubt, as well as the same terms to refer to different concepts. For example, Shīʿī jurists refer to the Ḥanafī category of *shubhat al-fiʿl* or *shubhat al-ishtibāh* as *shubha ḥukmiyya*, and to the Ḥanafī category of *shubhat al-maḥall* as *shubha mawḍūʿiyya*. The Ḥanafī *shubhat al-fiʿl* corresponds to the Shāfiʿī *shubhat al-fāʿil* or in *zinā* cases to *shubha fī 'l-mawṭūʾa*, where there is some mistake of fact on the part of the actor. Finally, *shubhat al-ʿaqd* for Abū Ḥanīfa refers to doubts that arise from the presence of a contract – albeit defective – and it typically gives rise to ḥudūd avoidance, whereas Shāfiʿīs and others take it to reflect a semblance of a contract, that is, a defective contract that *may* give rise to *ḥudūd*-averting doubts. In this book, I devise English terms to refer to these varied concepts in the text while identifying where and how jurists discussed them in their own terms in the margins.

62 In justifying *ḥudūd* aversion in such cases, including cases in which a father sleeps with his son's slave woman, jurists typically refer to the *ḥadīth* in which the Prophet declared to a young man that "you and your property belong to your father: *anta wa-māluk li-abīk*."

sanction, it was considered a "text" by consensus or by tacit endorsement, inasmuch as most jurists interpreted the foundational texts to allow it.[63]

As these two examples illustrate, Ḥanafī conceptions of legal doubt were typically subjective and offender-regarding. They called on judges to evaluate the offender's state of mind as to whether he had a reasonable, if mistaken, belief – substantiated through interpretation of text or early precedent – in the legality of his actions. Where they ascertained such belief and identified such texts, the doubt canon directed judges to avoid punishment.

b. Factual Doubt: Mistake of Fact Is Also an Excuse, if Reasonable

Ibn Nujaym's definition of factual doubt refers to cases in which the law is clear but the actor confuses the facts. It, too, emerges when a person has a *reasonable basis* for believing that he or she acted legally if the facts were as the person believed them to be. For instance, Islamic law unambiguously prohibits wine consumption. What would happen if a person found a reddish liquid in front of her? If she had strong reason to believe that the liquid was juice rather than wine and consumed it, even if she was mistaken, the doubt canon would require *ḥudūd* avoidance. But if she was unsure what the liquid was, the canon would not apply until and unless she had made diligent attempts to ascertain what the drink was.[64] With mistakes of fact, *reasonableness* means due diligence – that the actor has taken steps to ascertain the facts before engaging in potentially criminal behavior.

The classic scenarios that Ḥanafī jurists used to elaborate this principle were cases of mistaken identity in illicit sexual relations. What does the law say about a man who has sexual relations with a woman who he thinks is a legitimate partner, but she turns out not to be? For example, a man might go to bed at night and have sex with the woman lying there, mistakenly thinking that she is his wife. Or there might be an arranged marriage, in which the newlyweds do not meet until the wife arrives for the first time at the husband's house, and the couple does not discover until after consummation that the woman was not the one with whom the man had just entered into a marriage contract. In such scenarios, most

[63] See, for example, Ibn Rushd al-Ḥafīd, *Bidāyat al-mujtahid*, 2:79–80; Miqdād al-Suyūrī, *Naḍd al-qawāʿid*, 160.

[64] Qudūrī, *Tajrīd*, 11:5899.

non-Ḥanafī jurists would advise avoiding *ḥudūd* punishment.[65] But Ḥanafīs recognized only the latter scenario as a mistake reasonable enough to clearly give rise to *ḥudūd* avoidance.

For Ḥanafīs, mistakes of fact were reasonable only if made after attempts to investigate the situation, provided the agent had the necessary information to make an informed decision. In the arranged marriage scenario, the husband must rely on information received from those responsible for bringing his wife to him. Their announcement provides a reasonable basis for him to believe that the woman brought to him is his wife.[66] By contrast, the claim of mistake in the former scenario is not reasonable. It is unlikely that a man would not know his wife from another woman lying in his bed, as spouses are intimately familiar with one another – from their voices to their mannerisms and other identifying features. Moreover, as one fifth/eleventh-century jurist explained, the mistake claim would be especially unreasonable in his time in light of it being typical for a single household to house many unrelated women and female relatives who would not be legitimate sex partners for the master of the house. This housing situation would be enough to prompt the husband to inquire about a woman's identity if he could not readily distinguish his wife from the other women staying in his house.[67] In this context, failure to investigate would be negligence, which may not bar *ḥudūd* enforcement.[68]

[65] For Shāfiʿī discussions, see, for instance, Abū Isḥāq al-Shīrāzī (d. 476/1083), *al-Muhadhdhab fī fiqh al-Imām al-Shāfiʿī*, ed. Muhammad al-Zuḥaylī (Beirut: al-Dār al-Shāmiyya; Damascus: Dār al-Qalam, 1996); Abū Ḥāmid al-Ghazālī, *Wasīṭ*, 6:444. For Mālikī discussions, see, for example, Ibn ʿAbd al-Barr, *Kāfī*, 2:1074. Only Abū Ḥanīfa and those following his opinion in the Ḥanafī school questioned whether *ḥudūd* avoidance is automatically warranted here.

[66] Qudūrī, *Tajrīd*, 11:5900 (referencing external information as *biʾl-khabar*).

[67] Ibid. (analogizing the duty to inquire to situations in which a worshipper is trying to ascertain the proper direction for performing prescribed prayers: a visitor or newcomer to an area may not simply assume the direction, but for the prayers to be valid, he or she must ascertain the proper direction by going to a local mosque or asking those in the vicinity when possible).

[68] Ibid. This Islamic bar on ignorance as a defense in situations of negligence (*tafrīṭ*) is analogous to the bar on using willful blindness to excuse criminal liability in English and American law (often called "ostrich rules," referring to offenders who fail to investigate the circumstances surrounding suspicious activity that turns out to be criminal). See, for example, *United States v. Jewell*, 532 F.2d 697, 704 (9th Cir. 1976) (en banc) (calling deliberate ignorance a "calculated effort to avoid ... sanctions while violating" the law), *cert denied*, 426 U.S. 951 (1976). For a history and analysis of the doctrine, see, for example, Ira P. Robbins, "The Ostrich Instruction: Deliberate Ignorance as a Criminal *Mens Rea*," *Journal of Criminal Law and Criminology* 81, 2 (1990), 191–234.

In short, Ḥanafīs concluded that factual doubt has a reasonableness requirement, just like legal doubt. Moreover, inquiring about the facts produces information that provides a *legal basis* on par with other "texts" for the mistaken belief that a questionable act is in fact legal, also like legal doubt.[69] Judges were simply not to avoid punishment relying on baseless claims of mistake.[70]

c. Contractual Doubt: Defective Contracts Could Create Reasonable Doubt

As for contractual doubt, Ibn Nujaym did not at first take a position on the validity of using this type of mistake to trigger *ḥudūd* avoidance, and instead elucidated Abū Ḥanīfa's position on it. Contracts in any system create legal obligations and validate certain status relationships. Often, the law of contract provides some protection (or opportunity for correction) for transactions concluded even under color of a *defective* contract. On this score, Abū Ḥanīfa held that legal permissions normally flowing from a valid contract created doubt whenever a contract had been formed, even when it was materially defective. He considered marriage contracts between siblings, for example, as defective and thus voidable,[71] but they

[69] There is some dispute as to whether the case of mistaken identity in *zinā* is properly categorized as a mistake of fact or a mistake of law. Ibn Nujaym does not discuss this case in his work on legal maxims, *Ashbāh*, and does not place it in any category when he discusses it elsewhere. See Ibn Nujaym, *al-Baḥr al-rāʾiq*, 5:15. Kāsānī points out that mistaken identity is not a mistake of law (*shubhat al-fiʿl* or *al-ishtibāh*) – and presumably must be a mistake of fact instead – because legal consequences such as paternity flow from relations involving mistaken identity, whereas they do not in cases of mistakes of law. Kāsānī, *Badāʾiʿ al-ṣanāʾiʿ*, 9:4153. Zaylaʿī disagrees, saying that mistaken identity *is* an instance of mistake of law, except that the erroneous argument on which the offender relies is not a textual argument but an evidentiary one (that is, the information received from other women that the woman who came to his bed was his wife). This explains why paternity results here but not in mistake-of-law cases that rely on true textual arguments. For him, both, however, are mistakes of law in that they rely on some legal basis, whether textual or evidentiary. See Zaylaʿī, *Tabyīn al-ḥaqāʾiq*, 3:568; cf. Qudūrī, *Tajrīd*, 11:5900 (explaining that the key element to be considered in such situations is the legal cause that triggered the mistaken belief and concluding that reliance on external information in contexts of defective contracts creates *ḥadd*-averting doubt because the information provides some legal basis for the erroneous view of permissibility just as contracts typically do).

[70] Qudūrī, *Tajrīd*, 11:5899 (noting that a simple mistake is not automatically *ḥadd*-averting doubt: *mujarrad al-ishtibāh laysa bi-shubha*, said in response to the Shāfiʿī argument that the doubt canon applies to such cases generally).

[71] Jurists unanimously held that such contracts are defective, either because the subject of the contract is illegal or the contracting parties are legally ineligible to conclude a marriage

still created at least the *semblance* of a contract for which *zinā* punishments should be avoided.[72]

Elsewhere, Ibn Nujaym made clear that he rejected contractual doubt as a means of avoiding *ḥudūd* punishments.[73] He and most other Ḥanafīs found the type of "mistake" claimed by parties appealing to contractual doubt to be wholly unreasonable. The contract itself was per se *void* rather than *voidable*, and the parties to it were under an obligation to ascertain the facts before acting on a contract with such egregious material defects.[74] In short, whereas contract law took a place of primacy for Abū Ḥanīfa, for doubt to trigger *ḥudūd* avoidance, most later Ḥanafī jurists maintained that the contract in question had to be reasonable.

3. Doubt as Subjectivity?

Mainstream Ḥanafī law defined doubt in a way that included wide latitude for interpretations of the reasonableness required to render doubt exculpatory. Ḥanafī reasonableness entailed both objective and subjective elements. Objectively, strict adherence to clear *ḥudūd* laws meant rejection of deliberate, negligent, or unreasonable claims of mistake for violations of those laws. Ambiguous *ḥudūd* laws could tolerate varied interpretations and thus give rise to *ḥadd*-averting doubt. On the subjective scale, each category of Ḥanafī doubt contained an implicit *mens rea* requirement that was reasonable if the text was ambiguous enough to support a mistake. In other words, Ḥanafī doctrines of doubt encompassed both subjective notions of an offender's state of mind (he had to lack both actual criminal intent and constructive knowledge) *and* objective indications in the text (where the text itself tolerated multiple interpretations, entailed conflicting rules, or – for Abū Ḥanīfa – provided the semblance of a contract).

contract with one another. But they debated whether the contract is per se void (*bāṭil*) or merely voidable (*fāsid*). As we see here, this debate has implications for the determination of whether doubt exists and thus whether enforcement of the *ḥadd* punishment is warranted.

72 Ibn Nujaym, *Ashbāh*, 1:128 (noting Abū Ḥanīfa's rule of *ḥudūd* avoidance by contractual doubt (*shubhat al-ʿaqd*), even when the contracting parties know of the illegality of marrying a close relative (*maḥram*) and there is no mistake as to their identities). Abū Ḥanīfa applied a similar logic to the case of a man having sexual relations with a slave woman held as security and to other areas at the intersection of commercial law and family law. For a discussion of the primacy that he placed on contracts, see Chapter 5, section A.

73 Ibn Nujaym, *al-Baḥr al-rāʾiq*, 5:5 (recognizing only legal doubt and factual doubt).

74 Ibid. See also, for example, Ibn al-Humām, *Fatḥ al-qadīr*, 5:249–53 (rejecting Abū Ḥanīfa's category of contractual doubt).

B. MĀLIKĪ AND SHĀFIʿĪ DOUBT: ACCOMMODATION OF LEGAL PLURALISM

The doubt canon followed a very similar trajectory in the Mālikī and Shāfiʿī schools, marked by variations particular to the interpretive methodologies of each. Rather than plotting each difference, a more revealing way of mapping their school-specific and shared concepts of doubt is to identify convergence points of major jurists within each school.

1. Overview of Mālikī and Shāfiʿī Doubt

In Mālikī law, the generalization of doubt began in the early period in Andalusia with the legacy of famous jurists Ibn al-Qāsim, Ibn Ḥabīb, and their colleagues.[75] Their broad-ranging doubt jurisprudence was picked up by the Cordovan jurist Ibn ʿAbd al-Barr (d. 463/1071), the Egyptian scholar Shihāb al-Dīn Qarāfī (d. 684/1285), and subsequent Mālikī jurists elsewhere.[76] In their legal maxims treatises, each of these scholars detailed instances of doubt that drew on the common model cases introduced earlier in the discussions of Ḥanafī law but offered Mālikī rulings for each.[77]

[75] See Chapter 3.

[76] See, for example, Ibn ʿAbd al-Barr, *Kāfī*, 2:1069–73 (listing instances of doubt involving *zinā*), 1075–78 (same for defamation), 1079–87 (same for theft – listing mostly model cases of evidentiary doubt), 1088–89 (same for wine drinking). For discussions of the doubt canon and other legal maxims in the leading Mālikī treatises leading up to the legal maxims literature, see Bājī, *Muntaqā*, 9:168–71, 175–76, 232, esp. 9:175, explaining Mālik's and Saḥnūn's positions on *ḥudūd* avoidance with respect to early cases presented in *ḥadīth* sources with reference to the doubt canon: *wa-duriʾa ʿanh al-ḥadd bi-dhālik* (noting a rule of *ḥudūd* avoidance for the mistaken belief that a man may make it legal for another man to have sex with his slave woman just by giving verbal permission), *innahu yudraʾ ʿanh al-ḥadd* (noting that the mistaken belief in the legality of having sex with a son's or daughter's slave woman also warrants *ḥudūd* avoidance), and passim; Ibn Rushd al-Jadd, *Bayān*, 16:324 (detailing a scenario of *ḥudūd* avoidance from the early period and citing the doubt canon as a prophetic *ḥadīth*); Abū Bakr Ibn al-ʿArabī, *Aḥkām al-Qurʾān*, 2:604 (folding the "absence of doubt" into the meaning of theft), 632 (discussing differences of opinion on what constitutes *ḥadd*-averting doubt for *zinā* accusations: *ikhtilāfuhum fī-mā huwa shubha tudraʾ* [*bihā*] *ḥadd al-zinā*); Ibn Rushd al-Ḥafīd, *Bidāyat al-mujtahid*, 2:297 (citing the standard formula), 324 (citing the doubt canon as a prophetic *ḥadīth* and listing instances of its application); Qarāfī (d. 684/1285), *Dhakhīra*, 12:50–51, 60 (first principal author of a legal maxims treatise applying the doubt canon as a *ḥadīth* to several cases).

[77] The principal Mālikī compilers of legal maxims did not break down the categories of doubt, concerned as they were with detailing differences between legal principles as applied on a case-by-case basis rather than with overarching definitions of legal maxims

In Shāfiʿī law, the elaboration of doubt began in fifth/eleventh-century Iraq with Abū al-Ḥasan al-Māwardī (d. 450/1058) and Abū Ḥāmid al-Ghazālī (d. 505/1111).[78] Subsequent Shāfiʿī scholars built on their work,[79] further refining the categories of doubt in Shāfiʿī legal maxims literature of the seventh/thirteenth century and afterward.[80]

Notably, Mālikīs and Shāfiʿīs followed the two accepted categories of Ḥanafī factual and legal doubt – albeit with more expansive definitions – and, importantly, they added a third type of doubt. This new category of "interpretive doubt" referred to ambiguities that arose from differences in juristic opinions *within* and *across* Sunnī legal schools. The idea was that interpretive differences could give rise to *ḥadd*-averting doubt. This idea was not entirely new.[81] But among Mālikī and Shāfiʿī jurists of later periods, it became increasingly widespread as their social-historical and structural contexts caused them to subtly adjust their jurisprudence of doubt in order to better accommodate the demands of a regime of legal pluralism.

and their scope. See, for example, Abū ʿAbd Allāh al-Maqqarī (d. 758/1357), *al-Qawāʿid*, ed. Aḥmad b. ʿAbd Allāh b. Ḥamīd (Mecca: Jāmiʿat Umm al-Qurā, Maʿhad al-Buḥūth al-ʿIlmiyya wa-Iḥyāʾ al-Turāth al-Islāmī, 198-?); Wansharīsī,*ʿUdda*. As a result, there is less terminological diversity in Mālikī categories of doubt than in the Ḥanafī and Shāfiʿī contexts. One of the few jurists (and the earliest) to define the categories in the Mālikī context is Qarāfī; he does so with specific reference to the laws of *zinā*, though he means to include other crimes in his scheme: *shubha fī ʾl-mawṭūʾa* as mistake of law, *shubha fī ʾl-wāṭiʾ* as mistake of fact, and *shubha fī ʾl-ṭarīq* as interpretive doubt. See Qarāfī, *Furūq*, 4:1307–309 (*al-farq bayna qāʿidat mā huwa shubha tudraʾ bihā ʾl-ḥudūd waʾl-kaffārāt wa-qāʿidat mā laysa kadhālik*).

78 See Māwardī, *Kitāb al-ḥudūd min al-Ḥāwī*, 1:205, 207–15; Māwardī, *al-Aḥkām al-sulṭāniyya*, 250; Ghazālī, *Wasīṭ*, 6:443–46 (quoting the standard formula: *idraʾū ʾl-ḥudūd biʾl-shubahāt*, and outlining three categories of doubt under Shāfiʿī law as *shubha fī ʾl-maḥall, shubha fī ʾl-fāʿil*, and *shubha fī ṭarīq al-ibāḥa*); see also Ghazālī, *Wajīz*, 2:167.

79 For Shāfiʿī discussions of the doubt canon and for definitions of doubt among leading jurists during the period leading up to the rise of legal maxims literature, see Shīrāzī, *Muhadhdhab*, 5:385; al-Qaffāl al-Shāshī, *Ḥilyat al-ʿulamāʾ*, 8:7–15; Rāfiʿī, *ʿAzīz*, 11:144–50 (citing the doubt canon as a prophetic *ḥadīth*, for example, on p. 145); Nawawī, *Minhāj*, 3:206; Nawawī, *Majmūʿ*, 18:375, 385; Nawawī, *Rawḍa*, 7:306–13.

80 Shāfiʿī categories of doubt also go by different names, though they fall into the same three categories as in the Mālikī scheme. Suyūṭī identifies the following three substantive types of doubt: mistakes of law (*shubha fī ʾl-fāʿil*); mistakes of fact [elsewhere referred to as *shubha fī ʾl-maḥall*]; and juristic difference (*shubha fī ʾl-ṭarīq* or *shubhat al-khilāf*). Suyūṭī, *Ashbāh*, 237. For other labels, see legal maxims works, such as Ibn ʿAbd al-Salām, *Qawāʿid*, 2:279–80 (in the chapter entitled *qāʿida fī ʾl-shubahāt al-dāriʾa liʾl-ḥudūd: shubha fī ʾl-fāʿil, shubha fī ʾl-mawṭūʾa*, and *shubha fī ʾl-sabab al-mubīḥ liʾl-waṭʾ*), and *fiqh* works such as Ghazālī, *Wasīṭ*, 6:443–44 (*shubha fī ʾl-fāʿil, shubha fī ʾl-maḥall, shubha fī ṭarīq al-ibāḥa*); Rāfiʿī, *ʿAzīz*, 11:145–47 (*shubha fī ʾl-jiha waʾl-ṭarīq* for juristic difference); Nawawī, *Rawḍa*, 7:306–12 (*shubha fī ʾl-jiha* for juristic difference).

81 For Ḥanafī recognition of interpretive differences, see Chapter 5, note 56 and accompanying text.

a. Legal Doubt: Mistake of Law Is Always an Excuse

Mālikīs and Shāfiʿīs broadened the Ḥanafī conception of legal doubt from text-based claims of mistake. Recall the two model questions addressed in Ḥanafī law: (1) whether a father who takes money from his son has committed theft, and (2) whether a man who has sex with a partially owned slave woman has committed *zinā*. As in the Ḥanafī context, Mālikī and Shāfiʿī jurists concluded that textual ambiguities exist that could give rise to reasonable mistake-of-law claims, that is, the type of doubt that would caution punishment avoidance in these cases.[82]

What if the defendant in each case simply claimed ignorance of the law? For Mālikīs, ignorance would justify *ḥudūd* avoidance twice over. In his celebrated book on legal maxims and "distinctions" in Islamic law, the Egyptian Mālikī jurist Shihāb al-Dīn al-Qarāfī (d. 684/1285) explained why. Ignorance means, first, that the agent lacks the criminal intent to violate the law, and second, that she lacks knowledge that the law potentially or actually prohibits the act(s) in question.[83] Qarāfī added that ignorance of the law creates doubt for reasons having to do with the complexity of Islamic law. Simply put, Islamic law is too complex for it to be reasonable to expect a layperson to have notice of all its details and to hold him to account criminally if he does not.[84]

Qarāfī's concern no doubt came, in part, from the difficulties presented by the Mamlūk version of Islamic legal pluralism. The Mamlūk state, in which he operated as a jurist, had established a court system with four chief judges – one for each of the four main Sunnī schools of law.[85] Though he was not one of the state-appointed judges, the four-school judicial

[82] Mālikīs and Shāfiʿīs pointed to the same *ḥadīth* for the first case and the same precedential ruling on master-slave relations for the second case to support the mistaken beliefs. For Mālikī positions, see, for example, Ibn Rushd al-Ḥafīd, *Bidāyat al-mujtahid*, 2:261–62 (noting Mālik's position that the *ḥadd* punishment for theft applies to anyone who steals from a relative, except fathers taking from sons, in line with the "unanimous" opinion of the jurists); Qarāfī, *Furūq*, 4:1309. Cf. Ibn Rushd al-Ḥafīd, *Bidāyat al-mujtahid*, 2:633–34 (extending this rule to cover instances of a father having intimate relations with his son's slave woman, also as agreed upon by jurists). For Shāfiʿī positions, see, for example, Ibn ʿAbd al-Salām, *Qawāʿid*, 2:280 (in passing); Suyūṭī, *Ashbāh*, 237.

[83] Thus, Qarāfī explains in *Furūq*, 4:1307, mistake of law is an example of compound ignorance (*jahl murakkab*), which means being both ignorant about a matter (here: its legality) and unaware of one's own ignorance (here: the fact of one's violating the law). For further discussion of the concept in Islamic logic, see Muḥammad Riḍā Muẓaffar, *Manṭiq*, ed. Muṣṭafā Ḥusaynī Dashtī (Tehran: Mu'assasah-i Farhangī-i Ārāya, 1381/2002–3), 19–21.

[84] Qarāfī, *Furūq*, 4:1309.

[85] For the classic expositions of the four chief judgeships in the secondary literature, see J.H. Escovitz, "The Establishment of Four Chief Judgeships in the Mamlūk Empire,"

structure would have made Qarāfī particularly attentive to the realities of legal pluralism within the judiciary. As the leading Mālikī jurist of his time, he operated in a system where the Shāfiʿī-dominated judiciary often forced decisions based on non-Mālikī doctrines of law. Moreover, the political rulers often forced Mālikīs to impose exceedingly harsh punishments based on the dominant opinions in their school, which entry into the judiciary obliged them to apply.[86] The applicability of varied rules of law and harsh punishments prompted Qarāfī to determine what litigants knew or should have known in assessing criminal liability.[87] Accordingly, his conception of legal doubt revealed concern with a combination of objective elements (what the law is) and subjective elements (what a defendant perceives the law to be – whether based on a mistaken understanding of foundational legal texts or on rulings from other legal schools). Either mistake or ignorance, Qarāfī argued, sufficed to caution judges to avoid *ḥudūd* punishments.[88]

Likewise, Shāfiʿīs also grappled with how to conceptualize doubt in an era of legal pluralism. For most Shāfiʿīs, ignorance of the law meant that the material element of knowledge of a criminal prohibition was a missing implicit requirement for liability. For example, if a man were to marry a woman without her guardian present (which is prohibited under Shāfiʿī law), claiming ignorance about the Shāfiʿī prohibition, the groom would

Journal of the American Oriental Society 102, 3 (1982), 529–31; J. S. Nielsen, "Sultan al-Ẓāhir Baybars and the Appointment of Four Chief *Qāḍīs*, 663/1265," *Studia Islamica* 60 (1984), 167–76. For more in-depth treatments of the politics surrounding the institution, compare Sherman Jackson, "The Primacy of Domestic Politics: Ibn Bint al-Aʿazz and the Establishment of the Four Chief Judgeships in Mamlūk Egypt," *Journal of the American Oriental Society* 115, 1 (1995), 52–65 (arguing that the new Mamlūk sultan, Baybars, was obliged to create the four chief judgeships after the Shāfiʿī judge he installed to garner legitimacy threatened to alienate the other legal schools with his dogged assertion of Shāfiʿism that led to his own school's dominance in early Mamlūk Egypt), with Rapoport, "Legal Diversity," 210–28, esp. 212–13 (questioning Jackson's suggestion that the judicial reform was a matter of political expediency given the Fāṭimid antecedent to the Mamlūk judicial system and Sultan Baybars's longtime contemplation of the reform along with its long-lasting effects on the Mamlūk judicial system).

86 Mamlūk judicial politics not only required judges to follow the leading doctrines of their schools but also obligated Mālikī judges to impose death sentences on those accused of heresy accordingly. This was the scheme ultimately responsible for the execution of the famous scholar dubbed Shīʿī law's "First Martyr" – namely, al-Shahīd al-Awwal (d. 786/1384). See Rapoport, "Legal Diversity," 216, 218, and esp. 225 ("The Mālikī Chief *Qāḍī* initially refrained from issuing a judgment [in the heresy trial of al-Shahīd al-Awwal], but then the Shāfiʿī [judge] demanded strict adherence to Mālikī doctrine, and the Mālikī subsequently ordered Ibn Makkī's execution").

87 Cf. Jackson, *Islamic Law and the State*, 178–81.

88 Qarāfī, *Furūq*, 4:1307 (*shubha fī 'l-mawṭū'a*).

not be criminally liable.[89] In fact, in the Shāfiʿī view, this would not have been a criminal violation at all because of the specter of "elemental doubt," that is, the absence of a material element of the crime itself. In addition, the famous Shāfiʿī jurist Ibn ʿAbd al-Salām, a contemporary of Qarāfī, added a noteworthy moral component to the analysis in his work on legal maxims. He agreed that illicit master-slave sexual relations were not formally violations of sex crime laws in cases of ignorance.[90] But he maintained that such bad acts could nevertheless be considered undesirable or harmful under an umbrella principle that took Islamic law's purpose to be to "promote the best interests [of human agents] and avoid harm."[91] In other words, *ḥudūd* punishments were to be avoided in cases of ignorance, but legal agents were also to avoid border crimes – where they suspected illegality or immorality even if unsure of it.[92]

In practice, Shāfiʿīs approached the law of mistake and ignorance similarly to the Mālikīs. Both groups of jurists considered both kinds of claims to be legal doubt for which judges should avoid *ḥudūd* punishments,

[89] Shīrāzī, *Muhadhdhab*, 5:385. Cf. Rāfiʿī, *ʿAzīz*, 11:147 (noting one opinion removing *ḥadd* liability for offenders who claim ignorance of the bar against marrying various legally prohibited marriage partners); Ibn al-Naqīb, *ʿUmdat al-sālik*, 466 (noting a rule of non-liability for someone who drinks wine not knowing of its prohibition, as the person is "excused by his ignorance: *maʿdhūr fī jahlih*").

[90] Ibn ʿAbd al-Salām, *Qawāʿid*, 2:279; see also Suyūṭī, *Ashbāh*, 237.

[91] Ibn ʿAbd al-Salām, *Qawāʿid*, 1:6. Ibn ʿAbd al-Salām sought to outline this theory in his famous treatise on legal maxims – arguably the culmination of a long-standing attempt to reduce Islamic law to a set of principles that expresses the central spirit of the law, starting from the premise that Islamic law's core aim was to facilitate the welfare of the people (*li-maṣāliḥ al-anām*). Note that his definition follows other common definitions of the purposes of the law as serving the interest of the common good or that of human beings: *taḥqīq maṣāliḥ al-ʿibād*. For a discussion, see, for example, Khaled Abou El Fadl, *Speaking in God's Name: Islamic Law, Authority and Women* (Oxford: Oneworld, 2001), 32 ("The *Sharīʿah* is God's Will in an ideal and abstract fashion, but the *fiqh* is the product of the human attempt to understand God's Will. In this sense, the *Sharīʿah* is always fair, just and equitable, but the *fiqh* is only an attempt at reaching the ideals and purposes of *Sharīʿah* (*maqāṣid al-Sharīʿah*). According to the jurists, the purpose of *Sharīʿah* is to achieve the welfare of the people (*taḥqīq maṣāliḥ al-ʿibād*), and the purpose of *fiqh* is to understand and implement the *Sharīʿah*. The conceptual distinction between *Sharīʿah* and *fiqh* was the product of a recognition of the inevitable failures of human efforts at understanding the purposes or intentions of God.").

[92] This moral gloss has little practical effect in the case of joint slave ownership and similar cases. For example, if someone took property, claiming that the stolen item belonged to him (or mistakenly thinking that it did), or if a couple without a legally validating relationship claimed to have one (or mistakenly thought they did), the claim or mistaken belief is enough to avert the punishment for theft or *zinā*, respectively. The implication is that the mere claim of a lack of intent or mistaken belief suffices to create *ḥadd*-averting doubts. See, for example, Suyūṭī, *Ashbāh*, 237.

particularly inasmuch as Islamic law was a complex system made more complex by the reign of legal pluralism.

b. Factual Doubt: Mistake of Fact Is almost Always an Excuse

Mālikīs and Shāfiʿīs also broadened the Ḥanafī category of factual doubt, covering situations where the law is clear but the facts confused. Recall the model case discussed in Ḥanafī law: Did a man who had sexual relations with an illicit partner and claimed to have mistaken her for a valid partner commit the crime of *zinā*? Mālikī jurists answered no because of the doubt inherent in this mistake of fact (termed "doubt of mistaken identity"), which canceled criminal intent.[93] Qarāfī's rule was broader than that of Ḥanafī jurists: he imposed no additional requirements of diligence on the agent to ascertain the facts before being able to claim a mistake. This definition made mistake claims subjective, allowing a defendant to claim a mistake without the judge requiring objective means for verifying whether the mistake was reasonable.[94]

Shāfiʿīs also tended to be expansive in their mistake-of-fact doctrine, albeit with some difference of opinion regarding crimes for which both specific and general intent mattered. On the mistaken identity scenario, there was broad agreement. Like Ḥanafīs and Mālikīs, Shāfiʿīs held that criminal liability would not attach where the defendants lacked criminal intent.[95] This was a type of "elemental doubt," for which uncertainty about a material element of the crime triggered the doubt canon, which advised *ḥudūd* avoidance.[96] Ibn ʿAbd al-Salām further explained that young couples who found themselves in the contemplated situation could not be punished for engaging in otherwise lawful activity when the facts happened to be different from what they reasonably presumed them to be.[97]

When it came to homicide involving status differences, however, Shāfiʿī's disagreed as to whether the same mistake-of-fact doctrine applied

93 Qarāfī, *Furūq*, 4:3107 (*shubha fī 'l-wāṭi'*).

94 Ibid. However, as we will see, the broad Mālikī leeway for subjectivity was mitigated by permissive Mālikī laws of evidence to assess criminal liability.

95 See, for example, Shīrāzī, *Muhadhdhab*, 5:380; Ghazālī, *Wasīṭ*, 6:444.

96 Ibn ʿAbd al-Salām, *Qawāʿid*, 2:279 (noting that Islamic law will not punish a lack of sinful intent, which he read as the moral equivalent of a lack of *mens rea* to commit the crime).

97 Ibid. (noting that, for identical reasons, the same legal consequences that would have flowed from intimate relations under a valid marriage contract would attach in this case too: namely, paternity of a child born of the relations would attach to the man, the woman would be obliged to complete a divorce waiting period, and she would be entitled to a dowry (*mahr*/*ṣadāq*)).

to situations in which there was no *specific criminal intent*.[98] Recall that in the laws of homicide and retaliation, Islamic law imposes penalties for homicide that differ in severity according to the extent to which the killing was intentional, quasi-intentional, or accidental.[99] Recall also that, although they broadly were rejected as illegitimate, at least some status hierarchies made their way into at least some aspects of Islamic criminal law.[100] When a homicide was intentional, Shāfiʿīs maintained that the victim's family could petition courts for the death penalty on the perpetrator, provided the victim was of the same or higher social-legal status as the perpetrator. Alternatively, the victim's family could request blood money calculated according to the deceased's status. Under these rules, a Muslim who killed another Muslim was subject to the death penalty, whereas a Muslim who killed a non-Muslim was not.[101] According to formal Islamic legal doctrine here, lack of equality precluded application of the retaliatory penalty. But discussions of the practice show that some jurists also implicitly considered knowledge of lack of equality as part of the elements of crime and punishment. Extending the rule of factual mistake to this scenario meant that a person who intentionally committed murder could not be death-eligible if he mistakenly believed the victim's

98 This designation relates to distinctions in *mens rea* that Wayne LaFave has explained in the context of American common law: "Cases often distinguish 'general' from 'specific' intent .... The most common usage of 'specific intent' is to designate a special mental element which is required above and beyond any mental state required with respect to the *actus reus* of the crime. Common law larceny, for example, requires the taking and carrying away of the property of another [general intent] ..., but in addition it must be shown that there was an 'intent to steal' the property [specific intent]." Wayne R. LaFave, *Modern Criminal Law: Cases, Comments and Questions*, 5th ed. (St. Paul, MN: West, 2011), 122. Attempts tend to follow the categorization of the completed offense. Thus, murder is typically a specific intent crime, as is attempted murder. See, for example, *Braxton v. United States*, 500 U.S. 344, 351 (1991) (stating that "an attempt to commit murder requires a specific intent to kill").

99 For a succinct treatment of the various degrees of intent for homicide in Islamic law, see Peters, *Crime and Punishment*, 43–44.

100 See Chapter 3.

101 See, for example, Suyūṭī, *Ashbāh*, 237, for this baseline rule, shared by most early Muslim jurists but rejected by early Ḥanafīs. See, for example, Shaybānī, *Āthār*, 218–19 (ascribing to the first three caliphs the position that killing non-Muslims – including residents living in Muslim lands under a covenant of protection (*dhimmīs*), Christians, and Jews – rendered a Muslim perpetrator death-eligible, and noting Abū Ḥanīfa's extension of the rule to Zoroastrians (*Mājūs*)). The Ḥanafīs were criticized for this rule until Zufar, the third most prominent of Abū Ḥanīfa's companions, reportedly retracted it. Dhahabī, *Siyar*, 8:40–41 (entry for Zufar b. Hudhayl, reporting the story as related by ʿAbd al-Raḥmān b. Mahdī); Bayhaqī, *Sunan*, 8:31, no. 15700. For an English rendering of the story, see Fierro, "When Lawful Violence Meets Doubt," 222; see also Chapter 2, section A.

status to be subordinate to his own.[102] For Shāfiʿī jurists, the mistake about the victim's identity would signal a lack of *specific intent* even though the perpetrator had the *general intent* to commit homicide. Moreover, some Shāfiʿīs regarded this type of mistake to be a doubt sufficient to require a judge to avoid retaliatory *qiṣāṣ* sanctions.[103]

Other Shāfiʿīs considered this interpretation to be a bizarre divergence from general principles governing doubt. They insisted that "whoever is ignorant of the illegality of an act that obligates a *ḥadd* sanction ..., yet commits the act, is not to receive a *ḥadd* punishment; but if he knows of the illegality but is [simply] ignorant of the requisite *ḥadd* sanction or other punishment, he is to be punished."[104] In other words, perpetrators of homicide are to be punished if they formed a *general intent* to commit murder, regardless of whether they knew of the status of the victim or that capital punishment was a possible sanction.[105]

In this way, in their jurisprudence of legal and factual doubt, Mālikīs and Shāfiʿīs exposed the complexities of Islamic law and the fiction of comprehensive knowledge of it, given the indeterminate nature of the sources (foundational doubt) and the resultant regime of legal pluralism. These two features of Islamic law fed into a third type of doubt: interpretive doubt.

2. Interpretive Doubt

Muslim jurists' notion of "interpretive doubt" is the most inventive and perhaps characteristically "Islamic" category of doubt. Central to the notion is Islam's unique version of legal pluralism: all legal opinions issued

[102] Suyūṭī, *Ashbāh*, 237 (citing Nawawī's opinion in *Rawḍa*).

[103] For a discussion of general and specific intent drawn initially from common law, see *Braxton*, 500 U.S. at 351 (defining murder as a specific intent crime: "an attempt to commit murder requires a specific intent to kill"); see also *United States v. Kwong*, 14 F.3d 194 (2d Cir. 1994) (marking specific intent as an essential element of the crime such that "mere recklessness" does not suffice for either murder or attempted murder liability). See also LaFave, *Modern Criminal Law*, 112, 122 (defining intent as a necessary element of criminal culpability, and mistake as negation of a criminal element).

[104] For example, Tāj al-Dīn al-Subkī, *al-Ashbāh wa'l-naẓā'ir*, ed. ʿĀdil Aḥmad ʿAbd al-Mawjūd and ʿAlī Muḥammad ʿAwaḍ, 2nd ed. (Beirut: Dār al-Kutub al-ʿIlmiyya, 1991), 1:381, 882.

[105] Ibid., 1:382. Accordingly, if a Muslim murdered someone mistakenly thinking that there was no equality of status, his general intent to commit homicide would still be enough to render him death-eligible, because he knew that killing was impermissible. Subkī maintained – though other jurists disagreed – that this rule would hold even if evidence was subsequently produced to falsify that the defendant's belief about the *inequality* of status, such as if a victim thought to be a slave had in fact been freed before she was murdered, or if a victim thought to be a non-Muslim was in fact Muslim or had converted before he was murdered.

by qualified jurists and adopted by any of Islam's multiple legal schools were regarded as equally correct. That is, any rule that was valid in one Sunnī school was to be recognized as valid in all.[106]

Interpretive differences resulted easily from doubt as "textual ambiguity" – where the foundational texts either were silent or presented internal conflict as to the legality of particular acts.[107] Interpretive differences did not arise simply from varying degrees of openness to interpretation. As the discussion of Ḥanafī, Mālikī, and Shāfiʿī doubt jurisprudence so far makes clear, the main approaches to interpretation went beyond the two broad categories of "strict" and "pragmatic" textualism. Even within pragmatic textualism – to which jurists from each of these schools subscribed – the foundational sources tolerated wide differences of interpretation.

Such wide juristic differences and the resultant legal pluralism could become problematic in criminal law. What if an act regarded as licit in one school was considered illicit in another school, such that it gave rise to criminal sanctions in the other school? How could conflicting interpretations be regarded as equally correct? How could jurists accept legal pluralism in Islamic criminal law, which required clear statements of law and entailed harsh consequences for its violations? The notion of interpretive doubt was the Mālikī and Shāfiʿī answer: it represented their attempt to accommodate recognized, legitimate differences in interpretation among Sunnī jurists.

a. The Regime of Legal Pluralism

Interpretive doubt arose, in part, from the nature of the texts: a set of fixed Qur'ānic and sometimes fluctuating *ḥadīth* texts, the latter of which took

[106] See Jackson, *Islamic Law and the State*, 142 (quoting the definition of legal pluralism advanced by the distinguished Egyptian jurist Shihāb al-Dīn al-Qarāfī writing with respect to the multiple legal school jurisdictions of the Mamlūk era: "the ability to countenance the plurality of equally authoritative legal interpretations").

[107] A text is "ambiguous" when statements of general import engender uncertainty as to whether and how the law covers a new set of facts. Muṣṭafā Muḥaqqiq Dāmād, *Qavāʿid-i fiqh* (Tehran: Markaz-i Nashr-i ʿUlūm-i Islāmī, 1378/1999–2000), 4:54 (*ḥukm kullī-i chīzī mawrid-i tardīd bāshad*, noting that this type of ambiguity may occur when the law is silent: *fiqdān-i naṣṣ*, the scope of an existing and possibly related ruling is insufficiently clear: *ijmāl-i naṣṣ*, or two conflicting texts command contradictory rulings: *taʿāruḍ-i nuṣūṣ*). Cf. al-Murtaḍā al-Anṣārī (d. 1281/1864), *al-Rasāʾil al-jadīda waʾl-farāʾid al-ḥadītha*, ed. ʿAlī al-Mishkīnī al-Ardabīlī (Qum: n.p., 1390/1971), 150–51 (similarly defining textual doubt – that is, ambiguity – as uncertainty as to obligation or prohibition: *dawarān al-amr bayna ʾl-wujūb waʾl-taḥrīm*, based on silence of the text: *ʿadam al-naṣṣ*, generality of the text: *ijmāl*, or apparent conflicts between two texts: *taʿāruḍ*). For an analogous Sunnī definition, see, for example, Ibn ʿAbd al-Salām, *Qawāʿid*, 2:279–80 (describing textual conflicts as the operative scope of the doubt canon: *al-taʿāruḍ bayna adillat al-taḥrīm waʾl-taḥlīl*).

shape and gained authority over the course of several hundred years.[108] Even the Qur'ān contained criminal laws that jurists found ambiguous – as seen in the wildly divergent opinions of Ḥanafīs and Shāfiʿīs, respectively, on the legal status of male sodomy, for example.[109] The Ḥanafīs argued that the Qur'ān specified a punishment for *zinā*, defined as illicit male-female sexual relations, but was silent on male sodomy. Accordingly, for most of them, male sodomy could not be a *ḥadd* crime. The Shāfiʿīs disagreed. They argued that the Qur'ān labeled both *zinā* and male sodomy as a "gravely immoral act" (*fāḥisha*), meaning that the same fixed punishment – mentioned in connection to *zinā* – was mandated for both acts. In the alternative, they argued that the word *zinā* encompassed male-male sexual interactions as well as male-female sex offenses.[110] Where Ḥanafīs saw ambiguity, Shāfiʿīs saw clarity.[111] For Mālikīs and Shāfiʿīs, the interpretive difference between the various schools sufficed to create doubt about the legality of regarding sodomy as one of the *ḥudūd* crimes.[112]

Such textual ambiguities multiplied exponentially when it came to *ḥadīth* – because Muslim jurists could rarely agree on the authenticity, much less the meaning or normativity of thousands of often conflicting reports. Without a single authoritative corpus of *ḥadīth*, these jurists addressed questions of *ḥadīth* authenticity and meaning through elaborate rules of interpretation reflecting the particular hermeneutical principles of their schools. In this context, disagreements about *ḥadīth* created yet more interpretive differences among Islam's legal schools.[113]

108 On the gradually established authority of *ḥadīth* as a source of law and their canonization among Sunnīs, see generally Brown, *Canonization of al-Bukhārī and Muslim*.

109 For general legal treatments of male sodomy in Islam, see Arno Schmitt, "*Liwāṭ* im *Fiqh*: Männliche Homosexualität," *Journal of Arabic and Islamic Studies* 4 (2001–2002), 49–110 (defining the prohibition of *liwāṭ* as one against anal sex, not homosexuality or male sodomy); Khaled El-Rouayheb, *Before Homosexuality in the Arab-Islamic World, 1500–1800* (Chicago: University of Chicago Press, 2005), 118–28; Lange, *Justice*, 199–214.

110 See Ghazālī, *Wasīṭ*, 440; Rāfiʿī, *ʿAzīz*, 139–41; Nawawī, *Rawḍa*, 309.

111 Shīʿī law addressed this problem of ambiguity by citing *ḥadīth*, consensus, and rational arguments to the effect that, if *zinā* was a *ḥadd* crime, male sodomy as a graver moral offense should be punished even more harshly. See, for example, Mufīd (d. 413/1022), *Muqniʿa*, in *YF*, 23:31; al-Sharīf al-Murtaḍā (d. 436/1044), *Intiṣār*, in *YF*, 23:49–50; Ṭūsī, *Nihāya*, 2:723–24.

112 For detailed Ḥanafī responses to Shāfiʿī arguments in favor of counting male sodomy as a *ḥadd* crime, see Qudūrī, *Tajrīd*, 11:5910–16. Worth noting is that, although Ḥanafīs generally found that there was no *ḥadd* liability for male sodomy (with exceptions; see Ibn Nujaym, *al-Baḥr al-rāʾiq*, 5:17), they all regarded *public* male sodomy as immoral and thus punishable by death at the discretion of the caliph.

113 See, for example, Bernard Weiss, *Search for God's Law*, 151–258; Mottahedeh, *Lessons*, 10–13, 15–16.

In an attempt to manage the effect of these differences on criminal laws, some Muslim jurists elaborated a scheme that distinguished between two broad categories of Islamic law: "clearly established rules" and "debatable rules."[114] The former would be punishable and the latter subject to the realm of interpretive doubt.

Clearly established rules were laws so widespread that they could be presumed to be a matter of common knowledge in particular societies. Everyone in a Muslim society should know, for example, that Islamic law prohibits sex outside of marriage. In the earliest moments of the Muslim community, it may have been possible for new converts to claim that they were unaware of this prohibition, as occurred during the time of the second caliph, ʿUmar. The caliph ruled that a Yemeni man who had illicit sex was eligible for *ḥudūd* punishments only if he knew that his actions were prohibited. The implication is that the man's lack of awareness was indeed plausible, as Yemen was on the margins of the community at a time when Islamic law was not yet widespread. The man claimed ignorance of the law and was set free.[115]

While later jurists took ʿUmar's ruling as the basis for a *mens rea* requirement,[116] the case had implications for interpretive doubt as well. These same jurists also determined that Islamic law's clear prohibition against sex out of wedlock quickly became sufficiently widespread to fall

[114] For example, Qarāfī, *Furūq*, 4:1309 (defining the first category to be presumed, not actual, knowledge, as indicated by its label, *mashhūr*, meaning widespread or common).

[115] See Ibn Nujaym, *al-Baḥr al-rāʾiq*, 5:4. The implication is that the ability to claim ignorance of *zinā* prohibitions was limited to the first generations. Islamic prohibitions against *zinā* quickly became sufficiently widespread that they fell into the category of clearly established rules. See also Ibn Qudāma, *Mughnī*, 12:345. Cf. Paul R. Powers, *Intent in Islamic Law* (Leiden: Brill, 2006), 193–94.

[116] Prominent Ḥanafī jurists, including Ibn Māzah (d. 536/1141), ʿAynī (d. 855/1451), and Ibn ʿĀbidīn (d. 1252/1836), imposed a knowledge requirement for *zinā* liability based on ʿUmar's judgment, with Ibn ʿĀbidīn specifying that to enforce *ḥudūd* punishments without such a requirement would contravene the doubt canon. Other well-known Ḥanafīs rejected this view. For Ibn al-Humām, claims of ignorance were never appropriate in cases of sex offenses because all religions and communities had outlawed fornication and adultery. Similarly, Ibn Nujaym took a strict-liability approach, holding that *ḥudūd* punishments were to be enforced whenever *ḥudūd* laws were violated, regardless of publication of the law or the offender's knowledge. In an attempt to resolve the debate, Ibn Amīr al-Ḥājj argued that, in the early *Case of the Mysterious Pregnancy*, ʿUmar validly avoided punishment because of the lack of widespread knowledge of new Islamic laws just after Islam's advent, but thereafter, criminal liability attached to proved acts of fornication. For the various positions, see Ibn Nujaym, *al-Baḥr al-rāʾiq*, 5:4ff. and, on the margins, Ibn ʿĀbidīn's *Sharḥ*.

into the category of clearly established rules.[117] Accordingly, by the seventh/thirteenth century, interpretive doubt did not apply to one couple that claimed confusion about the legality of sex before marriage. (The couple argued that, because they *planned* to get married, they assumed that having sex beforehand was acceptable.) That claim, jurists concluded, did not constitute the type of doubt for which judges should avoid the *ḥudūd* sanctions, as the prohibition on extramarital sex had been clearly established by then.[118] In this way, jurists generally rejected claims of doubt for clearly established rules – which reflected the enduring core cultural-moral values of the expanding Muslim communities.

Debatable rules referred to the detailed, technical laws that had been the subject of juristic debate and that comprised most of Islamic law. "Only astute jurists can discern these rules," one jurist explained;[119] and even then, they often disagreed with each other. Muslim jurists have always acknowledged the probabilistic nature of legal interpretation and tried to account for it in various ways.[120] In Islamic criminal law, these jurists imposed a high burden of clarity before imposing criminal liability: any differences that arose from textual ambiguity as perceived by jurists gave rise to interpretive doubt that translated into the need to avoid enforcing *ḥudūd* punishments against the average person. In other words, if even jurists could reasonably disagree about the substance of the law, then a layperson should not be held criminally liable.[121]

One recurring example concerns the interpretive differences over valid forms of marriage. The sources suggest that the Prophet initially allowed "temporary marriages," whereby a couple specified a date upon which

[117] See Ibn Qudāma, *Mughnī*, 12:345, 7:307. The prohibition stems from the Qur'ān and prophetic reports, which advise that *zinā* is a grave moral offense and establish sanctions for its commission when the crime is proved by four male witnesses or by confession. In one passage, the Qur'ān advises Muslims to not even enter situations that might lead to *zinā*, characterized as a grave sin and a debaucherous way of life. In another, it states that God's (true) servants deserving reward are those who, among other things, refrain from polytheism, taking life unjustly, and *zinā* – all sins that will incur severe punishments in the hereafter. Qur'ān, 25:68–69. In addition, a prophetic report related on the authority of the early Kūfan jurist Ibn Mas'ūd states that the gravest sin after polytheism and infanticide is *zinā*. The first punishment that the Qur'ān set forth for *zinā* was life imprisonment for the married person; for the unmarried person (*bikr*), it was *adhā*, which meant verbal admonishment or discretionary physical punishments according to Ibn Qudāma, *Mughnī*, 7:307. Qur'ān, 4:15–16.

[118] Qarāfī, *Furūq*, 4:1309.

[119] Ibid. (*fa-lā ya'lamuh illā 'l-fuqahā' al-fuḥūl*).

[120] This insight is the major contribution of Zysow, *Economy of Certainty*, 90–91, 459–62.

[121] Qarāfī, *Furūq*, 4:1409 (explaining that ignorance of such laws creates an excuse).

their union would dissolve automatically without divorce proceedings. But Muslim jurists disagreed about whether the practice was subsequently outlawed. There is evidence that temporary marriages continued well into the second/eighth century. Ibn ʿAbbās (d. 68/687) and his followers in the Ḥijāz sanctioned them, as did the proto-Shīʿa in Medina, Kūfa, and Yemen.[122] Moreover, the head of the Meccan school, the famous jurist Ibn Jurayj (d. 150/767), gave firm support to the legality of temporary marriages throughout his lifetime.[123] Nevertheless, most Sunnī jurists came to a consensus by the late second/eighth century that temporary marriages were unlawful.[124] The century-long persistence of the practice suggests that any prohibition must have occurred well after the Prophet's death.[125] Indeed, Sunnī opponents to temporary marriage cited rules promulgated by ʿUmar, who reportedly prohibited the practice during his caliphate.[126]

[122] See Ibn Ḥazm, *Muḥallā*, 9:519.

[123] See Khayr al-Dīn al-Ziriklī, *al-Aʿlām: Qāmūs tarājim* (Beirut: Dār al-ʿIlm liʾl-Malāyīn, 1986), 4:160 (s.v. ʿAbd al-Malik b. ʿAbd al-ʿAzīz Ibn Jurayj); Dhahabī, *Siyar*, 6:331.

[124] For the settled Sunnī position of prohibition, see, for example, the editor's note in Qarāfī's *Furūq*, 4:1307 (citing Ibn Rushd al-Ḥafīd, *Bidāyat al-mujtahid*, 2:85, and saying that the reports that the Prophet prohibited temporary marriage were transmitted by many routes and thus certain); Māwardī, *Kitāb al-ḥudūd min al-Ḥāwī*, 11:449 (reporting a Sunnī consensus on the prohibition of temporary marriage).

[125] Temporary marriage continues to be a valid form of marriage in Shīʿī law today, with the argument that a caliph cannot permanently prohibit practices permitted by the Prophet or by one of the Imāms. There is evidence that the Shīʿa often adopted laws from Ibn ʿAbbās that diverged from the regulations issued by ʿUmar and applied by his son ʿAbd Allāh, who is a main source for Sunnī law. This adoption was not explicit, especially considering the ambiguous regard in which Shīʿī biographers held Ibn ʿAbbās. See Wilferd Madelung, "ʿAbd Allāh b. ʿAbbās and Shīʿite Law," in *Law, Christianity and Modernism in Islamic Society: Proceedings of the Eighteenth Congress of the Union Européenne des Arabisants et Islamisants, 1996* (Leuven, Netherlands: Katholieke Universiteit Leuven, 1998), 15–16, 23–25. Madelung's suggestion that the Shīʿa may have adopted readings from a pre-ʿUthmānic Qurʾānic codex of Ibn ʿAbbās to permit temporary marriage is not borne out by Shīʿī texts, which refer only to the ʿUthmānic reading as far as I can tell. Aside from appealing to independent sources of law preserved among the Prophet's close family members and their companions, the Shīʿī treatment of temporary marriage (*mutʿa*) may reflect a tendency to omit Ibn ʿAbbās as the true source, as Madelung posits. Ibid., 23–24. Alternatively, early Shīʿī jurists may have read Ibn ʿAbbās's additions as commentary rather than as variants, as they commonly did in other contexts, or it may be that they found no trouble interpreting the Qurʾān to support a continuing practice of the Prophet, the subsequent outlawing of which by non-Imāms was easily rejected in their theory of law and legal authority.

[126] For a discussion of first-century temporary marriage rulings and reports of ʿUmar's prohibition, see Motzki, *Origins*, 142–46. Contemporary scholars often dismiss the early opinions by which interpretive doubt would apply to temporary marriage. See, for example, the editor's note in Qarāfī's *Furūq*, 4:1307.

The disputed status of temporary marriage – particularly because of its sectarian dimensions, given its continuing acceptance in the Shīʿī community – created difficulties for Sunnī jurists trying to assess whether criminal liability attached to the consummation of marriages that they deemed invalid in the first place. Those jurists resolved such difficulties by appealing to interpretive doubt. That is, a law that deemed an act valid in one school was to be construed as creating the type of doubt that removed criminal liability from anyone accused of committing that same act when it was deemed illegal in another school. As jurists understood it in the temporary marriage context, punishment would be unfair because ambiguities about the legal status of that type of union did not give fair notice of criminal liability to temporarily married couples who were nonjurists and who believed their actions to be legal. In this way, through interpretive doubt, Sunnī jurists became proponents of equity and a version of fair notice.[127]

Juristic recognition of interpretive doubt in cases such as temporary marriage is a striking admission of the chimerical nature of a common legal fiction imputing knowledge of the law to laypeople in order to justify punishment. The fiction is a necessary pillar of the *principle of legality*, which requires that no act may be punished without first giving notice of the law (expressed by the well-known Roman law maxim, *nulla poena sine lege*).[128] At the same time, Muslim jurists acknowledged the particularly high stakes in Islam's fixed criminal laws – where punishment meant loss of life, limb, or liberty.[129] The epistemic justification for *ḥudūd* avoidance in cases of interpretive doubt was that the law would not tolerate harshly punishing people who had no notice of what the law was, given that even jurists could reasonably disagree about it. As we will see, Mālikīs and Shāfiʿīs in particular relied on an ever more robust understanding of doubt and fair notice to counsel against arbitrary or excessive punishment.

b. Mālikī Interpretive Doubt: Fictions of Legal Knowledge

The Mālikī jurist Qarāfī further elaborated notions of interpretive doubt and criminal liability under Islamic law's rubric of clearly established

[127] On values of fair notice and equity underlying the juristic invocations of the doubt canon, see my "Islamic Rule of Lenity," 1327–49.

[128] For further discussion of this principle with respect to Shīʿī law, see Chapter 8.

[129] See Chapter 1, section B.

versus debatable laws, detailed above.[130] With few exceptions, he agreed that the inhabitants of Muslim lands could fairly be presumed to know the clearly established laws – such as the criminal prohibition against extramarital sex. For this set of laws, doubt typically played no role and ignorance was not an excuse.[131]

But Qarāfī emphasized that debatable laws comprised the bulk of Islamic law and, given the unclear or ambiguous texts underlying them, most laypeople (and even many jurists) could not reliably determine a single right answer in this broad area of Islamic law – making ignorance of the law an excuse.[132] Sunnī jurists had long recognized that even the most Herculean of efforts to discover the law did not yield certain

[130] Qarāfī, *Furūq*, 4:1309. One should distinguish between this discussion and that of the first Mālikī type of doubt, in which only the general contours of the law are clear and settled, while a more detailed look at the law would provide reasonable bases for ignorance or mistakes of law. Such laws are more akin to the ones at issue in Qarāfī's second category of law, for which there is no easy translation. "Complex," "derived," or "not clearly established" would also be accurate descriptions; I settled on "debatable," because he means to suggest that these are rules derived from texts that bear different interpretations, as reflected by (reasonable) juristic debates about their meaning. Here, a comparable American law doctrine – which bears further study – is that of qualified immunity: an affirmative defense available to government officials accused of violating individual's fundamental rights while acting "under color of any statute, ordinance, regulation, custom, or usage" of a U.S. state, territory, or district; the success of which results in the officials' ability to avoid liability and punishment. See 42 U.S.C. § 1983 (providing a cause of action to individuals against state officials for violations of constitutional rights). Government officials cannot be held liable for rights violations if they acted with a reasonable belief in the constitutionality of the challenged conduct, unless their actions violated a "clearly established ... [constitutional] right." That is, they will have acted unreasonably, regardless of their subjective beliefs or knowledge of the law, if they violated "clearly established" laws "of which a reasonable person would have known." *Harlow v. Fitzgerald*, 457 U.S. 800, 818 (1982). See also *Anderson v. Creighton*, 483 U.S. 635 (1987) (specifying the standard for an objective judicial inquiry: that it "must be sufficiently clear that a reasonable official would understand that what he is doing violates that right"); *Pierson v. Ray*, 386 U.S. 547, 555–57 (1967) (laying the foundations for the qualified immunity doctrine). For more recent developments, see *Pearson v. Callanan*, 555 U.S. 223 (2009), overturning the mandatory application of the qualified immunity test outlined in *Saucier v. Katz*, 533 U.S. 194 (2001), which required courts to first decide complex constitutional law claims – in opposition to the constitutional avoidance canon (on which, see Appendix A, note 28) – and then decide whether the alleged violation of a constitutional right was "clearly established" at the time of the official's conduct in order to assess whether a government official was entitled to immunity. For discussion, see further Sheldon H. Nahmod, *Civil Rights and Civil Liberties Litigation: The Law of Section 1983*, 4th ed. (St. Paul, MN: West, 2010), chap. 8.

[131] Exceptions could be made for recent converts or Muslims born and raised elsewhere. But this, too, was a matter of debate, as illustrated by the Ḥanafī back-and-forth disputes on the matter, on which, see note 116.

[132] Qarāfī, *Furūq*, 4:1309 (*wa-taḥqīquh ʿasīr ʿalā akthar al-nās fa-kāna ʾl-labs fīh ʿudhran*).

conclusions or agreement among jurists.[133] For this reason, they readily admitted that their divergent interpretations of Islamic law were only *probably* correct. The corollary – that divergent opinions were not necessarily *in*correct – manifested as an extremely strong "clear statement rule" in criminal law. That is, only the clearest statements of prohibition could yield criminal liability.[134] Accordingly, Qarāfī extended the doubt canon to cover situations in which laypeople tried to interpret laws that jurists would have found to be clear, but got them wrong because the laws were not sufficiently widespread or clear enough to be counted as common knowledge.[135]

Following this logic, even sex crimes became subject to the doubt canon despite the law's seemingly clear-cut prohibitions. After all, Islam's various legal schools differed over the precise definition and elements of *zinā*: Does it encompass male sodomy, bestiality, and necrophilia? Is there extraterritorial liability? Do *zinā* laws apply to minors, the insane, and non-Muslims?[136] Does an act of *zinā* occur under circumstances – as in temporary marriage – that were once deemed legal?[137] For Qarāfī, the jurists' debates about even seemingly clear-cut laws translated easily into rules of interpretive doubt, for which *ḥudūd* punishments were to be avoided.

c. *Shāfiʿī Interpretive Doubt: Rules of Reasonableness*

Shāfiʿī jurists similarly recognized interpretive doubt, though they placed tight restrictions on its use and tried to tie it as closely as possible to textual authority.[138] They agreed that disputed forms of marriage deemed

[133] On Herculean interpretation as the model of exhaustive interpretation in a scheme that incorporates morality and political process into "law as integrity," see Ronald Dworkin, *Law's Empire* (Cambridge, MA: Belknap Press of Harvard University Press, 1986), 313–54.

[134] For a definition and examples of clear statement rules as fundamental law in the American context, see William N. Eskridge Jr. and Philip P. Frickey, "Quasi-Constitutional Law: Clear Statement Rules as Constitutional Lawmaking," *Vanderbilt Law Review* 45 (1992), 593–646.

[135] See Qarāfī, *Furūq*, 4:1309.

[136] Jurists agreed only on the most basic definition, which built doubt into the definition itself: *zinā* was defined as prohibited sexual relations between a man and a "woman [who have] no validating legal relationship or semblance of such a relationship" (*shubhat al-ʿaqd* or *shubhat al-milk*). Ibn Qudāma, *Mughnī*, 12:340.

[137] Qarāfī, *Furūq*, 4:1307 (calling this type of difference *shubha fī ʾl-ṭarīq* generally and *ikhtilāf al-ʿulamāʾ fī ibāḥat al-mawṭūʾa* specifically).

[138] Suyūṭī, *Ashbāh*, 237 (defining this type of doubt (*shubha fī ʾl-ṭarīq* or *shubhat al-khilāf*) as rules that "are licit according to some jurists but illicit according to others: *yakūn ḥalāl ʿinda qawm ḥarāman ʿinda ākharīn*").

permissible only in the earliest period of Islamic law created interpretive doubt: temporary marriage (as permitted in the early Meccan school and in proto-Shīʿī circles),[139] marriages – though not cohabitation – without witnesses (as permitted in the Medinan school of Mālik), and marriages without a guardian for the bride (as permitted in the Kūfan school of Abū Ḥanīfa).[140] Though Shāfiʿīs rejected these sorts of marriage in their own school, the fact that other early schools permitted them created a sort of precedential "text" that provided the basis for interpretive doubt.[141]

This Shāfiʿī willingness to recognize other schools' opinions was not absolute. For them, mere juristic disagreement, even if based on an early precedent, was not always enough to give rise to interpretive doubts. The disagreement also had to have some firm legal basis (preferably textual) that would pass muster according to specifically Shāfiʿī interpretive methods. That is, if a Shāfiʿī jurist examined the legal sources relied upon by other jurists to yield a divergent opinion, the Shāfiʿī jurists would be required to recognize only those divergent opinions whose underlying logic was so convincing that they suggested themselves to an astute Shāfiʿī jurist's mind.[142] Rather than differences arising from

139 According to Shāfiʿīs, temporary marriage was an ordinarily prohibited act made licit right at Islam's advent as a dispensation by necessity. They compared it to eating carrion to survive. According to them, the practice was forbidden in the year of the Battle of Khaybar, permitted in the year of the Meccan Conquest, then prohibited forever in the year of the Prophet's Farewell Pilgrimage, just before he died. In contrast to that narrative, the early Ḥijāzī scholar Ibn ʿAbbās ruled that it was permissible, and his opinion was followed in the Meccan and proto-Shīʿī schools. Based on the early Meccan recognition of the practice (though, notably, not the subsequent Shīʿī practice) in view of early interpretive differences surrounding its validity, Shāfiʿīs concluded that no *ḥadd* liability applied to Sunnī Muslims who practiced temporary marriage. See Ghazālī, *Wasīṭ*, 6:443–44; Rāfiʿī, *ʿAzīz*, 11:144; Nawawī, *Rawḍa*, 7:312; Ibn Ḥajar al-Haytamī, *Tuḥfa*, 4:120; Shirbīnī, *Mughnī*, 5:442.

140 The legal maxims literature commonly cites these types of marriage as examples of Sunnī jurists' application of the doubt canon to the rules of other schools even when they deemed those rules invalid in their own school. For example, Qarāfī, *Furūq*, 4:1307.

141 Suyūṭī, *Ashbāh*, 237. Likewise, they considered it improper to impose *ḥudūd* punishments for apostasy on people who intentionally abandoned the prescribed five daily prayers but had neither water nor sand (to make dry ablution) available to them, given the fact that use of one of the two was a necessary prerequisite for prayer. The jurists disputed the extent to which such people exercised choice and thus questioned the validity of apostasy determinations. See ibid.

142 See Ibn ʿAbd al-Salām, *Qawāʿid*, 2:279–80. It is for this reason that Shāfiʿīs flatly prohibited consumption of the alcoholic beverage *nabīdh* (see, for example, Ibn al-Naqīb, *ʿUmdat al-sālik*, 466–67) despite known interpretive disagreements about its legal status, with Ḥanafīs famously permitting it (see, for example, Marghīnānī, *Hidāya*, in Ibn Abī al-ʿIzz, *Tanbīh*, 4:175). See further discussion on the "drinking debate" in Chapter 5, Sections A and C.

any plausible interpretation of law, only differences based on "strong" legal arguments would create the kind of interpretive doubt that Shāfiʿīs would recognize.[143]

Going even further, one Shāfiʿī jurist recognized only those divergent conclusions that were adopted out of dire necessity. Ibn Surayj illustrated the point by analogy to the most extreme example of life-and-death straits: a Muslim could resort to eating carrion – ordinarily prohibited – only in order to survive. Likewise, he said, a jurist could accept a divergent opinion of law and authorize judges to apply the rule of interpretive doubt only when the legality of an act was unknown and the circumstances dire.[144]

This narrow interpretation of interpretive of doubt would bar judges from avoiding *ḥudūd* punishments in common cases of difference. Perhaps this was intentional, given the long-standing debate between Shāfiʿīs and Ḥanafīs over drinking the beerlike beverage *nabīdh*. One would expect a school's recognition of interpretive doubt to authorize judges to avoid *ḥudūd* punishments against Ḥanafī *nabīdh*-drinkers caught by non-Ḥanafī authorities. Indeed, the Mālikīs did just that, despite prohibiting the drink in their own school. But for the Shāfiʿīs, the clarity of the laws against drinking in the foundational texts left the Ḥanafīs with no reasonable basis for legalizing *nabīdh*. Accordingly, Shāfiʿī jurists rejected the operation of interpretive doubt here and advised judges to enforce *ḥudūd* punishments against Ḥanafī *nabīdh*-drinkers, even if they drank believing it to be lawful in their own legal school.[145]

In sum, after acknowledging early precedential rules from other schools of law, Shāfiʿī jurists restricted interpretive doubt to actual (or at least fairly

143 Suyūṭī, *Ashbāh*, 238 (*sharṭ al-shubha an takūn qawiyyan*).

144 Ibn al-Ahdal al-Yamanī (d. 1035/1626), *al-Farāʾid al-bahiyya*, quoted in Abū al-Fayḍ Muḥammad Yāsīn b. Muḥammad ʿĪsā al-Fādānī al-Makkī (d. 1334/1916–7), *al-Fawāʾid al-janiyya*, ed. Ramzī Saʿd al-Dīn Dimashqiyya (Beirut: Dār al-Bashāʾir, 1991), 2:133–34 (citing Ibn Surayj, *Wadāʾiʿ*).

145 See, for example, Ibn al-Naqīb, *ʿUmdat al-sālik*, 466–67 (defining the prohibition of drinking to cover any substance that would intoxicate if consumed in large quantity, based on the *ḥadīth* stating that a drink "that intoxicates in large quantity is prohibited in small quantity: *mā askara kathīruh fa-qalīluh ḥarām*"). For the rules prohibiting *nabīdh* in other Sunnī schools, see, for example, Abū al-Qāsim al-Khiraqī, *Mukhtaṣar* (Damascus: al-Maktab al-Islāmī, 1964), 196 (Ḥanbalī); Ibn Abī Zayd al-Qayrawānī, *Risāla* (Rabat: Wizārat al-Awqāf wa'l-Shu'ūn al-Islāmiyya, 1415/1995), 160 (Mālikī). Shīʿī law prohibits it, too, based on the *ḥadīth* rather than on analogy, and maintains that Ḥanafīs who drink *nabīdh* are *ḥadd*-eligible. See, for example, Ṭūsī, *Nihāya*, 2:731; Ibn Idrīs al-Ḥillī, *Sarāʾir*, 3:474; al-ʿAllāma al-Ḥillī, *Qawāʿid al-aḥkām*, in *YF*, 23:418.

plausible) ambiguities of legal texts based on their own interpretive methodology.[146] This limitation to Shāfiʿī rules and interpretive methods helped restrict potentially unwieldy claims of doubt based on the interpretations of other schools. It also aided Shāfiʿī jurists in interpreting the law more determinately and with respect to the text.

3. Doubt as Interpretive Difference?

Parallels between the Shāfiʿī and the Ḥanafī reluctance to embrace the category of interpretive doubt are perhaps telling about their respective positions of power. As the dominant legal system for centuries under ʿAbbāsid rule, Ḥanafism had an interest in expounding the law with respect to an *internal* jurisprudential logic that had no institutional need to recognize the divergent interpretations of minority schools, especially in public law spheres such as criminal law. Shāfiʿism developed initially as a minority school – that is, one without official state patronage – which may explain why Shāfiʿīs recognized interpretive doubt at all: it was their petition for self-recognition and an argument for their own relevance. Shāfiʿīs further developed their jurisprudence of legal maxims under the Seljūqs and Mamlūks, when their school was at the head of structurally diverse systems. Prominent Shāfiʿī figures such as Imām al-Ḥaramayn al-Juwaynī (d. 478/1085) and Abū Ḥāmid al-Ghazālī (d. 505/1111) led the spheres of learning in Seljūq Iraq and Persia. And Shāfiʿīs were dominant in Mamlūk Egypt and Syria, even as representatives of each school were officially recognized by the political authorities with the establishment of the four chief judgeships.[147] In those contexts, Shāfiʿīs – like early Ḥanafīs – would have had an interest in elaborating the law without being obliged to defer to the other schools. These dynamics may explain why – despite the early Shāfiʿī minoritarian embrace of interpretive doubt – later majoritarian Shāfiʿīs manifested a reluctance to invoke it easily.

C. FAULT LINES: STRICT LIABILITY AS DEFINITIONS OF MORAL VALUES

To be sure, doubt did not always produce the benefit of *ḥudūd* avoidance, and many jurists argued in favor of strict liability for certain crimes. On

[146] Ibn ʿAbd al-Salām describes interpretive doubt as referring to instances of conflict in legal texts, such as where one text indicates that a certain act is permissible and another that it is impermissible, without any indication of preference.

[147] See note 85.

balance, these were crimes in which the moral values at stake were so fundamental to Muslims that the doubt canon could not apply. In such cases, jurists advocated punishment regardless of legal doubt, factual doubt, or interpretive doubt.

1. Consensus Cases of Strict Liability

The main strict liability offense was rape. Muslim jurists across time agreed that doubt would not permit a judge to avoid punishment against the perpetrators of proved instances of rape. No claim of mistake or ignorance of the law could avert *ḥudūd* liability from the perpetrator because of the gravity and immorality of the crime and because of its severe harm to the victim.[148] The reverse was also true: the doubt canon was meant to uniformly prevent judges from punishing a rape victim. That is, the claim of a lack of voluntariness gave rise to doubt regarding the "material elements" – that is, to elemental doubt.[149]

Muslim jurists drew on an early precedent for support. During the reign of the second caliph, ʿUmar, recall that ʿUmar averted the sanction from a woman accused of *zinā* who claimed to have been sleeping and awoke to find a man atop her. ʿUmar determined the case to be one of rape, which lifted criminal culpability from the woman and presumably would have imposed it strictly on the man if he were known.[150] For Muslim jurists interpreting this case, the prohibition against rape was so clear and so well established that all legal agents were presumed aware of it and charged with respecting it. Accordingly, the jurists held that there was no room for doubt to aid the perpetrator in proved cases of rape.

[148] Ibn Qudāma, *Mughnī*, 12:347. Cf. Hina Azam, *Sexual Violence in Mālikī Legal Ideology: From Discursive Foundations to Classical Articulation* (PhD diss., Duke University, 2007) (discussing rape in early Islamic and medieval Mālikī law).

[149] Jurists based their uniform avoidance of enforcing the *ḥadd* sanction against rape victims on the *ḥadīth* in which the Prophet reportedly said that members of his community were not liable for matters arising from coercion. See Ibn Qudāma, *Mughnī*, 3:347–48 (citing the *ḥadīth*, "My community is not liable for [consequences arising from] mistake, forgetfulness, or coercion"). See also Muḥammad Bāqir al-Waḥīd al-Bihbahānī (d. 1206/1791–2), *Risālat aṣālat al-barāʾa,* in *al-Rasāʾil al-uṣūliyya* (Qum: Muʾassasat al-ʿAllāma al-Mujaddid al-Waḥīd al-Bihbahānī, 1416/[1996]), 354 (citing the *ḥadīth*, "My community is not liable in nine situations ... [among them] mistake, forgetfulness, coercion, ignorance, and incapacity"); Anṣārī, *Rasāʾil*, 154 (same). For further discussion, see Chapter 8.

[150] See Chapter 2 and Appendix B, case no. 14.

2. Against Contracting Ambiguity

Most jurists also imposed a rule of strict liability on couples who were clearly barred from marrying each other – such as siblings – but who did so anyway.[151] Abū Ḥanīfa attempted to counter that rule with his theory of contractual doubt, arguing that the legal permissions ordinarily flowing from a valid contract created *ḥadd*-averting doubt even when a contract was materially defective.[152] But this imaginative move fell flat. Even his successors rejected the rule, because Ḥanafīs as well as other jurists deemed the social-moral and political values inherent in maintaining the integrity of lineage too important to disregard in favor of contract law.[153]

3. Moral Values as Limits on *Ḥudūd* Avoidance

In these scenarios, Muslim jurists judged the moral imperatives against sexual violence and for preserving lineage to outweigh the interest in avoiding *ḥudūd* punishments. For them, although the sanctity of private agreements was a privileged value in Islamic law, it had to fit within rather than override the competing value of *ḥudūd* enforcement arising from the demand for judicial subservience to divine legislative supremacy. Core substantive moral values disallowed *ḥudūd* avoidance in these cases – no matter how strenuous the claims of mistake, ignorance, or doubt. All this had the effect of setting moral limits on otherwise expansive doctrines of doubt.

CONCLUSION

In sum, Muslim jurists after the early period developed a doctrine of doubt expressed in the legal maxims literature that blossomed most pronouncedly in the seventh/thirteenth through tenth/sixteenth centuries – a

[151] Many jurists dispensed with a *mens rea* requirement here, indicating the moral value they placed on this rule. Ibn Qudāma, *Mughnī*, 12:341 (citing late second/eighth- to mid-third/ninth-century jurists Abū Yūsuf, Muḥammad [al-Shaybānī], Isḥāq [Ibn Rāhawayh], and others, for whom the sensitive nature of such relationships and the moral depravity of crossing such lines warranted a strict-liability approach).

[152] Further examples in which Abū Ḥanīfa barred punishment even in cases where foundational Islamic legal texts clearly prohibited the acts in question include sexual relations with a slave woman held as security (see Ibn al-ʿAlāʾ al-Anṣārī, *al-Fatāwā al-Tātārkhāniyya*, 5:108–16; Ibn ʿĀbidīn, *Radd al-muḥtār*, 12:61–84; Qāḍī Khān, *Fatāwā*, 3:480–89) and contracts for the sale of wine (see Ibn Nujaym, *al-Baḥr al-rāʾiq*, 5:16).

[153] For further discussion, see Chapter 5.

literature that both restated and systematized the doubt jurisprudence in Islamic criminal law as a central feature of that law. In the law manuals and legal maxims treatises alike, the doubt canon not only featured prominently in criminal law discussions but also framed them. Jurists typically invoked the canon in their introductions to and definitions of each element of criminal law. They also cited the early *ḥadīth* reports of *ḥudūd* avoidance together with analogous cases from later periods, providing model cases meant to illustrate the scope of doubt from past cases and to offer normative guidance for future cases.

During this period, the rise and utility of the legal maxims literature signaled a move not only from traditions to law, but from common law–style case-by-case reasoning to principle-based theories of law. Importantly, the theories underlying the new expositions of law were neither uniform nor absolute. Jurists who readily accepted and invoked doubt jurisprudence differed significantly among themselves about what constituted doubt, what justified it, and what was the extent of limitations on it as they attempted to balance competing structural imperatives and moral values at play in discerning the contours of the jurisprudence of doubt.

Such was the jurisprudence of pragmatic textualists on doubt. Another strain of jurists, those who were more strictly textualist, approached the doubt canon and other legal maxims with caution and sometimes outright rejection. The next two chapters assess these strains and the rationales behind them in Sunnī and Shīʿī law.

PART IV

INTERPRETIVE AUTHORITY, SECOND/EIGHTH–TENTH/ SIXTEENTH CENTURIES

7

Against Doubt: Strict Textualism in Opposition to Doubt

Notwithstanding the development of a robust doubt jurisprudence in Islamic law, which typically counseled *ḥudūd* avoidance on the part of pragmatically textualist Sunnī jurists, the earlier, competing tendency toward *ḥudūd* enforcement did not disappear. Appealing to that tendency, a minority of Muslim jurists opposed the accommodation of doubt. The opposition from this group of more strictly textualist jurists appeared early and increased throughout the founding period.

Specifically, Ḥanbalī and Ẓāhirī jurists preferred appeals to clear statements, seeing doubt as an unwelcome intruder that compromised their ideal of textual certainty and facilitated human intervention in the divine law through encouraging the use of discretion. In their view, the doubt canon offended notions of certainty and divine legislative supremacy by granting a place of privilege to doubt and therefore to human interpretive authority. Accordingly, Ibn Ḥanbal exhibited discomfort with the doubt canon based on its dubious textual provenance. His followers adopted a similarly ambivalent stance toward the textual authenticity of the doubt canon, even when they concluded that it could be used in interpretation. For similar reasons, Dāwūd al-Ẓāhirī and his followers – who were even more strictly textualist and traditionist than their Ḥanbalī counterparts – rejected the canon outright. Their über-strict textualism led Ẓāhirīs to further object that the doubt canon was a dangerous tool in the hands of judges and jurists, who could invoke it much too capriciously to reflect their own preferences rather than those of the divine Lawgiver.

Yet doubt persisted in Islamic law. This chapter examines how Sunnī strict textualists responded to the textual concerns surrounding the doubt canon, and how they handled the inevitable persistence of doubt in Islamic criminal law.

A. ḤANBALĪ DOUBT: STRICT TEXTUALISM, CONSTRAINED DISCRETION

1. Overview of Ḥanbalī Traditionalism

Ibn Ḥanbal was a *ḥadīth* scholar and a jurist who adopted a fairly ambivalent attitude toward the doubt canon. As a *ḥadīth* scholar writing from Baghdad in the third/ninth century, he was part of the generations that did not regard the canon as an authentic *ḥadīth*. Moreover, as a jurist, he disagreed with doubt-framed practices of *ḥudūd* avoidance, seeing them often as an incoherent cover for reifying status hierarchies.

As for the canon's textual provenance, Ibn Ḥanbal – like other early *ḥadīth* scholars – thought that the standard version of the saying was of dubious authenticity. To be sure, he mentioned a version of the canon as a prophetic *ḥadīth* in his *Musnad*, but he never recognized the prophetic origins of the standard version claimed by other jurists, and he deemed the version of the *ḥadīth* that he did cite to be weak.[1] He noted nonetheless that the Prophet had avoided punishment against a woman suspected of *zinā* who claimed that she had been raped, given the lack of voluntariness on her part.[2]

As for status hierarchies, recall that Ibn Ḥanbal adopted the version of the elite-leniency maxim that allowed judges to "overlook the faults of the nobles except when they involve *ḥudūd* laws."[3] For serious moral offenses, he insisted on *ḥudūd* enforcement – emphasizing that those of high status were subject to punishment like everyone else.

In his discussions of the Prophet's avoidance of punishment and insistence on enforcement against criminal perpetrators, it is unclear to what extent Ibn Ḥanbal regarded these reports to have created a general precedent for accommodating doubt and avoiding punishment. His ambivalence revealed itself later in the strict textualist-traditionist jurisprudence of his followers, who adopted various positions on the validity of doubt.

Some subsequent Ḥanbalī scholars applied the doubt canon – albeit not always attributing it to the Prophet. In recognition of doubt, they

[1] For a discussion, see Chapter 3, section C.
[2] Ibn Ḥanbal, *Musnad*, 5:416.
[3] Ibid., 6:181. For further discussion, see Chapter 3, section C.

sometimes disagreed with Ibn Ḥanbal's rulings of *ḥudūd* enforcement in cases of doubt. For example, one of Ibn Ḥanbal's most prominent students, Isḥāq b. Ibrāhīm (d. 275/888–9), disagreed with his teacher's view that drinking intoxicating beverages warranted *ḥadd* punishment even if the person did not get drunk. Isḥāq perceived some degree of doubt as to whether the fixed punishment was for *drinking* intoxicants or for *intoxication*. To be sure, Isḥāq agreed with his teacher that drinking any intoxicant was illegal, based on the report, often cited by Shāfiʿīs, that "even small amounts of drinks that are intoxicating in abundance are prohibited."[4] But Isḥāq concluded that no punishment should attach to mere drinking because of the principle that *ḥudūd* sanctions are to "be avoided in cases of doubt."[5]

By contrast, the famous Iraqi jurist Abū al-Qāsim al-Khiraqī (d. 334/945) – who authored the main legal handbook relied upon in the Ḥanbalī school to this day – did not mention the doubt canon. Instead, he listed instances of mandatory *ḥudūd* enforcement on the one hand and of no *ḥudūd* liability on the other. In typical traditionalist-jurist style, each list was based on cases drawn from earlier *ḥadīth* rulings on specific scenarios in history.[6] In this way, Khiraqī's silence on the doubt canon stood in stark contrast to Isḥāq's invocation of it, although both jurists were Ḥanbalī.

These contrasting Ḥanbalī positions on doubt reflected the earlier tensions between policies of *ḥudūd* enforcement and policies of avoidance present in the early *ḥadīth* literature, and they presaged the later Ḥanbalī tendencies to offer mixed reviews of the concept of doubt. Ḥanbalī positions on doubt within Islamic criminal law were to become ever more diverse over time.

2. The Doubt Canon in Ḥanbalī Law: Limited *Ḥudūd* Avoidance

A few generations after the tenth- and eleventh-century textualization of doubt, some Ḥanbalī jurists began also to regard the doubt canon as a *ḥadīth* and to advocate broadly for *ḥudūd* avoidance. One might surmise

[4] See Isḥāq b. Ibrāhīm (d. 275/888–9), *Masāʾil al-Imām Aḥmad b. Ḥanbal*, ed. Zuhayr al-Shāwīsh (Beirut: al-Maktab al-Islāmī, 1400/1979), 2:265.

[5] Ibid.

[6] See, for example, Khiraqī, *Mukhtaṣar*, 193–94 (on theft: listing instances in which the *ḥadd* sanction for theft does not apply, including theft of dates or fruit, prohibited items, children's property by parents, and a master's property by a slave). His being an abridged handbook of law, Khiraqī did not cite the *ḥadīth* bases for these exceptions, but they were present in the *ḥadīth* literature from the collections of a century before – including Ibn Ḥanbal's *Musnad*, with which Khiraqī was familiar and upon which he presumably relied.

that Ḥanbalīs were merely mimicking the robust jurisprudence of doubt developed in the other Sunnī schools by that time. But there was more to it than that. The Ḥanbalī treatment of doubt did not reproduce the pragmatic jurists' jurisprudence of doubt, nor was the Ḥanbalī position on doubt uniform. The Ḥanbalīs' approach to doubt suggests a different set of textualist-traditionalist precepts altogether, best revealed through their alternate positions in favor of and in opposition to doubt.

In the camp of Ḥanbalī jurists unfavorably disposed to doubt was the prominent Ḥanbalī jurist and judge Qāḍī Abū Yaʿlā (d. 458/1066). Strikingly, he mentioned *ḥudūd* avoidance in his works only when defending Ḥanbalī views against divergent rulings from other law schools. This was a stark rejection not only of doubt but of legal pluralism itself, which reflected a larger vision of the extent to which he felt humans were constrained from interpreting God's law without respect to text. Accordingly, doubt receives no mention in his handbook of Ḥanbalī law, *al-Jāmiʿ al-ṣaghīr*.[7] By contrast, it features in his work *al-Aḥkām al-sulṭāniyya*,[8] a tract on political theory that responded to a work of the same title,[9] written by a famous Shāfiʿī contemporary, Māwardī.[10]

As Nimrod Hurvitz has argued, Abū Yaʿlā and Māwardī aimed to establish guidelines to ensure greater community cohesion and rule of law in the eleventh century's radically changed political landscape of

7 Qāḍī Abū Yaʿlā (d. 458/1066), *al-Jāmiʿ al-ṣaghīr fī fiqh ʿalā madhhab al-Imām Aḥmad b. Muḥammad b. Ḥanbal*, ed. Nāṣir b. Saʿūd b. ʿAbd Allāh al-Salāma (Riyadh: Dār Aṭlas, 2000), 305–309. Here he mostly presents the instances of *ḥadd* liability and nonliability in terms of mandatoriness. Abū Bakr al-Khallāl (d. 311/923) and Khiraqī (d. 334/945) had already noted most of these instances based on well-known *ḥadīth* reports and opinions attributed to Ibn Ḥanbal.

8 Nimrod Hurvitz, *Competing Texts: The Relationship Between al-Mawardi's and Abu Yaʿla's "al-Ahkam al-sultaniyya"* (Cambridge, MA: Islamic Legal Studies Program at Harvard Law School, 2007).

9 For the view that Abū Yaʿlā copied Māwardī's tract and "Ḥanbalized" it, see Muḥammad ʿAbd al-Qādir Abū Fāris, *al-Qāḍī Abū Yaʿlā al-Farrāʾ wa-kitābuh al-Aḥkām al-sulṭāniyya* (Beirut: Muʾassasat al-Risāla, 1983), esp. 499–523 (listing differences between the two and noting that Māwardī penned the original text). See also Donald Little, "A New Look at *al-Aḥkām al-sulṭāniyya*," *The Muslim World* 64 (1974), 1–15.

10 On Māwardī's work, see Hamilton A. R. Gibb, "Some Considerations on the Sunnī Theory of the Caliphate," in *Studies on the Civilization of Islam*, ed. Stanford J. Shaw and William R. Polk (London: Routledge, 2013) (orig. Boston: Beacon Press, 1962), 141–50; Hamilton A. R. Gibb, "Al-Māwardī's Theory of the Caliphate," in Shaw and Polk, *Studies on the Civilization of Islam*, 151–65. Gibb introduced Māwardī's scholarship to an English-speaking audience in the 1960s. For a comprehensive review some years later of the political context surrounding Māwardī and ideas about how it motivated the writing of this work, see Henri Laoust, "La pensée et l'action politiques d'al-Māwardī (364–450/974–1058)," *Revue des Études Islamiques* 36 (1968), 11–92 (repr., Paris: P. Geuthner, 1968).

increasingly decentralized rule.[11] Abū Yaʿlā and Māwardī were both "well-connected judges who had access to courtiers and caliphs and were therefore part of the ruling elite" to whom their works were explicitly addressed and whom their works had the effect of supporting.[12] They agreed that those in power – even if they achieved it by force – were owed near-total obedience, and the writings of both jurists accommodated that view. In that sense, their respective books of the same title were works "composed by members of the establishment for members of the establishment about the roles of the establishment."[13]

Viewed through the lens of doubt, however, the two works differ substantially. When discussing public jurisdiction over criminal law, Abū Yaʿlā noted limited permissions for *ḥudūd* avoidance – as had Ibn Ḥanbal, Khallāl, Khiraqī, and other Ḥanbalīs – based on specific scenarios presented in the early *ḥadīth* literature. In this context, Abū Yaʿlā was arguing *against* Māwardī – opposing what had become by then the widespread textualization and deployment of doubt. When he mentioned doubt, he decidedly avoided calling it prophetic and was at pains to limit its scope to the "correct" situations identified in Ḥanbalī jurisprudence. Thus, he maintained that if a man "claims plausible doubt as an excuse for committing *zinā*, such as [acting on the basis of] a defective contract, genuine confusion as to the identity of his wife, or ignorance that *zinā* is illegal in the first place, being a recent convert, then the *ḥadd* sanction is to be avoided."[14] This statement is a verbatim reproduction of the language of the other *Aḥkām* – minus Māwardī's citation of the doubt canon as a prophetic *ḥadīth* to bolster and explain the argument.[15]

11 See Hurvitz, *Competing Texts*, 5, 28, 38–39 (arguing that their views seemed to strengthen the position of regional rulers and further questioning the idea that there was wholesale copying between the two, noting significant differences between some sections, and arguing that the two works represented long-standing tensions between the juristic traditions of Māwardī and Abū Yaʿlā, with each excluding the legal school of the other in his analysis).

12 Ibid., 42 (citing the introduction to Māwardī's *Aḥkām*).

13 Ibid., 41. Hurvitz is agnostic on which *Aḥkām* was the original. Ibid., 42.

14 Abū Yaʿlā, *al-Aḥkām al-sulṭāniyya*, ed. Muḥammad Ḥāmid al-Fiqī (Cairo: Maktaba wa-Maṭbaʿat Muṣṭafā al-Bābī al-Ḥalabī, 1966), 265 (*wa-idhā ʾddaʿā fī ʾl-zinā shubha muḥtamala min nikāḥ fāsid aw ishtabahat ʿalayh bi-zawjatih aw jahila taḥrīm al-zinā wa-huwa ḥadīth al-Islām, duriʾa bihā shubha* [*sic* = *ʿanh*, as in Māwardī's *Aḥkām*, 254] *al-ḥadd*).

15 Māwardī explains that "the Prophet said: 'avoid punishments in cases of doubt.'" See his *Aḥkām*, 254 (*wa-idhā ʾddaʿā fī ʾl-zinā shubha muḥtamala min nikāḥ fāsid aw ishtabahat ʿalayh bi-zawjatih aw jahila taḥrīm al-zinā wa-hum* [*sic* = *huwa*, as in Abū Yaʿlā's *Aḥkām*, 265] *ḥadīth al-Islām, duriʾa bihā ʿanh al-ḥadd; qāla ʾl-Nabī ṣallā ʾllāhu ʿalayh wa-sallam: idraʾū ʾl-ḥudūd biʾl-shubahāt*).

Abū Yaʿlā's discussion on *ḥudūd* laws is replete with such direct references to doubt and oblique references to the doubt canon itself. This, along with the fact that he did not recognize the doubt canon in his other works, supports the notion that Abū Yaʿlā copied the work from Māwardī. In the copying process, Abū Yaʿlā was sure to delete the prophetic attributions appended to the doubt canon and to modify the rule to fit his school's doctrine.[16] Instead, Abū Yaʿlā drew only on anecdotes from the earliest generations (*salaf*) as authoritative. In short, Abū Yaʿlā's approach echoes Ibn Ḥanbal's ambivalence and his traditionist approach: he rejected the doubt canon as a *ḥadīth* and as a broad-ranging doctrine and accepted practices of *ḥudūd* avoidance only in situations backed by authoritative *ḥadīth* texts on a case-by-case basis.[17]

Abū Yaʿlā and Māwardī's differences on doubt stem from divergences in theological outlook on the scope of discretion that the divine Lawgiver had essentially "delegated" to jurists.[18] As a pragmatic textualist, Māwardī was willing to accommodate scholars of his ilk, who subscribed to a theology that saw jurists as the interpreters of God's law and doubt as the broad range of delegated interpretive discretion. That he shared this outlook with members of the Ḥanafī and Mālikī schools explains the intra-Sunnī comparative quality of the jurisprudence in his *Aḥkām* and his rich justification of the doubt canon as both a prophetic command and a rational principle. As a strict textualist and traditionalist who largely rejected that theology, Abū Yaʿlā restricted the law to textual rules of particular cases covered by the Prophet and the earliest community.[19]

[16] He did so while avoiding reference to Māwardī and to other schools' doctrines. See, for example, Abū Yaʿlā, *Aḥkām*, 263 (defining *zinā* as sex in the absence of a validating relationship or the semblance of one), 265 (noting the Ḥanbalī rule – against Abū Ḥanīfa – that if a man was to have sex with a prohibited partner (*maḥram*), even if the two were married, he would be *ḥadd*-eligible because such fatally defective contracts cannot overcome the textual prohibition against marriage to partners within prohibited degrees of relation in order to create a *ḥadd*-averting doubt: *lā yakūn al-ʿaqd maʿa taḥrīmihā biʾl-naṣṣ shubha fī darʾ al-ḥadd*), 266 (noting that intercession in a criminal trial is barred and cannot absolve *ḥudūd* liability, that is, *isqāṭ al-ḥadd*).

[17] By contrast, Māwardī cited political anecdotes from other periods, was rationally minded (believed in analogical reasoning (*qiyās*)), accepted the opinions of the other Sunnī schools – though not the Ḥanbalī school – as valid if not correct, and so argued with respect to the three major traditions (as Hurvitz points out); he viewed it as acceptable to appeal to doctrines external to the text. See Hurvitz, *Competing Texts*, 28.

[18] Hurvitz suggests that a long-standing theological dispute between the jurists was responsible for the differences between them. See ibid., 43 (referencing the *mutakallimūn* in Abū Yaʿlā's *Aḥkām*).

[19] Hurvitz is aware that Abū Yaʿlā does not cite historical anecdotes beyond the first few generations as authoritative, as in the chapter on *maẓālim* (extraordinary jurisdiction to address grievances, presided over by the caliph), he notes that Māwardī includes nine

Following Ibn Ḥanbal, Abū Yaʿlā rejected any theology that delegated to anyone but God the definition of law through the foundational texts. Moreover, he was more interested in finding the "one right answer" based on doctrines internal to the Ḥanbalī school than in accommodating legal pluralism or doubt. In his doubt jurisprudence, each jurist displayed fidelity to and thus revealed his respective theological and jurisprudential commitments.

a. Limited Doubt Jurisprudence

Abū Yaʿlā's immediate successors followed his textualist-traditionalist lead but disagreed on the textual status of doubt. Some had come to regard the doubt canon as a prophetic *ḥadīth*, in line with the consensus on its textualization among scholars of other schools. These Ḥanbalīs retained a distinctly textualist-traditionalist approach to criminal law and deployed a limited version of the doubt canon – as a *ḥadīth* – by drawing on traditions to define it.

For example, Ibn al-Bannāʾ (d. 471/1078–9) used the doubt canon to dispute Shāfiʿī's rejection of Khiraqī's rule that *ḥadd* liability for *zinā* requires four confessions or the testimony of four eyewitnesses. Ibn al-Bannāʾ argued that Shāfiʿī's position, which would impose *ḥadd* liability after only a single confession, was erroneous because it diverged from both the foundational texts imposing the rule of four eyewitnesses and from the doubt canon itself.[20] Moreover, he said, multiple precedents for *ḥudūd* avoidance, together with the prophet's direction to "avoid *ḥudūd* sanctions in cases of doubt"[21] supported Khiraqī's position – which he characterized as displaying a "general tendency to cancel *ḥudūd* liability," in contrast to that of Shāfiʿī.[22]

A generation later, the leading Ḥanbalī jurist of Baghdad, Abū al-Khaṭṭāb al-Kalwadhānī (d. 510/1116), similarly invoked the doubt canon to argue for avoiding fixed criminal punishments in situations

historical accounts that refer to caliphs, while Abū Yaʿlā includes none. Ibid., 25. Hurvitz does not, however, give Abū Yaʿlā's omissions of Māwardī's historical anecdotes much weight, commenting that both "integrate historical and contemporary political practice into the legal narrative of Islamic public law" to support their broader conclusions. Ibid., 47.

20 See Ibn al-Bannāʾ (d. 471/1078–9), *Kitāb al-Muqniʿ fī sharḥ Mukhtaṣar al-Khiraqī*, ed. ʿAbd al-ʿAzīz b. Sulaymān b. Ibrāhīm al-Baʿīmī (Riyadh: Maktabat al-Rushd, 1993), 3:1120 (noting that the Qurʾān requires four witnesses, that insane people and minors cannot be *ḥadd*-eligible, that an ill person convicted of a crime warranting a penalty lesser than death can request delayed punishment, that – contrary to Abū Ḥanīfa's rule – retracted confessions can remove *ḥadd* liability, etc.). Cf. Shāfiʿī, *Umm* (1961), 6:133.

21 Ibn al-Bannāʾ, *Muqniʿ*, 3:1120 (*idraʾū ʾl-ḥudūd biʾl-shubahāt*).

22 Ibid., 3:1120–21 (*taghlīban li-isqāṭ* [*al-ḥudūd*]).

where mere circumstantial evidence was used to prove an accusation of *zinā*.[23] The underlying question was one of ritual purity that could have criminal law implications if the same ritual law definitions were applied to criminal law. In ritual law, jurists debated whether a man who merely touched a woman as opposed to having sex with her invalidated the ritual purity of his ablution (*wuḍū'*). The uncertainty about the Qur'ānic text was part linguistic, part methodological: how were jurists to interpret the word "touch" in the verse instructing men who "touch women and do not find water [in order to purify themselves in preparation for prayer] to perform dry ablution [with clean dust]"?[24] Ḥanafīs and other jurists took the term "touch" to be a euphemism for sexual intimacy and read the verse to require ablution renewal only when a man and a woman had sex. By contrast, Ḥanbalīs argued that "touch" meant just what it said – touching with the hand, especially with desire – such that any male-female touch invalidated the ablution and required it to be redone.[25] But could "touching" have criminal implications when applied to other areas of law? Kalwadhānī said no.

Despite his position that any "touch" invalidated ritual purity, Kalwadhānī was careful to note that, in criminal proceedings adjudicating potential violations of *zinā* laws, mere touching would not give rise to criminal punishments. In criminal law, he considered the question as to whether a man and a woman unrelated to each other and lying together naked – with no other proof that they had had sex – could be criminally liable for *zinā*. Kalwadhānī noted that the couple's actions would be illegal, but not criminally liable. Even if they had committed *zinā*, Kalwadhānī cautioned *ḥudūd* avoidance based on "the Prophet's statement to 'avoid criminal punishments in cases of doubt.'"[26] Like Ibn al-Bannā', Kalwadhānī concluded from the doubt canon that – unlike ritual laws, which are to be read strictly and cautiously[27] – "*ḥudūd* laws are based on principles of avoidance and nonliability."[28]

23 Abū al-Khaṭṭāb al-Kalwadhānī (d. 510/1116), *al-Intiṣār fī 'l-masā'il al-kibār*, ed. Sulaymān b. 'Abd Allāh al-'Umayr (Riyadh: Maktabat al-'Ubaykān, 1993), 1:313–25.

24 Qur'ān, 4:43, 5:6 (*aw lāmastum al-nisā'a fa-lam tajidū mā'an fa-tayammamū*).

25 Kalwadhānī, *Intiṣār*, 1:313 (attributing the opinion that lustful touching breaks one's *wuḍū'* to mainstream Ḥanbalīs and to Mālik, noting that Abū Ḥanīfa and others held that mere touching – whether lustful or not – does not break the *wuḍū'*, and citing the Shāfi'ī view that any touching – whether lustful or not – does break the *wuḍū'*).

26 Ibid., 1:319–20 (*idra'ū 'l-ḥudūd bi'l-shubahāt*).

27 Ibid., 1:319 (noting that it was better to appeal to the *principle of precaution*, and thus be more stringent, in interpreting ritual law: *fa-ammā fī mas'alatinā fa-fīh iḥtiyāṭ li'l-'ibāda yaghlib*). For further elaboration of the precaution principle in the context of Shī'ī law, see Chapter 8.

28 Ibid. (*fa-ammā 'l-ḥudūd fa-mabnāhā 'alā 'l-dar' wa'l-isqāṭ*).

Accordingly, in cases where circumstantial evidence might otherwise trigger a punishment, he advocated following a general rule of avoiding a fixed punishment (though it could be replaced by a discretionary penalty).[29]

Ibn al-Bannāʾ, Kalwadhānī, and their generation of fifth/eleventh-century Ḥanbalī scholars were intent on defending Islamic law against the discretion-permitting pragmatic theories of the other Sunnī legal schools. Though these Ḥanbalī jurists accepted the doubt canon as a *ḥadīth*, they rejected what they regarded as the broad and unwieldy applications of the principle in the hands of jurists from the other schools.

b. Expanded Doubt Jurisprudence

The principal Ḥanbalī jurists of the next generation operating during the Mamlūk era followed the traditionalist approach but contested the textual basis of doubt. Specifically, Ibn Qudāma (d. 620/1223) and Ibn Abī al-Qāsim (d. 624/1226) accepted the doubt canon but did not regard it as a *ḥadīth*. They nevertheless deployed it broadly as had the Seljūq scholars of the generation before.[30]

Ibn Qudāma set a model for the later Mamlūk Ḥanbalī jurisprudence of doubt. He was the most influential Ḥanbalī jurist of his time, teaching and writing on Islamic law in an era of tremendous diversity, such that he readily engaged in comparative Sunnī law debates. In his lengthy comparative law treatise, he cited the doubt canon repeatedly throughout his extensive commentary on Khiraqī's (d. 334/945) earlier concise law manual. In essence, Ibn Qudāma announced that the doubt canon applied to every category to which its *non*-Ḥanbalī proponents applied it, with few (if any) Ḥanbalī-specific limitations. That is, he recognized legal and factual doubt, including claims of mistake of law,[31] ignorance

[29] Ibid. (mentioning other instances of seemingly arational rules in ritual and nonritual areas of law, such as the prohibition on buying wine because it is the means to drinking it, which is a *ḥadd*-eligible offense, and the requirement of making ablution after sleeping because the latter is a means or has the possibility of triggering an impurity (*khurūj al-ḥadath*)); see also ibid., 1:315 (*al-ḥaml ʿalā dhālik* [that is, "*lāmastum*" *ʿalā ʾl-lams biʾl-yad*] *aḥwaṭ liʾl-ʿibāda waʾl-bāb fī ʾl-ʿibādāt al-iḥtiyāṭ*).

[30] For a discussion of Ibn Qudāma's jurisprudence, see the next section. For Ibn Abī al-Qāsim, see his *Wāḍiḥ*, 4:413 (discussing *ḥadd*-averting doubt with reference to the *Case of Māʿiz* and applying the notion to retracted confessions: *li-anna rujūʿah shubha, waʾl-ḥudūd tudraʾ biʾl-shubahāt*), 416 (citing the doubt canon to explain why *ḥadd* liability for *zinā* requires male testimony based on the argument that Qurʾān, 2:282, signals that women's testimony raises the specter of doubt for which the *ḥadd* punishment should be avoided: *wa-li-anna fī shahādatihinna shubha li-taṭarruq al-ḍalāl ilayhinna … waʾl-ḥudūd tudraʾ biʾl-shubahāt*).

[31] See, for example, Ibn Qudāma, *Mughnī*, 12:345–46, 459–63 (noting that sex is not *ḥadd*-eligible when doubt is possible based on a purportedly validating legal text or status

of law,[32] mistake of fact,[33] coercion,[34] and questions about whether the criminal elements were present (that is, "elemental doubt").[35] He further found doubt in certain types of evidence, sometimes rejecting testimony based on gender or personal status as per se doubtful,[36] and at other times barring circumstantial evidence, such as the smell of alcohol, from creating *ḥadd* liability.[37] In contrast to scholars of previous generations, he appended the language of the doubt canon to each of these opinions to explain it.

The striking feature of Ibn Qudāma's doubt jurisprudence is the wide scope that he accorded to doubt. Namely, he extended doubt to cover new kinds of problems in law and evidence that earlier Ḥanbalīs had not previously recognized. Moreover, he incorporated a version of the late Shāfiʿī and Mālikī category of doubt, "interpretive doubt," to account for interschool and intraschool interpretive differences.[38] He explained that doubt arose in criminal accusations on acts subject to juristic disputes

relationship, for example, sex with a jointly owned slave woman or a father's taking of his son's property).

32 For example, ibid., 12:343, 345 (maintaining that sex within marriages the invalidity of which was a matter of juristic consensus would constitute *zinā* only if the parties involved had *knowledge* of the prohibition, and that ignorance of the law constitute a *ḥadd*-averting doubt, based on an earlier precedent from ʿUmar), 12:275–77 (giving examples indicating that to be *ḥadd*-averting, ignorance would have to be plausible based on circumstantial evidence of knowledge).

33 For example, ibid., 12:501 (giving the example of a person who mistakes an intoxicating beverage for a nonintoxicating one; the person would not be *ḥadd*-eligible).

34 For example, ibid., 12:347–48 (noting that there is no *ḥadd* liability for a rape victim based on the tradition of "lifted liability" – *ḥadīth al-rafʿ* – which stipulates rules against liability for acts committed or omitted out of mistake, forgetfulness, or coercion, and backed by the prophetic precedent cited by Ibn Ḥanbal, in which the Prophet avoided imposing the *ḥadd* sanction on a raped woman).

35 Ibid. (adding reasons of lack of voluntariness).

36 For example, ibid., 12:363–64, noting that the rules barring women's testimony in *zinā* proceedings and requiring two women for one man otherwise suggest there is perpetual doubt in women's testimony, such that it always constitutes the type of *ḥadd*-averting doubt that will drop *ḥudūd* liability (cf. note 30), and arguing that slave testimony also creates *ḥadd*-averting doubt (*annah* [that is, *al-ʿabd*] *mukhtalaf fī shahādatih fī sāʾir al-ḥuqūq fa-yakūn dhālika shubhatan tamnaʿ min qabūl shahādatih fī ʾl-ḥadd li-annah yandariʾ biʾl-shubahāt*).

37 See ibid., 12:501 (employing the doubt canon to support his view against *ḥadd* liability for the mere smell of alcohol on one's breath or for drunkenness, and citing an earlier precedent from ʿUmar for textual support).

38 Ibid., 12:472 (applying the doubt canon to avoid *ḥudūd* punishment in cases of theft backed by witness testimony where the accused denies having stolen, a situation on which three different Ḥanbalī opinions yield rulings of *ḥadd* liability, nonliability, and liability – the latter only if the thief had a reputation for lying or stealing, noting: *li-anna ʾl-ḥudūd tudraʾ biʾl-shubahāt*). Cf. ibid., 12:359 (applying the doubt canon to avoid punishment in view of the Ḥanafī rule that a mute person's confession through sign language constitutes *ḥadd*-averting doubt: *li-anna al-ḥadd lā yajib maʿa ʾl-shubha waʾl-ishāra lā tantafī maʿahā ʾl-shubahāt*).

because the very nature of the dispute generates doubt, for which the doubt canon directs judges to avoid ḥudūd *sanctions.*[39]

To be sure, Ibn Qudāma did not apply the doubt canon without limitation. Where the doubt canon would have conflicted directly with Khiraqī's unequivocal opinions, Ibn Qudāma usually did not invoke it. For example, a man might say to another man, "*zana'ta*," which literally means "you scaled [a mountain]," rather than "*zanayta*," which means "you committed fornication or adultery." Was the first man chargeable with the crime of defamation? Ibn Qudāma held – in line with Khiraqī – that the first statement would constitute defamation only if intended in the sense of the second statement. As had Shāfiʿī, Khiraqī – and, following him, Ibn Qudāma – read a *mens rea* requirement into defamation law. Judges were to avoid punishments in defamation cases unless there was the requisite criminal intent.[40] In addition, Ibn Qudāma rejected applications of the canon that went against community values of sexual mores. Case in point: like most other Sunnī jurists, he rejected Abū Ḥanīfa's infamous category of "contractual doubt" when it came to incestuous marriages.[41]

In short, Ibn Qudāma greatly expanded the Ḥanbalī recognition and application of doubt. For him, as for the jurists from the early period, the doubt canon was authoritative because it was a matter of consensus even if it was not a prophetic *ḥadīth*.[42] As such, it was the key governing principle of criminal law, pervading every area of his criminal law jurisprudence.

Most subsequent Ḥanbalī jurists followed suit – accepting the doubt canon not as a prophetic *ḥadīth* but as a guiding principle of criminal law. A notable example was Ibn al-Qayyim (d. 751/1350), who recognized the doubt canon as a judicial principle but severely limited its use. In his book

39 Ibid., 12:243–44 (emphasis added) (listing temporary marriage (*mutʿa*), an exchange marriage (*shighār*), validating marriage after a third divorce (*taḥlīl*), marriage without a guardian or witnesses, marrying the sister of one's divorced wife during the latter's waiting period, marrying a fifth wife during the waiting period of a divorced fourth, and marrying a Zoroastrian as issues subject to dispute, and noting that his position of *ḥudūd* avoidance is consistent with the opinion of most jurists given their interpretive differences as to the legality of such marriages: *al-ikhtilāf fī ibāḥat al-waṭʾ fīh shubha, waʾl-ḥudūd tudraʾ biʾl-shubahāt*). For further definitions of some of these types of marriage, see Chapter 5, note 191.

40 See ibid., 12:396.

41 See ibid., 12:341–42; cf. 12:348 (rejecting another of Abū Ḥanīfa's anomalous rulings – later billed as his expansive application of the doubt canon – that a man who is coerced into committing *zinā* is not *ḥadd*-eligible if the political authority does the coercing).

42 Ibid., 12:244 (pointing to Ibn al-Mundhir's statement to that effect three centuries before his time: *qāla Ibn al-Mundhir ajmaʿa kull man naḥfaẓ ʿanh min ahl al-ʿilm anna ʾl-ḥudūd tudraʾ biʾl-shubahāt*). See Ibn al-Mundhir, *Ijmāʿ*, 132 (*wa-ajmaʿū ʿalā darʾ al-ḥadd biʾl-shubahāt*).

on judging, *al-Ṭuruq al-ḥukmiyya fī ʾl-siyāsa al-sharʿiyya*, he asked a single question: Can a judge rule by his judicial acumen (*firāsa*), particularly when the evidence is insufficient by itself to dictate a clear decision?[43] In his answer, in the section addressing criminal law, he quoted the doubt canon, "Avoid criminal punishments in cases of doubt," and referenced an episode similar to the *Case of the Mysterious Pregnancy* in which ʿUmar, at the advice of ʿAlī, declined to enforce the *ḥadd* punishment against a woman accused of fornication.[44] Punishment avoidance in that case, Ibn al-Qayyim commented, was "the most subtle degree of judicial acumen."[45] He further mentioned the *Case of the Falsely Accused Butcher* as exemplary in this vein. Although he did not acknowledge the textual validity of the doubt canon, Ibn al-Qayyim embraced it as a general principle of criminal law.[46] His contemporaries agreed. For instance, like Ibn al-Qayyim, the slightly younger scholar Ibn Mufliḥ (d. 763/1361) accepted the doubt canon, albeit not its textual origins.[47]

c. *Rejected Doubt Jurisprudence*

The major exception to the broad Ḥanbalī acceptance of the doubt canon was espoused by Ibn Taymiyya (d. 728/1328). As usual, he bucked the Ḥanbalī

[43] Ibn al-Qayyim, *Ṭuruq* (2007), 3 (*fa-qad saʾalanī akhī ʿan al-ḥākim aw al-wālī yaḥkum biʾl-firāsa waʾl-qarāʾin allatī yaẓhar fīhā ʾl-ḥaqq waʾl-istidlāl biʾl-amārāt wa-lā yaqif maʿa mujarrad ẓawāhir al-bayyināt waʾl-iqrār* . . .).

[44] For the *Case of the Mysterious Pregnancy*, see Chapter 4, and Appendix B, case no. 14. Particularly noteworthy is that, in addition to quoting the mainstream Sunnī sources of his own tradition, the author cites ʿAlī's judgments from Shīʿī sources. See Ibn al-Qayyim, *Ṭuruq* (2007), 74–75 (quoting the Shīʿī jurist Ibrāhīm b. Hāshim al-Qummī's third/ninth-century collection of ʿAlī's judgments); for further instances of Ibn al-Qayyim's citations to ʿAlī's judgments from the Shīʿī traditionist and associate of ʿAlī in Kūfa, Aṣbagh b. Nubāta, see Modarressi, *Tradition and Survival*, 67–68.

[45] Ibn al-Qayyim, *Ṭuruq* (2007), 82 (*min daqīq al-firāsa*).

[46] Ibid., 89. See also Ibn al-Qayyim, *Iʿlām al-muwaqqiʿīn ʿan Rabb al-ʿālamīn*, ed. ʿAbd al-Raḥmān al-Wakīl (Cairo: Dār al-Kutub al-Ḥāditha, 1969), 1:104 (citing a version of the doubt canon that "punishments [rather than *ḥudūd* punishments] are to be avoided in cases of doubt: *al-ʿuqūbāt tudraʾ biʾl-shubahāt*").

[47] Ibn Mufliḥ (d. 763/1361), *Kitāb al-Furūʿ*, ed. ʿAbd Allāh b. ʿAbd al-Muḥsin al-Turkī (Beirut: Muʾassasat al-Risāla, 2003), 10:57 (noting that the absence of doubt is required for *ḥadd* liability for *zinā*: *wa-yushtaraṭ intifāʾ al-shubha*); see also 10:59, 61, and passim (making limited mention of *ḥadd*-averting and non-*ḥadd*-averting doubt). Most likely, the stripped-down doubt jurisprudence is deliberate, as Ibn Mufliḥ presents and elucidates his own preference for certain opinions of earlier Ḥanbalīs – some of whom quoted the doubt canon as a *ḥadīth* and/or adopted an expansive doubt jurisprudence, including Ibn Abī al-Qāsim in his *Wāḍiḥ*, Ibn Qudāma in his *Mughnī*, and Kalwadhānī in his *Intiṣār*. Ibn Mufliḥ, like Ibn al-Qayyim, was a student of Ibn Taymiyya, who largely ignores the doubt canon altogether.

trend – neither accepting nor incorporating the doubt canon, not as a prophetic *ḥadīth* and not as a consensus-based judicial principle.[48] Instead, he aimed to revert to what he perceived as the "original" and more constrained jurisprudence of *ḥudūd* laws that emphasized *ḥudūd* enforcement before the widespread textualization and generalization of the doubt canon.

Ibn Taymiyya typically argued for *ḥudūd* enforcement in response to various questions wherein a petitioner attempted to raise some measure of doubt.[49] For the limited instances in which he held there to be no *ḥadd* liability, he appealed for support to textual statements, not to doctrines of doubt.

For instance, on the question of whether repentance cancels *ḥadd* liability, Ibn Taymiyya pointed to an early precedent to conclude that liability would drop only if the perpetrator repented *before* the matter was brought to the court.[50] He further suggested that perpetrators conceal their crimes in line with other early reports, and thus encouraged private repentance.[51] In that vein, he cited the *Case of the Drunken Brother* – the early precedent in which ʿAbd al-Raḥmān, son of the caliph ʿUmar b. al-Khaṭṭāb, was dragged to court by his brother for drinking wine.[52] The governor and judge, ʿAmr b. al-ʿĀṣ, flogged him privately and drew censure from the caliph back in Medina. ʿUmar sent for his son and flogged him publicly.[53] The case was instructive for Ibn Taymiyya: he concluded that concealed crimes permitted private repentance. Yet public matters required *ḥudūd* enforcement rather than recognition of doubt of the kind that would lead to *ḥudūd* avoidance.

In large part, Ibn Taymiyya's narrowing of doubt had to do with his über-traditionalist orientation to law and theology.[54] He took a decidedly

48 In his collection of legal opinions (*fatāwā*), Ibn Taymiyya never acknowledges the doubt canon. See Ibn Taymiyya, *Majmūʿ al-fatāwā*, 34:177ff. (section on *ḥudūd* laws).

49 Ibid.

50 Ibid., 34:179–80 (on *zinā*, including the following texts: (1) *ḥadīth*: *man ibṭalā bi-shayʾ min hādhihi ʾl-qādhūrāt fa-ʾl-yastatir bi-satr Allāh, fa-innah man yubdi lanā ṣafḥatah naqim ʿalayh Kitāb Allāh*; (2) Qurʾān: *wa-ʾlladhīna idhā faʿalū fāḥishatan aw ẓalamū anfusahum dhakarū ʾllāh fa-ʾstaghfarū li-dhunūbihim*).

51 Ibid., 34:180, noting that repentance and concealment of the matter from the courts is preferable so long as it meets the requirements of "correct repentance," based on the *ḥadīth* encouraging as much (citing Qurʾān, 3:135, and two *ḥadīth* reports); cf. 15:302–303 (similar), 14:286–87 (similar).

52 See Appendix B, case no. 12 and sources cited therein.

53 Ibn Taymiyya, *Majmūʿ al-fatāwā*, 14:287 (commenting on Qurʾān, 24:2: *wa-lā taʾkhudhkum bihimā raʾfa*).

54 For studies examining Ibn Taymiyya's maverick theology and jurisprudence – which is beyond the scope of this book – see Ovamir Anjum, *Politics, Law, and Community in Islamic Thought: The Taymiyyan Moment* (Cambridge: Cambridge University Press,

strict textualist approach to law and adopted a traditionalist view of theology, which together manifested as a theory of legal authority that emphasized constrained human discretion and exclusive divine legislative supremacy located in foundational texts. Taking seriously the Islamic doctrine that all law was divine and explicated through the Qur'ān and Sunna, he sought to reduce the scope of human discretion in Islamic law to nil.[55]

3. Ḥanbalī Doubt

As the above discussion illustrates, Ḥanbalī jurists traveled in two different directions when dealing with doubt. Some jurists rejected the doubt canon and its textual provenance, some wholly embraced both, and most fell somewhere in the middle: accepting doubt but not viewing it as a *ḥadīth*. Over time, even Ḥanbalī jurists restating the law through legal maxims literature were unable to devise a consistent Ḥanbalī jurisprudence of doubt of the kind observed in other schools.[56] Instead, Ḥanbalīs took a case-by-case approach unified less by doctrine than by appeal to traditionalist strict textualism. These varied approaches to doubt reflected the ambivalence of the school's founder, and they encapsulated a traditionalist theology and theory of legal interpretation. In short, when it came to doubt, Ḥanbalī traditionalist theology gave primacy to textual over pragmatic or rational principles in attempts to subordinate human discretion to that of God.

2012); M. Shahab Ahmed and Yossef Rapoport, eds., *Ibn Taymiyya and His Times* (Karachi: Oxford University Press, 2010); Jon Hoover, *Ibn Taymiyya's Theodicy of Perpetual Optimism* (Leiden: Brill, 2007); Abdul-Hakim Matroudi, *The Ḥanbalī School of Law and Ibn Taymiyyah: Conflict or Conciliation* (London: Routledge, 2006).

55 Ibn Taymiyya, *Majmūʿ al-fatāwā*, 34:175 (on communal obligation, *farḍ kifāya*, noting that God addresses believers with "absolute" statements of law (*khiṭāban muṭlaqan*), signaling absolute obligation; citing the main *ḥudūd* verses: 5:38 on the penalty for theft; 24:2 on the penalty for *zinā*; 24:4, 32 on the penalty for defamation, etc.).

56 Of course, there is Ibn Rajab's work, entitled "Legal Maxims" (*Qawāʿid*), but it encapsulates Ḥanbalī substantive doctrines of law, rather than providing principles to guide future application. See Ibn Rajab (d. 795/1393), *Qawāʿid* (Mecca: Maktabat Nizār Muṣṭafā al-Bāz, 1999); see also ʿAbd al-Karīm b. Muḥammad Lāḥim, *Sharḥ Tuḥfat ahl al-ṭalab fī tajrīd uṣūl Qawāʿid Ibn Rajab*, ed. Muḥammad Ḥāmid al-Fiqī (Riyadh: Kunūz Ishbīliyā, 2006). Some later Ḥanbalī jurists, such as Ibn al-Laḥḥām (d. 803/1401–2), collected legal maxims and included the doubt canon. It may be that these works should be taken to have followed the larger trend of Ibn al-Laḥḥām's contemporaries from other schools composing legal maxims treatises. See Ibn al-Laḥḥām, *al-Qawāʿid wa'l-fawāʾid al-uṣūliyya* (Cairo: Maṭbaʿat al-Sunna al-Muḥammadiyya, 1956).

B. ẒĀHIRĪ DOUBT: STRICTER TEXTUALISM, BARRED DISCRETION

Going even further than Ḥanbalī textualists, Ẓāhirīs unequivocally rejected the doubt canon and any tendency toward *ḥudūd* avoidance. Dāwūd "the Literalist" established the school of strict textualism in the ninth century, with little to say about doubt.[57] It was his famously sharp-tongued and acerbic successor Ibn Ḥazm in the eleventh century who levied the most direct and hard-hitting attack on doubt.

1. Overview of Ẓāhirī Textualism

Dāwūd b. ʿAlī b. Khalaf al-Iṣbahānī al-Ẓāhirī (d. 270/833–4), dubbed "Dāwūd the Literalist" in medieval Islamic legal literature, laid the foundation for his followers' complete rejection of doubt. In essence, Ẓāhirīs maintained that there was a single right answer to any legal question, and that it was located in the text. Dāwūd had studied under the Ḥanbalī strict textualist jurist Ibn Rāhawayh and, adopting an even stricter view of interpretation, accepted only the apparent or plain meaning of authentic texts.[58] During his

57 For background references to Dāwūd b. ʿAlī and the Ẓāhirī school, see Chapter 1, note 52 and accompanying text. Notably, although Dāwūd and his disciples fell into the strict textualist camp generally, they fell to the extreme right of that camp and were thus historically characterized as "literalists." For a contrast between textualism and literalism in the American legal tradition, see, for example, Michael J. Gerhardt, "A Tale of Two Textualists," *Boston University Law Review* 74 (1994), 25–66, esp. 47, n. 126 (providing an example of former Justice Hugo Black's literalism in comparison and contrast with the textualism of Justice Antonin Scalia).

58 Dāwūd permitted inferences from textual bases, inference being "the fundamental principle on which [the Ẓāhirīs] built their doctrine." See Stewart, "Muḥammad b. Dāʾūd al-Ẓāhirī's Manual," 154; see also ibid., 153–54 ("What is explicitly mentioned in the Koran, set forth unambiguously by name and description, removes all doubt from the audience .... The meaning of texts in the Koran that indicate rulings implicitly, or present symbols and comparisons, may be determined by inference (*istidlāl*)."). But Dāwūd rejected the use of analogy, equity (*istiḥsān*), and other forms of *ijtihād* that other jurists used to extract rules not apparent in or inferred directly from the text. See ibid., 99–160, esp. 139–52 (against analogical reasoning (*qiyās*) and applying equitable principles (*istiḥsān*)), 154–58 (against *ijtihād*). Stewart notes that Ẓāhirī inference (*istidlāl*) seems to refer to non-analogical arguments that are "purely linguistic modes of inference, based entirely on the text itself," for example, *reductio ad absurdum*. Ibid., 154, n. 129. For later usage, see Adam Sabra, "Ibn Ḥazm's Literalism: A Critique of Islamic Legal Theory" (in two parts), *al-Qanṭara: Revista de Estudios Árabes* 28, 1 and 2 (2007), 7–40, 307–48 (cataloging Ibn Ḥazm's use of inference and other text-based interpretive strategies). This is the ordinary sense of inference, even among other jurists, and consistent with text-based canons of construction that all self-avowed textualists, medieval Muslim and modern

time, the doubt canon had yet to be textualized as an "authentic" *ḥadīth*, and as a result it fell outside the realm of his consideration.

For Dāwūd, the ideal of divine legislative supremacy required judges to appeal only to the Qurʾān and to authentic prophetic reports that made clear statements of law.[59] This rule applied with special relevance to substantive criminal law and punishment. For example, it was virtually axiomatic among other Sunnī schools that slaves who committed crimes were to receive half of the fixed punishment that would be incurred by free perpetrators. This rule extended the Qurʾānic directive to impose half of the punishment for sex crimes on married slave women who committed such crimes: "If [a slave woman] is married [or chaste] and commits a grave sin [that is, adultery], she is to receive half of the punishment of free, chaste women."[60] Dāwūd read this text narrowly to apply only to the married slave women mentioned in the verse. Unmarried slaves, whether male or female, were to receive the full punishment.[61] This was literalism par excellence.

Likewise, against the multiple interpretations of other Sunnī jurists,[62] Dāwūd read the Qurʾānic text requiring hand-amputation for theft literally and narrowly. For him, there was no minimum actionable amount required to trigger a punishment for theft because the text specified none. Instead, theft meant exactly what it said: those who took others' belongings were to be punished regardless of the value of the stolen goods or the manner of the theft.[63] This was literalism, again.

On evidentiary matters, Dāwūd maintained that whenever criminal violations were proved, judges were to strictly enforce criminal punishments.[64]

American – including Ẓāhirīs, Akhbārīs, and new textualists – readily accept. For an exposition from the latter point of view, see Scalia, *A Matter of Interpretation*, 23–29.

59 See Sabra, "Ibn Ḥazm's Literalism," 157–58. Although traditionalists and rationalists are typically put at complete odds with one another, and although their theological outlooks indeed differed in ways that affected their legal conclusions about the scope of human discretion to interpret the law, Dāwūd happened to share this position with the Sunnī Muʿtazilī rationalist theologians of Baṣra and their Shīʿī disciples such as the jurist al-Sharīf al-Murtaḍā. See Chapter 8, notes 48–76 and accompanying text.

60 Qurʾān, 4:25 (*fa-idhā uḥṣinna fa-in atayna bi-fāḥishatin fa-ʿalayhinna niṣfu mā ʿalā ʾl-muḥṣanāti min al-ʿadhāb*).

61 See Shaṭṭī, *Risāla*, 24–25 (collecting *masāʾil* – opinions on legal issues attributed to Dāwūd b. ʿAlī in various works). Recall that the Qurʾānic punishment for adultery was lashes, which could be divided, rather than stoning, which could not.

62 For varied Sunni interpretations, see Weiss, *Spirit of Islamic Law*, 101–109.

63 Shaṭṭī, *Risāla*, 25 (Dāwūd: *li-ʿumūm al-āya* [that is, *waʾl-sāriqu waʾl-sāriqatu fa-ʾqṭaʿū aydiyahumā* (Qurʾān, 5:38)] *wa-ẓāhir ḥadīth Abī Hurayra – laʿana ʾllāh ʾl-sāriq yasriq al-bayḍa fa-tuqṭaʿ yaduh wa-yasriq al-ḥabl fa-tuqṭaʿ yaduh*).

64 See ibid. (citing legal opinions attributed to Dāwūd b. ʿAlī from various works requiring the strict enforcement of criminal laws).

He applied this rule to require *ḥudūd* enforcement even in scenarios in which a defendant confessed to a crime but then retracted the confession.[65] Further, Dāwūd assessed evidence with an eye to the type of knowledge that would provide the most certain basis for *ḥudūd* enforcement: "The strongest evidence is the [judge's] own knowledge, then confession, then witness testimony (*bayyina*)."[66] In other words, he valued certainty over allowing for evidentiary doubt. For proof, Dāwūd cited a prophetic report of a case in which a woman named Hind, a Muslim convert and a former nemesis of the Prophet, had allegedly stolen money from her husband. Drawing on his own knowledge, the Prophet ruled that she had not committed theft as she had merely taken funds in order to meet the needs of herself and her son.[67] Because he had "judicial knowledge" of the facts, the Prophet did not require her to produce evidence to support her claim.[68] Dāwūd took this report to obligate judges to rely on their own knowledge of the facts when adjudicating criminal cases. His extraction of a general obligation to use judicial knowledge in criminal law is a radical inversion of the general aversion to that practice in Sunnī law.[69]

Moreover, Dāwūd and his followers emphasized that judges were not to exercise any interpretive discretion in criminal or other cases.[70] Three arguments stand out in the book written by his son, Muḥammad b. Dāwūd – the earliest written work of the Ẓāhirī school's jurisprudence. First, the Ẓāhirīs rejected the main *ḥadīth* on which other Sunnīs relied for the validity of interpretation (*ijtihād*). According to that report, the Prophet had sent the Companion Muʿādh b. Jabal to Yemen to serve as governor and judge. The Prophet questioned Muʿādh about his decision-making process, and Muʿādh responded that he would rule by the Qur'ān and the Sunna, and when those were exhausted, he would engage in interpretation and rely on his informed opinion (*ra'y*). Whereas other Sunnīs read the

[65] Ibid., 24.
[66] Ibid., 26 (specifying that the rule applies to *dimā'*, *amwāl*, *qiṣāṣ*, *furūj*, and *ḥudūd*).
[67] Ibid. (*bi'l-maʿrūf*).
[68] Ibid. For more on the Ẓāhirī position against any kind of nontextual argument, including rational legal interpretation (*ijtihād bi'l-ra'y*), see Maḥmūd, *Ittijāhāt*, 387–89.
[69] Māwardī, *Adab al-qāḍī*, 2:368–77 (noting diverse positions on the use of judicial knowledge in private law claims, but pointing out that the majority of Sunnī jurists (except for Ḥanafīs in many cases) disallowed reliance on judicial knowledge for *ḥudūd* laws), 2:376 (explaining the antipathy to using judicial knowledge to decide criminal cases, "because matters of public law [lit.: 'God's rights'] are established on the basis of leniency and forgiveness due to [the doctrine of] avoidance based on doubt: *li-anna ḥuqūq Allāh mawḍūʿa ʿalā 'l-takhfīf wa'l-musāmaḥa li-isqāṭihā bi'l-shubha*").
[70] See Stewart, "Muḥammad b. Dā'ūd al-Ẓāhirī's Manual," 156–57.

Prophet to have affirmed this process,[71] Ẓāhirīs criticized the report as weak with respect to both its authenticity and its meaning: the chain of transmission was unreliable and the content was contrary to the overarching, oft-emphasized principle of adherence to the text.[72]

Second, Ibn Dāwūd referred to the Qur'ān's explicit prohibitions on the use of human interpretation. The Prophet himself had pointed to the Qur'ān when instructing ʿUmar on dealing with a thorny inheritance issue. Elaborating on this, Ibn Dāwūd said:

> God – May His praise be manifest! – said, "We have revealed the Book unto you with the truth so that you may judge between mankind by that which God shows you. Do not be a pleader for the treacherous" (Q. 4:105). God did not say, "by that which you think for yourself" or "by that to which your choice and perception lead you." God – Blessed be His name! – said, "Who is more a miscreant than he who follows his own desire, with no guidance from God?" (Q 28:50).[73]

Finally, Ibn Dāwūd made a logical argument as well, using a type of inference that he considered valid as opposed to rational interpretation that accommodated personal or judicial preferences. He said: "If two people were to perform legal interpretation (*ijtihād*) and arrive at different opinions, [to accept both would be like saying that] the truth resided in two contradictory answers at the same time.... [However,] the truth is that which God, the Glorious and Almighty, enjoined upon us."[74]

With such arguments, Dāwūd and his followers maintained that each case had a single right answer located in clear foundational texts. Judicial interpretation that went beyond the text was "arbitrary personal opinion (*ra'y*) and human interpretation (*ijtihād*)" – technical terms that he gave a pejorative meaning – instead of divine law.[75] Against this backdrop it bears repeating that Dāwūd certainly did not consider the doubt canon to be an authentic text.

[71] See my "Islamic Legal Minimalism: Legal Maxims and Lawmaking When Jurists Disappear," in *Law and Tradition in Classical Islamic Thought*, ed. Michael Cook et al. (New York: Palgrave Macmillan, 2013), 145–66, and sources cited therein.

[72] Stewart, "Muḥammad b. Dā'ūd al-Ẓāhirī's Manual," 155–56 (as translated and quoted by Stewart).

[73] Ibid., 156.

[74] Ibid. He added that, was one to appeal to judges to decide matters according to "their own whims ... [each would] judge by his fancy, [giving a ruling] opposite to that determined by the fancy of his companion. According to this doctrine, the two rulings would be correct, despite their contradiction." Ibid., 157–58.

[75] Ibid., 157.

2. A Textualist Theory of Law and the Principle of Precaution

Two centuries after the founding of the Ẓāhirī school, the doubt canon had been textualized, making any form of textualism that excluded doubt in need of a stronger defender. Ibn Ḥazm, the infamously colorful Ẓāhirī spokesman of the eleventh century, filled that role.[76]

Ibn Ḥazm harshly criticized his Sunnī counterparts for textualizing the doubt canon in the first place, and for uncritically advocating *ḥudūd* avoidance on its basis.[77] His arguments against the doubt canon followed three lines of attack: (1) he challenged the textual authenticity of the doubt canon; (2) he emphasized the Islamic imperative to strictly enforce, rather than avoid, *ḥudūd* laws in deference to the Lawgiver and the divine legislative supremacy ideal; and (3) he highlighted what he took as emblematic of the dangers of human discretion in interpretation: the utter incoherence and arbitrariness of the Sunnī jurisprudence of doubt.

a. Against Textualization of Doubt

As for the textual authenticity of the doubt canon, Ibn Ḥazm argued that there was none. Contrary to the widespread notion among jurists of his time, he concluded that the canon was invalid, inauthentic, and definitely not prophetic.[78] One had only to look at the standard form of the canon as it appears in ʿAbd al-Razzāq's collection of reports, where he takes Ibrāhīm al-Nakhaʿī to have attributed the canon directly to ʿUmar, to see that the attribution was patently invalid. Ibrāhīm al-Nakhaʿī was born when ʿUmar had already died![79]

[76] Ibn Ḥazm was the last well-known leader of the Ẓāhirī (lit.: "literalist" or "apparent meaning") school, so named because its jurists insisted on accepting only the apparent or literal meaning of foundational texts, without regard for implicatures or contextual considerations. On the history of the Ẓāhirī school and its methodology, see the standard work by Ignaz Goldziher, *Die Ẓāhiriten* (1884), trans., *The Ẓāhirīs: Their Doctrine and Their History; A Contribution to the History of Islamic Theology*, trans. Wolfgang Behn (Leiden: Brill, 1971); see also Sabra, "Ibn Ḥazm's Literalism," 7–11 and nn. 2–14 (and sources cited therein), and 307. See also sources cited in note 133 and Chapter 1, note 52.

[77] See Ibn Ḥazm, *Muḥallā*, 12:57–63 (*mas'alat hal tudra' al-ḥudūd bi'l-shubahāt am lā*, specifically criticizing the Ḥanafīs, the Mālikīs, and the Shāfiʿīs, in that order, according to his estimation of their relative levels of support for the doubt canon).

[78] Ibid., 9:428, 8:252 (*mā jā'a ʿan al-Nabī qaṭṭu*). To be sure, some non-Ẓāhirī jurists realized this point as well, for example, the Mālikī jurist Ibn al-Shaṭṭ (d. 723/1323) in his *Idrār al-shurūq ʿalā Anwā' al-furūq*, on the margins of Qarāfī, *Furūq*, 4:316 (explaining that, even though the doubt canon is not authentic, it is nevertheless applicable because there is juristic consensus that *ḥudūd* punishments can only be enforced with the absence of doubt).

[79] Ibn Ḥazm, *Muḥallā*, 9:428, 8:252.

Moreover, even the authentic *ḥadīth* on which proponents of the doubt canon relied – such as the *Case of Māʿiz* – contained no evidence that *doubt* drove the Prophet's decision. The Prophet's questioning of Māʿiz was particular to his case at that time; it did not set forth a general precedent for criminal law that signaled a directive of *ḥudūd* avoidance. Sunnī jurists who took the opposite view were engaging in rather free readings that offered a post hoc explanation in line with their preferences. But in the end, their view was speculation, he accused, not law. The Prophet had made no mention of doubt. Instead, the foundational texts say only that *ḥudūd* enforcement is mandatory when someone has confessed to a crime or the crime has been otherwise proved.[80]

On consideration of the *Case of Ṣafwān*, Ibn Ḥazm also challenged the readings of the report that suggested the Prophet had avoided punishment. Recall that in that case, Ṣafwān attempted to stop the *ḥadd* punishment from being enforced after the Prophet came to a guilty verdict against a man whom Ṣafwān accused of stealing his cloak. Ibn Ḥazm rejected the idea that the Prophet even considered canceling *ḥadd* liability after the crime had been established. To the extent that the report suggested the contrary, he argued, it would contradict the known bar on intervening in criminal cases in an attempt to change the verdict after a conviction (drawn from other unquestionable reports, such as the *Case of the Makhzūmī Thief*). Moreover, an analysis of the report's chain of transmission revealed dubious provenance. Of the several versions recorded in *ḥadīth* collections, none had an unbroken chain of reliable transmission connecting back to the supposed events in question.[81] On these bases, Ibn Ḥazm affirmed that the Qur'ān and Sunnaic texts emphasized *ḥudūd* enforcement over the possibility of "doubt" once a crime had been litigated in court.[82]

In the same vein, Ibn Ḥazm examined the various versions of the elite-leniency maxim to conclude that only the version with the *ḥudūd* exception was authentic.[83] For him, that version of the maxim was acceptable because its chain was unproblematic. On that basis, but "without issuing

[80] Ibid., 8:252.

[81] Ibid., 12:54–57 (listing several versions, each with different narrations and chains of transmission, calling most truncated (*munqaṭiʿ*) – coming from ʿAṭāʾ, ʿIkrima, ʿAmr b. Dīnār, and Ibn Shihāb [al-Zuhrī], none of whom met Ṣafwān – and noting that the others include transmitters who were unreliable or unknown). On the treatment of *Ṣafwān's Case* in other circles, see discussion in Chapter 3 and Appendix B, case no. 9.

[82] Ibid.

[83] Ibid., 12:57 (citing the following version of the *ḥadīth*: *taʿāfaw al-ḥudūd fī-mā baynakum fa-mā balaghanī min ḥadd fa-qad wajab*).

a *fatwā* on the matter," Ibn Ḥazm maintained that judges could validly overlook the faults of nobles so long as they did not overlook *ḥudūd* violations.[84] If an act was truly criminal and caused harm to a victim, then, he reiterated, *ḥudūd* laws required bringing the matter to court and having the punishment enforced.[85]

In sum, in diametric opposition to pragmatic Sunnī jurists, Ibn Ḥazm rejected any report suggesting punishment avoidance solely on the basis of doubt. Instead, he placed a premium on certainty and authenticity, advocating a textualist reliance on plain meaning to avoid inserting doubt into the law.

b. In Favor of Ḥudūd *Enforcement*

Ibn Ḥazm also opposed *ḥudūd* avoidance in cases of doubt as a scheme marked with hierarchies that other jurists had let creep into *ḥudūd* laws. He argued that the majority Sunnī tendency to privilege those of high social status in criminal laws, often through arguments of doubt, contravened the letter and the spirit of the foundational texts. The Lawgiver had stipulated certain legal prescriptions and proscriptions, noted that His laws (*ḥudūd*) were not to be transgressed, and imposed fixed punishments for violations of those laws.[86] For Ibn Ḥazm, these rules applied across the board, without respect to social status or doubt.

One of Ibn Ḥazm's main criticisms concerned the majority Sunnī jurists' discrimination against those of low status backgrounds in criminal proceedings. This criticism arose in the recurring legal debate about whether defaming a slave woman constituted a criminal act subject to *ḥudūd* sanctions. Most Sunnī jurists held that it did not. They believed that a requisite element for the crime of defamation was a violation against the *honor* (*ḥurma*) of a person deserving respect.[87] The implication was that slaves' low station in life meant that they had none, or at best that the question was subject to doubt. Ibn Ḥazm argued to the contrary, rooting his arguments – as usual – in the foundational texts. He cited a series of *ḥadīth* reports that dealt with a related question regarding individual men

84 Ibid.

85 Ibid.

86 Ibid., 9:428 (citing a prophetic *ḥadīth* outlining that life, honor, and other fundamental values are sacred, and Qur'ān, 2:229, to the effect that God's laws (*ḥudūd*) are not to be transgressed). This is an equation of "*ḥudūd*" as divinely designated moral boundaries with "*ḥudūd*" in the sense of fixed criminal laws, which was the ordinary sense in which most Muslim jurists came to regard the term – though contemporary scholars have pointed out that the first sense is Qur'ānic while the second is not. See, for example, Kamali, "Punishment in Islamic Law."

87 Ibn Ḥazm, *Muḥallā*, 12:230–33.

who defamed slave women who had borne their masters children. The mother of a slave master's child (*umm walad*) was a special category of slave women, to be freed upon giving birth to the master's child or upon his death. In one of the texts on which Ibn Ḥazm relied, Ibn ʿUmar, the great jurist of seventh-century Medina, was asked about a man who defamed another man's *umm walad* and ruled that the defamer was indeed criminally liable.[88] For Ibn Ḥazm, the texts of the Sunna had settled the matter: judges were to enforce the *ḥudūd* punishments, and there was no basis for doubt.

More broadly, Ibn Ḥazm appealed to the early Islamic value of egalitarianism to shore up his argument against using doubt to avoid punishment where such notions of high-class honor were at issue. He cited the Qurʾān's specific instructions to address questions of honor on the basis of moral-religious distinction rather than blood lines: "O people! We have created you out of male and female . . . ; surely, the most honorable of you in God's eyes is the most God-conscious."[89] In other words, Ibn Ḥazm explained, it is clear that that "all people are born of a man and a woman [sharing the same origins]; people then rise in preference on the basis of their morals and religiosity, not their lineage or stature."[90] Ibn Ḥazm added that the Prophet had emphasized egalitarianism when he equated slaves to free people in advising his followers that "your lives, your property, your honor, and your 'bodily integrity' are sacred" to one another, without distinction by class or station.[91] On these textual grounds, every believer – slaves included – possessed the type of honor that could be violated by defamation.[92]

For Ibn Ḥazm, all of this was clear, textual evidence that Islam placed slaves on par with the free and regarded both as possessed of honor. This honor was so inviolate and backed by the threat of *ḥudūd* enforcement that for Ibn Ḥazm, it was simply "silly to suggest that slaves – men or women – lack dignity."[93] A general tendency toward *ḥudūd* avoidance for high-status individuals or anyone else was also potentially dangerous. It

88 Ibid., 12:232.

89 Qurʾān, 49:13 (*yā ayyuhā ʾl-nāsu innā khalaqnākum min dhakarin wa-unthā . . . inna akramakum ʿinda ʾllāhi atqākum*) (quoted in Ibn Ḥazm, *Muḥallā*, 12:232).

90 Ibn Ḥazm, *Muḥallā*, 12:232 (*thumma tafāḍala ʾl-nās bi-akhlāqihim wa-adyānihim lā bi-aʿrāqihim wa-lā bi-abdānihim*).

91 Ibid. (*ḥadīth*: *inna dimāʾakum wa-amwālakum wa-aʿrāḍakum wa-abshārakum ʿalaykum ḥarām*). Here, the term *abshārakum* refers to the inviolability of the body against physical assault or torture, and has thus been translated as "bodily integrity."

92 Ibid. (*waʾl-muʾmin lah ḥurma ʿaẓīma*).

93 Ibid. (*ammā qawluhum ʿlā ḥurma liʾl-ʿabd wa-lā liʾl-amaʾ fa-kalām sakhīf . . .*).

threatened the integrity of the entire Islamic legal system and of the divine legislative supremacy ideal, because anyone who *could* proffer claims of doubt to avoid punishment *would* do so by invoking the canon. This fear was enough for him to insist on policies of *ḥudūd* enforcement.[94]

Ibn Ḥazm was too much of a thoroughbred textualist to admit to being either pro- or anti-*ḥudūd* avoidance. Rather, he claimed that he was just following the text, saying, "it is impermissible [either] to avoid or to enforce criminal sanctions in cases of doubt." Judges were to enforce punishments when a crime was proved, and there was no criminal liability when it was not.[95] Yet in reality, Ibn Ḥazm's response to the other schools' emphasis on *ḥudūd* avoidance was to emphasize that the foundational texts counseled *ḥudūd* enforcement for criminal violations. Accordingly, he vehemently opposed the Sunnī majority's blanket policy of avoiding punishment, and characterized it as a departure from the texts of the Qur'ān, the Sunna, and the consensus of early Muslim jurists.[96]

c. On the Incoherence of Doubt Jurisprudence

Most bitingly and most extensively, Ibn Ḥazm objected to the doubt canon because it was an incoherent way of applying the law. In his view, doubt was a tool wielded by Sunnī jurists to justify their preferences for selective *ḥudūd* avoidance in contravention of the divine law and important Islamic mores. Although each school recognized doubt jurisprudence by his time, inasmuch as Shāfiʿī advocated for more strictly textualist approaches, Ibn Ḥazm found the explicitly pragmatist opinions of Ḥanafīs and Mālikīs particularly objectionable.

To begin with, he said, Mālikīs were among the staunchest proponents of doubt jurisprudence, but the harshest criminal law enforcers.[97] They advocated *ḥudūd* enforcement for fornication against unmarried women solely on the basis of the circumstantial evidence of pregnancy, even if she denied having committed a sex crime knowingly or voluntarily. If they were serious about recognizing doubt, he said, they would have found

94 Ibid.

95 Ibid., 12:57 (*al-ḥudūd lā yaḥill an tudraʾ wa-lā an tuqām bi-shubha wa-innamā huwa ʾl-ḥaqq li-ʾllāh taʿālā wa-lā mazīd, fa-in lam yathbut al-ḥadd lam yaḥill an yuqām bi-shubha* . . .). Strikingly, even though Ibn Ḥazm rejected the basis and formulation of the doubt canon, this statement virtually aligns his jurisprudence – albeit through other means – with that of doubt canon proponents.

96 Ibid., 9:428; for a similar criticism, see also Ibn Ḥazm, *al-Iḥkām fī uṣūl al-aḥkām* (Egypt: Dār al-Kutub al-ʿIlmiyya, 1968), 7:454–55.

97 This opinion had some resonance with Mālikī policies in Mamlūk Egypt. See Rapoport, "Legal Diversity," 216–25.

several bases for it in the circumstantial evidence – such as the possibility that the woman had been raped, that she had become pregnant during a valid marriage that was not publicized, or that she was temporarily insane.[98] To advocate *ḥudūd* avoidance on the basis of doubt and then enforce *ḥudūd* punishments on circumstantial evidence was, for Ibn Ḥazm, the epitome of incoherence.

Ḥanafīs bore the greatest brunt of Ibn Ḥazm's criticisms. He pointed out that they, too, advocated *ḥudūd* enforcement when their doubt jurisprudence should have led them to *ḥudūd* avoidance. For example, Ḥanafīs held that punishment for theft was due against accomplices who merely accompanied a thief into a house, regardless of whether the accomplice was a knowing and willing participant to the crime. If the lack of knowledge and voluntariness were not elements of Ḥanafī "doubt" relevant to establishing criminal liability in this scenario – as the Ḥanafīs claimed they were in others – then their entire conception of doubt was illogical.[99]

Ibn Ḥazm further took Abū Ḥanīfa himself to task for what he regarded as the outlandish notion of contractual doubt. Recall that Abū Ḥanīfa infamously advocated *ḥudūd* avoidance for a woman renting herself out to a man for sex.[100] Abū Ḥanīfa argued that the *semblance of a contract* created "doubt" about the legality of the act and pointed to an episode in the *ḥadīth* literature in which the caliph ʿUmar had avoided *ḥudūd* punishments in a scenario that could be understood as prostitution. Namely, when a woman who was starving approached a shepherd and begged desperately for food, the shepherd conditioned the "gift" of three bushels of dates on her agreement to let him have sex with her. She obliged, and when the story reached ʿUmar, he said, "[That is] dowry, dowry, dowry." That is, he interpreted the exchange as a "constructive marriage," thereby avoiding any *ḥadd* punishment.[101] Abū Ḥanīfa inferred from ʿUmar's decision that an agreement for sex with some consideration would be deemed a marriage contract; it did not warrant *ḥadd* liability and instead was a recognizable, though defective, contract that provided the semblance of legality.[102] The report served as the basis of his doctrine of contractual doubt. Ibn Ḥazm begged to differ.

98 Ibn Ḥazm, *Muḥallā*, 8:252.
99 Ibid.
100 Ibid., 12:195–98.
101 Ibid., 12:195 (reporting two versions of the story, with another about a woman in the marketplace).
102 As explained in Chapter 5, most other Sunnī jurists rejected Abū Ḥanīfa's view, including his two students Abū Yūsuf and Shaybānī and those following their line of opinions. See Ibn Ḥazm, *Muḥallā*, 12:195 (citing Abū Yūsuf, Shaybānī, Abū Thawr, Ẓāhirīs, Mālikīs,

In reaction, Ibn Ḥazm framed Abū Ḥanīfa's position on contractual doubt as advocating an immorality that starkly contradicted Islamic mores. In fact, he called it "one of the most anomalous opinions" that he had ever seen. Even on Abū Ḥanīfa's view of family law, a valid marriage dowry required a minimum of ten silver coins (*dirhams*). Three bushels of dates were worth less than that, so the "gift" would not have met the requirements of a marriage contract even in Ḥanafī law. How, then, was there any doubt about the illegality of the arrangement? Abū Ḥanīfa was selecting and rejecting Companion opinions to suit his own preferences, Ibn Ḥazm complained, and thereby "making a mockery [of the divine law]."[103] To avoid *ḥudūd* punishments for a paltry dowry but to not allow people to get married except with a sizable one "was providing an incentive to commit *zinā*."[104] The policy encouraged fornicators to have sex openly by simply paying a woman some paltry sum, such as a single silver coin, while requiring people who wanted to get married legitimately to pay a minimum of ten silver coins. In other words, Abū Ḥanīfa's policy meant legalizing prohibited sex-by-prostitution and placing obstacles in the way of legitimate sex-by-marriage.[105] If anything, for Ibn Ḥazm, both parties involved in prostitution agreements deserved punishment. Moreover, he considered their crime to be *more* serious than simple fornication: with the addition of money into the equation, the two parties added the sin of concluding an illegitimate financial transaction in an attempt to justify their crime of *zinā*.[106] Thus, to follow Abū Ḥanīfa's position on contractual doubt, he concluded, was clearly to violate the texts of the Qurʾān and the Sunna.

Finally, given the anomaly of Abū Ḥanīfa's position on contractual doubt even within his own school, Ibn Ḥazm also took mainstream Ḥanafīs and Shāfiʿīs to task for incoherent doctrines of evidentiary doubt. For example, what was the proper legal response to cases in which a man and a woman were found having sex and claimed to be married? Ḥanafī and Shāfiʿī jurists would avoid punishment on the basis of a report that ʿAlī did so in just such a scenario.[107] They surmised that doubt must have been the driving factor, analogizing that decision to scenarios in which a man had sex

Shāfiʿīs, and "all others" (*sāʾir al-nās*) to the effect that prostitution is *ḥadd*-incurring *zinā*).

103 Ibn Ḥazm, *Muḥallā*, 12:198 (*fa-hādhā huwa ʾl-istikhfāf ḥaqqan*).

104 Ibid. (*a-lā inna hādhā huwa ʾl-taṭrīq ilā ʾl-zinā*).

105 Ibid.

106 Ibid. (*akl al-māl biʾl-bāṭil*, as condemned by Qurʾān, 2:188: *wa-lā taʾkulū amwālakum baynakum biʾl-bāṭil* ...).

107 Ibid., 12:186 (*fa-daraʾa ʿanhā*).

with a slave woman known to belong to someone else but claimed to have bought her. If the actual owner and the slave woman affirmed the claim, there was no *ḥadd* liability – which suggested to these jurists that *claims* of legal relationships could provide a basis for doubt and therefore remove *ḥadd* liability.[108]

Ibn Ḥazm rejected that view as incoherent, arguing that several reasons cautioned against using doubt to avoid punishment in the scenario at issue. First, to hold otherwise would rely on the operation of the doubt canon, which Ibn Ḥazm – in his words – "had already demonstrated was apocryphal."[109] Second, the precedent cited in support of *ḥudūd* avoidance was a decision by a *Companion* of the Prophet, which was insufficient to create binding precedent in the manner of a decision made by or in the presence of the Prophet. Third, any question about *ḥadd* liability should have turned not on interpretation and extensions of analogy, but on facts. That is, evidence that *proved* claims of marriage with "truth and certainty" were required for *ḥadd* liability not to attach to sex out of wedlock.[110]

Ibn Ḥazm further explained that the burden of proof attached to the couple only in circumstances in which Islamic mores demanded it. To understand why, it should be remembered that during the Prophet's time, people used to emigrate to Medina in large waves from the farthest reaches of Yemen and other Arab lands together with their families and households, including free as well as slave women and men. If a man was found sleeping with a woman, his claim that she was his wife or slave was accepted, without any requirement to produce evidence to prove it. This should not surprise, said Ibn Ḥazm. "All Muslims" and indeed "all people" from the Prophet's time until the present were agreed that it was quite a normal state of affairs for people to travel with their families, without being asked for evidence to prove the validity of their associations at each turn.[111] In fact, Ibn Ḥazm argued that the practice was so universal and subject to consensus that it should be regarded as an authoritative and binding "text" (*naṣṣ*). Thus, whenever a couple found together claimed to be married, the claim was generally to be accepted, particularly – if somewhat paradoxically – if the partners were foreigners or unknown to a particular community.[112]

108 See ibid., 12:186–87.
109 Ibid.
110 Ibid., 12:187.
111 Ibid., 12:188 (*jamīʿ ahl al-islām wa-jamīʿ ahl al-arḍ*).
112 Ibid. (*gharībayn*).

Only in exceptional cases should a couple be asked to produce evidence of the marriage. For instance, if a couple was known in the community *not* to be married, judicial investigation of the claim would be warranted.[113] Or if an interested party produced solid evidence that the partners claiming to be married were not in fact married, a judge was to require them to produce evidence of their claim.[114] Likewise, if a judge was himself certain that the partners were lying about their claims to be married, he was required to enforce the *ḥadd* sanction, with no room for doubt and punishment avoidance.[115]

At bottom, Ibn Ḥazm opposed the blanket approach of the pragmatist Ḥanafīs and Shāfiʿīs, who saw doubt as a vehicle for *ḥudūd* avoidance as a matter of law. Ibn Ḥazm supported instead a more narrow approach that made questions surrounding *ḥudūd* avoidance contingent on apparent or contextual facts. This approach placed the burden of production on accused individuals to remove doubt in order to avoid punishment as a matter of fact, rather than opting for punishment avoidance based on doctrines of doubt as a matter of law.[116]

3. Ẓāhirī "Doubt"

Even as Ibn Ḥazm argued that the text should always control legal outcomes,[117] he, too, nevertheless acknowledged the presence of doubt. He

[113] Ibid., 12:187 (noting that even then, if a woman is *known* to be unmarried, her claim of this disputed fact should be accepted if plausible: *in amkana*).

[114] Ibid., 12:187–88. Interestingly, he also maintained that in cases of conflicting evidence, that is, where the man claims that they are married and the woman claims that she is his slave, no *ḥadd* sanction applies, because the testimony converges on the point of the validity of sexual relations (*ṣiḥḥat al-firāsh*), whether by marriage or a master-slave relationship.

[115] Ibid.

[116] The burden of production refers to the responsibility of a litigant or a defendant to produce sufficient evidence to back his or her claim in making out a prima facie case or establishing an affirmative defense, as a matter of law. The burden of proof refers to the obligation for litigating parties to prove or disprove a disputed fact – for example, the prosecution's burden to prove that the defendant committed a crime "beyond a reasonable doubt" for criminal trials or the plaintiff's burden to establish the respondent's liability by a "preponderance of the evidence" or by "clear and convincing evidence" for civil trials – as a matter of fact. For discussion in American law, see further Fleming James Jr., "Burdens of Proof," *Virginia Law Review* 47 (1961), 51–70; John T. McNaughton, "Burden of Production of Evidence: A Function of a Burden of Persuasion," *Harvard Law Review* 68 (1955), 1382–91; James B. Thayer, "The Burden of Proof," *Harvard Law Review* 4 (1890), 45–70.

[117] For a full catalog of his rulings on common criminal law matters, see Ibn Ḥazm, *Muḥallā*, 12:164–218 (*kitāb al-ḥudūd*).

identified at least three types. The first was the most common form: *textual ambiguity*, where words bore "more than one meaning." Interestingly, he maintained that the meaning of ambiguous phrases was not restricted to a single definition; instead, "all possible meanings [were] valid, provided they [did] not result in a logical absurdity."[118] This was the extent of Ẓāhirī legal pluralism, a version of "interpretive doubt" that took multiple semantic meanings of texts to be consistent with authorial intent.

Ibn Ḥazm also recognized a category that other jurists identified as *legal doubt*. He discussed this category as *ignorance of the law*, covering situations in which a layperson simply was unaware of the legal status of a given act with potentially criminal consequences.[119] In such cases, Ibn Ḥazm imposed a due diligence requirement: to be found nonliable for an act that turned out to be illegal, a defendant would have to demonstrate that he attempted to ascertain the correct rule either by himself or by asking a learned scholar. If he did the latter, he was to investigate the bases of that scholar's opinion to ensure that it followed the Qur'ān and Sunna rather than the interpretations of one of the Sunnī schools of law.[120] For strict textualism did not recognize the regime of *taqlīd*, that is, the authority of scholarly opinions based on what Ibn Ḥazm took to be the introduction of human discretion into the law.

Finally, Ibn Ḥazm conceded that *factual doubt* might arise where a layperson knew the law but was unsure of whether engaging in certain acts would result in a crime. To take the example of wine drinking, a person could know that wine was prohibited but be uncertain as to whether a reddish liquid in front of him or her was wine. In that scenario, Ibn Ḥazm opined that the person was to ask someone knowledgeable about what the liquid was before drinking it.[121]

In each of these instances of doubt, Ibn Ḥazm advocated against a blanket rule of *ḥudūd* avoidance. Aside from accommodating multiple

[118] See Ibn Ḥazm, *Nubdha*, in Sabra, "Ibn Ḥazm's Literalism." For a history and textualist critique of the absurdity doctrine's "strong intentionalist foundations" in American legal interpretation, see John F. Manning, "The Absurdity Doctrine," *Harvard Law Review* 116 (2002–2003), 2387–476, esp. 2390 and passim.

[119] See Ibn Ḥazm, *Muḥallā*, 12:60. Notably, both of these types correspond to legal doubt or *shubha ḥukmiyya* discussed in other schools.

[120] See Ibn Ḥazm, *Nubdha*, in Sabra, "Ibn Ḥazm's Literalism," 20. For more of Ibn Ḥazm's arguments against *taqlīd*, see Ibn Ḥazm, *Iḥkām*, 18, 793ff., 797ff.

[121] Or there could be doubt as to whether the evidence is sufficient to establish the crime. See, for example, Ibn Ḥazm, *Muḥallā*, 12:186–88 (detailing the case of a man and a woman arrested for *zinā* who claimed to be married). But he does not view this as one filled with "doubt" or "ambiguity." The crime, he says, either is established or is not.

interpretations of semantically ambiguous texts, he placed the burden in every instance on the actor to ascertain the facts or the law before engaging in acts with potentially criminal consequences. There was only one right answer, he insisted, and if the defendant missed it, he subjected himself to the rule of *ḥudūd* enforcement.

As for ambiguous texts or deficient evidence that did not immediately reveal the one right answer, jurists were to consider two textually grounded presumptions. The first was to ensure adherence to a set of *fundamental values*. A prophetic report had specified that Muslims' "blood, property, honor, and 'bodily integrity' are sacred,"[122] and had made the preservation of life a first-order principle on that list.[123] Thus, where there was lingering doubt in a *capital* case, judges were to decide the case in favor of life.

The second presumption was the *principle of precaution*, an across-the-board rule meant for jurists and laypeople alike. It stipulated that people must exercise caution against rendering permissible what God has prohibited, and they should do so, in part, by avoiding acting except on the basis of certainty – especially in serious matters involving criminal sanctions.[124] Just as the preservation of life and other fundamental values cautioned judges against enforcing capital punishment, those who were ignorant about the legality of acts that would bring about serious bodily injury were to refrain from such acts.[125]

Like Shīʿī strict textualists, discussed in the following chapter, Ibn Ḥazm adopted the principle of precaution not as a way of avoiding punishments, but as a way of avoiding doubt itself.[126] On his understanding, if a matter was clear, it was mandatory to enforce the *ḥudūd* punishments fixed by God, which no one had the license to avoid.[127] Thus, while he insisted that he adopted a presumption of neither legality nor illegality, Ibn Ḥazm in fact stipulated a presumption of liability if a person failed to avoid acts that were *potentially* unlawful.[128]

122 Ibid. For the report, see note 91, and accompanying text.
123 Ibid.
124 Ibid., 12:188 (*bi-yaqīn lā shakk fīh*).
125 Ibid., 12:60–61 (*wa-man jahila a-wajaba ʾl-ḥadd am lam yajib fa-farḍuh an lā yuqīmah li-anna ʾl-aʿrāḍ waʾl-dimāʾ ḥarām*).
126 On the Shīʿī positions, see Chapter 8.
127 Ibn Ḥazm, *Muḥallā*, 12:61 (*farḍ*).
128 This stance is similar to that of the Akhbārī Shīʿī textualists, as we will see in Chapter 8, elaborating on the principles and presumptions of legality and nonliability.

C. TEXTUALISM VS. DOUBT

The Ḥanbalīs and the Ẓāhirīs espoused different versions of strict textualism, and their respective stances toward doubt differed accordingly. Ibn Ḥanbal's ambivalent view of doubt allowed his traditionalist-textualist followers to adopt a range of positions that generally accommodated some form of *ḥudūd* avoidance. This made sense, given that the early precedents themselves seemed unclear and the Ḥanbalīs lived in regimes of legal pluralism, which likely made them especially keen on building a narrow doubt jurisprudence in response to the expansive notions of the other Sunnī schools. Dāwūd and Ibn Ḥazm, on the other hand, were textual purists, often – correctly – called literalists. Even more than the Ḥanbalīs, they insisted on a textualist approach to interpretation for which there was one right answer, God had not delegated the task of interpretation to any human, and the ideal of divine legislative supremacy meant adherence to God's law as represented in the texts. The texts, they found, in no way accommodated doubt.

Notwithstanding the narrowing or rejection of doubt jurisprudence, both Ḥanbalīs and Ẓāhirīs found ways to deal with doubt. For example, mainstream opinions in each of their schools maintained that necessity, duress, and other problems that canceled criminal culpability would bar punishment, as would questionable evidence in cases involving capital crimes. But when the law and the facts were clear, the most strictly textualist take on Islamic law saw other jurists' claims of doubt as no more than a means to circumvent the law. In view of the ideal of divine legislative supremacy, strict textualists held that punishments for crimes – once proved – were to be enforced, a rule that would later turn into a rule of broad criminal law enforcement with relaxed standards of proof.

CONCLUSION

Recall the American opponents to canons such as doubt, with Karl Llewellyn leading the charge among realists and Justice Antonin Scalia among textualists.[129] Like Llewellyn, Ibn Ḥazm posited that for every maxim there is a countermaxim, which jurists could use to flout the law. Like Scalia, Ibn Ḥazm was a textualist who favored interpretive canons, but unlike Scalia, Ibn Ḥazm made no exceptions for the doubt canon. In fact, he complained that the doubt canon was particularly

[129] See Introduction, notes 40–43 and accompanying text.

egregious, because it contravened the clear sense of *ḥudūd* laws as mandatory fixed criminal sanctions for serious crimes and, consequently, the intent of the Lawgiver that those laws not be transgressed.[130] Antiquity was no defense. Using a canon of dubious provenance to avoid observing the clear obligation to punish criminal law violations, he said, would run roughshod over the foundational sources of Islamic law, including the central ideal of divine legislative supremacy, which he found to be located in the texts.[131] Moreover, juristic applications of the canon were inconsistent and incoherent: it – like all substantive legal maxims – was a useful tool for anyone wishing to disregard the law, and it easily resulted in disparate application of the law.[132] His perspective was the most vehement expression of Sunnī opposition to doubt.

Instead of *avoiding punishment* in cases of doubt, strict textualists attempted to develop rules of *avoiding doubt* itself and insisted on authorizing legal action only in cases of certainty. This scheme turned out to be impracticable in the end, inasmuch as the foundational legal texts rarely addressed the myriad issues certain to arise in an ever-expanding and changing empire. To wit: Ẓāhirism did not survive long after Ibn Ḥazm, the last well-known representative of the most strictly textualist school of Islamic law.[133]

130 See Ibn Ḥazm, *Muḥallā*, 9:428.

131 Ibid. See also Ibn Ḥazm, *Iḥkām*, 7:454–55.

132 See Ibn Ḥazm, *Muḥallā*, 11:153; see also 9:428 (adding that there is no difference between *ḥudūd* laws and any other legal arena).

133 See Robert Gleave, *Islam and Literalism: Literal Meaning and Interpretation in Islamic Legal Theory* (Edinburgh: Edinburgh University Press, 2012), 174 ("Whilst a semi-institutional school did survive his death, it failed to gain a permanent foothold and was eventually swamped by Mālikī dominance. Ẓāhirism failed in both the East and the West."). On the continuation of Ẓāhirī thought, even if not as an operative legal school after Ibn Ḥazm, see Camilla Adang, "The Spread of Zahirism in al-Andalus in the Post-Caliphal Period: The Evidence from the Biographical Dictionaries," in *Ideas, Images, and Methods of Portrayal: Insights into Classical Arabic Literature and Islam*, ed. Sebastian Günther (Leiden: Brill, 2005), 297–346; Amr Osman, *The History and Doctrine of the Ẓāhirī* Madhhab (PhD diss., Princeton University, 2010), 349–53 (now published as The *Ẓāhirī* Madhhab *(3rd/9th–10th/16th Century): A Textualist Theory of Islamic Law* (Leiden: Brill, 2014)).

8

Shīʿī Doubt: Dueling Theories of Delegation and Interpretation

The same debates about doubt raging among Sunnīs played out in Shīʿī law as well. The discussion of doubt from the founding period in preceding chapters included Shīʿī cases – notably beginning with the *Case of the Falsely Accused Butcher*. That case was part of a collection put together by a ninth-century Shīʿī scholar and subsequently used by Sunnī jurists to expand their understanding of doubt.[1] This chapter seeks to trace what happened after that period, once the Imām had disappeared, leaving Shīʿī jurists once and for all to develop a jurisprudence that explicitly either acknowledged or sought to dispose of doubt.[2] The following discussion examines Shīʿī jurists mainly from the tenth century (when the Imām disappeared and when doubt was textualized in Shīʿī law alongside its textualization in Sunnī circles[3]) through the sixteenth century, with attention also to major figures of the seventeenth and eighteenth centuries who weighed in significantly on questions of doubt.

After the founding period, Shīʿī opponents of discretion and doubt increased in the vehemence of their opposition to both. Most significant was Muḥammad Amīn al-Astarābādī (d. 1036/1626–7), the vociferously strict textualist jurist arguing for a return to strict textualism in Shīʿī law by way of promoting the revival of the old Akhbārī legal school, which generally opposed the doubt canon. As a strict textualist who looked to the Qurʾān and *ḥadīth* as the sole sources of Islamic law, Astarābādī counted as valid only those legal maxims that had

[1] See Introduction, note 1; Chapter 7, note 44; and Appendix B, cases nos. 19–25.
[2] For elaboration of this argument, see my "Islamic Legal Minimalism."
[3] See Appendix A, versions 11 and 12.

firm grounding and precise meaning in those foundational texts.[4] From that starting point, he regarded the doubt canon as technically authentic, because it was a *ḥadīth* that appeared in Shīʿī law's authoritative collections of prophetic and imāmic reports.[5] But he did not regard its expansive use as legally valid. Just because it was a valid *ḥadīth* did not mean for him that jurists should apply the canon broadly. Like Sunnī strict textualists, he argued that it should apply narrowly.

In this way, doubt represented a major jurisprudential battleground between Shīʿī strict textualists such as Astarābādī, who saw texts as the only valid sources of Islamic law, and a group of Shīʿī pragmatic textualists, who also considered reason to be a valid source of Islamic law. In Shīʿī law, this battle was pitched around a theological question about the scope of divine delegation over "lawmaking" (or law-defining, as they put it) and adjudication: how much interpretive authority had God delegated to jurists to decide questions of law and to resolve doubt? Astarābādī believed that God had delegated little to no such authority to jurists. His pragmatic textualist counterparts disagreed.

Notably, Shīʿī debates about doubt are instructive for Islamic law as a whole, because they confront head-on the theological questions about reason versus revelation and the scope of divine delegation underlying all interpretive matters of Islamic law, Sunnī and Shīʿī alike. The structure of Sunnī law hides these questions behind the theory of four foundational sources that exclude reason, tackling them in works of theology only implicitly related to law. By contrast, the inclusion of reason and belief in Shīʿī law makes this legal system confront these questions directly within its jurisprudential considerations of doubt, adding a more theoretical tenor to debates about doubt. This chapter examines those debates.

THE BATTLEFIELD: THE SCOPE OF DIVINE DELEGATION

1. Reason vs. Revelation, Rationalists vs. Traditionalists

Shīʿī jurisprudence went through several successive stages that pitted rationalists, who believed in delegation, against traditionalists, who

[4] Astarābādī, *Fawāʾid* (198-?), 106.

[5] See al-Ḥurr al-ʿĀmilī (d. 1104/1693), *al-Fuṣūl al-muhimma*, 3rd ed. (Qum: Maktabat Baṣīratī, 198-?), 388; cf. al-Ḥurr al-ʿĀmilī, *Wasāʾil al-Shīʿa*, ed. ʿAbd al-Raḥīm al-Rabbānī al-Shīrāzī (Tehran: al-Maktaba al-Islāmiyya, 1383–89/1963–69), 28:48, no. 34179 (quoting the doubt canon as a *ḥadīth* from Ibn Bābawayh's treatise, *Kitāb man lā yaḥduruh al-faqīh*).

believed in the sole authority of the text of revelation, in debates about the meaning and scope of the law.[6] The rationalists, whom I also label pragmatic textualists, are commonly known in Shīʿī law for their recognition of a role for reason alongside foundational texts in interpreting Islamic law. The traditionalists, whom I also label strict textualists, are known for the exclusive authority they accorded to the texts of revelation and tradition as sources of Islamic law. Their age-old debate about the role of reason versus revelation appeared in varied discussions of doubt. The division began as a matter of theology, which, in Islamic contexts, was always intimately connected to issues of law.

Theology was worldview. It drove the interpretive philosophy of Islamic law. In contemplating a role for reason in Islamic legal interpretation, rationalists sought to include both pure and practical reason.[7] This use of reason translated into a *pragmatic jurisprudence* in which, as this chapter demonstrates, legal maxims – as both interpretive and substantive principles – gradually came to loom large.[8] Traditionalists, on the other hand, sought to banish all human discretion from Islamic law as a legal system that was supposed to be divine. Sticking closely to the words of the foundational texts, they advocated a *strict textualist jurisprudence*, which accommodated only a limited set of legal maxims – mostly grammatical

[6] For an overview, identifying eight stages or periods of Shīʿī legal history, see Modarressi, *Introduction to Shīʿī Law*, 23–58. For works detailing specific differences between rationalists and traditionalists, see ʿAbd Allāh b. Ṣāliḥ al-Samāhijī, *Munyat al-mumārisīn*, quoted and abridged in Muḥammad Bāqir b. Zayn al-ʿĀbidīn al-Khwansārī, *Rawḍāt al-jannāt*, ed. M. T. al-Kashfī and A. Ismāʿīliyyān (Tehran; Qum: Maktabat Ismāʿīliyyān, 1390–92/1970–73), 1:120–30; cf. Andrew Newman, "The Nature of the Akhbārī/Uṣūlī Dispute in Late Ṣafawid Iran, Part I: ʿAbd Allāh al-Samāhijī's '*Munyat al-mumārisīn*,'" *Bulletin of the School of Oriental and African Studies* (*BSOAS*) 55, 1 (1992), 24–51 and Part II, *BSOAS* 55, 2 (1992), 250–61 (reproducing and translating Samāhijī's work of 40 differences). See also Muḥammad b. Faraj Allāh al-Dizfūlī, *Fārūq al-ḥaqq fī 'l-farq bayna 'l-Uṣūliyyīn wa'l-Akhbāriyyīn*, on the margins of Jaʿfar b. Khaḍir al-Najafī Kāshif al-Ghiṭāʾ (d. 1228/1813), *al-Ḥaqq al-mubīn* (Tehran: n.p., 1319/1901), 2–97 (detailing 86 differences). For additional sources, see the bibliography "'Difference lists' between Akhbārīs and Uṣūlīs" in Robert Gleave, *Scripturalist Islam: The History and Doctrines of the Akhbārī Shīʿī School* (Leiden: Brill, 2007), 311–14.

[7] See Modarressi, *Introduction to Shīʿī Law*, 3–4, n. 1 (noting that by reason, rationalists referred to the "categorical judgments of both pure and practical reason," for instance, "the judgment of practical reason that justice is good and injustice is evil"). For brief definitions of these types of reason, see Donald M. Borchert, ed., *Encyclopedia of Philosophy*, 2nd ed. (Detroit: Macmillan Reference USA, 2006), 7:735–38 (s.v. "Practical Reason"); 8:279–82 (s.v. "Reason").

[8] For an analysis of "pragmatic" interpretation and legal maxims in American law, see Eskridge and Frickey, "Statutory Interpretation as Practical Reasoning," 321–84.

and linguistic interpretive canons. Substantive legal maxims based on rational precepts, they thought, could be unwieldy and arbitrary weapons in the hands of power-maximizing or willful judges. They feared that judges would use legal maxims to insert human discretion into divine law, which would compromise the ideal of divine legislative supremacy that all Muslims held up as paramount.

The two camps struggled for dominance in defining theories of delegation and interpretive authority when approaching questions of doubt and ambiguity. Was revelation comprehensive or was reason to play a role? Were legal maxims valid gap-filling tools for jurists to build on text-based norms when the text itself ran out, or were they limited canons of construction for a theory of law in which the text never ran out? Such questions were answered over time, beginning with the third/ninth-century initial disappearance of the Twelfth Imām, the last in the line of leaders of the mainstream Shīʿī community whose pronouncements carried the authority of a foundational text. The Imām's final disappearance in the fourth/tenth century, with the last of four agents said to have direct access to him, coincided with the textualization of doubt.

2. Historical Overview: Origins of the Debates

Until the early fourth/tenth century, the Shīʿī community could dogmatically claim that the Imāms were present to provide religious leadership following the Prophet's death in the first/seventh century. These Imāms, a line of the Prophet's descendants, were repositories of moral-legal guidance that passed from God to the community through them. To be sure, there were vibrant debates about legal rulings and the scope of interpretive authority even during the period when the Imāms were alive and present. For example, early rationalists insisted that the Imāms encouraged rational deliberation on general precepts of law by their students to derive particular details. Early traditionalists, in contrast, were adamant that adherence to religious law meant following only the text of revelation, that is, the Qurʾān and the reports of divinely inspired instructions from the Prophet and the Imāms.[9]

During the early period, the traditionalist approach became more salient, because its exponents could claim that they were merely deferring to

[9] On the rationalist, traditionalist, and "intermediate" tendencies in the second/eighth through early fourth/tenth centuries, see Modarressi, *Introduction to Shīʿī Law*, 26–35.

the living Imām – regardless of how much discretion they in fact employed in interpreting Islamic law. This claim led the once minority camp of traditionalists to gradually gain ascendancy over competing rationalist groups in the first few centuries of Shīʿī law.[10]

After the Imāms disappeared, the community was thrown into crisis. The eleventh Imām died in the mid-third/ninth century and – in what became the mainstream Imāmī view – left behind an infant son from whom the Shīʿī community continued to receive guidance through a series of representatives during a period dubbed this Twelfth Imām's "Minor Occultation." But the Imām's continued absence was disturbing. Rationalist scholars suggested that the answer to the Imām's absence lay in relying on reason to derive new legal opinions, as earlier scholars had done.[11] Meanwhile, traditionalist scholars articulated a separate doctrine – advocating reliance on the text of revelation and *ḥadīth* reports. By the turn of the fourth/tenth century, they had decided that the Twelfth Imām was a millennial figure called the *mahdī* or the *qāʾim*, who would establish truth and justice in the world in its Last Days, but who would until then remain hidden in "Major Occultation."[12] As far as legal matters were concerned, the community finally decided to rely more on legal interpretation and rational argument to arrive at answers to its ongoing concerns.

These developments would have particularly acute ramifications for criminal law. Just as in the Sunnī context, Shīʿī jurists understood *ḥudūd* laws to require divine authorization for their definition, interpretation, and

[10] See ibid., 27–29.

[11] One example was the Nawbakht family of prominent Shīʿī rationalist jurist-theologians – the most illustrious of whom included Abū Sahl b. Nawbakht (d. 311/923–4) and his nephew Abū Muḥammad al-Ḥasan b. Mūsā al-Nawbakhtī (d. between 300/912 and 316/923); see Martin McDermott, *Theology of al-Shaikh al-Mufīd* (d. 413/1022) (Beirut: Dār al-Mashriq; Librairie orientale, 1978), 22–24. See also ʿAbbās Iqbāl Āshtiyānī, *Khānadān-i Nawbakhtī*, 2nd ed. (Tehran: Kitābkhānah-i Ṭahūrī, 1966), available in Arabic translation as *Āl Nawbakht*, trans. ʿAlī Hāshim al-Asadī (Mashhad: Majmaʿ al-Buḥūth al-Islāmiyya, 1383/2004); Louis Massignon, *La Passion d'al-Ḥallāj [Ḥusayn ibn Mansour al-Ḥallāj], martyr, mystique de l'Islam* (Paris: Geuthner, 1927), 142–51. Another example is the prominent rationalist theologian from the same period, Ibn Qiba, on whom see Modarressi, *Introduction to Shīʿī Law*, part II.

[12] For a discussion, see Modarressi, *Crisis and Consolidation*, 92–98, 101–102 (discussing the four agents of the eleventh and twelfth Imāms – the last one of whom, ʿAlī b. Muḥammad al-Samarrī (d. 329/941), died without naming a successor – and noting that "it was, possibly, not until after 295/908, when the community started to realize that the situation was more unusual than they had originally thought and that possibly there would not be a manifest Imām for the foreseeable future, that the question of the number of Imāms came under serious consideration").

implementation.[13] The only Imām to exercise effective political authority to preside over *ḥudūd* laws had been the first, ʿAlī b. Abī Ṭālib (d. 41/661). The second Imām, ʿAlī's son Ḥasan al-Mujtabā (d. 49/669), did not have effective control during his brief six-month tenure. The other Imāms, while alive and actively leading the Shīʿī community, were monitored closely by the ruling authorities of the Sunnī majority – who saw ʿAlid claims to religious authority as a political threat. As a consequence, Shīʿī criminal law was not in force, and Shīʿīs regarded the legitimacy and content of the Sunnī criminal law that was in force as questionable to say the least.

Case in point: the illegitimacy that the Shīʿī minority attributed to the Sunnī majority prompted questions about whether the former could work for the latter as political aides. Shīʿī scholars answered that, before the early fourth/tenth-century Major Occultation, the Imāms had given permission to their Shīʿī followers to work with non-Shīʿī governments in specific cases.[14] But after the Occultation, these scholars could no longer claim to rely on the Imām's directives on specific cases, which led to a need for principles to guide general questions of public law.[15] As Wilferd Madelung has explained, "since the Imām could no longer be asked personally for permission to take up a post, the need to lay down generally applicable rules on the basis of the earlier dicta of the Imāms no doubt came to be felt more pressingly, as also happened in other areas of the law."[16] Leadership and the authority to work out these precepts had devolved onto the scholarly community. In criminal law, these precepts went in two different directions, one rationalist and the other traditionalist.

The rationalist approach was to assert that the community could continue to follow the Imām's guidance through elaborating general principles of law, which often took the form of legal maxims. In this vein, the doubt

[13] See, for example, Dāmād, *Qavāʿid*, 4:54; see also Abū Jaʿfar al-Ṭūsī, *ʿUddat al-uṣūl* (Tehran: n.p., 1314/1896–7); al-ʿAllāma al-Ḥillī, *Mabādiʾ al-wuṣūl ilā ʿilm al-uṣūl* (Qum: n.p., 1404/1985). Cf. Māwardī, *Kitāb al-ḥudūd min al-Ḥāwī*, 1:100–101.

[14] Wilferd Madelung, "A Treatise of the Sharīf al-Murtaḍā on the Legality of Working for the Government (*Masʾala fī ʾl-ʿamal maʿa ʾl- sulṭān*)," *Bulletin of the School of Oriental and African Studies* 43, 1 (1980), 18–31, at 18 (noting that this question arose in the second/eighth century, as a number of the disciples of the Imām worked for the early ʿAbbāsid caliphate, and referencing traditions of the sixth and seventh Imāms giving permission in specific cases on the basis that the government workers could help support and defend the interests of the Imām and the Shīʿī community).

[15] See Wilferd Madelung, "Authority in Twelver Shiism in the Absence of the Imam," in *La notion d'autorité au Moyen Age: Islam, Byzance, Occident; Colloques internationaux de la Napoule 1978* (Paris: Presses Universitaires de France, 1982), 168; Madelung, "Legality of Working for the Government," 18–31.

[16] Madelung, "Legality of Working for the Government," 20.

canon was an example of a general precept that provided guidance for resolving questions of Islamic criminal law. In elaborating its application, rationalists pointed to several early precedents from the time of ʿAlī and the other Imāms for support: the story of ʿAlī's pardon of the man in the *Case of the Falsely Accused Butcher*,[17] situations where people committed prohibited acts out of ignorance of the law or the facts,[18] and more generally, cases where the law itself was unclear.[19] For them, all of these instances were examples of the doubt canon in action.

The traditionalist approach maintained that in the Imām's absence, his followers were to avoid violating Islamic criminal laws by avoiding implementing Islamic criminal law altogether whenever it required corporal punishment. For these jurists, the doubt canon was valid only if sanctioned by tradition, and even then, it was of limited scope.

The following centuries saw attempts to resolve the debate between rationalists and traditionalists about the scope of human discretion for legal interpretation. The attempts centered on the interpretation of early traditions.

3. Ibn Bābawayh and Traditionalist Foundations

The rationalist-traditionalist duel largely centered on the meaning of a reported statement of the sixth Imām, Jaʿfar al-Ṣādiq (d. 148/765), that "everything is permissible unless specifically prohibited."[20] How was the community to interpret that tradition? Traditionalists answered this question narrowly.

Ibn Bābawayh (d. 381/991–2), "one of the greatest of [Shīʿī] authorities" and a prominent opponent of the rationalism of his time,[21] maintained that revelation was sufficient to govern human affairs and that it was to be understood primarily on the basis of traditions.[22] Implicitly rejecting the

17 See Introduction, note 1 and accompanying text. For other examples, see *Qaḍāyā ʿAlī*, 43–45, 52, 76–85, 139, 185, 189, 233, 236. See also Appendix B, case nos. 19–25.

18 For example, Ibn Idrīs, *Sarāʾir*, 4:438.

19 See, for example, Muḥammad al-Fāḍil al-Lankarānī, *al-Qawāʿid al-fiqhiyya* (Qum: Mihr, 1416/1995), 21 (describing *shubahāt ḥukmiyya*); Dāmād, *Qavāʿid*, 4:54–61 (same).

20 Ibn Bābawayh, *al-Iʿtiqādāt fī dīn al-Imāmiyya*, ed. Ghulām Riḍā al-Māzandarānī (Qum: G. R. al- Māzandarānī, 1412/1992), 8–9; see also Ibn Bābawayh, *Faqīh*, 1:202. For background on Ibn Bābawayh's challenges in Baghdad under al-Ṣāḥib Ibn ʿAbbād, see Wilferd Madelung, "Imāmism and Muʿtazilite Theology," in *Le Shîʿisme imâmite*, ed. Toufic Fahd (Paris: Presses Universitaires de France, 1979), 13–29 (repr. in Wilferd Madelung, Religious Schools and Sects in Medieval Islam (London: Variorum Reprints, 1985), no. VII).

21 See Asaf A. A. Fyzee, "Ibn Bābawayh," in *EI*^{2}, 3:726–27, and sources cited therein.

22 See Madelung, "Imāmism and Muʿtazilite Theology," 17–20.

notion of objective good and evil that reason can discern independently, Ibn Bābawayh rejected a central tenet of Muʿtazilī rationalist theologians,[23] namely, that people should not be held accountable for laws that were not within their capacity to know and thus apply.[24] When it comes to his answers to specific questions about the scope of divine delegation, his choice of traditions to cite in his work is instructive. The first among a number of foundational texts relevant to those questions has already been mentioned: Jaʿfar al-Ṣādiq's statement that "everything is permissible unless specifically prohibited."[25] Ibn Bābawayh further quoted the Qur'ānic verse that "God does not place a burden on any soul greater than it has strength to bear,"[26] and another report from Jaʿfar al-Ṣādiq: "I swear by God, God has not burdened His servants [humankind], save to what is within their capacities."[27]

Like other traditionists, Ibn Bābawayh placed a premium on *ḥadīth* authenticity and accordingly – as had the traditionist Kulaynī (d. 329/940–1) previously – advocated accepting only *ḥadīth* reports with verified chains of transmission and content that did not conflict with the Qur'ān.[28] He set about collecting textual sources for the law in his written works, most notably the legal treatise *Man lā yaḥḍuruh al-faqīh*, which – although intended to be a legal treatise – provides one of the four sources of Shīʿī *ḥadīth*.[29] Further, he aimed to reconcile those

23 For a general overview of Muʿtazilī theology and history, see Josef van Ess, *The Flowering of Muslim Theology*, trans. Jane Marie Todd (Cambridge, MA: Harvard University Press, 2006) (expansion by the author of *Prémices de la théologie musulmane* (2002)), esp. 6–7, 75–76, 79–115, 123–24; Tilman Nagel, *Geschichte der islamischen Theologie*, translated into English as *The History of Islamic Theology*, trans. Thomas Thornton (Princeton, NJ: Markus Wiener, 2000); D. Gimaret, "Muʿtazila," in *EI*², 7:783–93, and the sources cited therein.

24 See generally Ibn Bābawayh, *Kitāb al-Tawḥīd*, ed. Hāshim al-Ḥusaynī (Tehran: Maktabat al-Ṣadūq, 1387/1967); Ibn Bābawayh, *Iʿtiqādāt*; translated into English as *A Shiʿite Creed: A Translation of Risālatu 'l- iʿtiqādāt*, trans. Asaf A. A. Fyzee (London: Oxford University Press, 1942). Cf. Asaf. A. A. Fyzee, "The Creed of Ibn Bābawayhi," *Journal of Bombay University* 12 (1943), 70–86 (examining the creed and comparing it with the commentary and "correction," *Taṣḥīḥ al-Iʿtiqādāt*, by Mufīd).

25 See Ibn Bābawayh, *Iʿtiqādāt*, 8–9.

26 Qur'ān, 2:286.

27 Ibn Bābawayh, *Iʿtiqādāt*, 9.

28 On the body of early Shīʿī traditions, see Kohlberg, "*Al-Uṣūl al-Arbaʿumi'a*," 128–66 (identifying some of the four hundred or so notebooks, each conventionally called *kitāb* or *aṣl*, pl. *uṣūl*, purportedly recording the Imāms' sayings). For a review and bibliography of the written literature of the first three centuries, see generally Modarressi, *Tradition and Survival*.

29 The others are the *Kāfī* of Kulaynī and the *Istibṣār* and *Tahdhīb al-aḥkām* of Abū Jaʿfar al-Ṭūsī.

books to overcome what he called *apparent* conflicts. Ibn Bābawayh explained such conflicts first with reference to issues of authenticity – positing that some traditions could have resulted from imprecise narrations or even forgeries. In addition, he maintained that some conflicts could be resolved upon reflection: two traditions might simply provide alternative ways of satisfying a single obligation; they might offer instructions for successive stages; or they might provide rules applicable only when certain conditions are met.[30] In short, for Ibn Bābawayh, scholars were to appeal to the texts of the Qur'ān and traditions for legal doctrine, avoid reading incoherence into that doctrine by appealing only to reports of unassailable authenticity, and use reason to work out apparent conflicts. Ibn Bābawayh managed to amplify Shīʿism's earlier traditionalist tendencies, and the influence of his teachings and works was extensive.[31] Yet in ensuing generations, while subsequent Shīʿī jurists accepted his collected traditions as authentic, they viewed the meaning of those traditions as a matter of interpretation.

A. RATIONALIST THRUST: A PRESUMPTION OF NONLIABILITY AND LEGALITY

Ibn Bābawayh's influence was strong but of limited endurance, as the next generations of jurists moved Shīʿī jurisprudence in a more rationalist direction. Al-Shaykh al-Mufīd (d. 413/1022), al-Shaykh al-Ṭūsī (d. 460/1067), and al-ʿAllāma al-Ḥillī (d. 726/1325) were all prominent jurists who had a lasting effect on the trajectory of Shīʿī law and the course of legal maxims within it. Their entry point into the debate came through the tradition that Ibn Bābawayh had cited from Jaʿfar al-Ṣādiq, that "everything is permissible unless specifically prohibited."[32] This set of jurists interpreted the statement to designate a "presumption of nonliability," which they elaborated through a combination of traditions and rational arguments.

[30] See Ibn Bābawayh, *Iʿtiqādāt*, 59–63 (on the Qur'ān), 91–102 (on traditions). A more problematic cause of difference that Ibn Bābawayh suggests here and that cannot be countered by simply emphasizing authenticity is dissimulation (*taqiyya*), by which the Imāms did not always make known the "right" answers to legal questions when they feared that their lives or those of their followers might be in danger, normally because of sectarian disputes with the majority Sunnī government.

[31] Modarressi, *Introduction to Shīʿī Law*, 32.

[32] See note 20.

1. Narrow Rationalism

Reflecting on the oft-quoted Jaʿfar al-Ṣādiq tradition, Mufīd (d. 413/1022) concluded that a *presumption of nonliability* was a central precept of Shīʿī law. For him, because revelation was complete, it stood to reason that "the Law (fully) specifies the limits" that regulate human behavior – a notion that supports the conclusion that "any act not governed by a text explicitly indicating prohibition must be permissible."[33] By extension, people are "innocent" or free of legal liability for duties or prohibitions about which they have no knowledge.

This observation is immensely significant in that Mufīd offered one of the earliest formulations in Shīʿī law explicitly suggesting a tentatively rational basis for this nonliability presumption. Having studied under both rationalist and traditionalist scholars, Mufīd's approach fell somewhere between the two.[34] His turn toward rational bases for law rooted in tradition was a deliberate departure from his teacher Ibn Bābawayh's anti-rationalist stance on theology, and it was a deliberate attempt to displace the dominance of pure textualist-traditionalism.[35]

In a further effort to break the traditionalist grip on Shīʿī legal interpretation, Mufīd explained his position with appeal to explicitly rational principles.[36] The nonliability presumption itself rested on his formulation of the well-known Muʿtazilī theological *principle of legality*, that is, that God would not punish until He had given notice of the law.[37] In a

33 Mufīd, *Taṣḥīḥ al-iʿtiqād*, ed. ʿAbbās-Qūlī al-Wāʿiẓ al-Charandābī (Tabriz: Maṭbaʿat al-Riḍaʾī, 1364/1944), 69.

34 See Modarressi, *Introduction to Shīʿī Law*, 13–29 (listing borrowings as well as significant doctrinal differences between his and Muʿtazilī theology). See also W. Madelung, "Mufīd," in *EI*², 7:312–13 (noting that he had likely studied the doctrines of the Baghdādī "school" of Muʿtazilism, on which see Racha El Omari, *The Theology of Abū l-Qāsim al-Balḫī/al-Kaʿbī (d. 319/931): A Study of Its Sources and Reception* (PhD diss. Yale University, 2007).

35 On Mufīd, see, for example, Najāshī, *Rijāl* (Qum: Muʾassasat al-Nashr al-Islāmī al-Tābiʿa li-Jamāʿat al-Mudarrisīn, 1986) 399–403; Khwansārī, *Rawḍāt al-jannāt*, 536–43; Ibn Shahrāshūb, *Maʿālim al-ʿulamāʾ*, ed. ʿAbbās Iqbāl (Tehran: n.p., 1353/1954) [distribution by Maṭbaʿat Fardīn], 100–102. For his theological views, see Paul Sander, *Zwischen Charisma und Ratio: Entwicklungen in der frühen imāmitischen Theologie* (Berlin: K. Schwarz, 1994); McDermott, *Theology*; Madelung, "Mufīd," 7:312, and sources listed therein.

36 See Modarressi, *Introduction to Shīʿī Law*, 40 (describing elements of his rationalism and his criticism of traditionists in an approach designed to "pave the way for the return of rational analysis in Shīʿī doctrine").

37 See Mufīd, *Awāʾil al-maqālāt fī ʾl-madhāhib al-mukhtārāt*, ed. ʿAbbās-Qūlī al-Wāʿiẓ al-Charandābī (Tabriz: Maṭbaʿat al-Riḍaʾī, 1364/1944), 28–29 (*lā yuʿadhdhib aḥad illā ʿalā dhanb iktasabah aw jurm ijtaramah aw qabīḥ nahāh fa-ʾrtakabah*; noting general

"correction" to Ibn Bābawayh's position, Mufīd explained that the *ḥadīth*, "Everything is permissible unless specifically prohibited," really indicates that divine legal rulings are divided into two categories, roughly echoing *mala in se* and *mala prohibita*, respectively: (1) acts for which the intellect comprehends a ruling of prohibition because the mind immediately perceives them to be morally undesirable, such as acts of injustice;[38] and (2) acts for which reason can discern neither a ruling of prohibition nor one of permissibility, and which are therefore in need of revelation to clarify their legal status.[39] The latter category includes rulings that may have been subject to divine abrogation of laws that existed before Islam. "But after [Islam's] revelation, the governing principle is that 'everything for which there is no textual prohibition is permissible,' because the divine law establishes [its own] boundaries and specifies prohibitions."[40] On this basis, Mufīd limited the nonliability presumption to circumstances in which the text provided too little guidance.[41]

At the same time, Mufīd preferred a textualist approach that allowed for some, but not too much, rational analysis in legal interpretation. For him, pure reason-based arguments were faulty because they introduced human discretion into a legal system that was supposed to be guided solely by the divine Lawgiver.[42] Moreover, Mufīd believed that "reason does not render [people] free from the need for revelation" – which is why people are held fully accountable only with revelation: the Prophets and Imāms were conduits of divinely inspired

agreement among the Muʿtazila (*ahl al-tawḥīd*) on the presumption of nonliability (*aṣālat al-barāʾa*)). For the classic outline of the five tenets of (Baṣran) Muʿtazilism, see Mānkdīm Shashdīw (d. 425/1034), *Taʿlīq* [*ʿalā*] *sharḥ al-Uṣūl al-khamsa*, ed. ʿAbd al-Karīm ʿUthmān (Cairo: Maktabat Wahba, 1965), published as Qāḍī ʿAbd al-Jabbār (d. 415/1025), *Sharḥ al-Uṣūl al-khamsa*, as clarified by D. Gimaret in "Les *Uṣūl al-ḫamsa* du Qāḍī ʿAbd al-Gabbār et leurs commentaires," *Annales Islamologiques* 15 (1979), 47–96, at 49. In that tradition, the mainstream Muʿtazilī principle is that "it is morally wrong to punish without clarification (of the law): *qubḥ al-ʿiqāb bi-lā bayān*" [the principle of legality]. A second, usually related principle is that "it is morally wrong to impose moral-legal liability on those who lack capacity: *qubḥ taklīf mā lā yuṭāq*" [the principle of capacity]. Mufid does not mention the second principle, likely because he draws on the Baghdad school of Muʿtazilism, which rejected that principle. See El Omari, *Theology of Abū l-Qāsim al-Balḫī/al-Kaʿbī*.

38 Mufīd, *Taṣḥīḥ al-iʿtiqād*, published together with *Awāʾil*, 69 (*qabbaḥah al-ʿaql*).

39 Ibid. (*al-ākhar mawqūf fī ʾl-ʿaql; lā yaqḍī ʿalā ʾl-ḥaẓr wa-lā ʾl-ibāḥa*).

40 Ibid.

41 Indeed, he made efforts elsewhere to show that he relied on revelation alone. See Mufīd, *Tadhkira fī uṣūl al-fiqh*, in *Muṣannafāt al-Shaykh al-Mufīd* (Qum: al-Muʾtamar al-ʿĀlamī fī Alfiyyāt al-Shaykh al-Mufīd, 1413/1992–3), 9:43.

42 Ibid.

knowledge and provided a safeguard against the whims of human discretion in interpretation.[43]

Mufīd's uneasy tradition-based rationalism perhaps explains the rather short shrift that he gave to the doubt canon, which does not appear in his *fiqh* works at all. Moreover, when discussing criminal law, Mufīd privileged a traditionalist-textualist orientation and also excluded mention of the nonliability presumption. He did cite instances in which *ḥadd* liability was canceled, but those instances related mostly to cases of coercion (such as rape) and repentance, for which he found explicit foundational texts that lifted liability from the victim or the offender, respectively.[44] In addition, he noted instances in which strict *ḥadd* liability would apply (such as acts of male sodomy), again, as rooted in traditions.[45]

Notwithstanding Mufīd's focus on texts in *ḥudūd* discussions, he nevertheless paved the way for the maxims-accommodating stance that would come to dominate Shīʿī law by using rational arguments to complement and explicate the meaning of *ḥadīth* texts. His influence was extensive. Even before Ibn Bābawayh's death, Mufīd had begun gaining in scholarly stature in Baghdad, and he eventually became the leading theologian and spokesman for the Shīʿī community of his time.[46] Virtually all of the leading Shīʿī scholars of the following generation were students of Mufīd or of his teachings.[47] If Mufīd was trying to split the difference between rationalism and traditionalism, his students approached questions of divine delegation within that framework in different, sometimes unpredictable, ways. Of particular note are two divergent paths that stretched far into the horizon of Shīʿī law and theology: the adoption of a "broad-ranging" rationalism by Mufīd's highly influential student al-Sharīf al-Murtaḍā, and the adoption of a more "balanced" rationalism by his equally influential student Abū Jaʿfar al-Ṭūsī.

43 Mufīd, *Awāʾil*, published together with *Taṣḥīḥ*, 8, 11–12. Cf. ibid., 2–16 (distinguishing Twelver Shīʿī doctrine from Muʿtazilī rationalism).

44 See Mufīd, *al-Muqniʿa* (Qum: Muʾassasat al-Nashr al-Islāmī, 1410/1990), 787, 789 (applying the doubt canon – though not in its standard form – to instances of coercion, such as rape, and situations in which a defendant repents before his case is brought before the courts).

45 Mufīd, *Muqniʿa*, in *YF*, 23:31.

46 Madelung, "Imāmism and Muʿtazilite Theology," 21.

47 His students included those who, as noted in the text, would comment on the nonliability presumption and develop the law with respect to it: the two *naqīb*s (government-appointed chiefs of the ʿAlids, of whom he was tutor) al-Sharīf al-Raḍī (d. 406/1015) and al-Sharīf al-Murtaḍā (d. 436/1044), Abū Jaʿfar Muḥammad b. al-Ḥasan al-Ṭūsī (d. 460/1067), and others. For fuller lists, see Madelung, "Mufīd," 7:312; Devin Stewart, *Islamic Legal Orthodoxy: Twelver Shiite Responses to the Sunni Legal System* (Salt Lake City: University of Utah Press, 1998), 129.

2. Broad Rationalism

Toward the end of Mufīd's life, al-Sharīf al-Murtaḍā (d. 436/1044) assumed a leading role as both scholar and government-designated leader of the Shīʿī community in Baghdad.[48] He not only accepted the nonliability presumption, but greatly expanded its scope. Whereas Mufīd limited the presumption to matters of ritual, al-Sharīf al-Murtaḍā applied it to *ḥudūd* and other laws, whenever the import of foundational texts was uncertain.

The shift reflected al-Sharīf al-Murtaḍā's more rationalist brand of theology, which influenced his rationalist approach to law. In contrast to Mufīd's brand of Muʿtazilī-inspired rationalism drawn from the conservative "Baghdādī school" of Muʿtazilism, al-Sharīf al-Murtaḍā was inspired by the more enduring and liberal "Baṣran school," which he had studied under its head scholar, Qāḍī ʿAbd al-Jabbār, in their native Baghdad.[49] To be sure, al-Sharīf al-Murtaḍā agreed with Mufīd on the core Shīʿī theological and legal doctrines surrounding the Imāmate: its necessity, the designation of the twelve Imāms, and the logic of the Occultation.[50] But al-Sharīf al-Murtaḍā went further than his teacher in appeals to rational analysis in law. His aim was likely to place Imāmī thought on firmer rationalist bases precisely to counter the Muʿtazilī Sunnī detractors surrounding him who accepted the role of reason but rejected Shīʿī traditions.

The defining feature of al-Sharīf al-Murtaḍā's approach was his adoption of the Muʿtazilī rationalist principle that the basic truths of religion

[48] Al-Sharīf al-Murtaḍā succeeded his brother, al-Sharīf al-Raḍī, as chief of the ʿAlids. For his theological views, see McDermott, *Theology*, 373–94. On the office of the *naqīb* (government-designated ʿAlid chief), see C. E. Bosworth and J. Burton-Page, "Naḳīb," in *EI*[2], 7:926.

[49] Madelung, "Imāmism and Muʿtazilite Theology," 25–27 (noting that al-Sharīf al-Murtaḍā's writings drew on the works of his teacher, Qāḍī ʿAbd al-Jabbār). For a discussion of rationalist jurists who followed and further developed al-Sharīf al-Murtaḍā's approach, see Modarressi, *Introduction to Shīʿī Law*, 43–44. On the "conservatism" of the Baghdādī (traditionist) school and the "liberalism" of the Baṣran (rationalist) school, see discussions by Madelung and Modarressi in the works cited here.

[50] Al-Sharīf al-Murtaḍā adduced rational supports over and above – and often instead of – arguments based solely on revelation and traditions to support theological and legal doctrines. For examples, in defense of the Imāmate doctrine, see al-Sharīf al-Murtaḍā, *al-Uṣūl al-iʿtiqādiyya*, in *Nafāʾis al-makhṭūṭāt*, ed. Muḥammad Ḥasan Āl Yāsīn (Najaf: al-Maṭbaʿa al-Ḥaydariyya, 1954), 1:80–81; al-Sharīf al-Murtaḍā, *al-Dhakhīra fī ʿilm al-kalām*, ed. Aḥmad al-Ḥusaynī (Qum: Muʾassasat al-Nashr al-Islāmī, 1411/1990–1), 409–29, 502–504. Cf. Madelung, "Imāmism and Muʿtazilite Theology," 25–27.

can be established by reason.[51] The idea was that there is a moral system woven into the fabric of this world that humans could rationally discern, but that God made them free to follow or disregard the dictates of that morality and promised to judge them on that basis. Accordingly, al-Sharīf al-Murtaḍā maintained that whatever the human intellect perceives as morally good or morally wrong is indeed so before God.[52] This formulation was an expression of the enduring Shīʿī *principle of correlation*, a jurisprudential legal canon on revelation and reason, which states that "whatever reason dictates, so does the [divine] Law."[53] In other words, morality is objective, meaning that perceptions of moral value should not differ from God to human beings. However, because God's knowledge encompasses all things, He always perceives the true moral value of all acts, whereas the human mind may fall short in its ability to perceive facts fully.[54] Therefore, it behooves humans to look to God's revelation for legislation of perfect morality, in which God imposes obligations of only the morally good and beneficial, and punishes only the morally wrong and harmful.[55]

In addition to the *principle of correlation*, al-Sharīf al-Murtaḍā also incorporated two overarching Muʿtazilī precepts of moral-legal accountability as central to the entire structure of Islamic law. The first is the *principle of legality*, which we saw implicitly with Mufīd – the notion that it would be morally wrong for God to levy punishments without giving

[51] Madelung, "Imāmism and Muʿtazilite Theology," 25–27, esp. 25 ("[While Mufīd viewed theology] merely as a means of defending more effectively the Imāmite dogma derived from the teaching of the Imāms, al-Murtaḍā accepted the Muʿtazilite view that the basic truths of religion are to be established by reason alone.") (citing al-Sharīf al-Murtaḍā, *Masāʾil al-Sharīf Abī al-Ḥusayn al-Muḥsin b. Muḥammad b. Nāṣir* [now published in al-Sharīf al-Murtaḍā, *Rasāʾil*]). See also al-Sharīf al-Murtaḍā, *al-Uṣūl al-iʿtiqādiyya*, 1:80–81.

[52] Al-Sharīf al-Murtaḍā, *Rasāʾil*, 3:177–79 (contrasting *ḥasan* with *qabīḥ*).

[53] See al-Sharīf al-Murtaḍā, *Dhakhīra*, 105 (noting the correlation: *fa-tajrī lafẓat taklīf wa-mukallaf maʿa ʾl-qubḥ waʾl-ḥusn, waʾl-wājib wa-ghayr al-wājib*). See also Bihbahānī, *Risālat aṣālat al-barāʾa*, 392; Modarressi, *Introduction to Shīʿī Law*, 4 and citations therein (discussing the principle, called *qāʿidat al-mulāzama*, in the following form: *kull mā ḥakama bih al-ʿaql ḥakama bih al-sharʿ*).

[54] Al-Sharīf al-Murtaḍā, *Rasāʾil*, 3:179 (giving the frequently debated example of divergent perceptions regarding the morality of killing a child in the Qurʾānic story of Khiḍr and the prophet-to-be Moses; according to the story, it was deemed a morally sound act only with the benefit of the full divine knowledge that Khiḍr had but Moses lacked, see Qurʾān, 18:65–82). But see Muḥammad Bāqir al-Ṣadr, *Durūs fī ʿilm al-uṣūl*, trans. Mottahedeh, *Lessons*, 49–52 (discussing Ibn Bābawayh's and Mufīd's commentary on this same story to argue against the validity of interpretation (*ijtihād*) in the old sense, taken from Sunnī jurists, of taking speculative reasoning as a *source* of law rather than the developed sense among Shīʿī jurists pointing to such reason as a *process* of deriving the law from the texts).

[55] See al-Sharīf al-Murtaḍā, *Dhakhīra*, 295–302.

notice of the law. The second is the *principle of capacity* – that it would be morally wrong to punish anyone who had no capacity to follow the law.[56]

On these three premises – the principle of correlation, the principle of legality, and the principle of capacity – al-Sharif al-Murtaḍā viewed questions of legal-moral liability as running parallel with questions of moral value, which likewise matched revelatory rules of obligation and prohibition.[57] In this rubric, moral-legal liability attached only after a person had reached full intellectual maturity, the capacity to know the law fully, and the ability to choose freely whether to follow it.[58]

In principle, al-Sharīf al-Murtaḍā equated reason and revelation, but in practice, he defined morality with respect to revelation.[59] That is, he saw moral wrongs as those prohibited by God in the texts of revelation, by which he meant the foundational texts: the Qur'ān and Sunna.[60] Al-Sharīf al-Murtaḍā thus privileged the rules of revelation, viewed as the prerogative of the Lawgiver, whenever they seemed to diverge from the dictates of pure reason. Yet he limited the scope of revelation's exceptionalism to particular cases, justifying the divergence otherwise in terms of God's all-encompassing knowledge of the facts and the notion of divine justice.[61]

For al-Sharīf al-Murtaḍā, revelation provided moral-legal guidance to cover all acts through general precepts if not specific textual rules. Accordingly, jurists were to take recourse first to authoritative foundational texts: the Qur'ān, widely transmitted *ḥadīth*, and individually transmitted *ḥadīth* – that is, "single-source" reports known to be authentic by

[56] Ibid., 105 ("It is morally wrong to enforce legal-moral accountability for acts beyond a person's capacity: *taklīf mā lā yuṭāq qabīḥ*"). For sources on this principle, referred to in shorthand as "no liability without capacity: *qubḥ* or *ʿadam taklīf mā lā yuṭāq*," see above, note 37.

[57] Ibid. (discussing *ḥusn* and *qubḥ*).

[58] Ibid. (specifying that *taklīf* is not *ḥasan* until after a person reaches full intellectual maturity (*ikmāl al-ʿaql*) and comprehends the law (*ḥaṣb al-adilla*)), 121 (noting that the knowledge of the law can be actual or constructive, that is, that a person either knows or has the means to discover the law: *ʿāliman bi-mā kullifa aw mutamakkinan min al-ʿilm bi-dhālik*), 295 (noting that punishment is due for immoral acts of commission of prohibitions or omission of obligations "so long as the person freely chooses the [prohibited] action or is able to avoid abandoning the [obligated] action").

[59] Al-Sharīf al-Murtaḍā is by no means unique in this regard. Jurist-theologians typically opposed philosophical principles that disagreed with their theological dogmas from scripture. Yet they tended increasingly to adopt philosophical terminology and concepts, which they folded into their writings. See, for example, Sabine Schmidtke, *The Theology of al-ʿAllāma al-Ḥillī (d. 726/1325)* (Berlin: K. Schwarz, 1991).

[60] Al-Sharīf al-Murtaḍā, *Dhakhīra*, 81.

[61] See discussion in ibid., 295–302.

virtue of community consensus and contextual clues.[62] He exhibited a deep skepticism – more so than Mufīd – about the utility of the latter type of text for resolving questions of theology and of law. To overcome those doubts, he imposed stringent criteria for accepting single-source reports by evaluating each with rational assessments and with reference to reliable textual evidence such as that of the Qur'ān.[63]

If these foundational texts did not provide clear rules, al-Sharīf al-Murtaḍā argued that jurists were then to take recourse to rulings derived through reason, which – according to the principle of correlation – accords with divine law.[64] While insisting that revelation was comprehensive, he readily admitted that "situations are infinite but the [foundational] texts finite."[65] In this way, al-Sharīf al-Murtaḍā brought the equation of reason to revelation full circle: he believed that revelation provided *general* principles to cover all aspects of life, but where the *specific* rules were non-explicit or undiscoverable, reason's dictates could fill the gaps based on the general principles.

One such principle is, of course, the presumption of nonliability. For al-Sharif al-Murtaḍā, its scope of operation was as wide as the domain of doubt. The caveat was that he rarely, if ever, found the texts to be ambiguous or doubtful, particularly in the domain of *ḥudūd* laws – which he saw to be, by definition, specifically and clearly designated by God.

In criminal law, al-Sharif al-Murtaḍā typically followed the foundational texts and used rational arguments to explain or justify them. Consider his treatment of male sodomy. In his book distinguishing unique positions of Shīʿī law and defending them against Sunnī critics, he relied on a report of ʿAlī's decision that the death penalty applied to male sodomites, bolstered by reference to Shīʿī scholarly consensus on that ruling.[66] He further noted contextual indications drawn from the Sunnī literature, confirming similar contemporaneous developments in the proto-Sunnī

62 Ibid., 315.

63 See Madelung, "Imāmism and Muʿtazilite Theology," 25, n. 4 (citing al-Sharīf al-Murtaḍā, *al-Masāʾil al-Ṭarābulusiyya al-thālitha*, describing the Shīʿī books of *ḥadīth* as being full of errors for which strict criteria for discerning authentic reports are needed).

64 Al-Sharīf al-Murtaḍā, *Rasāʾil*, 1:318 (*ḥukm al-aṣl fī ʾl-ʿaql*). This statement is an affirmation of the nonliability presumption, *aṣālat al-barāʾa* – that is, that people are to appeal to the original presumptive state.

65 Ibid., 1:316 (*fa-qad tadull mā yatanāhā fī nafsih* [*al-nuṣūṣ al-mutanāhiya*] *ʿalā ḥukm ḥawādith lā tatanāhā*).

66 Al-Sharīf al-Murtaḍā, *Intiṣār*, in *YF*, 23:49–50 (citing the tradition of ʿAlī (*man wajadtumūh ʿalā ʿamal qawm Lūṭ fa-ʾqtulū ʾl-fāʿil waʾl-mafʿūl bih*), and adducing claims of consensus to head off objections that single-source traditions are invalid).

context.[67] Finally, he listed rational arguments, perhaps designed to defend his position against possible Sunnī Muʿtazilī opponents. He argued that "*ḥudūd* laws were legislated for deterrence of serious moral offenses (*fawāḥish*) and other serious crimes. The more morally corrupt the act (*afḥash*), the greater the measure of deterrence required."[68] From this premise, al-Sharīf al-Murtaḍā suggested that male sodomy was morally more corrupt than were ordinary sex crimes, given Qur'ānic discussions of how the penchant for sodomy on the part of Lot's people brought about the destruction of Sodom and Gomorrah. For him, the act therefore rationally required harsher criminal punishment. He was careful to note that his exercise of legal analysis was not a form of analogical reasoning (*qiyās*), which his fellow Imāmī Shīʿa readily rejected as yielding questionable and uncertain conclusions; rather, it was a type of logical argumentation from inference (*istidlāl*) to provide a supporting rationale for the unambiguous Shīʿī textual rule.[69]

What about doubt in criminal law? Al-Sharīf al-Murtaḍā did not invoke the doubt canon in its standard formulation in his legal works. Although Sunnīs during his time were beginning to regard the doubt canon as a prophetic *ḥadīth*,[70] and although Ibn Bābawayh had deemed it an authentic *ḥadīth* in the Shīʿī corpus decades earlier,[71] al-Sharīf al-Murtaḍā – along with Mufīd – does not seem to have followed suit. The latter two scholars' skepticism toward single-source reports may well have made the doubt canon fall short of their higher standards of authenticity. Moreover, that they privileged revelation particularly when defining crimes meant that they placed a premium on *ḥudūd* enforcement over avoidance.[72]

[67] Ibid. (citing sources stating that Ibn ʿAbbās and Abū Bakr agreed with ʿAlī, and that the sources recorded no disagreement contemporaneous to their times; also noting reports from the early proto-Sunnī jurists, Mālik and al-Layth b. Saʿd, that male sodomizers were to be stoned to death).

[68] Ibid.

[69] Ibid. For a comparison of the Sunnī treatment of the same issue, see Lange, *Justice*, 199–214.

[70] Recall that the Ḥanafī jurist from Rayy, Abū Bakr Aḥmad b. ʿAlī al-Rāzī (d. 370/981), known as Jaṣṣāṣ, was the first Sunnī jurist we know of to cite the doubt canon as a prophetic *ḥadīth*. See Jaṣṣāṣ, *Aḥkām al-Qur'ān*, 3:330. See further Chapter 2, note 31 and accompanying text.

[71] He includes it in his *Muqniʿ*, 147, and his *Faqīh*, 4:53, no. 90.

[72] For instance, when speaking of otherworldly consequences, al-Sharīf al-Murtaḍā gathers from foundational texts that punishments for crimes can be canceled by pardon (that is, God's grace) as the result of sincere repentance, increased good works, etc. Al-Sharīf al-Murtaḍā, *Dhakhīra*, 302. Perhaps his focus on just deserts in the afterlife can explain his jurisprudence in this worldly contexts of *ḥudūd* laws, which favors *ḥudūd* enforcement over avoidance.

After al-Sharīf al-Murtaḍā, Shīʿī law and theology more or less filled in the rationalist approach to law that he had framed: an equation of revelation to reason with a thumb on the revelation side of the scale, and adherence to the principle of legality and the principle of capacity.[73] Beginning with the leading students of Mufīd and al-Sharīf al-Murtaḍā, the generations of Shīʿī theologians and jurists following these two scholars developed this framework into a fuller edifice, constructing different points of emphasis as to the operational scope of reason alongside revelation in Shīʿī law.[74]

3. Balanced Rationalism

The next turn in the meaning of the nonliability presumption came through scholars who tried to smooth out the link between reason and revelation. After al-Sharīf al-Murtaḍā, most Shīʿī jurists continued to both defend and demand a central role for reason in interpreting Islamic law. As had al-Sharīf al-Murtaḍā, they incorporated the two central Muʿtazilī presumptions that provided the theoretical framework for their rationalist-pragmatist interpretive philosophy of law: the principle of legality (that it would be morally unjust to punish without clarifying the law) and the principle of capacity (that it would be morally unjust to punish anyone lacking the capacity to follow the law). On these bases, Shīʿī jurists maintained that for liability, especially criminal liability, to attach, the law had to be clear and it had to fall within the human capacity to apply it – outlining a sort of clear statement rule. These jurists further maintained that clarity required certainty.[75] Absent these conditions, the default rule was the presumption of nonliability and exemption from moral-legal liability.

In rationalist circles over time, the nonliability presumption became firmly entrenched as the rule of first resort whenever the import of the text was in doubt.[76] Once this presumption was firmly in place, the scope of the doubt canon was at its widest, and it proliferated in new juristic works on Islamic substantive law and legal maxims alike. But before that

[73] See Madelung, "Imāmism and Muʿtazilite Theology," 27.

[74] For an accessible list of al-Sharīf al-Murtaḍā's students, see Stewart, *Islamic Legal Orthodoxy*, 129–30.

[75] That is, the authoritativeness of certainty (*ḥujjiyyat al-qaṭʿ*, that is, *ʿilm*). For further discussion, see Mottahedeh/Ṣadr, *Lessons*, 58–62 (translated as the "probativity of assurance").

[76] An exception is Muḥammad Bāqir al-Ṣadr, who privileged the precautionary principle (*iḥtiyāṭ*) above the nonliability presumption. See ibid., 120–25, and discussion below.

point, Shīʿī jurisprudence took several turns. Along the way, it became clear that the grounds for assessing textual clarity, human capacity, and legal certainty were themselves in dispute.

Abū Jaʿfar al-Ṭūsī (d. 460/1067) attempted to develop Shīʿī jurisprudence in a slightly different direction from that laid out by his teachers Mufīd and al-Sharīf al-Murtaḍā.[77] Though committed to rationalist methods of interpretation, he relied on single-source reports as authoritative sources of law, provided they accompanied intrinsic or extrinsic clues indicating reliability. Such clues could include being well known in the community, though not rising to the level of consensus as al-Sharīf al-Murtaḍā required. Toward that end, Ṭūsī copied *ḥadīth* reports from the individual notebooks produced by the early transmitters, and thereby collected more traditions than were available in the early "comprehensive" collections. He placed his collected reports in two works that came to round out the corpus of authoritative Imāmī Shīʿī *ḥadīth*: *al-Istibṣār* and *Tahdhīb al-aḥkām*. In those works, Ṭūsī did not include the doubt canon; but in his works of law, he emphatically did. For example, in his legal treatise *Nihāya*, Ṭūsī applied the doubt canon to cases of ignorance, repentance, and coercion.[78] But where his predecessors had exempted accused offenders from legal liability in those instances based on individual traditions, Ṭūsī applied the doubt canon expansively to those and other scenarios, sometimes in surprising ways. For example, he posited that mere claims denying wrongdoing were enough to create doubt sufficient to warrant *ḥudūd* avoidance – such as the scenario in which a man and a woman are found together and arrested on charges of sex crimes but claim to be married; or the scenario in which someone steals from a secure location but upon arrest claims that the owner gifted the stolen item to him or her.[79] Ṭūsī even articulated a theory of *partial doubt* and proportional application of the doubt canon along with proportional punishment. For instance, if a man slept with a slave woman whom he owned only partially, judges were to avoid punishment (ordinarily 100 lashes), in amounts proportionate to his ownership interest; for although the act was 100 percent illicit, only that fraction for which there was no

[77] On Ṭūsī's jurisprudence, see Modarressi, *Introduction to Shīʿī Law*, 44. Cf. Mohammad Ali Amir-Moezzi, "Al-Ṭūsī, Muḥammad b. al-Ḥasan," in *EI*², 10:745–46, and sources cited therein.

[78] See Ṭūsī, *Nihāya*, 2:708, 716, 725. This work became the most authoritative Shīʿī text for the next two centuries. See Modarressi, *Introduction to Shīʿī Law*, 44.

[79] Ṭūsī, *Nihāya*, 2:711, 746.

ownership was conceivably subject to *ḥudūd* avoidance on the basis of doubt.[80] In this way, in the *Nihāya* and other works, Ṭūsī relied on the nonliability presumption for his general tendency to identify doubt and to advocate avoidance of *ḥudūd* sanctions accordingly.[81]

These scenarios illustrate how Ṭūsī's approach to interpretation resulted in a criminal law jurisprudence that was neither fully textualist-traditionalist nor fully pragmatic-rationalist. He rejected the textual form of the doubt canon but expanded the doctrine on rational bases. This amalgamated approach, perhaps inspired by his earlier studies of Sunnī law,[82] gained him significant criticism from rationalists and traditionalists alike.[83] According to one scholar, his borrowings from Sunnī law expanded Shīʿī interpretive methods but also allowed inconsistencies with basic Shīʿī precepts to creep into the substance of the law.[84]

Lingering inconsistencies in Ṭūsī's jurisprudence were addressed by a series of prominent jurist-theologians culminating in al-ʿAllāma al-Ḥillī (d. 726/1325),[85] who has been said to represent "the last school of original thought" in Shīʿī theology.[86] He and his teachers applied technical, philosophical concepts to substantive Shīʿī law and theology, aiming to devise a

80 Ibid., 2:717. Later jurists disputed this proportionality approach. For example, Ibn Idrīs, *Sarāʾir*, 3:446 (recognizing but rejecting the proportionality theory in favor of total avoidance of *ḥudūd* punishment in cases of disputed or joint ownership, in part on the basis of the nonliability presumption).

81 See Ibn Idrīs, *Sarāʾir*, 3:432–33 (noting his disagreement with Ṭūsī's reliance on the nonliability presumption, especially in his *Khilāf*, at which point he had apparently lessened his reliance on single-source reports); cf. 3:433–34 (noting his agreement with Ṭūsī's later opinion, in the *Khilāf*, that in cases of mistaken identity where a woman masquerades falsely as a man's wife, the rule of *ḥudūd* avoidance applies to avert the *ḥadd* punishment from the man).

82 He initially studied Shāfiʿī law, and Subkī included him in his biographical dictionary of Shāfiʿī jurists. See Tāj al-Dīn al-Subkī, *Ṭabaqāt al-Shāfiʿiyya al-kubrā*, ed. Maḥmūd Muḥammad al-Ṭanāḥī and ʿAbd al-Fattāḥ Muḥammad al-Ḥilw (Cairo: Maktaba wa-Maṭbaʿat ʿĪsā al-Bābī al-Ḥalabī, 1964–76), 4:126–27, no. 315.

83 Purebred traditionists accused him of practicing Sunnī-style analogical reasoning, while mainstream rationalists criticized him for reasoning on the basis of weak traditions. Modarressi, *Introduction to Shīʿī Law*, 45.

84 Ibid., 47.

85 Al-ʿAllāma al-Ḥillī's most important legal works include *Mukhtalaf al-Shīʿa*, *Tadhkirat al-fuqahāʾ*, *Muntahā ʾl-maṭlab*, *Taḥrīr al-aḥkām al-sharʿiyya*, *Qawāʿid al-aḥkām*, *Irshād al-adhhān*, *Nihāyat al-iḥkām*, *Tabṣirat al-mutaʿallimīn* and *Talkhīṣ al-marām*. For his contributions to Shīʿī law, see Modarressi, *Introduction to Shīʿī Law*, 44, 47–48. For his theological views, see generally Schmidtke, *Theology*.

86 See Madelung, "Imāmism and Muʿtazilite Theology," 27 (observing that after him, Shīʿī theology developed through commentaries, abstractions, and restatements of his works and those of his teachers Nāṣir al-Dīn al-Ṭūsī (d. 672/1274) and al-Muḥaqqiq al-Ḥillī (d. 676/1277)). Compare Modarressi, *Introduction to Shīʿī Law*, 23 (noting that he

coherent and systematic theory that emphasized the authoritativeness of *ḥadīth* as a form of revelation while preserving reason as an analytical tool required for legal interpretation.[87]

Al-ʿAllāma al-Ḥillī's students and intellectual descendants followed the same track. Al-Shahīd al-Awwal (d. 786/1389), who had studied under the ʿAllāma's son, was the first to distill the principles identified by the elder scholar into an exclusively Shīʿī formula and to collect the theological precepts and jurisprudential principles that guided the law. To that end, he produced the first work of Shīʿī legal and other maxims, *al-Qawāʿid wa'l-fawā'id*,[88] which was enormously influential.[89] These developments, beginning with Ṭūsī and coming to fruition in al-ʿAllāma al-Ḥillī, completed the rationalist reconciliation between reason and revelation in Shīʿī law, and gave form to a rationalist-traditionalist combination that held sway during their time and – after a one century-long interruption – endures in Shīʿī law to this day.[90]

Like his predecessors, al-ʿAllāma al-Ḥillī was a staunch supporter of an objective theory of morality along with the principles of legality and capacity that reason required.[91] He and other rationalists also continued to espouse the principle of correlation between revelation and reason and emphasized that it gave form to the theory of objective values, allowing rules to be "inferred from the sole verdict of reason."[92] Through reason, he maintained,

represents a turning point in Shīʿī law, with some sources referring to scholars preceding him as the "ancients" and those after him as the "moderns").

87 Madelung, "Imāmism and Muʿtazilite Theology," 27 (calling this a new phase of Shīʿī theology, which had been espoused during al-Sharīf al-Murtaḍā's lifetime but was not fully incorporated into Shīʿī scholarship until Nāṣir al-Dīn Ṭūsī and al-ʿAllāma al-Ḥillī). Unlike al-Sharīf al-Murtaḍā, al-ʿAllāma al-Ḥillī regarded traditions less skeptically. He accepted *ḥadīth* as sources for law, evaluating them more on the basis of the reliability of their chains of transmission (*isnād*) – an approach that became a standard feature of Shīʿī jurisprudence. See, for example, Bihbahānī, *Risālat aṣālat al-barā'a*, 361–64.

88 This is the common view among scholars working on Shīʿī legal maxims. See, for example, Ḥasan al-Bujnūrdī, *al-Qawāʿid al-fiqhiyya*, ed. Mahdī al-Mihrīzī and Muḥammad Ḥusayn al-Dirāyatī (Qum: al-Hādī, 1419/1998), 1:9. Some erroneously list al-ʿAllāma's work *Qawāʿid al-aḥkām* (*fī maʿrifat al-ḥalāl wa'l-ḥarām*) among works of legal maxims that would prefigure that of al-Shahīd al-Awwal; see, for example, Muḥammad ʿAlī al-Tashkīrī et al., *al-Qawāʿid al-uṣūliyya wa'l-fiqhiyya ʿalā madhhab al-Imāmiyya* (Tehran: al-Majmaʿ al-ʿĀlamī li'l-Taqrīb al-Madhāhib al-Islāmiyya, 2004), 592 (bibliography). A review of *Qawāʿid al-aḥkām* shows that it is more a standard *fiqh* work detailing legal rulings than one dealing with principles governing the law.

89 It dominated the field until the rise of the traditionists during the Ṣafavid period in the mid-eleventh/seventeenth century. See Modarressi, *Introduction to Shīʿī Law*, 49–50.

90 See ibid., 44.

91 See Schmidtke, *Theology*, 99.

92 Modarressi, *Introduction to Shīʿī Law*, 4.

humans could discern the general contours of good and bad acts. Yet as Mufīd, al-Sharīf al-Murtaḍā, and other Shīʿī jurists had long held, al-ʿAllāma al-Ḥillī also maintained that there were some areas of law where rules of obligation (and therefore good acts) could not be known by reason alone. Revelation was required, for example, to instruct humans on how to perform ritual acts of worship. In addition, revelation was required for the details of Islamic law: rational deliberation could discern general rulings but access to the detailed rulings could be gained only with the help of revelation. Accordingly, al-ʿAllāma al-Ḥillī viewed revelation as a shortcut: "Through revelation, God therefore assists man in gaining access to the full knowledge about objective values to which He is Himself subject."[93]

In his criminal law jurisprudence, al-ʿAllāma al-Ḥillī appears to have adopted both the nonliability presumption and doctrines of doubt. Though he did not cite the doubt canon directly, he devoted considerable space to outlining areas of doubt that cancel *ḥudūd* liability. For example, he maintained that in cases where individuals were confused about the legality of a certain act (thinking it permissible when it was in fact not), the confusion and resulting mistake would be the type of doubt that required avoidance of *ḥudūd* sanctions.[94] He abstracted from that ruling a general principle that closely echoed the doubt canon for uncertainties confronting legal agents: "In any case where a person believes that [an act] is permissible [when in fact it is not], *ḥadd* liability is [to be] removed."[95] And he applied the principle liberally to cover cases of mistakes of fact, inadvertence, and other types of doubt.[96] Extending that principle to questions of voluntariness, proof,[97] and other forms of evidentiary doubt spawned a second statement of the general principle, also echoing the doubt canon closely for procedural aspects of the law: "Whenever a judge faces doubt, the [*ḥudūd* sanction] will not apply."[98]

[93] Schmidtke, *Theology*, 100.

[94] For example, al-ʿAllāma al-Ḥillī, *Qawāʿid*, in *YF*, 23:397 (avoiding punishment in the case of a man who married a prohibited woman by mistake, on the basis that his mistaken belief in the legality of the marriage (*iʿtaqadah shubhatan wa-jahila ʾl-taḥrīm*) was a *ḥadd*-averting doubt), 422 (on theft, on the mistaken belief in ownership).

[95] Ibid., 23:397 (in the context of marriage and *zinā*: *kull mawḍiʿ yuʿtaqad fīh ibāḥat al-nikāḥ yasquṭ fīh al-ḥadd*).

[96] Ibid. He also adopts Ṭūsī's proportionality rule for cases in which a person enjoys full "property" benefits when ownership or right of access is in fact partial, including sex with slave women and use of property. See ibid. (slave women), 23:423–24 (theft from war spoils (*ghanīma*)).

[97] Ibid., 23:398 (witnesses), 406 (claims of marriage, if plausible (*muḥtamal*), in cases of alleged *zinā*), 422 (claims of ownership in cases of alleged theft).

[98] Ibid., 23:422–23 (on theft: *law ḥaṣala al-shubha liʾl-ḥākim saqaṭa al-qaṭʿ*).

This approach – reliance on the nonliability presumption and other rationalist precepts of Shīʿī jurisprudence, including broad application of the doubt doctrine as another rational precept – proved enduring. In this way, the nonliability presumption and the doubt doctrine together became core features of Shīʿī criminal law.[99] The presumption was in fact so central to the entire structure of the law and to the theory of doubt that rationalists later found themselves emphatically defending the presumption of nonliability against traditionalists who would wage a full-on attack against it and against the doctrine of doubt.

B. TRADITIONALIST PARRY: ONE RIGHT ANSWER AS TEXT

Rationalism's steady rise over traditionalism since the fourth/tenth century was overshadowed and almost eclipsed in the eleventh/seventeenth century at the hands of Muḥammad Amīn al-Astarābādī, who sought to revive and restore the textualist-traditionalist school.[100] The rise of the traditionalists accompanied dramatic new political developments in the Shīʿī community. Namely, in 907/1501, a group of military leaders under the banner of Shāh Ismāʿīl seized power over Persian lands and established the first large, independent Imāmī Shīʿī polity: the Ṣafavid Empire.[101]

[99] With the exception of Ibn Idrīs, Shīʿī jurists rarely cited the doubt canon as a *ḥadīth*, but they applied it nonetheless, in ways similar to al-ʿAllāma al-Ḥillī's articulation and application of that canon. By contrast, contemporary Shīʿī jurists accept the doubt canon as a *ḥadīth* and a core precept of Shīʿī criminal law. See, for example, Dāmād, *Qavāʿid*, 4:44; Taskhīrī et al., *Qawāʿid*, 359.

[100] On developments that laid the groundwork for Astarābādī's rise, see Modarressi, *Introduction to Shīʿī Law*, 52–54. See also Rula Jurdi Abisaab, *Converting Persia: Religion and Power in the Safavid Empire* (London: I. B. Tauris, 2004), 105–12.

[101] On the consolidation, production, and transmission of Shīʿī religious knowledge in Ṣafavid Iran and surrounding lands, see generally Abisaab, *Converting Persia*, esp. 53–87 (on Shāh ʿAbbās's reign, 1587–1629). See also Albert Hourani, "From Jabal ʿĀmil to Iran," *Bulletin of the School of Oriental and African Studies* 49, 1 (1986), 133–40. But see Andrew J. Newman, "The Myth of the Clerical Migration to Safawid Iran," *Die Welt des Islams* 33, 1 (1993), 66–112 (challenging Hourani). But see, in turn, Devin Stewart, "Notes on the Migration of ʿĀmilī Scholars to Safavid Iran," *Journal of Near Eastern Studies* 55, 2 (1996), 81–103 (refuting Newman's refutation of Hourani). For a more general Ṣafavid history (r. 907–1135/1501–1722), see H. R. Roemer, "The Safavid Period," in *The Cambridge History of Iran*, vol. 6, ed. Peter Jackson and Lawrence Lockhart (Cambridge: Cambridge University Press, 1986), 189–350; see also Roger M. Savory, "Safawid Persia," in *The Cambridge History of Islam*, ed. Peter Holt et al. (Cambridge: Cambridge University Press, 1970), 1:349–429.

Under the Ṣafavids, Astarābādī inaugurated a new form of Shīʿī traditionalism.[102] In his seminal work, *al-Fawāʾid al-Madaniyya*, he responded pointedly to rationalists' claims of a role for reason in the law. He attacked them not only for adopting the nonliability presumption but also for what he regarded as their selective use of traditions to support a priori positions within a severely flawed theory of law when it came to dealing with doubt. For Astarābādī, rationalists had fundamentally misunderstood the *ḥadīth* cited by Ibn Bābawayh, which states that "everything is permissible unless specifically prohibited," as well as other traditions they frequently cited in support of the nonliability presumption.[103] Their error had to do with a failure to defer to revelation over reason and therefore to comprehend the true nature of doubt, morality, and the interpretive process. His arguments addressed each of these themes.

1. Doubt between Law and Fact, Obligation and Prohibition

When Astarābādī wrote, he well understood that Shīʿī legal texts outlined several types of doubt that continuously arose in legal interpretation – from questions of law and questions of fact to questions of morality.[104]

[102] While there is some evidence of cordial relations between Astarābādī and the Ṣafavid regime (see Gleave, *Scripturalist Islam*, 97 (describing the *fatwā* that he gave to Shāh ʿAbbās I on the purity of wine), 315–19 (text and translation of the *fatwā*)), it is not clear that Astarābādī's success came from official Ṣafavid patronage or support – especially inasmuch as Shāh ʿAbbās I clearly favored the two staunch "rationalists" of his day, the philosopher-lawyer Bahāʾ al-Dīn al-ʿĀmilī (d. 1030/1621) and Mīr Dāmād (d. 1040/1631–2). For the biographies and status of these two figures, see Abisaab, *Converting Persia*, 71–79, 95–96, 112–13; Devin J. Stewart, "A Biographical Notice on Bahāʾ al-Dīn al-ʿĀmilī (d. 1030/1621)," *Journal of the American Oriental Society* 111, 3 (1991), 563–71; Said Amir Arjomand, "The Clerical Estate and the Emergence of a Shiʿite Hierocracy in Safavid Iran: A Study in Historical Sociology," *Journal of the Economic and Social History of the Orient*, 28, 2 (1985),169–219, esp. 202.

[103] Muḥammad Amīn al-Astarābādī, *al-Fawāʾid al-Madaniyya* (Qum: Muʾassasat al-Nashr al-Islāmī, 1424/2003), 326, mentioning the "*ḥadīth* of lifted liability" (*ḥadīth al-rafʿ*), the "*ḥadīth* of barred liability" (*ḥadīth al-ḥajb*), and others, discussed below.

[104] See for example, Muẓaffar, *Uṣūl al-fiqh*, ed. Raḥmat Allāh Raḥmatī al-Arākī (Qum: Muʾassasat al-Nashr al-Islāmī, 1423/2002–3), 4:314–15 (distinguishing legal doubt (*shubha ḥukmiyya*, addressing situations where the import of the text is unclear or how it applies to a certain set of facts is unknown) from factual doubt (*shubha mawḍūʿiyya*, including mistake and ignorance)); cf. Abū al-Qāsim al-Qummī (d. 1231/1816), *Qawānīn al-uṣūl* (Tabriz: n.p., 1275/1858–9), 269–70; Muḥammad Kāẓim al-Khurāsānī (d. 1329/1911), *Kifāyat al-uṣūl*, ed. ʿAbbās ʿAlī al-Zāriʿī al-Sabzawārī (Qum: Muʾassasat al-Nashr al-Islāmī al-Tābiʿa li-Jamāʿat al-Mudarrisīn, 2006–7), 387; Bihbahānī, *Risālat aṣālat al-barāʾa*, 403–404 (noting that the categories are also called *shubha fī nafs al-ḥukm* (that is, *shubha ḥukmiyya*) and *shubha fī ṭarīq al-ḥukm* (that is, *shubha mawḍūʿiyya*) and quoting

In questions of law, the main concern here, Shīʿī treatment covered two basic types of legal rules: obligations and prohibitions. Shīʿī jurists treated these types of legal rules as giving rise to two separate spheres of legal doubt – uncertainties regarding obligations (*shubahāt wujūbiyya*) and uncertainties regarding prohibitions (*shubahāt taḥrīmiyya*).[105] The latter was germane to the question of doubt that surfaced in discussions of *ḥudūd* laws. Relatedly, the nonliability presumption applied to both spheres according to rationalists, but was restricted to the former according to traditionalists. Why the difference?

The divergence arose from fundamental differences over Shīʿī concepts of doubt and the scope of divinely delegated interpretive authority to resolve doubt. For both traditionalists and rationalists, ambiguities regarding obligations emerged when foundational texts did not *clearly* impose an obligation. In the absence of such a text, both groups maintained that the law presumes the agent to be exempt from any legal duty, because only clear revelation can impose obligations. Traditionalists argued on the basis of their textualist doctrine that all laws – whether of obligation or prohibition – proceed directly from the text; absent a clear textual obligation, one need not, indeed *must not*, act.[106] Rationalists agreed with the basic textualist requirement but added that punishment for acts of omission in cases of ambiguously worded *putative* rules would be unjust. To suppose the opposite would violate both textualist requirements and the rational principles of legality and capacity.[107] In the realm of putative obligations, then, traditionalists and rationalists agreed that no liability could attach without a clear statement of law imposing an obligation. The result, if not the reasoning, on whether the nonliability presumption applied to this type of doubt was relatively uncontroversial: both camps agreed that it did.

al-Ḥurr al-ʿĀmilī). Some traditionist jurists identified a separate category of doubt: "intrinsic doubt" (*qism ākhar mutaraddad bayna ʾl-qismayn … ishtibāhuhā bi-sabab amr dhātī*), for example, al-Ḥurr al-ʿĀmilī, as noted in Bihbahānī, *Risālat aṣālat al-barāʾa*, 403; other rationalist jurists identified separate categories of doubt arising from coercion and mistake, for example, Dāmād, *Qavāʿid*, 4:54–61 (*shubhah-i khaṭaʾ* and *shubhah-i ikrāh*).

105 See Muẓaffar, *Uṣūl al-fiqh*, 4:314–15; Aḥmad al-Ghurayfī al-Baḥrānī, *Aṣālat al-barāʾa fī ʾl-sharīʿa al-Islāmiyya* (Qum: Dār al-Ḥifẓ al-Turāth al-Baḥrānī, 1427/2006–7), 230.

106 See, for example, Qummī, *Qawānīn*, 266 (noting that the *aṣālat al-barāʾa* may be also called a *aṣālat al-nafy*, more clearly conveying the sense of nonliability or the absence of a legal rule, that is, to indicate that there can be no punishment for acts of omission in the absence of a clear text imposing an obligation); cf. ʿAbd Allāh b. Muḥammad al-Fāḍil al-Tūnī, *al-Wāfiya fī uṣūl al-fiqh*, ed. Muḥammad Ḥusayn al-Raḍawī al-Kashmīrī (Qum: Majmaʿ al-Fikr al-Islāmī, 1412/1992), 178.

107 See, for example, Bihbahānī, *Risālat aṣālat al-barāʾa*, 350 (joining the two, that is, *qubḥ al-ʿiqāb bi-lā bayān* and *qubḥ taklīf mā lā yuṭāq*); Anṣārī, *Rasāʾil*, 151.

The major controversy surrounded situations in which doubts about the law involved rules of prohibition, which of course encompassed *ḥudūd* laws. The rationalist-traditionalist debates here are thus key to understanding the validity and scope of the doubt canon. That is, these debates provide the backdrop for discussions about doubt related to the prohibitions of criminal law. For rationalists, the principles of legality and capacity applied across the board, meaning that the nonliability presumption would apply to prohibitions just as it did to obligations. Without this presumption, they reasoned, the possibility of an obscure prohibition lurking behind an ambiguous text might require certain precautionary measures to help individuals avoid transgressing the law's unknown prohibitions. That lurking possibility was precisely what led traditionalists to reject the broad, rationalist version of the nonliability presumption in attempts to avoid doubt altogether. Astarābādī explained why in his parry to the rationalist claims.

2. Ambiguity and Avoidance: One Right Answer as Text

To begin with, Astarābādī complained that rationalists did not truly take the foundational texts as their starting point. If they did, they would conclude, as had traditionalist-textualists, that the law itself requires avoidance of doubt. Instead, Astarābādī added, rationalist jurists attempted to attack doubt with unwieldy tools such as the broad nonliability presumption, expansive readings of the doubt canon, and reliance on other rational analyses of the law that diverged from the dictates of the text.

Astarābādī and his fellow traditionalists subscribed to a monist theory of law, according to which there was one right answer: a uniform law expressing a single, definitive legal ruling for any given act – a reflection of the rule always present in the mind of God.[108] Accordingly, human beings subject to Islamic law were required to follow it by adhering to areas of clear legality and avoiding areas of clear illegality as spelled out in revelation. As one *ḥadīth* reports:

> The lawful is clear, the unlawful is clear, and there is ambiguity (*shubahāt*) between the two. Whoever avoids ambiguity will be saved from violating prohibitions, and whoever operates in the realm of ambiguity may commit a prohibited act and thereby [fall into] self-destruction unknowingly.[109]

108 Astarābādī, *al-Fawā'id al-Madaniyya* (n.p.: Dār al-Nashr li-Ahl al-Bayt, [198-?]), 106; al-Ḥurr al-ʿĀmilī, *al-Fuṣūl al-muhimma*, 180–99.

109 Astarābādī, *Fawā'id* (2003), 325. For the tradition, see Muḥammad b. Yaʿqūb al-Kulaynī (d. 329/940–1), *al-Kāfī* (Tehran: Dār al-Uswa, 1418/1997–8), 1:68. Compare, in the Sunnī sources, Bukhārī, *Ṣaḥīḥ*, 1:20, 3:52; Muslim, *Ṣaḥīḥ*, 3:1219; Tirmidhī, *Sunan*, 2:340.

Thus, he concluded, *in the absence of revelation*, it would make sense to recognize a broad presumption of nonliability, because ordinary human beings would be unable to gain access to certain knowledge of the law.[110] In that scenario, people would have no choice but to appeal to their own reasoning merely to approximate rules for moral conduct. But *with revelation*, these presumptions no longer apply "because the actual laws have been revealed to govern all situations, even if [those laws] have not always been preserved," given the various episodes of book burning and other losses of Shīʿī works.[111] In other words, revelation obviates the need to devise so-called objective moral values or reason-based laws. In fact, Astarābādī suggested that such objectivity did not even exist as a basis for law: "Objective morality and immorality are one thing; objective obligations and prohibitions are something else."[112] For him, the trigger for legal-moral liability was revelation, meaning that human beings would never be held accountable for law on the basis of reason alone.[113]

So far, the picture that Astarābādī and his fellow traditionalists have painted of legality appears rather black and white: matters are either lawful or unlawful, as spelled out in the text of revelation. But what about the gray area in between – the hazy realm of doubt? Traditionalists recognized that a consequence of the notion that the correct laws were known perfectly only in the mind of God and by those whom He guided was that laypeople in the age of a hidden Imām could not always know or access the full contours of the law. Yet doubt of this sort was not an invitation to appeal to reason. Instead, people were to respect the unambiguous Qurʾānic instruction to "obey God and His messenger and those in authority over you" and to appeal to them for guidance toward resolving any disputes.[114]

110 Muslim jurists explored this idea by considering questions of legal liability in the period before revelation, that is, by debating whether there was moral-legal accountability in the period prior to the Prophets. See further A. Kevin Reinhart, *Before Revelation: The Boundaries of Muslim Moral Thought* (Albany: State University of New York Press, 1995).

111 Yūsuf al-Baḥrānī (d. 1186/1772), *al-Ḥadāʾiq al-nāḍira* (Najaf: Dār al-Kutub al-ʿIlmiyya, 1377–/1957–), 1:75.

112 Astarābādī, *Fawāʾid* (2003), 328 (*hunā masʾalatān … al-ḥusn waʾl-qubḥ al-dhātiyyān wa … ʾl-wujūb waʾl-ḥurma al-dhātiyyān*).

113 Ibid., 330 ("Legal-moral liability does not attach to anyone until and unless revelation has reached them: *baʿd bulūgh al-khiṭāb*."). Cf. al-Ḥurr al-ʿĀmilī, *Wasāʾil al-Shīʿa*, 18:127; Baḥrānī, *Ḥadāʾiq*, 1:49; Baḥrānī, *al-Durar al-Najafiyya min al-multaqaṭāt al-Yūsufiyya* (Beirut: Sharikat Dār al-Muṣṭafā li-Iḥyāʾ al-Turāth, 2002), 34.

114 Astarābādī, *Fawāʾid* (2003), 330 (citing Qurʾān, 4:59: *yā ayyuhā ʾlladhīna āmanū aṭīʿū ʾllāha wa-aṭīʿū ʾl-rasūla wa-ulī ʾl-amri minkum fa-in tanāzaʿtum fī shayʾin fa-ruddūhu ilā ʾllāhi waʾl-rasūl*). For a discussion with similar citations, see Ghurayfī, *Aṣāla*, 311 (citing

Even rationalists recognized this much.[115] The question, though, was how to carry out those instructions. Unsurprisingly, Astarābādī and his cohorts looked to the text.

They often cited the report of tripartite legality (*ḥadīth al-tathlīth*) dividing the world into the legal, the illegal, and the ambiguous – interpreting that report to mean that all matters of doubt were off-limits for jurists and laypeople alike to engage. Both groups were to avoid whatever was not mentioned in the foundational texts in order to avoid committing acts that were *potentially* prohibited, because the true legal status of the acts was unknown if the texts were silent about them.[116] Traditionalists further drew support from several other reports to impose an explicit obligation to exercise precaution in the face of doubt – giving shape to what we may call the abiding traditionalist *principle of precaution*. For example, one report known in both Shīʿī and Sunnī circles advised Muslims to "avoid what makes you doubt for that which does not."[117] Read in juxtaposition with the tripartite legality report, this report prompted traditionalists to conclude that – logically – doubtful matters did not fall into the first two categories of clear statements of law, so they must fall into a third category of doubt, which was to be avoided. Their conclusion amounted to a blanket rule covering all matters of law, which they declined to subordinate to a non-liability presumption as did the rationalists.[118] To do otherwise, they maintained, would be to render the third category of the tripartite report a nullity, which would violate basic rules of textual construction.[119] In sum,

Qur'ān, 16:43 and 21:7: "If you do not know [about a matter], ask those who know [that is, to whom God sent revelation before]: *fa-'s'alū ahla 'l-dhikri in kuntum lā taʿlamūn*").

115 Indeed, rationalist jurists cited these same verses but interpreted them differently, as discussed later. See, for example, Anṣārī, *Rasā'il*, 205.

116 Al-Ḥurr al-ʿĀmilī, *al-Fuṣūl al-muhimma*, 180–99; Astarābādī, *Fawā'id* (198-), 106. For additional arguments, see Ghurayfī, *Aṣāla*, 311.

117 Baḥrānī, *Ḥadā'iq*, 1:76 (interpreting this *ḥadīth* to require precautionary measures (*iḥtiyāṭ*)). Cf. Anṣārī, *Rasā'il*, 209 (with variations, noting that al-Shahīd al-Thānī mentioned this *ḥadīth* report, copying it from Sunnī sources); Ibn Ḥajar, *Fatḥ al-bārī*, 5:196 (noting that the *ḥadīth* appears in the canonical Sunnī collections by Bukhārī, Tirmidhī, Nasā'ī, et al.).

118 Baḥrānī, *al-Durar al-Najafiyya*, 24.

119 See Astarābādī, *Fawā'id* (198-?), 106. Cf. Ibn Ḥazm, *Iḥkām*, 6:745 (arguing that the bipartite and tripartite traditions of legality express the same idea and that the latter should be read in light of the former to mean that those confused about the status of an act should avoid it). While Astarābādī appealed to a common pragmatic canon of construction (compare to the American "presumption against redundancy"), Ibn Ḥazm was recognizing another textual canon premised on reading texts together as if part of a contiguous law to avoid reading legal texts as conflicting with one another (compare to the American "whole act rule"). See Eskridge et al., *Legislation*, appendix B, 21–23 ("textual canons").

traditionalists read these reports to impose not just advisory, but mandatory rules of avoidance of doubt on jurists and laypeople alike. That is, jurists *had to* avoid ruling on matters of ambiguous import (*tawaqquf*), and laypeople were likewise to avoid engaging in acts that had an ambiguous legal status out of an exercise of precaution (*iḥtiyāṭ*).[120]

Traditionalist arguments for mandatory precaution in the face of doubt abound.[121] Some identified early cases in which the practice of the Imāms themselves suggested a precautionary stance. In one case, two people who had violated a ritual rule were unsure whether the amount of financial compensation due in expiation was to be shared between them or whether each was obliged to pay the full amount. The fifth Imām, Muḥammad al-Bāqir, clarified that each owed the full amount. Upon further deliberation, he instructed his followers in future situations of doubt to "adopt a precautionary stance until you are able to inquire about the correct ruling." Clearly, for traditionalists, this directive rendered the principle of precaution mandatory in cases of doubt, ignorance, or inability to ascertain the law.[122]

[120] Astarābādī, *Fawā'id* (2003), 325. Traditionalist legal literature distinguishes the rule of *tawaqquf* (suspended judgment) – which Astarābādī defined as the obligation on jurists to "avoid rulings on every positive act about whose legality humans lack certainty: *tark kull fi'l wujūdī lam naqṭa' bi-jawāzih*" – from *iḥtiyāṭ* (suspended action out of precaution) – which Tūnī defines as the obligation for laypeople to avoid acts whose legal status is potentially one of prohibition rather than another of the five possible rulings, that is, obligatory, encouraged, neutral, discouraged, or prohibited (*tark al-amr al-muḥtamal li'l-ḥurma wa-ḥukm ākhar min al-aḥkām al-khamsa*). See Ghurayfī, *Aṣāla*, 309, n. 1. For similar definitions, see ibid., 321 (citing Majlisī, *Mir'āt al-'uqūl* [for published edition, see Muḥammad Bāqir al-Majlisī, *Mir'āt al-'uqūl fī sharḥ akhbār Āl al-Rasūl: sharḥ Kitāb al-Kāfī* [by Kulaynī], ed. Murtaḍā al-'Askarī and Hāshim al-Rasūlī (Tehran: Dār al-Kutub al-Islāmiyya, 1404–11/1984–91)], 309 (citing Qummī, *Qawānīn*, 2:17: *al-tawaqquf huwa 'l-sukūt 'an al-fatwā fī 'l-wāqi'a al-khāṣṣa wa-'adam al-idh'ān bi'l-maṭlūbiyya aw al-mabghūḍiyya*). In the more technical and developed usage of rationalist jurists, a further distinction is made between *tawaqquf* and *iḥtiyāṭ*. *Tawaqquf* refers to the juristic obligation to avoid pronouncing a definitive ruling in cases of legal doubt (*'adam iltizām bi-ḥukm min al-aḥkām al-khamsa fī-mā idhā lam yaqum dalīl mu'tabar 'alā ithbātih*), and *iḥtiyāṭ* refers to the individual obligation to avoid acting (*waẓīfa 'amaliyya*) on a matter in which the legal ruling or the factual state of the situation is uncertain. See Ghurayfī, *Aṣāla*, 309; cf. Bihbahānī, *Risālat aṣālat al-barā'a*, 396 (noting that Akhbārī *ḥadīth* supports for the precaution principle may, at most, lend credence to the idea that suspension and avoidance of judgment on the part of the jurist (*al-tawaqquf wa'l-tark*) is the "safer way," but they do not require suspension of the juristic interpretive process or avoiding certain acts on the part of the layperson out of an [exaggerated] sense of precaution). Cf. Anṣārī, *Rasā'il*, 151 (discussing and rejecting the Akhbārī position of *wujūb al-iḥtiyāṭ bi'l-tark*).

[121] The fullest list that I have found is in al-Ḥurr al-'Āmilī, *Wasā'il al-Shī'a*, 18:111–29 (collecting sixty *ḥadīth* reports in support of the obligation of the precaution principle).

[122] Baḥrānī, *Ḥadā'iq*, 1:76 (*fa-'alaykum bi'l-iḥtiyāṭ ḥattā tas'alū 'anh*). Compare Astarābādī, *Fawā'id* (2003), 325 (cited above, note 120, defining *wujūb al-tawaqquf* as the requirement

After Astarābādī, al-Ḥurr al-ʿĀmilī took up the mantle of defending the traditionalist worldview with particular emphasis against reading a broad nonliability presumption into the contested *ḥadīth* cited by Ibn Bābawayh – that "everything is permissible unless specifically prohibited." Against the rationalist insistence that the report had a clear, broad meaning, al-Ḥurr al-ʿĀmilī insisted that it "[bore] multiple interpretations," the strongest of which indicated that the statement was limited and text-bound, and subordinate to the precaution principle rather than being a broad and reason-based approach to doctrines of doubt:

> First, the report may be interpreted to be an instance of dissimulation (*taqiyya*). Sunnīs [by contrast] take this [nonliability] presumption as authoritative (*ḥujjiyyat al-aṣl*). But this position [and their interpretation, to the extent that it supports the nonliability presumption] is challenged by the strength of the preceding [traditions, indicating the primacy of the precaution principle]. Moreover, this single-source report cannot trump widely diffused reports [that require precaution].
>
> Second, the report may be interpreted to apply specifically to revelatory texts. That is, any [statement] contained in revelatory texts is to be taken in an absolute and general sense unless there is also [another text that outlines] a prohibition qualifying some matters [as exceptional] and removing [them] from the purview of the general instruction. Take, for example, the *ḥadīth* report [stating] that "all water is pure until you know that it has been made impure." This is to be understood as a general proposition. [At the same time,] there is a prohibition [in the law] against using either of two containers if one has been made impure but the individual is confused about which one. This [second] ruling has qualified [the matter and] taken it out of the purview of the general instruction [such that in like scenarios, one cannot presume that water is pure even when there is no certain knowledge about which of the two containers is impure]. For this reason, Ṣadūq [Ibn Bābawayh] cited [the above *ḥadīth* report] [specifically] to indicate the permissibility of performing prayer supplications in Persian. That is, the instruction to perform supplication in prayer was general and absolute, and he was aware of no prohibition on performing the supplication in Persian that would remove [that option] from the purview of the general instruction [of permissibility].
>
> Third, the report may be interpreted specifically to apply to matters other than those contained in the revelatory rulings themselves, though they may

to "avoid any positive act, concerning the legality of which we have no [textual] certainty"). Notably, some scholars took a contrary view, maintaining that *fa-ʿalaykum al-iḥtiyāṭ* refers to taking precautions in issuing rulings about areas of clearly established rules, that is, taking a stance against issuing *fatwā*s where the text of the Qur'ān or authentic *ḥadīth* are clear. However, if after a duly diligent attempt to ascertain the law doubt remains, he held that this directive does not apply because of the *ḥadīth* instructing people that the law is flexible when it comes to areas of "debatable rules," that is, matters that lack certain knowledge (*al-nās fī saʿat mā lam yaʿlamū*). Ibid.

relate to legal subjects and related areas [governed by the divine law], as when a person doubts whether the [land] grants of an unjust ruler (*maghṣūba*, lit.: "usurped") are in fact illegal. [They are to presume that they are not unless the divine law specifically states that they are.]

Fourth, [the report may be interpreted to mean] that the prohibition at issue refers to both general and specific types of prohibition. We are aware of the general prohibition on **operating in cases of doubt (*irtikāb al-shubahāt*) about the law.** [We also are aware] of the command not to pass any judgment and to instead practice precaution (*al-amr bi-tawaqquf wa'l-iḥtiyāṭ*) regarding [legal uncertainties] and any matter on which the [foundational] texts are silent. [In other words, legal agents are on notice that there is no leeway for exercising discretion whether there is clarity or textual (legal) ambiguity about the extent of prohibitions. Accordingly, they should regard the statement in question, that "everything is permissible unless specifically prohibited," to be restricted to issues of fact rather than issues of law.]

Fifth, [the report may be interpreted] to refer specifically to the period before the completion of the law [as contained in revelation]. After [the completion of revelation], the nonliability presumption would not apply.

Sixth, [the report may be interpreted] to refer specifically to those who are unaware of the *ḥadīth* reports [spelling out] the **prohibition on operating in the realm of doubt (*man lam tablughhu aḥādīth al-nahy ʿan irtikāb al-shubahāt*)** or the command to practice precaution (*al-amr bi'l-iḥtiyāṭ*) cited above. Holding such an uninformed person liable is contrary to both reason and revelation.

Seventh, [the report may be interpreted] to relate specifically to matters for which there is no reason to believe that a rule of prohibition might apply. For example, [suppose that] a certain matter is known to be permissible, but then there is doubt as to whether it is obligatory. In that case, the ruling of permissibility applies generally (*muṭlaq*) until a text is found that prohibits *not* doing it [that is, that obligates it]. This is because the implication of the traditions [cited above] does not call for applications of the precaution principle upon the mere possibility of a ruling of obligation, even if that possibility might be the preferred position otherwise, wherever a ruling of prohibition is not at issue.

Eighth, [the report may be interpreted] to apply specifically to significant matters that affect the entire [or at least a large portion of the] community, and where it is known that, if there were a ruling contrary to the existing [known] laws, [the ruling] would have been [clearly] transmitted. This much is understood from ʿAlī's statement: "Know, O son, that if there were another God, His messengers would have come to you, and you would have seen the effects of His dominion."[123]

All of this was to demonstrate that the traditionalist position that the *ḥadīth* report on which rationalists so heavily relied to provide textual support for their broad nonliability presumption was not so clearly in support of that presumption after all, at least from a textualist standpoint.

123 Al-Ḥurr al-ʿĀmilī, *Wasāʾil al-Shīʿa*, 18:127–29 (emphasis added).

By listing no fewer than eight alternative interpretations for the text, al-Ḥurr al-ʿĀmilī sought to prove the generality and superiority of the precaution principle over the nonliability presumption. In all but one of his alternative interpretations of Ibn Bābawayh's *ḥadīth*, al-Ḥurr al-ʿĀmilī constructed arguments that limited its permissive import – to the extent that it might support a nonliability presumption – by interpreting it to refer to specific situations. Accordingly, for him, the nonliability presumption applied to doubts about prohibitions only on factual grounds, not on legal ones.

This move was typical of traditionalist arguments against rationalist interpretations: Where rationalists saw generality, traditionalists saw specificity. Moreover, traditionalists argued that all the rationalist so-called textual proofs for the authority of general principles of law (expressed in the form of legal maxims) typically referred to specific factual matters. For traditionalists, any general directive related to *factual*, not *legal*, doubt.[124]

In the one instance in which al-Ḥurr al-ʿĀmilī did not limit the *ḥadīth* in this way, he attacked its validity altogether; and this was the argument with which he began. In his opening salvo, he went back to an old principle that Ibn Bābawayh himself had noted to explain why traditions may *appear* to be in conflict: some of them are not to be acted on literally, as the Imāms may have made the statements out of fear for their own lives or those of their followers, that is, the known practice of dissimulation (*taqiyya*). This practice was deemed appropriate for situations in which there was an official position of the caliphate, usually attributed to the Prophet's Companions, that went against an opinion that the Shīʿī community understood to be that of ʿAlī, thereby turning the matter into a cause for a sectarian rift. Al-Ḥurr al-ʿĀmilī argued that to use Ibn Bābawayh's *ḥadīth* to support rationalist general principles was both anomalous and weak next to the overwhelming evidence in support of the precaution principle.

Interestingly, al-Ḥurr al-ʿĀmilī slightly reformulated the traditionalist position that precaution means avoidance of *questionable acts* on the basis that they might be prohibited to mean avoidance of *doubt* altogether. In fact, the phrase he used – highlighted above – indicates that the precaution

124 Cf. al-Ḥurr al-ʿĀmilī, *al-Fuṣūl al-muhimma*, 235 (arguing that many of the *ḥadīth* indicating the permissibility of acts in cases of doubt until a prohibition is known relate to *shubahāt mawḍūʿiyya*); see also Astarābādī, *Fawāʾid* (198-), 160; Baḥrānī, *Ḥadāʾiq*, 1:49; Baḥrānī, *al-Durar al-Najafiyya*, 34; al-Ḥurr al-ʿĀmilī, *al-Fawāʾid al-Ṭūsiyya*, ed. Mahdī al-Lājwardī al-Ḥusaynī and Muḥammad Darūdī (Qum: al-Maṭbaʿa al-ʿIlmiyya, 1403/1983), 253.

principle requires avoidance of the "*commission* of doubt: *irtikāb al-shubahāt*," which is a term typically employed for crimes or sins. He thus equated *doubt* with the specter of *crime* or *sin* to the point that he linguistically and conceptually elided the latter into the former. He then used this formulation to support his view that the precaution principle requires avoidance of doubt itself.

Furthermore, al-Ḥurr al-ʿĀmilī rejected reliance on the so-called correlation between reason and revelation as a basis for moral-legal accountability. He pointed out that the law does not prohibit many objectively immoral acts (*al-qabāʾiḥ al-ʿaqliyya*), nor does it obligate all objectively moral acts.[125] That is enough to conclude that there is no objective morality, much less a one-to-one correlation between it and revelation. Rationalist attempts to establish some correlation between revelation and reason and to read into the law a broad nonliability presumption were misguided, in al-Ḥurr al-ʿĀmilī's view, precisely because they diverged from the text. Such broad presumptions "have no textual basis (*naṣṣ*)," and this automatically bars them from consideration in the law.[126]

Like their earlier counterparts, al-Ḥurr al-ʿĀmilī and this set of "new traditionalists" emphasized certainty and a single right answer, both of which they located in the text. For support, they cited the Qurʾānic command, "And do not follow that about which you have no knowledge; for you will all be questioned about matters of hearing, of sight, and of the heart."[127] They pointed to a *ḥadīth* stating that one of God's rights is that human beings speak only from knowledge and that they suspend action when they have no knowledge.[128] And they referenced several other *ḥadīth* reports advising people not to reject certain directives simply because they did not understand the *reasoning* of the reports containing them.[129] In short, traditionalists placed a premium on the authenticity of *ḥadīth* as a measure for the authority and content of the law. They found the rationale behind legal rules to be irrelevant so long as a report was authentic.

[125] Astarābādī, *Fawāʾid* (2003), 328.

[126] Ibid. (noting that the adoption of these presumptions would rest on the "basis of a lack of knowledge, or worse, mere speculation (*ẓann*)," which deference to divine sovereignty does not allow); Baḥrānī, *Ḥadāʾiq*, 1:75 (same).

[127] Qurʾān, 17:36 (*wa-lā taqfu mā laysa laka bihi ʿilmun inna ʾl-samʿa waʾl-baṣara waʾl-fuʾāda kullu ulāʾika kāna ʿanhu masʾūlan*), cited in Kulaynī, *Kāfī* (1997–8), 1:50. See also Ghuraytī, *Aṣāla*, 310.

[128] Al-Ḥurr al-ʿĀmilī, *Wasāʾil al-Shīʿa*, 18:112; see also Kulaynī, *Kāfī* (1997–8), 1:50.

[129] See, for example, Astarābādī, *Fawāʾid* (2003), 325–26 (listing *ḥadīth* reports).

3. Interpretive Process: Textual Canons and Constrained Discretion

It is clear from the traditionalist jurisprudence that doubt was emphatically *not* an invitation for juridical interventions based on reason. Doubt was instead a prompt for restraint. Astarābādī noted that God gave assurances that He would clarify the law to a select group and would prevent them from making errors in delivering the message: "We will guide to Our path(s) those who strive for Our cause."[130] Clearly, for him, that was an announcement of divine guidance through the Prophet and the Imāms, who well performed their task of clarifying the law when they were alive and present.[131]

So if doubt remained, it was not because the law had not been made clear. Rather, it may simply have been that an individual jurist or layperson was unable to understand the clarifying statements contained in the traditions, did not have access to the full text of the laws (given that many works were lost in the course of history in book-burning episodes and other forms of intermittent persecution of the Shīʿa), or simply was not exhaustive in his research and deliberation.[132] In a retort to the rationalist claim that doubt tolerates juridical resolution rather than requiring avoidance of a questionable act, Astarābādī maintained that "failure to discover the rule does not mean that the rule does not exist."[133]

This understanding guided the traditionalist orientation to the nonliability presumption, the doubt canon, and all other canons of construction that arose in the interpretive process. To be sure, traditionalists did not reject all legal canons outright. They applied linguistic canons and rejected or narrowed substantive legal maxims where they perceived no textual basis, consistent with the broader traditionalist theology that envisioned a legal rule for everything, one right answer contained in the text, and a principle of precaution in cases of doubt. It was on these bases, ultimately, that Astarābādī and other traditionalists rejected a broad reading of the nonliability presumption. They applied a similar analysis to narrow the doubt canon – which, like the basis for the nonliability presumption, had been recorded in an authoritative Shīʿī collection for the first and only time

130 Astarābādī, *Fawāʾid* (2003), 321, 329–30 (discussing the primordial "day of eternity," *yawm alastu* (see Qurʾān, 7:172) as a time when obedience was obligated through God's presentation of Himself to all humankind and solicitation of an acknowledgment from them that He was the Lord to whom they owed obedience).

131 Ibid., 321 (*al-ʿaqāʾid waʾl-aʿmāl*).

132 Ibid. (citing Qurʾān, 29:69: *wa-ʾlladhīna jāhadū fīnā la-nahdiyannahum subulanā*).

133 Ibid., 350.

by Ibn Bābawayh.[134] Ibn Bābawayh's inclusion of the canon gave it a textual purchase that traditionalists had to acknowledge, but they approached it based on prior commitments from a particular theology that informed their textualist worldview and interpretive philosophy of law.

Al-Ḥurr al-ʿĀmilī's treatment of the doubt canon was typical of the traditionalist approach. He included the canon in *Wasāʾil al-Shīʿa*, his massive collection of traditions that doubled as his *fiqh* compendium, as was typical of traditionalist jurisprudence. But instead of citing the standard version, "Avoid criminal punishments in cases of doubt," he preferred a version with the addition, "but there is to be no intercession, nor bail, nor oaths in *ḥadd* [proceedings]." Ibn Bābawayh had recorded both in his works.[135] In the longer version, the text itself places limitations on *ḥudūd* avoidance by cautioning against circumventing criminal laws through the common mitigating strategies of intercession, bail, or even oaths (of innocence). At least one of these strategies – claims of innocence – had been understood by rationalist jurists such as al-ʿAllāma al-Ḥillī as giving rise to *ḥadd*-averting doubt, in consonance with the general rationalist tendency to construe the canon broadly. By contrast, al-Ḥurr al-ʿĀmilī and other traditionalists rejected the nonliability presumption for uncertainties regarding all prohibitions, especially *ḥudūd* laws, and would require any reading of the doubt canon to fit with the many texts requiring precaution.[136]

To that end, traditionalists gave the doubt canon as stingy a reading as possible. Al-Ḥurr al-ʿĀmilī did not therefore even remotely entertain the idea that the canon requires *ḥudūd* avoidance in expansive cases of doubt. Like other traditionalists, he omitted it completely from the section with traditions governing substantive criminal law. Instead, he cited the canon only in the section on judicial procedure to support a doctrine of *ḥudūd enforcement* – that there could be no intercession or other maneuvers to avoid punishment once a crime had been established.[137]

[134] See Ibn Bābawayh, *Faqīh*, 1:202.

[135] Ibn Bābawayh attributed the longer version to the Prophet without an *isnād* (see Ibn Bābawayh, *Faqīh*, 4:53, no. 90: *idraʾū ʾl-ḥudūd biʾl-shubahāt wa-lā shafāʿa wa-lā kafāla wa-lā yamīn fī ḥadd*), and the shorter, standard version to ʿAlī – as noted above – also without an *isnād* (Ibn Bābawayh, *Muqniʿ*, 437 (*idraʾū ʾl-ḥudūd biʾl-shubahāt*)). Notably, the standard version is ignored by traditionalists but taken up by rationalists. See Appendix A, version 12.

[136] See al-Ḥurr al-ʿĀmilī, *Wasāʾil al-Shīʿa*, 18:111–29 (listing sixty *ḥadīth* supports for the precaution principle).

[137] Many traditionists tended not to write works on *fiqh* topics, as they viewed the text of *ḥadīth* to be the law itself. Accordingly, they organized *ḥadīth* reports around legal topics,

It is likely that the doubt canon signaled more trouble than it was worth in the traditionalist scheme. In the traditionalists' theory of doubt, the first part of the *ḥadīth* (the standard version of the canon: "Avoid criminal punishments in cases of doubt") seems to have had no meaning in criminal adjudication. A traditionalist would have already decided that a nonliability presumption or avoidance principle could not apply to legal doubt surrounding prohibitions (such as *ḥudūd* laws). And in any case, *ḥudūd* laws were by definition clear statements of prohibitions. So, if anything, "doubt" here would refer to matters of fact such as issues of evidence or *mens rea*, but not to the texts of *ḥudūd* laws, and certainly not to questions about the morality of punishment. Moreover, the precaution principle would have already obligated avoidance of any act a person suspected to be prohibited because of confusion about facts. There was no joining the two: the precaution principle and the doubt canon were in opposition. Accordingly, in the sixty traditions that al-Ḥurr al-ʿĀmilī compiled in what seems to have been his attempt at a comprehensive listing of all traditions supporting the precaution principle, the doubt canon does not appear.[138]

In the end, the presence of both the nonliability presumption and the doubt canon as *ḥadīth* reports in Ibn Bābawayh's collection meant that al-Ḥurr al-ʿĀmilī and other traditionalist jurists had to accept both as authentic. But their emphasis on the right answer as text led them to reject the nonliability presumption as applied to uncertainties regarding prohibitions, and to accord primacy to the precaution principle for all other doubt. Accordingly, they severely curtailed the interpretation and application of problematic textual traditions such as the doubt canon and the other, "Everything is permissible" *ḥadīth* cited by Ibn Bābawayh. In other words, traditionalists regarded the sayings with the same eye of authenticity, but they did not regard the doubt canon with the same liberal eye as did the rationalists because they rejected the interpretation of the nonliability presumption that drove a wide application of the canon.

Traditionalists viewed other interpretive and substantive legal maxims similarly. They did not reject all legal maxims outright, as has

that organization providing an indication of their interpretations of the law (*fiqh*). Al-Ḥurr al-ʿĀmilī wrote works consistent with that more general traditionist trend. See, for example, al-Ḥurr al-ʿĀmilī's section on criminal law (esp. *muqaddamāt al-ḥudūd*) and compare it with his section on judicial procedure: al-Ḥurr al-ʿĀmilī, *Wasāʾil al-Shīʿa*, vol. 18.

138 See ibid., 18:111–29.

been supposed.[139] Rather, they accepted a set of legal maxims, provided they were rooted in some textual grounding, then interpreted them narrowly in the context of their emphasis on textual authority, a limited theory of doubt, and the primacy they accorded to ideas of certainty and one right answer. From these maxims came the principles of their textualist jurisprudence, with the precaution principle at its core. In addition to that principle, examples of other interpretive legal maxims that Astarābādī identified include the following:

- Illegality primacy canon: If the legal and illegal mix, the illegal takes precedence.[140]
- Illegality avoidance canon: Any matter that has legal and illegal aspects is legal unless you know that it is illegal, in which case you should avoid it.[141]
- Completion canon: Any doubt [that befalls a person] after completing a matter is to be ignored.[142]
- Certainty primacy canon: It is improper to cancel out certainty by way of doubt; certainty can be canceled only by way of another certainty.[143]

Thus, traditionalists accepted legal maxims, but even these text-based legal maxims did not easily hang together, at least not according to their rationalist critics. As we will see, this fact fueled the response of the rationalists, who objected that these maxims, if taken at face value, were contradictory and would lead to an incoherent legal system if applied without any rational construction or without a more robust theory of doubt.

[139] Gleave has noted that "Astarābādī was not devoid of hermeneutic awareness, and required the scholar . . . to be able, not only to know *ḥadīth*, but also to understand the procedures relating to *iḥtiyāṭ* [precaution]." But that awareness was limited, inasmuch as Astarābādī glossed over or ignored major jurisprudential issues treated by rationalist jurists, such as the relationship among *muftī*s (in cases of disagreement among them over the import of traditions) and how laypeople recognize a true *ḥadīth* expert (and hence legitimate *muftī*). See Gleave, *Scripturalist Islam*, 86–88.

[140] Astarābādī, *Fawā'id* (2003), 313 (citing the *ḥadīth* "*idhā 'khtalaṭa 'l-ḥalāl wa'l-ḥarām, ghalaba 'l-ḥarām*" from Ibn Abī Jumhūr, *'Awālī 'l-la'ālī*, 3:466, no. 17; Ṭūsī, *Tahdhīb al-aḥkām*, 1:29, no. 72).

[141] Ibid. (citing the *ḥadīth* "*kull shay' fīh ḥalāl wa-ḥarām fa-huwa lak ḥalāl ḥattā ta'rif al-ḥarām bi-'aynih fa-tada'ah*" from Ṭūsī, *Tahdhīb al-aḥkām fī sharḥ al-Muqni'a*, ed. 'Alī Akbar al-Ghaffārī (Tehran: Maktabat al-Ṣadūq, 1997), 9:79, with slight variations).

[142] Ibid. (citing the *ḥadīth* "*al-shakk ba'd al-inṣirāf lā yultafat ilayh*" from Ṭūsī, *Tahdhīb al-aḥkām*, 2:248, no. 31).

[143] Ibid. (citing the *ḥadīth* "*laysa yanbaghī lak an tanquḍ yaqīnan bi-shakk abadan wa-innamā tanquḍuh bi-yaqīn ākhar*" from Ṭūsī, *Tahdhīb al-aḥkām*, 1:8, no. 11).

Astarābādī's and al-Ḥurr al-ʿĀmilī's writings reflect interpretive principles typical of the traditionalist school: they relied on the text of traditions as the only authoritative sources of law next to the Qur'ān. They completely rejected the use of rational analysis in construing texts and in deriving legal norms, and likewise rejected the basic presumptions of law that rationalist jurists had devised as lacking in strong textual foundation. Moreover, Astarābādī pointedly honed in on doubt as a *problem* that, in his view, necessarily arose in the use of Aristotelian logic – the rationalists' prime tool in their interpretive exercises. That fact alone required appeal to the authority of authentic and unassailably reliable traditions, he argued, and he was enormously successful in making his case – that is, until his rationalist opponents counterattacked. The first significant move came from Astarābādī's rationalist critic, al-Waḥīd al-Bihbahānī (d. 1206/1791–2), whose camp dealt a decisive blow to traditionalism in the mid-thirteenth/nineteenth century through the pen of Murtaḍā al-Anṣārī (d. 1281/1864).

C. RATIONALIST RIPOSTE: ONE RIGHT ANSWER AS REVELATION BEFORE REASON

Rationalists objected strongly to traditionalist attempts to characterize them as atextualist, even as they insisted on significantly incorporating rational elements into legal interpretation to construct a pragmatic jurisprudence. In the same spirit as the quip among contemporary American legal scholars that "we are all textualists now," in Islamic law, medieval Muslim rationalist jurists insisted that their process of interpretation began always with the text.[144] Their interpretations typically started with the Qur'ān and Sunna before moving to arguments about juridical consensus and other rational bases for law. By following this methodology, they were reinforcing the formal hierarchy of Islamic legal sources outlined in the developed works of legal theory. Theirs was an attempt to create a system that was

[144] See Jonathan T. Molot, "The Rise and Fall of Textualism," *Columbia Law Review* 106 (2006), 1–58, at 43; William N. Eskridge, "All about Words," *Columbia Law Review* 101 (2001), 990–1106, at 1090 (noting that pragmatist and textualist jurists alike begin first and foremost with the text); Jonathan R. Siegel, "Textualism and Contextualism in Administrative Law," *Boston University Law Review* 78 (1998), 1023–112, at 1057 ("In a significant sense, we are all textualists now"). This statement is drawn from an earlier observation that "we are all realists now," in recognition of the mainstreaming of the idea that judges and lawyers openly consider policy or political implications of legal rules and that legal opinions reflect certain political, economic, and historical contexts. See Dennis Patterson, *A Companion to Philosophy of Law and Legal Theory* (Cambridge, MA: Blackwell, 1996), 261.

at once coherent with respect to *existing* legal texts and juristic precedents and capable of providing *prospective* guidance for dealing with new issues.

After Astarābādī's damaging traditionalist blows, the challenge for rationalists was to reassess their own jurisprudence and approach to doubt in light of the strict textualist attacks. Toward that end, they revisited the foundational texts as well as the question of reason's role in construing them. They concluded, all the more strongly, that both supported the nonliability presumption, a key aspect of which in contemplating potential prohibitions was a general *permissibility presumption* (*aṣālat al-ibāḥa*): that all acts are presumed permissible (or legal) unless proven otherwise. Moreover, they reformulated the entire jurisprudential structure to include a certain core of interpretive legal canons designed to address lingering doubts not resolved directly in the text itself. In the end, this restructuring led to what has been dubbed rationalism's victory over the traditionalist challenge. It also undergirds the expansive room for the doubt canon and other substantive legal maxims that enjoy a place of authority in the education circles and interpretive debates surrounding the application of Shīʿī law in the present day.[145]

1. Defensive Theories of Nonliability and Interpretive Discretion

a. In Defense of Presumed Nonliability

To root the nonliability presumption more firmly in foundational texts, Anṣārī and other rationalists pointed to several Qurʾānic verses and traditions.[146] Three verses in particular double as supports for the principles of legality and capacity that rationalists had previously discussed in terms of pure reason. The first is the verse, "God does not hold people accountable

[145] For an influential legal treatise that is used as a textbook in Shīʿī institutions of study for Islamic law and that includes mention of the doubt canon, see Muḥammad Ḥasan al-Najafī (d. 1266/1850), *Jawāhir al-kalām fī sharḥ Sharāʾiʿ al-Islām*, ed. Riḍā al-Ustādī (Najaf: Dār al-Kutub al-Islāmiyya, 1378/1958–9), 41:157; cf. ʿAlī Muḥammadī, "Naqd-i sākhtār-i qānūn-i mujāzāt-i Islāmī" (a critique of the structure of the [Iranian] Islamic Penal Code), *Fiqh va ḥuqūq* 1, 1 (2004), 157–74 (criticizing Iran's post-revolutionary penal code for, among other things, codifying rules without laying out general principles such as the doubt canon). The code was revised in 2013, after much debate. The new code includes the doubt canon. See the *Iranian Penal Code* (*Qānūn-i mujāzāt-i Islāmī*) (1392/2013), arts. 120–21 (in the section entitled "Operation of the Doubt Canon: *iʿmāl qāʿidah-i dar*'").

[146] Bihbahānī, *Risālat aṣālat al-barāʾa*, 353–54 (citing Qurʾān, 17:15, 8:42, 65:7, 9:115, 7:33, 2:173, 16:115); Anṣārī, *Rasāʾil*, 151–68 (same, and adding Qurʾān, 6:145 and 6:119).

except for what He has given them (or: what is within their capacities to act upon)."[147] Anṣārī noted that the general meaning of the verse is clear, though the specific phrase "what He has given" may be open to interpretation. If this verse is placed in the context of the phrase preceding it, "Whoever has his sustenance measured out to him should spend from what God has given him,"[148] then the "gift" refers to wealth, and the subsequent phrase means that God requires people to give only when they have the financial capacity to do so. But "what He has given" could also refer to the freedom of each person to act according to his or her sense of moral-legal liability; the "gift" would then be an allusion to a human's general capacity to act, with the result that the verse indicates the *absence of liability for those who have no capacity*. This latter sense accords better with the prima facie meaning of the text, Anṣārī said, and it is the more comprehensive reading, because spending when one has the means is already understood from the command to spend "what God has given." So to understand the verse in that way would be redundant; one cannot spend what one does not have. But it is not typically beyond a person's capacity to decide to commit or omit certain acts from the moral wherewithal that God has given. Thus, the verse is better understood to mean that people are not accountable for acting beyond their capacity.[149] In other words, this verse supports the formerly rational principle of capacity, Anṣārī argued, exempting those without the capacity to know or follow the law from liability for failing to do so.

This interpretation accords with a second often cited verse, stating the matter more clearly: "God does not hold anyone accountable except for what is within their capacity."[150] Anṣārī also cited traditions from the Imāms to support his view that this verse and the verse above support a general presumption of nonliability:

> Jaʿfar al-Ṣādiq was asked, "Are people liable for [discovering] the Truth (*maʿrifa*)?" He responded, "No, it is upon God to clarify the law, for 'God does not hold anyone accountable except for what is within their capacity: *lā yukallifu 'llāhu nafsan illā wusʿahā*' [Qur'ān, 2:286], and 'God does not hold anyone accountable except for what He has given them: *lā yukallifu 'llāhu nafsan illā mā ātāhā* . . .' [Qur'ān, 65:7]."[151]

147 Qur'ān, 65:7 (*lā yukallifu 'llāhu nafsan illā mā ātāhā*).

148 Qur'ān, 65:6 (*wa-man qudira ʿalayhi rizquhu fa'l-yunfiq mimmā ātāhu 'llāh*).

149 Anṣārī, *Rasā'il*, 151 (citing Qur'ān, 65:7); cf. Bihbahānī, *Risālat aṣālat al-barā'a*, 353, 356 (same, with *ḥadīth* exegesis giving a similar meaning).

150 Anṣārī, *Rasā'il*, 152 (citing Qur'ān, 2:286: *lā yukallifu 'llāhu nafsan illā wusʿahā*).

151 Ibid. (citing, *inter alia*, Qur'ān, 9:115: "God does not allow a people to stray after having guided them until he clarifies for them what they must be mindful of: *wa-mā kāna 'llāhu*

A third verse states the principle even more clearly: "We never punish until We send a messenger."[152] Anṣārī further explained that "sending messengers" is another way of expressing clarification of the law – whether by reason or revelation.[153] This verse, along with others, he maintained, therefore "explicitly provides support for the principle of legality (*nafy al-ʿiqāb qabl al-bayān*)" and the presumption of nonliability.[154] Further, it supports the notion, important for *ḥudūd* laws in particular, that to follow Islamic law was to obey God, and consequently people must be notified of what the law is so that they know what God has prohibited and thus which acts they must avoid.[155] Together, these verses underline the rationalist stance that not only does reason require clear statements of law before liability can attach, but the implicit promise of God's justice requires it as well.

Rationalists pointed to traditions, too, which was especially important to counter traditionalist claims inasmuch as that group tended to privilege traditions over the Qurʾān. The most important supporting tradition for rationalists was the oft-quoted *ḥadīth of lifted liability* (*ḥadīth al-rafʿ*). In fact, this *ḥadīth*, more than any other, was the mainstay (*ʿumda*) of late rationalist juristic arguments in favor of the nonliability presumption.[156] It states that liability is lifted from members of the community in nine situations, among them mistake, forgetfulness, coercion, ignorance, and incapacity.[157] Commenting on this tradition at length, Anṣārī rejected any

li-yuḍilla qawman baʿda idh hadāhum ḥattā yubayyina lahum mā yattaqūn." Cf. Bihbahānī, *Risālat aṣālat al-barāʾa*, 356 (similar, with *ḥadīth* exegeses).

152 Qurʾān, 17:15 (*wa-mā kunnā muʿadhdhibīna ḥattā nabʿatha rasūlan*).

153 Anṣārī, *Rasāʾil*, 152 (arguing that *baʿth al-rusul* is a figurative term of speech (*kināya*) for clarifying legal liability whether by revelation or reason: *bayān al-taklīf naqlan aw ʿaqlan*).

154 Ibid., 152–53; Bihbahānī, *Risālat aṣālat al-barāʾa*, 353; Khurāsānī, *Kifāya*, 385 (explaining that this principle invalidates punishment without clearly stated law [as contained in revelation] brought by prophets: *nafy al-taʿdhīb qabl itmām al-ḥujja bi-baʿth al-rusul*).

155 Anṣārī, *Rasāʾil*, 153. This is an expression of the Shīʿī doctrine of God's justice, whereby He would not punish except after making the law, including prohibitions, clear – for which purpose He sent prophets out of His grace. See, for example, Khurāsānī, *Kifāya*, 385 (explaining that this principle of no punishment without sending prophets to clarify the law is a function of divine grace or mercy (*minna*)).

156 Al-Waḥīd al-Bihbahānī, *al-Fawāʾid al-Ḥāʾiriyya* (Qum: Majmaʿ al-Fikr al-Islāmī, 1995), 239; cf. Ghurayfī, *Aṣāla*, 253.

157 See citations in, for example, Anṣārī, *Rasāʾil*, 154; Bihbahānī, *Risālat aṣālat al-barāʾa*, 354; Khurāsānī, *Kifāya*, 2:168; Muḥammad Ḥusayn al-Nāʾinī (d. 1355/1936), *Fawāʾid al-uṣūl*, ed. Raḥmat Allāh Raḥmatī al-Arākī (Qum: Muʾassasat al-Nashr al-Islāmī al-Tābiʿa li-Jamāʿat al-Mudarrisīn, 1404/1983–4), 2:205. For the *ḥadīth*, see Ibn Bābawayh, *Faqīh*, 1:19 ("[Liability for] nine things is 'lifted' from my community: mistake, forgetfulness, what [people] are forced to do, what they have no knowledge of, what they have no capacity for, what they do by necessity . . . : *rufiʿa ʿan ummatī tisʿat ashyāʾ: al-khaṭaʾ wa'l-nisyān wa-mā ukrihū ʿalayhā wa-mā lā yaʿlamūn wa-mā lā yuṭīqūn wa-mā ʾḍṭurrū ilayh*

arguments limiting its scope. He argued by way of working through a question of Islamic criminal law, namely, how to view a violation of the prohibition on wine drinking by those who fall into one of the categories mentioned in the *ḥadīth*. Traditionalists argued that "those who do not know" should be read alongside the neighboring categories of people,[158] and surmised on that basis that the report would exempt people from liability only in specific cases of factual mistake or ignorance. That is, if an individual drank a reddish liquid, unaware that it was actually wine, no liability would attach because of the mistake of fact. Whether the mistake was genuine or the ignorance reasonable would be a determination that a judge would make on a case-by-case basis. In other words, the *ḥadīth* applies only to ambiguities of fact, not law.[159]

Anṣārī regarded this as an atomistic approach that was excessively limited and terribly mistaken. To be sure, he agreed with traditionalists that the *ḥadīth* did cover situations of factual doubt. For example, it is widely accepted by many jurists, both Sunnī and Shīʿī, that ignorance is exculpating when someone lacks notice of the law and is unaware that he or she might be violating it.[160] But beyond that, Anṣārī argued that the *ḥadīth* on the whole must be read alongside all the other textual sources, namely myriad Qurʾānic verses as noted above, specifying that liability exists only when there are clear statements of prohibitions. These verses would have no meaning if the *ḥadīth* of lifted liability applied to facts alone. That is, both text and reason provide evidence supporting the presumption of nonliability as a general principle applying to doubt about both law and fact.[161] Finally, Anṣārī added that, in a battle of the

waʾl-ḥasad waʾl-tafakkur fī ʾl-waswasa fī ʾl-khalq mā lam yanṭiqū bi-shafa"); cf. Kulaynī, *Kāfī* (1957–8), 1:463; al-Ḥurr al-ʿĀmilī, *Wasāʾil al-Shīʿa*, 6:295.

158 Anṣārī, *Rasāʾil*, 154–63. These principles echo parallel legal maxims used in Anglo-American law: *noscitur a sociis* ("known from associates"), that is, the meaning of a statutory term must be ascertained from the surrounding words, and *ejusdem generis* ("of the same kind"), that is, when a list of two or more specific descriptors are followed by more general descriptors, the otherwise broad meaning of the general descriptors must be restricted to the same class, if any, as that of the specific words that precede them. See Miller, "Pragmatics and the Maxims of Interpretation," 1226; Eskridge et al., *Legislation*, appendix B, 20.

159 See, for example, Astarābādī, *Fawāʾid*. This is an example of factual doubt (*shubha mawḍūʿiyya*), to which Astarābādī acknowledged that the nonliability presumption and the *ḥadīth* of lifted liability may apply.

160 Ghurayfī, *Aṣāla*, 255–56 (that is, "someone who has encountered no authoritative basis for [or has no notice of] the law: *man lam taqum ʿindah al-ḥujja ʿalā ʾl-ḥukm*").

161 Anṣārī, *Rasāʾil*, 154–56. Some later rationalists agreed with the limitation of the nonliability presumption to doubt that arises from issues of fact (*shubha mawḍūʿiyya*); but this is not the majority position. See Ghurayfī, *Aṣāla*, 294.

textual evidence, the permissive reports would win, for they were more reliably authentic than the reports indicating the opposite.[162]

In sum, the rationalists argued strongly that the Qur'ān and the *ḥadīth* corpus both supported the nonliability presumption unambiguously. But against traditionalist restrictions of the principle to issues of factual doubt, how could rationalists extend the presumption to cover various types of doubt relating to Islamic law generally, especially if those uncertainties touched on potential prohibitions? How could they assume that there were no lurking prohibitions? Would not the safer path be to avoid those types of doubt entirely?[163] To answer these challenges, rationalists had to specifically address the question of the default status of legal rules. They recognized that if it were possible or even likely that acts about which the texts were doubtful were illegal, then traditionalists might have a point – that to presume nonliability would be risky. Accordingly, alongside the presumption of nonliability – which applied to obligations – they further elaborated the corollary *presumption of permissibility*.

b. In Defense of Presumed Legality

Seeing it as part and parcel of the nonliability presumption, rationalists made arguments to root the permissibility presumption in the text as well: that everything is permissible until or unless the law clearly states otherwise.[164] They pointed to texts such as the Qur'ānic announcement that "[God] created everything in the earth for you [humans]."[165] Whereas traditionalists saw this verse merely as a call for people to reflect on God's existence as seen through His creation,[166] rationalists interpreted this and

162 Anṣārī, *Rasā'il*, 154–63.

163 Cf. Whitman, *Reasonable Doubt*, 116–17, 180, 189–202 (on the "safer path" doctrine in Christian moral theology and its reverberations in medieval English and Continental criminal law).

164 There is some confusion in the juristic literature between rationalist and traditionalist positions about the nonliability presumption because the two camps often conflated it with the permissibility presumption (*al-aṣl fī 'l-ashyā' al-ibāḥa*), which traditionists definitively rejected. See Ghuraythī, *Aṣāla*, 230, 269–71.

165 Qur'ān, 2:29 (*huwa 'lladhī khalaqa lakum mā fī 'l-arḍi jamī'an*).

166 See Ghuraythī, *Aṣāla*, 269 (noting that the verse indicates that humans should use reason only to the extent that it allows them to discover God's existence, after which they should rely on texts for the content of the law). Cf. Ṭūsī, *al-Tibyān fī tafsīr al-Qur'ān* (Najaf: al-Maṭba'a al-'Ilmiyya, 1957–63), 1:124 (explaining that the verse addresses non-Muslims, asking them to reflect on the fact that God created everything on earth for humans out of His grace and questioning how they could then deny His existence).

other verses of similar import to mean that everything on earth was placed here for the benefit – and therefore free use – of human beings.[167]

On this point, rationalists once again invoked Ibn Bābawayh's permissibility *ḥadīth*: "Everything is permissible unless specifically prohibited."[168] Rationalists took this to mean that a person need not avoid acts on which the law does not make clear statements of illegality.[169] Anṣārī even argued that this was Ibn Bābawayh's intended meaning when he cited the *ḥadīth* – namely, that the earlier jurists expounded this argument – while another work of his meant to render the presumption of permissibility a fundamental and unqualified principle of Shīʿī law.[170] For Anṣārī, that Ibn Bābawayh himself had made the case for this presumption more clearly than anyone else made for a powerful argument against the traditionalist insistence on a general obligation of precaution in the face of doubt. Moreover, Anṣārī elaborated the implications of that principle to reach a conclusion quite opposite to that of the traditionalists. He concluded that *in cases of doubt, no precautionary measures are due.*[171] Instead, the jurist and the layperson were to adopt the default presumption of permissibility, as supported by Ibn Bābawayh's *ḥadīth* and by Qurʾānic instructions. In this way, he maintained that the textual basis for the permissibility presumption placed the burden of production on those maintaining that there was a prohibition or potential for one.

Anṣārī's formulation of the permissibility presumption in this jurisprudential discussion sounds remarkably similar to the wording of the doubt canon in the judicial context: in cases of doubt, avoid imposing criminal sanctions. Whereas Anṣārī's formulation is a negative one, against precaution, the doubt canon is an affirmative directive, specifying avoidance. But the two have complementary import.

167 For example, al-Miqdād al-Suyūrī, *Kanz al-ʿirfān fī fiqh al-Qurʾān*, ed. Muḥammad Bāqir al-Bahbūdī (Tehran: al-Maktaba al-Murtaḍawiyya, 1384/1964), 2:300 (citing Qurʾān, 2:168 for support for a doctrine of general permissibility without clear statements of illegality); Ṭabāṭabāʾī, *Mīzān*, 1:425 (criticizing avoidance of ambiguous matters as an act of *disobedience* to divine law by prohibiting what God has made permissible). For further discussion of the permissibility presumption, see Ghuraylī, *Aṣāla*, 275–78 (citing Qurʾān, 6:145, 2:173, 2:168, 6:119).

168 Cited in Bihbahānī, *Risālat aṣālat al-barāʾa*, 354–57; Anṣārī, *Rasāʾil*, 164–65.

169 Ibid., 164–65 (that is, permissibility of things, not acts: *ibāḥat al-ashyāʾ ḥattā yathbut al-ḥaẓr*).

170 Ibid. (citing Ibn Bābawayh's *Kitāb al-Amālī*).

171 Ibid.

c. In Defense of Reason's Dictates: Revelation and the Principle of Legality

Reason, too, Anṣārī claimed, dictates that it would be unjust to punish violations of the law without first offering a clear statement of it; hence the principle of legality, the starting point of rationalist jurisprudence on prohibitions.[172] The simplest example suffices: the master-servant metaphor. If a master punished a servant for failing to carry out a command that the master did not make clear in the first place, any reasonable person would conclude that the master had acted arbitrarily and unjustly.[173] Using this metaphor, rationalists insisted on the idea of divine justice as *fairness*: God, the master, would not take humans, the servants, to task for failing to carry out commands and prohibitions that He did not clarify. Reason, then, requires that He would not punish humans for failing to avoid criminal prohibitions outlined in texts that lacked clarity.[174]

Rationalist arguments for the principle of legality proceeded from both rational and revelatory grounds, both trying to define morality. Recall that rationalists adopted a principle of correlation between revelation and reason: whatever reason requires, so does the Law. They understood this principle to be, in some sense, both descriptive and prescriptive. That is, not only did revelation map on to reason, but reason was also to play a role in discovering the rule. To explain how that should play out, Anṣārī drew on arguments from both reason and revelation to offer a sophisticated, pragmatist theory aiming – successfully – to displace the dominant traditionalist narrative of his time in favor of a "new rationalism."[175]

[172] See Bihbahānī, *Risālat aṣālat al-barā'a*, 349–50 (beginning with this rationalist argument).

[173] Anṣārī, *Rasā'il*, 168–69 (referencing the practice of "rational people" (*ʿuqalā'*)). Not every rationalist jurist adopted this stance. Muḥammad Bāqir al-Ṣadr, a leading twentieth-century jurist, for example, famously rejected it. See Mottahedeh/Ṣadr, *Lessons*, 122 (discussing but rejecting the principle of "rational exemption" with reference to the master-servant metaphor – that "in the opinion of rational people punishment is wrong without a clear statement" of the pertinent injunction – for matters of divine law (on which, see further note 196)). For a comparable example arising in later Gadamerian legal hermeneutics, see William N. Eskridge Jr., "Fetch Some Soupmeat," *Cardozo Law Review* 16 (1995), 2209–24.

[174] Anṣārī, *Rasā'il*, 168–69 (*ḥukm al-ʿaql bi-qubḥ al-ʿiqāb ʿalā shay' min dūn bayān al-taklīf*); see also Bihbahānī, *Fawā'id*, 240–41 (*ḥukm al-ʿaql bi-qubḥ al-taklīf wa'l-mu'ākhadha mā lam yakun bayān*); Bihbahānī, *Risālat aṣālat al-barā'a*, 350 (same). Note that the sense of justice as fairness here is quite different from the modern Anglo-American Rawlsian sense.

[175] See Anṣārī, *Rasā'il*, 151–70 (presenting seven verses and eight *ḥadīth* reports before providing the purely rational arguments in support of the principle of legality and the

2. Doubt and Ignorance: Due Diligence and Constraint

The rationalists also responded to strong traditionalist objections that they relied on the nonliability presumption whenever they failed to locate the actual rule. Traditionalists were certain that there was one right answer, that it was clear, and that it would be reflected in the text if anywhere. For them, the only scenario in which one would not find the answer would be if it were somehow lost, *not* because God had not clarified it through foundational texts. Earlier rationalist jurists had made themselves susceptible to this attack because they had indeed made arguments for a rational nonliability presumption on the grounds that their failure to find the rule indicated that it did not exist. In contrast, as we see here, later rationalists argued in favor of the nonliability presumption on the basis of *textual* arguments, not a lack of guiding texts.[176] That is, in the rationalist view, it was not that the presumption applied because of textual silence, but it applied because the text itself had indicated as much for cases of textual ambiguity and had further delegated to jurists the task of ascertaining which principle was pertinent in each case.[177] Rationalist jurists concluded that the nonliability presumption was the first of the principles to which the text directed them in cases of doubt.[178]

Importantly, as if in response to the strict textualist critiques of Astarābādī and other traditionalists, rationalists were keen to insist that the nonliability presumption was not an unconstrained principle that permitted jurists to follow their whims freely. The presumption arose only when there was genuine doubt as to what the texts of the law required.[179] When was doubt genuine? As Anṣārī put it, before jurists could conclude that a matter was irresolvably doubtful from the text alone, they had to exercise due diligence in ascertaining the legal rule

nonliability presumption); see esp. 168–69 on the principle of legality. While Bihbahānī began with the principle of legality in his discussions of the presumption of nonliability (*aṣālat al-barā'a*) (see his *Risālat aṣālat al-barā'a*, 349, 350), Anṣārī flipped the order – perhaps in recognition of the importance of starting with the text as a means of neutralizing traditionist claims that rationalists strayed from the text to pull rules out of their own pockets.

176 Anṣārī, *Rasā'il*, 268 (*ḥujjiyyat al-barā'a al-sharʿiyya*).

177 Ibid. Compare Bihbahānī, *Fawā'id*, 253 (affirming that the nonliability presumption exists based on the doctrine that the Prophet delivered God's complete message, per Qur'ān, 5:3, but that particular rules – instead of always being clearly stated in the texts – might, by divine delegation, require rational analysis to ascertain).

178 An exception was the influential Muḥammad Bāqir al-Ṣadr, who inverted the order of the nonliability presumption and the precaution principle. For further discussion, see Mottahedeh/Ṣadr, *Lessons*, 165.

179 Anṣārī, *Rasā'il*, 150–51 (defining legal doubt as "uncertainty as to whether the rule is one of prohibition or of obligation").

through an exhaustive investigation of all of the foundational and other texts. Only then would the presumption of nonliability apply, and even then, the circumstances of its application were limited to genuine doubt or ignorance of the law.[180] Anṣārī again pointed to several Qur'ānic verses and *ḥadīth* requiring people to support the notion that absolution from legal liability required first seeking knowledge and inquiring in cases of ignorance.[181] Accordingly, *negligent* ignorance was not an excuse; the nonliability presumption would not apply to a jurist who failed to investigate the matter or to a layperson who failed to ask a jurist or someone knowledgeable about the law when they had reason to suspect that some ruling beyond the default state of permissibility might apply.[182] Even in mundane matters, people typically had constructive knowledge of social norms – being generally aware of the acceptability of certain behaviors with social cues to help signal the boundaries of Islamic behavioral norms. No reasonable person would conclude that diverging wildly from those norms was excusable based on mere claims of ignorance that concealed a deliberate disregard for observing the norms. Likewise in the law, rationalists presumed that all legal agents had at least a general awareness of the existence of obligations and prohibitions and that they should ascertain what these were whenever a set of facts caused them to doubt the default status of permissibility.[183] Accordingly, where the law was clearly stated and clearly discoverable, legal violations suggested that the agent was acting out of willful ignorance, and no rational mind would conclude that punishment was unjust, claims of ignorance notwithstanding.[184]

How much investigation was enough? Anṣārī noted that the standard changed over time but that at the very least, it meant investigating so thoroughly "that one concludes (lit.: "despairs") that one will not find

[180] Ibid., 312 (noting that this discussion applies to doubt about the law (*shubha ḥukmiyya*), as there is no need to search *legal* texts for resolution to *factual* doubt (*shubha mawḍūʿiyya*)). Traditionalists agreed that the nonliability presumption could apply to the realm of factual doubt if it applied anywhere.

[181] Ibid. (citing both Qur'ānic verses and traditions).

[182] Ibid. (*ʿadam maʿdhūriyyat al-jāhil al-muqaṣṣir*); cf. Dāmād, *Qavāʿid*, 4:57, contrasting excusable ignorance (*jahl-i quṣūrī*), to which the nonliability presumption would apply – as in the case of someone who duly tried to ascertain the law but was unable to because that person lived far away from the centers of knowledge – with inexcusable ignorance (*jahl-i taqṣīrī*), to which the nonliability presumption would not apply – as when a layperson would have been able to ascertain the law by simply asking a jurist, but failed to do so for fear that the act might be prohibited; this is called ignorance by way of negligence, here a form of willful blindness.

[183] Anṣārī, *Rasāʾil*, 313.

[184] Ibid., 312–13.

a relevant text [to guide the matter decisively] from the available sources."[185] Specifically, the search includes examining the texts of the Qur'ān and the four main *ḥadīth* collections, as well as other relied-upon and easy-to-access *ḥadīth* collections.[186] If, after searching through all of these sources, the expert jurist finds no clear textual guidance, he or she then has "strong reason to believe" that there is no clear statement in the texts. This belief is the legal doubt required to move him or her into the realm of the nonliability presumption.[187] Here, Anṣārī admitted that "strong reason to believe" is not certainty – the standard typically required for inferring a legal obligation. But both for pragmatic reasons and in light of the directives of other texts, he maintained that the jurist need not engage in further research: doing so would impose an undue burden (*ḥaraj*), which a "universal legal maxim" forbids,[188] and would render the interpretive process excessively cumbersome in a way that would prevent jurists from investigating or articulating other areas of Islamic law.[189] But he also pointed out that the jurists' strong belief is not the basis for the rule. Rather, the basis is in the text itself, which is certain and which directs jurists to apply the nonliability presumption in the face of ambiguities precisely to resolve such instances of doubt.[190]

In short, the nonliability presumption is applicable only after the interpretive process has been exhausted to the point that the search has revealed that there is no clear statement of law and thus no moral-legal liability.[191] This is the definition of doubt. The texts had defined the process, and it was as if God in His foundational texts had *delegated* to jurists the interpretive task of saying what the law is, based on a rational analysis informed by the nonliability presumption and a hierarchy of other interpretive legal maxims designed to resolve doubt.

3. Doubt and Resolution: One Right Answer as Process

Roy Mottahedeh has provided the most succinct outline of this delegated interpretive process in his translation of Muḥammad Bāqir al-Ṣadr's

185 Ibid., 327 (*ḥadd al-faḥṣ huwa 'l-ya's 'an wijdān al-dalīl fī-mā bi-aydīnā min al-adilla, wa-yakhtalif dhālik bi-'khtilāf al-a'ṣār*).
186 Ibid.
187 Ibid. (*ẓann*).
188 For a taxonomy of Islamic legal maxims, see Appendix C.
189 Anṣārī, *Rasā'il*, 327.
190 See ibid., 151–68 (identifying textual bases).
191 Bihbahānī, *Fawā'id*, 253 (that is, *ba'd badhl al-juhd wa-'stifrāgh wus'ih fī 'l-adilla, wa-taḥṣīl al-ḥukm, fa-in lam yajid dalīl 'alā 'l-taklīf tamassaka bih* [*aṣl al-barā'a*]).

influential and widely read contemporary work on Shīʿī jurisprudence.[192] In Ṣadr's scheme, rationalist jurisprudence comprises three main areas of inquiry: textualist bases, interpretive presumptions, and conflicts of arguments.

The strict textualist bases are by now familiar. The texts of the Qurʾān and the Sunna provide the basic building blocks for Islamic law. These texts are clarified by contextual indicators that elaborate the meaning of revelation in situations in which the texts alone are unclear or of dubious authenticity. The contextual indicators include modes of consensus, the wide prevalence of a particular legal opinion, and continuous community practice that lends support to accounts in traditions that would otherwise fall short of the technical standards of reliability when related by a single source.

The presumptions are familiar as well: the nonliability presumption, the precaution principle, and other interpretive legal maxims that rationalists and traditionalists so vehemently debated. These Ṣadr called shared elements of jurisprudence,[193] or common linguistic canons of construction.[194] Such interpretive presumptions led to knowledge of the *practical duty* (if not the ideal that remained in the mind of God), which applied when "no substantiating [textual] argument can be found and the proper ruling remains in doubt."[195]

Finally, at times different methods of deriving the law might point to different conclusions, such as in conflicts between texts or interpretive

[192] See Mottahedeh/Ṣadr, *Lessons*, 137.

[193] Examples include the following: that the specific takes precedence over or qualifies the general import of a text; that the existence of a "mandatory" ruling depends on certain necessary preliminaries; that injunctive legal rulings are of five basic types: mandatory, recommended, permissible, discouraged, and prohibited; and that declaratory rulings (concerning the effects of legal instruments designed to change or create a certain status, such as marriage contracts) are of three types: valid, invalid, and defective. For discussions, see, for example, Mottahedeh/Ṣadr, *Lessons*, 55–56. For lists, see, for example, Taskhīrī et al., *Qawāʿid*, 1:213–64 (*qawāʿid al-ʿāmm waʾl-khāṣṣ waʾl-muṭlaq waʾl-muqayyad*), 265–303 (*qawāʿid al-qaṭʿ wa-wasāʾil al-iḥrāz al-wijdānī*), 311–50 (*qawāʿid al-ẓann*).

[194] Examples include the following: that words are to be taken according to their conventional meanings unless some textual clue indicates otherwise (the *canon of conventional meaning*), and that commands are to be understood to mean mandatoriness unless some other clue indicates that they are advisory (the *canon of mandatoriness of commands*). For discussions, see Mottahedeh/Ṣadr, *Lessons*, 72–73, 82–88. For lists, see, for example, Taskhīrī et al., *Qawāʿid*, 1:15–42 (linguistic canons, *qawāʿid al-alfāẓ*), 423.

[195] Mottahedeh/Ṣadr, *Lessons*, 36, 165.

presumptions. In such cases, Islamic jurisprudence further lays out ways to resolve these conflicts between interpretive principles.

This framework, and the elaboration of the interpretive legal maxims called "procedural principles" that gave it concrete shape, had been Anṣārī's major contribution to jurisprudence, which Ṣadr then built upon and popularized. Through them, Ṣadr advanced a text-based, standards-governed mechanism to resolve instances of doubt. He proposed the following hierarchy of interpretive rules of thumb whenever a jurist faced legal doubt:[196]

- **The Nonliability Presumption** (*aṣālat al-barāʾa*). This principle has been discussed at length here. In essence, it applies as an interpretive rule of thumb to resolve uncertainties about both obligation and prohibition and about questions of law and fact.[197]
- **The Precaution Principle** (*qāʿidat al-iḥtiyāṭ* or *ishtighāl al-dhimma*). This principle refers to situations in which a legal agent is aware that there is certainly some legal duty to either perform or avoid a certain act but is confused as to the correct duty among two or more possibilities. In such cases, the "safer way" is for the agent to perform or to avoid both or all acts in question in order to avoid negligently falling short of performing the *potential* duty. For example, if a person knows that there is a duty not to drink wine and is presented with two glasses – one of which the person knows to be wine but is unsure which one – that person must avoid both. Likewise, if a legal agent believes that there may be a duty to perform the congregational Friday prayer or a duty to perform the ordinary midday prayer on Fridays, but there is uncertainty about which is a firm duty, this principle requires the person to perform both. In this case, one should choose the "safer way," usually by avoiding both

196 As a theoretical proposition, Ṣadr initially accords primacy to the precaution principle over the nonliability presumption, calling the former the fundamental principle (*al-qāʿida al-ʿamaliyya al-asāsiyya*) on the notion that a servant owes the master complete obedience. With any guiding texts, logic might lead the servant to conclude that precaution is warranted because avoiding all *possible* prohibitions and following all *likely* commands would certainly bring his or her acts within the scope of the master's wishes. Ibid., 120–23. Yet the texts and the principle of legality (*qubḥ al-ʿiqāb bi-lā bayān*) within them suggest otherwise, namely, that the nonliability presumption is primary rather than secondary (*al-qāʿida al-ʿamaliyya al-thānawiyya*). Ibid., 123–25. The typical order (and the order with which Ṣadr himself agrees in the end) has been followed here, placing the nonliability presumption first.

197 Ibid., 123–25.

in the case of prohibitions and performing both in the case of obligations. This principle is the traditionalists' sole guiding principle for dealing with doubt.[198]

- **The "Either-Or Principle": Duty to Perform One of Two Obligations (*takhyīr*).** This principle refers to situations in which a legal agent is aware of a duty to perform one of two unknown obligations but is unsure which of the two alternatives is due. That is, a person is presented with two rulings that lead to polar opposites, as in one ruling commanding to perform an action and another prohibiting it. For example, a person has firm reason to believe that either the Friday prayer is obligatory and the midday prayer is prohibited that day, or vice versa – that the midday prayer is obligatory and the Friday prayer is prohibited. In such cases, the agent can neither perform both the Friday prayer and the midday prayer nor abandon both without sinning. This principle advises the person to perform one of them, rather than to perform or abandon both.[199]
- **The Presumption of Continuity (*qāʿidat al-istiṣḥāb*).** This principle stipulates that the agent should continue to rely on his or her knowledge about the legal status of any practice "about which he was formerly certain but then subsequently has come to doubt that [the previously applicable ruling or fact] persists."[200] For example, he knows that water in large amounts is intrinsically pure for ritual purposes. However, he then doubts whether contact with an impure substance that, for example, falls into a small pool of water is sufficient to render the entire body of water impure.[201] This principle directs the agent to assume that the small body of water remains

198 Ibid., 120–23; see also Khurāsānī, *Kifāya*, 406–35.

199 Ṣadr calls this "the principle of the inculpatoriness of nonspecific knowledge (*qāʿidat munajjiziyyat al-ʿilm al-ijmālī*)." Mottahedeh/Ṣadr, *Lessons*, 119–32, 165–69.

200 Ibid., 133.

201 That is, an amount of water equal to or less than the minimum for which the status of purity will not change if touched by a ritually unclean substance or if a ritually unclean object falls into it. For Sunnīs, one way of measuring is by an amount called *qullatān*, which amounts to 500 Baghdādī units of measurement (*raṭl*) according to the eighth/fourteenth-century Shāfiʿī jurist Ibn al-Naqīb; this is estimated to fill a space with a volume of two to three feet by a square meter. The Shīʿa, who call the amount *kurr*, measure it as 383.06 kilograms, which fills a space of three and a half feet by a square meter. Like slavery, issues of ritual purity related to standing water are an example of an early legal issue from a medieval desert context that – while largely inapplicable today – continues to feature in contemporary works of Islamic law because of the authoritative pull of tradition from the founding period.

> pure. This example involves factual doubt. As for legal doubt, an individual may doubt, for instance, whether congregational Friday prayers – which he or she knew were obligatory during the age of the Imāms' presence – continue to be obligatory in their absence; does the caliph or modern state stand in the place of the Imām? This principle directs her to assume that the obligation to pray congregational Friday prayers continues. It is based on a broadly stated tradition – a universal legal maxim – that "certainty [regarding the existing situation] is not superseded by doubt [regarding whether the circumstances have changed]." That is, she should change her understanding about purity, ritual law obligations, or any other factual or legal issue only based on *certain* knowledge of a material change that changes one's fundamental obligations before the law.[202]

For rationalist jurists, following this interpretive process yields "a practical position vis-à-vis th[e] unascertainable ruling as a substitute for the discovery of the ruling itself."[203] The important point to note is that rationalists did not disagree with the traditionalist insistence that there was one right answer: most said that there was.[204] Rather, they were disagreeing about whether it was always possible to ascertain the correct legal rule in the text itself and about what a legal agent's obligations were if not. For traditionalists, for whom the text was the starting and end point, the right answer was contained in the clear *text* and required complete *avoidance* of matters of continuing doubt. For rationalists, for whom the text was also the starting point, the right answer had to be reached through the *interpretive process*. This brought about the resolution of doubt through the

202 Mottahedeh/Ṣadr, *Lessons*, 132–36, esp. 133 (citing the well-known *ḥadīth*, here from Zurāra b. Aʿyan al-Kūfī – on whom see Modarressi, *Tradition and Survival*, 404–405 – that is counted as one of the universal legal maxims of both Sunnī and Shīʿī law: "Certainty is not superseded by doubt.").

203 Ibid., 119.

204 See Khurāsānī, *Kifāya*, 468–69. He notes the consensus Shīʿī position, called *takhtaʾa*, that God has for every matter a ruling, which jurists sometimes ascertain through the interpretive process but sometimes miss. This is the majority position in Sunnism as well, as against a minority Sunnī position called *taṣwīb*, which holds that God does not have a single right answer for every matter and that the correct ruling shifts according to the conclusion at which jurists arrive through their interpretive processes. This is principally a theological question that has been brought into and underlies legal discussions about obligation and juristic interpretive authority. For a brief analysis presenting arguments on both sides and evaluating the relationship between those positions and questions of interpretive authority, see Birgit Krawietz, *Hierarchie der Rechtsquellen im tradierten sunnitischen Islam* (Berlin: Duncker und Humblot, 2002), 337–53. For further discussion, see my "Islamic Legal Minimalism."

interpretive legal maxims contained in, including presumptions indicated by, the foundational texts. This same framework of differences governed the application of the doubt canon and other legal maxims that had both interpretive and practical, substantive aspects.

CONCLUSION

In their search for clarity and certainty in the law, rationalists and traditionalists alike had to admit that doubt persisted, a reality to which each camp had to respond. Doubt was, from the beginning, the central battleground for the debates about reason and revelation in the law, inasmuch as legal questions were to be grounded in the revealed foundational texts. In criminal law, rationalist and traditionalist approaches to interpretation revealed theologically informed conceptions about the scope of human discretion to resolve doubt in this most contentious area of law. These different approaches resulted in a back-and-forth between stances favoring punishment avoidance based on the recognition of doubt and those favoring enforcement out of strict adherence to understandings of foundational texts.[205]

Turning back to analogous American contexts, it is useful to take stock of parallel arguments about the rule of lenity. In that context, even textualists joined the hostilities against the expansive use of legal maxims that did not belong to the text-based, interpretive variety.[206] For them, such "substantive canons" that went beyond the text to express particular policy preferences – such as those urging judges to read statutes in light of an unstated statutory purpose (the "purpose canon") – risked judicial lawmaking of the worst sort.[207] Legal realists, legal process scholars, public choice theorists, and textualists differed radically in their accounts of legal interpretation, but they all agreed that courts should apply the law and that substantive legal maxims were an easy way to circumvent it.

205 Murtaḍā al-Anṣārī is credited with advancing the law to provide a decisive "victory" for rationalism over traditionalism in Shīʿī law. Modarressi, *Introduction to Shīʿī Law*, 57–58; J. J. G. Jansen and Andrew Newman, "Uṣūliyya," in *EI*², 10:935; Abdul-Hadi Hairi, "Anṣārī, Shaykh Murtaḍā," in *EI*², 12:75 and sources cited therein. Subsequent Shīʿī jurists have subscribed to rationalist views, except for small pockets in the Gulf countries of Bahrain and Saudi Arabia (that is, Qaṭīf and Aḥsāʾ) and in the Indian subcontinent.

206 See Scalia, *A Matter of Interpretation*, 25–26 (noting that judges' use of legal maxims (especially of the substantive kind) is extremely selective and self-serving, akin to a person looking out over a crowd to pick out their friends).

207 Ibid. Cf. John F. Manning, "Textualism and the Equity of the Statute," *Columbia Law Review* 101 (2001), 1–127.

The rule of lenity has been a legal maxim of central concern (and controversy): the storied canon of American criminal law,[208] which stipulates that judges are to avoid criminal sanctions in cases of doubt or ambiguity. Many American legal scholars have called for the elimination of the lenity rule because it seems to exemplify a form of atextualism and arbitrariness of the very kind to which Llewellyn objected in his attack on legal maxims. The lenity rule, these scholars contend, is a convenient tool for judges to flout express legislative intent to punish crime. Moreover, they claim that its inconsistent application reflects the rule of judges' personal preferences rather than the rule of law, and it does so in the sensitive area of criminal law – where the structural imperatives of the legal system dictate that deference to the legislature should be most pronounced.[209]

American textualists accept the lenity rule only reluctantly, and then only because of its long-standing presence in the law. For the Supreme Court's self-identified archtextualist, Justice Antonin Scalia, lenity is "as old as the common law itself, so I suppose that it is validated by sheer antiquity."[210] With this thinnest of justifications,[211] the lenity rule persists – with Justice Scalia, surprisingly, as its greatest proponent.[212]

208 The famous jurist and legal theorist Jeremy Bentham (d. 1832) commented that the rule had become, even in his time, "the subject of more constant controversy than perhaps of any in the whole circle of the Law." Jeremy Bentham, *A Comment on the Commentaries: A Criticism of William Blackstone's Commentaries on the Laws of England*, ed. Charles Warren Everett (Oxford: Clarendon Press, 1928) (orig. 1776) (cited in Antonin Scalia and Bryan A. Garner, *Reading Law: The Interpretation of Legal Texts* (St. Paul, MN: Thompson/West, 2012), 297).

209 See, for example, Zachary Price, "The Rule of Lenity as a Rule of Structure," *Fordham Law Review* 72 (2004), 885–942, at 887 (arguing that lenity should be rehabilitated); Philip M. Spector, "The Sentencing Rule of Lenity," *University of Toledo Law Review* 33 (2002), 511–80, at 512 (arguing for modification through limitation); Dan M. Kahan, "Lenity and Federal Common Law Crimes," *Supreme Court Review* 1994 (1994), 345–428 (arguing for abolition altogether). But see Dan M. Kahan, "Is Chevron Relevant to Federal Criminal Law?" *Harvard Law Review* 110 (1996), 469–521 (arguing, instead, for wider application through paying deference to Department of Justice interpretations).

210 Scalia, *A Matter of Interpretation*, 26–27; cf. *United States v. Wiltberger*, 18 U.S. at 43 ("The rule that penal laws are to be construed strictly is perhaps not much less old than construction itself.").

211 To be sure, Justice Scalia's new co-authored treatise on textualist legal interpretation seeks to place lenity alongside all other acceptable "textualist" canons on firmer ground; but the authors do not offer a more explicit justification for lenity beyond rejecting its constitutional fair-notice rationale and labeling it a "private-right canon." See Scalia and Garner, *Reading Law*, 296–302.

212 See Sarah Newland, "The Mercy of Scalia: Statutory Construction and the Rule of Lenity," *Harvard Civil Rights-Civil Liberties Law Review* 29 (1994), 197–230; Kahan, "Lenity and Federal Common Law Crimes," 390–96.

In the context of Islamic interpretive debates surrounding legal maxims, my study reveals that the doubt canon was the locus of similar controversies with analogously serious consequences for less well documented theories of Islamic legal interpretation involving legal maxims such as the doubt canon. Muḥammad Amīn al-Astarābādī, as the leading textualist jurist of seventeenth-century Shīʿī law, had announced his opposition to doubt in urgent tones. For him, substantive legal maxims, which he called rational presumptions (*uṣūl*), were a means to subordinate revelation to reason rather than vice versa. Legal validity and legitimacy required appeal to foundational texts as the sole source of law, and thus any legal maxim had to have a textual basis to be valid.[213] From his perspective, most likely, if the doubt canon was at all valid, it was so not out of reason's dictates but because it appeared in the law's foundational texts.[214] Moreover, he viewed other constraining interpretive principles as taking priority over that malleable canon and as severely curtailing its scope – barring jurists from exercising discretion and thereby inserting their own preferences into the law. Like Scalia, Shīʿī textualists found that antiquity (in the guise of the prophetic authority behind a foundational text) justified the canon. Unlike Scalia, they held that its textual basis did not translate into wide discretion in legal interpretation and therefore in the application of the canon. For them, as for Ibn Ḥazm, sheer antiquity was no defense.

Throughout this discussion, we have seen that Islamic legal maxims themselves were not necessarily in a duel – as if enlivened, armed, and viciously on the attack against one another. Instead, *jurists* breathed life into legal maxims in response to ongoing societal and political demands, as a means of ameliorating moral concerns, and through executing their own interpretive philosophies arising out of their theological worldviews about the nature and scope of interpretive authority. It is the jurists' varied underlying understandings of Islamic law implicitly based on these three factors that created fundamental differences in Sunnī and Shīʿī methods of legal interpretation and uses of legal maxims.

The dueling camps exhibited heightened concern for certainty and aimed to constrain discretion in the area of criminal law, but each manifested those concerns differently. When rationalist jurists adopted theology-based

[213] Astarābādī, *Fawāʾid* (198-), 106.

[214] See al-Ḥurr al-ʿĀmilī, *al-Fuṣūl al-muhimma*, 388 (referencing the doubt canon as a prophetic *ḥadīth*); cf. al-Ḥurr al-ʿĀmilī, *Wasāʾil al-Shīʿa*, 28:48, no. 34179 (quoting the doubt canon as a *ḥadīth* from Ibn Bābawayh's *Faqīh*).

presumptions of nonliability and permissibility in law (even if de facto, as in the Sunnī context), they considered acts legal unless otherwise specified. This orientation yielded a pragmatist conception of the legality principle that undergirded the expansive reach of the doubt canon. When traditionalists adopted theology-based presumptions of *potential* culpability, all doubtful acts and legal judgments were to be avoided unless otherwise specified. This orientation, by contrast, yielded a highly textualist legality principle, one for which all that is legal was to be spelled out in the text. The battle tactics, then, on the two sides can fairly be summed up as follows: *Rationalists sought to resolve ambiguity, while traditionalists preferred to preempt it.*

A duel there was. But it was not one between legal maxims as Llewellyn had presumed in American law, and perhaps before him Ibn Ḥazm and Shīʿī traditionalists in Islamic law. Nor was it one in which jurists simply used opposing legal maxims to adjudicate in outcome-determinative ways. Instead, the field of Islamic legal interpretation was a battleground of complex theoretical, theological, and practical concerns surrounding the emergence and application of doubt. The duel was between groups of jurists with different interpretive approaches to the question of the scope of divine delegation for human interpretation of Islamic law. Divergences in their approaches stemmed from a host of sociopolitical considerations, theological presuppositions, and moral concerns about the nature of Islamic law and interpretive authority to confront doubt.

CONCLUSION

Doubt in Comparative and Contemporary Context

Recall the *Case of the Falsely Accused Butcher* with which this book began. That case depicted one early episode of the factual, legal, and moral doubt that Muslim jurists faced when adjudicating questions of criminal law. The history of doubt that followed it traced the process by which, on the basis of that case and other early precedents, Muslim jurists dealt with doubt. Externally, they canonized, textualized, and generalized doubt in their struggle with the ruling authorities outside of their ranks for power over definitions of Islamic law and legitimate forms of criminal punishment. Internally, and against the backdrop of changing sociopolitical contexts, these same jurists debated one another over how best to accomplish that task on moral, procedural, and interpretive grounds. In the process, they defined both the rules and the institutional structures required for legitimate definitions of Islamic criminal law, definitions that sought to maintain fidelity to the will of the divine Lawgiver.

I chose to begin with the *Case of the Falsely Accused Butcher* because it spanned both Sunnī and Shīʿī law discussions, as well as legal issues that were both substantive and procedural arising out of that scenario, as an extreme case of doubt.[1] Muslim jurists' evolving approach to doubt was neither simple nor uncontested. However, the *interpretive process* used to

[1] Notably, the case also relates to criminal law discussions in other legal traditions, secular and religious. In all traditions, the story is highly stylized. It appears as a familiar trope in sources for Jewish criminal law in discussions rejecting circumstantial evidence. See Moses Maimonides, *Maimonides' Commentary on the Mishnah, Tractate Sanhedrin*, trans. Fred Rosner (New York: Sepher-Hermon Press, 1981), Sanhedrin 20:1. I thank Moshe Halbertal and Daniel Greenwood for references to this episode in Jewish criminal law and to that law's corresponding rule against circumstantial evidence in criminal cases.

deal (or duel) with doubt was a constant across all schools of Islamic law, and indeed across other text-based legal traditions considered comparatively.

Alongside the external and internal factors driving these discussions were important developments in the eleventh century that further helped make sense of the canonization, textualization, and generalization of doubt: the accelerating breakup of the Muslim empire and the accompanying text-based systematization of Islamic law. That is, the transformation of doubt from a recognized legal maxim based on judicial practice into a prophetic *ḥadīth*, putatively located in the textual corpus, tracked the systematization of distinct interpretive legal schools toward the end of the long founding period of Islamic law. This period included an ever-increasing reliance on the authority of foundational texts for legitimate legal interpretation. As a textual rule, even if it could not definitively constrain political rulers, the doubt canon could at the very least help Muslim jurists draw the contours of criminal law that they deemed legitimate.

In that vein, now recall also the controversies over the role and validity of the doubt canon and, returning to the comparative perspectives from the modern American context, consider again Karl Llewellyn's infamous portrayal of dueling maxims. For decades, Llewellyn's critique in the American context crippled the once robust intellectual discourse on legal maxims.[2] But Llewellyn's attack never fully expunged legal maxims from the courtroom or the classroom, nor did the strict textualist disdain for substantive legal maxims accomplish that end either.[3] Over the past few decades, the persistence of legal maxims in American legal education and interpretation has forced scholars to pay attention to various uses of legal maxims in order to explain why they persist or, for opponents, to redouble their efforts to persuade courts to discard them once and for all.[4]

Regardless of whether the Islamic version of the story once had a historical basis, alongside other early cases in the Islamic legal tradition, it was nevertheless important for Muslim jurists' interpretation of it and for the role such cases therefore played in helping to construct the Islamic law of doubt and related institutions.

2 See, for example, Jonathan R. Macey and Geoffrey P. Miller, "The Canons of Statutory Construction and Judicial Preferences," *Vanderbilt Law Review* 45 (1992), 647–72 ("A regrettable side-effect of Karl Llewellyn's interesting critique of the canons of statutory construction was that intellectual debate about the canons was derailed for almost a quarter of a century.").

3 See, for example, Eskridge et al., *Legislation*, 97–108, app. B, 1–41 (collecting the legal canons used or cited by the Rehnquist Court from 1986 through 1993); James J. Brudney and Corey Ditslear, "Canons of Construction and the Elusive Quest for Neutral Reasoning," *Vanderbilt Law Review* 58 (2005), 1–120, at 106–107 (cataloging the use of some legal maxims subsequently in that same Court).

4 Since the 1980s, the study of legal canons has become a central part of debates about statutory and constitutional interpretation. Reflecting that trend, the same journal that

Similarly, the rise of Islamic law over the past few decades in the Muslim world has fueled ongoing scholarly conversations about various features of Islamic law, including the role and validity of legal maxims. The vehement attacks on doubt leveled by Muslim strict textualists, with Ibn Ḥazm and Astarābādī leading the charge, failed to defeat the doubt canon in Islamic law. Just as with legal maxims in American law, the doubt canon invites questions about the form and function of interpretive canons in Islamic criminal law. This book alone will not provide answers to questions of the modern construction of Islamic law. But given the importance of Islam's founding period to legitimate interpretations of Islamic law today, this history at least provides a starting point for understanding such inquiries. In short, this book contributes a framework for investigating how one legal maxim, the doubt canon, historically operated in Islamic criminal law and why it was endemic to the construction of that system of law.

In fact, the medieval Muslim jurists' near-ubiquitous use of the doubt canon – and the debates with the minority who opposed it – were striking. So were the rationales that the majority used to justify their use of this and other canons, and those that the minority used to oppose them. Although these canons have been marginal so far to most histories of Islamic law and legal theory, the history of doubt shows how Islamic legal maxims were a crucially important vehicle by which Muslim jurists implemented their power to "say what Islamic law is" from the very beginning of Islamic legal history.

More pointedly, the trajectory of doubt demonstrates that no student of Islamic legal history should be fooled by the relatively late appearance of treatises on legal maxims into thinking that those maxims were not devised or deployed until the fourteenth century. The doubt canon was there from the start of Islamic law, with the earliest sources recording its circulation, and it was already canonized as common judicial practice by the seventh or early eighth century. The doubt canon was then textualized and generalized in the eleventh century, as the main schools of Islamic law matured, the empire broke up, and the Muslim world witnessed a shift from judicial practice to legal text as the authoritative basis for legitimate interpretations

published Llewellyn's chafing critique in 1950 – the *Vanderbilt Law Review* – published a symposium issue in 1992 (vol. 45) highlighting the renewed interest in legal maxims, and there have been other symposia on the subject since (for example, *Cardozo Law Review* 16 (1995)). For a representative sample of the 1980s scholarship, see Macey and Miller, "Canons and Judicial Preferences," 648, n. 4 (listing citations). For a review of canons scholarship since, see Eskridge et al., *Legislation*.

of Islamic law. The form and function of the doubt canon – and along with it, of Muslim jurists' interpretive authority among both Sunnī and Shīʿī jurists – continued to be a matter of debate thereafter, as the use of legal maxims and the literature recording them grew from the eleventh century until the sixteenth, where the main focus of this book ends.

After the sixteenth century, legal maxims literature continued to grow largely undisturbed in the Sunnī Ottoman and Mughal lands as well as the Shīʿī world, well into the eighteenth century. The sections on criminal law in these collections of legal maxims contained a restatement of the earlier definitions of doubt jurisprudence in ways that seemed often to serve pedagogical aims for legal education and deliberative ones for adjudication – though more work is required to detail the precise role of doubt in those arenas.

This history of doubt provides a backdrop to assess the sharp decline of legal maxims in the modern world, particularly after the fall of the Ottoman Empire – with the 99-maxim introduction to the 1869 Ottoman Commercial Code (the *Mecelle*) marking one of the last great heydays of legal maxims in Islamic law's classical period. Legal maxims generally fell into disuse in the Muslim world following a period of European colonialism and codification in the eighteenth and nineteenth centuries, as new governing structures brought drastic changes to legal education and juristic authority over law in the Muslim world. Modern legal codes were designed to sideline jurists, as was the dismantling of the traditional educational system in favor of Western modes. Codification of civil and criminal laws accompanied Western-inspired models of government in the Middle East: new legislatures, state-controlled courts, and stronger executives. Indeed, this shift from the dynamic interpretive tradition of medieval Islamic law to European-style codes and courts in modern contexts allowed new state-appointed judges to dispense with Islamic legal maxims and adopt more strictly textualist approaches to law. Moreover, these judges likely drew on *ḥadīth* collections and other texts that did not necessarily include legal maxims such as the doubt canon, which was textualized only toward the end of Islam's founding period and thus did not appear in the corpus of Islam's foundational texts.

Continuing foreign influence had the unintended effect of creating nostalgia for an imagined golden era when Muslims, sovereign over their own affairs, were able to implement a criminal law regime ostensibly marked by broad enforcement of Islam's criminal punishments. Appeals to such ahistoric notions of this imagined golden era brought symbolic legitimacy to actors in West African countries, to name one example, such as Nigeria and Mali. There, these actors have sought to rhetorically restore the rule of Islamic law by enforcing Islamic *criminal* law through a modern state apparatus or as non-state actors, respectively. Yet these Islamists are not legal scholars, nor are they historians. They tend to be unfamiliar with Islamic law beyond basic texts, which typically contain singular formulations of the substance but not the extensive procedure of Islamic criminal law, as it developed through the doubt canon. In short, the most vehement advocates for Islamic criminal law exhibit little to no understanding of its historical contours, and certainly not of the contextual definitions, functions, and uses of doubt.

Perhaps it is for this reason that, in the twentieth and twenty-first centuries, attention to Islamic legal maxims has reemerged from scholarly pockets in the Muslim world – with new attention given to excavating medieval legal maxims in order to examine their relationship to modern legal questions. As one scholar suggested almost three decades ago, it may well be that considering Islamic law without legal maxims blocks avenues for grasping the nature of Islamic law and legal interpretation both historically and in the contemporary world.[5]

Indeed, the popular notion of Islamic law highlighted at the start of this book – as a divinely revealed textual ideal endowed with certainty, dismissive of doubt – seems not only ahistorical and incorrect but also an unfortunately pervasive way of approaching Islamic law in the modern world. In pursuit of clarity, that notion instead tends to produce legal doctrines that are far more rigid, explicitly harsh, and resistant to change than Islam's historical tradition would have it – especially in criminal law. There is no getting around it: the history of Islamic criminal law suggests that Muslim jurists of any age must grapple with doubt.

[5] See Hossein Modarressi, "The Legal Basis for the Validity of the Majority Opinion in Islamic Legislation," in *Under Siege: Islam and Democracy (Conference Proceedings)*, ed. Richard Bulliet (New York: Middle East Institute, Columbia University, 1993), 81–92, esp. 82–86. The chapter in question was published from a paper delivered at the John M. Olin Center for Inquiry into the Theory and Practice of Democracy at the University of Chicago in 1985.

APPENDICES

Appendix A

Ḥadīth *Versions of the Doubt Canon (with* isnāds/ *chains of transmission)*

Version 1

"Avoid *ḥudūd* [punishments] wherever you find an opportunity to do so." (*Idfaʿū ʾl-ḥudūd mā wajadtum lah madfaʿan.*)

Ibn Mājah (d. 303/915)[1]	ʿAbd Allāh b. al-Jarrāḥ – Wakīʿ – Ibrāhīm b. [al-]Faḍl – Saʿīd b. Abī Saʿīd – Abū Hurayra – Muḥammad

Version 2

"Avoid *ḥudūd* [punishments] involving Muslims to the extent possible; if there is an exculpating cause for [the accused], then release him, as it is better that the *imām* make a mistake in pardoning than in punishing." (*Idraʾū ʾl-ḥudūd ʿan al-muslimīn mā ʾstaṭaʿtum fa-in kāna lah makhrajan fa-khallū sabīlah fa-inna ʾl-imām in yukhṭiʾ fī ʾl-ʿafw khayr min an yukhṭiʾ fī ʾl-ʿuqūba.*)

[1] Ibn Mājah, *Sunan* (1998), 4:161, no. 2545 (*bāb satr ʿalā ʾl-muʾmin wa-dafʿ al-ḥudūd biʾl-shubahāt*); Bashshār ʿAwwād Maʿrūf et al., eds., *al-Musnad al-jāmiʿ* (Beirut: Dār al-Jīl; Kuwait: Sharikat al-Muttaḥida, 1993–96), 17:344, no. 13743. For an English translation, see Muhammad b. Yazeed et al., ed. and trans., *English Translation of Sunan Ibn Mājah* (Riyadh: Dār al-Salām, 2007). *Ḥadīth* critics concluded that this report was extremely weak, as Ibrāhīm b. [al-]Faḍl's narrations were rejected. See, with accompanying footnotes, Abū Yaʿlā, *Musnad*, 11:494, no. 6618; Mizzī, *Tuḥfat al-ashrāf bi-maʿrifat al-aṭrāf* (Beirut: Dār al-Gharb al-Islāmī, 1999), 9:468, no. 12945; Muḥammad Nāṣir al-Dīn al-Albānī, *Ḍaʿīf Ibn Mājah*, ed. Zuhayr al-Shāwīsh (Beirut: al-Maktab al-Islāmī, 1988), 554; Muḥammad Nāṣir al-Dīn al-Albānī, *Irwāʾ al-ghalīl fī takhrīj aḥādīth Manār al-sabīl* (Beirut: al-Maktab al-Islāmī, 1979), 2:356.

ʿAbd al-Razzāq (d. 211/826)[2]	(1) Thawrī – Ḥammād – Ibrāhīm [al-Nakhaʿī] – [anonymous]
Ibn Abī Shayba (d. 235/849)[3]	(2) Wakīʿ [b. al-Jarrāḥ] – Yazīd b. Ziyād **al-Baṣrī** – Zuhrī – ʿUrwa – ʿĀʾisha
Tirmidhī (d. 279/892)[4]	(3) Abū ʿAmr ʿAbd al-Raḥmān b. al-Aswad al-Baṣrī – Muḥammad [b.] Rabīʿa – Yazīd b. Ziyād **al-Dimashqī** – Zuhrī – ʿUrwa – ʿĀʾisha – Muḥammad
	(4) Hannād – Wakīʿ – Yazīd b. Ziyād [**al-Kūfī?**] – . . . – [ʿĀʾisha]
Dāraquṭnī (d. 385/995)[5]	(5) ʿAbd Allāh b. Muḥammad b. ʿAbd al-ʿAzīz – Dāwūd b. Rashīd – Muḥammad b. Rabīʿa – Yazīd b. Ziyād **al-Shāmī** – Zuhrī – ʿUrwa – ʿĀʾisha – Muḥammad
	(6) Ibrāhīm b. Ḥammād – al-Ḥasan b. ʿArafa – Muḥammad b. Rabīʿa – Yazīd b. Ziyād **al-Shāmī** – Zuhrī – ʿUrwa – ʿĀʾisha – Muḥammad
Bayhaqī (d. 458/1066)[6]	(7) Abū al-Ḥasan ʿAlī Shaqīr b. Yaʿqūb – Abū Jaʿfar Aḥmad b. ʿĪsā b. Hārūn al-ʿIjlī – Muḥammad b. ʿAbd al-ʿAzīz b. Abī Razma – al-Faḍl b. Mūsā and [his father] Mūsā – Yazīd b.

[2] ʿAbd al-Razzāq, *Muṣannaf* (1972), 10:166, no. 18698 (with variations in the Arabic text: *fa-idhā wajadtum liʾl-Muslim* instead of *fa-in kāna lah, fa-ʾdraʾ ʿanh* instead of *fa-khallū sabīlah; fa-innah in yukhṭiʾ ḥākim min ḥukkām al-muslimīn* instead of *fa-inna ʾl-imām*).

[3] Ibn Abī Shayba, *Muṣannaf*, 9:362, no. 28972 (with variations in the Arabic text: *ʿibād Allāh* instead of *muslimīn*).

[4] Tirmidhī, *Sunan*, 5:112–13, no. 1424; *al-Musnad al-jāmiʿ*, 2:41–42, no. 16799. Tirmidhī points out that the first chain is likely inauthentic because it alone attributes the saying to the Prophet and does so through Yazīd b. Ziyād from Damascus, who was unreliable (*ḍaʿīf al-ḥadīth*). Tirmidhī deems the second chain (which he suggests goes back only to ʿĀʾisha) to be more reliable (*aṣaḥḥ*), as it was transmitted by Wakīʿ b. Jarrāḥ, likely by way of Yazīd b. Ziyād the Iraqi, who was older and more reliable (*aqdam wa-athbat*) than the Damascene Yazīd. Moreover, attribution to a Companion rather than the Prophet himself is to be expected, as this canon was a known saying among the Companions. Tirmidhī, *Sunan*, 5:112 (noting additional attributions to Abū Hurayra [as noted by Ibn Mājah] and to ʿAbd Allāh b. ʿAmr [b. al-ʿĀṣ], without complete chains). Note that "Muḥammad Rabīʿa" in this edition should be Muḥammad *b.* Rabīʿa, the Kufan paternal cousin of Wakīʿ (see Mizzī, *Tahdhīb al-kamāl*, 25:196–99, no. 5210), as in *al-Musnad al-jāmiʿ*, 2:41–42, no. 16799.

[5] Dāraquṭnī, *Sunan*, 4:62–63, no. 3097 (with variations in the Arabic text: transposition of *mā ʾstaṭaʿtum* and *ʿan al-Muslimīn*; *fa-in wajadtum liʾl-muslim makhrajan* instead of *fa-in kāna lah makhrajan*). Note that this edition clarifies that what the 1966 edition presents as a single chain at 3:84 is in fact two chains. Like Tirmidhī, Dāraquṭnī has a problem with Yazīd b. Ziyād al-Dimashqī, whom he deems weak, based on Bukhārī's assessment that this Yazīd's *ḥadīth* narrations are to be rejected (that is, that he is *munkar al-ḥadīth*) and Nasāʾī's similar conclusion (that is, that he is *matrūk* [*al-ḥadīth*]). Dāraquṭnī adds that Wakīʿ narrated the saying on the authority of Yazīd in a chain that did not trace back to the Prophet (*mawqūf*) and agreed with Tirmidhī that this chain was more reliable.

[6] Bayhaqī, *Sunan*, 8:413, nos. 17057–58 (with variations in the Arabic text from the first version (chain nos. 7–9): same as Dāraquṭnī's version above, with the addition of *lah* after *fa-inna ʾl-imām in yukhṭiʾ fī ʾl-ʿafw khayr*). Like Tirmidhī and Dāraquṭnī, Bayhaqī finds the chain ending in ʿĀʾisha (chain no. 8) to be inauthentic because of Yazīd b. Ziyād's unreliability (*fīh ḍaʿf*). He

Ziyād [al-ʿIrāqī?] – Zuhrī [al-ʿIrāqī?] – ʿUrwa – ʿĀʾisha – Muḥammad

(8) Wakīʿ – Yazīd b. Ziyād [al-ʿIrāqī?] – [Zuhrī] – [ʿUrwa] – ʿĀʾisha

(9) Rishdīn b. Saʿd – ʿUqayl – Zuhrī – . . . – [Muḥammad: *marfūʿ*[*an*]]

(10) Abū Ḥāzim al-Ḥāfiẓ – Abū al-Faḍl Khamīrawayh – Aḥmad b. Najda – Saʿīd b. Manṣūr – Hushaym – ʿUbayda – Ibrāhīm [al-Nakhaʿī] – [ʿAbd Allāh] Ibn Masʿūd

Version 3

"Avoid *ḥudūd* [punishments] among the people as much as possible." (***Idraʾū ʾl-ḥudūd ʿan ʿibād Allāh mā ʾstaṭaʿtum.***)[7]

Ibn Abī Shayba (d. 235/849)[8]	Ibn Fuḍayl – al-Aʿmash – Ibrāhīm [al-Nakhaʿī] – [anonymous: *kānū yaqūlūn*]

Version 4

"If *ḥadd* [liability] is doubtful [to you], then avoid [the punishment]." (***Idhā ʾshtabaha* [*ʿalayk*] *al-ḥadd fa-ʾdraʾah.***)

also finds weak the chain reported by Rishdīn (chain no. 9), which also traces back to the Prophet, because of Rishdīn's unreliability (that is, that he is *ḍaʿīf*). The more sound chain (*aqrab ilā ʾl-ṣawāb*), then, is that containing Wakīʿ (chain no. 4), as Tirmidhī and Dāraquṭnī concluded. Note that Tirmidhī reports that this chain contains and stops with Yazīd b. Ziyād [likely, the Iraqi rather than the Damascene]. Bayhaqī traces that chain back to ʿĀʾisha via Yazīd b. Ziyād – Zuhrī – ʿUrwa. There is some confusion as to whether the Yazīd b. Ziyād in this chain is Iraqi or Damascene. Bayhaqī's editor says that he is Damascene, and Dāraquṭnī labeled him as Shāmī; but Tirmidhī notes that there was a difference between the two Yazīd b. Ziyāds and says that the one who appeared in this chain was Iraqi, calling him Kūfan (while others have called the Iraqi Yazīd b. Ziyād Baṣran). Fierro has suggested that the juxtaposition was deliberate, a matter that requires further study. Finally, see also Bayhaqī, *Sunan*, 8:414, no. 17062 (with variations in the Arabic text from the second version accompanying chain no. 10: *ʿan al-muslimīn* omitted; *innakum* and appropriate forms of the verbs instead of *imām*; *darʾ al-ḥadd* repeated twice, and the first and second parts of the canon transposed). This version of the report is not attributed to the Prophet, but to the Companion and Kufan jurist Ibn Masʿūd (*mawqūf*). Bayhaqī has no comment on it, apparently accepting the attribution of the saying to Ibn Masʿūd through Ibrāhīm al-Nakhaʿī.

7 The Arabic phrase *ʿibād Allāh* literally means "servants of God," but it has been translated as "the people" in order to capture its intended general meaning in classical Arabic-Islamic usage. The phrase takes on the literal meaning, connoting "believers," only if juxtaposed with statements specifically mentioning Muslims, as in version 5 below.

8 Ibn Abī Shayba, *Muṣannaf*, 9:359, no. 28966. This version is similar to the one recorded in Ibn Mājah (version 1), using different phrasing (*idraʾū* instead of *idfaʿū* and *idhā ʾstaṭaʿtum* instead of *mā wajadtum lah makhrajan*), and similar to the version recorded by Tirmidhī (version 2), except that it excludes the second part of that *ḥadīth*. The author does not comment on the authenticity of the chain, as it is an anonymous saying adopted by Ibrāhīm al-Nakhaʿī.

Ibn Abī Shayba (d. 235/849)[9]	(1) ʿAbd al-Salām [b. Ḥarb] – Isḥaq b. Farwa [= Isḥāq b. ʿAbd Allāh b. Abī Farwa] – ʿAmr b. Shuʿayb – his father [= Shuʿayb b. Muḥammad] – Muʿādh [b. Jabal], [ʿAbd Allāh] Ibn Masʿūd, and ʿUqba b. ʿĀmir [al-Juhanī]
Dāraquṭnī (d. 385/995)[10]	(2) Muḥammad b. ʿAbd Allāh b. Ghaylān – Abū Hishām al-Rafāʿī – ʿAbd al-Salām b. Ḥarb – Isḥāq b. ʿAbd Allāh b. Abī Farwa – ʿAmr b. Shuʿayb – his father [= Shuʿayb b. Muḥammad] – Muʿādh b. Jabal, ʿAbd Allāh Ibn Masʿūd, and ʿUqba b. ʿĀmir al-Juhanī
Bayhaqī (d. 458/1066)[11]	(3) Abu Ḥāzim al-Ḥāfiẓ – Abū al-Walīd al-Faqīh – al-Ḥasan b. Sufyān – Abū Bakr b. Abī Shayba – ʿAbd al-Salām b. Ḥarb – Isḥāq b. Abī Farwa [= Isḥāq b. ʿAbd Allāh b. Abī Farwa] – ʿAmr b. Shuʿayb – his father [= Shuʿayb b. Muḥammad] – Muʿādh [Ibn Jabal], ʿAbd Allāh Ibn Masʿūd, and ʿUqba b. ʿĀmir [al-Juhanī]

Version 5

"Avoid [sentences of] death and flogging involving Muslims to the extent possible." (*Idraʾū ʾl-qatl waʾl-jald ʿan al-muslimīn mā ʾstaṭaʿtum.*)

Ibn Abī Shayba (d. 235/849)[12]	(1) Wakīʿ – Sufyān – ʿĀṣim – Abū Wāʾil – ʿAbd Allāh [b. Masʿūd]
Bayhaqī (d. 458/1066)[13]	(2) Abū ʿAbd Allāh al-Ḥāfiẓ – Abū al-Walīd al-Faqīh – Muḥammad b. Zuhayr – ʿAbd Allāh b. Hāshim – Wakīʿ – Sufyān – ʿĀṣim [b. Bahdala] – Abū Wāʾil – ʿAbd Allāh [Ibn Masʿūd]

Version 6

"Avoid *ḥudūd* [punishments] wherever there is doubt." (*Idfaʿū ʾl-ḥudūd li-kull shubha.*)

Ibn Abī Shayba (d. 235/849)[14]	ʿAbd al-Aʿlā – Burd – Zuhrī

[9] Ibid., 9:359, no. 28964. The author does not comment on the authenticity of the chain.

[10] Dāraquṭnī records the same text (with the addition of *mā ʾstaṭaʿt*) and the same chain, as far back as ʿAbd al-Salām b. Ḥarb, who then transmits the statement to Abū Hishām al-Rifāʿī (rather than to Ibn Abī Shayba, as in Bayhaqī's version below). Dāraquṭnī, *Sunan*, 4:63–64, no. 3099 (reporting that this chain is weak because of the presence of Isḥāq b. Farwa, whose *ḥadīth*s are to be rejected (*matrūk qawluh*)).

[11] Bayhaqī, *Sunan*, 8:414, no. 17063 (Arabic text: *idhā ʾshtabaha ʾl-ḥadd fa-ʾdraʾūh*). The author does not trace this report back to the Prophet and has no comment.

[12] Ibn Abī Shayba, *Muṣannaf*, 9:360, no. 28968. The author records this chain, which ends in a Companion, without commenting on its authenticity.

[13] Bayhaqī, *Sunan*, 8:414, no. 17064 (transposing *jald* and *qatl*).

[14] Ibn Abī Shayba, *Muṣannaf*, 9:360, no. 28967 (or *bi-kull shubha*, according to the editor's footnote). The author does not comment on the authenticity of the report, which is attributed to Zuhrī.

Version 7

"That I suspend *ḥudūd* [punishments] where there is doubt is more preferable to me than imposing them where there is doubt." (*La-an uʿaṭṭil al-ḥudūd biʾl-shubahāt aḥabb ilayya min* [*an*] *uqīmahā fī ʾl-shubahāt.*)

Ibn Abī Shayba (d. 235/849)[15]	(1) Hushaym – Manṣūr – al-Ḥārith – Ibrāhīm [al-Nakhaʿī] – [. . .] – ʿUmar b. al-Khaṭṭāb
Bayhaqī (d. 485/1066)[16]	(2) Abū Ṭāhir al-Faqīh – Abū Bakr al-Qaṭṭān – Ibrāhīm b. al-Ḥārith – Yaḥyā b. Abī Bukayr – Ḥasan b. Ṣāliḥ – his father [= Ṣāliḥ b. Ḥayy] – [. . .] – ʿUmar

Version 8

"If 'perhaps' and 'maybe' apply to [determining liability for] *ḥudūd* [crimes], there is no *ḥadd* [liability]." (*Idhā balagha fī ʾl-ḥudūd laʿalla wa-ʿasā fa-ʾl-ḥadd muʿaṭṭal.*)

ʿAbd al-Razzāq (d. 211/826)[17]	Ibrāhīm b. Muḥammad – an associate (*ṣāḥib lah*) – al-Ḍaḥḥāk b. Muzāḥim – ʿAlī

Version 9

"Avoid *ḥudūd* [punishments]." (*Idraʾū ʾl-ḥudūd.*)

Dāraquṭnī (d. 385/995)[18]	(1) Muḥammad b. al-Qāsim b. Zakariyyā – Abū Kurayb – Muʿāwiya b. Hishām – Mukhtār al-Tammār – Abū Maṭar – ʿAlī – Muḥammad
Bayhaqī (d. 458/1066)[19]	(2) Abū Bakr b. al-Ḥārith al-Iṣbahānī – ʿAlī b. ʿUmar – Muḥammad b. al-Qāsim b. Zakariyyā – Abū

15 Ibid., 9:359, no. 28963.

16 Bayhaqī has a similar version, also attributed to ʿUmar, but with slightly different language. See Bayhaqī, *Sunan*, 8:414, no. 17061 (Arabic text: *idhā ḥaḍartumūnā fa-ʾsʾalū fī ʾl-ʿahd* [sic=*al-afw*?] *juhdakum fa-innī in ukhṭiʾ fī ʾl-ʿafw aḥabb ilayya min an ukhṭiʾ fī ʾl-ʿuqūba*). Bayhaqī has no critical comments, though Ṣāliḥ b. Ḥayy does not transmit directly from ʿUmar. There is likely a link missing in the chain to ʿUmar, as Ṣāliḥ was an adult before his son Ḥasan (d. 168–9/785–6) was born in the year 100/718–9. See Mizzī, *Tahdhīb al-kamāl*, 13:54–56 (Ṣāliḥ b. Ḥayy); ibid., 6:177–91 (Ḥasan b. Ṣāliḥ). See also Modarressi, *Tradition and Survival*, 256, no. 84 (s.v. Ibn Ḥayy), and sources cited therein.

17 ʿAbd al-Razzāq, *Muṣannaf* (1972), 7:340–41.

18 Dāraquṭnī, *Sunan*, 4:63, no. 3098. The author notes that the report is not sound because Mukhtār al-Tammār is unreliable. Although this version seems to be a truncated form of previous ones, I have counted it separately because its chain, uniquely for this particular phrasing among Sunnī collections, attributes it to the Prophet via ʿAlī. This formulation is also the beginning of other versions in Shīʿī collections that attribute the standard version of the doubt canon to ʿAlī.

19 Bayhaqī, *Sunan*, 8:414, no. 17059. The content and the chain are the same as the record above, except that the report comes to Bayhaqī through Muḥammad b. al-Qāsim to ʿAlī b. ʿUmar rather than Dāraquṭnī. Bayhaqī rejects this as well, saying that the chain is not sound.

	Kurayb – Muʿāwiya b. Hishām – Mukhtār al-Tammār – Abū Maṭar – ʿAlī – [Muḥammad: *marfūʿ*]

Version 10

"Avoid *ḥudūd* [punishments], although it is improper for the *imām* to neglect them [completely]." (*Idraʾū ʾl-ḥudūd wa-lā yanbaghī liʾl-imām an yuʿaṭṭil al-ḥudūd.*)

Bayhaqī (d. 458/1066)[20]	Abū Bakr b. al-Ḥārith – Muḥammad b. Ḥayyān – Ibn Abī ʿĀṣim – al-Ḥasan b. ʿAlī – Sahl b. Ḥammād – al-Mukhtār b. Nāfiʿ – Abū Ḥayyān al-Taymī – his father [Saʿīd b. Ḥayyān] – ʿAlī – Muḥammad

Version 11

"Avoid *ḥudūd* [punishments] in cases of doubt, and overlook the faults of the nobles except in *ḥudūd* [crimes]." (*Idraʾū ʾl-ḥudūd biʾl-shubahāt wa-aqīlū ʾl-kirām ʿatharātihim illā fī ḥudūd Allāh.*)

Qāḍī Nuʿmān (d. 363/974)[21]	(1) [no *isnād*]

[20] Ibid., no. 17060. Bayhaqī considers this report unreliable, because Bukhārī determined that Mukhtār b. Nāfiʿ's narrations are to be rejected (*munkar al-ḥadīth*). Cf. Shawkānī, *Nayl al-awṭār*, 7:109, who rejects *ḥadīth*s such as this one with Mukhtār b. Nāfiʿ in the chain for the same reason. (Shawkānī gives the standard version, but he must mean version 9, where this Mukhtār appears.) The word I have translated as "neglect completely" (*yuʿaṭṭil*) also means *to void*, *cancel out*, *discontinue*, or (permanently) *suspend*. This version is interesting because it combines *ḥudūd* avoidance as in version 9 (or all other versions in truncated form) with a principle that seems to conflict with the rationale offered in versions 2 and 7. In those versions, the exponents of the doubt canon (variously the Companions Ibn Masʿūd, ʿĀʾisha, and ʿUmar plus the traditionist Zuhrī and jurist Ibrāhīm al-Nakhaʿī) err on the side of caution, warning that it is better to pardon offenders mistakenly than to punish non offenders falsely. Versions 7 and 8 (which offer no rationale) use language that parallels language here (*taʿṭīl al-ḥudūd*, *muʿaṭṭal*); I have translated it differently in version 8 ("suspend") to reflect its implicit reference to case-by-case individual determinations of *ḥudūd* liability. In this version, by contrast, the exponent – said to be the Prophet through ʿAlī – warns against completely neglecting *ḥudūd* laws. The subtext is that *ḥudūd* punishments are necessary to give effect to God's prerogative and His will in legislating them in the first place, as Ibn Ḥazm reasons above. See Chapter 7.

[21] Qāḍī Nuʿmān, *Daʿāʾim*, 2:463 (variation in Arabic text: adds *ḥadd min* before *ḥudūd Allāh*) (cited in al-Nūrī al-Ṭabarsī, *Mustadrak al-Wasāʾil*, 18:26, no. 21911 (in *bāb annah lā yamīn fī ʾl-ḥudūd wa-anna ʾl-ḥudūd tudraʾ biʾl-shubahāt*)). Notably, Qāḍī Nuʿmān also lists two other versions with wording that echoes the doubt canon but does not mention *ḥudūd* in his chapter by that title: "avoid [punishing] the believer as much as you can … (*dāriʾ ʿan al-muʾmin mā ʾstaṭaʿt* …)," *Daʿāʾim*, 2:442–43, as well as a similar report mentioning doubt, ibid., 1:417 (*wa-lā tarkabanna ʾl-shubha*). The latter formulation comes in Qāḍī Nuʿmān's version of the letter that ʿAlī wrote to

Ibn ʿAdī (d. 365/976)[22]	(2) Ibn Lahīʿa – Yazīd b. Abī Ḥabīb – ʿIkrima – Ibn ʿAbbās (3) Ibn ʿAbbās [no *isnād*]

Version 12

"Avoid *ḥudūd* [punishments] in cases of doubt, but there is to be no intercession, nor bail, nor oaths in *ḥadd* [proceedings]." (*Idraʾū ʾl-ḥudūd biʾl-shubahāt wa-lā shafāʿa wa-lā kafāla wa-lā yamīna fī ḥadd.*)

Ibn Bābawayh (d. 381/991–2)[23]	(1) Prophet Muḥammad [no *isnād*]
al-Ḥurr al-ʿĀmilī (d. 1104/1693)[24]	(2) Muḥammad b. ʿAlī b. al-Ḥusayn [Ibn Bābawayh] – . . . – Muḥammad

Mālik al-Ashtar upon appointment to the governorship over Egypt, and it stands in place of the doubt canon itself in the version of the letter recorded by Ibn Shuʿba al-Ḥarrānī in *Tuḥaf al-ʿuqūl*, 126–49. Neither formulation appears in the version of that letter in al-Sharīf al-Rāḍī's *Nahj al-balāgha*, 426–45. For a comparison of the letters, see Muḥammad Bāqir al-Maḥmūdī, *Nahj al-saʿāda fī mustadrak Nahj al-balāgha*, ed. ʿAzīz Āl Ṭālib (Tehran: Mu'assasat al-Ṭibāʿa wa'l-Nashr, Wizārat al-Thaqāfa wa'l-Irshād al-Islāmī, 1418–1422/1997–8 to 2001–2), 5:57–109; Muḥammad al-Rayshahrī, *Mawsūʿat al-Imām ʿAlī b. Abī Ṭālib*, ed. Maḥmūd al-Ṭabāṭabāʾī and Muḥammad Kāẓim al-Ṭabāṭabāʾī (Beirut: Dār al-Ḥadīth, 2000), 7:54–76.

22 See ʿAynī, *ʿUmdat al-qārī*, 20:259; see also Suyūṭī, *Jāmiʿ*, 1:135, no. 793. One issue worth mentioning is that this version appears only in the fourth/tenth century. It may be tempting to think that Ibn ʿAdī, or whoever formulated the combined maxim, copied it and attributed it to Ibn ʿAbbās from Abū Ḥanīfa's *Musnad* by Ḥārithī (same formula). Indeed, Albānī suggests that such a borrowing is possible, surmising that Ibn ʿAdī's record of the *ḥadīth* matches Ḥārithī's records from Abū Ḥanīfa in both content and chain of transmission. Albānī, *Irwāʾ al-ghalīl*, 7:345. However, this is not what occurred. The two are in fact different, as Ḥārithī never mentions the elite-leniency maxim. Albānī may have conflated Abū Ḥanīfa's version with this combined version, based on attributions of this version to Ibn ʿAbbās (by Ḥārithī in Abū Ḥanīfa's *Musnad* and by Suyūṭī and later scholars elsewhere), without having compared the content or the transmission chain. Finally, one might also suppose that Ibn ʿAdī and Qāḍī Nuʿmān, who were contemporaries, copied the *ḥadīth* from a source common to both Sunnī and Shīʿī (Ismāʿīlī) traditionists. However, there were no known interactions between them, and Qāḍī Nuʿmān – who was a Mālikī Sunnī turned Ismāʿīlī Shīʿī – copied from a limited amount of books available to him, none of which, according to Madelung's list of those sources, would have included Ibn ʿAdī's sources. See Madelung, "Sources of Ismāʿīlī Law," 29. For further analysis of the difficulties involved in tracing this version to Ibn ʿAdī and on Qāḍī Nuʿmān's sources, see Chapter 3, notes 46, 54–61 and accompanying text.

23 Ibn Bābawayh, *Faqīh*, 4:53; see also Ibn Bābawayh, *Muqniʿ*, 437 (standard version, with no *isnād*).

24 Al-Ḥurr al-ʿĀmilī, *Wasāʾil al-Shīʿa*, 28:48, no. 34179. The source of this attribution is unclear, as Ibn Bābawayh attributes the saying directly to the Prophet in his *Faqīh*.

Standard Version

"Avoid *ḥudūd* [punishments] in cases of doubt." (*Idraʾū ʾl-ḥudūd biʾl-shubahāt.*)

Ḥārithī (d. 340/951–2)[25]	(1) Abū Saʿīd – Yaḥyā b. Farrūkh – Muḥammad b. Bishr – Abū Ḥanīfa – Miqsam – Ibn ʿAbbās
Ibn Bābawayh (d. 381/991–2)[26]	(2) Amīr al-Muʾminīn [= ʿAlī b. Abī Ṭālib] [no *isnād*]

A Note on Translations: Doubt and Avoidance

Throughout this book, I have translated *shubha* (pl. *shubahāt*) as "doubt" or "ambiguity" to cover two senses in which jurists use the term: uncertainties concerning questions of fact and uncertainties concerning questions of law. I have generally translated *darʾ* as "avoidance" to reflect the fact that Muslim jurists actively determined whether doubt existed in making decisions about the legitimacy of enforcing (or alternatively, avoiding) criminal punishment. That is to say, the conception of doubt was not self-executing. Rather, a Muslim judge or jurist typically acted as both agent and addressee of the doubt canon[27] – first recognizing (or designating) the legally cognizable types of doubt, then avoiding enforcing criminal punishments wherever they perceived it. In addition, "avoidance" better captures the sense of an analogous usage of the term in the corpus of American legal maxims: the "constitutional avoidance canon," whereby judges presented with doubt about the constitutionality of one interpretation are to avoid the serious consequences of making a decision that *may* tread on constitutional norms in favor of an equally plausible interpretation decided on other, narrower grounds.[28] In similar ways, especially for the

[25] ʿAbd Allāh b. Muḥammad al-Ḥārithī, *Musnad Abī Ḥanīfa*, ed. Abū Muḥammad al-Asyūṭī (Beirut: Dār al-Kutub al-ʿIlmiyya, 1971), 39, no. 70.

[26] Ibn Bābawayh, *Muqniʿ*, 437.

[27] Where authors of relevant legal texts seem to focus on doubt as the operative term, I have retained some form of the word "aversion" (for example, *ḥadd*-averting doubt). Alternative translations that are more literal, but also more awkward and less communicative of the sense of the doubt canon, include "avert *ḥudūd* punishments with doubts and ambiguities," or even "use doubts and ambiguities to avert *ḥudūd* punishments."

[28] For path-setting studies of the canon of constitutional avoidance in American law, see Adrian Vermeule, "Saving Constructions," *Georgetown Law Journal* 85 (1997), 1945–77 (providing a general overview); Eskridge and Frickey, "Quasi-Constitutional Law," esp. 599–600 (identifying clear statement rules used by the U.S. Supreme Court in the 1970s and 1980s as constitutional norms, derogation from which was to be avoided); Trevor W. Morrison, "Constitutional Avoidance in the Executive Branch," *Columbia Law Review* 106, 6 (2006), 1189–259, esp. 1193, n. 10 (citing cases of applications of the constitutional avoidance canon) and 1202, nn. 42–48 (listing variations in definitions of

category of "interpretive doubt," when Muslim judges and jurists were presented with doubt about the validity of enforcing punishment on one interpretation of the foundational texts, they were to avoid enforcing punishment in favor of a plausible interpretation that did not invoke criminal liability.

Key

The following map includes the chains of transmission of the *ḥadīth* versions of the doubt canon from collections circulating in the first three centuries (as listed above). Fourth/tenth- and fifth/eleventh-century chains are included only if discussed in the text.

	Published collection
	Problematic transmitter (see notes in main body)
——————→	Unbroken chain/direct attribution
---------------→	Broken chain/indirect attribution
Bold Name	Significant figure (discussed in the text and notes)

the constitutional avoidance canon). For the U.S. Supreme Court's definitions and applications of the constitutional avoidance canon, see, for example, *Crowell v. Benson*, 285 U.S. 22, 62 (1932) ("When the validity of an act of Congress is drawn in question, and even if a serious doubt of constitutionality is raised, it is a cardinal principle that this Court will first ascertain whether a construction of the statute is fairly possible by which the question may be avoided."); see also *Gonzales v. Oregon*, 546 U.S. 243, 268–69 (2006); *Zadvydas v. Davis*, 535 U.S. 678, 689 (2001). In Islamic law, the closest ideal to this norm is arguably a principle – which also manifests in deliberations on doubt – by which jurists avoid interpretations that create theological difficulties regarding the nature of God or foundational values in favor of interpretations that present no such difficulties. Intimations of these norms appear throughout this book with respect to the doubt canon, especially in Parts II and IV; but a more targeted inquiry into this phenomenon deserves more direct attention as the subject of further study.

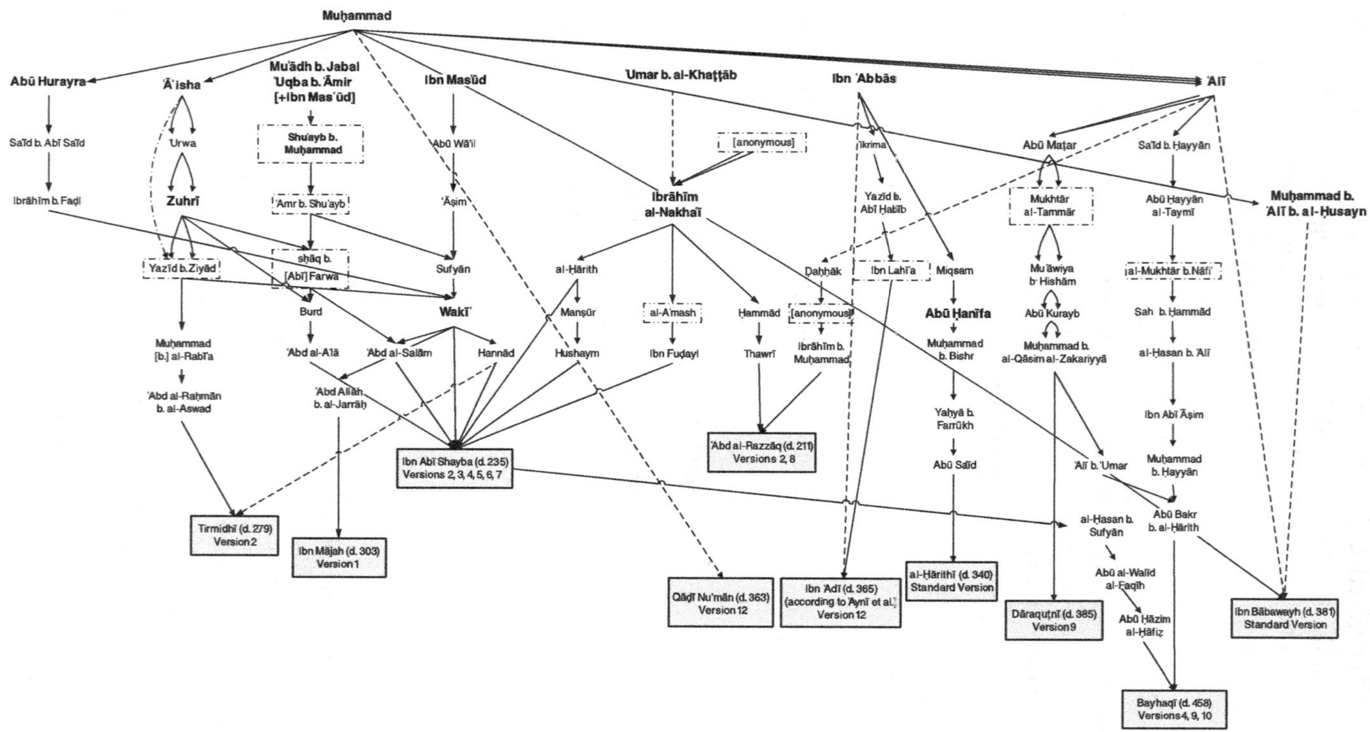

Early Spread of the Doubt Canon as a *Ḥadīth*
(Map of the Chains of Transmission from Muḥammad to Published Third/Ninth-Century *Ḥadīth* Collections)

APPENDIX B

Early Cases on *Ḥudūd* Enforcement and Avoidance

Summary and Explanatory Note

The following list of 25 cases provides a sample of the types of cases that arose in the developing doubt jurisprudence among early Muslim jurists, as discussed throughout this book. These cases fall into three groups: (1) Those reported in literary sources, including historical chronicles, biographical dictionaries (sometimes absorbed in *fatwā* collections), and collections of anecdotes. Most of these cases feature elite judges and high-status offenders citing the doubt canon to avoid punishment. See further Chapter 3. (2) The "landmark cases" from Sunnī *ḥadīth* collections and other legal sources. These cases fall into two categories: those aimed at *ḥudūd* enforcement and those aimed at *ḥudūd* avoidance. These cases are dubbed "landmark" because they are central to and repeated in later juristic discussions of criminal law and the jurisprudence of doubt; they are also typical of a broader panoply of cases in the early literature. See further Chapter 4, esp. note 8 and accompanying text. (3) ʿAlī's judgments recorded in early Shīʿī sources – some of which also came to be "landmark cases" in both Sunnī and Shīʿī law. Here, the cases uniformly pursue a path of *ḥudūd* avoidance, typically reflecting moral concerns with the death penalty and other severe punishments. In all groups, for ease of reference, each case has been given a case name along with citations to discussions of the case in this book. The table further offers the brief facts of each case, the judge presiding, the place where the events presumably took place [in brackets where surmised from the likely location of those involved], the *ḥadd* charge, the decision (whether avoidance or enforcement) and the legislated *ḥadd* sanction (according to *fiqh* opinions), the rationales (both stated ones, where available, and presumed ones on the basis of the surrounding context and implications of the statements of the actors in each case), and the sources in which each case is found.

1. *Literary Sources*

Mixed *Ḥudūd* Enforcement and Avoidance

Case: Short Name and Facts	Judge	Place	*Ḥadd* Charge	Decision	Rationales	Sources
CASE **1–Case of the Secret Lovers** A young nobleman is accused of theft, having been caught inside a house with clothes belonging to the house's owner. It is later discovered that the young man is seeing the young woman who lives in the house. See Ch. 3, note 80.	Khālid al-Qasrī (d. 126/743), Umayyad governor and judge	Iraq	Theft, *zinā*	**Avoidance** *Ḥadd* sanction: 100 lashes for fornication; death by stoning for adultery Sentence: no sentence imposed; instead, the two are married to each other	Stated rationale: actual innocence Imputed rationale [Fierro]: avoidance because of high status (both for theft accusation and for the possible *zinā* accusation)	*Arabian Nights* or *One Thousand and One Nights* (*Alf Layla wa-Layla*) Itlīdī (d. late 11th/17th c.), *Nawādir al-khulafā'*
CASE **2–Case of the Blaspheming Poet: The Ṣāliḥ b. ʿAbd al-Quddūs Episode** ʿAbbāsid caliph al-Mahdī presides over accusations that the poet Ṣāliḥ b. ʿAbd al-Quddūs (d. 167/783) is a "crypto-infidel" or masked unbeliever (*zindīq*) and has made blasphemous statements. See Ch. 3, 93–94.	Muḥammad b. Manṣūr al-Mahdī (r. 158–169/775–785), ʿAbbāsid caliph	Baghdad	Blasphemy	**Avoidance, then Enforcement** *Ḥadd* sanction: death penalty Sentence: execution, crucifixion over a bridge	Stated rationale for avoidance: the doubt canon as a *ḥadīth* Stated rationale for enforcement: "admission" that the poet would continue to blaspheme Imputed rationale [Fierro]: harshness for low-status offender	Al-Khaṭīb al-Baghdādī (d. 463/1071), *Ta'rīkh Baghdād* Ibn ʿAsākir (d. 571/1176), *Ta'rīkh Madīnat Dimashq* Ibn Khallikān (d. 681/1282), *Wafayāt al-aʿyān*

I. (*continued*)

Case: Short Name and Facts	Judge	Place	*Ḥadd* Charge	Decision	Rationales	Sources
CASE **3–Case of Royal Indiscretions: The Abū Yūsuf Episode** Hārūn al-Rashīd (r. 170–193/786–809) witnesses a member of his household committing *zinā* and calls in Abū Yūsuf to adjudicate. See Intro., note 34; Ch. 3, 89–90.	Abū Yūsuf (d. 182/798), ʿAbbāsid judge and Ḥanafī jurist	Baghdad	*Zinā*	**Avoidance** *Ḥadd* sanction: 100 lashes or stoning Sentence: no punishment mentioned	Stated rationale: insufficient evidence (in judge's or *imām*'s knowledge alone) Imputed rationale [Fierro]: lenience for high-status offender	al-Qāḍī al-Tanūkhī (d. 384/994), *Nishwār al-muḥāḍara* Ibn Khallikān (d. 681/1282), *Wafayāt al-aʿyān* Ibn al-Wardī (d. 749/1349), *Taʾrīkh Ibn al-Wardī* Yāfiʿī (d. 768/1366–7), *Mirʾāt al-jinān*
CASE **4–Andalusian Blasphemy Case: The Ibn Ḥabīb Episode** Hārūn b. Ḥabīb criticizes Muslims in favor of Christians, for which he is accused of blasphemy. The caliph, ʿAbd al-Raḥmān II, appeals to Hārūn's brother, ʿAbd al-Malik Ibn Ḥabīb, and others to adjudicate. See Ch. 3, 90–93.	ʿAbd al-Malik Ibn Ḥabīb (d. 238/853), Andalusian judge and jurist	Cordova	Blasphemy	**Avoidance** *Ḥadd* sanction: death penalty Sentence: no *ḥadd* punishment, but imprisonment	Stated rationale: the statement was ill-advised, but not a *ḥadd* crime of blasphemy Presumed rationale [Fierro]: lenience for high-status offender	Khushanī (d. 361/971–2 or 371/981), *Akhbār al-fuqahāʾ* Qāḍī ʿIyāḍ (d. 544/1149), *Madārik*; idem, *Shifāʾ* [whence Wansharīsī (d. 915/1508), *Miʿyār*]

CASE **5–Case of the Royal Concubine's Naughty Nephew** The nephew of the royal concubine ʿAjab is accused of blasphemy. The caliph [ʿAbd al-Raḥmān II?] appeals to Ibn Ḥabīb and others to adjudicate. See Ch. 3, 93.	ʿAbd al-Malik Ibn Ḥabīb (d. 238/853), Andalusian judge and jurist	Cordoba	Blasphemy	**Enforcement** *Ḥadd* sanction: death penalty Sentence: execution	Stated rationale: n/a Imputed rationale [Fierro]: status hierarchies (The concubine was not of high status.)	Khushanī (d. 361/971–2 or 371/981), *Akhbār al-fuqahā'* Qāḍī ʿIyāḍ (d. 544/1149), *Madārik*; idem, *Shifā'* [whence Wansharīsī (d. 915/1508), *Miʿyār*] Nubāhī (d. 713/1313–4), *Marqaba*
CASE **6–Case of the Drunken Noble I** The Andalusian judge Ibn Abī ʿĪsā spots a young nobleman and poet who is drunk and claims not to know of the Qur'ānic prohibition of wine drinking but also threatens to revile the judge with negative poetry if punished. See Ch. 3, note 80.	Ibn Abī ʿĪsā (d. 339/950), Andalusian judge and jurist	Andalusia	Wine drinking	**Avoidance** *Ḥadd* sanction: 80 lashes Sentence: no punishment imposed	Stated rationale: n/a Imputed rationale [Nubāhī]: insufficiency of a single confession or of circumstantial evidence Imputed rationale [Fierro]: status hierarchies (The young man was of high status.)	Nubāhī (d. 713/1313–4), *Marqaba*
CASE **7–Case of the Drunken Noble II** Similar to above scenario. See Ch. 3, note 80.	Simāja al-Sanhājī (d. ca. 482/1090), Zīrid vizier	Ifrīqiya [Tunisia]	Wine drinking	**Avoidance** *Ḥadd* sanction: 80 lashes Sentence: no sentence imposed	Stated rationale: n/a Imputed rationale [Fierro]: the young man was of high status	Ibn al-Khaṭīb, *Kitāb aʿmāl aʿlām*

11. *"Landmark" Cases: Early Sunnī Sources*

Ḥudūd Enforcement

Case: Short Name and Facts	Judge	Place	*Ḥadd* Charge	Decision	Rationales	Sources
CASE **8–Case of the Makhzūmī Thief** A woman of the Makhzūmī clan in the Qurashī tribe steals (or borrows and then denies it); Usāma b. Zayd, son of the Prophet's adopted son, attempts to intervene on her behalf. See Ch. 1, 42–43; Ch. 4, 104–105; Ch. 7, 248.	The Prophet	[Medina]	Theft	**Enforcement** *Ḥadd* sanction: hand-amputation Sentence: hand-amputation	Stated rationale: equal justice for high- and low-status offenders Imputed rationale: judicial subservience	*ḥadīth* collections; *fiqh* treatises
CASE **9–Case of Ṣafwān** A man steals a cloak from Ṣafwān b. Umayya on his way to Medina, after the Hijra. After the Prophet has sentenced the man, Ṣafwān attempts to intervene on his behalf, by gifting the cloak to him. See Ch. 4, 105–107; Ch. 5, 148–50,	The Prophet	[Medina]	Theft	**Enforcement [or Avoidance?]*** *See Qudūrī, *Tajrīd*, 11:5986–87 (that the *ḥadd* sanction was avoided) *Ḥadd* sanction: hand-amputation	Stated rationale: impossibility of changing legal facts of the case after adjudication Imputed rationale: judicial subservience	*ḥadīth* collections; *fiqh* treatises

170–71; Ch. 6, 189; Ch. 7, 248.						
CASE **10–Case of the Yemeni Servant** A house servant in Yemen is accused of committing *zinā* with the house owner's wife. See Ch. 4, note 32.	The Prophet	Yemen, Medina	*Zinā*	**Enforcement** *Ḥadd* sanction: 100 lashes for fornication; death by stoning for adultery Sentence: 100 lashes are likely imposed, but no information regarding stoning	Stated rationale: the appropriate punishment for *zinā* is 100 lashes for the servant, death by stoning for the wife if she confesses Imputed rationale: judicial subservience	*ḥadīth* collections; *fiqh* treatises
CASE **11–Case of the Drunken Orphan** A man brings his orphaned nephew to Ibn Masʿūd on an accusation – and admission – of wine drinking. See Ch. 4, 107–108.	Ibn Masʿūd (d. 32/652–3), Prophetic Companion, judge, and jurist	Kūfa	Wine drinking	**Enforcement** *Ḥadd* sanction: 40 or 80 lashes Sentence: not mentioned	Stated rationale: qualms about severity do not lift *ḥadd* liability; judicial subservience Imputed rationale: judicial subservience and publicity	*ḥadīth* collections; *fiqh* treatises
CASE **12–Case of the Drunken Brother** The caliph ʿUmar b. al-Khaṭṭāb's son brings his brother ʿAbd al-Raḥmān before ʿAmr b. al-ʿĀṣ on charges – and presumed admission – of wine drinking. See Ch. 4, note 20; Ch. 7, 241.	ʿAmr b. al-ʿĀṣ (d. 43/663–4), governor and judge of Egyptian capital at Fusṭāṭ	Egypt, Medina	Wine drinking	**Enforcement** *Ḥadd* sanction: 40 or 80 lashes Sentence: lashes (number unknown) administered privately by ʿAmr in Egypt, then again publicly by ʿUmar in Medina	Stated rationale: n/a Imputed rationale: compassion or status do not lift *ḥadd* liability; judicial subservience; publicity	*ḥadīth* collections; *fiqh* treatises

Case: Short Name and Facts	Judge	Place	*Ḥadd* Charge	Decision	Rationales	Sources
CASE **13–Case of Māʿiz** Māʿiz b. Mālik confesses to the Prophet multiple times that he committed *zinā*, knowingly, and was of sound mind when he did so. See Ch. 1, 25–27, 38–41, 43–46; Ch. 4, 115, 117, 121, 124–25; Ch. 5, 143, 163; Ch. 6, 196; Ch. 7, 248.	The Prophet	[Medina]	*Zinā*	**Enforcement outcome/ Avoidance principle** *Ḥadd* sanction: death by stoning Sentence: reportedly enforced, though the Prophet says that the people should not have carried out the sentence	Stated rationale for enforcement: criminal elements completed Imputed rationale: judicial subservience Stated rationale for avoidance: he may have repented Imputed rationale: moral discomfort with the death penalty	*ḥadīth* collections; *fiqh* treatises
CASE **14–Case of the Mysterious Pregnancy** A woman comes to Abū Mūsā al-Ashʿarī, who submits the case to ʿUmar b. al-Khaṭṭāb (version 1), or the woman comes to ʿUmar b. al-Khaṭṭāb directly (version 2), acknowledging that she had sex resulting in a pregnancy, but claiming that she had been assaulted while asleep. See Ch. 4, 115–17; Ch. 6, note 116.	ʿUmar b. al-Khaṭṭāb (d. 23/644), second caliph	[Medina or Minā] and Yemen	*Zinā*	**Avoidance** *Ḥadd* sanction: 100 lashes or death by stoning Sentence: no punishment imposed; the people are told to feed and clothe her	Stated rationale for enforcement: actual innocence in that she may have been raped; fear of God's wrath Imputed rationale: moral discomfort with enforcing the death penalty	*ḥadīth* collections; *fiqh* treatises

CASE **15–Case of the Falsely Accused Passerby** A woman is raped on her way to the mosque and accuses the wrong person of assailing her. Her story is corroborated by bystanders attempting to help her, but denied by the accused. The real perpetrator admits culpability. See Ch. 4, note 60.	[Baghdādī governor] *Attributed to the Prophet, but Baghdad was founded in the mid-second/eighth century	[Baghdad]	*Zinā* (rape)	**Avoidance*** *Ḥadd* sanction: death by stoning for the rapist Sentence: no punishment imposed on the rapist *But see Ibn al-Qayyim, *Ṭuruq*, 86 (reporting but rejecting opinions that the *ḥadd* sanction was enforced)	Stated rationale: repentance Imputed rationale: moral discomfort with enforcing the death penalty	*ḥadīth* collections; *fiqh* treatises
CASE **16–Case of ʿAmmār's Thief** A man steals a bag from the Companion ʿAmmār, for which ʿAmmār himself pursues, catches, and releases the thief [alt. version: Ibn ʿAbbās and Zubayr chase him to retrieve the bag but then release the thief]. See Ch. 4, 109.	Ibn ʿAbbās (d. 68/687), Prophetic Companion and jurist	Ḥijāz [Mecca?]	Theft	**Avoidance** *Ḥadd* sanction: hand-amputation Sentence: no punishment imposed	Stated rationale: value of concealment (*satr*); compassion Imputed rationale: publicity element; moral discomfort with hand-amputation	*ḥadīth* collections; *fiqh* treatises
CASE **17–Case of Private Drinking** The first Umayyad caliph Muʿāwiya's governor-judge in Egypt, ʿUqba b. ʿĀmir, is brought a complaint by	ʿUqba b. ʿĀmir (d. 58/677–8), governor and judge in Egypt	Egypt	Wine drinking	**Avoidance** *Ḥadd* sanction: 80 lashes Sentence: no punishment imposed; ʿUqba advises Dukhayn not to call the police but to admonish the offenders verbally	Stated rationale: value of concealment (*satr*) Imputed rationale: publicity element; moral discomfort	*ḥadīth* collections; *fiqh* treatises

II. (*continued*)

Case: Short Name and Facts	Judge	Place	*Ḥadd* Charge	Decision	Rationales	Sources
his secretary, Dukhayn al-Ḥajrī, of drinking neighbors. See Ch. 4, 110.						

III. *ʿAlī's Judgments: Shīʿī Sources*

Case: Short Name and Facts	Judge	Place	*Ḥadd* Charge	Decision	Rationales	Sources
CASE **18–Case of the Falsely Accused Butcher** A man murders another man for money in Medina. A butcher found near the scene of the crime is arrested and convicted, until the real perpetrator admits culpability. See Intro., 1–3; Ch. 4, 120–21; Ch. 7, 240; Ch. 8, 266; Conc., 317.	ʿAlī b. Abī Ṭālib (d. 40/661), fourth caliph and first Imām	Medina	Murder	**Avoidance** *Ḥadd* [here: *qiṣāṣ*] sanction: death penalty in retaliation for the perpetrator's act Sentence: no punishment imposed	Stated rationale: n/a Imputed rationale: moral discomfort with enforcing the death penalty	Ibrāhīm b. Hāshim al-Qummī (d. mid-3rd/9th c.), *Qaḍāyā ʿAlī* [whence Ibn al-Qayyim (d. 751/1350), *Ṭuruq*]
CASE **19–Case of the Absentee Husband** A woman becomes pregnant [alt. version: remarries] after her husband has been absent for two years and has a child. The husband [or first husband] returns and accuses her of committing *zinā*. See Ch. 4, 118–20.	ʿUmar → Enforcement ʿAlī → Avoidance	[Medina]	*Zinā*	**Avoidance** *Ḥadd* sanction: death by stoning Sentence: no punishment of stoning imposed; the child stays with the wife and the husband eventually claims paternity	Stated rationale for enforcement: criminal elements completed Imputed rationale: judicial subservience Stated rationale for avoidance: n/a Imputed rationale: moral discomfort with enforcing the death penalty; superior judicial acumen	Ibrāhīm b. Hāshim al-Qummī (d. mid-3rd/9th c.), *Qaḍāyā ʿAlī*; Shīʿī *ḥadīth* collections

III. (*continued*)

Case: Short Name and Facts	Judge	Place	*Ḥadd* Charge	Decision	Rationales	Sources
CASE **20–Case of the Absent Slave Owner** A slave driver has sex with a slave woman in his care while the master-owner is absent (traveling). The owner returns and accuses the slave driver of *zinā*. See Ch. 4, note 55.	ʿUmar → Enforcement ʿAlī → Avoidance	[Medina]	*Zinā*	**Avoidance** *Ḥadd* sanction: 100 lashes or death by stoning Sentence: no punishment imposed; the child stays with the slave driver, to whom paternity is assigned	Stated rationale for enforcement: n/a Imputed rationale: ʿUmar's tendency for harsh punishment Stated rationale for avoidance: n/a Imputed rationale: moral discomfort with enforcing the death penalty [or lashes]; superior judicial acumen	Ibrāhīm b. Hāshim al-Qummī (d. mid-3rd/9th c.), *Qaḍāyā ʿAlī*; Shīʿī *ḥadīth* collections
CASE **21–Case of a Framed Rape** A woman frames a man whom she wants to either attract or punish if he will not give her attention. She accuses him of rape. See Ch. 4, note 55.	ʿUmar → Enforcement ʿAlī → Avoidance	Medina	*Zinā*	**Avoidance** *Ḥadd* sanction: 100 lashes or death by stoning Sentence: no punishment imposed	Stated rationale for enforcement: n/a Imputed rationale: portrayal of ʿUmar as harsh and lacking in judicial acumen Stated rationale for avoidance: insufficient evidence [fear of false testimony] Imputed rationale: moral discomfort with enforcing the death penalty [or lashes]; superior judicial acumen	Ibrāhīm b. Hāshim al-Qummī (d. mid-3rd/9th c.), *Qaḍāyā ʿAlī*; Shīʿī *ḥadīth* collections

CASE **22–Case of the Orphan and the Jealous Wife** A wife fears that her traveling husband will be attracted to their maturing foster daughter when he returns. She enlists her neighbors' help in framing the orphan by puncturing her hymen and then accusing her of having committed *zinā*. See Ch. 4, note 55.	ʿUmar → Enforcement ʿAlī → Avoidance	[Medina]	*Zinā*	**Avoidance** *Ḥadd* sanction: 100 lashes or death by stoning Sentence: no punishment imposed on the orphan; wife is sentenced to the *ḥadd* punishment for defamation [80 lashes] and payment of 400 silver coins [for puncturing the orphan's hymen, and thus compromising her virginity]	Stated rationale for enforcement: n/a Imputed rationale: portrayal of ʿUmar as harsh and lacking in judicial acumen Stated rationale for avoidance: evidentiary infirmity Imputed rationale: moral discomfort with enforcing the death penalty; superior judicial acumen	Ibrāhīm b. Hāshim al-Qummī (d. mid-3rd/9th c.), *Qaḍāyā ʿAlī*; Shīʿī *ḥadīth* collections
CASE **23–Case of Sex with a Wife's Slave Woman** A wife accuses her husband of having intimate relations with her slave woman, against which he counters he had her permission. ʿAlī tells her of the consequences – stoning for the husband or the *ḥadd* punishment for defamation for the wife if she is lying (version 1) – or sentences the man to death, upon	ʿAlī [ʿUmar in Sunnī sources]	Kūfa or Medina	*Zinā*	**Avoidance** *Ḥadd* sanction: 100 lashes or death by stoning for *zinā* [depending on whether construed as fornication or adultery]; 80 lashes for defamation Sentence: no punishment for the husband (all versions); no punishment for the wife (version 1), or wife is sentenced to the punishment for	Stated rationale: [constructed] false testimony/perjury Imputed rationale: moral discomfort with enforcing the death penalty and with severity in punishment in light of evidentiary infirmities; superior judicial acumen	Ibrāhīm b. Hāshim al-Qummī (d. mid-3rd/9th c.), *Qaḍāyā ʿAlī*; Shīʿī *ḥadīth* collections; Mālik (d. 179/795), *Muwaṭṭaʾ* (citing ʿUmar as judge who avoided punishment)

Case: Short Name and Facts	Judge	Place	*Ḥadd* Charge	Decision	Rationales	Sources
which the wife perjures herself (version 2). [In version 3, ʿUmar tells the wife that he will stone the man for adultery, prompting the woman to perjure herself.] See Ch. 2, 54; Ch. 4, note 55.				defamation (versions 2, 3)		
CASE **24–Case of Sex in Prison** A married man commits *zinā* in prison; guilt is not at issue. See Ch. 4, note 55.	ʿAlī	[Kūfa]	*Zinā*	**Avoidance** *Ḥadd* sanction: death by stoning for adultery Sentence: 100 lashes for fornication, but avoidance of stoning for adultery	Stated rationale: diminished culpability (no access to licit sex while imprisoned) Imputed rationale: moral discomfort with enforcing the death penalty; stance against excessive severity; superior judicial acumen	Ibrāhīm b. Hāshim al-Qummī (d. mid-3rd/9th c.), *Qaḍāyā ʿAlī*; Shīʿī *ḥadīth* collections
CASE **25–Case of Sex while Traveling** A married man from Yemen commits *zinā* while traveling in	ʿUmar → Enforcement ʿAlī → Avoidance	Medina	*Zinā*	**Avoidance** *Ḥadd* sanction: death by stoning for adultery Sentence: 100 lashes for fornication, but	Stated rationale for enforcement: n/a Imputed rationale: portrayal of ʿUmar as harsh and lacking in judicial acumen	Ibrāhīm b. Hāshim al-Qummī (d. mid-3rd/9th c.), *Qaḍāyā ʿAlī*; Shīʿī *ḥadīth* collections

Medina. See Ch. 4, note 55.		avoidance of stoning for adultery	Stated rationale for avoidance: diminished culpability (no access to licit sex while traveling) Imputed rationale: moral discomfort with enforcing the death penalty; stance against excessive severity; superior judicial acumen

APPENDIX C

On the Rise of Islamic Legal Maxims: A Prehistory of Doubt

This book traces medieval Muslim jurists' conceptions and deployment of doubt in criminal law as one manifestation of the role of Islamic legal maxims in constructing Islamic law and its institutions. A broader history of Islamic legal maxims awaits a future project. However, provided below is a short history designed to orient the reader wanting a general overview of where the doubt canon and related legal maxims discussed here – the paternity maxim, the elite-leniency maxim, etc. – fit within that broader history.

The emergence of doubt as a recognized maxim of Islamic law and as a prophetic *ḥadīth* tracked the systematization of distinct interpretive legal schools of Islamic law beginning in the fourth/tenth century and the production of the first treatises on legal maxims in the fifth/eleventh century. By this time, jurists had grouped themselves into discrete associations and coalesced around distinct substantive doctrines and interpretive methodologies of law, which now increasingly focused on *textual* authority, with *ḥadīth* as central. Likewise, these groups of jurists had settled on shared theological principles that undergirded their interpretive philosophies of law. In addition, this same period saw the further breakup of the Muslim empire following the fourth/tenth-century period of Būyid dominance over the ʿAbbāsid caliphate and the subsequent fifth/eleventh-century Seljūq control – all of which were factors in and presaged the end of the ʿAbbāsid caliphate in 656/1258 with the coming of the Mongols. As suggested in the Introduction, the efforts at legal systematization and the growth of legal maxims during this period arguably reflected juristic attempts to regain order, and a sense of legitimacy, through law.

1 The Growth of Islamic Legal Maxims

Legal maxims as they originated in the founding period of Islamic legal history (from the first/seventh to the fifth/eleventh century) differ from their subsequent incarnation as a separate, self-conscious field of Islamic law in collections dedicated to cataloging maxims (after the fifth/eleventh century). In fact, legal maxims can fairly be said to have played a central role in the development and spread of Islamic law itself in the first few centuries and afterward.[1]

During the early period (first/seventh to third/ninth century), Muslim jurists drew no particular distinctions among legal maxims but rather used them in the course of legal interpretation, adjudication, and pedagogy. Legal maxims appeared in the earliest *ḥadīth* collections, judicial manuals, substantive law treatises, Qur'ān commentaries, historical chronicles, and even literary works. Not all were *ḥadīth* – even if later jurists understood them to be so.

By the fourth/tenth and fifth/eleventh centuries, jurists had developed a sophisticated and internally regulated system of legal interpretation, as manifested in distinct schools of law and jurisprudence. Of multiple schools from that period, only a handful endured: four major schools in Sunnī law and three in Shīʿī law. The jurists of these schools continued the earlier practice of invoking legal maxims in various fields of law and legal education, but they now identified certain formulations as school-specific and began to collect them in independent works. The doubt canon featured in several of these collections.

After this long founding period and over the next several centuries, Muslim jurists refined their treatments of legal maxims, collecting them and authoring treatises on them until their works acquired a firm place as the third major genre of Islamic law.[2] After the seventh/thirteenth and eighth/fourteenth centuries, a rich literature on legal maxims flourished in every legal school, the use of legal maxims as authoritative "texts" in adjudication and legal pedagogy grew, and jurists offered more technical definitions and treatments of various legal maxims as they placed them into categories that tracked and attempted to organize the major divisions of Islamic law itself.[3]

[1] Bujnūrdī, *al-Qawāʿid al-fiqhiyya*, 1:9.

[2] Catalogs collecting legal maxims began to be compiled into the fourth/tenth century, blossomed during the seventh/thirteenth to tenth/sixteenth centuries, and have reemerged in the twentieth and twenty-first centuries. See Heinrichs, "*Qawāʿid* as a Genre of Legal Literature," 366–84, for a partial list.

[3] For example, the Mālikī jurist Shihāb al-Dīn al-Qarāfī penned what is now hailed as the most relied-upon work of legal maxims in his school, *Anwār al-burūq fī anwāʾ al-furūq*,

The history of doubt and related legal maxims illustrates the unfolding of this process along with varied, contested approaches to Islamic legal interpretation. Though not created by legal maxims, these approaches are clearly visible through them. The founding period featured *contextual* and *jurisprudentially pragmatic bases* for Islamic law and legal authority, and during this period, maxims existed as uncodified but instructive principles of law that arose from judicial practice. The end of the founding period and the beginning of the next period (fifth/eleventh to seventh/thirteenth centuries) saw a shift to *textualist bases* of Islamic law and legal authority and, with it, a systematic elaboration of Islamic law and legal maxims through the addition of prophetic authority to legal maxims – as illustrated by the way in which jurists transformed the doubt canon into a prophetic text. Finally, a third period (eighth/fourteenth to tenth/sixteenth centuries) witnessed the rise of a robust legal maxims literature, which can viewed as having attempted to combine the pragmatist and textualist approaches.[4]

2 Types of Islamic Legal Maxims

Legal maxims constitute the third major genre of Islamic law, alongside legal theory or jurisprudence (*uṣūl al-fiqh*) and substantive law (*furūʿ al-fiqh*). Following these two major divisions of Islamic law, medieval Muslim jurists categorized legal maxims as either jurisprudential or substantive legal

and his rival Ibn ʿAbd al-Salām (d. 660/1262) did the same in the Shāfiʿī context, in *al-Qawāʿid al-kubrā*. Some time later, the Ḥanbalī scholar Ibn Rajab (d. 795/1392) wrote his school's central work of legal maxims, *Taqrīr al-qawāʿid wa-taḥrīr al-fawāʾid*, followed by Ibn al-Mibrad al-Ṣāliḥī (d. 909/1502), *al-Qawāʿid al-kulliyya waʾl-ḍawābiṭ al-fiqhiyya*. Meanwhile, the Shīʿī legal luminary and martyr al-Shahīd al-Awwal (d. 786/1384) wrote what is regarded as his school's first work of maxims, *al-Qawāʿid waʾl-fawāʾid*, followed by works by al-Fāḍil al-Miqdād al-Suyūrī (d. 826/1423), *Naḍd al-qawāʿid al-fiqhiyya*, and al-Shahīd al-Thānī (d. 996/1559), *Tamhīd al-qawāʿid al-uṣūliyya waʾl-ʿarabiyya li-tafrīʿ fawāʾid al-aḥkām al-sharʿiyya*. As for the Ḥanafīs, the jurist Sharaf al-Dīn al-Ḥanafī (d. 799/1390) was an early treatise-writer on legal maxims from the second, "Mamlūk phase" of maxims collections, and his work was followed by a proliferation of writing on legal maxims during the Ottoman era by the likes of Ibn Nujaym (d. 970/1563) and Ibn ʿĀbidīn (d. 1252/1836). Significantly, a committee of Ottoman jurists composed a commercial code (the *Mecelle*) in 1286/1869 that codified principles of that area of law, with a framework of some 99 legal maxims that drew primarily on Ibn Nujaym's and Ibn ʿĀbidīn's formulations. That collection was meant to guide applications of Islamic law by judges not trained in the classical tradition, and it was implemented throughout the Ottoman Empire until its replacement by European and British legal codes in the mid-twentieth century.

4 For alternative accounts of major periods of Islamic legal history in the Sunnī context, see generally Hallaq, *Origins and Evolution of Islamic Law*; Maḥmaṣānī, *Falsafat al-tashrīʿ*, 325–76. For the standard work in the Shīʿī context, see generally Modarressi, *Introduction to Shīʿī Law*.

principles. To that bipartite division, they added a set of five "universal legal maxims" and also deployed a number of uncategorized procedural and other maxims. A more detailed outline of categories of legal maxims follows.

2.1 *Jurisprudential Canons, Interpretive Legal Maxims (qawāʿid uṣūliyya)*

Jurisprudential maxims may be called "interpretive canons" or "canons of construction," as they are commonly known in the American legal lexicon when referring to established rules for construing legal texts. In Islamic law, these canons address the relationship between textual sources and legal rulings, according to recognized linguistic principles of construction and approaches to weighing legal authority (especially *ḥadīth*). These canons also help make the move from jurisprudential principles to substantive legal rules. For example, jurists used the canon that "a negative command indicates prohibition [of a particular act]: *al-nahy liʾl-taḥrīm*" [the "negative command canon"] to derive the legal ruling that fornication and adultery are prohibited, based on the negative command in the Qurʾānic text "Do not approach fornication or adultery: *wa-lā taqrabū ʾl-zinā*" (Q. 17:32). Other common interpretive canons include rules advising judges to assume the literal meaning of texts unless contextual clues indicate that a different reading is merited (*al-aṣl fī ʾl-kalām al-ḥaqīqa*) [the "literal meaning canon"] and indicating that exceptional cases do not create precedent and are not generalizable (*mā thabata ʿalā khilāf al-qiyās fa-ghayruh lā yuqās ʿalayh*) [the "non-precedential exceptionalism canon"].

In Imāmī Shīʿī jurisprudence, a set of four "procedural principles" (*uṣūl ʿamaliyya*) are central to the process of interpretation when foundational texts are ambiguous. These principles may also be regarded as interpretive canons: (1) the nonliability presumption, *aṣālat al-barāʾa* – which directs jurists to presume that there is no legal obligation or liability where texts do not make clear statements creating legal duties or imposing prohibitions; (2) the precaution principle, *qāʿidat al-iḥtiyāṭ* – which advises people who are uncertain about whether they are obliged to perform one or two acts (or to avoid one or two acts) to perform both (or avoid both) out of an abundance of caution; (3) the either-or principle, *takhyīr* – which suggests that people perform one of two acts when they know that at least one but not both are required; and (4) the presumption of continuity, *qāʿidat al-istiṣḥāb* – which authorizes a reliance on existing knowledge about legal duties on the presumption that a known rule of Islamic law continues to apply as is unless it has been changed through a clear statement of law.

Like many other legal maxims, these procedural principles are presumptions derived from foundational and other texts. Although they are treated separately in Shīʿī law, in Sunnī law, similar procedural principles are included within discussions of substantive canons. For instance, the first Shīʿī procedural principle (the nonliability presumption) is counted as a common substantive law maxim among Sunnī jurists. It is reflected in Article 8 of the *Mecelle*, the 1869 Ottoman legal code that begins with 99 key legal maxims of Ḥanafī law: *al-aṣl barāʾat al-dhimma*.[5]

2.2 *Substantive Canons (qawāʿid fiqhiyya)*

Muslim jurists divided substantive canons by their scope and range of application to particular areas of law. They specified a set of "universal legal maxims" of general application, "substantive legal maxims" of more limited application to particular legal fields, and "procedural presumptions" governing laws of judicial procedure and evidence.

2.2.1 *Universal Legal Maxims (qawāʿid fiqhiyya kulliyya)*

By the fifth/eleventh century, Muslim jurists had identified a set of five universally applicable legal maxims that they took to apply to all aspects of Islamic law. Jalāl al-Dīn al-Suyūṭī (d. 911/1505) and other scholars of legal maxims credit the Shāfiʿī judge of Baghdad, Qāḍī Ḥusayn al-Marwazī (d. 462/1069), as the first to record this initial handful of universal maxims. His list included four maxims, to which a fifth was later added.[6] Subsequent jurists – Sunnī and Shīʿī alike – settled on this short list of five maxims as universal and reflective of very spirit of Islamic law:

(1) **The Harm Principle** – Harm is to be removed: *al-ḍarar yuzāl.*

(2) **The Custom Principle** – Custom is legally authoritative: *al-ʿāda muḥakkima.*

(3) **The Hardship Accommodation Principle** – Hardship requires accommodation [of strict legal rules]: *al-mashaqqa tajlib al-taysīr.*

[5] For further elucidation of the Shīʿī divisions, see Chapter 8.

[6] Though his work is no longer extant, most scholars of legal maxims recording the history of the genre identify Qāḍī Ḥusayn's work as the first to list four of these universal legal maxims. See, for example, Maqqarī, *Qawāʿid*, 1:133; Suyūṭī, *Ashbāh*, 7. The fifth maxim was belated likely because it came from a *ḥadīth* that referred to spiritual reward (*innamā ʾl-aʿmāl biʾl-niyyāt*), not intention in law, and the former was not heavily or widely recognized in Islamic legal precepts (especially those outside of the Shāfiʿī ritual law context), which focused more on objective indicia of intent rather than subjective intent itself.

(4) **The Certainty Primacy Principle** – Certainty is not superseded by doubt: *al-yaqīn lā yazūl bi'l-shakk*.
(5) **The Intentionality Principle** – Acts are to be evaluated according to their aims: *al-umūr bi-maqāṣidihā*.[7]

2.2.2 *Substantive Legal Maxims, Specific Legal Maxims* (*qawāʿid fiqhiyya juzʾiyya, ḍawābiṭ fiqhiyya*)

"Substantive legal maxims" or "specific legal maxims" may be regarded as a subset of the broader category of "substantive canons," and they comprise expressions of settled doctrines and policies governing particular areas of law, including commercial law, family law, criminal law, and the like. Some scholars differentiate between various types of substantive legal maxims by pointing to a smaller subset of "subject-specific presumptions" of even more limited scope (*ḍawābiṭ* or *uṣūl*), which further specify the operation of these substantive canons. For instance, a substantive legal maxim of commercial law specifies that "Muslims [are to] honor contractual stipulations: *al-muslimūn ʿinda shurūṭihim*." This is a maxim of general import for interpreting contracts, while an accompanying subject-specific presumption clarifies that a condition is valid only if it does not go against the Qurʾān or the Sunna. Another famous maxim of family law – the "paternity maxim" – stipulates that "the child belongs to the [marital] bed: *al-walad liʾl-firāsh*," that is, paternity is assigned based on the known marital relationship of a contested child's mother.[8] Judges use

[7] See, for example, Maqqarī, *Qawāʿid*, 212; Miqdād al-Suyūrī, *Naḍd al-qawāʿid*, 90–114; Ibn Nujaym, *Ashbāh*, 1:17–19; Muḥammad Ḥusayn Kāshif al-Ghiṭāʾ (d. 1373/1954), *Taḥrīr al-Majalla*, ed. Muḥammad Mahdī al-Āṣifī and Muḥammad al-Sāʿidī (Iran: al-Majmaʿ al-ʿĀlamī liʾl-Taqrīb bayna ʾl-Madhāhib al-Islāmiyya, 1422/2001–2), 1:129–32, 139–42, 153–56 (critical commentary on *Mecelle* articles 2, 4, 17, 19, and 36). For other divisions, see, for example, Suyūṭī, *Ashbāh*, 35, 201, 299, 337; Nāṣir Makārim Shīrāzī, *al-Qawāʿid al-fiqhiyya* (Qum: Madrasat al-Imām ʿAlī b. Abī Ṭālib, 1416/1995–6), 1:26–27 (five categories).

[8] For contrasting studies on the origins of this maxim, see Schacht, *Origins*, 181–88 (arguing that the paternity maxim originated in Roman law and transferred to the Iraqis either before Islam's advent or in the second century, and that it was introduced as a *ḥadīth* in the generation preceding Ibrāhīm b. Saʿd (a contemporary of Mālik (d. 179/795)), who was responsible for putting the maxim in the form of a tradition); Motzki, *Ḥadīth*, xlv (offering a general overview); Motzki, *Origins*, 91, 125–27 (noting that several early jurists quoted the maxim as an early legal opinion or a prophetic dictum, including Ibn Jurayj quoting ʿAṭāʾ, Mālik in his *Muwaṭṭaʾ*, and ʿAbd al-Razzāq in his *Muṣannaf*, while acknowledging that it may also have been in pre-Islamic usage by the judge Aktham b. Ṣayfī); Motzki, "The *Muṣannaf* of ʿAbd al-Razzāq al-Ṣanʿānī," 18. For additional origins studies of this maxim, see Crone, *Roman, Provincial and Islamic Law*, 10, 96ff.; G. H. A. Juynboll, "Notes on Islam's First *Fuqahāʾ*," 287–314; Rubin, "Al-Walad li-l-Firāsh," 5–26. The maxim applies

this paternity maxim to make determinations about child custody, inheritance, and other issues of contested paternity. A third maxim specifies that people are liable for property destruction: "Whoever destroys property is liable for its replacement: *man atlafa shay'an fa-'alayh ḍamānuh*."

Importantly, substantive legal maxims in one area of law often operated alongside other substantive legal maxims with implications for other areas of law. For instance, judges have invoked the family-law paternity maxim alongside the criminal-law doubt canon, instructing judges to "avoid criminal punishments in cases of doubt: *idra'ū 'l-ḥudūd bi'l-shubahāt*." The juxtaposition of these two canons resulted in judges avoiding punishment for a husband's unproven and dubious allegations of adultery against his pregnant wife. That is, in view of both canons, even though the husband might accuse his wife of marital infidelity, without certain proof of such infidelity, the paternity maxim led judges to ascribe paternity to the husband and the doubt canon led them to avoid punishment of both the wife for adultery and the husband for defamation.[9]

2.2.3 *Procedural Legal Maxims, Evidentiary Presumptions (qawā'id fiqhiyya juz'iyya, qawā'id qaḍā'iyya)*

This category is typically undifferentiated from substantive legal maxims in much of the relevant Islamic legal literature. Nevertheless, to be discerned from the same literature together with historical sources is a significant set of legal canons that address Islamic laws of evidence and judicial procedure, some of which are set apart in judicial manuals. An example is the well-known law of evidence placing the burden of proof on the plaintiff: "The burden of proof is on the claimant and the respondent may swear an oath of denial: *al-bayyina 'alā 'l-mudda'ī wa'l-yamīn 'alā man ankar*" (*Mecelle*, Art. 76). Another example is the presumption that "written evidence is as probative as oral testimony: *al-kitāb ka'l-khiṭāb*" (*Mecelle*, Art. 69).

2.3. Other Categories: Administrative, Governance, and Other Canons

A review of the legal maxims literature reveals additional categories of maxims that govern other aspects of Islamic law and society, from legal theory and the relationship between law and governance to public values

to legal relationships, including both marital and slave relationships. See Chapter 2, note 6, and Chapter 5, note 78.

9 See generally Ya'qūb b. 'Abd al-Wahhāb al-Bā Ḥusayn, *al-Qawā'id al-fiqhiyya: al-mabādi', al-muqawwimāt, al-maṣādir al-dalīliyya, al-taṭawwur – dirāsa naẓariyya taḥlīliyya ta'ṣīliyya ta'rīkhiyya* (Riyadh: Maktabat al-Rushd, 1998).

and rules of propriety. For example, one maxim related to matters of administration specifies that "[government] relations with the people should be based on the public interest: *al-taṣarruf ʿalā ʾl-raʿiyya manūṭ biʾl-maṣlaḥa*" (Mecelle, Art. 58).[10] Besides *qawāʿid*, the literature employs several other terms for legal maxims, including *ʿanāwīn*, *al-ashbāh waʾl-naẓāʾir*, *ḍawābiṭ*, *mabādiʾ*, *qawānīn*, and *uṣūl*, and for related concepts, such as *fawāʾid* and *furūq* and even *amārāt* and *ʿawāʾid*. One should be careful to distinguish between legal maxims proper and other statements that are quite distinct from the technical sense of Islamic legal maxims elaborated here, including terms from the preceding list of related concepts, as well as the genre of *takhrīj al-uṣūl ʿalā ʾl-furūʿ* and *maqāṣid*, the latter of which are "objectives of law" that do not typically operate within legal interpretation and instead describe metavalues governing the law.

In short, scholars of Islamic legal maxims have yet to develop a comprehensive understanding of the field as it operated historically or in modern times, nor have they categorized legal maxims in ways that take account of their full spread. In the growing contemporary literature on legal maxims in the Arabic- and Persian-speaking world, legal scholars have categorized maxims in various ways. The most common strategy is to follow medieval divisions between *fiqh* and *uṣūl al-fiqh*, and to divide maxims between substantive legal maxims (*qawāʿid fiqhiyya*) and interpretive canons (*qawāʿid uṣūliyya*), though this bipartite division fails to identify the evidentiary and procedural presumptions that in medieval legal usage formed a distinctive area of maxims. Table 1 represents a preliminary attempt at addressing this lack by depicting the more detailed categorization above.

3 The Doubt Canon as a Jurisprudential and Substantive Canon

Where does the doubt canon fit into this scheme? The answer involves more than one category. Methodologically, jurists found it difficult to apply the universal legal maxims to resolve doubt or to determine the outcomes of concrete situations. This is because those maxims read more like broad statements of meta-Islamic *fundamental values* (that is, akin to *maqāṣid*) than like interpretive principles of *law* useful for judges or jurists needing to resolve doubt. Instead, jurists typically appealed to *jurisprudential canons* to guide textual construction of ambiguous laws, to *substantive canons* when they harbored legal doubts as to particular areas of

[10] In this vein, Bā Ḥusayn has identified a fourth category of "legislative maxims" (*qawāʿid qānūniyya*), which he defines as rules of administration that govern the relationship between the state and the people. Bā Ḥusayn, *Qawāʿid*, 153.

TABLE 1. *Divisions of Islamic Legal Maxims*

		Substantive canons: *qawāʿid fiqhiyya*	
Jurisprudential canons: *qawāʿid uṣūliyya*		**1 Universal legal maxims (*qawāʿid fiqhiyya kulliyya*)** **2 Specific legal maxims (*qawāʿid fiqhiyya juzʾiyya*)**	
Text-based canons • Source-critical canons • Textual construction canons • Reference canons	**Extratextual or procedural principles** • Sunnī law: equitable principles (*uṣūl*, *istiḥsān*, *istiṣlāḥ*) • Shīʿī law: procedural principles (*uṣūl ʿamaliyya*)	**Substantive legal maxims** • Subject-specific legal maxims (*qawāʿid fiqhiyya*) • Subject-specific presumptions (*ḍawābiṭ*)	**Judicial presumptions** • Procedural rules of thumb (*qawāʿid fiqhiyya qaḍāʾiyya*) • Evidentiary presumptions (*uṣūl*)

Key: This table depicts the classical categories in the first row, my general categories in the second half-row (which seek to identify the major types of legal maxims as jurists used them historically), and a proposal for further divisions of these same maxims in the third row (based on the sources of authority for each maxim, with reference to understandings of the genre as it has recently developed in leading works of American legal statutory interpretation).
Note: For a comparable division of American legal maxims into categories of substantive, textual, and reference canons, see Eskridge et al., *Legislation*, 848, as well as the discussion throughout his chapter 8 (847–1115) and the examples by category in his appendix B (19–41).

law, and to *procedural canons* to guide adjudication in the face of evidentiary and factual doubt. The doubt canon traversed all three categories. It thus offers a site of particularly valuable insights for the study of the range of Islamic legal maxims – deployed as it was to theorize the bases for criminal liability; to define the contours of criminal laws; to increase juristic power and constrain that of the ruling authorities; to confer legitimacy; and to guide judges with legal, moral, and theological concerns on issues of interpretation and adjudication surrounding convictions and sentencing in cases of doubt.

Bibliography

Notes on Citations and Style

Citation and Punctuation

For citations and punctuation, this book largely follows the *Chicago Manual of Style* (*CMOS*), 15th edition for articles, books, and manuscripts, and the *Bluebook* style of citation for modern legal sources. Modifications are as follows: Dissertation titles are italicized, rather than placed in quotation marks. Where I have used more than one edition of a source, I group them in the bibliography and parenthetically note the year of the edition used in the footnotes. The three editions of the *Encyclopaedia of Islam* are shortened to *EI*¹, *EI*², and *EI*³. Where I have used the work collecting major works of Shīʿī law (Murwārīd's *Silsilat al-yanābīʿ al-fiqhiyya* (1993)), I refer to the individual work by title and add "in *YF*." As for punctuation, following the *Bluebook*, I use internal parentheses inside parentheses (not brackets) for all references, reserving brackets for interpolated text. Rather than compress all number ranges to a minimum of two digits, as recommended by *CMOS* and the *Bluebook*, I use one digit for alternative years given as date ranges, that is, successive CE years that represent the equivalent of a Hijrī date to a Gregorian calendar date (for example, d. 471/1078–9). I use two for page ranges, for example, pp. 463–64. For both, I use three or four digits when the second part of the range would begin with a zero. Finally, multiple works by the same author(s) are listed in chronological rather than alphabetical order.

Transliteration

For Arabic and Persian transliterations, I generally follow the *International Journal of Middle East Studies* (*IJMES*). Exceptions and unique stylistic matters are as follows: I omit the initial definite article from proper names or places when mentioned alone except when that article is a commonly known part of the proper name. Thus, al-Mahdī (to refer to the proper name of the ʿAbbāsid caliph), but otherwise, Mahdī. Except in personal names, such as Abū al-Ḥasan, the silent "a" (*alif*) of the definite article *al-* and the place-holding *alifs* at the start of certain verb forms are elided and replaced by a *hamza* character (similar to an apostrophe) when preceded by a vowel (for example, *idraʾū ʾl-ḥudūd* not *idraʾū al-ḥudūd*). The conjunctions *wa* (and) and *fa* (and or then) and prepositions *bi* (in or with) and *li* (to) are typically assimilated into the silent "a" (*alif*) of the definite article *al* without the hyphen that normally separates them from following words (for example, *waʾl-sāriq*, *biʾl-shubahāt* and *liʾl-imām*, but *wa-ajmaʿū* and *li-abīk;* the dropped hyphen does not apply to elisions of alifs that are not articles (thus, *wa-ʾkhtilāf*, *fa-ʿlam*, and *qul li-ʾlladhīna*). Only Qurʾānic verses are fully vowelled. I typically use lower case "b." for ibn ("son of") where it is part of a longer name, but write out Ibn when it is part of the popularized name by which the figure is normally referred; thus Aḥmad Ibn Ḥanbal or Ibn Ḥanbal, not Aḥmad b. Ḥanbal.

Terms of Art and Other Stylistic Matters

Though the doubt canon uses the form *ḥudūd* (pl. of *ḥadd*) for "criminal sanction," the two forms of the word are used interchangeably to match grammatical context (thus, *ḥadd*-eligible, but *ḥudūd* avoidance). *Ḥadīth* is used as a collective noun to refer to both plural and singular instances of prophetic reports. Where potentially unclear or grammatically awkward, I have used "*ḥadīth* reports" or traditions to refer to the plural. I have also attempted to provide dates for both AH (after the Hijra) and CE (Common Era) upon first mention and where relevant in the text and the margins. I have provided death dates in the bibliography in that style (for example, 786/1384) for noncontemporary authors of Islamic sources (whereas other authors are better known by the publication dates of their authored works). Unless otherwise specified, references to a single date (for example, "the tenth century") are typically to the Common Era.

Encyclopedias and Other Reference Material

Dānishnāmah-i jahān-i Islām, ed. Ghulām-ʿAlī Ḥaddād ʿĀdil. Tehran: Bunyād-i Dāʾirat al-Maʿārif, 1375/1996–7.

Encyclopaedia Iranica, ed. Ehsan Yarshater. London and Boston: Routledge and Kegan Paul, 1982–.

Encyclopaedia of Islam, First Edition (*EI*[1]), ed. T. W. Arnold, R. Basset, H. A. R. Gibb, R. Hartmann, W. Heffening, M. Th. Houtsma, E. Lévi-Provençal, and A. J. Wensinck. Leiden: Brill, 1913–38.

Encyclopaedia of Islam, Second Edition (*EI*[2]), ed. P. Bearman, Th. Bianquis, C. E. Bosworth, E. van Donzel, and W. P. Heinrichs. Leiden: Brill, 1960–.

Encyclopaedia of Islam THREE (*EI*[3]), ed. G. Krämer, D. Matringe, J. Nawas, and E. Rowson. Brill Online, 2007–.

Encyclopedia of Philosophy, ed. Donald M. Borchert. 2nd ed. Detroit: Macmillan Reference USA, 2006.

al-Mawsūʿa al-fiqhiyya. Kuwait: Wizārat al-Awqāf wa'l-Shu'ūn al-Islāmiyya, 1987–.

Model Penal Code: Official Draft and Explanatory Notes [Complete text of model penal code as adopted at the 1962 Annual Meeting of the American Law Institute at Washington, DC, May 24, 1962]. Philadelphia, PA: American Law Institute, 1985.

Silsilat al-yanābīʿ al-fiqhiyya (*YF*), ed. ʿAlī Aṣghar Murwārīd. Beirut: Dār al-Turāth; al-Dār al-Islāmiyya (vols. 1–25); Mu'assasat Fiqh al-Shīʿa (vols. 26–40), 1990–3.

Constitutions, Statutes, Court Cases, and Administrative Decisions

United States

Constitution of the United States (1789) (as amended 1789, 1795, 1804, 1865, 1868, 1870, 1913, 1920, 1933, 1951, 1961, 1964, 1967, 1971, 1992).

42 U.S.C. § 1983

Abdul-Kabir v. Quarterman, 550 U.S. 233 (2007).

Anderson v. Creighton, 483 U.S. 635 (1987).

Atkins v. Virginia, 536 U.S. 304 (2002).

Baze v. Rees, 553 U.S. 35 (2008).

Bell v. State, 668 P.2d 829, 833 (Alaska Ct. App. 1983).

Booth v. Maryland, 482 U.S. 496 (1987).

Braxton v. United States, 500 U.S. 344 (1991).

Burrage v. United States, 134 S. Ct. 881, 891 (2014).

Church of Holy Trinity v. United States, 143 U.S. 457 (1892).

Crowell v. Benson, 285 U.S. 22, 62 (1932).

Furman v. Georgia, 408 U.S. 238 (1972).

Gardner v. Florida, 430 U.S. 349 (1977).

Godfrey v. Georgia, 446 U.S. 433 (1980).

Gonzales v. Oregon, 546 U.S. 243 (2006).

Gregg v. Georgia, 428 U.S. 153 (1976).

Harlow v. Fitzgerald, 457 U.S. 800, 818 (1982).

Harmelin v. Michigan, 501 U.S. 957 (1991).

Hyde v. United States, 225 U.S. 347 (1912)

In re Winship, 397 U.S. 358 (1970).

Kansas v. Marsh, 548 U.S. 163 (2006).

Kelly v. California, 55 U.S. 1020 (2008).

Lawrence v. Texas, 539 U.S. 558 (2003).

Lockett v. Ohio, 438 U.S. 586 (1978).

Marbury v. Madison, 5 U.S. (1 Cranch) 137 (1803).
McBoyle v. United States, 283 U.S. 25 (1931).
McCleskey v. Kemp, 481 U.S. 279 (1987).
OCC *Interpretive Letter No. 806*. Office of the Comptroller of the Currency (Dec. 1997).
OCC *Interpretive Letter No. 867*. Office of the Comptroller of the Currency (Nov. 1999).
Payne v. Tennessee, 501 U.S. 808 (1991).
Pearson v. Callanan, 555 U.S. 223 (2009).
People v. Rizzo, 246 N.Y. 334 (1927).
Pierson v. Ray, 386 U.S. 547 (1967).
Ring v. Arizona, 536 U.S. 584 (2002).
Saucier v. Katz, 533 U.S. 194 (2001).
Schriro v. Summerlin, 542 U.S. 348 (2004).
Spaziano v. Florida, 468 U.S. 447 (1984).
United States v. Bass, 404 U.S. 336 (1971).
United States v. Elashyi, 544 F.3d 48 (5th Cir. 2008).
United States v. Hudson & Goodwin, 11 U.S. (7 Cranch) 32 (1812).
United States v. Jewell, 532 F.2d 697 (9th Cir. 1976).
United States v. Kwong, 14 F.3d 194 (2d Cir. 1994).
United States v. Santos, 553 U.S. 507 (2008).
United States v. Wiltberger, 18 U.S. 35 (1820).
Vinewood Capital LLC v. Sheppard Mullin Richter and Hampton LLP. 735 F. Supp. 2d 503 (N.D. Tex. 2010).
Wainwright v. Witt, 469 U.S. 412 (1985).
Woodson v. North Carolina, 428 U.S. 280 (1976).
Zadvydas v. Davis, 535 U.S. 678, 689 (2001).

United Kingdom and Commonwealth Countries

A Minor v. Director of Public Prosecutions, [2000] A.C. 428 (H.L.).
King v. Barker, [1924] N.Z.L.R. 865.
Regina v. Prince, L.R. 2 Cr. Cas. Res. 154 (1875).

Egypt

Constitution of the Arab Republic of Egypt (1971, 1980, 2011, 2012, 2014).
Egyptian Supreme Constitutional Court Case No. 8, Judicial Year 17, 21 *al-Jarīda al-Rasmiyya* 1026 (May 1996).

Egyptian Supreme Constitutional Court Case No. 62, Judicial Year 19, 12 SCC 92–110 (Nov. 2006).

Egyptian Supreme Constitutional Court Case No. 23, Judicial Year 19, 12 SCC 307–13 (Apr. 2007).

Egyptian Supreme Constitutional Court Case No. 45, Judicial Year 28, 12 SCC 1359–72 (Nov. 2009).

Iran

Iranian Penal Code (*Qānūn-i mujāzāt-i Islāmī*), revised (1392/2013)

Primary and Secondary Sources

Abd-Allah Wymann-Landgraf, Umar Faruq. *Mālik and Medina: Islamic Legal Reasoning in the Formative Period*. Leiden: Brill, 2013.

ʿAbd al-Majīd, ʿAbd al-Majīd Maḥmūd. *al-Ittijāhāt al-fiqhiyya ʿinda aṣḥāb al-ḥadīth fī ʾl-qarn al-thālith al-hijrī*. Cairo: Maktabat al-Khānjī, 1399/1979.

ʿAbd al-Qāhir al-Baghdādī (d. 429/1037) = Abū Manṣūr ʿAbd al-Qāhir b. Ṭāhir al-Tamīmī. *Kitāb Uṣūl al-dīn*, ed. Lajnat Iḥyāʾ al-Turāth al-ʿArabī fī Dār al-Āfāq al-Jadīda. Beirut: Dār al-Āfāq al-Jadīda, 1981.

——*al-Farq bayna ʾl-firaq*, ed. Muḥammad Muḥyī al-Dīn ʿAbd al-Ḥamīd. Cairo: Maktabat Muḥammad ʿAlī Ṣabīḥ, n.d.

ʿAbd al-Razzāq al-Ṣanʿānī (d. 211/826) = ʿAbd al-Razzāq b. Hammām al-Ṣanʿānī al-Ḥimyarī. *al-Muṣannaf fī ʾl-ḥadīth*, ed. Ayman Naṣr al-Dīn al-Azharī. Beirut: Manshūrāt Muḥammad ʿAlī Bayḍūn; Dār al-Kutub al-ʿIlmiyya, 2000. Also 1972 edition: Edited by Ḥabīb al-Raḥmān al-Aʿẓamī. Beirut: Dār al-Kutub al-ʿIlmiyya, 1972.

Ābī, Ṣāliḥ b. ʿAbd al-Samīʿ al-Azharī al-. *al-Thamar al-dānī ʿalā Risālat al-Qayrawānī*, ed. Aḥmad Muṣṭafā Qāsim al-Ṭaḥṭāwī. Cairo: Dār al-Faḍīla, 2007.

Abisaab, Rula Jurdi. *Converting Persia: Religion and Power in the Safavid Empire*. London: I. B. Tauris, 2004.

Abou El Fadl, Khaled. "The Common and Islamic Law of Duress." *Arab Law Quarterly* 6, 2 (1991): 121–59.

——*Rebellion and Violence in Islamic Law*. Cambridge: Cambridge University Press, 2001.

——*Speaking in God's Name: Islamic Law, Authority and Women*. Oxford: Oneworld, 2001.

Abū Dāwūd (d. 275/889) = Sulaymān b. al-Ashʿath al-Sijistānī. *Sunan*, ed. Muḥammad ʿAbd al-ʿAzīz al-Khālidī. Beirut: Dār al-Kutub al-ʿIlmiyya, 1996. Also 1935 edition: Edited by Muḥammad Muḥyī al-Dīn ʿAbd al-Ḥamīd. Cairo: al-Maktaba al-Tijāriyya al-Kubrā, 1935.

Abū Fāris, Muḥammad ʿAbd al-Qādir. *al-Qāḍī Abū Yaʿlā al-Farrāʾ wa-kitābuh al-Aḥkām al-sulṭāniyya*. Beirut: Muʾassasat al-Risāla, 1983.

Abū ʿĪd, ʿĀrif Khalīl Muḥammad. *Imām Dāwūd al-Ẓāhirī wa-atharuh fī ʾl-fiqh al-Islāmī*. Kuwait: Dār al-Arqam, 1984.

Abū ʿUbayd (d. 224/838) = al-Qāsim b. Sallām. *Kitāb al-Amthāl*, ed. ʿAbd al-Majīd Qaṭāmish. Mecca: Jāmiʿat al-Malik ʿAbd al-ʿAzīz, 1980.

Abū Yaʿlā (d. 307/918) = Aḥmad b. ʿAlī al-Mawṣilī. *Musnad*, ed. Ḥusayn Salīm Asad. Damascus: Dār al-Maʾmūn liʾl-Turāth, 1984–94.

Abū Yaʿlā, Ibn al-Farrāʾ, al-Qāḍī (d. 458/1066) = Muḥammad b. al-Ḥusayn b. Khalaf. *al-Aḥkām al-sulṭāniyya*, ed. Muḥammad Ḥāmid al-Fiqī. Cairo: Maktaba wa-Maṭbaʿat Muṣṭafā al-Bābī al-Ḥalabī, 1966.

——*al-Jāmiʿ al-ṣaghīr fī fiqh ʿalā madhhab al-Imām Aḥmad b. Muḥammad b. Ḥanbal*, ed. Nāṣir b. Saʿūd ibn ʿAbd Allāh al-Salāma. Riyadh: Dār Aṭlas, 2000.

Abū Yūsuf (d. 182/798) = Abū al-Ḥajjāj Yaʿqūb b. Ibrāhīm al-Anṣārī. *Ikhtilāf Abī Ḥanīfa wa-Ibn Abī Laylā*, ed. Abū al-Wafāʾ al-Afghānī. Silsilat al-Maṭbūʿāt, no. 6. Hyderabad: Maṭbaʿat al-Wafāʾ, 1357/1938–9.

——*Kitāb al-Āthār*, ed. Abū al-Wafāʾ al-Afghānī. Hyderabad: Lajnat Iḥyāʾ al-Maʿārif al-Nuʿmāniyya, 1355/1936–7.

——*Kitāb al-Kharāj*, ed. Muḥammad Ibrāhīm al-Bannāʾ. Cairo: Dār al-Iṣlāḥ, 1981.

Abū Zahra, Muḥammad. *Abū Ḥanīfa: Ḥayātuh wa-ʿaṣruh, ārāʾuh wa-fiqhuh*. 2nd ed. Cairo: Dār al-Fikr al-ʿArabī, 1965.

Adang, Camilla. "The Spread of Zahirism in al-Andalus in the Post-Caliphal Period: The Evidence from the Biographical Dictionaries." In *Ideas, Images, and Methods of Portrayal: Insights into Classical Arabic Literature and Islam*, ed. Sebastian Günther. Leiden: Brill, 2005: 297–346.

Āghā Buzurg al-Ṭihrānī (d. 1389/1970) = Muḥammad Muḥsin. *al-Dharīʿa ilā taṣānīf al-Shīʿa*. Najaf: Maṭbaʿat al-Gharī, 1936.

Ahmad, Ahmad Atif. *Structural Interrelations of Theory and Practice in Islamic Law: A Study of Six Works of Medieval Islamic Jurisprudence*. Leiden: Brill, 2006.

Aḥmad b. ʿĪsā b. Zayd (d. 248/862). *Amālī* (also known as *Kitāb al-ʿUlūm*). Collected and commented upon by Muḥammad b. Manṣūr b. Yazīd al-Murādī al-Kūfī. [Yemen]: Yūsuf b. al-Sayyid Muḥammad al-Muʾayyad al-Ḥasanī, 1401/1981. Also preserved in ʿAlī b. Ismāʿīl b. ʿAbd Allāh al-Muʾayyad al-Ṣanʿānī, *Kitāb Raʾb al-ṣadʿ*. Beirut: Dār al-Nafāʾis, 1990.

Ahmed, Asad. *The Religious Elite of the Early Islamic Ḥijāz: Five Prosopographical Case Studies*. Oxford: Unit for Prosopographical Research, 2011.

Ahmed, M. Shahab, and Yossef Rapoport, eds. *Ibn Taymiyya and His Times*. Karachi: Oxford University Press, 2010.

Albānī, Muḥammad Nāṣir al-Dīn al-. *Irwāʾ al-ghalīl fī takhrīj aḥādīth Manār al-sabīl*. Beirut: al-Maktab al-Islāmī, 1979.

——*Ḍaʿīf Sunan Ibn Mājah*, ed. Zuhayr al-Shāwīsh. Beirut: al-Maktab al-Islāmī, 1988.

Ali, Kecia. *Marriage and Slavery in Early Islam*. Cambridge, MA: Harvard University Press, 2010.

al-ʿAllāma al-Ḥillī (d. 726/1325) = Abū Manṣūr al-Ḥasan b. Yūsuf b. al-Muṭahhar. *Mabādiʾ al-wuṣūl ilā ʿilm al-uṣūl*. Qum: n.p., 1404/1985.

——*Irshād al-adhhān ilā aḥkām al-īmān*, ed. Fāris Ḥassūn. Qum: Muʾassasat al-Nashr al-Islāmī, 1410/1989–90.

——*Qawāʿid al-aḥkām*. Qum: Muʾassasat al-Nashr al-Islāmī, 1413–19/1992–99. Also edition in *YF*, ed. ʿAlī Aṣghar Murwārīd. Beirut: Dār al-Turāth; al-Dār al-Islāmiyya, 1990. Volume 23.

Alshech, Eli. "'Do Not Enter Houses Other Than Your Own': The Evolution of the Notion of a Private Domestic Sphere in Early Sunnī Islamic Thought." *Islamic Law and Society* 11, 3 (2004): 291–332.

ʿĀmilī (d. 1373/1953–4) = Muḥsin al-Amīn al-. *Aʿyān al-Shīʿa*. 4th ed. Beirut: Maṭbaʿat al-Inṣāf, 1945–63.

——*ʿAjāʾib aḥkām Amīr al-Muʾminīn ʿAlī b. Abī Ṭālib*, ed. Fāris Ḥassūn Karīm. Qum?: Markaz al-Ghadīr liʾl-Dirāsāt al-Islāmiyya, 2000.

Amir-Moezzi, Mohammad Ali. "Al-Ṭūsī, Muḥammad b. al-Ḥasan." In *EI*[2]. Leiden and London: Brill, 1960–: 10:745–46.

Anderson, J. N. D. "Homicide in Islamic Law." *Bulletin of the School of Oriental and African Studies* 13 (1951): 811–28.

——*Law Reform in the Muslim World*. London: Athlone Press, 1976.

Anjum, Ovamir. *Politics, Law, and Community in Islamic Thought: The Taymiyyan Moment*. Cambridge: Cambridge University Press, 2012.

Anṣārī, al-Shaykh al-; al-Murtaḍā al-Anṣārī (d. 1281/1864) = Murtaḍā b. Muḥammad Amīn al-Tustarī. *al-Rasāʾil al-jadīda waʾl-farāʾid al-ḥadītha: Talkhīṣ li-Farāʾid Murtaḍā al-Anṣārī*, ed. ʿAlī al-Mishkīnī al-Ardabīlī. Qum, n.p.: 1390/1971.

Arjomand, Said Amir. "The Clerical Estate and the Emergence of a Shiʿite Hierocracy in Safavid Iran: A Study in Historical Sociology." *Journal of the Economic and Social History of the Orient* 28, 2 (1985): 169–219.

——"Middle Eastern Constitutional and Ideological Revolutions and the Rise of Juristocracy." *Constellations* 19 (2012): 204–15.

Ashʿarī (d. 324/936) = Abū al-Ḥasan ʿAlī b. Ismāʿīl al-. *Maqālāt al-Islāmiyyīn wa-ʾkhtilāf al-muṣallīn*, ed. Muḥyī al-Dīn ʿAbd al-Ḥamīd. Beirut: al-Maktaba al-ʿAṣriyya, 1990.

Āshtiyānī, ʿAbbās Iqbāl. *Khānadān-i Nawbakhtī*. 2nd ed. Tehran: Kitābkhānah-i Ṭahūrī, 1966. Arabic translation: *Āl Nawbakht*, trans. ʿAlī Hāshim al-Asadī. Mashhad: Majmaʿ al-Buḥūth al-Islāmiyya, 1383/2004.

Astarābādī (d. 1036/1626–7) = Muḥammad Amīn al-. *al-Fawāʾid al-Madaniyya*. N.p.: Dār al-Nashr li-Ahl al-Bayt, 198-?. Also 2003 edition: Qum: Muʾassasat al-Nashr al-Islāmī, 1424/2003.

El Awa, Mohamed S. *Punishment in Islamic Law*. Indianapolis: American Trust Publications, 1993.

ʿAwda, ʿAbd al-Qādir. *al-Tashrīʿ al-jināʾī al-Islāmī*. Beirut: Dār al-Kitāb al-ʿArabī, 1968.

ʿAynī (d. 855/1451) = Badr al-Dīn Abū Muḥammad Maḥmūd b. Aḥmad al-. *ʿUmdat al-qārī: sharḥ Ṣaḥīḥ al-Bukhārī*. Cairo: Idārat al-Ṭibāʿa al-Munīriyya, 1348/1929–30.

——*Ramz al-ḥaqāʾiq fī sharḥ Kanz al-daqāʾiq*. Sakkhar, India: al-Maktaba al-Nūriyya al-Raḍawiyya, 1982.

——*al-Bināya: sharḥ al-Hidāya*, ed. Ayman Ṣāliḥ Shaʿbān. Beirut: Manshūrāt Muḥammad ʿAlī Bayḍūn, 2000.

Ayoub, Mahmoud M. *The Crisis of Muslim History: Religion and Politics in Early Islam*. Oxford: Oneworld, 2003.

Azam, Hina. *Sexual Violence in Mālikī Legal Ideology: From Discursive Foundations to Classical Articulation*. PhD dissertation, Duke University, 2007.

Azami, M. Mustafa al-. *On Schacht's Origins of Muhammadan Jurisprudence*. Riyadh: King Saud University; New York: John Wiley & Sons, Inc., 1985.

Bahrāmī, Muḥammad. "Barrasī va taḥlīl-i fiqhī va ḥuqūqī-i qāʿidah-i '*Tudraʾ al-ḥudūd biʾl-shubahāt*.'" *Dīdgāhhā-yi ḥuqūqī* 5–6 (1376/1997–8): 19–56.

Baḥrānī (d. 1186 /1772) = Yūsuf b. Aḥmad al-. *al-Ḥadāʾiq al-nādira fī aḥkām al-ʿitra al-ṭāhira*. Najaf: Dār al-Kutub al-ʿIlmiyya, 1377–/1957–.

——*al-Durar al-Najafiyya min al-multaqaṭāt al-Yūsufiyya*. Beirut: Sharikat Dār al-Muṣṭafā li-Iḥyāʾ al-Turāth, 2002.

Baḥr al-ʿUlūm, Muḥammad Taqī Āl. *Risāla fī ʾl-farq bayna ʾl-ḥaqq waʾl-ḥukm*. Published in his *Bulghat al-faqīh*. Tehran?: n.p., 1329/1911–2.

Bā Ḥusayn, Yaʿqūb b. ʿAbd al-Wahhāb al-. *al-Qawāʿid al-fiqhiyya: al-mabādiʾ, al-muqawwimāt, al-maṣādir al-dalīliyya, al-taṭawwur – dirāsa naẓariyya taḥlīliyya taʾṣīliyya taʾrīkhiyya*. Riyadh: Maktabat al-Rushd, 1998.

Bājī (d. 474/1081) = Abū al-Walīd Sulaymān b. Khalaf b. Saʿd al-. *al-Muntaqā: sharḥ Muwaṭṭaʾ Mālik*, ed. Muḥammad ʿAbd al-Qādir Aḥmad ʿAṭāʾ. Beirut: Dār al-Kutub al-ʿIlmiyya, 1999.

Bājūrī (d. 1277/1860) = Ibrāhīm b. Muḥammad al-. *Ḥāshiyat Fatḥ al-qarīb*. Beirut: Dār al-Maʿārif, 1974.

Baker, John Hamilton. *An Introduction to English Legal History*. 4th ed. London: Butterworths, 2002. [Orig. 1971.]

Bâli, Aslı. "The Perils of Judicial Independence: Constitutional Transition and the Turkish Example." *Virginia Journal of International Law* 52 (2012): 235–320.

Bālṭayyib, Ṭāwūs Ḥājjī, ed. *Alf layla wa-layla*. Tunis: Wizārat Shuʾūn al-Marʾa waʾl-Usra, n.d.

Balūshī, ʿAbd al-Ghafūr b. ʿAbd al-Ḥaqq al-. *al-Imām Isḥāq b. Rāhawayh wa-kitābuh al-Musnad*. Medina: Maktabat al-Īmān, 1990.

Bassiouni, M. Cherif, ed. *The Islamic Criminal Justice System*. London: Oceana, 1982.

——"Crimes and the Criminal Process." *Arab Law Quarterly* 12 (1997): 269–86.

Bauer, Thomas. *Die Kultur der Ambiguität: Eine andere Geschichte des Islams*. Berlin: Verlag der Weltreligionen, 2011.

Bayhaqī (d. 458/1066) = Abū Bakr Aḥmad b. al-Ḥusayn b. ʿAlī al-. *al-Sunan al-kubrā*, ed. Muḥammad ʿAbd al-Qādir ʿAṭāʾ. Beirut: Dār al-Kutub al-ʿIlmiyya, 1994.

Bearman, Peri, et al. "Ḥasab wa-nasab." In *EI*². Leiden: Brill, 1960–: 3:238–39.

——"Ḥuḳūḳ, pl. of ḥaḳḳ." In *EI*². Leiden: Brill, 1960–: 3:551.

Beattie, J.M. *Crime and the Courts in England, 1660–1800*. Princeton, NJ: Princeton University Press, 1986.

Behnām, Ramsīs. *al-Naẓariyya al-ʿāmma liʾl-qānūn al-jināʾī*. Alexandria: Munshaʾāt al-Maʿārif, 1968.

Bencherifa, M. "al-Bunnāhī lā al-Nubāhī." *Académia: Revue de l'Académie du Royaume du Maroc* 8 (1998): 71–89.

Bentham, Jeremy. *A Comment on the Commentaries: A Criticism of William Blackstone's Commentaries on the Laws of England*, ed. Charles Warren Everett. Oxford: Clarendon Press, 1928. [Orig. 1776.]

Berkey, Jonathan P. *The Formation of Islam: Religion and Society in the Near East, 600–1800*. Cambridge: Cambridge University Press, 2003.

Bernheimer, Teresa. *The ʿAlids: The First Family of Islam, 750–1200*. Edinburgh: Edinburgh University Press, 2013.

Bihbahānī, al-Waḥīd al- (d. 1206/1791–2) = Muḥammad Bāqir b. Muḥammad. *al-Fawāʾid al-Ḥāʾiriyya*. Qum: Majmaʿ al-Fikr al-Islāmī, 1995.

——*Risālat aṣālat al-barāʾa*. In *al-Rasāʾil al-uṣūliyya*. Qum: Muʾassasat al-ʿAllāma al-Mujaddid al-Waḥīd al-Bihbahānī, 1416/1996.

Biqāʿī, Yūsuf, ed. *Muʿjam aḥādīth ḍuʿafāʾ al-rijāl min Kitāb al-Kāmil*. Beirut: Dār al-Fikr, 1988.

Blackstone, William. *Commentaries on the Laws of England*. Oxford: Clarendon Press, 1765–69.

Bosworth, Clifford E. "Siyāsa." In *EI*². Leiden: Brill, 1960–: 9:693–94.

——*The New Islamic Dynasties*. 2nd ed. New York: Columbia University Press, 2004.

Bosworth, Clifford E., and J. Burton-Page. "Naḳīb." In *EI*². Leiden: Brill, 1960–: 7:926.

Brockelmann, Carl. *Geschichte der arabischen Litteratur*. Leiden: Brill, 1996–.

Brockopp, Jonathan. *Early Mālikī Law: Ibn ʿAbd al-Ḥakam and His Major Compendium of Jurisprudence*. Leiden: Brill, 2000.

Brown, Jonathan A.C. *The Canonization of al-Bukhārī and Muslim: The Formation and Function of the Sunnī Ḥadīth Canon*. Leiden: Brill, 2007.

——"Critical Rigor vs. Juridical Pragmatism: How Legal Theorists and *Ḥadīth* Scholars Approached the Backgrowth of *Isnād*s in the Genre of *ʿIlal al-ḥadīth*." *Islamic Law and Society* 14, 1 (2008): 1–41.

Brown, Nathan. *When Victory Is Not an Option: Islamist Movements in Arab Politics*. Ithaca, NY: Cornell University Press, 2012.

——"Egypt: A Constitutional Court in an Unconstitutional Setting." Unpublished paper presented at New York University Law School Constitutional Transitions Colloquium, Oct. 23, 2013.

——*Arab Constitutions in the 21st Century: A New Beginning or an Unhappy Ending?* New Haven, CT: Yale Law School Dallah Albaraka Lectures on Islamic Law and Civilization, 2014.

Brown, Nathan J., and Clark B. Lombardi. "Translation: The Supreme Constitutional Court of Egypt on Islamic Law, Veiling and Civil Rights: An Annotated Translation of Supreme Constitutional Court of Egypt Case No. 8 of Judicial Year 17 (May 18, 1996)." *American University International Law Review* 23 (2006): 379–460.

Brown, Peter. "The Saint as Exemplar in Late Antiquity." *Representations* 2 (1983): 1–25.

Brudney, James J., and Corey Ditslear. "Canons of Construction and the Elusive Quest for Neutral Reasoning." *Vanderbilt Law Review* 58 (2005): 1–120.

Buhūtī (d. 1051/1641) = Manṣūr b. Yūnus al-. *Kashshāf al-qināʿ ʿan matn al-Iqnāʿ*, ed. Hilāl Muṣayliḥī Muṣṭafā Hilāl. Riyadh: Maktabat al-Naṣr al-Ḥadītha, 196-?.

Bujnūrdī, Ḥasan. *al-Qawāʿid al-fiqhiyya*, ed. Mahdī al-Mihrīzī and Muḥammad Ḥusayn al-Dirāyatī. Qum: Hādī, 1419/1998.

Bujnūrdī, [Muḥammad] Mūsawī. "Dū qāʿidah-i fiqhī: Qāʿidah-i '*Tudraʾ al-ḥudūd biʾl-shubahāt*.'" *Faṣlnāmah-i dīdgāhhā-yi ḥuqūqī* 8 (1365/1986–7): 11–36.

Bukhārī (d. 256/870) = Muḥammad b. Ismāʿīl al-. *al-Adab al-mufrad*, ed. Muḥammad Fuʾād ʿAbd al-Bāqī. Beirut: Dār al-Bashāʾir, 1409/1989.

——*Ṣaḥīḥ*, ed. Ṭāhā ʿAbd al-Raʾūf Saʿd, Muṣṭafā Muḥammad al-Hawārī, and Muḥammad ʿAbd al-Muʿṭī. Cairo: Maktabat al-Kulliyyāt al-Azhariyya, 1994.

Burūjirdī, Ḥusayn al-Ṭabāṭabāʾī al-. *Jāmiʿ aḥādīth al-Shīʿa*. Qum: Maṭbaʿat Mihr, 1992.

Calder, Norman. *Studies in Early Muslim Jurisprudence*. Oxford: Clarendon Press, 1993.

Carmona, Alfonso. "Al-Nubāhī (or more probably, al-Bunnāhī)." In *EI*[2] Supplement. Leiden: Brill, 1960–: 7:679.

——"The Introduction of Mālik's Teachings in Al-Andalus." In *The Islamic School of Law: Evolution, Devolution, and Progress*, ed. Peri Bearman, Rudolph Peters, and Frank Vogel. Cambridge, MA: Islamic Legal Studies Program at Harvard Law School, 2005: 41–56.

Chokr, Melhem. *Zandaqa et zindiqs en Islam au second siècle de l'hégire.* Damascus: Institut français de Damas, 1993.

Cohen, Mark. "The Trias of Maimonides." In *Studia Judaica: Forschungen zur Wissenschaft des Judentums*, ed. Georges Tamer. Berlin: Walter de Gruyter, 2005: 65–81.

Cook, Michael A. *Commanding Right and Forbidding Wrong in Islamic Thought.* Cambridge: Cambridge University Press, 2000.

Coulson, Noel. *A History of Islamic Law.* Edinburgh: Edinburgh University Press, 1964.

Crone, Patricia. *Slaves on Horses: The Evolution of the Islamic Polity.* Cambridge: Cambridge University Press, 1980.

——*Meccan Trade and the Rise of Islam.* Princeton, NJ: Princeton University Press, 1987.

——*Roman, Provincial and Islamic Law: The Origins of the Islamic Patronate.* Cambridge: Cambridge University Press, 2002.

Crone, Patricia, and Martin Hinds. *God's Caliph: Religious Authority in the First Centuries of Islam.* Cambridge: Cambridge University Press, 1986.

Dabūsī (d. 430/1039) = Abū Zayd ʿUbayd Allāh b. ʿUmar al-. *Taʾsīs al-naẓar*, ed. Muṣṭafā Muḥammad al-Qabbānī al-Dimashqī. Beirut: Dār Ibn Zaydūn; Cairo: Maktabat al-Kulliyyāt al-Azhariyya, n.d. Also edited by Zakariyyā ʿAlī Yūsuf. Cairo: Maṭbaʿ al-Imām, 1972?.

——*Kitāb al-Asrār.* In *Debbusi'nin "El-Esrar fi'l-Usul ve'l-furuʿ" Adlı Eserinin Tahkik ve Tahlili*, ed. Salim Özer. PhD dissertation, Erciyes Üniversitesi [in Kayseri, Turkey], 1997: 151–1945.

Dāmād, Muṣṭafā Muḥaqqiq. "The Codification of Islamic Juridical Principles." *Ḥikmat* 1, 1 (1995): 89–107.

——*Qavāʿid-i fiqh.* Tehran: Markaz-i ʿUlūm-i Islāmī, 1378–/1999–.

Dāraquṭnī (d. 385/995) = ʿAlī b. ʿUmar al-. *Sunan*, ed. Shuʿayb al-Arnaʾūṭ, Ḥasan ʿAbd al-Munʿim Shalabī, and Haytham ʿAbd al-Ghafūr. Beirut: Muʾassasat al-Risāla, 2004.

Dārimī (d. 255/869) = Abū Muḥammad ʿAbd Allāh b. ʿAbd al-Raḥmān al-. *Sunan*, ed. ʿAbd Allāh Hāshim Yamānī al-Madanī. Cairo: Dār al-Maḥāsin li'l-Ṭibāʿa, 1966.

Dasūqī (d. 1230/1815) = Shams al-Dīn Muḥammad b. Aḥmad al-. *Ḥāshiya* [*t al-Dasūqī ʿalā ʾl-Sharḥ al-kabīr*]. Cairo: Dār Iḥyāʾ al-Kutub al-ʿArabiyya, 198-?.

Dāwūd al-Ẓāhirī (d. 270/883–4) = Dāwūd b. ʿAlī b. Khalaf al-Iṣbahānī. *ʿUyūn al-masāʾil.* In *Risāla fī ʾl-madhhab al-Imām Dāwūd al-Ẓāhirī* (in *Majmūʿ yashtamilu ʿalā risālatayn*), ed. Muḥammad al-Shaṭṭī. Damascus: Maṭbaʿat Rawḍat al-Shām, 1330/1911–2).

Ḍayf Allāh, Muḥammad Ḥasan. *Fayḍ al-qadīr li-tartīb wa-sharḥ al-Jāmiʿ al-ṣaghīr.* Cairo: Maktaba wa-Maṭbaʿat Muṣṭafā al-Bābī al-Ḥalabī, 1964.

Demko, Daniela. "*In dubio pro reo* – im Zweifel für den Angeklagten." In *Zweifelsfälle*, ed. Christine Abbt and Oliver Diggelmann. Bern: Stämpfli, 2007: 15–70.

Dhahabī (d. 748/1348) = Shams al-Dīn Muḥammad b. Aḥmad b. ʿUthmān al-. *Siyar aʿlām al-nubalāʾ*, ed. Ḥusayn al-Asad and Shuʿayb al-Arnaʾūṭ. Beirut: Muʾassasat al-Risāla, 1981.

——*Tadhkirat al-ḥuffāẓ*, ed. Zakariyyā ʿUmayrāt. Beirut: Dār al-Kutub al-ʿIlmiyya; Muḥammad ʿAlī Bayḍūn, 1998.

Dizfūlī, al-Qāḍī al- (d. thirteenth/nineteenth century) = Muḥammad b. Faraj Allāh. *Fārūq al-ḥaqq fī ʾl-farq bayna ʾl-Uṣūliyyīn waʾl-Akhbāriyyīn*. On the margins of Jaʿfar b. Khaḍir al-Najafī Āl Kāshif al-Ghiṭāʾ (d. 1228/1813), *al-Ḥaqq al-mubīn*. Tehran: n.p., 1319/1901.

Donahue, Charles, Jr. "Proof by Witnesses in the Church Courts of Medieval England: An Imperfect Reception of the Learned Law." In *On the Laws and Customs of England: Essays in Honor of Samuel E. Thorne*, ed. Morris S. Arnold, Thomas A. Green, Sally A. Scully, and Stephen D. White. Chapel Hill: University of North Carolina Press, 1981: 127–58.

Donner, Fred M. *Early Islamic Conquests*. Princeton, NJ: Princeton University Press, 1981.

——*Narratives of Islamic Origins: The Beginnings of Islamic Historical Writing*. Princeton, NJ: Darwin Press, 1998.

Dutton, Yasin. "*ʿAmal* v. *Ḥadīth* in Islamic Law: The Case of *Sadl al-Yadayn* (Holding One's Hands by One's Sides) When Doing the Prayer." *Islamic Law and Society* 3, 1 (1996): 13–40.

——*Original Islam: Malik and the Madhhab of Madina*. London: Routledge, 2007.

Dressler, Joshua. *Understanding Criminal Law*. 6th ed. Danvers, MA: LexisNexis, 2012.

Dworkin, Ronald. *Law's Empire*. Cambridge, MA: Belknap Press of Harvard University Press, 1986.

Easterbrook, Frank. "Statutes' Domains." *University of Chicago Law Review* 50 (1983): 533–52.

Elhauge, Einer. *Statutory Default Rules: How to Interpret Unclear Legislation*. Cambridge, MA: Harvard University Press, 2008.

El-Hibri, Tayeb. *Reinterpreting Islamic Historiography: Hārūn Al-Rashīd and the Narrative of the ʿAbbāsid Caliphate*. Cambridge: Cambridge University Press, 1999.

Emon, Anver. "*Ḥuqūq Allāh* and *Ḥuqūq al-ʿIbād*: A Legal Heuristic for a Natural Rights Regime." *Islamic Law and Society* 13, 3 (2006): 325–91.

Escovitz, J.H. "The Establishment of Four Chief Judgeships in the Mamlūk Empire." *Journal of the American Oriental Society* 102, 3 (1982): 529–31.

Eskridge, William N., Jr. *Dynamic Statutory Interpretation*. Cambridge, MA: Harvard University Press, 1994.

——"Fetch Some Soupmeat." *Cardozo Law Review* 16 (1995): 2209–24.

——"All about Words: Early Understandings of 'Judicial Power' in Statutory Interpretation, 1776–1806." *Columbia Law Review* 101 (2001): 990–1106.

——"No Frills Textualism." *Harvard Law Review* 119 (2005–2006): 2014–76.

Eskridge, William N., Jr., and John Ferejohn. "Super-Statutes." *Duke Law Journal* 50 (2001): 1215–76.

——*A Republic of Statutes: The New American Constitution*. New Haven, CT: Yale University Press, 2010.

Eskridge, William N., Jr., and Philip P. Frickey. "Statutory Interpretation as Practical Reasoning." *Stanford Law Review* 42 (1990): 321–84.

——"Quasi-Constitutional Law: Clear Statement Rules as Constitutional Law Making." *Vanderbilt Law Review* 45 (1992): 593–646.

Eskridge, William N., Jr., Philip Frickey, and Elizabeth Garrett. *Legislation: Statutes and the Creation of Public Policy*. 4th ed. St. Paul, MN: West, 2006.

van Ess, Josef. *Theologie und Gesellschaft im 2. und 3. Jahrhundert Hidschra: Eine Geschichte des religiösen Denkens im frühen Islam*. Berlin: Walter de Gruyter, 1991–97.

——*The Flowering of Muslim Theology*, trans. Jane Marie Todd. Cambridge, MA: Harvard University Press, 2006.

Estrich, Susan. *Real Rape: How the Legal System Victimizes Women Who Say No*. Cambridge, MA: Harvard University Press, 1987.

Fadel, Mohammad. *Adjudication in the Mālikī Madhhab: A Study of Legal Process in Medieval Islamic Law*. PhD dissertation, University of Chicago, 1995.

——"The Social Logic of *Taqlīd* and the Rise of the *Mukhtaṣar*." *Islamic Law and Society* 3, 2 (1996): 195–233.

——"Two Women, One Man: Knowledge, Power and Gender in Medieval Sunni Legal Thought." *International Journal of Middle East Studies* 29 (1997): 185–204.

——"Public Authority (*Sulṭān*) in Islamic Law." In *Oxford International Encyclopedia of Legal History*, ed. Stanley N. Katz (Baber Johansen, Islamic Law editor). Oxford: Oxford University Press, 2009: 5:3–6.

al-Fāḍil al-Lankarānī, Muḥammad. *al-Qawāʿid al-fiqhiyya*. Qum: Mihr, 1416/1995.

Fähndrich, H. "Al-Tanūkhī." In *EI*[2]. Leiden: Brill, 1960–: 10:192.

Fallon, Richard H., Jr. "Legitimacy and the Constitution." *Harvard Law Review* 118 (2005): 1787–852.

Feldman, Noah. *Fall and Rise of the Islamic State*. Princeton, NJ: Princeton University Press, 2008.

Fernández Félix, Ana. *Cuestiones legales del islam temprano: La ʿUtbiyya y el proceso de formación de la sociedad islámica andalusí*. Madrid: Consejo Superior de Investigaciones Científicas, 2003.

Fierro, Maribel. *La Heterodoxia en al-Andalus durante el periodo Omeya*. Madrid: Instituto Hispano-Arabe de Cultura, 1987.

——"Proto-Malikis, Malikis, and Reformed Malikis in al-Andalus." In *The Islamic School of Law: Evolution, Devolution, and Progress*, ed. Peri Bearman,

Rudolph Peters, and Frank Vogel. Cambridge, MA: Islamic Legal Studies Program at Harvard Law School, 2005: 57–76.

——"Idra'ū l-ḥudūd bi-l-shubuhāt: When Lawful Violence Meets Doubt." *Hawwa* 5, 2–3 (2007): 208–38.

Friedman, Lawrence. *A History of American Law*. 3rd ed. New York: Simon and Schuster, 2005.

Friendly, Henry J. "Mr. Justice Frankfurter and the Reading of Statutes." Reprinted in Henry J. Friendly, *Benchmarks*. Chicago: University of Chicago Press, 1967: 196–234.

Frijda, Nico H. "Lex Talionis: On Vengeance." In *Emotions: Essays in Emotion Theory*, ed. Stephanie H. M. van Goozen, Nanne van de Poll, and Joseph A. Sergeant. Oxford: Psychology Press, 1994: 263–89.

Fyzee, Asaf A. A. "The Creed of Ibn Bābawayhi." *Journal of Bombay University* 12 (1943): 70–86.

——"Ibn Bābawayh, Abū Dja'far Muḥammad b. Abu 'l Ḥasan 'Alī b. Ḥusayn b. Mūsā al-Ḳummī." In *EI*². Leiden: Brill, 1960–: 3:726–27.

Gabel, Leona Christine. *Benefit of Clergy in England in the Later Middle Ages*. New York: Octagon Books, 1969. [Orig. 1929.]

García Gómez, E. "Sobre la diferencia en el castigo de plebeyos y nobles." *Al-Andalus* 36 (1971): 71–79.

Gerhardt, Michael J. "A Tale of Two Textualists." *Boston University Law Review* 74 (1994): 25–66.

——"Super Precedent." *Minnesota Law Review* 90 (2006): 1294–331.

——*The Power of Precedent*. New York: Oxford University Press, 2008.

Ghaffār, 'Abd al-Ḥasan al-. *al-Kulaynī wa'l-Kāfī*. Qum: Mu'assasat al-Nashr al-Islāmī al-Tābi'a li-Jamā'at al-Mudarrisīn, 1416/1995–6.

Ghamrāwī, Muḥammad al-Zuhrī al-. *Anwār al-masālik: sharḥ 'Umdat al-sālik*, ed. Yūsuf 'Alī Badīwī. Damascus: Dār al-Ṭabbā', 1996.

Gharāwī, Muḥammad 'Abd al-Ḥasan Muḥsin al-. *Maṣādir al-istinbāṭ bayna 'l-Uṣūliyyīn wa'l-Akhbāriyyīn*. Qum: Markaz al-Nashr; Maktab al-I'lām al-Islāmī, 1413/1992–3.

Ghazālī (d. 505/1111) = Abū Ḥamīd al-. *al-Mustaṣfā min 'ilm al-uṣūl*, ed. Ibrāhīm Muḥammad Ramaḍān. Beirut: Dār al-Arqam, 1997.

——*al-Wajīz fī fiqh al-Imām al-Shāfi'ī*, ed. 'Alī Mu'awwaḍ and 'Ādil 'Abd al-Mawjūd. Beirut: Dār al-Arqam, 1997.

——*al-Wasīṭ fī 'l-madhhab*, ed. Aḥmad Maḥmūd Ibrāhīm and Muḥammad Muḥammad Tāmir. Cairo?: Dār al-Salām, 1997.

Ghurayfī al-Baḥrānī, Aḥmad al-. *Aṣālat al-barā'a fī 'l-sharī'a al-Islāmiyya*. Qum: Dār Ḥifẓ al-Turāth al-Baḥrānī, 1427/2006–7.

Gibb, Hamilton A. R. "Some Considerations on the Sunnī Theory of the Caliphate." In *Studies on the Civilization of Islam*, ed. Stanford J. Shaw and

William R. Polk. London: Routledge, 2013: 141–50. [Orig. Boston: Beacon Press, 1962.]

——"Al-Māwardī's Theory of the Caliphate." In *Studies on the Civilization of Islam*, ed. Stanford J. Shaw and William R. Polk. London: Routledge, 2013: 151–65. [Orig. Boston: Beacon Press, 1962.]

Gīlānī, Muḥammad Muḥammadī. "Āshināʾī bā qāʿidah-i *'al-Ḥudūd tudraʾ biʾl-shubahāt.'" Majallah-i qaḍāʾī va ḥuqūqī-i dādgustarī-i Jumhūrī-i Islāmī-i Īrān* 5, 15–16 (1375/1996–7): 25–30.

Gimaret, Daniel. "Muʿtazila." In *EI*². Leiden: Brill, 1960–: 7:783–93.

——"Les *Uṣūl al-ḫamsa* du Qāḍī ʿAbd al-Gabbār et leurs commentaires." *Annales Islamologiques* 15 (1979): 47–96.

Gleave, Robert. *Scripturalist Islam: The History and Doctrines of the Akhbārī Shīʿī School*. Leiden: Brill, 2007.

——*Islam and Literalism: Literal Meaning and Interpretation in Islamic Legal Theory*. Edinburgh: Edinburgh University Press, 2012.

Goldsmith, Jack, and Daryl Levinson. "Law for States: International Law, Constitutional Law, Public Law." *Harvard Law Review* 122 (2009): 1791–868.

Goldziher, Ignaz. *The Ẓāhirīs: Their Doctrine and Their History; A Contribution to the History of Islamic Theology*, trans. Wolfgang Behn. Leiden: Brill, 1971. [Orig. Ignác Goldziher, *Die Ẓāhiriten: Ihr Lehrsystem und ihre Geschichte; Ein Beitrag zur Geschichte der muhammedanischen Theologie*. Leipzig: O. Schulze, 1884.]

——"Sâlih b. ʿAbd al-Kuddus und das Zindîkthum während der Regierung des Chalifen al-Mahdî." In *Transactions of the Ninth International Congress of Orientalists* (London, September 1892), ed. E. Delmar Morgan. London: printed for the Committee of Congress, 1893: 104–29.

——*Muslim Studies*, ed. and trans. S.M. Stern and C.R. Barber. Chicago: Aldine Atherton, 1971.

Haider, Najam. *The Origins of the Shīʿa: Identity, Ritual, and Sacred Space in Eighth-Century Kūfa*. Cambridge: Cambridge University Press, 2011.

Hairi, Abdul-Hadi. "Anṣārī, Shaykh Murtaḍā." In *EI*². Leiden: Brill, 1960–: 12:75.

Ḥājjī Khalīfa, Kâtip Çelebi (d. 1067/1657) = Muṣṭafā b. ʿAbd Allāh. *Kashf al-ẓunūn ʿan asāmī ʾl-kutub waʾl-funūn*, ed. Muḥammad Sharaf al-Dīn Yāltaqāyā and Rifʿat Bīlga al-Kilīsī. 3rd ed. Tehran: al-Maktaba al-Islāmiyya waʾl-Maktaba al-Jaʿfarī, 1967.

al-Ḥākim al-Naysābūrī (d. 405/1015–6) = Muḥammad b. ʿAbd Allāh. *al-Mustadrak ʿalā ʾl-Ṣaḥīḥayn*. Cairo: Dār al-Ḥaramayn, 1997.

Ḥalabī, Abū al-Ṣalāḥ (d. 447/1055) = Taqī al-Dīn b. Najm al-Dīn al-. *al-Kāfī fī ʾl-fiqh*, ed. Riḍā Ustādī. Iṣfahān: Maktabat al-Imām Amīr al-Muʾminīn ʿAlī al-ʿĀmma, 1980.

Hall, Jerome. *Theft, Law, and Society*. Boston, MA: Little, Brown, 1935.

Hall, Livingston. "Strict of Liberal Construction of Penal Statutes." *Harvard Law Review* 48 (1935): 748–74.

Hallaq, Wael. "Was the Gate of *Ijtihād* Closed?" *International Journal of Middle East Studies* 16, 1 (1984): 3–41.

—"On the Origins of the Controversy about the Existence of Mujtahids and the Gate of *Ijtihād*." *Studia Islamica* 63 (1986): 129–41.

—"Was al-Shāfiʿī the Master Architect of Islamic Jurisprudence?" *International Journal of Middle East Studies* 25, 4 (1993): 587–605.

—*A History of Islamic Legal Theories: An Introduction to Sunnī Uṣūl al-Fiqh*. Cambridge: Cambridge University Press, 1997.

—*Authority, Continuity, and Change in Islamic Law*. Cambridge: Cambridge University Press, 2001.

—*The Origins and Evolution of Islamic Law*. Cambridge: Cambridge University Press, 2005.

—"Can the Sharīʿa be Restored?" In *Islamic Law and the Challenges of Modernity*, ed. Yvonne Yazbeck Haddad and Barbara Freyer Stowasser. Walnut Creek, CA: AltaMira Press, 2004: 21–53.

—*Sharīʿa: Theory, Practice, Transformations*. Cambridge: Cambridge University Press, 2009.

—*The Impossible State: Islam, Politics, and Modernity's Moral Predicament*. New York: Columbia University Press, 2012.

Handler, Andrew. *The Zīrids of Granada*. Coral Gables, FL: University of Miami Press, 1974.

Ḥārithī (d. after second/eighth century) = Abū Muḥammad ʿAbd Allāh b. Muḥammad b. Yaʿqūb. *Musnad Abī Ḥanīfa*, ed. Abū Muḥammad al-Asyūṭī. Beirut: Dār al-Kutub al-ʿIlmiyya, 2008.

Harmūsh, Maḥmūd Muṣṭafā ʿAbbūd Āl. *Muʿjam al-qawāʿid al-fiqhiyya al-Ibāḍiyya*. Oman: Wizārat al-Awqāf wa'l-Shu'ūn al-Dīniyya, 2010?.

Hart, Henry M., Jr., and Albert M. Sacks. *The Legal Process*. 10th ed., ed. William N. Eskridge Jr. and Philip P. Frickey. Eagan, MN: Foundation Press, 1994. [Orig. 1958.]

Hart, H. L. A. *The Concept of Law*. 2nd ed. Oxford: Oxford University Press, 1994. [Orig. 1961.]

Hāshimī, Sayyid Muḥammad Amīn. "Taʿzīr dūn al-ḥadd." *Fiqh-i Ahl-i Bayt* 57 (2010): 178–228.

Ḥaskafī (d. 1088/1677) = ʿAlāʾ al-Dīn Muḥammad b. ʿAlī b. Muḥammad al-Dimashqī al-. *al-Durr al-mukhtār*. N.p., n.d.

Haykel, Bernard. *Revival and Reform in Islam: The Legacy of Muḥammad Al-Shawkānī*. Cambridge: Cambridge University Press, 2003.

Haythamī (d. 807/1405) = ʿAlī b. Abī Bakr al-. *Majmaʿ al-zawāʾid*. Cairo: Dār al-Rayyān li'l-Turāth; Beirut: Dār al-Kutub al-ʿIlmiyya, 1407/1986–7.

——*Mawārid al-ẓam'ān*, ed. Muḥammad 'Abd al-Razzāq Ḥamza. Beirut: Dār al-Kutub al-'Ilmiyya, n.d.

Heine, P. "Nabīdh." In *EI²*. Leiden: Brill, 1960–: 7:840.

Heinrichs, Wolfhart. "*Qawā'id* as a Genre of Legal Literature." In *Studies in Islamic Legal Theory*, ed. Bernard Weiss. Leiden: Brill, 2002: 365–84.

——"Ḳawā'id Fiḳhiyya." *EI²* Supplement. Online edition: Brill, 2008–.

Ḥillī (d. 698/1298–9) = Yaḥyā b. al-Ḥasan b. Sa'īd al-. *Nuzhat al-nāẓir fī 'l-jam' bayna 'l-ashbāh wa'l-naẓā'ir*. In *YF*, ed. 'Alī Aṣghar Murwārīd. Beirut: Mu'assasat Fiqh al-Shī'a, 1990. Volume 40.

Hinds, Martin. "Makhzūm, Banū." In *EI²*. Leiden: Brill, 1960–: 6:137–40.

——"Kufan Political Alignments and Their Background in the Mid-Seventh Century A.D." *International Journal of Middle East Studies* 2, 4 (1971): 346–67.

——"The Murder of the Caliph 'Uthmān." In *Studies in Early Islamic History*, ed. Jere Bacharach, Lawrence Conrad, and Patricia Crone. Princeton, NJ: Darwin Press, 1996: 29–55.

Hodgson, Marshall. *The Venture of Islam*. Rev. ed. Chicago: University of Chicago Press, 1974. [Orig. 1961.]

Hoexter, M. "*Ḥuqūq Allāh* and *Ḥuqūq al-'Ibād* as Reflected in the *Waqf* Institution." *Jerusalem Studies in Arabic and Islam* 19 (1995): 133–56.

Hoexter, Miriam, Shmuel N. Eisenstadt, and Nehemia, Levtzion, eds. *The Public Sphere in Muslim Societies*. Albany, NY: State University of New York Press, 2002.

Hoover, Jon. *Ibn Taymiyya's Theodicy of Perpetual Optimism*. Leiden: Brill, 2007.

Hourani, Albert. "From Jabal 'Āmil to Persia." *Bulletin of the School of Oriental and African Studies* 49, 1 (1986): 133–40.

Hoyland, Robert. *Seeing Islam as the Others Saw It: A Survey and Evaluation of Christian, Jewish, and Zoroastrian Writings on Early Islam*. Princeton, NJ: Darwin Press, 1997.

Humphreys, Stephen. *Islamic History: A Framework for Inquiry*. Rev. ed. Princeton, NJ: Princeton University Press, 1991. [Orig. 1983.]

al-Ḥurr al-'Āmilī (d. 1104/1692) = Muḥammad b. al-Ḥasan. *al-Fawā'id al-Ṭūsiyya*, ed. Mahdī al-Lājwardī al-Ḥusaynī and Muḥammad Darūdī. Qum: al-Maṭba'a al-'Ilmiyya, 1403/1983.

——*Wasā'il al-Shī'a*, ed. 'Abd al-Raḥīm al-Rabbānī al-Shīrāzī. Tehran: al-Maktaba al-Islāmiyya, 1383–89/1963–69). Also 1988–89 edition: Edited by Mu'assasat Āl al-Bayt li-Iḥyā' al-Turāth. Qum: Mu'assasat Āl al-Bayt li-Iḥyā' al-Turāth, 1409/1988–9.

——*al-Fuṣūl al-muhimma fī uṣūl al-a'imma*. Qum: Maktabat Baṣīratī, 198-.

Hurvitz, Nimrod. *Competing Texts: The Relationship between Al-Mawardi's and Abu Ya'la's "al-Ahkam al-sultaniyya."* Occasional Publications. Cambridge, MA: Islamic Legal Studies Program at Harvard Law School, 2007.

Ḥusayn, ʿAqīla. *al-Shubahāt al-musqiṭa liʾl-ḥudūd aw al-ẓurūf al-mukhaffifa waʾl-aʿdhār al-musqiṭa liʾl-ʿuqūbāt al-mutarattaba ʿalā jarāʾim al-ḥudūd: Dirāsa fiqhiyya muqārana ʿalā ʾl-madhāhib al-Sunniyya*. Beirut: Dār Ibn Ḥazm, 2003.

Ibn ʿAbd al-Barr (d. 463/1071) = Yūsuf b. ʿAbd Allāh. *al-Kāfī fī fiqh ahl al-Madīna al-Mālikī*. Beirut: Dār al-Kutub al-ʿIlmiyya, 2002?.

Ibn ʿAbd al-Salām (d. 660/1262) = ʿIzz al-Dīn ʿAbd al-ʿAzīz. *al-Qawāʿid al-kubrā* (also known as *Qawāʿid al-aḥkām fī iṣlāḥ* [or *maṣāliḥ*] *al-anām*). 2nd ed., ed. Nazīh Kamāl Ḥammād and ʿUthmān Jumuʿa Ḍumayriyya. Damascus: Dār al-Qalam, 2007.

Ibn Abī al-Dunyā (d. 281/894) = Abū Bakr ʿAbd Allāh b. Muḥammad b. ʿUbayd Ibn Abī al-Dunyā al-Qurashī al-Baghdādī. *Makārim al-akhlāq*, ed. Majdī al-Sayyid Ibrāhīm. Cairo: Maktabat al-Qurʾān, 1411/1990.

Ibn Abī Ḥātim (d. 327/939) = ʿAbd al-Raḥmān b. Muḥammad. *al-Jarḥ waʾl-taʿdīl*. Hyderabad: Maṭbaʿat Jamʿiyyat Dāʾirat al-Maʿārif al-ʿUthmāniyya, 1970.

Ibn Abī al-ʿIzz (d. 792/1390) = Ṣadr al-Dīn ʿAlī b. ʿAlī. *al-Tanbīh ʿalā mushkilāt al-Hidāya*. On the margins of Burhān al-Dīn al-Marghīnānī, *Hidāya*, ed. Anwar Ṣāliḥ Abū Zayd. Beirut: Dār al-Kutub al-ʿIlmiyya, 2007.

Ibn Abī al-Qāsim (d. 624/1226) = ʿAbd al-Raḥmān b. ʿUmar. *al-Wāḍiḥ fī sharḥ Mukhtaṣar al-Khiraqī*, ed. ʿAbd al-Malik b. ʿAbd Allāh b. Duhaysh. Beirut: Dār Khiḍr, 2000.

Ibn Abī Shayba (d. 235/849) = Abū Bakr ʿAbd Allāh b. Muḥammad. *Muṣannaf*, ed. Ḥamad b. ʿAbd Allāh al-Jumuʿa and Muḥammad b. Ibrāhīm al-Laḥīdān. Riyadh: Maktabat al-Rushd, 2004.

Ibn Abī Zayd al-Qayrawānī (d. 386/996) = Abū Muḥammad ʿAbd Allāh b. ʿAbd al-Raḥmān. *Risāla*. Rabat: Wizārat al-Awqāf waʾl-Shuʾūn al-Islāmiyya, 1415/1995.

——*al-Nawādir waʾl-ziyādāt*, ed. ʿAbd al-Fattāḥ Muḥammad al-Ḥilw. Beirut: Dār al-Gharb al-Islāmī, 1999.

Ibn ʿĀbidīn (d. 1252/1836) = Muḥammad Amīn b. ʿUmar. *Minḥat al-Khāliq ʿalā ʾl-Baḥr al-rāʾiq*. On the margins of Ibn Nujaym, *al-Baḥr al-rāʾiq*. Cairo: n.p., 1893?.

——*Nuzhat al-nawāẓir ʿalā ʾl-Ashbāh waʾl-naẓāʾir*. On the margins of Ibn Nujaym, *al-Ashbāh waʾl-naẓāʾir*, ed. Muḥammad Muṭīʿ al-Ḥāfiẓ. Damascus: Dār al-Fikr, 1983.

——*Radd al-muḥtār ʿalā ʾl-Durr al-mukhtār*, ed. ʿĀdil Aḥmad ʿAbd al-Mawjūd and ʿAlī Muḥammad Muʿawwaḍ. Beirut: Dār al-Kutub al-ʿIlmiyya, 1994–98.

Ibn ʿAdī (d. 365/976) = Abū Aḥmad ʿAbd Allāh Ibn ʿAdī al-Jurjānī. *al-Kāmil fī ḍuʿafāʾ al-rijāl*. Beirut: Dār al-Fikr, 1984. See also *Muʿjam aḥādīth ḍuʿafāʾ al-rijāl min Kitāb al-Kāmil* (organized alphabetically), ed. Yūsuf Biqāʿī. Beirut: Dār al-Fikr, 1988.

Ibn al-Ahdal al-Yamanī (d. 1035/1626) = Abū Bakr b. Abī al-Qāsim b. Aḥmad b. Muḥammad al-Ḥusaynī. *al-Farāʾid al-bahiyya*. Quoted in Abū al-Fayḍ

Muḥammad Yāsīn b. Muḥammad ʿĪsā al-Fādānī al-Makkī (d. 1334/1916–7), *al-Fawāʾid al-janiyya*, ed. Ramzī Saʿd al-Dīn Dimashqiyya. Beirut: Dār al-Bashāʾir, 1991.

Ibn al-ʿAlāʾ al-Anṣārī (d. 786/1384–5) = Ibn al-ʿAlāʾ al-Anṣārī al-Andarabtī al-Dihlawī al-Hindī. *al-Fatāwā al-Tātārkhāniyya*, ed. Sajjād Ḥusayn. Karachi: Idārat al-Qurʾān waʾl-ʿUlūm al-Islāmiyya, 1990–.

Ibn al-ʿArabī (d. 543/1148) = Abū Bakr Muḥammad b. ʿAbd Allāh. *Aḥkām al-Qurʾān*. Beirut: Dār al-Fikr, n.d.

Ibn ʿAsākir (d. 571/1176) = Abū al-Qāsim ʿAlī b. al-Ḥasan. *Taʾrīkh madīnat Dimashq*. Beirut: Dār al-Fikr, 1995.

Ibn Bābawayh, Ṣadūq (d. 381/991–2) = Muḥammad b. ʿAlī b. al-Ḥusayn al-Qummī. *al-Iʿtiqādāt fī dīn al-Imāmiyya*, ed. Ghulām Riḍā al-Māzandarānī. Qum: Ghulām Riḍā al-Māzandarānī, 1412/1992. English translation: *A Shīʾite Creed: A Translation of Risālatu ʾl-Iʿtiqādāt*, trans. Asaf A. A. Fyzee. London: Oxford University Press, 1942.

—*Kitāb al-Tawḥīd*, ed. Hāshim al-Ḥusaynī. Tehran: Maktabat al-Ṣadūq, 1387/1967.

—*Hidāya*. In *YF*, ed. ʿAlī Aṣghar Murwārīd. Beirut: Dār al-Turāth; al-Dār al-Islāmiyya, 1990. Volume 23.

—*Kitāb man lā yaḥḍuruh al-faqīh*, ed. ʿAlī Akbar al-Ghaffārī. Qum: Jamāʿat al-Mudarrisīn fī ʾl-Ḥawza al-ʿIlmiyya, 1994.

—*Muqniʿ*. Qum: Muʾassasat al-Imām al-Hādī, 1994.

Ibn Bakkār (d. 256/870) = Abū ʿAbd Allāh Zubayr. *Jamharat nasab Quraysh*, ed. Maḥmūd Muḥammad Shākir. Cairo: Maktabat Dār al-ʿUrūba, 1381/1962.

Ibn al-Bannāʾ (d. 471/1078–9) = Ḥasan b. Aḥmad. *Kitāb al-Muqniʿ fī sharḥ Mukhtaṣar al-Khiraqī*, ed. ʿAbd al-ʿAzīz b. Sulaymān b. Ibrāhīm al-Baʿīmī. Riyadh: Maktabat al-Rushd, 1993.

Ibn Dāwūd al-Ẓāhirī (d. 297/909) = Abū Bakr Muḥammad (attributed). *al-Wuṣūl ilā maʿrifat al-uṣūl*. Reproduced and translated in Devin Stewart, "Muḥammad b. Dāʾūd al-Ẓāhirī's Manual of Jurisprudence: *al-Wuṣūl ilā maʿrifat al-uṣūl*," in *Studies in Islamic Legal Theory*, ed. Bernard Weiss. Leiden: Brill, 2002: 99–160.

Ibn Farḥūn (d. 799/1396–7) = Abū Isḥāq Ibrāhīm b. ʿAlī b. Muḥammad al-Yaʿmurī. *Tabṣirat al-ḥukkām*, ed. Jamāl Marʿashlī. Beirut: Dār al-Kutub al-ʿIlmiyya, 2001.

Ibn Ḥajar al-ʿAsqalānī (d. 852/1449) = Aḥmad b. ʿAlī. *Fatḥ al-bārī: sharḥ Ṣaḥīḥ al-Bukhārī*, ed. Ṭāhā ʿAbd al-Raʾūf Saʿd, Muṣṭafā Muḥammad al-Hawārī, and Muḥammad ʿAbd al-Muṭīʿ. Cairo: Maktabat al-Kulliyyāt al-Azhariyya, 1994.

—*Tahdhīb al-Tahdhīb*, ed. Muṣṭafā ʿAbd al-Qādir ʿAṭāʾ. Beirut: Dār al-Kutub al-ʿIlmiyya, 1994.

Ibn Ḥajar al-Haytamī (d. 974/1567) = Aḥmad b. Muḥammad b. Muḥammad b. ʿAlī. *Tuḥfat al-muḥtāj bi-sharḥ al-Minhāj*, ed. ʿAbd Allāh Maḥmūd Muḥammad ʿUmar. Beirut: Dār al-Kutub al-ʿIlmiyya, 2001.

Ibn Ḥanbal (d. 241/855) = Aḥmad b. Ḥanbal. *Musnad*, ed. ʿAbd Allāh al-Darwīsh. Beirut: Dār al-Fikr, 1991.

Ibn Ḥazm (d. 456/1064) = ʿAlī b. Aḥmad. *Jamharat ansāb al-ʿArab*, ed. ʿAbd al-Salām Muḥammad Hārūn. Cairo: Dār al-Maʿārif, 1962.

——*al-Iḥkām fī uṣūl al-aḥkām*. Egypt: Dār al-Kutub al-ʿIlmiyya, 1968.

——*al-Muḥallā biʾl-āthār*, ed. ʿAbd al-Ghaffār Sulaymān al-Bandārī. Beirut: Dār al-Kutub al-ʿIlmiyya, 1988.

——*Nubdha*. In Adam Sabra, "Ibn Ḥazm's Literalism: A Critique of Islamic Legal Theory." *Al-Qanṭara: Revista de Estudios Árabes* 28, 1–2 (2007): 7–40, 307–48.

Ibn Ḥibbān (d. 354/965) = Abū Ḥātim Muḥammad b. Ḥibbān al-Bustī. *Ṣaḥīḥ*. Arranged by ʿAlāʾ al-Dīn ʿAlī b. Balabān al-Fārisī, ed. Shuʿayb al-Arnaʾūṭ and Ḥusayn Asad. Beirut: Muʾassasat al-Risāla, 1407/1987.

Ibn al-Humām (d. 861/1457) = Kamāl al-Dīn Muḥammad b. ʿAbd al-Wāḥid. *Fatḥ al-qadīr*, published together with his commentary, *Sharḥ Fatḥ al-qadīr liʾl-ʿājiz al-faqīr*. Beirut: Dār Ṣādir, 1972?.

Ibn Idrīs al-Ḥillī (d. 598/1202) = Abū Jaʿfar Muḥammad b. Manṣūr. *Kitāb al-Sarāʾir*. Qum: Muʾassasat al-Nashr al-Islāmī, 1410/1989–90.

Ibn al-Jawzī (d. 597/1200) = Abū al-Faraj ʿAbd al-Raḥmān b. ʿAlī. *Al-Ḍuʿafāʾ waʾl-matrūkīn*, ed. Abū al-Fidāʾ ʿAbd Allāh al-Qāḍī. Beirut: Dār al-Kutub al-ʿIlmiyya, 1986.

——*al-Muntaẓam fī tawārīkh al-mulūk waʾl-umam*, ed. Muḥammad ʿAbd al-Qādir ʿAṭāʾ and Muṣṭafā ʿAbd al-Qādir ʿAṭāʾ. Beirut: Dār al-Fikr, 1992.

Ibn Kathīr (d. 774/1373) = Ismāʿīl b. ʿUmar. *Tafsīr*. N.p.: Dār al-Fikr, 1401/1980–1.

Ibn Khallikān (d. 681/1282) = Aḥmad b. Muḥammad b. Ibrāhīm. *Wafāyāt al-aʿyān wa-anbāʾ abnāʾ al-zamān*. Beirut: Dār al-Thaqāfa, 1968. Also 1998 edition: Edited by Maryam Qāsim Ṭawīl and Yūsuf ʿAlī Ṭawīl. Beirut: Dār al-Kutub al-ʿIlmiyya, Muḥammad ʿAlī Bayḍūn, 1998.

Ibn al-Khaṭīb (d. 776/1374) = Muḥammad b. ʿAbd Allāh. *Kitāb aʿmāl al-aʿlām* [*fī man būyiʿa qabla ʾl-iḥtilām min mulūk al-Islām wa-mā yataʿallaq bi-dhālika min al-kalām*], ed. Évariste Lévi-Provençal. Rabat: al-Maṭbaʿa al-Jadīda, 1353/1934.

Ibn al-Laḥḥām (d. 803/1401–2) = ʿAlī b. ʿAbbās al-Baʿlī. *al-Qawāʿid waʾl-fawāʾid al-uṣūliyya*, ed. Muḥammad Ḥāmid al-Fiqī. Cairo: Maṭbaʿat al-Sunna al-Muḥammadiyya, 1956.

Ibn Mājah (d. 303/915) = Abū ʿAbd Allāh Muḥammad b. Yazīd al-Qazwīnī. *Sunan*, ed. Muḥammad Fuʾād ʿAbd al-Bāqī. Cairo: Dār Iḥyāʾ al-Kutub al-ʿArabiyya, 1952–53. Also 1998 edition: Edited by Maḥmūd Muḥammad Maḥmūd Ḥasan Naṣṣār. Beirut: Dār al-Kutub al-ʿIlmiyya, 1998.

Ibn al-Malāḥimī (d. 536/1141) = Rukn al-Dīn Maḥmūd b. Muḥammad. *al-Muʿtamad fī uṣūl al-dīn*, ed. Wilferd Madelung and Martin McDermott. London: al-Hoda, 1991.

Ibn Manẓūr (d. 711/1311) = Abū al-Faḍl Muḥammad b. Mukarram. *Lisān al-ʿArab*. Beirut: Dār Ṣādir, 1997.

Ibn al-Mibrad al-Ṣāliḥī (d. 909/1502) = Yūsuf b. Ḥasan b. Aḥmad b. ʿAbd al-Hādī. *al-Qawāʿid al-kulliyya waʾl-ḍawābiṭ al-fiqhiyya*, ed. Jāsim b. Sulaymān al-Fuhayd al-Dawsarī. Beirut: Dār al-Bashāʾir, 1415/1994.

Ibn Mufliḥ (d. 763/1361) = Shams al-Dīn Muḥammad. *Kitāb al-Furūʿ*, ed. ʿAbd Allāh b. ʿAbd al-Muḥsin al-Turkī. Beirut: Muʾassasat al-Risāla, 2003.

Ibn al-Mundhir (d. 319/930) = Abū Bakr Muḥammad b. Ibrāhīm. *al-Ijmāʿ*, ed. ʿAbd Allāh ʿUmar al-Bārūdī. Beirut: Dār al-Jinān, 1986.

Ibn al-Murtaḍā (d. 840/1437) = Aḥmad b. Yaḥyā al-Ḥusaynī al-Yamanī. *al-Baḥr al-zakhkhār al-jāmiʿ li-madhhab ʿulamāʾ al-amṣār*. 2nd ed. Beirut: Muʾassasat al-Risāla, 1975.

——*Kitāb al-Azhār fī fiqh al-aʾimmat al-aṭhār*. N.p.: n.p., 198-.

Ibn al-Naqīb, Ibn Luʾluʾ (d. 769/1367) = Aḥmad b. al-Naqīb al-Miṣrī. *ʿUmdat al-sālik wa-ʿuddat al-nāsik*. On the margins of Muḥammad al-Zuhrī al-Ghamrāwī, *Anwār al-masālik: sharḥ ʿUmdat al-sālik*, ed. Yūsuf ʿAlī Badīwī. Damascus: Dār al-Ṭabbāʿ, 1996.

Ibn Nujaym (d. 970/1563) = Zayn al-Dīn b. Ibrāhīm. *al-Ashbāh waʾl-naẓāʾir*, ed. Muḥammad Muṭīʿ al-Ḥāfiẓ. Damascus: Dār al-Fikr, 1983.

——*al-Baḥr al-rāʾiq: sharḥ Kanz al-daqāʾiq*. Cairo: n.p., 1983?.

Ibn Qayyim al-Jawziyya (d. 751/1350) = Shams al-Dīn Abū ʿAbd Allāh Muḥammad b. Abī Bakr. *Iʿlām al-muwaqqiʿīn ʿan Rabb al-ʿālamīn*, ed. ʿAbd al-Raḥmān al-Wakīl. Cairo: Dār al-Kutub al-Ḥadītha, 1969.

——*al-Ṭuruq al-ḥukmiyya fī ʾl-siyāsa al-sharʿiyya*, ed. Muḥammad Jamīl Ghāzī. Cairo: Maṭbaʿat al-Madanī, 1978. Also 2007 edition: Edited by Nāyif b. Aḥmad al-Ḥamad. Mecca: Dār ʿĀlam al-Fawāʾid, 1428/2007.

——*Jāmiʿ al-fiqh* (Collected works of Ibn al-Qayyim), ed. Yusrī al-Sayyid Muḥammad. Mansoura, Egypt: Dār al-Wafāʾ, 1428/2007.

Ibn Qudāma (d. 620/1223) = Muwaffaq al-Dīn ʿAbd Allāh. *al-Kāfī fī fiqh Ibn Ḥanbal*, ed. Zuhayr al-Shāwīsh. Beirut: al-Maktab al-Islāmī, 1979.

——*al-Mughnī ʿalā Mukhtaṣar Abī al-Qāsim al-Khiraqī*, ed. ʿAbd Allāh b. ʿAbd al-Muḥsin al-Turkī and ʿAbd al-Fattāḥ Muḥammad al-Ḥilw. Cairo: Hajar, 1986.

Ibn Qundus (d. ninth/fifteenth century) = Abū Bakr Ibrāhīm b. Yūsuf al-Baʿlī. *Ḥāshiya* [*ʿalā Kitāb al-Furūʿ*]. On the margins of Ibn Mufliḥ, *Kitāb al-Furūʿ*, ed. ʿAbd Allāh b. ʿAbd al-Muḥsin al-Turkī. Beirut: Muʾassasat al-Risāla, 2003.

Ibn Rāhawayh (d. 238/853) = Isḥāq b. Rāhawayh. *Musnad*, ed. ʿAbd al-Ghafūr b. ʿAbd al-Ḥaqq al-Balūshī. Medina: Maktabat al-Īmān, 1412/1990–1.

Ibn Rajab (d. 795/1393) = Abū al-Faraj Zayn al-Dīn ʿAbd al-Raḥmān b. Aḥmad. *Qawāʿid*. 2nd ed. Mecca: Maktabat Nizār Muṣṭafā al-Bāz, 1999.

Ibn Rushd al-Ḥafīd, Ibn Rushd II, Averroës (d. 595/1198) = Abū al-Walīd Muḥammad b. Aḥmad b. Muḥammad al-Qurṭubī. *Bidāyat al-mujtahid*, ed.

ʿAlī Muḥammad Muʿawwaḍ and ʿĀdil Aḥmad ʿAbd al-Mawjūd. Beirut: Dār al-Kutub al-ʿIlmiyya, 2000. English translation: *The Distinguished Jurist's Primer : A Translation of Bidāyat Al-Mujtahid*, trans. Imran Ahsan Khan Nyazee. Reading: Garnet, 1999.

Ibn Rushd al-Jadd, Ibn Rushd I (d. 520/1126) = Abū al-Walīd Muḥammad b. Aḥmad b. Rushd al-Qurṭubī. *al-Bayān wa'l-taḥṣīl*, ed. Muḥammad Ḥajjī. Beirut: Dār al-Gharb al-Islāmī, 1984.

——*al-Muqaddimāt al-mumahhidāt*, ed. Muḥammad Ḥajjī. Beirut: Dār al-Gharb al-Islāmī, 1988.

Ibn Saʿd (d. 230/844–5) = Abū ʿAbd Allāh Muḥammad b. Saʿd. *al-Ṭabaqāt al-kubrā* (or *Kitāb al-Ṭabaqāt al-kabīr*), ed. ʿAlī Muḥammad ʿUmar. Cairo: Maktabat al-Khānjī, 2001.

Ibn Shahrāshūb (d. 588/1192) = Rashīd al-Dīn Muḥammad b. ʿAlī al-Sarawī. *Maʿālim al-ʿulamāʾ*, ed. ʿAbbās Iqbāl. Tehran: n.p., 1353/1954 [distribution by Maṭbaʿat Fardīn].

Ibn al-Shaṭṭ (d. 723/1323) = Sirāj al-Dīn Abū al-Qāsim b. ʿAbd Allāh b. al-Shaṭṭ. *Idrār al-shurūq ʿalā Anwāʾ al-furūq*. On the margins of Shihāb al-Dīn al-Qarāfī, *Furūq*. Beirut: Dār al-Maʿrifa, 197-?.

Ibn Shuʿba al-Ḥarrānī (d. fifth/eleventh century?) = Abū Muḥammad al-Ḥasan b. ʿAlī b. al-Ḥusayn b. Shuʿba al-Ḥarrānī al-Ḥalabī. *Tuḥaf al-ʿuqūl fī-mā jāʾa min al-ḥikam wa'l-mawāʿiẓ ʿan Āl al-Rasūl*, ed. ʿAlī Akbar al-Ghaffārī. Tehran: Maktabat al-Ṣadūq, 1376/1956–7.

Ibn Taymiyya (d. 728/1328) = Aḥmad b. ʿAbd al-Ḥalīm. *Majmūʿ al-fatāwā*, ed. ʿAbd al-Raḥmān b. Muḥammad b. Qāsim al-ʿĀṣimī al-Najdī al-Ḥanbalī and (his son) Muḥammad. Beirut: Maṭābiʿ Muʾassasat al-Risāla, 1997.

Ibn al-Wardī (d. 749/1349) = Zayn al-Dīn ʿUmar b. al-Muẓaffar. *Taʾrīkh Ibn al-Wardī*. Najaf: al-Maṭbaʿa al-Ḥaydariyya, 1969.

Iṣbahānī, Abū al-Faraj (d. 356/967) = ʿAlī b. al-Ḥusayn b. Muḥammad al-. *Maqātil al-Ṭālibiyyīn*, ed. Aḥmad Ṣaqr. N.p.: al-Maktaba al-Ḥaydariyya, 1423/2002–3. [Orig. ed. Aḥmad Ṣaqr. Cairo: Dār Iḥyāʾ al-Kutub al-ʿArabiyya, 1949.]

Iṣfahānī, Muḥammad Taqī b. Ḥasan al-Mudarris. *Risāla fī 'l-farq bayna 'l-ḥaqq wa'l-ḥukm*. In his *Rasāʾil al-taqawiyya fī 'l-masāʾil al-fiqhiyya*. Tehran?: n.p., 1363/1943–4.

Isḥāq b. Ibrāhīm (d. 275/888–9) = Isḥāq b. Ibrāhīm b. Hāniʾ al-Naysābūrī. *Masāʾil al-Imām Aḥmad b. Ḥanbal*, ed. Zuhayr al-Shāwīsh. Beirut: al-Maktab al-Islāmī, 1400/1979.

Itlīdī (d. late eleventh/seventeenth century) = Muḥammad b. Diyāb al-. *Nawādir al-khulafāʾ* (also known as *Iʿlām al-nās bi-mā waqaʿa li'l-Barāmika maʿa Banī al-ʿAbbās*), ed. Ayman ʿAbd al-Jābir al-Buḥayrī. Cairo: Dār al-Āfāq al-ʿArabiyya, 1998.

Izzi Dien, M. Y. "Taʿzīr." In *EI*[2]. Leiden: Brill, 1960–: 10:406.

Jackson, Sherman. "The Primacy of Domestic Politics: Ibn Bint al-A'azz and the Establishment of the Four Chief Judgeships in Mamlūk Egypt." *Journal of the American Oriental Society* 115, 1 (1995): 52–65.

—*Islamic Law and the State: The Constitutional Jurisprudence of Shihāb al-Dīn al-Qarāfī.* New York: Brill, 1996.

—"Taqlīd, Legal Scaffolding and the Scope of Legal Injunctions in Post-Formative Theory: Muṭlaq and 'Āmm in the Jurisprudence of Shihāb al-Dīn al-Qarāfī." *Islamic Law and Society* 3, 2 (1996): 165–92.

—"Domestic Terrorism in the Islamic Legal Tradition." *The Muslim World* 91, 3–4 (2001): 293–310.

Jahangir, A., and H. Jilani. *The Hudood Ordinances: A Divine Sanction?* Lahore: Rhotac Books, 1988.

James, Fleming, Jr. "Burdens of Proof." *Virginia Law Review* 47 (1961): 51–70.

Jaṣṣāṣ (d. 370/981) = Abū Bakr Aḥmad b. 'Alī al-Rāzī al-. *Aḥkām al-Qur'ān*, ed. Muḥammad al-Ṣādiq Qamḥawī. Beirut: Dār Iḥyā' al-Turāth al-'Arabī, n.d.

Jīdī, 'Umar b. 'Abd al-Karīm al-. *Mabāḥith fī 'l-madhhab al-Mālikī bi'l-Maghrib.* Rabat: Dār al-Hilāl al-'Arabiyya, 1993.

Johansen, Baber. "Claims of Men and Claims of God: The Limits of Government Authority in Hanafite Law." In *Pluriformiteit en Verdeling van de Macht in het Midden-Oosten.* Nijmegen: Vereniging voor de Studie van het Midden-Oosten en de Islam, 1980: 60–104.

—"Sacred and Religious Elements in Hanafite Law: Function and Limits of the Absolute Character of Government Authority." In *Islam et politique au Maghreb*, ed. Abdallah Hammoudi, Ernest Gellner, and Jean-Claude Vatin. Paris: Éditions du Centre National de la Recherche Scientifique, 1981: 281–303.

—"Legal Literature and the Problem of Change: The Case of the Land Rent." In *Islam and Public Law*, ed. Chibli Mallat. London: Graham and Trotman, 1993: 29–47. Reprinted in Baber Johansen, *Contingency in a Sacred Law: Legal and Ethical Norms in the Muslim Fiqh.* Leiden: Brill, 1999: 446–64.

—"The Valorization of the Human Body in Muslim Sunnī Law." In *Law and Society in Islam*, ed. Baber Johansen, Amy Singer, and Devin Stewart. Princeton, NJ: Markus Wiener, 1996: 71–112.

—"Vom Wort- zum Indizienbeweis: Die Anerkennung des richterlichen Folter in islamischen Rechtsdoctrinen des 13. und 14. Jahrhunderts." *Ius Commune* 28 (2001): 11–12.

Jubūrī, 'Abd Allāh Muḥammad al-. *Fiqh al-Imām al-Awzā'ī* [d. 157/774]. Baghdad: Maṭba'at al-Irshād, 1977.

Juynboll, G. H. A. *Muslim Tradition: Studies in Chronology, Provenance, and Authorship of Early Ḥadīth.* Cambridge: Cambridge University Press, 1983.

—"Some Notes on Islam's First *Fuqahā'* Distilled from Early *Ḥadīṯ* Literature." *Arabica* 39 (1992): 287–314.

——"Some *Isnād*-Analytical Methods Illustrated on the Basis of Several Woman-Demeaning Sayings from *Ḥadīth* Literature." In *Ḥadīth*, ed. Harald Motzki. Aldershot; Burlington, VT: Ashgate/Variorum, 2004: 175–216.

Kadi, Wadad al-. "An Early Fāṭimid Political Document." *Studia Islamica* 48 (1978): 71–108.

Kahan, Dan M. "Lenity and Federal Common Law Crimes." *Supreme Court Review* 1994 (1994): 345–428.

——"Is Chevron Relevant to Federal Criminal Law?" *Harvard Law Review* 110 (1996): 469–521.

Kaḥḥāla, ʿUmar Riḍā. *Muʿjam al-muʾallifīn*. Damascus: al-Maktaba al-ʿArabiyya, 1957–61.

Kalwadhānī (d. 510/1116) = Abū al-Khaṭṭāb Maḥfūẓ b. Aḥmad al-. *al-Intiṣār fī ʾl-masāʾil al-kibār*, ed. Sulaymān b. ʿAbd Allāh al-ʿUmayr. Riyadh: Maktabat al-ʿUbaykān, 1993.

Kamali, Mohammad Hashim. *Principles of Islamic Jurisprudence*. Rev. ed. Cambridge: Islamic Texts Society, 1991.

——"Fundamental Rights of the Individual: An Analysis of *Haqq* (Right) in Islamic Law." *American Journal of Social Sciences* 10, 3 (1993): 340–65.

——"Punishment in Islamic Law: A Critique of the Hudud Bill of Kelantan, Malaysia." *Arab Law Quarterly* 13, 3 (1998): 203–34.

——"Legal Maxims and Other Genres of Literature in Islamic Jurisprudence." *Arab Law Quarterly* 20, 1 (2006): 77–101.

——*Sharīʿah Law: An Introduction*. Oxford: Oneworld, 2008.

Karkhī (d. 340/952) = Abū al-Ḥasan ʿUbayd Allāh b. al-Ḥusayn al-. *Uṣūl*. In Abū Zayd al-Dabūsī, *Taʾsīs al-naẓar*, ed. Muṣṭafā Muḥammad al-Qabbānī al-Dimashqī. Beirut: Dār Ibn Zaydūn; Cairo: Maktabat al-Kulliyyāt al-Azhariyya, n.d.: 161–75. Also edition by Zakariyyā ʿAlī Yūsuf. Cairo: Maṭbaʿ al-Imām, 1972?.

Kāsānī (d. 587/1191) = Abū Bakr b. Masʿūd al-. *Badāʾiʿ al-ṣanāʾiʿ fī tartīb al-sharāʾiʿ*, ed. Aḥmad Mukhtār ʿUthmān. Cairo: Zakariyyā ʿAlī Yūsuf, 1968.

Kāshif al-Ghiṭāʾ (d. 1228/1813) = Jaʿfar b. Khaḍir al-Najafī. *al-Ḥaqq al-mubīn*. Tehran: n.p., 1319/1901.

Kāshif al-Ghiṭāʾ (d. 1373/1954) = Muḥammad Ḥusayn. *Taḥrīr al-Majalla*, ed. Muḥammad Mahdī al-Āṣifī and Muḥammad al-Sāʿidī. Iran: al-Majmaʿ al-ʿĀlamī liʾl-Taqrīb bayna ʾl-Madhāhib al-Islāmiyya, 1422/2001–2.

Katz, Marion Holmes. "The *Ḥadd* Penalty for *Zinā*: Symbol or Deterrent? Texts from the Early Sixteenth Century." In *The Lineaments of Islam: Studies in Honor of Fred McGraw Donner*. Leiden: Brill 2012: 351–76.

Kennedy, Hugh. *The Prophet and the Age of the Caliphates: The Islamic Near East from the Sixth to the Eleventh Century*. Harlow: Pearson Education, 1986.

Khadduri, Majid. "Nature and Sources of Islamic Law." *George Washington Law Review* 22 (1953): 3–23.

——"Introduction." In his *Al-Imām Muḥammad ibn Idrīs al-Shāfiʿī's "al-Risāla fī Uṣūl al-Fiqh": Treatise on the Foundations of Islamic Jurisprudence*. Cambridge: Islamic Texts Society, 1987: 3–54.

Khalidi, Tarif. *Islamic Historiography: The Histories of Masʿūdī*. Albany: State University of New York Press, 1975.

Khalīl (d. 776/1374) = Khalīl b. Isḥāq al-Jundī. *Mukhtaṣar*, ed. Ṭāhir Aḥmad al-Zāwī. Cairo: Dār Iḥyāʾ al-Kutub al-ʿArabiyya, 198-.

Khaṭīb, ʿAbd Allāh al-. *Ṣāliḥ b. ʿAbd al-Quddūs al-Baṣrī*. Baghdad: Dār Manshūrāt al-Baṣrī, 1967.

Khaṭīb, ʿAbd al-Zahrāʾ al-Ḥusaynī al-. *Maṣādir Nahj al-balāgha wa-asānīduh*. 2nd ed. Beirut: Muʾassasat al-Aʿlamī liʾl-Maṭbūʿāt, 1975.

al-Khaṭīb al-Baghdādī (d. 463/1071) = Abū Bakr Aḥmad b. ʿAlī. *Taʾrīkh Baghdād*, ed. Muṣṭafā ʿAbd al-Qādir ʿAṭāʾ. Beirut: Dār al-Kutub al-ʿIlmiyya, 1997.

Khiraqī (d. 334/945) = Abū al-Qāsim ʿUmar b. Ḥusayn al-. *Mukhtaṣar*. Damascus: al-Maktab al-Islāmī, 1964.

Khurāsānī (d. 1329/1911) = Muḥammad Kāẓim al-. *Kifāyat al-uṣūl*, ed. ʿAbbās ʿAlī al-Zāriʿī al-Sabzawārī. Muʾassasat al-Nashr al-Islāmī al-Tābiʿa li-Jamāʿat al-Mudarrisīn, 2006–7.

Khushanī (d. 361/971 or 371/981) = Muḥammad b. al-Ḥārith al-Qayrawānī. *Akhbār al-fuqahāʾ waʾl-muḥaddithīn*, ed. Sālim Muṣṭafā al-Badrī. Beirut: Dār al-Kutub al-ʿIlmiyya, 1999.

Kim, Yung Suk. "Lex Talionis in Exodus 21:22–25: Its Origin and Context." *Journal of Hebrew Scriptures* 6, 3 (2006): 2–11.

Kinports, Kit. "Rape and Force: The Forgotten *Mens Rea*." *Buffalo Criminal Law Review* 4 (2001): 755–99.

Kohlberg, Etan. "The Evolution of the Shīʿa." *The Jerusalem Quarterly* 27 (1983): 109–26. Reprinted in Etan Kohlberg, *Belief and Law in Imāmī Shīʿism*. Aldershot: Variorum, 1991: no. I.

——"*Al-Uṣūl al-Arbaʿumiʾa*." *Jerusalem Studies in Arabic and Islam* 10 (1987): 128–66. Reprinted in Etan Kohlberg, *Belief and Law in Imāmī Shīʿism*. Aldershot: Variorum, 1991: no. VII.

——"Imām and Community in the Pre-Ghayba Period." In *Authority and Political Culture in Shīʿism*, ed. Said Amir Arjomand. Albany: State University of New York Press, 1988. Reprinted in Etan Kohlberg, *Belief and Law in Imāmī Shīʿism*. Aldershot: Variorum, 1991: no. XIII.

——*Belief and Law in Imāmī Shīʿism*. Aldershot: Variorum, 1991.

Krawietz, Birgit. *Hierarchie der Rechtsquellen im tradierten sunnitischen Islam.* Berlin: Duncker und Humblot, 2002.

Kulaynī (d. 329/940–1) = Muḥammad b. Yaʿqūb al-. *al-Kāfī.* 5th ed. Tehran: Dār al-Uswa, 1418/1997–8. Also 1957–8 edition: Edited by ʿAlī Akbar al-Ghaffārī. Tehran: n.p., 1377/1957–8.

LaFave, Wayne R. *Modern Criminal Law: Cases, Comments and Questions.* 5th ed. St. Paul, MN: West, 2011.

Lāḥim, ʿAbd al-Karīm b. Muḥammad al-. *Sharḥ Tuḥfat ahl al-ṭalab fī tajrīd uṣūl Qawāʿid Ibn Rajab.* Riyadh: Kunūz Ishbīliyyā, 2006.

Laknawī (d. 1304/1887) = Abū al-Ḥasanāt ʿAbd al-Ḥayy b. Muḥammad al-Anṣārī. *al-Nāfiʿ al-kabīr.* On the margins of Muḥammad b. al-Ḥasan al-Shaybānī, *al-Jāmiʿ al-ṣaghīr.* Karachi: Idārat al-Qurʾān waʾl-ʿUlūm al-Islāmiyya, 1407/1987.

Lane, Edward William. *Arabic-English Lexicon.* Cambridge: Islamic Texts Society, 1984. [Orig. London: Williams and Norgate, 1863.]

Langbein, John H. "Shaping the Eighteenth-Century Criminal Trial: A View from the Ryder Sources." *University of Chicago Law Review* 59 (1983): 1–136.

——*The Origins of Adversary Criminal Trial.* Oxford: Oxford University Press, 2003.

Langbein, John H., Renee Lettow Lerner, and Bruce P. Smith. *A History of the Common Law: The Development of Anglo-American Legal Institutions.* New York: Aspen Publishers, 2009.

Lange, Christian. *Justice, Punishment and the Medieval Muslim Imagination.* Cambridge: Cambridge University Press, 2008.

Lambton, A. K. S. *State and Government in Islam – An Introduction to the Study of Islamic Political Theory: The Jurists.* Oxford: Oxford University Press, 1981.

Laoust, Henri. "La pensée et l'action politiques d'al-Māwardī (364–450/974–1058)." *Revue des Études Islamiques* 38 (1968): 11–92. Reprint: Paris: P. Geuthner, 1968.

Lapidus, Ira. "The Arab Conquests and the Formation of Islamic Society." In *Studies on the First Century of Islamic Society*, ed. G. H. A. Juynboll. Carbondale: Southern Illinois University Press, 1982: 49–72.

——*A History of Islamic Societies.* Rev. ed. Cambridge: Cambridge University Press, 2002. [Orig. 1988.]

Leiter, Brian. "American Legal Realism." In *The Blackwell Guide to the Philosophy of Law and Legal Theory*, ed. Martin P. Golding and William A. Edmundson. Malden, MA: Blackwell, 2005: 50–66.

Levy, Reuben. *The Social Structure of Islam.* Cambridge: Cambridge University Press, 1957. [Orig. *The Sociology of Islam* (1931–33).]

Lewicki, Tadeusz. "The Ibādites in Arabia and Africa." *Cahiers d'histoire mondiale* 13, 1 (1971): 51–130.

Lewis, Bernard. "Siyāsa." In *In Quest of an Islamic Humanism: Arabic and Islamic Studies in Memory of Mohamed al-Nowaihi*, ed. A.H. Green. Cairo: American University in Cairo Press, 1984: 3–14.

Lindholm, Charles. "Kinship Structure and Political Authority: The Middle East and Central Asia." *Comparative Studies in Society and History* 28, 2 (1986): 334–55.

Linzer, Peter. "The Comfort of Certainty: Plain Meaning and the Parol Evidence Rule." *Fordham Law Review* 71 (2002): 799–839.

Lippman, Matthew, Sean McConville, and Mordechai Yerushalmi, eds. *Islamic Criminal Law and Procedure: An Introduction*. New York: Praeger, 1988.

Little, Donald. "A New Look at *al-Aḥkām al-sulṭāniyya*." *The Muslim World* 64 (1974): 1–15.

Llewellyn, Karl N. "A Realistic Jurisprudence – The Next Step." *Columbia Law Review* 30 (1930): 431–44.

—"Remarks on the Theory of Appellate Decision and the Rules or Canons about How Statutes Are to be Construed." *Vanderbilt Law Review* 3 (1950): 396–406.

Lombardi, Clark. *State Law as Islamic Law in Modern Egypt: The Incorporation of the Sharīʿa into Egyptian Constitutional Law*. Leiden: Brill, 2006.

—"Egypt's Supreme Constitutional Court: Managing Constitutional Conflict in an Authoritarian, Aspirationally 'Islamic' State." *Journal of Comparative Law* 3 (2008): 234–53.

Lowry, Joseph E. "Does Shāfiʿī Have a Theory of 'Four Sources' of Law?" In *Studies in Islamic Legal Theory*, ed. Bernard Weiss. Leiden: Brill, 2002: 23–50.

—*Early Islamic Legal History: The Risāla of Muḥammad Ibn Idrīs al-Shāfiʿī*. Leiden; Boston: Brill, 2007.

—ed. and trans. *The Epistle on Legal Theory* [by Muḥammad b. Idrīs al-Shāfiʿī]. New York: New York University Press, 2013.

Macey, Jonathan R., and Geoffrey P. Miller. "The Canons of Statutory Construction and Judicial Preferences." *Vanderbilt Law Review* 45 (1992): 647–72.

Madelung, Wilferd. "Imāma." In *EI*². Leiden: Brill, 1960: 3:1163–69.

—"Mufīd." In *EI*². Leiden: Brill, 1960: 7:312–13.

—"The Early Murjiʾa in Khurāsān and Transoxania and the Spread of Ḥanafism." *Der Islam* 59 (1971): 32–39.

—"The Sources of Ismāʿīlī Law." *Journal of Near Eastern Studies* 35 (1976): 29–40.

—"Imāmism and Muʿtazilite Theology." In *Le Shîʿisme Imâmite*, ed. Toufic Fahd. Paris: Presses Universitaires de France, 1979: 13–39. Reprinted in Wilferd Madelung, *Religious Schools and Sects in Medieval Islam*. London: Variorum, 1985: no. VII.

—"A Treatise of the Sharīf al-Murtaḍā on the Legality of Working for the Government (*Masʾala fī ʾl-ʿamal maʿa ʾl-sulṭān*)." *Bulletin of the School of Oriental and African Studies* 43, 1 (1980): 18–31.

—"Authority in Twelver Shiism in the Absence of the Imam." In *La notion d'autorité au Moyen Age: Islam, Byzance, Occident; Colloques internationaux de la Napoule 1978*. Paris: Presses Universitaires de France, 1982.

——*Religious Schools and Sects in Medieval Islam*. London: Variorum, 1985.

——*Religious Trends in Early Islamic Iran*. Albany, NY: Bibliotheca Persica, 1988.

——*The Succession to Muḥammad: A Study of the Early Caliphate*. Cambridge: Cambridge University Press, 1996.

——"ʿAbd Allāh b. ʿAbbās and Shiʿite Law." In *Law, Christianity and Modernism in Islamic Society in 1996: Proceedings of the Eighteenth Congress of the Union Européenne des Arabisants et Islamisants*. Leuven, Netherlands: Katholieke Universiteit Leuven, 1998.

Maḥmaṣānī, Ṣubḥī. *Falsafat al-tashrīʿ fī ʾl-Islām*. 5th ed. Beirut: Dār al-ʿIlm liʾl-Malāyīn, 1980. [Orig. 1946.] English translation: *The Philosophy of Jurisprudence in Islam*, trans. Farhat Ziadeh. Leiden: Brill, 1961.

Maḥmūdī, Muḥammad Bāqir al-. *Nahj al-saʿāda fī mustadrak Nahj al-balāgha*, ed. ʿAzīz Āl Ṭālib. Tehran: Muʾassasat al-Ṭibāʿa waʾl-Nashr, Wizārat al-Thaqāfa waʾl-Irshād al-Islāmī, 1418–1422/1997–8 to 2001–2.

Maimonides, Moses. *Maimonides' Commentary on the Mishnah, Tractate Sanhedrin*, trans. Fred Rosner. New York: Sepher-Hermon Press, 1981.

Majlisī (d. 1110/1698) = Muḥammad Bāqir b. Muḥammad Taqī al-. *Biḥār al-anwār*, ed. Jawād al-ʿAlawī. Tehran: Dār al-Kutub al-Islāmiyya, 1376–92/1957–73.

——*Mirʾāt al-ʿuqūl fī sharḥ akhbār Āl al-Rasūl: sharḥ Kitāb al-Kāfī* [by Kulaynī], ed. Murtaḍā al-ʿAskarī and Hāshim al-Rasūlī. Tehran: Dār al-Kutub al-Islāmiyya, 1404–11/1984–91.

Makārim Shīrāzī, Nāṣir. *al-Qawāʿid al-fiqhiyya*. Qum: Madrasat al-Imām ʿAlī b. Abī Ṭālib, 1416/1995–6. [Orig. 1382/1963.]

Makdisi, George. *Ibn ʿAqīl et la Résurgence de l'islām au XIe siècle (Ve siècle de l'hégire)*. Damascus: n.p., 1963.

——"The Significance of the Sunnī Schools of Law in Islamic Religious History." *International Journal of Middle East Studies* 10, 1 (1979): 1–8.

——"Hanbalite Islam." In *Studies on Islam*, ed. M. L. Swarz. New York: Oxford University Press, 1981: 215–73.

Makkī (d. 1334/1916–7) = Abū al-Fayḍ Muḥammad Yāsīn b. Muḥammad ʿĪsā al-Fādānī al-. *al-Fawāʾid al-janiyya*, ed. Ramzī Saʿd al-Dīn Dimashqiyya. Beirut: Dār al-Bashāʾir, 1991.

Mālik b. Anas (d. 179/795) = Mālik b. Anas al-Aṣbaḥī al-Ḥimyarī. *al-Muwaṭṭaʾ*. Narrated by Yaḥyā b. Yaḥyā al-Laythī al-Andalusī, ed. Bashshār ʿAwwād Maʿrūf. Beirut: Dār al-Gharb al-Islāmī, 1996.

Mallat, Chibli. *The Renewal of Islamic Law: Muhammad Baqer as-Sadr, Najaf, and the Shi'i International*. Cambridge: Cambridge University Press, 1993.

Manning, John. "Textualism and the Equity of the Statute." *Columbia Law Review* 101 (2001): 1–127.

——"The Absurdity Doctrine." *Harvard Law Review* 116 (2002–2003): 2387–476.

——"Second-Generation Textualism." *California Law Review* 98 (2010): 1287–318.

Manṣūrī, Saʿīd. *Qavāʿid-i fiqh: Bakhsh-i jazāʾī – fiqh-i taṭbīqī-i qāʿidah-i darʾ*. Tehran: Tadbīr, 1375/1997.

Maqqarī (d. 758/1357) = Abū ʿAbd Allāh Muḥammad b. Muḥammad al-. *al-Qawāʿid*, ed. Aḥmad b. ʿAbd Allāh b. Ḥamīd. Mecca: Jāmiʿat Umm al-Qurā, Maʿhad al-Buḥūth al-ʿIlmiyya wa-Iḥyāʾ al-Turāth al-Islāmī, 198-.

Marāghī (d. 1250/1835) = ʿAbd al-Fattāḥ al-Ḥusaynī al-. *al-ʿAnāwīn*. Qum: Muʾassasat al-Nashr al-Islāmī, 1417–18/1996–98.

Mardāwī (d. 885/1480) = ʿAlī b. Sulaymān al-. *Taṣḥīḥ al-furūʿ*. In Ibn Mufliḥ, *Kitāb al-Furūʿ*, ed. ʿAbd Allāh b. ʿAbd al-Muḥsin al-Turkī. Beirut: Muʾassasat al-Risāla, 2003.

Marghīnānī (d. 593/1197) = Burhān al-Dīn ʿAlī b. Abī Bakr al-. *al-Hidāya: sharḥ Bidāyat al-mubtadiʾ*, ed. Muḥammad Muḥammad Tāmir and Ḥāfiz ʿĀshūr Ḥāfiẓ. Cairo: Dār al-Salām, 2000. Also 1966 edition. Edited by Muḥammad ʿAdnān Darwīsh. Cairo: Muḥammad ʿAlī Ṣabīḥ, 1966. English translation: *The Hedàya, or Guide: A Commentary on the Mussulman Laws*, trans. Charles Hamilton (by the Order of the Governor-General and Council of Bengal [Warren Hastings]). London: T. Bensley, 1791. Reprinted as *The Hedaya: Commentary on the Islamic Law*. New Delhi: Kitāb Bhavan, 1985.

Marghīnānī (d. 616/1219) Burhān al-Dīn Maḥmūd b. Aḥmad al-Bukhārī al-. *al-Muḥīṭ al-burhānī fī ʾl-fiqh al-Nuʿmānī*, ed. Aḥmad ʿIzzū ʿInāya. Beirut: Dār Iḥyāʾ al-Turāth al-ʿArabī, 2003.

Marín, Manuela, et al., eds. *Estudios onomástico-biográficos de al-Andalus*. Madrid: Consejo Superior de Investigaciones Científicas, Instituto de Filología, Departamento de Estudios Arabes, 1988–.

Marlow, Louise. *Hierarchy and Egalitarianism in Islamic Thought*. Cambridge: Cambridge University Press, 1997.

Maʿrūf, Bashshār ʿAwwād, et al. *al-Musnad al-jāmiʿ li-aḥādīth al-kutub al-sitta*. Beirut; Kuwait: al-Sharika al-Muttaḥida, 1993–6.

Martyn, Georges, Anthony Musson, and Heikki Pihlajamäki, eds. *From the Judge's Arbitrium to the Legality Principle: Legislation as a Source of Law in Criminal Trials*. Berlin: Duncker und Humblot, 2013.

Masud, Muhammad Khalid. *Islamic Legal Philosophy: A Study of Abū Isḥāq al-Shāṭibī's Life and Thought*. Islamabad: Islamic Research Institute, 1977.

——"A Study of Wakīʿ's (d. 306/917) *Akhbār al-quḍāt*." In *The Law Applied: Contextualizing the Islamic Sharīʿa*, ed. Wolfhart Heinrichs, Peri Bearman, and Bernard G. Weiss. London: I. B. Tauris, 2008: 116–27.

Masʿūdī (d. 345/956) = Abū ʿAlī b. al-Ḥusayn b. ʿAlī al-. *Murūj al-dhahab wa-maʿādin al-jawhar*, ed. Yūsuf Asʿad Dāghir. Beirut: Dār al-Andalus, 1965–66.

Massignon, Louis. *La Passion d'al-Ḥallāj [Ḥusayn ibn Mansour al-Ḥallāj], martyr, mystique de l'Islam*. Paris: Geuthner, 1927.

Matroudi, Abdul Hakim I. Al-. *The Ḥanbalī School of Law and Ibn Taymiyyah: Conflict or Conciliation*. London: Routledge, 2006.

Māwardī (d. 450/1058) = Abū al-Ḥasan ʿAlī b. Muḥammad al-. *Adab al-qāḍī*, ed. Muḥyī Hilāl al-Sarḥān. Baghdad: Riʾāsat Dīwān al-Awqāf; Maṭbaʿat al-ʿĀnī, 1392/1972.

——*al-Aḥkām al-sulṭāniyya waʾl-wilāyāt al-dīniyya*, ed. Muḥammad Fahmī al-Sirjānī. Cairo: al-Maktaba al-Tawfīqiyya, 1978.

——*Kitāb al-ḥudūd min al-Ḥāwī al-kabīr*, ed. Ibrāhīm b. ʿAlī Ṣanduqjī. Beirut: n.p., 1995.

Mawṣilī (d. 683/1284) = ʿAbd Allāh b. Maḥmūd al-. *al-Ikhtiyār li-taʿlīl al-mukhtār*. Cairo: Maktaba wa-Maṭbaʿat Muṣṭafā al-Bābī al-Ḥalabī, 1951?.

Maxwell, Peter Benson. *On the Interpretation of Statutes*. London: W. Maxwell & Son, 1875.

Māzandarānī, Bashīr al-Muḥammadī al-, ed. *Musnad Muḥammad b. Qays al-Bajalī*. Qum: al-Markaz al-ʿĀlamī liʾl-Dirāsāt al-Islāmiyya, 1409/1989.

McDermott, Martin J. *The Theology of al-Shaikh al-Mufīd (d. 413/1022)*. Beirut: Dār al-Mashriq; Librairie orientale, 1978. Arabic translation: *Āl Nawbakht*, trans. ʿAlī Hāshim al-Asadī. Mashhad: Majmaʿ al-Buḥūth al-Islāmiyya, 1383/2004.

McNaughton, John T. "Burden of Production of Evidence: A Function of a Burden of Persuasion." *Harvard Law Review* 68 (1955): 1382–91.

Melchert, Christopher. *The Formation of the Sunni Schools of Law, 9th–10th Centuries C.E.* Leiden: Brill, 1997.

——"Traditionist-Jurisprudents and the Framing of Islamic Law." *Islamic Law and Society* 8, 3 (2001): 383–406.

——*Ahmad ibn Hanbal*. Oxford: Oneworld, 2006.

Meron, Y. "Marghīnānī: His Method and His Legacy." *Islamic Law and Society* 9, 3 (2002): 410–16.

Mezran, Karim. "Constitutionalism and Islam in Libya." In *Constitutionalism in Islamic Countries: Between Upheaval and Continuity*, ed. Rainer Grote and Tillman J. Röder. Oxford: Oxford University Press, 2012: 513–33.

Miller, Geoffrey P. "Pragmatics and the Maxims of Interpretation." *1990 Wisconsin Law Review* (1990): 1179–227.

Minow, Martha. *Between Vengeance and Forgiveness*. Boston: Beacon Press, 1998.

Mir-Hosseini, Ziba. "Criminalising Sexuality: Zinā Laws as Violence against Women in Muslim Contexts." *Sur* 8, 15 (2011): 7–34.

Mizzī (d. 742/1341) = Jamāl al-Dīn Abū al-Ḥajjāj Yūsuf b. ʿAbd al-Raḥmān al-. *Tahdhīb al-kamāl fī asmāʾ al-rijāl*, ed. Bashshār ʿAwwād Maʿrūf. Beirut: Muʾassasat al-Risāla, 1992.

——*Tuḥfat al-ashrāf bi-maʿrifat al-aṭrāf*. Beirut: Dār al-Gharb al-Islāmī, 1999.

Modarressi, Hossein. *An Introduction to Shīʿī Law: A Bibliographical Study*. London: Ithaca Press, 1984.

——*Crisis and Consolidation in the Formative Period of Shīʿite Islam: Abū Jaʿfar Ibn Qiba al-Rāzī and His Contribution to Imāmite Shīʿite Thought*. Princeton, NJ: Darwin Press, 1993.

——"Early Debates on the Integrity of the Qurʾān: A Brief Survey." *Studia Islamica* 77 (1993): 5–39.

——"The Legal Basis for the Validity of the Majority Opinion in Islamic Legislation." In *Under Siege: Islam and Democracy*, ed. Richard Bulliet. New York: Middle East Institute, Columbia University, 1993: 81–92.

——*Tradition and Survival: A Bibliographical Survey of Early Shīʿite Literature*. London: Oneworld, 2003.

——*Tārīkhiyyāt: Majmūʿah-i maqālāt va taḥqīqāt-i tārīkhī*. New Jersey: Zagros, 2009.

Moin, A. Azfar. "Partisan Dreams and Prophetic Visions: Shīʿī Critique in Masʿūdī's History of the ʿAbbāsids." *Journal of the American Oriental Society* 127, 4 (2007): 415–28.

Molot, Jonathan T. "The Rise and Fall of Textualism." *Columbia Law Review* 106 (2006): 1–58.

Morony, Michael. *Iraq after the Muslim Conquest*. Princeton, NJ: Princeton University Press, 1984.

Morrison, Trevor W. "Constitutional Avoidance in the Executive Branch." *Columbia Law Review* 106, 6 (2006): 1189–259.

Mottahedeh, Roy P. "The Shuʿûbîyah Controversy and the Social History of Early Islamic Iran." *International Journal of Middle East Studies* 7, 2 (1976): 161–82.

——*Loyalty and Leadership in an Early Islamic Society*. Princeton, NJ: Princeton University Press, 1980. Also rev. ed: London: I. B. Tauris, 2001.

——trans. *Lessons in Islamic Jurisprudence* (English translation of *Durūs fī ʿilm al-uṣūl* by Muḥammad Bāqir al-Ṣadr). Oxford: Oneworld, 2003.

Motzki, Harald. "*Wal-Muḥṣanātu mina n-Nisāʾi illā mā malakat aimānukum* (Koran 4:24) und die koranische Sexualethik." *Der Islam* 63 (1986): 192–218.

——"The *Muṣannaf* of ʿAbd al-Razzāq al-Ṣanʿānī as a Source of Authentic *Aḥādīth* of the First Century A. H." *Journal of Near Eastern Studies* 50, 1 (1991): 1–21.

——*Die Anfänge der Islamischen Jurisprudenz: Ihre Entwicklung in Mekka bis zur Mitte des 2./8. Jahrhunderts*. Stuttgart; Leiden: Brill, 1997. English translation: *The Origins of Islamic Jurisprudence: Meccan Fiqh before the Classical Schools*, trans. Marion Katz. Leiden: Brill, 2002.

——ed. *Ḥadīth: Origins and Developments*. Aldershot: Ashgate Variorum, 2004.

Mufīd (d. 413/1022) = Abū ʿAbd Allāh Muḥammad b. al-Nuʿmān al-ʿUkbarī al-Baghdādī, Ibn al-Muʿallim. *Awāʾil al-maqālāt fī ʾl-madhāhib al-mukhtārāt*, ed. ʿAbbās-Qūlī al-Wāʿiẓ al-Charandābī. Tabriz: Maṭbaʿat al-Riḍaʾī, 1364/1944.

——*Taṣḥīḥ al-iʿtiqād*, ed. ʿAbbās-Qūlī al-Wāʿiẓ al-Charandābī. Tabriz: Maṭbaʿat al-Riḍaʾī, 1364/1944.

——*al-Muqniʿa*. Qum: Muʾassasat al-Nashr al-Islāmī, 1410/1990. Also published in *YF*, ed. ʿAlī Aṣghar Murwārīd. Beirut: Dār al-Turāth; al-Dār al-Islāmiyya, 1990. Volume 23.

——*Tadhkira fī uṣūl al-fiqh*. In *Muṣannafāt al-Shaykh al-Mufīd*. Qum: al-Muʾtamar al-ʿĀlamī fī Alfiyyāt al-Shaykh al-Mufīd, 1413/1992–3. Volume 9.

——*Qavāʿid-i fiqh*. Tehran: Markaz-i Nashr-i ʿUlūm-i Islāmī, 1378/1999–2000.

Muḥammad b. Sulaymān al-Kūfī (d. fourth/tenth century). *Muntakhab*. Ṣanʿāʾ, Yemen: Dār al-Ḥikma al-Yamāniyya, 1993.

Muḥammadī, ʿAlī. "Naqd-i sākhtār-i qānūn-i mujāzāt-i Islāmī." *Fiqh va ḥuqūq* 1, 1 (2004): 157–74.

Muḥammadī Gīlānī, Muḥammad. "Āshināʾī bā qāʿidah-i *'al-Ḥudūd tudraʾ biʾl-shubahāt.'" Majallah-i qaḍāʾī va ḥuqūqī-i dādgustarī-i Jumhūrī-i Islāmī-i Īrān* 5, 15–16 (1375/1996–7): 25–30.

Muḥibbī (d. 1111/1699) = Muḥammad Amīn b. Faḍl Allāh al-. *Khulāṣat al-athar fī aʿyān al-qarn al-ḥādī ʿashar*. Beirut: Maktabat Khayyāṭ, 1966.

Munāwī (d. 1030/1621) = ʿAbd al-Raʾūf al-. *al-Taysīr: sharḥ al-Jāmiʿ al-ṣaghīr*, ed. Muṣṭafā Muḥammad al-Dhahabī. Cairo: Dār al-Ḥadīth, 2000.

Muranyi, Miklos. *Beiträge zur Geschichte der Ḥadīṯ und Rechtsgelehrsamkeit der Mālikiyya in Nordafrika bis zum 5. Jh. d. H.: Bio-bibliographische Notizen aus der Moscheebibliothek von Qairawān*. Wiesbaden: Harrassowitz, 1997.

——*Die Rechtsbücher des Qairawāners Saḥnūn b. Saʿīd: Entstehungsgeschichte und Werküberlieferung*. Stuttgart: Deutsche Morgenländische Gesellschaft; Kommissionsverlag F. Steiner, 1999.

Muslim (d. 261/875) = Muslim b. al-Ḥajjāj al-Qushayrī. *Ṣaḥīḥ*, ed. Muḥammad Fuʾād ʿAbd al-Bāqī. Cairo: Dār Iḥyāʾ al-Kutub al-ʿArabiyya, 1375/1955–6.

Mustafa, Abdul-Rahman. *On Taqlīd: Ibn al Qayyim's Critique of Authority in Islamic Law*. Oxford: Oxford University Press, 2013.

al-Muttaqī al-Hindī (d. 975/1567) = ʿAlāʾ al-Dīn ʿAlī b. Ḥusām al-Dīn al-Burhān al-Fawrī. *Kanz al-ʿummāl li-sunan al-aqwāl waʾl-afʿāl*. Aleppo: Maktabat al-Turāth al-Islāmī, 1969?.

Muẓaffar, Muḥammad Riḍā. *Manṭiq*, ed. Muṣṭafā Ḥusaynī Dashtī. Tehran: Muʾassasah-i Farhangī-i Ārāya, 1381/2002–3).

——*Uṣūl al-fiqh*, ed. Raḥmat Allāh Raḥmatī al-Arākī. Qum: Muʾassasat al-Nashr al-Islāmī, 1423/2002–3.

Muzanī (d. 264/878) = Abū Ibrāhīm Ismāʿīl b. Yaḥyā al-. *Mukhtaṣar*. Beirut: Dār al-Kutub al-ʿIlmiyya, 1993.

Nadwī, ʿAlī Aḥmad al-. *al-Qawāʿid al-fiqhiyya*. Damascus: Dar al-Qalam, 1418/1998.

Nagel, Tilman. *Geschichte der islamischen Theologie*. English translation: *The History of Islamic Theology: From Muhammad to the Present*, trans. Thomas Thornton. Princeton, NJ: Markus Wiener, 2000.

Nahmod, Sheldon H. *Civil Rights and Civil Liberties Litigation: The Law of Section 1983*. 4th ed. St. Paul, MN: West, 2010.

Nā'inī (d. 1355/1936) = Muḥammad Ḥusayn b. ʿAbd al-Raḥīm al-Gharawī al-. *Fawā'id al-uṣūl*. Compiled by Muḥammad ʿAlī al-Kāẓimī al-Khurāsānī (d. 1363/1945–6), ed. Raḥmat Allāh Raḥmatī al-Arākī. Qum: Mu'assasat al-Nashr al-Islāmī al-Tābiʿa li-Jamāʿat al-Mudarrisīn, 1404/1983–4.

Najafī (d. 1266/1850) = Muḥammad Ḥasan b. Muḥammad Bāqir. *Jawāhir al-kalām fī sharḥ Sharā'iʿ al-Islām*, ed. Riḍā al-Ustādī. Najaf: Dār al-Kutub al-Islāmiyya, 1378/1958–9.

Najāshī (d. 450/1058) = Aḥmad b. ʿAlī al-Najāshī al-Asadī al-Kūfī. *Rijāl* (also known as *Fihrist asmā' muṣannafī 'l-Shīʿa*), ed. M. Sh. al-Zanjānī. Qum: Mu'assasat al-Nashr al-Islāmī al-Tābiʿa li-Jamāʿat al-Mudarrisīn, 1988.

Nasafī (d. 710/1310) = ʿAbd Allāh b. Aḥmad b. Maḥmūd al-. *Kanz al-daqā'iq*, ed. Abū al-Ḥusayn ʿAbd al-Majīd al-Murādzihī al-Khāshī. Zāhidān, Iran: Mu'assasat Usāma, 2003.

Nasā'ī (d. 303/915) = Aḥmad b. Shuʿayb b. ʿAlī al-Khurāsānī. *al-Sunan al-kubrā*, ed. Ḥasan ʿAbd al-Munʿim al-Shalabī. Beirut: Mu'assasat al-Risāla, 2001.

Pseudo-Nāshi' (d. 293/905–6) = ʿAbd Allāh b. Muḥammad al-Anbarī, al-Nāshi' al-Akbar (attributed). *Masā'il al-imāma*, ed. Josef van Ess as *Frühe muʿtazilitische Häresiographie: Zwei Werke des Nāšī' al-Akbar* (attributed). Beirut; Wiesbaden: Kommissionsverlag F. Steiner, 1971.

al-Nāṭiq bi'l-Ḥaqq (d. 424/1033) = Abū Ṭālib Yaḥyā b. al-Ḥusayn. *Kitāb al-Taḥrīr*, ed. Muḥammad Yaḥyā Sālim ʿAzzān. Ṣanʿā', Yemen: Maktabat Badr, 1997.

Nawawī (d. 676/1277) = Yaḥyā b. Sharaf b. Marrī al-. *al-Majmūʿ: sharḥ al-Muhadhdhab*, ed. Muḥammad Najīb al-Muṭīʿī. Cairo: al-Maktaba al-ʿĀlamiyya, 1971.

——*Rawḍat al-ṭālibīn*, ed. ʿĀdil Aḥmad ʿAbd al-Mawjūd and ʿAlī Muḥammad Muʿawwaḍ. Beirut: Dār al-Kutub al-ʿIlmiyya, 1992.

——*Minhāj al-ṭālibīn*, ed. Aḥmad b. ʿAbd al-ʿAzīz al-Ḥaddād. Beirut: Dār al-Bashā'ir, 2000.

Newland, Sarah. "The Mercy of Scalia: Statutory Construction and the Rule of Lenity." *Harvard Civil Rights and Civil Liberties Law Review* 29 (1994): 197–230.

Newman, Andrew J. *The Development and Political Significance of the Rationalist (Uṣūlī) and Traditionist (Akhbārī) Schools in Imāmī Shīʿī History from the Third/Ninth to the Tenth/Sixteenth Century A.D.* PhD dissertation, UCLA, 1987.

——"The Nature of the Akhbārī/Uṣūlī Dispute in Late Ṣafawid Iran." *Bulletin of the School of Oriental and African Studies* 55, 1–2 (1992): 22–51 (Part I), 250–61 (Part II).

——"The Myth of the Clerical Migration to Safawid Iran: Arab Shiite Opposition to ʿAlī al-Karakī and Safawid Shiism." *Die Welt des Islams* 33, 1 (1993): 66–112.

Newman, Andrew, and Jansen, J. J. G. "*Uṣūliyya*." In *EI*[2]. Leiden: Brill, 1960–: 10:935–38.

Nielsen, J. S. "Sultan al-Ẓāhir Baybars and the Appointment of Four Chief *Qāḍīs*, 663/1265." *Studia Islamica* 60 (1984): 167–76.

al-Niẓām, al-Shaykh, et al. (fl. eleventh/seventeenth century). *al-Fatāwā al-ʿĀlamgīriyya* (also known as *al-Fatāwā al-Hindiyya*), ed. ʿAbd al-Laṭīf Ḥasan ʿAbd al-Raḥmān. Beirut: Dār al-Kutub al-ʿIlmiyya, 2000. Also 1975 edition: Bulaq: n.p., 1975.

Nubāhī (d. after 798/1389–90), ʿAlī b. ʿAbd Allāh al-. *al-Marqaba al-ʿulyā de al-Nubahi: La atalaya suprema sobre el cadiazgo y el muftiazgo*. Edited and translated into Spanish by Arsenio Cuellas Marqués and Celia del Moral. Granada: Universidad de Granada, 2005.

Nūrī al-Ṭabarsī (d. 1320/1908) = Ḥusayn b. Muḥammad Taqī al-. *Mustadrak al-Wasāʾil wa-mustanbaṭ al-masāʾil*. Qum: Muʾassasat Āl al-Bayt li-Iḥyāʾ al-Turāth, 1407/1986–7.

El Omari, Racha. *The Theology of Abū l-Qāsim al-Balḫī/al-Kaʿbī (d. 319/931): A Study of Its Sources and Reception*. PhD dissertation, Yale University, 2007.

Osman, Amr. *The History and Doctrine of the Ẓāhirī Madhhab*. PhD dissertation, Princeton University, 2010. [Published as *The Ẓāhirī Madhhab (3rd/9th–10th/16th Century): A Textualist Theory of Islamic Law*. Leiden: Brill, 2014.]

Ostien, Philip, ed. *Sharia Implementation in Northern Nigeria, 1999–2006: A Sourcebook*. Ibadan, Nigeria: Spectrum Books, 2007.

Patterson, Dennis. *A Companion to Philosophy of Law and Legal Theory*. Cambridge, MA: Blackwell, 1996.

Peters, Rudolph. "The Islamization of Criminal Law: A Comparative Analysis." *Die Welt Des Islams* 34 (1994): 246–74.

——"Murder in Khaybar: Some Thoughts on the Origins of the *Qasāma* Procedure in Islamic Law." *Islamic Law and Society* 9, 2 (2002): 132–67.

——*Crime and Punishment in Islamic Law*. Cambridge: Cambridge University Press, 2005.

Peters, Rudolph, and Gert J. J. de Vries. "Apostasy in Islam." *Die Welt des Islams* 17, 1/4 (1976–7): 1–25.

Poonawala, Ismail K. "Al-Qāḍī al-Nuʿmān and Ismāʿīlī Jurisprudence." In *Mediaeval Ismāʿīlī History and Thought*, ed. Farhad Daftary. Cambridge: Cambridge University Press, 1996: 117–43.

——"The Beginning of the Ismaili Daʿwa and the Establishment of the Fatimid Dynasty as Commemorated by al-Qāḍī al-Nuʿmān." In *Culture and Memory in Medieval Islam: Studies in Honor of Wilferd Madelung*, ed. Farhad Daftary and Josef Meri. London: I. B. Tauris, 2003: 338–63.

Posner, Richard A. "Statutory Interpretation – In the Classroom and in the Courtroom." *University of Chicago Law Review* 50 (1983): 800–23.

——"Legal Formalism, Legal Realism, and the Interpretations of Statutes and the Constitution." *Case Western Law Review* 37 (1986–87): 179–217.

Powers, David S. *Studies in Qur'ān and Ḥadīth: The Formation of the Islamic Law of Inheritance*. Berkeley: University of California Press, 1986.

——*Law, Society, and Culture in the Maghrib, 1300–1500*. Cambridge: Cambridge University Press, 2002.

Powers, Paul R. *Intent in Islamic Law: Motive and Meaning in Medieval Sunnī Fiqh*. Leiden: Brill, 2006.

Price, Zachary. "The Rule of Lenity as a Rule of Structure." *Fordham Law Review* 72 (2004): 885–942.

Qāḍī Khān (d. 592/1196) = al-Ḥasan b. Manṣūr al-Ūzjandī al-Farghānī. *Fatāwā Qāḍī Khān*. Cairo: Maṭba'at Muḥammad Shāhīn, 1282/1865.

Qāḍī Nu'mān (d. 363/974) = Abū Ḥanīfa Nu'mān b. Muḥammad b. Manṣūr. *Da'ā'im al-Islām*, ed. A. A. A. Fyzee. Cairo: Dār al-Ma'ārif, 1951 and 1960.

——*Kitāb al-Iqtiṣār*, ed. 'Ārif Tāmir. Beirut: Dār al-Aḍwā', 1996.

——*Īḍāḥ*, ed. Muḥammad Kāẓim Raḥmatī. Beirut: Mu'assasat al-A'lamī li'l-Maṭbū'āt, 2007.

al-Qaffāl al-Shāshī (d. 507/1113) = Abū Bakr Muḥammad b. Aḥmad. *Ḥilyat al-'ulamā' fī ma'rifat madhāhib al-fuqahā'*, ed. Yāsīn Aḥmad Ibrāhīm Darādika. Amman: Maktabat al-Risāla al-Ḥadītha; Mecca: Dār al-Bāz, 1998.

Qal'ahjī, Muḥammad Rawwās. *Mawsū'at fiqh Abī Bakr al-Ṣiddīq*. Damascus: Dār al-Fikr, 1983.

——*Mawsū'at fiqh 'Alī b. Abī Ṭālib*. Damascus: Dār al-Fikr, 1983.

——*Mawsū'at fiqh 'Uthmān b. 'Affān*. Mecca: Jāmi'at Umm al-Qurā, Kulliyyat al-Sharī'a wa'l-Dirāsāt al-Islāmiyya, Markaz al-Baḥth al-'Ilmī wa-Iḥyā' al-Turāth al-Islāmī, 1983.

——*Mawsū'at fiqh 'Abd Allāh b. 'Umar*. Beirut: Dār al-Nafā'is, 1986.

——*Mawsū'at fiqh Ibrāhīm al-Nakha'ī*. 2nd ed. Beirut: Dār al-Nafā'is, 1986–.

——*Mawsū'at fiqh al-Ḥasan al-Baṣrī*. Beirut: Dār al-Nafā'is, 1989.

——*Mawsū'at fiqh Sufyān al-Thawrī*. Beirut: Dār al-Nafā'is, 1990.

——*Mawsū'at fiqh 'Umar b. 'Abd al-'Azīz*. Kuwait: Jāmi'at al-Kuwayt, 1990.

——*Mawsū'at fiqh Zayd b. Thābit wa-Abī Hurayra*. Beirut: Dār al-Nafā'is, 1993.

——*Mawsū'at fiqh 'Abd Allāh b. 'Abbās*. 2nd ed. Beirut: Dār al-Nafā'is, 1996.

——*Mawsū'at fiqh 'Abd Allāh b. Mas'ūd*. 2nd ed. Beirut: Dār al-Nafā'is, 1996.

——*Mawsū'at fiqh al-Layth b. Sa'd*. Kuwait: Jāmi'at al-Kuwayt, 2002.

——*Mawsū'at fiqh 'Abd al-Raḥmān al-Awzā'ī*. Kuwait: Majlis al-Nashr al-'Ilmī, 2003.

Qalqashandī (d. 821/1418) = Abū al-ʿAbbās Aḥmad b. ʿAlī al-. *Ṣubḥ al-aʿshā fī ṣināʿāt al-inshāʾ*. Cairo: al-Muʾassasa al-Miṣriyya al-ʿĀmma, 1964.

Qarāfī (d. 684/1285) = Shihāb al-Dīn Abū al-ʿAbbās al-Ṣanhājī al-. *Anwār al-burūq fī anwāʾ al-furūq*. Beirut: Dār al-Maʿrifa, 197-?.

——*al-Dhakhīra fī furūʿ al-Mālikiyya*. Beirut: Dār al-Gharb al-Islāmī, 1994.

Qubānchī, Ḥasan al-. *Musnad al-Imām ʿAlī*, ed. Ṭāhir al-Sallāmī. Beirut: Muʾassasat al-Aʿlamī, 2000.

Qudūrī (d. 428/1037) = Abū al-Ḥusayn Aḥmad b. Muḥammad al-. *Tajrīd: al-Mawsūʿa al-fiqhiyya al-muqārana*, ed. Muḥammad Aḥmad al-Sirāj and ʿAlī Jumuʿa Muḥammad. Cairo: Dār al-Salām, 2004.

Quinn, Rob. "U.S. Firm Calls for Islamic Law in Lawsuit: Blackwater Boss Seeks Sharia Law to Dodge Afghan Crash Suit." *Newser*, June 19, 2008.

Qummī (d. 1231/1816) = Abū al-Qāsim al-. *Qawānīn al-uṣūl*. Tabriz: n.p., 1275/1858–9.

Qummī (d. mid-third/ninth century) = Ibrāhīm b. Hāshim al-Kūfī al-. *Qaḍāyā Amīr al-Muʾminīn ʿAlī b. Abī Ṭālib*, ed. Fāris Ḥassūn Karīm. Qum: Muʾassasat Amīr al-Muʾminīn, 1382/2003. Also 1947 and 2000 editions: *ʿAjāʾib aḥkām Amīr Al-Muʾminīn*. Collected by Muḥsin al-Amīnī al-ʿĀmilī, ed. Fāris Ḥassūn Karīm. 2nd ed. Qum?: Markaz al-Ghadīr liʾl-Dirāsāt al-Islāmiyya, 2000. [Orig. 1947.]

Quraishi, Asifa. "Her Honor: An Islamic Critique of the Rape Laws of Pakistan from a Woman-Sensitive Perspective." *Michigan Journal of International Law* 18 (1997): 287–320.

Qurṭubī (d. 543/1143) = Abū Bakr Muḥammad b. Aḥmad al-. *al-Jāmiʿ li-aḥkām al-Qurʾān*. Cairo: Dār al-Shāʿb, 1961?.

Rabb, Intisar A. "We the Jurists: Islamic Constitutionalism in Iraq." *University of Pennsylvania Journal of Constitutional Law* 10 (2008): 527–79.

——"Islamic Legal Maxims as Substantive Canons of Construction: *Ḥudūd*-Avoidance in Cases of Doubt." *Islamic Law and Society* 17, 1 (2010): 63–125.

——"The Islamic Rule of Lenity: Judicial Discretion and Legal Canons." *Vanderbilt Journal of Transnational Law* 44, 5 (2011): 1299–351.

——"Negotiating Speech in Islamic Law and Politics: Flipped Traditions of Expression." In *Islamic Law and International Human Rights*, ed. Anver M. Emon, Mark S. Ellis, and Benjamin Glahn. Oxford: Oxford University Press, 2012: 144–67.

——"Islamic Legal Minimalism: Legal Maxims and Lawmaking When Jurists Disappear." In *Law and Tradition in Classical Islamic Thought*, ed. Michael Cook, Najam Haider, Intisar Rabb, and Asma Sayeed. New York: Palgrave Macmillan, 2013: 145–66.

——"The Least Religious Branch? Judicial Review and the New Islamic Constitutionalism." *UCLA Journal of International and Foreign Affairs* 17 (2013): 72–132.

Rabbānī, Muḥammad Ḥasan al-. *Qāʿidat al-darʾ*. Qum: Muʾassasat al-Nashr al-Islāmī al-Tābiʿa li-Jāmiʿat al-Mudarrisīn, 1428/2007–2008.

Radin, Max. "The Theory of Judicial Decision: Or How Judges Think." *American Bar Association Journal* 11 (1925): 357–62.

Radzinowicz, Leon. *A History of English Law and Its Administration from 1750*. London: Stevens & Sons, 1948.

Rāfiʿī (d. 623/1226) = Abū al-Qāsim ʿAbd al-Karīm b. Muḥammad. *al-ʿAzīz: sharḥ al-Wajīz* (also known as *al-Sharḥ al-kabīr*), ed. ʿAlī Muḥammad Muʿawwaḍ and ʿĀdil Aḥmad ʿAbd al-Mawjūd. Beirut: Dār al-Kutub al-ʿIlmiyya, 1997.

Rahman, Fazlur. *Islam*. 2nd ed. Chicago: University of Chicago Press, 1979. [Orig. London, 1966.]

Ramlī (d. 1004/1596) = Muḥammad b. Aḥmad al-Anṣārī al-Manūfī al-. *Nihāyat al-muḥtāj ilā sharḥ al-Minhāj*. Cairo: [Maktaba wa-Maṭbaʿat] Muṣṭafā al-Bābī al-Ḥalabī, 1938.

Rapoport, Yossef. "Legal Diversity in the Age of Taqlīd: The Four Chief Qāḍīs under the Mamlūks." *Islamic Law and Society* 10, 2 (2003): 210–28.

Rayshahrī, Muḥammad al-. *Mawsūʿat al-Imām ʿAlī b. Abī Ṭālib*, ed. Maḥmūd al-Ṭabāṭabāʾī and Muḥammad Kāẓim al-Ṭabāṭabāʾī. Beirut: Dār al-Ḥadīth, 2000.

Reinhart, A. Kevin. *Before Revelation: The Boundaries of Muslim Moral Thought*. Albany: State University of New York Press, 1995.

Robbins, Ira P. "The Ostrich Instruction: Deliberate Ignorance as a Criminal *Mens Rea*." *Journal of Criminal Law and Criminology* 81, 2 (1990): 191–234.

Robinson, Chase. *Islamic Historiography*. Cambridge: Cambridge University Press, 2003.

Robinson, Paul H., Adnan Zulfiqar, Margaret Kammerud, and Michael Orchowski. "Codifying Sharīʿa: International Norms, Legality & the Freedom to Invent New Forms." *Journal of Comparative Law* 2, 1 (2007): 1–53.

Roemer, H. R. "The Safavid Period." In *The Cambridge History of Iran*, vol. 6, ed. Peter Jackson and Lawrence Lockhart. Cambridge: Cambridge University Press, 1986: 189–350.

El-Rouayheb, Khaled. *Before Homosexuality in the Arab-Islamic World, 1500–1800*. Chicago: University of Chicago Press, 2005.

Rubin, Edward L. "Modern Statutes, Loose Canons, and the Limits of Practical Reason: A Response to Farber and Ross." *Vanderbilt Law Review* 45 (1992): 579–91.

Rubin, Uri. "'Al-Walad li-l-Firāsh': On the Islamic Campaign against 'Zinā.'" *Studia Islamica* 78 (1993): 5–26.

Sabra, Adam. "Ibn Ḥazm's Literalism: A Critique of Islamic Legal Theory." *Al-Qanṭara: Revista de Estudios Árabes* 28, 1–2 (2007): 7–40 (Part I), 307–48 (Part II).

Ṣadr, Muḥammad Bāqir al-. *Durūs fī ʿilm al-uṣūl*. Qum: Majmaʿ al-Fikr al-Islāmī, 1419/1998. English translation: *Lessons in Islamic Jurisprudence*, trans. Roy P. Mottahedeh. Oxford: Oneworld, 2003.

Saḥnūn (d. 240/854) = ʿAbd al-Salām b. Saʿīd. *al-Mudawwana al-kubrā*. Beirut: Dār Ṣādir, n.d.

Saifee, Seema. "Penumbras, Privacy, and the Death of Morals-Based Legislation: Comparing U.S. Constitutional Law with the Inherent Right of Privacy in Islamic Jurisprudence." *Fordham International Law Journal* 27 (2003): 370–454.

Samāhijī (d. 1135/1723) = ʿAbd Allāh b. Ṣāliḥ al-Samāhijī al-Baḥrānī. *Munyat al-mumārisīn*. In Muḥammad Bāqir B. Zayn al-ʿĀbidīn al-Khwansārī (d. 1313/1895), *Rawḍāt al-jannāt*, ed. M. T. al-Kashfī and A. Ismāʿīliyyān. Tehran; Qum: Maktabat Ismāʿīliyyān, 1390–92/1970–73.

Ṣanʿānī, ʿAlī b. Ismāʿīl b. ʿAbd Allāh al-Muʾayyad. *Kitāb Raʾb al-ṣadʿ*. Beirut: Dār al-Nafāʾis, 1990.

Sander, Paul. *Zwischen Charisma und Ratio: Entwicklungen in der frühen imāmitischen Theologie*. Berlin: K. Schwarz, 1994.

Sarakhsī (d. 483/1090) = Shams al-Aʾimma Muḥammad b. Aḥmad b. Sahl al-. *Mabsūṭ*, ed. Abū ʿAbd Allāh Muḥammad Ḥasan Ismāʿīl al-Shāfiʿī. Beirut: Dār al-Kutub al-ʿIlmiyya, 2001.

——*Uṣūl*, ed. Abū al-Wafāʾ al-Afghānī. Beirut: Dār al-Maʿrifa, 2001.

Savory, Roger M. "Safawid Persia." In *The Cambridge History of Islam*, ed. P. M. Holt, Ann K. S. Lambton, and Bernard Lewis. Cambridge: Cambridge University Press, 1970: 1:349–429.

Sayeed, Asma. "Gender and Legal Authority: An Examination of Early Juristic Opposition to Women's Ḥadīth Transmission." *Islamic Law and Society* 16, 2 (2009): 115–50.

——*Women and the Transmission of Religious Knowledge in Islam*. Cambridge: Cambridge University Press, 2013.

Sayyid, Riḍwān al-. *al-Umma wa'l-jamāʿa wa'l-ṣulṭa*. Beirut: Dār al-Iqraʾ, 1984.

Scalia, Antonin. *A Matter of Interpretation: Federal Courts and the Law*. Princeton, NJ: Princeton University Press, 1997.

Scalia, Antonin, and Bryan A. Garner. *Reading Law: The Interpretation of Legal Texts*. St. Paul, MN: Thompson/West, 2012.

Schacht, Joseph. "A Revaluation of Islamic Traditions." *Journal of the Royal Asiatic Society* 81, 3–4 (1949): 143–54.

——*The Origins of Muhammadan Jurisprudence*. Oxford: Clarendon Press, 1950.

——"Abū Ḥanīfa, al-Nuʿmān b. Thābit." In *EI*². Leiden: Brill, 1960–: 1:123–24.

——"Abū Yūsuf, Yaʿḳūb b. Ibrāhīm al-Anṣārī al-Kūfī." In *EI*². Leiden: Brill, 1960–: 1:164–65.

——"Ibn Abī Laylā." In *EI*². Leiden: Brill, 1960–: 3:687–88.

——*An Introduction to Islamic Law*. Oxford: Clarendon Press, 1964.

——"On Some Manuscripts in the Libraries of Kairouan and Tunis." *Arabica* 14 (1967): 225–58.

Schacter, Jane. "The Changing Structure of Legitimacy in Statutory Interpretation." *Harvard Law Review* 108 (1995): 593–663.

Schauer, Frederick. "An Essay on Constitutional Language." In *Interpretive Law and Literature: A Hermeneutic Reader*, ed. Sanford Levinson and Steven Mailloux. Evanston, IL: Northwestern University Press, 1988: 133–54.

——"Constitutional Invocations." *Fordham Law Review* 65 (1997): 1295–312.

Scheppele, Kim Lane. *Legal Secrets: Equality and Efficiency in the Common Law*. Chicago: University of Chicago Press, 1988.

——"Facing Facts in Legal Interpretation." *Representations* 30 (1988): 42–77.

Schmidtke, Sabine. *The Theology of al-ʿAllāma al-Ḥillī (d. 726/1325)*. Berlin: K. Schwarz, 1991.

Schmitt, Arno. "*Liwāṭ* im *Fiqh*: Männliche Homosexualität." *Journal of Arabic and Islamic Studies* 4 (2001–2002): 49–110.

Schottlaender, Adolf. *Die geschichtliche Entwicklung des Satzes*: Nulla poena sine lege. Breslau: n.p., 1911.

Schulhofer, Stephen. "Attempt." In *Encyclopedia of Crime and Justice*, ed. Sanford H. Kadish. New York: Free Press, 1983: 1:97.

Serrano, Delfina. "Twelve Cases on the Application of Penal Law under the Moravids." In *Dispensing Justice in Islam: Qadis and Their Judgments*, ed. Muhammad Khalid Masud, Rudolph Peters, and David S. Powers. Leiden: Brill, 2006: 473–93.

Sezgin, Fuat. *Geschichte des arabischen Schrifttums*. Leiden: Brill, 1967–2007.

Shāfiʿī (d. 204/820) = Muḥammad b. Idrīs al-. *Risāla*, ed. Muḥammad Nabīl Ghanāyim and ʿAbd al-Ṣabūr Shāhīn. Cairo: Markaz al-Ahrām li'l-Tarjama wa'l-Nashr, Mu'assasat al-Ahrām, 1988. English translation: *The Epistle on Legal Theory*. Edited and translated by Joseph Lowry. New York: New York University Press, 2013. Also English translation: *Al-Imām Muḥammad ibn Idrīs al-Shāfiʿī's "al-Risāla fi Uṣūl al-Fiqh": Treatise on the Foundations of Islamic Jurisprudence*. Translated by Majid Khadduri. Cambridge: Islamic Texts Society, 1987.

——*Kitāb al-Umm*, ed. Rifʿat Fawzī ʿAbd al-Muṭṭalib. [Mansoura]: Dār al-Wafā', 2008. Also 1961 edition: Edited by Muḥammad Zuhrī al-Najjār. Cairo: Maktabat al-Kulliyyāt al-Azhariyya, 1961. Also 1996 edition: Edited by Aḥmad Badr al-Dīn Ḥassūn. N.p.: Dār Qutayba, 1996.

al-Shahīd al-Awwal (d. 786/1389) = Shams al-Dīn Muḥammad b. Makkī al-ʿĀmilī. *al-Qawāʿid wa'l-fawā'id*. Tehran: n.p., 1308/1929–30.

al-Shahīd al-Thānī (d. 996/1558) = Zayn al-Dīn b. ʿAlī Jubaʿī al-ʿĀmilī. *Tamhīd al-qawāʿid al-uṣūliyya wa'l-ʿarabiyya li-tafrīʿ fawā'id al-aḥkām al-sharʿiyya*. Qum: Maktab al-Iʿlām al-Islāmī, 1374/1995.

Shahrastānī (d. 548/1153) = Abū al-Fatḥ Muḥammad b. ʿAbd al-Karīm al-. *al-Milal waʾl-niḥal*, ed. ʿAbd al-Amīr ʿAlī Muhannā and ʿAlī Ḥasan Fāʿūr. Beirut: Dār al-Maʿrifa, 1990.

Shāljī, ʿAbbūd al-. *Mawsūʿat al-ʿadhāb*. Beirut: al-Dār al-ʿArabiyya liʾl-Mawsūʿāt, 198–.

El Shamsy, Ahmed. *From Tradition to Law: The Origins and Early Development of the Shāfiʿī School of Law in Ninth-Century Egypt*. PhD dissertation, Harvard University, 2009. [Published as *The Canonization of Islamic Law: A Social and Intellectual History*. Cambridge: Cambridge University Press, 2013.]

Shantarīnī (d. 542/1147) = Abū al-Ḥasan ʿAlī b. Bassām al-. *al-Dhakhīra fī maḥāsin ahl al-Jazīra*, ed. Iḥsān ʿAbbās. Beirut: Dār al-Thaqāfa, 1979.

Shapiro, David L. "Community and Change in Statutory Interpretation." *New York University Law Review* 67 (1992): 921–60.

al-Sharīf al-Murtaḍā (d. 436/1044) = ʿAlam al-Hudā ʿAlī b. al-Ḥusayn al-Mūsawī. *al-Uṣūl al-iʿtiqādiyya*. In *Nafāʾis al-makhṭūṭāt*, ed. Muḥammad Ḥasan Āl Yāsīn. Najaf: al-Maṭbaʿa al-Ḥaydariyya, 1954.

——*Intiṣār*, ed. Muḥammad Riḍā al-Sayyid Ḥasan al-Kharsān. Najaf: al-Maṭbaʿa al-Ḥaydariyya, 1971.

——*Rasāʾil*, ed. Aḥmad al-Ḥusaynī and Mahdī Rajāʾī. Qum: Dār al-Qurʾān al-Karīm, 1405–/1984 or 1985–.

——*al-Dhakhīra fī ʿilm al-kalām*, ed. Aḥmad al-Ḥusaynī. Qum: Muʾassasat al-Nashr al-Islāmī, 1411/1990–1.

al-Sharīf al-Raḍī (d. 406/1015) = Muḥammad b. al-Ḥusayn al-Mūsawī. *Nahj al-balāgha*, ed. Ṣubḥī al-Ṣāliḥ. Beirut: Dār al-Kitāb al-Lubnānī, 1967.

Shashdīw (d. 425/1034) = Mānkdīm Shashdīw. *Taʿlīq* [*ʿalā*] *sharḥ al-Uṣūl al-khamsa*, ed. ʿAbd al-Karīm ʿUthmān. Cairo: Maktabat Wahba, 1965. [Published as ʿAbd al-Jabbār b. Aḥmad (d. 415/1025), *Sharḥ al-uṣūl al-khamsa*, as clarified by D. Gimaret in "Les *Uṣūl al-ḫamsa* du Qāḍī ʿAbd al-Gabbār et leurs commentaires," *Annales Islamologiques* 15 (1979): 47–96.]

Shāṭibī (d. 790/1388) = Abū Isḥāq Ibrāhīm b. Mūsā al-. *al-Muwāfaqāt fī uṣūl al-aḥkām*, ed. Muḥammad Muḥyī al-Dīn ʿAbd al-Ḥamīd. Cairo: Muḥammad ʿAlī Ṣabīḥ, 1969–70.

Shaṭṭī (d. 1307/1890) = Muḥammad b. Ḥasan al-Shaṭṭī al-Ḥanbalī. *Risāla fī madhhab al-Imām Dāwūd al-Ẓāhirī*. Damascus: Maṭbaʿat Rawḍat al-Shām, 1330/1911–2.

Shawkānī (d. 1255/1839) = Muḥammad b. ʿAlī al-. *Nayl al-awṭār: sharḥ Muntaqā al-akhbār min aḥādīth Sayyid al-Akhyār*, ed. Muḥammad Ḥallāq and ʿIzz al-Dīn Khaṭṭāb. Beirut: Dār Iḥyāʾ al-Turāth al-ʿArabī, 1999.

Shaybānī (d. 189/804) = Muḥammad b. al-Ḥasan al-. *al-Jāmiʿ al-kabīr*, ed. Abū al-Wafāʾ al-Afghānī. India: Maṭbaʿat al-Istiqāma, 1357/1938.

——*al-Jāmiʿ al-ṣaghīr*. Karachi: Idārat al-Qurʾān waʾl-ʿUlūm al-Islāmiyya, 1407/1987.

——*Kitāb al-Āthār*, ed. Khadīja Muḥammad Kāmil. Karachi: Idārat al-Qur'ān wa'l-'Ulūm al-Islāmiyya, 1419/1998–9.

Shboul, Ahmad M. H. *Al-Mas'ūdī and His World: A Muslim Humanist and His Interest in Non-Muslims*. London: Ithaca Press, 1979.

Shīrāzī (d. 476/1083) = Ibrāhīm b. 'Alī al-. *al-Tabṣira fī uṣūl al-fiqh*, ed. Muḥammad Ḥasan Haytū. Damascus: Dār al-Fikr, 1980.

——*al-Muhadhdhab fī fiqh al-Imām al-Shāfi'ī*, ed. Muḥammad al-Zuḥaylī. Beirut: al-Dār al-Shāmiyya; Damascus: Dār al-Qalam, 1996.

Shirbīnī (d. 922/1560) = Muḥammad b. Aḥmad al-Khaṭīb al-. *al-Mughnī al-muḥtāj ilā ma'rifat ma'ānī alfāẓ al-Minhāj*, ed. 'Alī Muḥammad Mu'awwaḍ and 'Ādil Aḥmad 'Abd al-Mawjūd. Beirut: Dār al-Kutub al-'Ilmiyya, 1994.

Shoshan, Boaz. *The Poetics of Islamic Historiography*. Leiden: Brill, 2004.

Sidahmed, Abdel Salam. "Problems in Contemporary Applications of Islamic Criminal Sanctions: The Penalty for Adultery in Relation to Women." *British Journal of Middle Eastern Studies* 28 (2001): 187–204.

Siegel, Jonathan R. "Textualism and Contextualism in Administrative Law." *Boston University Law Review* 78 (1998): 1023–112.

Soufi, Denise L. *The Image of Fatima in Classical Muslim Thought*. PhD dissertation, Princeton University, 1997.

Spector, Philip M. "The Sentencing Rule of Lenity." *University of Toledo Law Review* 33 (2002): 511–80.

Spectorsky, Susan. *Chapters on Marriage and Divorce: Responses of Ibn Ḥanbal and Ibn Rāhwayh*. Austin: University of Texas Press, 1993.

——"*Ḥadīth* in the Responses of Isḥāq B. Rāhwayh." *Islamic Law and Society* 8, 3 (2001): 407–31.

Steiker, Carol S., and Jordan M. Steiker. *Entrenchment and/or Destabilization? Reflections on (Another) Two Decades of Constitutional Regulation of Capital Punishment*. Forthcoming.

Stein, Peter. *Regulae Iuris: From Juristic Rules to Legal Maxims*. Edinburgh: Edinburgh University Press, 1966.

Stephen, James Fitzjames. *A History of the Criminal Law of England*. London: Routledge, 1996. [Orig. 1883.]

Stewart, Devin J. "A Biographical Notice on Bahā' al-Dīn al-'Āmilī (d. 1030/1621)." *Journal of the American Oriental Society* 111, 3 (1991): 563–71.

——"The First Shaykh al-Islām of the Safavid Capital Qazvin." *Journal of the American Oriental Society* 116, 3 (1996): 387–405.

——"Notes on the Migration of 'Āmilī Scholars to Safavid Iran." *Journal of Near Eastern Studies* 55, 2 (1996): 81–103.

——*Islamic Legal Orthodoxy: Twelver Shiite Responses to the Sunni Legal System*. Salt Lake City: University of Utah Press, 1998.

——"Muḥammad b. Dāwūd al-Ẓāhirī's Manual of Jurisprudence, *al-Wuṣūl ilā maʿrifat al-uṣūl*." In *Studies in Islamic Legal Theory*, ed. Bernard Weiss. Leiden: Brill, 2002: 99–160.

Stewart, Potter. "The Road to *Mapp v. Ohio* and Beyond: The Origins, Development, and Future of the Exclusionary Rule in Search-and-Seizure Cases." *Columbia Law Review* 83 (1983): 1365–404.

Stilt, Kristen. *Islamic Law in Action: Authority, Discretion, and Everyday Experiences in Mamluk Egypt*. Oxford: Oxford University Press, 2011.

Stree, Walter. *In dubio pro reo*. Tübingen: Mohr, 1962.

Subkī, Tāj al-Dīn (d. 771/1370) = ʿAbd al-Wahhāb b. ʿAlī al-. *Ṭabaqāt al-Shāfiʿiyya al-kubrā*, ed. Maḥmūd Muḥammad al-Ṭanāḥī and ʿAbd al-Fattāḥ Muḥammad al-Ḥilw. Cairo: [Maktaba wa-Maṭbaʿat] ʿĪsā al-Bābī al-Ḥalabī, 1964–76.

——*al-Ashbāh wa'l-naẓā'ir*, ed. ʿĀdil Aḥmad ʿAbd al-Mawjūd and ʿAlī Muḥammad ʿAwaḍ. 2nd ed. Beirut: Dār al-Kutub al-ʿIlmiyya, 1991.

Sutherland, Jabez Gridley. *Statutes and Statutory Construction*, ed. Norman J. Singer. 5th ed. Chicago: Callaghan, 1992. [Orig. 1891.]

Suyūrī, al-Fāḍil al-Miqdād (d. 826/1423) = Jamāl al-Dīn al-Miqdād b. ʿAbd Allāh al-Ḥillī. *Kanz al-ʿirfān fī fiqh al-Qur'ān*, ed. Muḥammad Bāqir al-Bahbūdī. Tehran: al-Maktaba al-Murtaḍawiyya, 1384/1964.

——*Naḍd al-qawāʿid al-fiqhiyya ʿalā madhhab al-Imāmiyya*, ed. ʿAbd al-Laṭīf al-Kūhkamarī et al. Qum: Maktabat Āyat Allāh al-ʿUẓmā al-Marʿashī, 1403/1982–3.

Suyūṭī (d. 911/1505) = Jalāl al-Dīn ʿAbd al-Raḥmān al-. *al-Ashbāh wa'l-naẓā'ir*, ed. Muḥammad al-Muʿtaṣim bi'llāh al-Baghdādī. Beirut: Dār al-Kitāb al-ʿArabī, 1998.

——*Jāmiʿ al-aḥādīth: al-Jāmiʿ al-ṣaghīr wa-zawā'idih wa'l-jāmiʿ al-kabīr*, ed. Aḥmad ʿAbd al-Jawwād and ʿAbbās Aḥmad Ṣaqr. Beirut: Dār al-Fikr, 1998.

Syed, Mairaj. *Coercion in Classical Islamic Law and Theology*. PhD dissertation, Princeton University, 2011.

Ṭabarānī (d. 360/970) = Sulaymān b. Aḥmad al-. *al-Muʿjam al-awsaṭ*, ed. Ṭāriq b. ʿIwaḍ Allāh b. Muḥammad and ʿAbd al-Muḥsin b. Ibrāhīm al-Ḥusaynī. Cairo: Dār al-Ḥaramayn, 1995.

Ṭabarī (d. 310/923) = Abū Jaʿfar Muḥammad b. Jarīr al-. *Ta'rīkh al-rusul wa'l-mulūk*, ed. Muḥammad Abū al-Faḍl Ibrāhīm. Cairo: Dār al-Maʿārif, 1960. English translation: *History of al-Ṭabarī*, trans. various scholars (40 vols.). Albany: State University of New York Press, 1989–2007.

——*Jāmiʿ al-bayān ʿan ta'wīl āy al-Qur'ān* (also known as *Tafsīr al-Ṭabarī*), ed. Ṣalāḥ ʿAbd al-Fattāḥ al-Khālidī and Ibrāhīm Muḥammad al-ʿAlī. Damascus: Dār al-Qalam; Beirut: al-Dār al-Shāmiyya, 1997.

Ṭabāṭabā'ī (d. 1403/1983) = al-ʿAllāma, Muḥammad Ḥusayn al-. *al-Mīzān fī tafsīr al-Qur'ān*. Beirut: Mu'assasat al-Aʿlamī li'l-Maṭbūʿāt, n.d.

Ṭaḥāwī (d. 321/933) = Abū Jaʿfar Aḥmad b. Muḥammad al-. *Sharḥ maʿānī ʾl-āthār*, ed. Muḥammad Sayyid Jād al-Ḥaqq, Muḥammad Zuhrī al-Najjār, and Yūsuf ʿAbd al-Raḥmān al-Marʿashlī. Beirut: ʿĀlam al-Kutub, 1994.

Takim, Liyakat N. *The Heirs of the Prophet: Charisma and Religious Authority in Shi'ite Islam*. Albany: State University of New York Press, 2006.

Tanūkhī (d. 384/933) = al-Qāḍī al-Muḥassin b. ʿAlī. *Nishwār al-muḥāḍara wa-akhbār al-mudhākara*, ed. ʿAbbūd al-Shāljī. Beirut: Dār Ṣādir, 1971. English translation: *The Table Talk of a Mesopotamian Judge*, trans. D. S. Margoliouth. London: Royal Asiatic Society, 1922.

Tashkīrī, Muḥammad ʿAlī al-, et al. *al-Qawāʿid al-uṣūliyya waʾl-fiqhiyya ʿalā madhhab al-Imāmiyya*. Distributed under the rubric of Lajnat ʿIlmiyya fī ʾl-Ḥawza al-Dīniyya. Tehran: al-Majmaʿ al-ʿĀlamī liʾl-Taqrīb bayna ʾl-Madhāhib al-Islāmiyya, 2004.

Thayer, James B. "The Burden of Proof." *Harvard Law Review* 4 (1890): 45–70.

Tillier, Mathieu. "La société abbasside au miroir du tribunal: Égalité juridique et hiérarchie sociale." *Annales islamologiques* 42 (2008): 157–86.

Tirmidhī (d. 279/892) = Muḥammad b. ʿĪsā al-. *Sunan*. N.p.: n.p., 1965–69.

Tsafrir, Nurit. *The History of an Islamic School of Law: The Early Spread of Ḥanafism*. Cambridge, MA: Islamic Legal Studies Program at Harvard Law School, 2004.

Tūnī (d. 1070/1660–1) = ʿAbd Allāh b. Muḥammad al-Fāḍil al-. *al-Wāfiya fī uṣūl al-fiqh*, ed. Muḥammad Ḥusayn al-Riḍawī al-Kashmīrī. Qum: Majmaʿ al-Fikr al-Islāmī, 1412/1912.

Ṭūsī (d. 460/1067) = Abū Jaʿfar Muḥammad b. al-Ḥasan b. ʿAlī al-, Shaykh al-Ṭāʾifa. *ʿUddat al-uṣūl*. Tehran: n.p., 1314/1896–7.

——*al-Tibyān fī tafsīr al-Qurʾān*. Najaf: al-Maṭbaʿa al-ʿIlmiyya, 1957–63.

——*al-Nihāya fī mujarrad al-fiqh waʾl-fatāwā*. Tehran: Chāpkhānah-i Dānishgāh, 1342/1963.

——*Amālī*, ed. Muḥammad Ṣādiq Baḥr al-ʿUlūm. Qum: Maktabat al-Dāwarī, 197-.

——*Rijāl*, ed. Jawād al-Qayyūmī al-Iṣfahānī. Qum: Muʾassasat al-Nashr al-Islāmī al-Tābiʿa li-Jamāʿat al-Mudarrisīn, 1315/1994.

——*Fihrist*. Qum: Muʾassasat Nashr al-Fiqāha, 1417/1996–7.

——*Tahdhīb al-aḥkām fī sharḥ al-Muqniʿa*, ed. ʿAlī Akbar al-Ghaffārī. Tehran: Maktabat al-Ṣadūq, 1997.

——*al-Istibṣār fī-mā ikhtalafa min al-akhbār*, ed. ʿAlī Akbar al-Ghaffārī. Qum: Dār al-Ḥadīth, 1380/2001–2.

Tyan, Emile. *Histoire de l'organisation judiciaire en pays d'islam*. Leiden: n.p., 1960.

Urban, Elizabeth. "The Identity of Crisis of Abū Bakra: *Mawlā* of the Prophet, or Polemical Tool?" In *The Lineaments of Islam: Studies in Honor of Fred McGraw Donner*, ed. Paul Cobb. Leiden: Brill, 2012.

Ustādī, Riḍā al-. "Qāʿidah-i darʾ." *Fiqh-i Ahl-i Bayt* 32 (1382–3/2005): 209–24 (Part I); 37 (1382–3/2005): 169–85 (Part II).

ʿUthmān b. ʿAbd Allāh al-ʿIrāqī (mid-sixth/twelfth century) = Abū Muḥammad. *al-Firaq al-muftaraqa*. Ankara: n.p., 1961.

Vermeule, Adrian. "Saving Constructions." *Georgetown Law Journal* 85 (1997): 1945–77.

——*Judging Under Uncertainty: An Institutional Theory of Legal Interpretation.* Cambridge, MA: Harvard University Press, 2006.

Vogenauer, Stefan, and Stephen Weatherill, eds. *The Harmonisation of European Contract Law: Implications for European Private Laws, Business and Legal Practice*. Oxford; Portland, OR: Hart, 2006.

Wādiʿī, Saʿīd b. Misfir al-Daghghār al-. *Athar al-shubahāt fī darʾ al-ḥudūd*. Riyadh: Maktabat al-Tawba, 1998.

Wakīʿ (d. 306/917) = Muḥammad b. Khalaf b. Ḥayyān. *Akhbār al-quḍāt*, ed. Saʿīd Muḥammad al-Laḥḥām. Beirut: ʿĀlam al-Kutub, 2001.

Waismann, Friedrich. "Verifiability." *Proceedings of the Aristotelian Society*, Supplementary Volume 19 (1945): 119–50.

Waldron, Jeremy. "Lex Talionis." *Arizona Law Review* 34 (1992): 25–52.

Walzer, Michael. *Just and Unjust Wars: A Moral Argument with Historical Illustrations*. New York: Basic Books, 1977.

Wansharīsī (d. 915/1508) = Aḥmad b. Yaḥyā al-. *al-Miʿyār al-muʿrib waʾl-jāmiʿ al-mughrib ʿan fatāwā ahl Ifrīqiya waʾl-Andalus waʾl-Maghrib*, ed. Muḥammad Ḥajjī. Rabat: Wizārat al-Awqāf waʾl-Shuʾūn al-Islāmiyya, 1981.

——*ʿUddat al-burūq fī jamʿ mā fī ʾl-madhhab min al-jumūʿ waʾl-furūq*, ed. Ḥamza Abū Fāris. Beirut: Dār al-Gharb al-Islāmī, 1990.

Warren, Alex, and Lin Noueihed. *The Battle for the Arab Spring: Revolution, Counter-Revolution and the Making of a New Era*. New Haven, CT: Yale University Press, 2012.

Watson, Alan. *Society and Legal Change*. 2nd ed. Philadelphia: Temple University Press, 2001. [Orig. Edinburgh, 1977.]

Watt, Montgomery. "The Closing of the Door of Iǧtihād." In *Orientalia Hispanica*, ed. J. M. Barral. Leiden: Brill, 1974: 675–78.

Weiss, Bernard. "Language and the Law: The Linguistic Premises of Islamic Legal Science." In *In Quest of an Islamic Humanism: Arabic and Islamic Studies in Memory of Mohamed al-Nowaihi*, ed. A. H. Green. Cairo: American University of Cairo Press, 1984: 15–21.

——*The Search for God's Law*. Salt Lake City: University of Utah Press, 1992.

——*The Spirit of Islamic Law*. Salt Lake City: University of Utah Press, 1998.

Whitman, James Q. *The Origins of Reasonable Doubt: Theological Roots of the Criminal Trial*. New Haven, CT: Yale University Press, 2008.

Wilke, Martina, and Heike Pfann. *In dubio pro reo: Risikoklassifikation und risikospezifische Suche nach Risikoentschärfungsoperatoren*. MA thesis, Heidelberg University, 2006.

Wilkinson, John C. *The Imamate Tradition of Oman*. Cambridge: Cambridge University Press, 1987.

Yāfiʿī (d. 768/1366–7) = Abū ʿAbd Allāh b. Asʿad al-. *Mirʾāt al-jinān wa-ʿibrat al-yaqẓān fī maʿrifat ḥawādith al-zamān*. Beirut: Muʾassasat al-Aʿlamī liʾl-Maṭbūʿāt, 1390/1970.

Yanagihashi, Hiroyuki. "Abū Ḥanīfa." In *EI*[3]. Leiden: Brill Online, 2009.

Zakariyah, Luqman. *Applications of Legal Maxims in Islamic Criminal Law with Special Reference to Shariah Law in Northern Nigeria (1999–2007)*. PhD dissertation, University of Wales, 2009.

Zamakhsharī (d. 538/1144) = Abū al-Qāsim Maḥmūd b. ʿUmar al-, Jār Allāh. *al-Kashshāf ʿan haqāʾiq al-tanzīl*. Beirut: Dār al-Kitāb al-ʿArabī, 1965?.

Zaman, M. Qasim. *Religion and Politics under the Early ʿAbbāsids: The Emergence of the Proto-Sunnī Elite*. Leiden: Brill, 1997.

——"The Caliphs, the ʿUlamāʾ, and the Law: Defining the Role and Function of the Caliph in the Early ʿAbbāsid Period." *Islamic Law and Society* 4, 1 (1997): 1–36.

Zarkashī (d. 772/1370) = Badr al-Dīn Muḥammad b. Bahādur b. ʿAbd Allāh al-. *Sharḥ al-Zarkashī ʿalā Mukhtaṣar al-Khiraqī*, ed. ʿAbd al-Munʿim Khalīl Ibrāhīm. Beirut: Dār al-Kutub al-ʿIlmiyya, 2002. Also 1993 edition: Edited by ʿAbd Allāh b. ʿAbd al-Raḥmān b. ʿAbd Allāh al-Jibrīn. Riyadh: Maktabat al-ʿUbaykān, 1993.

Zayd b. ʿAlī (d. 122/740). *Musnad* (also known as *al-Majmūʿ al-fiqhī*). Collected and compiled by ʿAbd al-ʿAzīz b. Isḥāq al-Baghdādī (d. 363/973–4). Ṣanʿāʾ, Yemen: Maktabat al-Irshād, 1990.

Zaylaʿī (d. 743/1343) = Fakhr al-Dīn ʿUthmān b. ʿAlī b. Miḥjan al-. *Tabyīn al-ḥaqāʾiq*, ed. Aḥmad ʿIzzū ʿInāya. Beirut: Dār al-Kutub al-ʿIlmiyya, 2000.

Zaylaʿī (d. 762/1361) = Jamāl al-Dīn Abū Muḥammad ʿAbd Allāh b. Yūsuf al-. *Naṣb al-rāya: Takhrīj aḥādīth al-Hidāya*, ed. Aḥmad Shams al-Dīn. Beirut: Dār al-Kutub al-ʿIlmiyya, 1996.

Zeghal, Malika. *Constitution-Drafting and Islam in Tunisia*. Forthcoming.

Ziriklī, Khayr al-Dīn al-. *al-Aʿlam: Qāmūs tarājim*. Beirut: Dār al-ʿIlm liʾl-Malāyīn, 1986.

Zubayrī (d. 236/850) = Abū ʿAbd Allāh Muṣʿab b. ʿAbd Allāh al-. *Nasab Quraysh*, ed. E. Lévi-Provençal. Cairo: Dār al-Maʿārif, 1953.

Zuḥaylī, Wahba al-. *al-Wasīṭ fī uṣūl al-fiqh al-Islāmī*. Damascus: Maṭbaʿat Jāmiʿat Dimashq, 1965.

Zysow, Aron. *The Economy of Certainty: An Introduction to the Typology of Islamic Legal Theory*. Atlanta, GA: Lockwood Press, 2013.

Index A. Names and Terms

NB. References to notes are marked with "n."

Index B. Types and Bases of Doubt

Index C. Legal Maxims

Other Legal Maxims (Anglo-American, Latin)

Other titles in the series

Popular Culture in Medieval Cairo Boaz Shoshan
Early Philosophical Shiism: The Ismaili Neoplatonism of Abū Ya'qūb al-Sijistānī Paul E. Walker
Indian Merchants and Eurasian Trade, 1600–1750 Stephen Frederic Dale
Palestinian Peasants and Ottoman Officials: Rural Administration around Sixteenth-Century Jerusalem Amy Singer
Arabic Historical Thought in the Classical Period Tarif Khalidi
Mongols and Mamluks: The Mamluk – Īlkhānid War, 1260–1281 Reuven Amitai-Preiss
Hierarchy and Egalitarianism in Islamic Thought Louise Marlow
The Politics of Households in Ottoman Egypt: The Rise of the Qazdağlis Jane Hathaway
Commodity and Exchange in the Mongol Empire: A Cultural History of Islamic Textiles Thomas T. Allsen
State and Provincial Society in the Ottoman Empire: Mosul, 1540–1834 Dina Rizk Khoury
The Mamluks in Egyptian Politics and Socieity Thomas Philipp and Ulrich Haarmann (eds.)
The Delhi Sultanate: A Political and Military History Peter Jackson
European and Islamic Trade in the Early Ottoman State: The Merchants of Genoa and Turkey Kate Fleet
Reinterpreting Islamic Historiography: Hārūn Al-Rashīd and the Narrative of the 'Abbāsid Caliphate Tayeb El-Hibri
The Ottoman City between East and West: Aleppo, Izmir, and Istanbul Edhem Eldem, Daniel Goffman, and Bruce Masters
A Monetary History of the Ottoman Empire Şevket Pamuk
The Politics of Trade in Safavid Iran: Silk for Silver, 1600–1730 Rudolph P. Matthee
The Idea of Idolatry and the Emergence of Islam: From Polemic to History G. R. Hawting
Classical Arabic Biography: the Heirs of the Prophets in the Age of al-Ma'mūn Michael Cooperson
Empire and Elites After the Muslim Conquest: The Transformation of Northern Mesopotamia Chase F. Robinson
Poverty and Charity in Medieval Islam: Mamluk Egypt, 1250–1517 Adam Sabra
Christians and Jews in the Ottoman Arab World: The Roots of Sectarianism Bruce Masters
Culture and Conquest in Mongol Eurasia Thomas T. Allsen
Revival and Reform in Islam: The Legacy of Muhammad al-Shawkani Bernard Haykel
Tolerance and Coercion in Islam: Interfaith Relations in the Muslim Tradition Yohanan Friedmann
Guns for the Sultan: Military Power and the Weapons Industry in the Ottoman Empire Gábor Ágoston

Marriage, Money and Divorce in Medieval Islamic Society Yossef Rapoport
The Empire of the Qara Khitai in Eurasian History: Between China and the Islamic World Michal Biran
Domesticity and Power in the Early Mughal World Ruby Lal
Power, Politics and Religion in Timurid Iran Beatrice Forbes Manz
Postal Systems in the Pre-Modern Islamic World Adam J. Silverstein
Kingship and Ideology in the Islamic and Mongol Worlds Anne F. Broadbridge
Justice, Punishment and the Medieval Muslim Imagination Christian Lange
The Shiites of Lebanon under Ottoman Rule, 1516–1788 Stefan Winter
Women and Slavery in the Late Ottoman Empire Madeline Zilfi
The Second Ottoman Empire: Political and Social Transformation in the Early Modern World Baki Tezcan
Non-Muslims in the Early Islamic Empire: From Surrender to Coexistence Milka Levy-Rubin
The Legendary Biographies of Tamerlane: Islam and Heroic Apocrypha in Central Asia Ron Sela
Law and Piety in Medieval Islam Megan Reid
The Origins of the Shīʿa: Identity, Ritual, and Sacred Space in Eighth-Century Kūfa Najam Haider
Politics, Law, and Community in Islamic Thought: The Taymiyyan Moment Ovamir Anjum
The Power of Oratory in the Medieval Muslim World Linda G. Jones
Animals in the Qur'an Sarra Tlili
The Logic of Law Making in Islam: Women and Prayer in the Legal Tradition Behnam Sadeghi
Empire and Power in the Reign of Süleyman: Narrating the Sixteenth-Century Ottoman World Kaya Şahin
Women and the Transmission of Religious Knowledge in Islam Asma Sayeed
The New Muslims of Post-Conquest Iran: Tradition, Memory, and Conversion Sarah Bowen Savant
The Mamluk City in the Middle East: History, Culture, and the Urban Landscape Nimrod Luz
Disability in the Arab Ottoman World, 1500–1800 Sara Scalenghe
The Holy City of Medina: Sacred Space in Early Islamic Arabia Harry Munt
Muslim Midwives: The Craft of Birthing in the Premodern Middle East Avner Giladi
Doubt in Islamic Law: A History of Legal Maxims, Interpretation, and Islamic Criminal Law Intisar A. Rabb